Tiferet Yisrael

תפארת ישראל

Tiferet Yisrael

Translation and Commentary
by
Rabbi Ramon Widmonte

VOLUME 1

Introduction and
Chapters 1–9

THE MAHARAL OF PRAGUE
{HARAV YEHUDA LOEW}

URIM PUBLICATIONS
Jerusalem • New York

Tiferet Yisrael: Translation and Commentary
by Rabbi Ramon Widmonte

Typeset by Ariel Walden

Printed in Israel

First Edition

ISBN 978-965-524-147-1

Urim Publications
P.O. Box 52287
Jerusalem 9152102 Israel

www.UrimPublications.com

Library of Congress Cataloging-in-Publication Data

Names: Judah Loew ben Bezalel, approximately 1525–1609, author. | Widmonte, Ramon, translator. | Judah Loew ben Bezalel, approximately 1525–1609. Tiferet Yisrael. | Judah Loew ben Bezalel, approximately 1525–1609. Tiferet Yisrael. English.

Title: Tiferet Yisrael : translation and commentary / the Maharal of Prague (Harav Yehuda Loew) ; translated by Ramon Widmonte.

Other titles: Tiferet Yisrael. English

Description: First edition. | Jerusalem : Urim Publications, [2017–]

Identifiers: LCCN 2016039022 | ISBN 9789655241471 (hardback)

Subjects: LCSH: Talmud Torah (Judaism) | Commandments, Six hundred and thirteen. | Judah Loew ben Bezalel, approximately 1525-1609. Tiferet Yisrael. | BISAC: RELIGION / Judaism / Sacred Writings. | RELIGION / Judaism / Kabbalah & Mysticism.

Classification: LCC BM71.J8313 2017 | DDC 296.3–dc23 LC record available at https://lccn.loc.gov/2016039022

CONTENTS

Commentary

Appendix

DEDICATIONS

In loving memory of

our special Dad and Zaida

WILFRED SCHNAID

who lived for his children and grandchildren.
We love and miss you every day,
you are and forever will be
in our hearts.

BONNIE, ALAN, KIRA, TALIA
and JACOB POLLARD

In memory of

CAROLINE JANE KATZ

beloved wife, mother,
grandmother, sister and friend.

Through your spirituality you have merited
that your children and grandchildren
follow in the path of Hashem.

In honour of

our 44th Wedding Anniversary

Wishing you strength and success in all your endeavours

JUDY and MARTIN MORITZ

The MAHARAL OF PRAGUE championed the fierce, passionate love of HASHEM and the Jewish people. In his leadership roles, he placed this love at the forefront of every deed, no matter the personal cost, and became known as an unwavering standard bearer of integrity and authenticity.

Our beloved GREG ROSENBERG, *z"l*, מרדכי בן שליט, was also driven by an unbounded *ahavat Hashem* and *ahavat Yisrael*; placing all his energies, creativity and abilities in the service of Hashem and the Jewish community.

May his memory continue to be a blessing, inspiration and example for all who follow in his stead.

Fondly remembered,
ROS ROSENBERG *&* family

In loving memory of

GLYNNIS SHER, גיטל בת אליהו

and

Rabbi MOSHE SHER, הרב משה יונה בן יעקב

In loving memory of

ברוך בן אליהו שמואל, Basil Wunsh

Our dear father and grandfather.
A man of extreme intellect, ethics
and the embodiment of a klal mensch.
Your life and example continue to inspire us.

Emma, Laurence, Daniel, Alexa and David

To our parents and grandparents

Michael and Gloria Hoff,
Ivan and Linda Stone,
Rafael and Janice Melmed

who continue to guide us and allow our
family to thrive in our Yiddishkeit.

Damon, Robyn, Sara, Leah, Avigayil,
Michal and Tamar Hoff.

In memory of

my late grandfather

Joseph Sindelman

לעילוי נשמת
אליהו בן משה יוסף

*

In memory of
the late RONNIE ROSEN

Stan, Claudette and family

*

In loving memory of
our dear MOTHER and BOBBA DESRE

Love
Mark, Jacqui, Sarit, Tali and Yakira Bregman

*

In loving memory of
our beloved parents
LESLIE KAPLAN (Eliezer ben Tuvia HaCohen)
CHARLIE KRUGER (Elchanan ben Zorach) and
FANNY KRUGER (Feigel bat Moshe HaCohen)

*

Dedicated to the memories of
MEIR BEN SHIMON HALEVI, *z"l*
and ELIYAHU BEN YISROEL, *z"l*

*

We dedicate this *sefer* to our children
YONATAN SHLOMO and TOVA MALKA

Ilan and Janine Rabinowitz

*

לעילוי נשמת
ישראל יוסף בן הלל אהרון ובשה אסתר

*

In loving memory of
SHARON BERENICE DIAMOND
שרה בת יצחק יעקב וולד

*

THE SASSOON FOUNDATION

In memory of NEIL GLATT, *z"l*
יהי זכרו ברוך

Melanie and Martin Glatt

*

In loving memory of
our late father, father-in-law and grandfather
SELWYN LIONEL PRICE

*

With *shevach* and *hoda'ah*
to *HaKadosh Baruch Hu*

Sean, Leila, Azriel and Chaya Sara Lederman

*

Dedicated to
JACQUI FELDMAN
who had a great love, drive, understanding
and respect for TALMUD TORAH.

Her loving family,
Alon, Kim, Solomon and Saphira Feldman

*

In loving memory of
JILLIAN PAUWEN, *z"l*
You taught us the value of being a mensch
and all who knew you were touched by your
warmth, kindness and integrity.
לע"נ יוכבד בת אדל הכהן ז"ל

*

לעילוי נשמת
חיים ברוך ב"ר הירש יהודה ליב ע"ה

*

For *Kavod HaTorah*
and for *achdus* among KLAL YISRAEL

*

L'iluy nishmat
DEVORAH BAT ABBA HA'LEVI

*

לזכר נשמת
יעקב בן עזריאל

*

Dedicated to AHARON BEN BRACHA

Dedicated to our children
YAKIRA and GADIEL SHEPHERD
May you always be inspired by our rich heritage.

*

In loving honour to the *iluy neshama* of
AVRAHAM BEN PERETZ, STANLEY FROOM

*

Dedicated to the memory of
Rabbi A.C. GOLDFEIN,
who was my spiritual mentor for many years and was also
the one who introduced me to the Maharal's works.
יהי זכרו ברוך

Adrian and Elana Chiger

*

In loving memory of
BERNARD FRIEDMAN, Dov ben Ya'akov HaKohen, *z"l*,
an old-school lawyer, family man and friend to many.
He instinctively lived Torah values and lived his life to the full.

*

In loving memory of
STEVEN and TAMARA WIDMONTE
JEFFREY and GREG GRUNEBAUM
SELWYN and RABBI MICHAEL ORELOWITZ
MARC WEINBERG

*

Dedicated to Brocha Bat Shlomo Yisrael ז"ל,
BERYL GOLDMAN,
our precious and beloved Wife, Mother and Nana, who had
a heart of gold, a woman filled with compassion, endless
care and good advice, chesed, deep emunah and love.

In our hearts forever.

*From her husband Solly; children, Sharyn, Andy, Earle,
Jonny and Marianne; and grandchildren, Joshua,
Saul, Ben, Adam, Asher, Yakira and Jasmine.*

*

In loving memory of
YAAKOV BEN CHAIM LEIB and MIRIAM BAT YOSEF

APPROBATIONS

Rabbi MOSHEH LICHTENSTEIN שליט"א,
Rosh Yeshivah of Yeshivat Har Etzion

RABBI JUDAH LOEW, the MAHARAL OF PRAGUE, is one of the seminal figures in the field of Jewish thought. Although primarily known to a popular audience through the provinces of folklore, MAHARAL was a rabbinic leader of great stature and a thinker who made a major contribution to the field of Jewish thought. From RAV KOOK to RAV HUTNER and their followers, contemporary thinkers continue to draw upon his work, to engage in dialogue with his ideas and to be influenced by his approach to the Jewish religious experience.

Several characteristics combine to make MAHARAL's work so rewarding of study and his contribution to Jewish religious thought so interesting and important. MAHARAL was a transitional figure who lived at the threshold of the modern world, yet whose literary and spiritual roots were in medieval Jewish philosophy. Active in 16th century Central Europe in a traditional setting, both culturally and philosophically, his work is informed by a creative tension between the old and the new.

A major characteristic of MAHARAL's thought is its focus upon the particular Jewish element within the religious life. There are Jewish philosophers who mainly deal with universal questions, common to believers of all faiths and stripes. While their treatment presents the perspective of the Torah, the dilemmas and issues that they raise relate to the universal religious experience. These include discussions of issues such as faith and belief, theodicy, prayer and many other such questions of universal nature. What is common to most of these discussions is that they focus upon the individual and his encounter with God as an individual. Other thinkers, in contrast, emphasize the particularly Jewish element, and focus upon those expressions of faith which are unique to us, either in the life of the individual such as mitzvoth or Jewish holidays or through our collective relationship with the KBH as the God of Israel.

MAHARAL clearly belongs in the second category. His major works revolve around the Jewish experience, a fact that can be gleaned even by a cursory glance at some of their titles (Tiferet Yisrael, Netzach Yisrael and not Lonely Man of Faith), and deal extensively with the Jewish historical experience and festivals (Pesach, Purim, Chanukah and Tisha B'Av all have dedicated works) as well as the individual's religious life in its Jewish context.

If one were to add the observation that systematic medieval Jewish philosophy tended to focus upon the universal issues, as any reader of MAIMONIDES's *Guide to the Perplexed* is well aware, comprehensive works of Jewish philosophy that related to the more particular elements were in short supply. Thus, MAHARAL's work fulfilled, and continues to fulfill a real need, by providing analysis and insight into those areas of ritual and observance that the rhythm of Jewish religious life revolves around, as well as addressing universal dilemmas from within a very particular Jewish context.

No less important for an understanding of MAHARAL's achievement is a recognition of the novelty of the sources that he placed at the center of his oeuvre. Classical Jewish philosophy was based upon a dialogue and/or confrontation with rationalistic philosophy and its framework of reference was either biblical or philosophical. Medrash and other sources of classic rabbinical thought from Chazal were utilized sporadically and were treated to isolated observations and insight. Be it the Kuzari or the Guide, this is the general state of affairs in MAHARAL's predecessors. MAHARAL, though, placed Chazal and their literature at the center of his work. He made massive use of Medrash and Agaddah and made them into the cornerstone of his writings. Thousands upon thousands of Medrashim are quoted and discussed by MAHARAL; by doing so, he not only mined a rich source of material for valuable insights, but he also transformed Medrash from secondary to primary material, worthy of evaluation and treatment in its own right.

Thus, great benefit can be derived from study of MAHARAL's work. The contemporary Jewish learner and worshipper, although living his life in a different historical setting, can still learn a great deal by confronting the issues that MAHARAL analyzed and by contemplating the answers that he offered. The fact that his work remains a vibrant part of the contemporary Jewish religious scene is a testimony to its relevance and vitality.

The blessed initiative of Rabbi RAMON WIDMONTE, a dear and beloved student of mine, to present MAHARAL's thought to the English-reading public is a great service that will provide the intelligent and interested reader a window into the thought of this great thinker. Rabbi WIDMONTE is to be commended and thanked for initiating this project and for engaging in the difficult and often frustrating task of translation and organization. His reward, undoubtedly, were the many hours that he spent in MAHARAL's company and the depths to which he was exposed by virtue of his tireless work.

As the reader will see for himself, Rabbi WIDMONTE has succeeded in the mission that he took upon himself and has done an excellent job of presenting the material to the reader in a clear and lucid manner. This is not surprising since he is both a serious learner and an experienced educator. These qualities, combined with his personal seriousness and deep introspection which have made him into a true man of faith, provide him with the necessary tools to succeed in this task. May the KBH grant him the strength and wisdom to continue producing such works alongside his wonderful educational work, and may He provide the WIDMONTE family with the bounty of His divine blessings.

Rabbi Yehoshua Hartman שליט"א,
Author of the Machon Yerushalayim editions of the works of the Maharal

בס"ד, יום ב, ו' חשון, התשע"ג

לכבוד ידידי היקר, מרביץ תורה לרבים,
הרב ישראל זלמן ווידמונט שליט"א

בנועם מיוחד קבלתי את הידיעה שהנך עומד הכן להוציא לאור כרך ראשון של תפארת ישראל למרנא ורבנא אור עולם המהר"ל זיע"א, מלווה בהערות והארות ומקבילות משאר ספריו הקדושים. מפאת לחץ הזמן לא עלה בידי לעבור על כל הספר, אלא רק כפי מסת הפנאי, אך הקצת שראיתי הוא ראיה על טיב עבודתך המשובחה, המענג את הנפש. ניכרת היטב היגיעה הרבה שלך, כי רק על ידה היה ניתן להגיש ספר נפלא כזה לקהל הלומדים.

המיוחד בעבודתך הוא שהצלחת לבאר את דברי המהר"ל באופן השוה לכל נפש. הסתייעת בעבודת הקודש שלך, שהנך מרביץ תורה לעדרים בק"ק יוהנסבורג, ומתוך כך הגעת למידה זאת, לבאר דברי המהר"ל למבקשים והצמאים. ולא רק זאת, אלא רשמת טבלאות והשוואות מתוך דברי המהר"ל מיניה וביה, ובכך עלה בידך להמחיש את הדברים. וכבר השריש המהר"ל בספרו גור אריה [ויקרא פי"א אות ג] "שצריך להראות לתלמידו לחוש העין, כדי שיהיה בקי בהן". והנני לברכך מקרב לב שבעזרת ה' יתברך תמשיך ותתמיד ביתר שאת וביתר עוז להדיר ספר זה עד גמירא, ויאותו רבים לאור הגדול הגנוז בהם, שבין בתריו נתבאר נוראותיה של תורה ומעלתה העליונה והנבדלת.

הכותב וחותם לכבוד לומדי התורה
יהושע הרטמן

Rabbi Yehoshua Hartman שליט"א,

Author of the Machon Yerushalayim editions of the works of the Maharal

Translation by the Author

BS"D

Monday, 6 Cheshvan 5773

To my dear friend, disseminator of Torah to the public,
Rabbi Widmonte שליט"א,

It is with special pleasure that I was informed that you are about to publish the first volume of the *Tiferet Yisrael*, authored by our Master and Teacher, light of the world, the Maharal, may his merit protect us, accompanied with comments from his other holy works.

Due to time pressures I could not go over the entire work, but the parts that I saw attest to the praiseworthy nature of your work which is a delight to the soul. Your great toil is visible – which is the only way you could present such a wonderful work as this to the learning public.

What is unique in your work is that you have succeeded in clarifying the words of the Maharal in a manner that benefits everyone. You have been aided in this holy work, since you disseminate Torah to students in Johannesburg through which you reached the stage of explaining the words of the Maharal to those who seek them and thirst for them.

Moreover, you created tables and comparisons from within the Maharal's works and you succeeded in making these ideas tangible. The Maharal already planted this idea in his work Gur Aryeh [Vayikra 11:3*] where he wrote, "One must demonstrate to one's students using the visual sense so that he will become an expert in the subject matter."

I bless you from within my heart, that with Hashem's help (may He be Blessed) you may continue and you will be consistent, with great power to complete this work and that the public will benefit from the hidden light concealed herein, for it contains the wonders of the Torah and its transcendent and elevated level.

One who writes and signs for the honor of those who learn Torah,
Yehoshua Hartman

* *In regular editions this is Vayikra 11:1.*

Chief Rabbi Dr. Warren Goldstein שליט"א,
Chief Rabbi of South Africa

בס"ד

Any community dedicated to heaven will endure forever
TALMUD, Ethics of the Fathers 4:14

כל כנסיה שהיא לשם שמים סופה להתקיים
פרקי אבות ד:יד

19 July 2011
17 Tammuz 5771

To whom it may concern

I was delighted to receive Rabbi Ramon Widmonte's manuscript which elucidates one of the great books of the Maharal of Prague, תפארת ישראל. I perused the document and was most impressed with the important contribution it makes to understanding תפארת ישראל.

The philosophical depth and the vast conceptual framework of the Maharal make a deep and true understanding of the Maharal's writings a serious challenge even for a seasoned scholar. Rabbi Widmonte's manuscript sets out very clearly the flow of the Maharal's ideas, as well as how they connect to the Maharal's broader philosophy and ideas. The unique combination of the text and diagrams of Rabbi Widmonte's manuscript illuminate תפארת ישראל in a comprehensive and excellent manner.

Rabbi Widmonte is a respected and admired member of the South African Rabbinate and it therefore gives me great pleasure to wish him Hashem's abundant blessings for much success with the publication of this manuscript. May this work bring the light of the Maharal's Torah into the world, and in this merit may Hashem bless us all.

Yours sincerely

Rabbi Warren Goldstein

Office of the Chief Rabbi | Union of Orthodox Synagogues of South Africa
58 Oaklands Road, Orchards 2192 Johannesburg, South Africa | P.O. Box 46559, Orange Grove 2119
T +27 11 640 9669 | F +27 11 485 1497 | E office@chiefrabbi.co.za

Rabbi Avraham Tanzer שליט"א
Rosh Yeshiva of Yeshiva College

בס"ד

YESHIVA COLLEGE
The Torah School of Excellence

Playschool | Pre-Primary | Primary | Girls High | Boys High

1 August 2013 / 25 Av 5773

To our dear friends

Rabbi Ramon Widmonte, one of the Talmedai Chachamim, who serve our Kehillah, has shown me the manuscript of his work on the Maharal's Teferes Yisroel.

Rabbi Widmonte has translated the Maharal's words, as well as writing a commentary on the more challenging sections in the Maharal's thoughts.

The Maharal of Prague was a seminal figure in the world of Jewish thought, whose ideas have served as a springboard for many of the major currents of mussar, chassidus and *machsheves Yisroel* (Jewish thought).

Moreinu HaRav Yehudah Loew of Prague, known as Maharal Me-Prague, lived over 400 years ago, from 1512 to 1609. He was a contemporary of Rav Yosef Karo, author of the *Shulchan Aruch*, and the master of Torah's secrets, Rav Yitzchok Luria, *Ari'zal*. Maharal taught a metaphysical system that draws upon the Zohar and later Kabbalistic works. Using that method, his explanations of Talmudic and Midrashic homiletics are systematic, consistent and relevant. Maharal's teachings have provided a framework for authentic Jewish philosophy down to our generation.

One of the major novel approaches that Rabbi Widmonte has taken is to create a method of synthesizing the Maharal's thought and summarizing them, utilizing summaries and graphics devices. These are elements which assist majorly with acquiring an overall understanding of how the Maharal's Torah flows together to become the magnificent edifice of Torah that it is.

Rabbi Widmonte has played a major educational role here on the Yeshiva College campus within the school, Bnei Akiva and the adult community and his pedagogic skills are evident in the work before us which should be a tremendous aid to all those who wish to learn and teach the Maharal. Additionally, the material he has made available for educators, will be a great help to teachers and their students.

May Hashem bless this work and all those who learn it that they should attain a deeper understanding of the Maharal's Torah and grow in their Yiras Hashem and Ahavas Hashem.

We congratulate Rabbi Widmonte on his important contribution in helping us to understand the words of the Holy Maharal. May Hashem bless him and his family with every Bracha and Hatzlacha.

With warm personal regards

RABBI AVRAHAM TANZER
Rosh Yeshiva

ACKNOWLEDGEMENTS

My thanks are due first and foremost to Hashem who has graced me with the opportunity to be amongst those who are enriched by the *beit midrash*; who both "dwell in the home of Hashem" and also "visit His sanctuary." מה אשיב לה' כל תגמולוהי עלי.

I bear immense gratitude to my teachers who imbued me with the knowledge and inspiration to learn and teach Torah – my *Rashei Yeshivah*, Rabbi Yehuda Amital, *z"l*, and Rabbi Aharon Lichtenstein, *z"l*. At the time of going to press, the Jewish people received the bitter news of Rav Aharon's passing and as I write here, I have had to change the notation after his name from "*shlit"a*" to "*z"l*," the most devastating change this manuscript has required. I have been inspired and guided "by his light" for twenty years now, and my world and that of so many others is now darkened immensely: it was my hope and prayer to be able to present this volume to him, but now he will read it *miShamayim*. I would also like to thank my Rav, Rabbi Mosheh Lichtenstein, *shlit"a*, and all my teachers in Yeshivat Har Etzion. The more I learn and grow, the more I appreciate their wisdom, guidance and being.

I am also grateful for everything that the Maharal, *z"l*, Rav Hutner, *z"l*, and להבחל"ח Rav Hartman, *shlit"a*, have contributed to my life and this work. Rav Hartman, in particular, has spent time encouraging me in the arduous process of publishing a book as well as making himself available to aid me in understanding the Maharal – all this is deeply appreciated.

I thank my family for their support: my parents who supported me for many years in following the path of learning and teaching Torah; and in particular, I thank my wife, Julie, תבלח"ט, the bastion of our shared life who has supported me and offered valuable guidance at every step of the journey. I also thank my daughter, Batya, and my sons Yonatan and Aryeh, יבלח"ט, for their patience with me while I teach and write. I pray that Hashem bless our family in all ways and enable us to grow closer to Him, to one another, *Am Yisrael* and all of humanity.

Any fault or error is of course my own and I kindly ask any reader with a constructive criticism to contact me on the website, www.ravramon.net, in order to afford me with the opportunity to correct these errors.

My thanks go to all the wonderful people at Urim Publications – Tzvi Mauer, Michal Alatin, Batsheva Pomerantz, my editor, and Ariel Walden. Shoshana Hurwitz and Marc Sherman prepared the indices with great effort and attention to detail. Their care, efforts, devotion, professionalism and desire to produce holy works which sound and appear graceful are a testament to them all. Batsheva's lavish attention to detail has impacted on its readability and quality immensely. Additionally, Jonathan Cohen's masterful work on the graphic summaries has transformed my original basic ideas into works of art and thought.

Many people enabled the publication process of this work through generous financial support and I am deeply grateful that they have chosen to invest in spreading the words of the Maharal.

It is my fervent hope that this work provides the general public with a view into the Torah's depths and excite those who learn it to further and deepen their Torah study and to strive to reach the pinnacle of all – to bond with Hashem in awe and love.

The Maharal's Torah, powerful ideas and striking words have changed my life immeasurably for the better, I hope he does the same for you.

I end with a paraphrasing of the prayer of the Maharal himself at the end of his Introduction.

ובכן התפלה ... שיהיו לרצון אמרי פי לפני כל קוראי ויורני דרך אמת ויסעדני בימין צדקו נצח אמן.

This is my prayer to Hashem . . . that He will guide my pen so that my words will find favor before you, dear reader, and that Hashem will teach me the path of truth and will sustain me with His right hand of righteousness, forever. Amen.

OVERVIEW & DIAGRAMMATIC SUMMARIES

Introduction and Chapters 1–9 as a whole

Human beings are made in Hashem's image and thus Hashem wishes to connect with each of us, no matter how small we are in our own eyes. This connection is our life's purpose and will encompass every part of our physical and spiritual life. Each Jewish person, in particular, can achieve this connection through Torah learning and performing mitzvot, both of which should stem from a love for Hashem; and the nation, as a whole, achieves its connection through these too. Such a bond is due to the *process* we undergo of reaching for a relationship with Hashem.

Introduction

The best way to bond with Hashem is through Torah learning undertaken out of love for Hashem. Conversely, the only way one can understand Torah is by having a bond of love with Hashem. This creates a virtuous cycle: more love of Hashem aids one in learning Torah better which enables one to bond with Hashem more deeply and so on. A person involved in such a cycle will be guided in his understanding and communication of Torah, and even if he errs, Hashem will aid him in perceiving and correcting his error.

Chapter 1

Each creation in the world has a unique activity which expresses its unique destiny. Humanity's unique actions *should be* the learning of Torah and performance of mitzvot. However, unlike the rest of the animate and inanimate world, our essential actions are not automatic, because we have free choice. Since the Jewish nation is not embedded in nature, it resonates innately with the Torah and mitzvot which are also above nature. The Jewish people has the latent potential necessary for the fulfillment of Torah and mitzvot; this potential can only exist in people who are not at any extreme in life.

Chapter 2

A person can rise above his/her purely natural existence through mitzvot. The best example of this is *milah*, circumcision. It is performed on the eighth day because the natural world is symbolized by the number seven (seven days of creation and seven perspectives to space/time). Hashem purposefully left the natural world unfinished so that we could partner with Him in perfection and so that we could transcend our purely physical aspects.

Chapter 3

Humans bear infinite potential and we should live life in reaching for perfection. We toil in converting that infinite potential to actuality through the choice to do good, which is the only way to satiate our souls. Human *choice* (even if we don't actually reach all of our goals) is the ultimate barometer of who we are, and although perfecting the physical and societal realms of life are both necessary and important in and of themselves, the crown jewel is perfecting society and the world through Torah learning and sharing.

Chapter 4

There are two categories of mitzvot: prohibitions and *mitzvot aseh*. There are two parts of physical reality: humanity (made in G-d's image with the choice to actualize that) and the rest of the natural world (bounded by the Sun as a representative of time). The two categories of mitzvot mirror the structure of reality: the prohibitions maintain the preset moral order, which is echoed by the sun which maintains the order of the natural world through time; on the other hand, the *mitzvot aseh* allow a person to perfect him or herself and thus become a true reflection of G-d's image. Thus, the four general results of proper mitzvah observance are: they actualize one's potential, allow one to rise above the natural world, refine one and allow one to bond with Hashem.

Chapter 5

Mitzvot ultimately do benefit individuals and the Jewish nation even though being obligated in more mitzvot does automatically entail more scope for failing to observe those mitzvot. The reason that the benefits outweigh the disadvantages is that before Hashem obligates anyone in a mitzvah, He adds a concomitant strength and capacity to that person. Thus, having more mitzvot must mean that the Jewish people have been given extra capacity to fulfill them; and it is this capacity and depth which always benefits us. Additionally, since Hashem runs the world through fairness and justice, the only way a person can grow is if he or she achieves that growth independently, thus there is no way that we could achieve greatness without the risk of failure.

Chapter 6

When we say (in Chapter 5) that mitzvot benefit a person, we don't mean that this is the *reason* that Hashem gave us the mitzvot. Rather, Hashem decreed that we do the mitzvot because it is just and correct for us to fulfill them. Now, since Hashem is good, everything He does results in goodness and thus the mitzvot definitely benefit us, but this is a subsequent side-benefit. Even mitzvot which appear to flow from Hashem's mercy on humans or animals actually flow from His attribute of Justice. Ultimately, when a person performs a mitzvah, he or she is replacing his/her own set of motivations with Hashem's transcendent mindset; this binds one to Hashem, even without an understanding of the mitzvah (although deeper understanding deepens the bond).

Chapter 7

Mitzvot and all their details have reasons. The general reason for all mitzvot is that a human adopts Hashem's transcendent system of thinking and actions. This system replaces one's natural desires and binds one to Hashem. *Mitzvot aseh* allow a person to grow beyond their current state to reflect his/her being in G-d's "Form" by self-actualization.

Chapter 8

Mitzvot do have positive practical consequences; however, those consequences are not the *reason* for the mitzvot. Rather, the mitzvot are part of Hashem's transcendent system whereby a person assimilates G-d's will. A person should never perform mitzvot in order to accrue practical benefits, but to bond with Hashem.

Chapter 9

The consequence of doing mitzvot is closeness to Hashem, which is the greatest possible pleasure and success. We term this, inaccurately, "reward." The most abject failure and pain is separation from Hashem, which can be the direct consequence of a person's actions if that person chooses to do evil. We term this, inaccurately, "punishment." Performing *mitzvot aseh* enables the creation of a bond with Hashem, whilst violating prohibitions distances one from Hashem. A person is worthy of bonding with Hashem because each person is made in Hashem's image.

The components of the mitzvah of learning Torah

Tighter bond leads to better Torah study

Passionate immersion in Torah

Abstract, disconnected understanding of Torah

PRACTICAL APPLICATIONS OF THIS IDEA

e.g. The prayer said on entering the *Beit Midrash*

Two challenges in learning Torah:

1 Understanding truly
2 Communicating the truth

When one intends to bond with Hashem in Torah learning, Hashem ensures one avoids these challenges.

e.g. The *b'rachah* said on the mitzvah of learning Torah = "to immerse oneself"

One learns in order to be immersed in a relationship with Hashem through the Torah.

e.g. The "Reason" for the destruction of the First Temple

N'darim 81a
The reason for the destruction = Not saying the blessings before learning Torah.

There is no bonding with Hashem during one's Torah learning

The "Reason" for something both brings it into existence and maintains its existence.
E.g., the root is the reason for the tree.

Hashem is the "Reason" for the Torah

With a bond, even if one errs, Hashem remains the reason for the Torah and He will help one repair the error.

Without a bond with Hashem in one's Torah learning, one lacks the "Reason" for the Torah and it cannot continue to exist, thus it fades.

In the First Temple, despite the fact that they learned Torah, they were not bonding with Hashem through the learning, thus their Torah faded and they disintegrated morally.

A sage who doesn't bond with Hashem through his Torah is unable to create students who are sages, since the students connect to the sage only and not to Hashem.

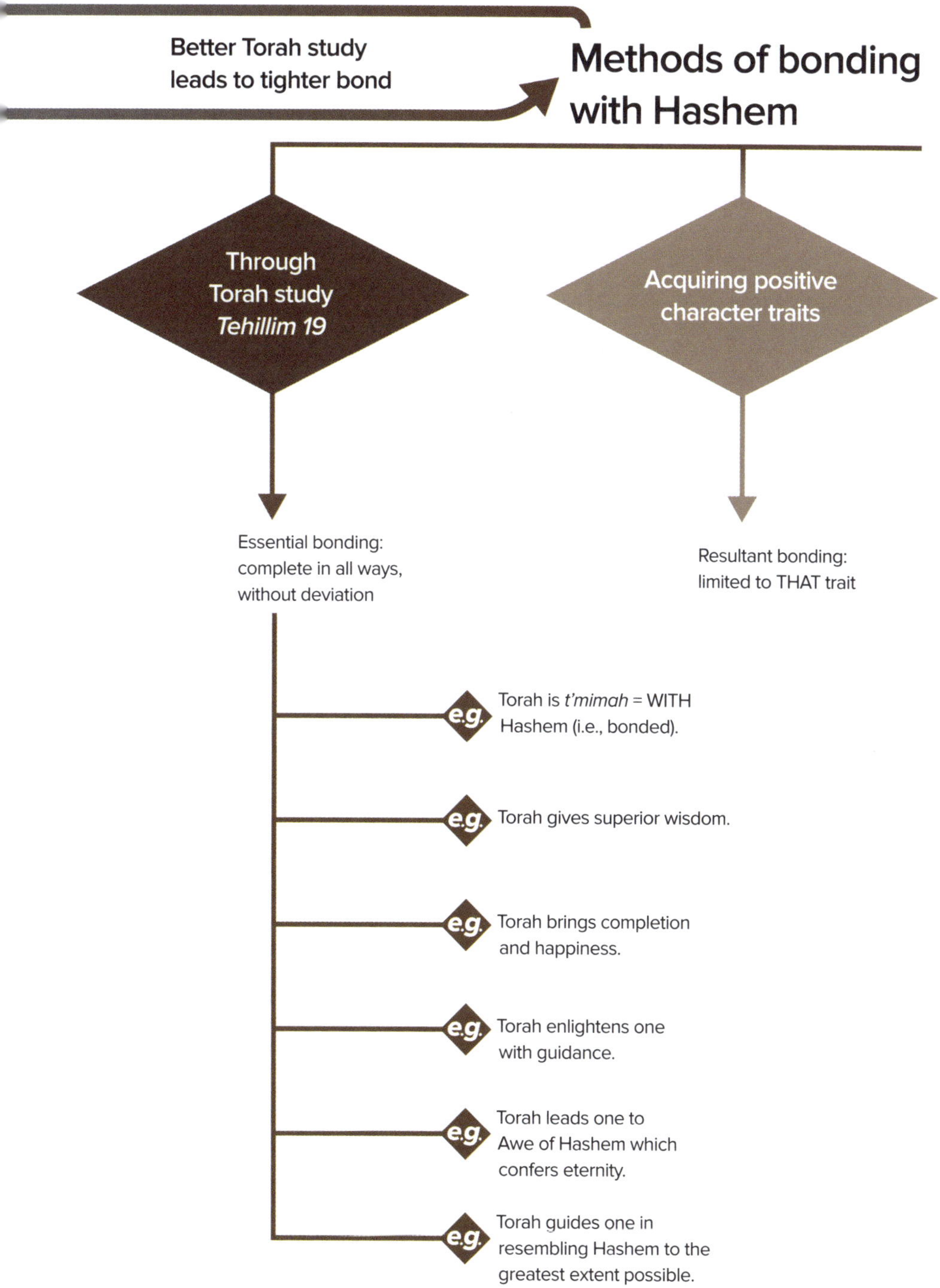
Better Torah study
leads to tighter bond
Methods of bonding
with Hashem
Through
Torah study
Tehillim 19
Acquiring positive
character traits
Essential bonding:
complete in all ways,
without deviation
Resultant bonding:
limited to THAT trait
e.g.
Torah is *t'mimah* = WITH
Hashem (i.e., bonded).
e.g.
Torah gives superior wisdom.
e.g.
Torah brings completion
and happiness.
e.g.
Torah enlightens one
with guidance.
e.g.
Torah leads one to
Awe of Hashem which
confers eternity.
e.g.
Torah guides one in
resembling Hashem to the
greatest extent possible.

Each creation has an essential uniqueness

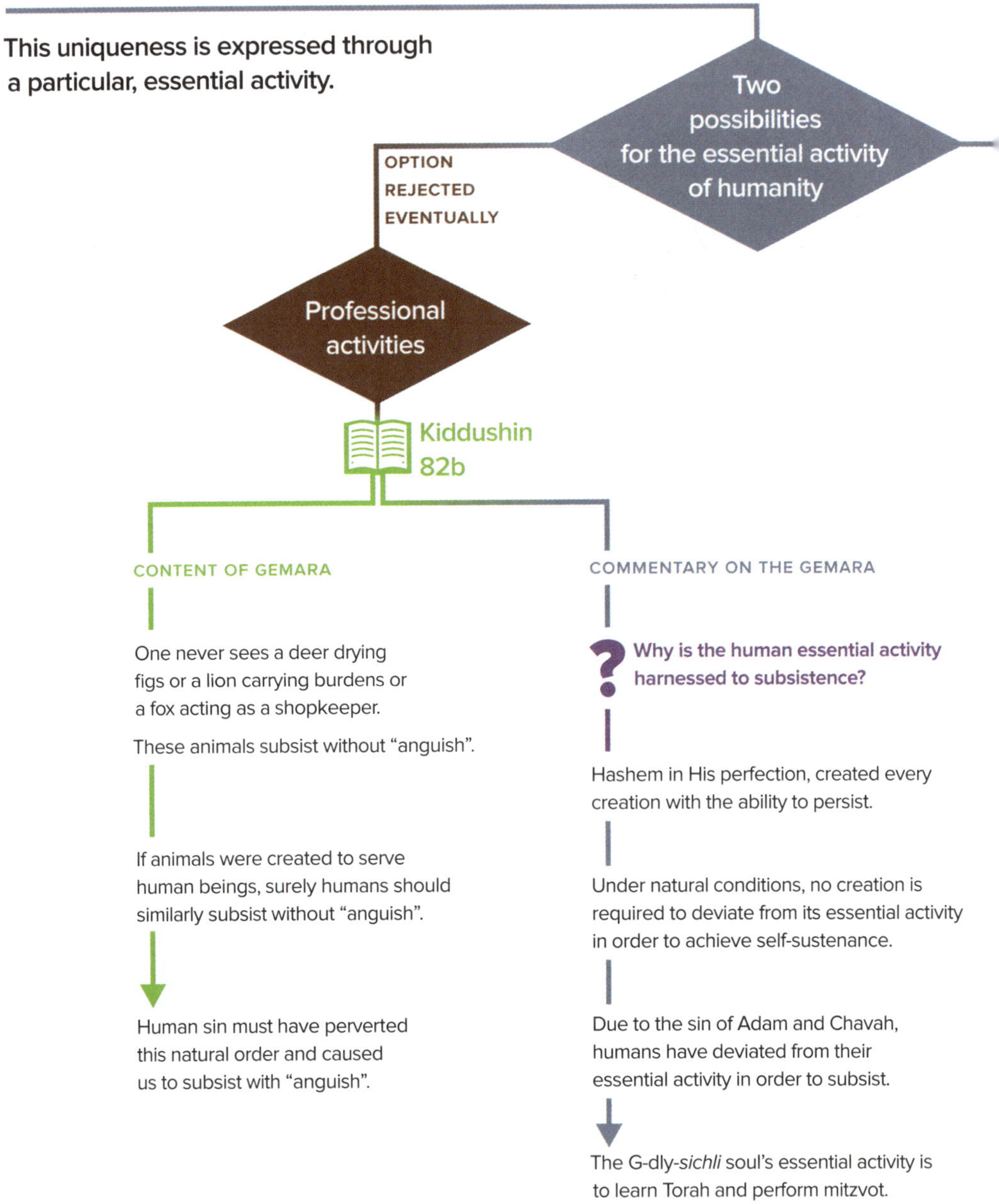

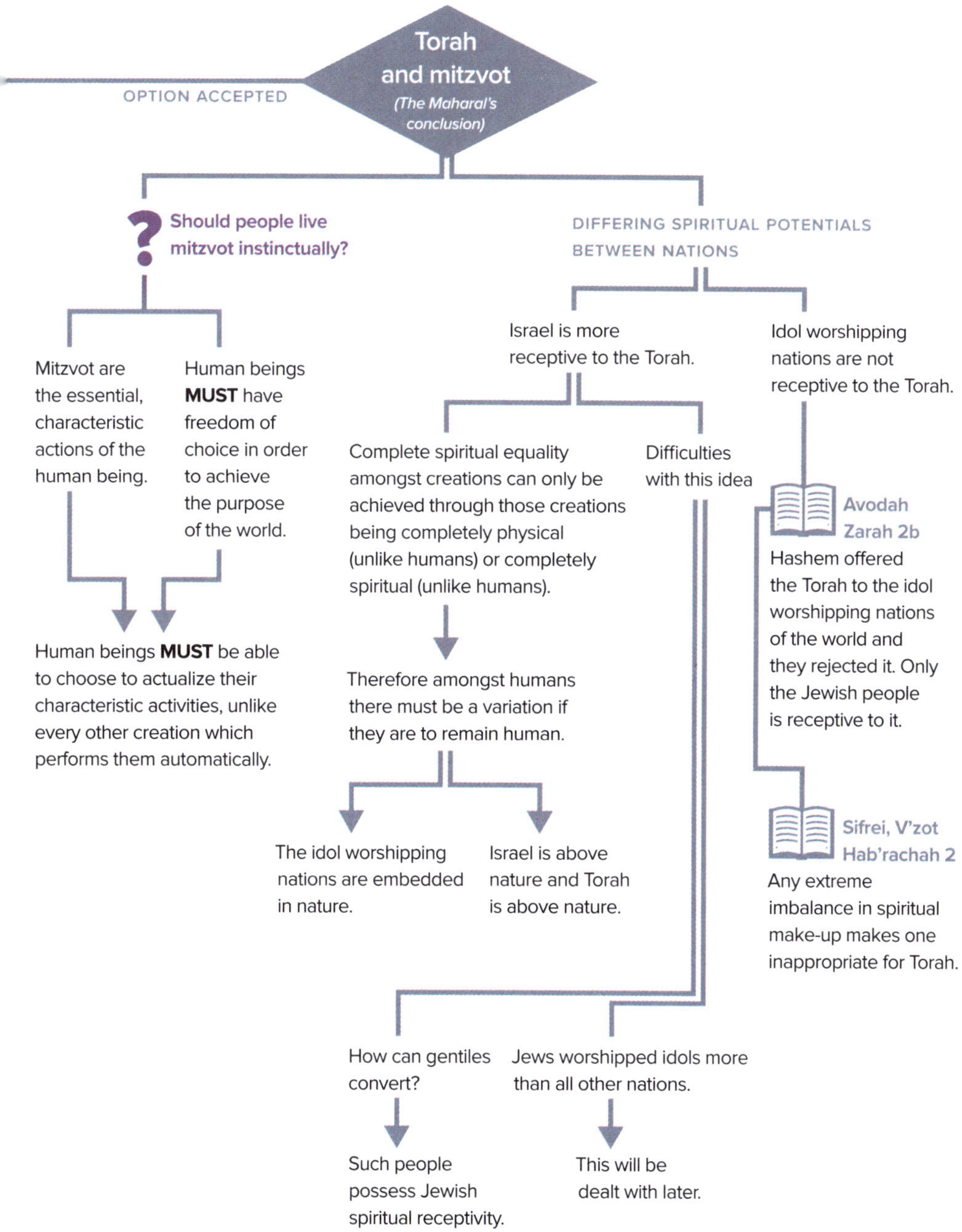
Torah and mitzvot
(The Maharal's conclusion)
OPTION ACCEPTED
Should people live mitzvot instinctually?
Mitzvot are the essential, characteristic actions of the human being.
Human beings MUST have freedom of choice in order to achieve the purpose of the world.
Human beings MUST be able to choose to actualize their characteristic activities, unlike every other creation which performs them automatically.
DIFFERING SPIRITUAL POTENTIALS BETWEEN NATIONS
Israel is more receptive to the Torah.
Idol worshipping nations are not receptive to the Torah.
Complete spiritual equality amongst creations can only be achieved through those creations being completely physical (unlike humans) or completely spiritual (unlike humans).
Therefore amongst humans there must be a variation if they are to remain human.
The idol worshipping nations are embedded in nature.
Israel is above nature and Torah is above nature.
Difficulties with this idea
How can gentiles convert?
Such people possess Jewish spiritual receptivity.
Jews worshipped idols more than all other nations.
This will be dealt with later.
Avodah Zarah 2b
Hashem offered the Torah to the idol worshipping nations of the world and they rejected it. Only the Jewish people is receptive to it.
Sifrei, V'zot Hab'rachah 2
Any extreme imbalance in spiritual make-up makes one inappropriate for Torah.

The nature of mitzvot: A general overview

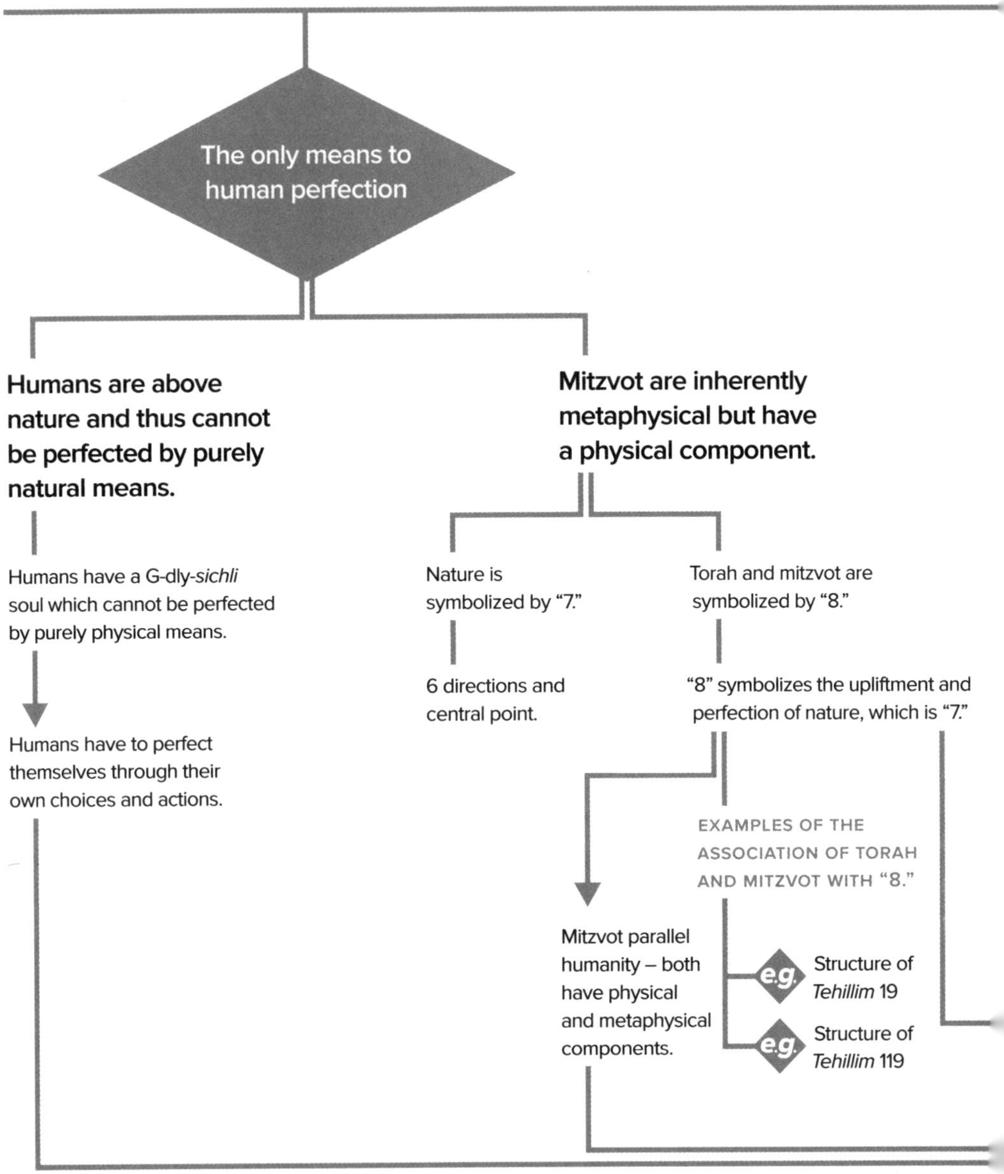

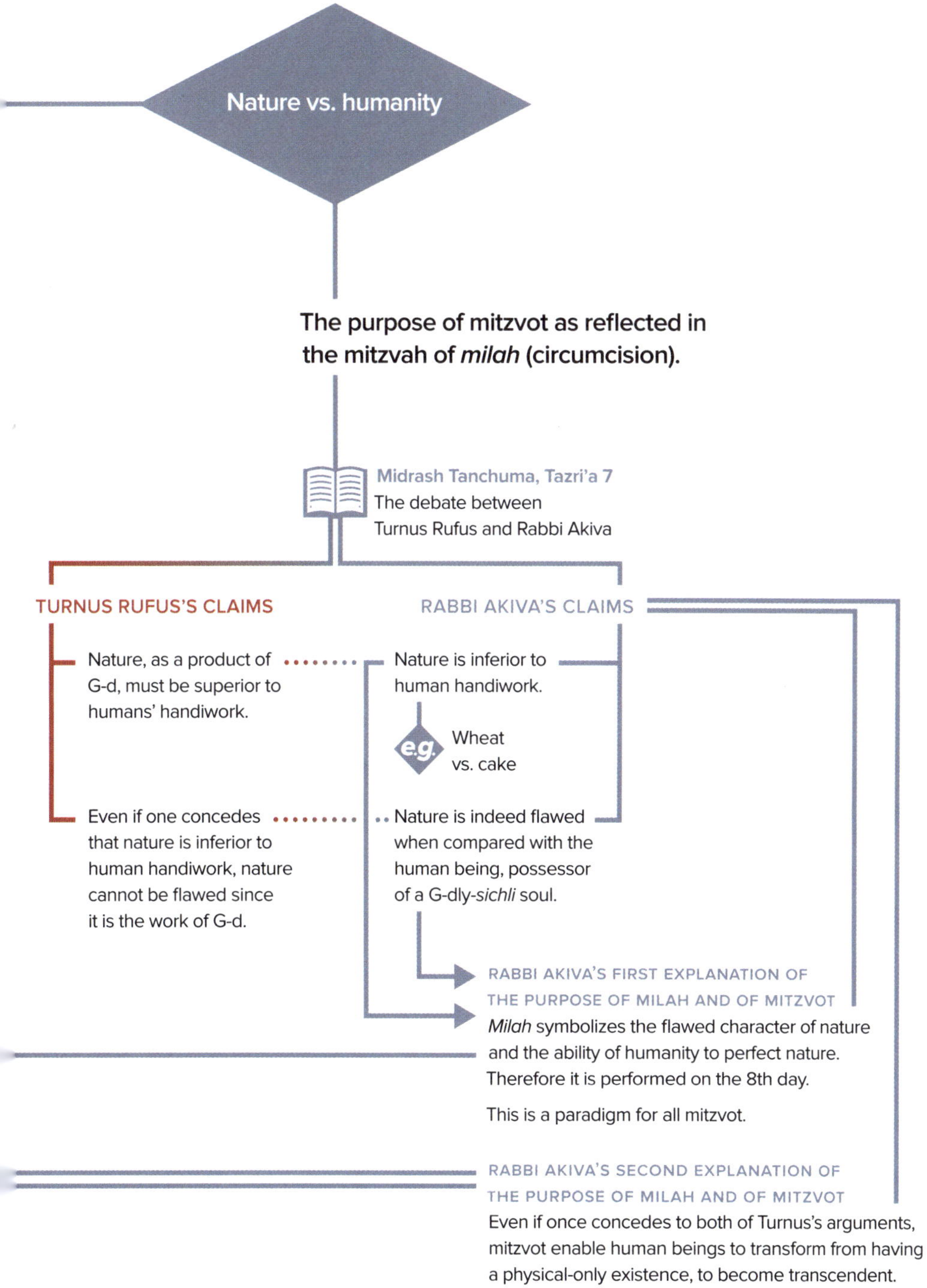
Nature vs. humanity
The purpose of mitzvot as reflected in the mitzvah of *milah* (circumcision).
Midrash Tanchuma, Tazri'a 7
The debate between Turnus Rufus and Rabbi Akiva
TURNUS RUFUS'S CLAIMS
Nature, as a product of G-d, must be superior to humans' handiwork.
Even if one concedes that nature is inferior to human handiwork, nature cannot be flawed since it is the work of G-d.
RABBI AKIVA'S CLAIMS
Nature is inferior to human handiwork.
e.g.
Wheat vs. cake
Nature is indeed flawed when compared with the human being, possessor of a G-dly-*sichli* soul.
RABBI AKIVA'S FIRST EXPLANATION OF THE PURPOSE OF MILAH AND OF MITZVOT
Milah symbolizes the flawed character of nature and the ability of humanity to perfect nature. Therefore it is performed on the 8th day.
This is a paradigm for all mitzvot.
RABBI AKIVA'S SECOND EXPLANATION OF THE PURPOSE OF MILAH AND OF MITZVOT
Even if once concedes to both of Turnus's arguments, mitzvot enable human beings to transform from having a physical-only existence, to become transcendent.

Diagrammatic summary: Chapter 3

Living life as reaching for potential

The need for effort

Humanity = potential perfection

EVERYTHING ELSE

Other physical creations

No potential perfection to be actualized

Animals are called *b'h mah (b'heimah)* = everything is already in it.

Angels and other inhabitants of the transcendent world

All their perfection is completely actualized – this is the definition of the transcendent world.

HUMANITY

Humans are potential perfection, awaiting actualization.

Parallel to Earth
Both the earth and humanity are agents of conversion of potential to reality.

PARALLEL TERMS

adam — adamah;

fruit

Actualizing perfection through choice

After death, there is no actualization – the transcendent world is completely actualized.

Actualization of perfection can only occur through freedom of choice to act and actualize; or the choice to remain unactualized, G-d forbid.

A person who chooses not to fulfill mitzvot (choosing not to actualize his perfection).

Has a choice but refuses it

Potential perfection exists and is unactualized.

A person who is coerced not to fulfill mitzvot (so he/she cannot actualize perfection).

e.g. One who tries to act but is stopped

e.g. One who dies young

The soul's choice or lack of choice to fulfill mitzvot and to actualize perfection is the critical factor; the practical outcome is less critical.

The infinity of human potential

Purposes of life

Sanhedrin 99b
"A person will be born to toil"
(Iyov 5:7)

Future tense, "will be born," connotes never-ending potential for growth.

THREE POSSIBILITIES

NECESSARY FOR PERFECTION — Verbal toil in Torah

INSUFFICIENT — Verbal toil = inter-human communication

INSUFFICIENT — Physical toil

The soul's yearning for perfection

Vayikra Rabbah 4:2
Parable: A princess (the soul) married to a commoner (physical body) can never be satisfied with luxuries (Torah and mitzvot) because her potential as a queen (transcendent being) is always unfulfilled as long as she remains with the commoner.

The soul is constantly yearning for its true place – the transcendent world = complete actualization of perfection.

The only avenues for actualization of the soul's potential are mitzvot and Torah. However, whilst it is lodged in this world, even they leave it thirsting for more.

General effects and purposes of mitzvot by category

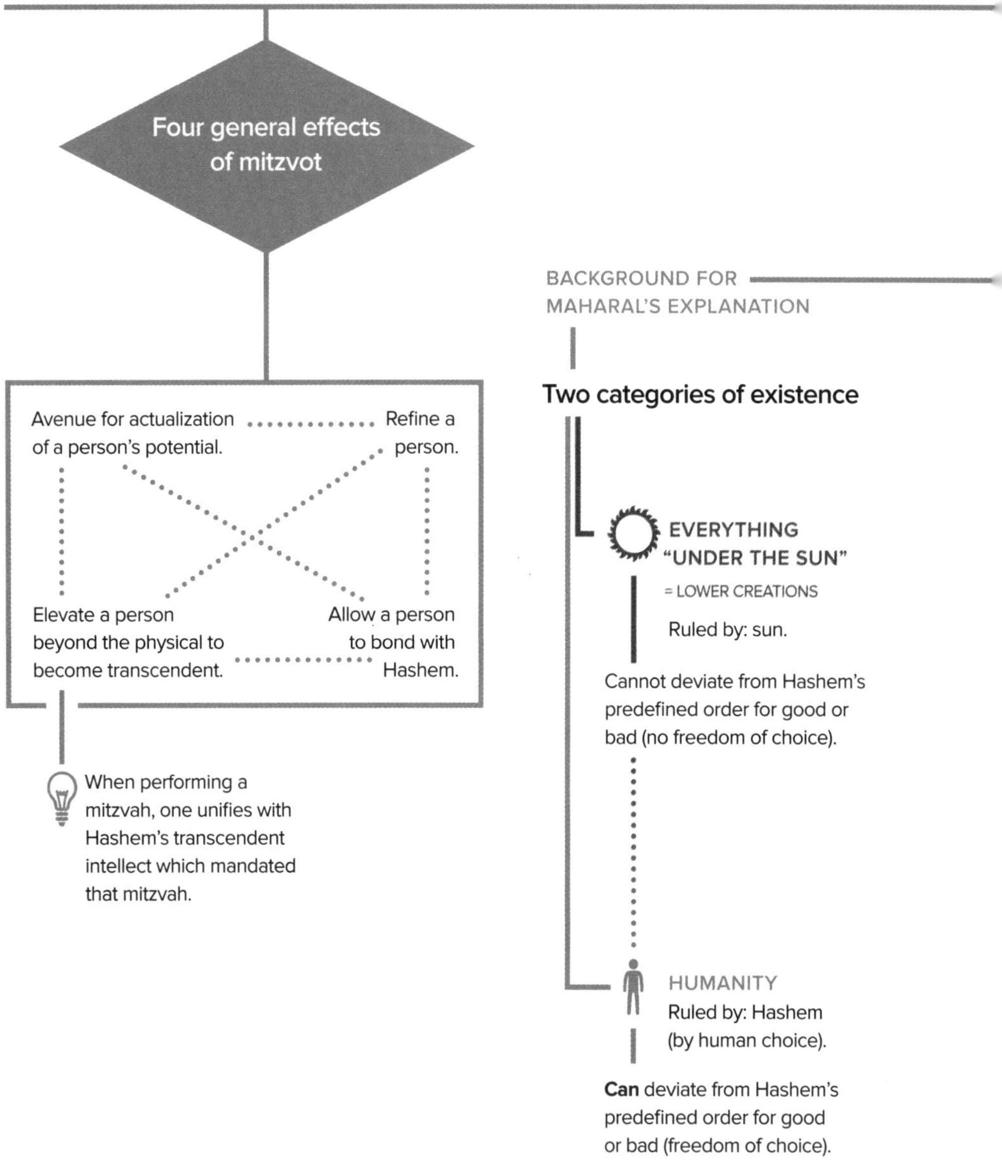

The number and purpose of mitzvot by category

CORRESPONDENCES

The Torah generates reality.

Sun is king of physical world. — Female spiritual dynamic — Matter

365 prohibitions

Prohibitions in Torah maintain Hashem's preset moral order for the universe.

Makkot 23b

Sun **maintains Hashem's preset order** for the universe and prevents deviation through its regulation of time:

365 DAYS A YEAR

Zohar

Sinews in human body maintain **order of body**:

365 SINEWS

Humanity is **potentially** transcendent = can be perfected. — Male spiritual dynamic — Form

248 *mitzvot aseh*

Mitzvot aseh in the Torah allow humanity to perfect itself and become transcendent by actualizing its Form.

Makkot 23b, Zohar

The Human Form is in the image of Hashem which confers upon humans the **ability to perfect themselves**. This Form has:

248 COMPONENT-LIMBS

Do mitzvot ultimately benefit individuals and the Jewish people?

Two primary sources

Avodah Zarah 18a
Rabbi Chaninah ben Tradyon

Used his money for the Purim feast for charity, in error, and afterwards did not claim recompense. As a result of this "one mitzvah" he was told he would gain entry to the World to Come.

Makkot 23b
Rabbi Chanani'ah ben Akashi'ah

Hashem multiplied the mitzvot so that He could bestow merit on Israel.

Rambam

One mitzvah, when done properly, with the sole intention of serving Hashem out of love, gains a person entry to the World to Come. → Rabbi Chaninah did his one mitzvah perfectly which gained him entry into the World to Come.

The more mitzvot there are, the greater the opportunities to find a mitzvah to do perfectly. → Therefore, more mitzvot means more merit.

ORIGINAL QUESTION

? How can the mitzvot just supply merit, surely they must also supply an equal demerit, since people have more ways to sin and fail?

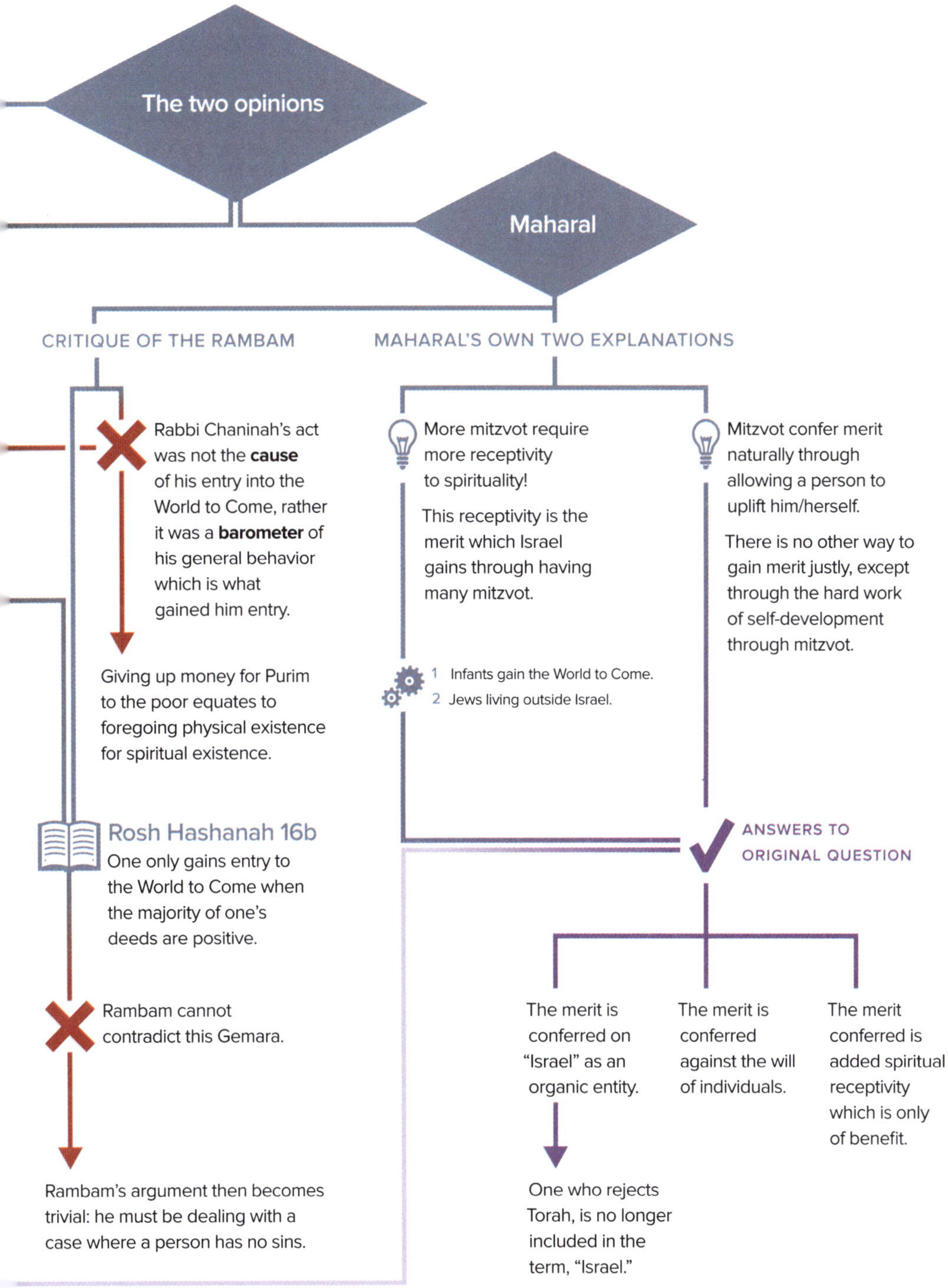

The two opinions
Maharal
CRITIQUE OF THE RAMBAM
MAHARAL'S OWN TWO EXPLANATIONS
Rabbi Chaninah's act was not the **cause** of his entry into the World to Come, rather it was a **barometer** of his general behavior which is what gained him entry.
Giving up money for Purim to the poor equates to foregoing physical existence for spiritual existence.
Rosh Hashanah 16b
One only gains entry to the World to Come when the majority of one's deeds are positive.
Rambam cannot contradict this Gemara.
Rambam's argument then becomes trivial: he must be dealing with a case where a person has no sins.
More mitzvot require more receptivity to spirituality!
This receptivity is the merit which Israel gains through having many mitzvot.
1 Infants gain the World to Come.
2 Jews living outside Israel.
Mitzvot confer merit naturally through allowing a person to uplift him/herself.
There is no other way to gain merit justly, except through the hard work of self-development through mitzvot.
ANSWERS TO ORIGINAL QUESTION
The merit is conferred on "Israel" as an organic entity.
One who rejects Torah, is no longer included in the term, "Israel."
The merit is conferred against the will of individuals.
The merit conferred is added spiritual receptivity which is only of benefit.

Diagrammatic summary: Chapter 6

The purpose of mitzvot (part 1): Rooted in G-d's Mercy or Justice?

The philosophers' questions

THE TWO QUESTIONS

? How can physical mitzvot affect a person's spiritual destiny?

? Many of the mitzvot seem to generate no concrete improvement in character. What is their purpose?

THE MAHARAL'S RESPONSE

There is no need to respond, as the philosophers' method is deficient.

Nevertheless, the Maharal will respond.

The answer spans Chapters 6–9 of *Tiferet Yisrael*.

The key text

Mishnah and Gemara B'rachot 5:3 (33b)

"One silences a person who says that G-d's mercy extends to the mother bird."

Referring to the mitzvah to send away the mother bird.

Gemara's Explanation 1: "He places jealousy amongst the creations."

Gemara's Explanation 2: "He turns G-d's attributes into Mercy when they are solely decrees."

The three opinions

Ramban

Such mitzvot are not generated by Hashem's mercy on animals, but out of his desire that humans become merciful and not cruel.

In fact, Hashem does take mercy on the mother bird and animals, and this mercy generates this mitzvah.

Maharal's rejections

1 This explanation places jealousy amongst the creations, contradicting Explanation 1 in the Gemara, since we only have mercy on certain animals.

2 The details of all such mitzvot do not always ensure that mercy is learned.

3 The Ramban ignores the conclusion of Explanation 2 in the Gemara, "they are only decrees".

Maharal says Ramban is reconcilable with the Maharal's theory if we say that it is Hashem's decree that we learn kindness.

Rambam

The Mishnah is not accepted as normative, therefore we do **not** silence such a person.

Maharal's rejection

There is no indication anywhere that the Mishnah is not accepted.

Maharal

MAHARAL'S KEY PRINCIPLE

The world was created and mitzvot were given through Hashem's attribute of Justice decreeing that this happen, it is not due to His attribute of Mercy.

The **reason** for mitzvot is not to benefit humans or animals.

Nevertheless, since Hashem is absolutely good, there is goodness and benefit accrued from fulfilling mitzvot, as a natural consequence.

This benefit is decreed and cannot be refused.

Rosh Hashanah 28a

"Mitzvot were not given for benefit."

M'nachot 65a

Dispute between R' Yochanan ben Zakai and the Baytosim.

Oaths to prevent benefit from an object do not prevent one using them for mitzvot.

The purpose of mitzvot (part 2): The mechanism by which they impact humanity

The key text – the Midrash

B'reishit Rabbah 44:1

"Does it matter to the Holy One, blessed be He, whether one slaughters from the throat or the [back of the] neck? Rather, the mitzvot were only given to refine humans, as the verse says, 'The statement of Hashem is refined.'"

THREE OPINIONS ON THE REASON FOR MITZVOT

Rambam

Moreh N'vuchim 3:26

All mitzvot have reasons. The details of the mitzvot have no reasons and only come to refine the human being through teaching obedience.

Maharal's rejection: He believes that the details also have reasons.

Ramban

Commentary to D'varim 22:6

All mitzvot have reasons as well as their details. However, no mitzvah is for G-d's benefit. They are all for human benefit to refine the human being by developing positive character traits within him/her.

Maharal's rejection: There are many mitzvot for which reasons are unknown and which therefore cannot develop any positive traits within a person.

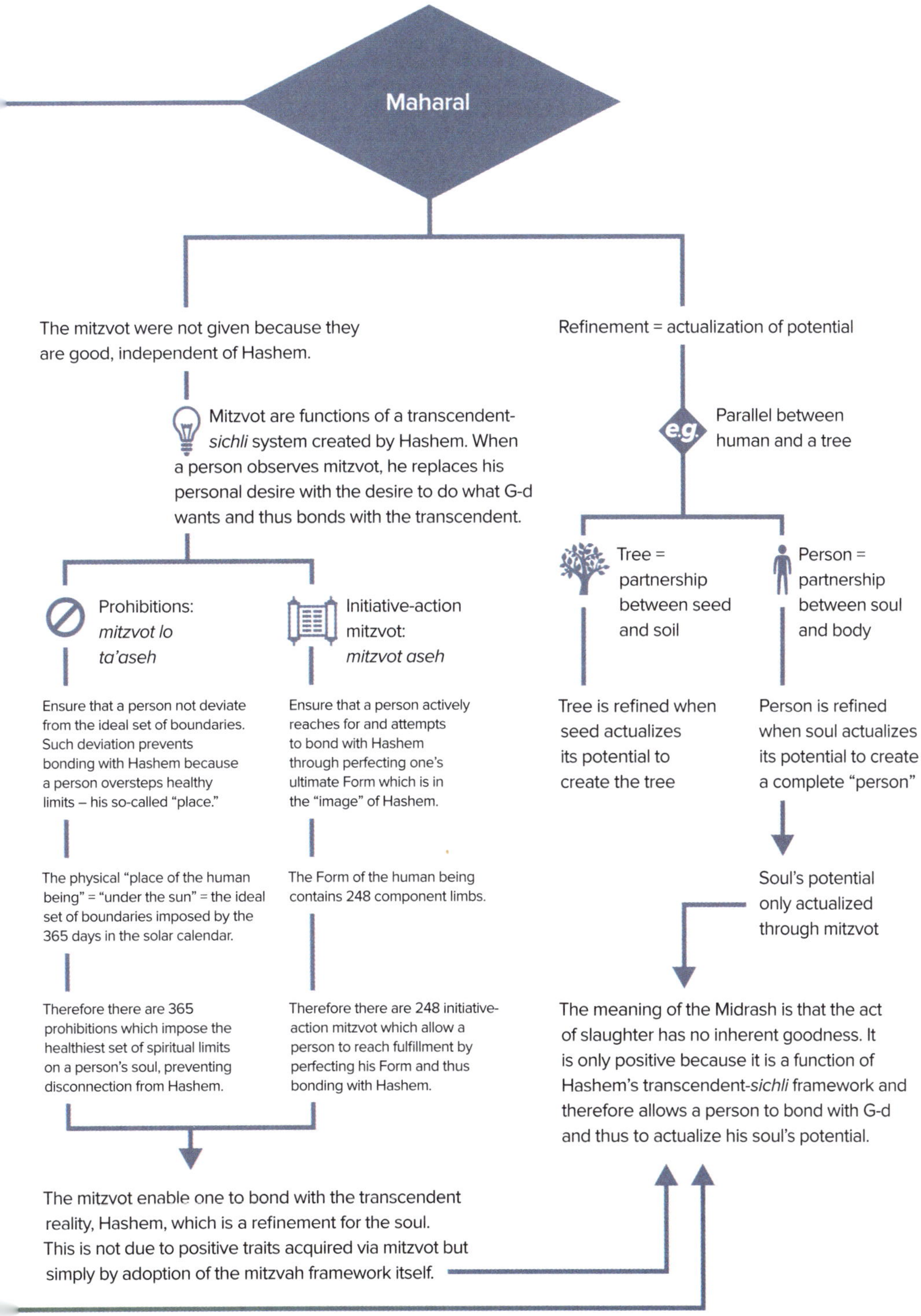
Maharal
The mitzvot were not given because they are good, independent of Hashem.
Mitzvot are functions of a transcendent-*sichli* system created by Hashem. When a person observes mitzvot, he replaces his personal desire with the desire to do what G-d wants and thus bonds with the transcendent.
Prohibitions: *mitzvot lo ta'aseh*
Ensure that a person not deviate from the ideal set of boundaries. Such deviation prevents bonding with Hashem because a person oversteps healthy limits – his so-called "place."
The physical "place of the human being" = "under the sun" = the ideal set of boundaries imposed by the 365 days in the solar calendar.
Therefore there are 365 prohibitions which impose the healthiest set of spiritual limits on a person's soul, preventing disconnection from Hashem.
Initiative-action mitzvot: *mitzvot aseh*
Ensure that a person actively reaches for and attempts to bond with Hashem through perfecting one's ultimate Form which is in the "image" of Hashem.
The Form of the human being contains 248 component limbs.
Therefore there are 248 initiative-action mitzvot which allow a person to reach fulfillment by perfecting his Form and thus bonding with Hashem.
The mitzvot enable one to bond with the transcendent reality, Hashem, which is a refinement for the soul. This is not due to positive traits acquired via mitzvot but simply by adoption of the mitzvah framework itself.
Refinement = actualization of potential
e.g.
Parallel between human and a tree
Tree = partnership between seed and soil
Tree is refined when seed actualizes its potential to create the tree
Person = partnership between soul and body
Person is refined when soul actualizes its potential to create a complete "person"
Soul's potential only actualized through mitzvot
The meaning of the Midrash is that the act of slaughter has no inherent goodness. It is only positive because it is a function of Hashem's transcendent-*sichli* framework and therefore allows a person to bond with G-d and thus to actualize his soul's potential.

Diagrammatic summary: Chapter 8

The purpose of mitzvot (part 3): Natural vs. essential reasons

Mitzvot have no *natural* reasons.

Two primary sources

B'midbar Rabbah 19:8

Rabbi Yochanan ben Zakai concedes that the rationale behind the laws of *tumah* and *taharah* are not natural and causational.

Yoma 39a

Any negative effect induced by eating non-kosher animals is due to the fact that one has transgressed a prohibition and not due to an innate blemish in the food.

The purpose of mitzvot is not to achieve any practical aim.

Rather, they are part of Hashem's transcendent, intellectual framework which He has decreed. He crafted this framework with His wisdom.

Mitzvot definitely have practical benefits but this is not their ultimate reason.

Naturalistic explanations

EXAMPLES

Violating prohibitions induces a negative character trait within oneself.

e.g. Eating non-kosher foods (including pork, *cheilev*, blood).

e.g. Eating meat from an animal which was not properly slaughtered.

Awareness of the reasons for mitzvot

FUNCTION OF THE MITZVOT
The mitzvot allow one to bond with Hashem regardless of whether one knows the reason.

THERE *ARE* REASONS
Even if we do not know the reasons for a mitzvah, it doesn't mean there is no reason for it.

MAHARAL'S REJECTIONS

There are halachic exceptions to these prohibitions – which would seem to encourage the development of these negative character traits.

e.g. When the Jewish people entered Israel, they were allowed to eat anything they found in the homes they captured.

e.g. A *ben paku'ah* does not require slaughtering and one may eat its *cheilev*.

Sifra, K'doshim 10
"A person should not say, 'I do not desire pork, I do not desire something forbidden.' Rather, he should say, 'I do desire! But what can I do, for my Father in Heaven has decreed on me.'"

One should not default to naturalistic explanations for mitzvot.

Diagrammatic summary: Chapter 9

The purpose of mitzvot (part 4): How physical mitzvot help one achieve spiritual success

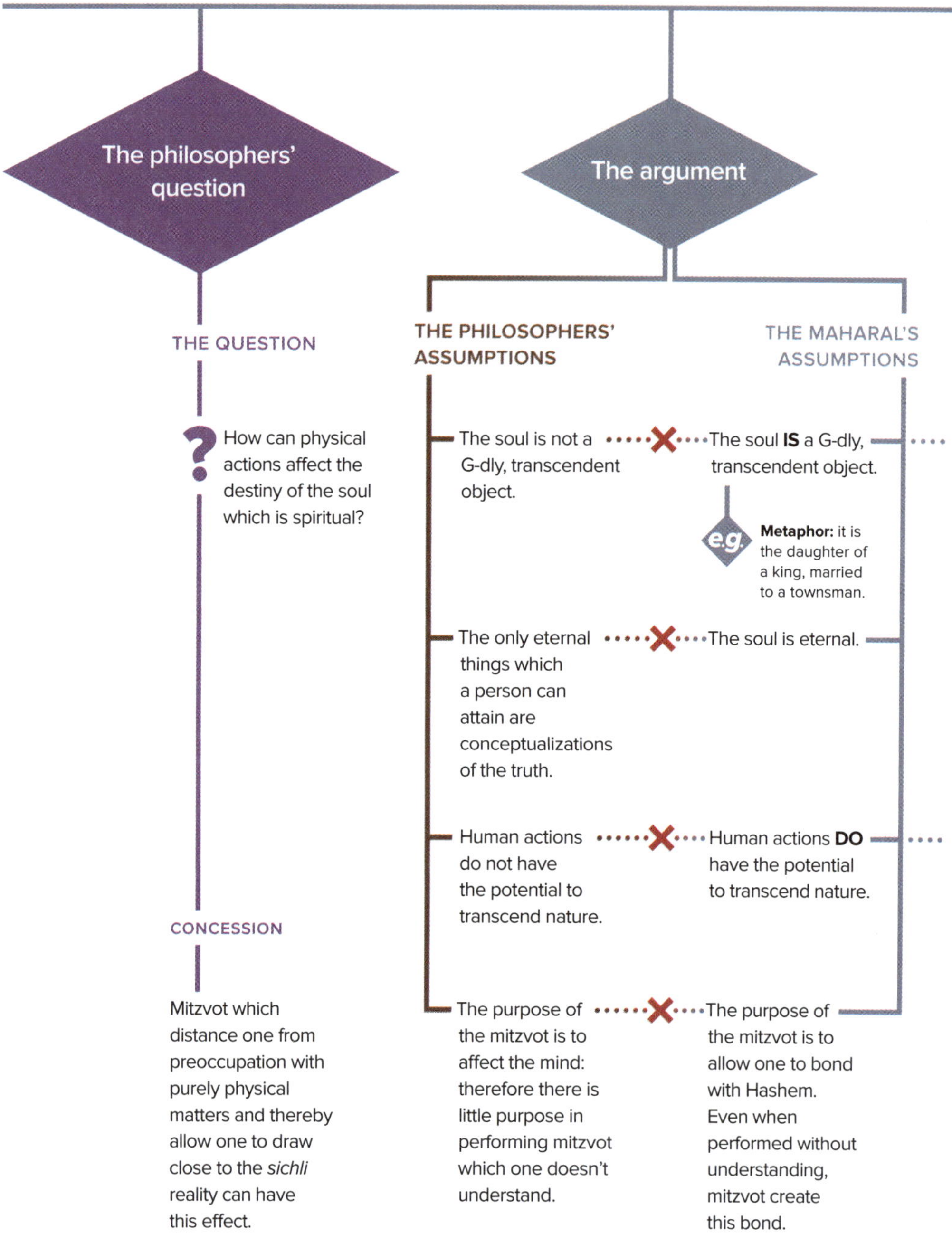

The Maharal's response

PRINCIPLES

Success/"Reward"
The greatest success is bonding with Hashem. Even though this comes as a natural consequence of a person's choice of actions in life, we term it "reward." It is the greatest possible pleasure.

Failure/"Punishment"
The greatest failure is being separated from Hashem. Even though this also comes as a natural consequence of a person's choice of actions in life, we term it "punishment." It is the greatest possible pain.

IMPLEMENTATION

Mitzvot aseh enable one to bond with Hashem.

HOW THIS BOND IS ACHIEVED

Sotah 14a
Certain mitzvot are emulations of Hashem's attributes.

- The mitzvot are the *sichli* framework which Hashem has created. Adopting it allows one to "adopt" Hashem's will.
- Mitzvot allow us to create a relationship with Hashem as our king. This only happens when we accept and fulfill His commands.
- Since the soul is "the King's daughter," physical actions can transcend nature, refining the body and soul and allowing a person to bond with Hashem.

WHY HUMANS ARE WORTHY OF THIS BONDING

Humans are made in Hashem's image.

Mitzvot lo ta'aseh prevent one from distancing him/herself from Hashem.

WHAT PREVENTS THIS BONDING?

Sh'vu'ot 13a
Actions which demonstrate clearly that a person wishes to disconnect from Hashem.

- **Atheism:** Clearly one disconnects from Hashem if one believes He does not exist, G-d forbid.
- **One who denigrates the Torah:** One cannot connect to Hashem except through the Torah.
- **One who does not give himself a covenantal circumcision:** The covenant is the archetypal model of bonding with Hashem – similar to a marriage. One who rejects the covenant is rejecting the most basic level of bond.

CHAPTER OUTLINES

As I describe in the Preface to this work, the Tiferet Yisrael is distinguished by many factors. In my opinion, the outstanding facet of this work is the way it addresses many of life's key questions through the prism of Torah. Below is a somewhat different content structure, which highlights the issues which appear in each chapter.

Also, as I outline in the Preface, the Maharal utilizes parts of our everyday mitzvot in his explanations, with the net result that these mitzvot are explained in a way that helps us grasp their profundity and which makes the everyday much more meaningful. So, as a product of learning the Maharal, one gains not just an amazing framework for Torah philosophy, but many mitzvot and basic concepts gain greater meaning along the way. This is the purpose of the right-most column below – to illustrate which mitzvot and basic ideas are addressed in each chapter. Enjoy!

Chap.	**Foundational concepts and questions addressed**		**Mitzvot and ideas elucidated**
	General concept	**Details**	
Intro	**Morality**	Why are there outwardly observant ("*frum*") people who end up doing terrible things?	The blessings we say in the morning over learning Torah. The prayer we say before studying Torah.
		Why was the First Temple destroyed if the people at that time learned so much Torah?	
		How should we define our successes – relative to the failures of others or independent of others?	
		How is it that the students of a great sage don't always end up with spiritual achievements?	
	Creating a connection with Hashem	What is the best way (and secondary ways) to create a connection to Hashem?	Torah learning and developing one's character traits.
		The truth of Hashem's connection to reality and to the Torah in particular.	
		A person who is connected to Hashem will be aided in reaching the truth and in mending the errors of his/her ways.	

Chap.	Foundational concepts and questions addressed		Mitzvot and ideas elucidated
	General concept	Details	
Intro	Learning Torah	Why should I learn Torah, especially if I'm not the most gifted intellectually and others seem to understand far quicker than I do? Who am I to do this?	The blessings we say in the morning over learning Torah. The meaning of Psalm 19 (said on Shabbat mornings.)
		If a person makes an error in their Torah learning, does the learning have any value?	
		What is the best way to ensure I reach the truth in my Torah learning and that I communicate that truth correctly?	
		How can and should Torah learning impact me?	
	The effects of performing mitzvot in the correct manner	Performing mitzvot in the correct manner has an infinitely positive effect on a person physically and spiritually.	

Chap.	General concept	Details	Mitzvot and ideas elucidated
Chap. 1	Meaning of life	What is the general meaning of human life?	
		The relationship between one's professional life and spiritual life.	
		There are actions which are unique to a person.	
	Character	The danger of any extreme in life.	
	Free choice	Why do we need to *choose* to do good? Why isn't it instinctual?	
		The difference between the souls of a person and an animal.	
	Nature of idolatry and of the Jewish people	The embeddedness of idolatry within nature on all levels.	
		What is the difference between Jews and idolaters on the level of spiritual receptivity? The natural vs. the supernatural ideas.	The significance of "8" in Torah thought.
		Different peoples are spiritually receptive to different ideals.	
		Why is it that at certain times Jewish people are found on the absolute extreme of negative behavior – steeped in the worst of idolatry and other evil deeds?	
	Converts	How does conversion to Judaism work on a spiritual level?	Conversion

Chap.	Foundational concepts and questions addressed		Mitzvot and ideas elucidated
	General concept	**Details**	
Chap. 2	**The purpose of human life in the natural world**	Partnering with Hashem by perfecting what He intentionally left imperfect – first and foremost ourselves.	*Brit milah.* Meaning and structure of Psalms 19 (said on Shabbat) and 119.
		Brit Milah (the covenant of circumcision) as the primary symbol of self-perfection and perfection of the world.	
		Humans can rise above nature which has been left for us to perfect. Humans share their physicality with animals, but through our choices we can become more.	The numerology of "7" vs. "8" in Torah thought.

Chap.	General concept	Details	Mitzvot and ideas elucidated
Chap. 3	**The potential of every person**	Human beings have infinite potential and all of life is a journey to uncover and actualize more and more of what we have inside us. Life is the never-ending process of mining one's flaws into the jewels of perfection. Humans are born to toil in converting their infinite potential to actuality through mitzvot.	Why humans are called "*adam*" in Hebrew and why animals are termed "*b'heimah.*"
		What is the ultimate fruit of human life? Physical descendants or moral effects?	Developing one's character (*middot*).
		Choosing to perfect yourself has a significantly positive effect whether or not you reach your goal.	
		The soul can never be satisfied with this world – Torah and mitzvot are the closest it gets to self-fulfillment.	The need to push oneself in spiritual goals.
	The goal of humanity: perfecting 3 aspects of the world	3 areas of life which we should strive to perfect: all of physicality, inter-human verbal communication, verbal Torah communication.	The importance of physicality and inter-human communication in the Torah's view.
	The place of speech in human destiny	The importance of speech in Torah thought.	Speech: secular and holy uses.
		The need (Halachic and metaphysical) to verbalize Torah.	

<table>
<tr><th rowspan="2">Chap.</th><th colspan="2">Foundational concepts and questions addressed</th><th rowspan="2">Mitzvot and ideas elucidated</th></tr>
<tr><th>General concept</th><th>Details</th></tr>
<tr><td rowspan="9">Chap. 4</td><td rowspan="3">Effect of mitzvot</td><td>4 general effects which mitzvot should have on a person: actualize one's potential, allow one to rise above the natural, refine one and allow one to bond with Hashem.</td><td rowspan="2">Why do mitzvot?</td></tr>
<tr><td>Mitzvot enable a person to "resemble" G-d in full.</td></tr>
<tr><td>Two categories of mitzvot and their complementary effects: boundaries and enabling perfection.</td><td>Why 365 prohibitions and 248 mitzvot aseh?</td></tr>
<tr><td rowspan="4">Metaphysics</td><td>Three categories of reality: nature (time-bound), transcendent beings (angels) and humanity (choice enabled).</td><td rowspan="4"></td></tr>
<tr><td>The Torah definition of "kingship."</td></tr>
<tr><td>Form and Matter in Torah thought – the male and female spiritual dynamics.</td></tr>
<tr><td>Humanity and the Jewish people are microcosms of all reality.</td></tr>
<tr><td>Gender differences in Torah thought</td><td>The exemption of women from time-bound mitzvot aseh and the gender dynamics behind this.</td><td>Why are women exempt from time-bound mitzvot aseh?</td></tr>
</table>

<table>
<tr><td rowspan="5">Chap. 5</td><td rowspan="3">Pros and cons of having to keep mitzvot</td><td>Surely as much as mitzvot offer a chance for achievement, they offer an equal opportunity for failure? So maybe an obligation to keep 613 mitzvot is worse than just having to keep 7 (as non-Jews do).</td><td rowspan="5"></td></tr>
<tr><td>One mitzvah done correctly, can gain a person entry to the World to Come. (Rambam)</td></tr>
<tr><td>G-d pre-equips a person with the tools necessary to fulfill a greater responsibility in life, so more mitzvot means more ability. (Maharal)</td></tr>
<tr><td rowspan="2">G-d works on 100% justice</td><td>Growth can never be bestowed, it has to be organically earned by each individual. A person's actions (physical and spiritual) have effects.</td></tr>
<tr><td>Mitzvot can be viewed as "points" earned and conversely as growth attained.</td></tr>
</table>

<table>
<tr><th rowspan="2">Chap.</th><th colspan="2">Foundational concepts and questions addressed</th><th rowspan="2">Mitzvot and ideas elucidated</th></tr>
<tr><th>General concept</th><th>Details</th></tr>
<tr><td rowspan="2">Chap. 5</td><td rowspan="2">The individual Jew vs. the Jewish nation</td><td>What is beneficial for the nation of Israel is not always beneficial to certain individual Jews and sometimes, it can even be harmful to individuals.</td><td rowspan="2"></td></tr>
<tr><td>A Jew can partially disconnect himself from the Jewish nation (and from Hashem) through his active decision to reject Torah and mitzvot.</td></tr>
</table>

<table>
<tr><td rowspan="10">Chap. 6</td><td rowspan="5">The possible effects of mitzvot on a person and the reasons for mitzvot</td><td>How can mitzvot affect a person spiritually if they are physical actions?</td><td rowspan="5">Sending away the mother bird (shilu'ach haken).
The requirement and method of kosher slaughter (sh'chitah).
Not slaughtering a dam and its progeny on the same day (oto v'et b'no).
Giving tz'dakkah (Jewish social support.)
Eating kosher food (kashrut)
The date of Shavu'ot.</td></tr>
<tr><td>How can a mitzvah affect someone if he/she doesn't understand the mitzvah?</td></tr>
<tr><td>Mitzvot channel Hashem's mercy (and His other traits) on all of creation. (Rambam)</td></tr>
<tr><td>Mitzvot habituate people to behaving with mercy (and other positive traits). (Ramban)</td></tr>
<tr><td>Mitzvot allow people to adopt Hashem's framework of Thought and Will.
Mitzvot flow from Hashem's attribute of Justice. They always benefit people but this is a subsidiary effect, not the reason they were given, and this benefit is not optional. (Maharal)</td></tr>
<tr><td rowspan="4">Metaphysics</td><td>The attribute of Hashem which predominates in His directing of cosmic affairs is His attribute of Justice.</td><td rowspan="2"></td></tr>
<tr><td>Absolute goodness flows from Hashem.</td></tr>
<tr><td>The names we have for Hashem as reflecting His different attributes. In particular, Y-H-V-H and Elokim.</td><td>Intention when praying.</td></tr>
<tr><td>How can Hashem, Who is wholly unified have different "attributes"? Is this only how it looks from a human perspective?</td><td></td></tr>
</table>

Chap.	Foundational concepts and questions addressed		Mitzvot and ideas elucidated
	General concept	Details	
Chap. 6	Miracles	The parallels between Hashem's moral law and His rule of the physical laws which govern this universe. What happens when there are exceptions to these rules?	
	Philosophy	The shortcomings of the philosophical and empirical methods.	
Chap. 7	The reasons for mitzvot	Do mitzvot have "reasons"?	
		Mitzvot in general have reasons but not their details, which serve to instill obedience to Hashem. (Rambam)	
		Mitzvot and their details all have reasons. The general reason for all mitzvot is to refine humans by nurturing the development of positive traits within them. (Ramban)	
		Mitzvot and all their details have reasons. The general reason for all mitzvot is that a human adopts a transcendent system of thinking and action which replaces his natural desires. The more a person adopts this system, the more he is really adopting G-d's thinking and desires. The subsequent result of this is that a person bonds with Hashem and actualizes his own potential. (Maharal)	Non-Jews who keep Shabbat are liable.
	The function of prohibitions and *mitzvot aseh*	Prohibitions (*mitzvot lo ta'aseh*) ensure that a person remains within healthy boundaries to preserve his/her equilibrium in all areas of life. They preserve one's bond with G-d. They allow one to achieve "peace."	
		Mitzvot aseh allow a person to grow beyond their current state to reflect his being in G-d's "Form." This allows a wider and deeper bond with Hashem. This is a person's self-actualization by which the soul achieves as much as it can while it dwells within the physical world.	
	Metaphysics	The concept of "place" as it applies to every part of reality and, in particular, to people.	
		The concept of the "Form" of G-d, in which humans were created.	
	Metaphysics	The spatial coordinate system with 6 or 7 factors as a paradigm for spiritual existence.	

<table>
<tr><th rowspan="2">Chap.</th><th colspan="2">Foundational concepts and questions addressed</th><th rowspan="2">Mitzvot and ideas elucidated</th></tr>
<tr><th>General concept</th><th>Details</th></tr>
<tr><td rowspan="3">Chap. 7</td><td rowspan="2">The seven Noahide mitzvot</td><td>The function of the seven Noahide mitzvot.</td><td rowspan="2">Noahide prohibitions against: murder, theft, idolatry, blasphemy, consuming an animal's limb prior to its death, perversion of justice, sexual immorality.</td></tr>
<tr><td>The numerology of the seven Noahide mitzvot.</td></tr>
<tr><td>Human-tree comparison</td><td>Parallels and differences between trees (partnership of seed and soil) and humans (partnership of soul and body).
The key difference is that the soul's natural place is not the body and thus the partnership is not automatic and requires active choice.</td><td></td></tr>
</table>

<table>
<tr><td rowspan="6">Chap. 8</td><td rowspan="5">The reasons for mitzvot and the impact of mitzvah performance</td><td>Mitzvot have positive practical consequences; however, those consequences are not the reason for the Mitzvot. Rather, they are part of Hashem's transcendent system whereby a person assimilates G-d's will.</td><td rowspan="2">Eating kosher food (and the exceptional times when one can eat non-kosher food).
Tumah caused by a corpse.</td></tr>
<tr><td>A person should state that he is not performing mitzvot because they concur with his natural desires or to achieve some practical end; on the contrary, a person should perform mitzvot because they are G-d's decree.</td></tr>
<tr><td>Mitzvot allow one to bond with Hashem regardless of whether a person fully understands the mitzvah (although greater understanding allows greater bonding.)</td><td></td></tr>
<tr><td>The ideal approach to mitzvot which are readily comprehended.</td><td>Tz'dakkah, prayer, honoring parents, theft, robbery.</td></tr>
<tr><td>The ideal approach to mitzvot which are not readily comprehended.</td><td></td></tr>
<tr><td>Kashrut</td><td>The impact that eating non-kosher food has on a person's body and soul. Divergent views of Maharal, Ramban and Rambam.</td><td>Kashrut
Sh'chitah</td></tr>
</table>

Chap.	Foundational concepts and questions addressed		Mitzvot and ideas elucidated
	General concept	**Details**	
Chap. 9	**Meta-physics: 4 differences with the philosophers**	1. The soul is a G-dly, transcendent object. 2. The soul is eternal. 3. Human actions do have the potential to transcend nature. 4. The general purpose of mitzvot is to allow one to bond with Hashem, a link which is created even if the mitzvot are performed without understanding.	
	"Reward" and "punishment"	The consequence of doing mitzvot is closeness to Hashem, which is the greatest possible pleasure and success. We term this inaccurately, "reward." The most abject failure and pain is separation from Hashem, which can be the direct consequence of a person's actions if that person chooses to do evil. We term this, inaccurately, "punishment."	"Reward" and "punishment."
	How *mitzvot aseh* create a bond with Hashem	*Mitzvot aseh* allow one to create a bond with Hashem in four ways: emulating Hashem's attributes, adopting the *sichli* framework as one's will, accepting Hashem as a king through accepting His decrees (both this and the previous goal can be achieved even without understanding the mitzvot), and transcending nature via refining the soul and body.	*Tz'dakkah*, implementing justice (preventing robbery, murder, kidnapping and sexual immorality.)
	How violation of mitzvot separates one from Hashem	In general, when a person violates a mitzvah, it is a statement that the person wishes to disconnect from Hashem. There are three archetypal categories of disconnection: atheism, denigration of the Torah and rejecting the Jewish people's covenant with Hashem.	Atheism. Deriding the Torah. Not having a *brit milah*.
	WHY YOU ARE WORTH IT!	Human beings were made in Hashem's image and that means we are worthy of the ultimate intimacy with Hashem which one can achieve through Torah and mitzvot. You don't have to be the world's biggest genius!	

PREFACE

With thanks to Hashem.

While this preface serves as a guide to this translation and commentary of the Maharal's Tiferet Yisrael, should you wish to, you can plunge in right away and begin learning this powerful Torah – this work aims to be as user-friendly and self-explanatory as possible. Should you wish to clarify any technical aspect of this work, please feel free to refer back later to this Preface.

If you are still reading, below you will find an outline of how this work can aid you in your encounter with the Splendor of Israel – our holy Torah, as presented by the Maharal. You'll also find some technical and stylistic details.

Our motivation

The Maharal is one of the giants of Torah thought whose works have influenced many spheres of Jewish thought. His ideas and words are sometimes so powerful and majestic, they leave the reader speechless, awestruck and thirsting for more Torah. It is our hope that we will manage to reproduce this majesty in this work and thus to expose the English-speaking world to Torah through the prism of the Maharal's genius.

One of the difficulties in learning the Maharal is his complexity of thought which often leaves the reader grasping for an overall structure. We have attempted to address this in several ways, as will be explained further.

There are several outstanding features, in my opinion, to the Maharal's Torah in general.

Firstly, is quite simply his breadth and rigor. When I began learning the Maharal, I had the sense of encountering a larger Torah – a Torah which sought to encompass all of reality, all of physicality, all of spirituality; his canvas was broader than most. Moreover, his approach always requires a return to first principles – he is just never content with supplying a superficial answer, he always digs down to reveal an interlocking framework of profound principles on which he builds his thought. The Maharal may take many chapters building up a complete, sufficient set of principles; but if that's what it takes to explain the profundity of Torah, he will do so.

Secondly, the Maharal's Torah is superbly balanced. He presents the competing demands of a balanced spiritual life and he doesn't shy away from confronting the paradoxes with which a Torah Jew must battle.

Thirdly, there is a gritty reality in his writings which demonstrates how close he was to the same experiences we all share in our growth in Torah and service of Hashem. He asks the questions we all ask and provides answers that have stayed with me since I first learned them.

Fourthly, the Maharal utilizes parts of our everyday mitzvot in his explanations, with the net result that these mitzvot are explained in a way that helps one understand their profundity and that makes the everyday much more meaningful. So, as a product of learning the Maharal, one gains not just an amazing framework for Jewish thought, but many mitzvot and basic concepts gain greater meaning as implementations of his Torah.

Fifthly, the Maharal provides a great background to learning the opinions of many of our other luminaries, whom the Maharal introduces in the course of his writing.

*

I chose to present this work, the Tiferet Yisrael, in particular, for a number of reasons.

Firstly, it's a great example of all that I mentioned above.

Secondly, as is evident from the contents of this work, the Tiferet Yisrael deals in depth with a group of foundational concepts and questions in Torah, which I have yet to see dealt with in as cohesive and consistent manner in any other work. Some of these are listed by chapter above. Moreover, the issues addressed in the Tiferet are perhaps the broadest and most necessary for spiritual life: "Why we do mitzvot" is not just a question amongst others, it is one of *the* questions which undergird all of Torah life. The general theme of the Tiferet is "Torah" which of course stands at the very center of Jewish life.

This edition

This edition serves to translate the Maharal's text as accurately as possible.

We have still taken to heart the Rambam's timeless advice to translators, "It is inappropriate for a translator to translate word for word, preserving the original sentence structure. Rather, the translator must first understand the original text and thereafter he should explain and relate the subject according to his understanding" (*Letter to Rabbi Sh'mu'el Ibn Tibbon*). Therefore, we have added bridging phrases where necessary in the body of the text in order to ensure the translation is easier to read.

Footnotes and commentary

We have provided extensive footnotes to guide the reader in locating the sources of the Maharal's thoughts.

Where there is a particularly challenging idea in the Maharal, we have attempted to explain it in the Commentary for each chapter, which can be found at the back of the book. The Commentary is divided by the Chapters of the book, to facilitate location of comments on each chapter. We do not claim to have plumbed the profound depths of the Maharal in any way, and thus, in the Commentary, we humbly offer parallel writings of the Maharal and citations from other sages which shed some light on the Maharal's intent.

Each chapter of commentary contains several numbered points and we have further directed the reader to the appropriate point in the Commentary section by using the following notation in the body of the work and in the footnotes: "See the Commentary, Introduction § Point 1".

Additionally, it is apparent to all that much of what the Maharal writes can only be understood through the prism of Kabbalah – the esoteric tradition of the Torah. We are in no way qualified or able to provide the complete background in such areas and as such, at times, there will be a limit in understanding beyond which we will not forge.

Internal structure

We have striven to ensure that the structure of the Maharal's Torah is made as clear as possible through various means:

A. Subdividing each chapter

Each chapter is subdivided into manageable sections, usually two or three sections per chapter.

B. Summaries

Summaries are provided:

i. Within the text (see "In-line summaries" below).
ii. After each section.

C. Graphic Summaries, which enable the reader to grasp the structure of the chapter as a whole, are placed after the Overview.

D. We have utilized different print type and different colors (shading) to assist the reader in understanding the Maharal, as follows:

i. Body of translation
The body of the translation is in the following type:

> A person should never say that the Torah was given only to the greatest of sages who are far from ever making a mistake. Rather, the Torah was given to everyone.

ii. Citations
Citations are in a smaller type to the main body of the text and are slightly indented, as follows:

> The verse in Shir Hashirim states, "The King brought me to the house of wine, and his banner over me was in love!"

iii. Footnotes
There are extensive footnotes which are indicated through superscripts in the text:

> This is the Torah which Moshe placed before the children of Yisrael.[1]

E. In-line summaries
We have included partial summaries within the English text in order to guide the reader in navigating the Maharal. These comments are highlighted in gray and look as follows:

> The Maharal begins by explaining the complete accessibility of Torah to all, regardless of their intellectual ability.

F. In-line explanatory notes
In certain citations, such as from the Gemara and some Midrashim, much of the internal logic of argument is taken for granted by the Gemara and the Midrashim. We have added comments containing this logic inside square parentheses as follows:

> [The Midrash asks,] What is the deeper meaning of this verse?

G. Bridging phrases
Where added words are clearly necessary to render the text into English, we have added bridging phrases within square parentheses, as follows:

> Therefore, the verse did not say, "[which Moshe] gave to the children

Stylistic points

A. Phoneticization of Hebrew terms
We have used a Sephardic transliteration of Hebrew terms.

B. Use of the apostrophe
We have used the apostrophe to indicate:

i. The *sh'va na*
For example, *pos'kim.*
Certain Hebrew words have achieved almost universally accepted

English transliterations and thus we have not altered the spelling in these, for example: Gemara, Tehillim.

ii. Diphthongs
For example, *Yishma'el.*
Certain Hebrew words have achieved almost universally accepted English transliterations and thus we have not altered the spelling in these, for example: *Yisrael.*

C. Use of italics

i. Phoneticized Hebrew words
We have used italics primarily for phoneticized Hebrew words. For example, *pos'kim*.
We have not italicized:
- Names of books (though we have italicized the names of chapters or subsections within a work).
- Names of authors
- Certain select words which have become commonplace in English:
  - Halachah (and the plural, "Halachot").
  - Torah
  - Midrash (and the plural, "Midrashim").
  - Mitzvah (and the plural, "mitzvot"). However, where this word is used in a construct, we have italicized it, for example, *mitzvot aseh*.

ii. Emphasis
We have also used italics for emphasis in the body of the text and in citations, and all such emphases are our own and are *not* to be found in the original Hebrew or Aramaic.

iii. In-line summaries
Our in-line summaries are also italicized.

D. Use of bold

We have also used bold type for emphasis on occasion, particularly within a text already italicized, and again, all such emphases are our own and are not to be found in the original Hebrew or Aramaic texts.

E. Masculine and feminine gender

We have remained true to Hebrew which, in general, lacks a neuter gender and we have attempted to minimize the use of cumbersome phrases such as "One should," "one says" and so on.

Thus, we use the masculine gender in general and, unless indicated otherwise by context, this is intended to include the feminine as well.

F. The spelling used throughout the text is American English.

G. Printings and Editions
The first edition of the Tiferet Yisrael was printed by the renowned Daniel Zanetti in Venice in 1598. It was reprinted by Zanetti thirteen times in 1599; however, the next edition was only printed in 1793 in Slavuta (today in Western Ukraine), probably by the famed Shapiro printing house. These sporadic printings mark the history of the publication of the Maharal's works, with the next burst of interest in the 1950–1960's when more than twenty-six printings took place.

Works consulted

The primary work we have utilized is Rabbi Yehoshua Hartman's edition of Tiferet Yisrael (Machon Yerushalayim, 5760). We are completely indebted to Rabbi Hartman for this work which has guided both the text of the Maharal we have used as well as our commentary. We are also tremendously appreciative of the guidance Rabbi Hartman rendered during the preparation of this work and for his approbation. May Hashem bless him and his family to continue in the dissemination of Torah.

Additionally, everything we understand about the Maharal has been imbued with the ideas of Rabbi Yitzchak Hutner, *zt"l*, and his monumental work, *Pachad Yitzchak* in which he regularly introduces and explains the Maharal's foundational concepts.

Use of Hebrew terms and glossary

We have chosen to translate certain terms into English and others we have retained in the Hebrew (e.g., mitzvah). These latter terms have been chosen due to their being key concepts in the Torah or their being virtually untranslatable. In the latter case, we have included a note on terminology at the beginning of the Commentary for that chapter.

We have also included a Glossary which includes all words – those translated and those not.

Citations

Citation conventions are as follows:

a. "Rambam" refers to the Yad Chazakah.
b. When a tractate of Gemara is cited without qualification, it is from the Talmud Bavli.
c. All works cited, unless specified otherwise, are the standard editions. For example, the Gemara used is the Vilna Shas.

Overall Structure of the contents of the Tiferet Yisrael

The Tiferet Yisrael contains 70 chapters.

Clearly, as Rabbi Hartman (Volume 1, pp. 18–19) notes, given the Maharal's focus on numerology, this number is not coincidental, and immediately reminds one of the famous statement that the Torah has seventy facets (B'midbar Rabbah 13:15); which is entirely appropriate, given that this work deals with the nature of Torah.

Rabbi Hartman also cites there a proposition of the internal structure of these seventy chapters, suggested by Rabbi Uzi Kalcheim zt"l, that there are nine topics dealt with in the work, all of which contain eight chapters, except the last two which contain seven chapters each, as follows:

1. The utility of the mitzvot to one who performs them: Chapters 1–8
2. The acquisition of a bond with Hashem and of eternal life, granted by the performance of mitzvot: Chapters 9–16
3. Those who receive the Torah: Chapters 17–24
4. The preparations undertaken for the original receiving of the Torah at Sinai: Chapters 25–32
5. The giving of the Torah at Sinai and the 10 commandments from the perspective of Hashem (the Primal Cause) as it were – until the fourth commandment: Chapters 33–40
6. The giving of the Torah at Sinai and the 10 commandments from the perspective of the recipients, as well as the golden calf: Chapters 41–48
7. The eternity of Torah: Chapters 49–56
8. The reward for mitzvot in this world and the world to come: Chapters 57–63
9. The Written and Oral Torah: Chapters 64–70

It is for this reason that this first volume contains the Introduction as well as the first nine chapters. In including the ninth chapter here, I have deviated somewhat from Rabbi Kalcheim's suggestion for several reasons. Firstly, as one will note from the beginning of Chapter Nine, in referring to the original question of the philosophers, the Maharal seems to be very clearly linking Chapter Nine into the unit spanning from Chapter Six (which was where the original question was raised). Secondly, as one will note from the beginning of Chapter Ten, it seems clear that Chapter Ten begins a new unit with a new question.

Upcoming volume

This volume is the first in our edition of the Maharal's Tiferet Yisrael; with Hashem's blessing we will be publishing the next volume in good time.

A BRIEF BIOGRAPHY OF THE MAHARAL[1]

The righteous even in their death are termed "living" (B'rachot 18a)

One of the notable features of our greatest sages is the paucity of biographical detail that remains after they have left this world.

Primarily, this is a simple sign of the impact their lives and Torah made on the world – people were not interested in the details of their birth and their careers since all of that paled into insignificance when compared with the magnitude of their Torah and the example they led. The Torah itself sets this trend when discussing Avraham Avinu, Abraham our forefather, of whose early life the written Torah says almost nothing.

This is similarly true for the Maharal. The central source for biographical material on his life, Sefer Hayuchasin, was first published over one hundred years after the Maharal's passing and was a reconstruction from second- or third-hand sources. Sadly, most people recognize his name in association with the legend of the Golem, an automaton allegedly constructed from clay by the Maharal to protect the Jewish community. This legend is almost certainly just that.

Despite this lack of detail about his earthly life, we have been gifted with the ultimate record of his spiritual life – his works and impact. This short biography seeks to describe the key milestones as we know them.

Early Life

The Maharal's family hailed from Worms, but he was born in Posen in 1512 (or 1522) to Reb Betzalel Loew. Maharal is an acronym for **M**oreinu **HaR**av **L**oew but his full name was Rabbi Yehudah Loew, son of Reb Betzalel. The surname, Loew is derived from the German, "*Löwe*," meaning, "lion."

We know little of his early education. He was married in 1544 to Perl, daughter of Shmelke the Rich, one of the prominent citizens of Prague. They had six daughters and one son. It seems that the Maharal started life as an independently wealthy man, something which enabled him to write, publish and teach in the manner of his choosing.

---

1. This brief biography has been compiled from a number of sources – primarily, *Megillat Yuchasin* (Warsaw: 1864); the introduction by Rabbi Avraham Chaim Carmell to *Maharal, Emerging Patterns*, Rabbi Yaakov Rosenblatt (Feldheim: 2001), as well as the works of Chaim Freedman.

Public Career

In 1553, he was elected to his first position – as Chief Rabbi of Nikolsburg and all of Moravia, where he stayed for twenty years. He was renowned throughout greater Moravia not only for his erudition but for his sage construction of communal policy, something for which many sought his guidance throughout his life.

He took issue with several negative behavior patterns in the varying communities in which he served and it is from his principled leadership in these areas that he became known as a powerful, unswerving Torah leader; someone who was not always popular with the lay leadership.

He took issue time and again with the potential assimilatory tendencies latent in certain practices, in particular Jews drinking *stam yeinam* (wine produced by non-Jews – not in accordance with Jewish law). The wealthy were particularly sensitive to this campaign. He also made a point of stopping people talking in *shul*, which may bring a wry smile to many a rabbinical face.

He moved to Prague after twenty years in Nikolsburg, in 1573. He did not take up an official position there, and as a financially independent man, had no need for one.

In 1578, he published his first work, the Gur Aryeh (The Lion Cub), a commentary on Rashi (which is in turn, the central commentary on the Chumash). The title contains a hint to his name, since his surname was Loew, meaning, "lion"; additionally, his first name was Yehudah (Judah) and the title, Gur Aryeh comes from the blessing which Ya'akov (Jacob) bestowed on Yehudah (B'reishit 49:9).

In 1582, he published G'vurot Hashem (The Power of G-d), a large work discussing the original enslavement and redemption from Egypt and related themes.

In 1583, the position of Chief Rabbi of Prague became vacant with the passing of the incumbent, Rabbi Mellnick. The Maharal was the natural successor (at perhaps more than seventy years of age). He was invited to deliver the famous sermon on the Shabbat between Rosh Hashanah and Yom Kippur. One might think that he would have utilized this as a platform to ingratiate himself with the selection committee; however, this was not the Maharal, a person who saw himself as tasked with the mission to lead. Instead, he delivered a blistering, critical sermon focusing heavily on the terrible plague of slander which was then wracking the Prague community. At that time, certain people were circulating vicious rumors of illegitimacy about many prominent families. This was the so-called *Nadler* issue. At the end of the sermon, the Maharal issued a ban of excommunication on anyone engaged in *Nadler* slander. After the sermon, someone else was elected to the position of Chief Rabbi and the Maharal returned to Posen in 1584.

In 1588, the position of Chief Rabbi became vacant again and the Maharal returned to Prague.

In 1589, he published his commentary on Pirkei Avot (the Ethics of the Fathers), titled, Derech Chaim[2] (The Way of Life, probably a tribute to his brother, Chaim, who had passed away that year).

Some time after 1592 (and his famous audience with Emperor Rudolf II, reportedly discussing esoteric matters), he moved back to Posen and while there, he occupied the position of Chief Rabbi of Poland. While there, in 1596, he published a work of ethical character development, Netivot Olam (Paths of the World).

Finally, after four or five years in Posen, the Maharal returned to Prague to serve as the Chief Rabbi. In 1598 he published his Tiferet Yisrael (The Splendor of Israel – this work) and in the same year, B'er Hagolah (The Wellspring of the Exile) which was a thinly veiled rebuttal of the works of certain scholars (most prominently Azariah De Rossi) who had attacked the Aggadah (philosophical and exegetic sections of the Oral Torah).

His other published works are:

- *Netzach Yisrael* (The Eternity of Israel) – dealing with the themes of destruction and exile, published in 1599.
- *Ohr Chadash* (A New Light) – dealing with the festival of Purim, published in 1599 or 1600.
- *Ner Mitzvah* (A Mitzvah Candle) – dealing with the festival of Chanukah, published for the first time in 1798, to the best of my knowledge.
- *Chiddushei Aggadot* (Novel interpretations of Aggadah), published for the first time in 1957, to the best of my knowledge.
- *Chiddushei Halachot* (Novel interpretations of Halachah), published from 2006 onwards on various tractates.
- A collection of sermons, published for the first time in 1958, to the best of my knowledge.
- A commentary on the Tur (*Yoreh De'ah*) published in 1775.

In 1604, the Maharal resigned his position as Chief Rabbi, and on the 18th of Elul 5369 (1609) he passed away.

Impact

Almost unique to the Maharal is the impact he had on non-Jewish society, entering the folklore, theater and literature of the citizens of Prague. In 1917, when the new town-hall was erected, a statue of him was erected adjacent thereto. The legend of the Golem (which seems to have originated in the early 1800s) played no small part in this, as did his audience with the Em-

2. The frontispiece of the 1589 Krakow edition gives the name of this book as "Derech *Ha*Chaim", whilst in the Maharal's own introduction to this edition, we find the name he gives the work to be "Derech Chaim". We will use the Maharal's given title in this work.

peror. In 1592, he reportedly had an audience with Emperor Rudolf II, which he attended together with his brother Sinai and his son-in-law Yitzchak Cohen. The Emperor was known to be interested in alchemy, magic and Kabbalah, and this audience was reputedly a discussion regarding Kabbalah.

The Maharal's greatest impact of course was on the Torah world. As such an outstanding and controversial leader, however, his works were immediately overshadowed by his presence and much of his Torah languished in relative obscurity for close to 150 years. It was the leaders of several streams in the Chassidic world who revived the study of the Maharal and ensured that the study of his works was taken up by the Mussar (Ethics) movement and the religious-Zionist movement.

Another important legacy was his views on the correct methods of educating children in Torah. Although his ideas were never implemented in full in his lifetime or in the following century, slowly they gained popularity. The core of the Maharal's view is that children should be educated in an incremental manner, gaining mastery over Tanach (the Bible), then Mishnah (the first component of the Oral law), and then only thereafter should they turn to Gemara (the central component of the Oral law, and the most difficult). He also writes against the method of *pilpul* learning (a type of study which strayed far from the simple principles of Jewish law) which was so prevalent at the time.

As part of his educational outlook, he introduced the systematic study of Mishnah (the basis of the Oral Torah), something which did catch on fairly quickly and is a staple of Torah study till this day. His student, Rabbi Yom Tov Lipman Heller, wrote a commentary on the entire Mishnah (known as the Tos'fot Yom Tov) which is now printed as part of the standard editions of Mishnah.

The Nature of the Maharal's Torah

It is apparent from the Maharal's writings that he was learned in so many different disciplines in both the secular and holy worlds.

The golden thread which runs throughout all his works however, is the manner in which he related to Aggadah (the non-Halachic sections of Torah). The Maharal elevated the study of Aggadah to unprecedented heights, creating out of the seemingly disconnected statements of our sages a coherent, consistent Torah Hashkafah (philosophy).

As Rabbi Pinchas Gruman puts it so pithily,[3]

> Maharal's writings are beyond simple classification: They are not Kabbalah, yet there is a significant element of Kabbalah within them. They are not Torah

---

3. Approbation to *Maharal, Emerging Patterns*, Rabbi Yaakov Rosenblatt (Feldheim: 2001)

> exegeses, yet there is a significant amount of Torah exegeses within them. They are not philosophy, yet there is a significant element of philosophy within them. Indeed, they are all of the above, yet none of the above exclusively.

Indeed, quite simply, he is the Maharal; and I invite you to partake in his unique Torah.

TIFERET YISRAEL

INTRODUCTION

INTRODUCTION

Part 1 of 4

The Maharal begins by explaining the complete accessibility of Torah to all, regardless of their intellectual ability.

וזאת התורה אשר שם משה לפני בני ישראל (דברים ד׳) הכתוב הזה רוצה לומר, כי התורה חפץ מונח כל הרוצה לזכות בה יזכה בה, ולכך לא אמר אשר שם לבני ישראל רק לפני בני ישראל, כמו דבר המונח לפני כל הרוצה לזכות זוכה בה. ולא יאמר האדם כי התורה לא נתנה רק לגדולי החכמים שהם רחוקים מן הטעות, אבל התורה נתנה לכל.

"This is the Torah which Moshe placed before the children of Yisrael."[1] This verse means that the Torah is something which is placed in the open: any person who wishes to merit and possess it, can do so. Therefore, the verse did not say, "[which Moshe] *gave* to the children of Yisrael" but rather, "[which Moshe] *placed* before the children of Yisrael," like something which has been placed in the open, and any person wishing to merit and own it, can come and take it. A person should never say that the Torah was given only to the greatest of sages who are far from ever making a mistake. Rather, the Torah was given to everyone.

The Maharal now relates to people who feel they will make mistakes and are not smart enough to learn Torah. He cites a Midrash which proves that Hashem values the learning of a person who doesn't reach the deepest understanding of Torah, as long as that person is learning out of a desire to connect to Hashem in love. The Midrash also demonstrates that Hashem values the words of a person who loves Hashem but who is so ignorant that he doesn't even know enough Hebrew to say the words, "I love you Hashem," and instead ends up saying, "I hate you!" In both cases, the Maharal's point is that the foundation of learning Torah must be a motive of love for Hashem coupled with sincere effort, even if a person makes errors.

ולא יאמר גם כן אולי אשגה בתורה. ודבר זה פירשו במדרש (שה"ש רבה רפ"ב):

A person should also *not* say, "Perhaps I will make a mistake in [my understanding of] the Torah [and so I should rather not learn Torah]." This issue was explained by our sages in the Midrash:[2]

---

1. D'varim 4:44.
2. Shir Hashirim Rabbah 2:4.

הביאני אל בית היין ודגלו עלי אהבה.

רבי יונה אמר שני חברים העוסקים בהלכה זה אומר בית אב של הלכה וזה אינו אומר בית אב של הלכה אומר הקב"ה ודגלו עלי אהבה.

אמר רב אחא עם הארץ שקורא לאהבה איבה כגון ואהבת ואיבת אמר הקב"ה ודגלו עלי אהבה, ע"כ.

The verse states, "He brought Me to the house of wine, and his banner over Me was in love!"[3,4]

Rabbi Yonah said, "If two friends are *immersed* in Halachah[5] and one of them articulates an overarching principle of Halachah and the other does not, then [regarding the one who *doesn't* reach a complete understanding of the Halachah, but due to his dedication and love for Hashem,] Hashem says, 'his banner over Me was in love!'"

Rav Acha says, "[This verse applies to another, even more extreme case – where] an ignoramus misreads [the Sh'ma prayer,[6] and instead of reading], 'you shall love Hashem,'[7] he reads, 'you shall be an enemy of Hashem.'[8] This is when Hashem says [due to the ignoramus's love for Hashem, despite his error], 'his banner over Me was in love!'"[9]

Based on the Midrash above, the Maharal now begins explaining the wording of the blessing which Jews make before learning Torah (a blessing which we make each morning). The Maharal's idea is that the blessing's wording teaches us what the essence of Torah learning is. His explanation will begin with the description in the Midrash above of people who are *immersed* in learning Torah. It is the immersion which the Maharal will define as what Hashem really wants of us. (See the Commentary, Introduction § Point 2 and 3).

The Maharal will bring two explanations for the wording of the blessing made before learning Torah. His second explanation is that which will address his concern above – that people may not learn Torah for fear of misunderstanding and it will also address the question of the key thrust and purpose of Torah learning.

---

3. Shir Hashirim 2:4.

4. The use of uppercase or lowercase for the pronouns "me" and "his" reflects the Midrash's understanding of this verse, which has this sentence stated by G-d regarding Himself.

5. Torah Law.

6. D'varim 6:5.

7. In Hebrew, "*v'ahavta*," ואהבת.

8. In Hebrew, "*v'ayavta*," ואיבת. This is almost a homophone for the correct phrase and thus the error.

9. In our version of the Midrash, the verse here is actually paraphrased and it reads "*v'dilugo alay ahavah*," ודלוגו עלי אהבה, meaning, "and his skipping over me was in love." This is a pun, substituting "*v'dilugo*," ודלוגו, for "*v'diglo*," ודגלו, by swapping the *dalet* ד, and *gimmel*, ג, in the Hebrew so that the meaning now becomes, "his omission of the proper word, his skipping over the proper meaning, was in love."

פי׳ בית אב של הלכה שרש הלכה וטעמה. ומפני זה נראה כי הברכה על למוד התורה לעסוק בדברי תורה, ואין מברכין ללמוד תורה.

What is the "overarching principle of Halachah" mentioned in the Midrash? It is the root of the Halachah and its reason. It seems that [the ideas raised in] this [Midrash, regarding people who are immersed in Torah learning but who just don't manage to reach the deepest understanding of the root of the Halachah and its reason] is why the blessing we make over learning Torah [contains the phrase] "to be *immersed*[10] in the words of Torah" and we do not say "to *learn*[11] Torah."

The Maharal now brings his first explanation for the wording of the blessing made before learning Torah, which focuses on the technical requirements of fulfilling the mitzvah. Every mitzvah requires some type of physical action and in the case of learning Torah, that action is verbalizing the Torah which one learns. This is a type of "immersion" since human speech reflects the entirety of a human being, employing the mind and body; an idea we discuss in the Commentary, Ch. 3 § Point 6.

ועם שיש לפרש שלכך אנו מברכין לעסוק בדברי תורה, מפני שהברכה הזאת היא ברכת המצוות שחייב לברך על כל מצוות עשה, ואין מצות עשה רק בדבר שיש בו מעשה שהרי נקרא מצות עשה שחייב לעשות, ולכך יש לברך לעסוק דהיינו למוד תורה במעשה, וזה כאשר הוא מוציא הדבור זה נקרא עסק בתורה שהדבור נחשב מעשה, אבל למוד נקרא הבנת הדבר מה שלמד ואין הברכה רק על מעשה המצוה, ואם למד בעיון לבד אין לו לברך לעסוק בדברי תורה שזה נאמר על המעשה.

It is possible to explain that the reason for this specific wording of the blessing on learning Torah is rather, "to be immersed in the words of Torah," because this blessing is one which is said on a commandment and one is required to recite such a blessing before the performance of a *mitzvat aseh*.[12] Now a *mitzvat aseh* can only be fulfilled through some physical action – which is why its Hebrew name is "*mitzvat aseh*"[13] because a person is obligated to perform a specific action. Therefore, one could explain that the reason the blessing is, "to be immersed in the words of Torah," is that the commandment is to have one's learning of Torah actioned – which [only] happens when a person articulates *words* of Torah. This is called "immersing oneself" – the verbal framing of sentences of Torah is considered an action as opposed to the [purely intellectual] learning itself which is not called an action but is simply an

10. In Hebrew, "*la'asok*," לעסוק.

11. In Hebrew, "*lilmod*," ללמוד.

12. In Hebrew, "*mitzvat aseh*," מצוות עשה, literally "a commandment of action," as opposed to a command to refrain from some action, prohibition. For a discussion of this terminology, see the Commentary, Introduction § Point 1.

13. Lit., "commandment of doing."

intellectual understanding. The blessing, however, can only be recited over the action of the mitzvah,[14] so if a person just learned in-depth, and did not articulate a single word of his learning, he cannot say the blessing since the blessing is only said over the action [i.e., speaking the words of Torah].

The Maharal now brings a second, preferred explanation for the wording of the blessing made before learning Torah. This is his substantive proof that no person should ever refrain from learning Torah due to fear of error and it also begins to explain what Torah learning is really about.

אמנם נראה לומר כמו שאמרנו, כי לכך מברכין לעסוק בדברי תורה, כי ללמוד תורה לא שייך רק על מי שלמד תורה ומכוין ההלכה לאמיתתה שבזה שייך למוד תורה, אבל מי שאינו מכוין ההלכה על אמיתתה אין זה למוד. לכך מברכין לעסוק בדברי תורה, בין שהוא מכוין ההלכה או שאינו מכוין ההלכה, רק שיכוין ללמוד האמת אע"ג ששגג.

הרי כי למוד התורה לעצמו נקל מאד ואין צריך לחוש לשום דבר.

However, it seems that the reason for the blessing's wording is connected to the Midrash above – that the definition of a person who has "learned Torah" is one who has studied and in the process of that study, has actually arrived at the true [understanding of] Halachah. But, when a person studies and does not arrive at a true understanding of the Halachah, this is not defined as "learning." Therefore, the wording of the blessing is rather "to be *immersed* in the words of Torah" because this [term, "immersion"] includes both a person who arrives at a true understanding of the Halachah as well as one who does not, *as long as he intends to learn truth regardless of whether he errs.*

You can see from this that immersion in Torah, in and of itself, is very easy, since there is nothing to fear.[15]

The Maharal now explores the challenges of learning with a partner. In such a case, there is a greater need to reach a true understanding in one's learning as well as a need to communicate adequately; therefore, here there might be substantial

14. A blessing is usually recited prior to the performance of a *mitzvat aseh*, but it must be recited before the specific halachic action which constitutes fulfillment of that commandment. If one is not actually going to perform that action satisfactorily, one may not recite the blessing beforehand since one will not be fulfilling the mitzvah. See the Commentary, Introduction § Point 4 for an exploration of the Maharal's Halachic stance on the mitzvah of learning Torah.

15. Thus, to achieve the level of "immersion" one needs simply to immerse oneself in the study of Torah in an attempt to reach truth and one need not live in fear of falling short of that goal – one is still considered to be "immersed." See the Commentary, Introduction § Point 6 regarding the connection to Hashem bestowed by such immersion.

reasons to doubt whether one should learn Torah with a partner. Here, too, the Maharal will eventually supply a solution to these apprehensions which will prevent them from becoming realistic fears.

אמנם לשום דברי תורה לפני זולתו הוא קשה מב׳ פנים, האחד כי אם אינו מכוין ההלכה להאיר עיני זולתו בדבר אמת למה לה כי תכלית מה שיכוין המניח דברי תורה לפני זולתו להחכים אותו בדברי אמת ויושר, ודרך האמת רחוק משימצא ומכל שכן בדורות האלו שאבדה חכמה מבני אדם.

השני אף אם הוא מכוין ההלכה מי יודע אם יהיו לרצון אמרי פיו לזולתו, ואם לא יהיו לרצון עדיין לא הועיל דבר, ואין ספק כי כל פעולה אשר רחוק שיגיע הפועל אל תכלית כוונתו, אין ראוי שיפעל אותה פעולה שלא יהיה פעולתו לריק ולבטלה.

והדבר הזה אשר אמרנו אף בדורות השלמים היה צריך לאדם זירוז יתירה שלא יהיה נכשל בזה.

However, when you are learning with someone else and you need to present your conclusions before them, it is more challenging for two reasons. Firstly, if you don't arrive at a true understanding of Halachah, why are you bothering to say anything, since the whole purpose of learning with a fellow is to share wisdom with him through words of truth and correctness? (And the way of truth is generally difficult to find, how much more so in these generations when wisdom has been lost from people.)

The second reason that learning with a fellow is a greater challenge is that even if you do arrive at the correct understanding of the Halachah, who knows if the *way* you present [your understanding] to him will find favor in his eyes; and if he doesn't like what you say [even if it is only due to problems in communication], once again, there's no point in learning with him – [since] there's no doubt that it makes no sense to perform any action which is unlikely to achieve its purpose, since it will wind up being wasted and be pointless.[16]

All this was true even in the [previous,] more perfect generations – that a person would need huge energy not to fail in these two areas [– achieving true understanding and communicating it acceptably].

The Maharal now brings a Gemara which addresses the two difficulties raised above in connection with learning with a partner. He also begins to suggest a solution to these problems.

16. Therefore, learning with a partner can be so much harder and one might question whether it's worthwhile – it can be so difficult to understand Torah and then on top of that it's difficult to communicate certain ideas and the whole exercise can end up being wasted.

בפ׳ ד׳ דברכות (כ״ח ע״ב):

בכניסתו לב״ה מתפלל י״ר שלא אכשל בדבר הלכה ולא אומר על טהור טמא וישמחו בי חברי ולא יכשלו חברי בדבר הלכה ואשמח בהם ע״כ.

In the fourth chapter of Tractate B'rachot it states,[17]

> When one enters the academy,[18] one should pray, "May it be Your will, Hashem, that I do not stumble in a matter of Halachah and that I not rule that something which is really pure is impure and my friends will rejoice over me, and that my friends not stumble in a matter of Halachah and I rejoice over them."

The Maharal begins analyzing this prayer, which is different from the blessing on the Torah which he mentioned previously. His initial understanding (which he questions but eventually retains) is that this prayer is expressing the hope that when one does err in learning Torah, that his companions not rejoice in his error and that similarly he not rejoice when they stumble. Such pettiness reflects deeper issues regarding one's motivation for learning Torah and it is in this sphere – that of one's ultimate motivation – that the Maharal will locate the solution to the concerns one might have when learning Torah.

הרי שאף בת״ח גדול לב האדם נוטה לשמוח כאשר ימצא בדברי זולתו חסרון, כי כל אדם בטבעו ששמח בשלימות אשר יש לו על זולתו ולכך מתפלל שלא ילך אחר טבעו וישמח כשחברו נכשל בדבר הלכה והוא אינו נכשל.

Even in a great sage, the heart of a person tends to be happy when he finds a lacking in the words of his fellow because every person is happy in the relative perfection he has above his fellow. Therefore, the prayer we say before we enter the Beit Midrash is that we not follow our nature and not rejoice when our fellow stumbles, yet we don't stumble.

The Maharal now offers an alternative explanation for this Gemara in B'rachot, which he subsequently rejects.

ואם כי יש לפרש ההפך מה שאמר וישמחו חברי בי, תפלה שישמחו חבריו בו כאשר לא יכשל הוא בדבר הלכה. אין המאמר סובל זה, שעדיין לא אמר שיאמר דבר הלכה, רק שאמר בדרך שלילה שלא אכשל בדבר הלכה, ואולי לא יאמר דבר הלכה כלל כי לא כל אדם יאמר דבר הלכה בבית

One could suggest that really, when the Gemara states, "that I not rule that something which is really pure is impure and my friends will rejoice over me . . ." it doesn't mean that the rejoicing is over your failure, but rather that this phrase [regarding rejoicing] is not connected to the phrase regarding failure in render-

17. B'rachot 28b.

18. In Hebrew, "*Beit HaMidrash*," בית המדרש.

המדרש, והיה לו לומר יהי רצון שאומר על טהור טהור ועל טמא טמא וישמחו חברי בי, ופירוש רש"י ז"ל יוכיח.

ing judgment. Thus the meaning of the prayer is, rather, that when one *succeeds* in rendering correct judgment that he prays that his friends will rejoice over him and vice versa.

However, this doesn't fit the plain meaning of the prayer[19] since till this point the Gemara only spoke in the negative, "that I *not* rule that something which is really pure is impure" [and made no mention of a correct ruling] – perhaps this person will not say any word of Halachah at all, not everyone in the Beit Midrash does! If this [second] explanation were correct, the text of the prayer should have been, "May it be Your will, Hashem, that I rule that something which is really pure is pure and that something which is really impure is impure and that [subsequent to my successful decisions] my friends will rejoice over me . . ." The explanation of Rashi proves [that the Maharal's rejection of this second explanation is correct].[20]

Having raised the real apprehension people might have in learning Torah (both as individuals and with partners), the Maharal now offers his profound solution. He explains that Torah learning is not some isolated encounter between a person and a Holy Text; rather it is fundamentally a setting and means for an intimate relationship between a person (or people) and Hashem. If this is one's motivation, Hashem becomes part of the process of learning Torah and both concerns raised previously (achieving true understanding and communicating it) will not materialize.

ואם הדבר הוא כך בשלמי המעלה מכ"ש בדור הבלתי שלם אשר כל דברי זולתו אינם לו לרצון, כי לא ילמוד זכות על האומר והרי הקושי מצד שני פנים.

אמנם להנצל מזה, כאשר יכוין מעשיו אל השי"ת אשר הוריש אל האדם התורה והחכמה גם עתה, יתן לו תורתו וידריך אותו בנתיבות אמת כי מאתו תצא תורה.

If all this is true regarding people who were complete in their stature [in previous generations], how much more so is it true for our imperfect generation in which nothing anyone else says finds favor in one's eyes since no one evaluates others' words with the benefit of the doubt. So today the difficulty in learning with a fellow lies in both reasons mentioned above.

19. Since according to such an explanation there is a clause missing which should change the prayer to, "that I not rule that something which is really pure is impure *and that when I do render a correct judgment* my friends will rejoice over me . . ."

20. Rashi writes (B'rachot 28b, s.v. *v'lo ekashel*), "What is the meaning of the phrase in the text of the prayer, 'that I not stumble?' It means that one prays that one not stumble and that one's friends not rejoice at this failure." Thus Rashi concurs with the Maharal's explanation that the rejoicing here is at a fellow's failure to understand.

How then can one be saved from this [misunderstanding and G-d forbid, rejoicing at another's misunderstanding]?

A person needs to intend that all his actions be performed for the sake of Hashem who bequeathed His Torah and wisdom to humans and continues to do so till this day; and that Hashem should give him His Torah and guide him in the paths of truth because from Him comes Torah.

The idea mentioned above – that the true learning of Torah only happens through a constant, current relationship of love with Hashem – forms the backbone of the Maharal's solution to the challenges of reaching a true understanding of Torah and to being able to communicate it effectively. The rest of the Introduction is pretty much an elaboration and expansion of this idea. The Maharal now brings his first example of an application of this idea – the true reason for the destruction of the First Temple.

ובפרק אלו נדרים (דף פ"א.):

אמר רב יהודה אמר רב מאי דכתיב מי האיש החכם ויבין את זאת על מה אבדה הארץ וגו' דבר זה נשאל לחכמים ולנביאים ולמלאכים ולא פירשוהו עד שפירשו הקב"ה בעצמו שנאמר ויאמר ה' על עזבם תורתי ולא הלכו בה.

היינו ולא שמעו בקולי היינו ולא הלכו בה!

אמר רב שלא ברכו בתורה תחלה, ע"כ.

In Tractate N'darim it states,[21]

Rav Yehudah said in the name of Rav, "What does the Torah mean when it says, 'Who is the wise person who will understand this? . . . Why was the Land of Israel destroyed?'[22] Well, this question [why the Land of Israel was destroyed at the time of the First Temple] was asked to sages, prophets and even angels, but none of them could explain it until Hashem Himself explained it [as the verse continues, citing Hashem's answer to this question], Hashem said, 'Because they left My Torah which I placed before them and they did not listen to My voice and they did not walk in its way.'"

[The Gemara asks,] But what does this verse mean? [It seems to have redundancies] – surely "they did not listen to My voice" means the same thing as "they did not walk in its way"?

Rav answered this redundancy by saying, "What this [extra phrase, 'they did not walk in its way'] means is that the Jews at the time [of the First Temple] did not make the blessing on the Torah before they learned. That is why the Temple and the Land of Israel were destroyed."

ודבר זה מן התימה שיהיה חרבן הארץ בשביל שלא ברכו בתורה תחלה, ולא בשביל עכו"ם וגלוי עריות ושפיכת דמים שהיו בבית ראשון.

Now such a statement is astonishing. How could the destruction of the land have been due to them not making a blessing on the Torah beforehand? [The

21. N'darim 81a.
22. Yirmiyahu 9:11.

Gemara in Yoma says that] the destruction was due to the three cardinal sins which were widespread at that time in Israel – idol worship, sexual immorality and murder![23]

The Maharal's answer to his own question first requires an analysis of what "a reason" for something is. He explains that "a reason" for something accomplishes two tasks: it brings that thing into existence and then sustains it in existence.

אמנם ביאור זה כי הדבר שהוא סבה אל מציאות דבר אחר הוא ג"כ סבה אל קיום מציאותו. ואל יקשה לך כי הנגר הוא סבה לבנין הבית, ועם כל זה בהעדר הנגר ישאר הבית קיים. דבר זה אינו, כי אין הנגר סבה לבית רק שהוא מקרב העצים יחד, ודבר זה הנגר פועל לא עצם הבית והבית נעשה מן הנגר במקרה. אבל דבר שהוא סבה בעצם אל מציאות דבר אחר כל שכן שהוא סבה לקיום שלו שהרי היה סבה שיהיה נמצא וכן גם כן הוא סבה לקיום שלו ודבר זה מבואר במופת.

However, the explanation of this is as follows. If something is the reason for the existence of something else, it is also the reason for the *continued existence* of the second thing. Don't think, for example, that a carpenter is the "reason" for the building of a house and yet without him, the house still stands. This is incorrect, because a carpenter is not the reason for the house's existence, he only links the beams together – he does not create the essence of the house. But, when one says that something is the reason for something else it is clear that it is also the reason for its continued existence, since the reason created it in the first place. This can be easily demonstrated by experiment.

Using this foundation, the Maharal explains that Hashem is the "reason" for the Torah which means that He not only gives us the Torah initially, but that His presence is required in order for the Torah's existence to be sustained within a person.

ולפיכך אם היו מברכין על התורה תחלה לומר ברוך נותן תורה לישראל, והיה אהבה אל הש"י במה שנתן תורה לישראל, כי זה ענין הברכה על התורה שהוא יתברך מבורך על זה ואוהב השי"ת בשביל הטוב שנתן לו התורה, ואז היה זה סבה ג"כ שתהיה התורה מתקיימת בישראל, שהיה השי"ת נותן בלבם לשמור ולעשות ולקיים אף אם

Therefore, if the people [at the time of the First Temple] had first made the blessing on the Torah, saying, "Blessed is the One who *gives*[24] Torah to Israel," they would thereby have [expressed their] love towards Hashem for giving the Torah to Israel; this is because the idea behind the blessing is that Hashem is blessed [by a person] for giving him the

23. Yoma 9b.

24. This word is in the present tense which buttresses the Maharal's claim that a relationship with Hashem is needed at every moment if a person wishes to have Torah, because even now it is still Hashem who *gives* the Torah.

היו עוברים לפעמים מצוה אחת, היו חוזרים מיד לשמור ולעשות ולקיים, וזה היה מן השי"ת אשר הוא סבה לתורה והוא גם כן סבה שלא תתבטל.

דומה לזה, כאשר הגיע נזק אל ענף היוצא מן האילן, אז העקר שממנו יצא חוזר וגודל גדולו מן השרש אשר היה סבה לגדול שלו שיצא, ובלא השורש אין קיום לאילן כלל.

ולפיכך אילו היו מברכין בתורה תחלה, מה שהוא יתברך סבה לתורה ונתן להם התורה, והיו דבקים בו יתברך באהבה במה שנתן תורה לישראל, מצד הדבקות הזה היה השי"ת סבה גם כן שלא תתבטל התורה. אבל מפני שלא ברכו בתורה תחלה, שלא היו דבקים בו יתברך באהבה במה שנתן תורה לישראל, לא היה כאן סבה מקיימת את התורה בישראל, ובאו לידי זה שעברו על התורה ודבר זה גורם שאבדה הארץ.

Torah and that a person loves Hashem because of the goodness of His giving him the Torah. This then becomes the reason that Torah would have continued to exist within Israel, because Hashem would have implanted in their heart to guard, perform and observe the Torah. And even if sometimes they transgressed, they would have immediately returned to guard, perform and observe the Torah which would be due to Hashem, Who is the reason for the Torah's primal existence and Who is also the reason for its continued existence.

A parable for this is as follows: if a branch, growing from a tree, is damaged then the trunk (from which that branch grew) renews itself and develops new growth [all ultimately] emanating from the root which is the reason for its original growth. But without the root, a tree cannot exist at all.

Therefore, if [at the time of the First Temple] people had first made the blessing over the Torah (before they learned) and had acknowledged that Hashem is the reason for Torah and gave them the Torah, *and if they had bonded with Hashem because He gave us the Torah, then that very bonding with Hashem would have prevented the Torah's nullification [within their society.]* But, since they did not first make the blessing on the Torah and they did not bond with Hashem in love out of recognition that He gave us the Torah, there was no connection to the reason which sustains Torah in Israel,[25] and therefore, they arrived at a situation wherein they transgressed the [whole] Torah and this caused the destruction of the Land.

The Maharal here concludes his first example of how Torah is learned and sustained. His thesis is that Torah is not abstract knowledge, disconnected from Hashem. Rather, Torah is a vibrant, vital part of our loving relationship and bonding with Hashem. Without this relationship, true Torah is unattainable. Furthermore, as the Maharal explains here, Torah cannot be sustained without this relationship and as he illustrated before, the only way one can attain a true understanding of Torah and an ability to communicate Torah is if Hashem is part of the process, giving one that

25. I.e., Hashem.

true understanding and helping one communicate, every step of the way. This is a virtuous cycle: a loving relationship with Hashem enables one to acquire a more profound Torah; and a deeper Torah further weaves a greater depth into one's relationship with Hashem. The Pachad Yitzchak has a profound analysis of this dynamic which we outline in the Commentary, Introduction § Point 8.

SUMMARY

Introduction 1/4

I. The Torah is accessible to every Jew

A. A person should never avoid learning and spiritual growth for fear of misunderstanding.

1. The Midrash in Shir Hashirim Rabbah teaches us that Hashem values the Torah study even of a person who doesn't reach a true understanding of Torah.
2. Two ways to explain the wording of the Blessing on the Torah, "to be immersed in the words of Torah":
    a. "Immersion in words of Torah" refers to the physical action of the mitzvah.
        (1) There is a blessing said before the performance of mitzvot, but it is always said prior to the physical action of that mitzvah.
        (2) In learning Torah, the action is the articulation of words of Torah studied.
        (3) Therefore, the blessing can only be said prior to the action, which is articulation.
        (4) This is why the blessing is, "to be immersed in the words of Torah" (which emphasizes the articulation) as opposed to "to learn Torah" (which emphasizes the silent, inward, intellectual experience).
    b. "Learning" refers to understanding truly; "Immersion" can happen even without true understanding.
        (1) The Maharal explains that the mitzvah of studying Torah is not fulfilled exclusively by those who reach a true understanding of Torah (referred to as "learning Torah") but also by those who strive for that Truth, even if they fall short of true understanding (referred to as "being immersed in Torah").
        (2) The blessing includes everyone, even those who do not understand, as long as their aim is to reach truth and Hashem.
        (3) Thus, it is relatively easy to reach a level of "immersion" in Torah and one should not refrain from Torah study for fear of misunderstanding, since Torah study goes beyond just getting a true understanding and is, at the most basic level, about being immersed in a loving relationship with Hashem.

II. The difficulty and the necessity of learning with someone else

A. Two difficulties
   1. One's conclusions must be true – not just learning regardless of the truth of outcomes.
   2. Even true conclusions must be presented favorably to a second party.

B. Overcoming these difficulties using the prayer said upon entering the Beit Midrash.
   1. This is not the blessing on the Torah mentioned above, but a prayer said just before entering the Beit Midrash.
   2. The prayer addresses the need to overcome one's "natural" joy at seeing one's own relative perfection reflected in the relative imperfection of someone else. This "natural" joy is a symptom of the greatest impediment to Torah study: disconnection from Hashem.
   3. The prayer said on entering the Beit Midrash lays out one's aim in learning which should be to join with Hashem and be guided by Him in all ways.
   4. This will aid one in overcoming both difficulties:
      a. Hashem will help the person better understand Torah.
      b. Hashem will help the person communicate his ideas to his fellow.

C. Once again, the necessity for striving to have a relationship with Hashem (within the context of Torah) is the basis for Torah study and with it, one need have no fear of misunderstandings or miscommunications.

III. The reason for destruction of First Temple = Not having a connection to Hashem through Torah study

A. N'darim 81a
   1. The Gemara teaches us that the reason for the destruction of the First Temple was that people did not make the blessing before learning Torah.
   2. The Maharal questions this statement:
      a. How could something so seemingly trivial have caused such utter destruction?
      b. The Gemara in Yoma (9b) contradicts ours by saying that the cause of the destruction of the First Temple was that the Jewish people committed idolatry, sexual immorality and murder.

B. The Maharal's explanation
   1. The Reason for something's existence
      a. Reason = primal existence + continued existence
         (1) The Maharal defines the "reason" for something as being the initiator of that object's existence, as well as the continuing sustainer of that object's existence.

(2) Therefore, if the reason is removed, the object cannot exist any more.

b. Analogy: Branch on a tree with a root

(1) The root is the real reason for the branch, the root caused the branch to sprout initially, and without the root, the branch will wither and die.

2. The Reason for Torah = Hashem

a. The Blessings on the Torah ensure that we are connected to the Reason for Torah (i.e., Hashem).

C. Without connecting to Hashem, Torah dissolves and Torah life is not sustainable. This is why the land was destroyed at the time of the First Temple, because even though people learned Torah, they were disconnected from Hashem and thus their Torah dissolved.

D. Once again, if one strives to have a relationship with Hashem through Torah study, one need not fear the challenges of learning, communicating or retaining one's Torah, either personally or societally. Their not saying the blessing on the Torah was a symptom of their disconnection from Hashem.

INTRODUCTION

Part 2 of 4

The Maharal continues with his explanation of the Gemara in N'darim (cited earlier in the Introduction) and of his main thesis: the need for bonding with Hashem through the Torah.

In the Gemara above[1] it states that the question [as to why the First Temple and the Land of Israel were destroyed] was asked to three different groups – sages, prophets and angels – none of whom could answer it.

The explanation of this is that there is a hint to three different levels here. There is the level of wisdom which relates to a human's intellectual ability (while living in the lower, physical world) to understand and grasp concepts [this is symbolized by the sages.] The second level is that of prophecy, which prophets achieve. Prophets are people who live in this lower, physical world but they receive heavenly, spiritual guidance from the upper worlds. The third level is that of the comprehension achieved amongst those who dwell in the upper worlds – for example, angels.

That Hashem is the *reason*[2] for the Torah, is out of reach of the level of sages, prophets and angels, too; because all of these levels are manifestations[3] and results[4] [of G-d's existence, Who is the

ואמרו דבר זה נשאל וכו'.

פירוש שג' מדרגות הם, המדרגה האחת היא מדרגת החכמה שיש לאדם בתחתונים מה שיכול האדם להשיג, המדרגה השניה היא מדרגת הנבואה שהיא על הנביאים, שהם בני אדם שהם בעוה"ז ובא להם רוה"ק מעליונים, המדרגה הג' היא ההשגה שהיא בעליונים כי המלאכים הם עליונים.

וזה שאמר דבר זה נשאל וכו', כי מה שהוא יתברך סבה לתורה הוא יותר עליון מן מדרגת חכמים נביאים ומלאכים, כי אלו כולם הם עלולים ומסובבים, ואינם מגיעים אל דבר שהוא מצד העלה דוקא, ומצד העלולים אין ידיעה לזה. כי אף אם היו נותנים הסבה שאבדה הארץ בשביל שחטאו לא היה זה סיבה לאבוד הארץ, כי אם חטאו היה הש"י מקיים התורה בהם והיו חוזרים למוטב.

רק הסבה היה שלא ברכו בתורה תחלה ובזה בא להם אבוד הארץ, ואלו היו דבקים בו יתברך במה שנתן תורה אז היה השם יתברך עמהם במה שנתן התורה להם. וכמו שהיה הוא יתברך

1. Cited earlier.
2. The Maharal explained his understanding of the concept of a "reason" earlier in this chapter.
3. To use the Maharal's metaphor, they are all like the leaves on a tree.
4. See the Commentary, Introduction § Points 1 and 7 for a note on terminology and a broader discussion.

הסבה למציאות התורה בהם היה גם כן סבה לקיום התורה בהם ולא אבדה הארץ. אבל עתה שלא היו מברכים בתורה תחלה ולא היו דבקים בו יתברך במה שנתן תורה לישראל, ג"כ לא היה השם יתברך עמהם לקיים התורה, וזה היה גורם שאבדה הארץ.

Primal Cause[5]], and they do not reach the level of that which is the Primal Cause[6] and [thus] they have no knowledge [of what happens at Hashem's level – the level of the Primal Cause]. So even if the sages, prophets or angels had said that the reason that the destruction [of the Temple and land] occurred was that the Jews sinned, this alone would not be a sufficient reason to explain the destruction – because as we explained above, if the Jews were really connected to Hashem, He would have sustained the Torah within them and they would have returned to the good [even if they had sinned].

Rather, the real reason for the destruction was, as we explained before,[7] that they did not say the blessing over the Torah before learning, and this is how the land was destroyed. However, had the Jews at the time bonded with Hashem through His giving of the Torah to them, Hashem would have been with them through this recognition. Then, just as Hashem would have been the reason for the Torah's initial existence within them, so, too, would He have been the reason for its sustained existence within them and the land would not have been destroyed. But since they did not make the blessing over the Torah before they learned, and therefore did not bond with Hashem through His act of giving the Torah to Israel, Hashem was not with them to sustain the Torah within them and this is what caused the destruction of the land.[8]

The Maharal clarifies that the meaning of the Gemara is not that the people at the time of the First Temple did not say the words of the blessing before learning Torah; they did say the words of the blessing, but there was no emotional or spiritual connection to Hashem – it was just empty words.

ואל יקשה לך למה לא היו מברכין בתורה תחלה, שאין פירוש הברכה

Don't think that this means that they didn't say the words of the blessing;

5. See the Commentary, Introduction § Points 1 and 7 for a note on terminology and a broader discussion.

6. The leaves on a tree are sustained by the root, which is (originally and sometimes permanently) independent of the leaves.

7. Earlier in this chapter.

8. As we saw in the first part of the Introduction, the Maharal explains that the fundamental flaw of the people at the time of the First Temple was that they did not understand that Hashem is the *reason* of the Torah, and while they did learn Torah, they did not connect to G-d. Due to this lack of connection, the Torah could not endure amongst them since the Torah's existence requires G-d's presence.

they definitely did! Rather, they had no connection to the blessing itself, which is the absolute love and bonding with Hashem, loving Hashem for giving us the Torah – this is the essence of the blessing.

Now, not all loves are equal – true love is the love with *all* [one's] heart and soul, as the Torah writes, "You shall love Hashem your G-d with all your heart and with all your soul and with all your might."[9] The Jews at that time, however, did not have this complete love for Hashem for His giving us the Torah – which was especially wrong since the Torah is the greatest goodness possible (therefore, a person should bless Hashem for this with all one's heart) – so they did not bless Hashem with all their heart, which they should have done in accordance with this superior goodness [which is the Torah].

הדבור בפה בלבד, דודאי הדבור בפה היו מברכים, אבל הכוונה על הברכה בעצמה היא האהבה הגמורה והדבקות אל השם יתברך, לאהוב השם יתברך במה שנתן תורה, וזהו ענין הברכה.

ואין כל האהבות שוות, כי האהבה האמתית היא האהבה בכל לב ובכל נפש, וכדכתיב (דברים ו׳) ואהבת את ה׳ א-להיך בכל לבבך ובכל נפשך ובכל מאדך, ולא היה להם האהבה הגמורה אל השם יתברך במה שנתן התורה לישראל, ובפרט על הטובה הגדולה שהיא התורה שהיא טובה על הכל, שיש לברך הש״י ויתעלה שמו על זה בכל לבו וכפי הטובה העליונה לא היו מברכים בכל לבם.

The Maharal introduces his thesis that even Torah scholars find it challenging to bond with Hashem while learning Torah, since one can truly bond with only one significant other, in this case, the Torah or Hashem. This then impacts heavily on the nature of one's Torah learning.

This idea also explains another statement of our sages, of blessed memory,[10] in N'darim,[11]

> Why do some sages not have students who become sages themselves? Because [the teaching sages] do not say the blessing before learning Torah.

Here, too, this doesn't mean that these sages don't say the words with their mouths, they do; but it means that for this thing – the giving of the Torah – one

וזה שאמרו שם (נדרים פ״א ע״א) ג״כ:

> מפני מה אין תלמידי חכמים מצויים שיוצאים מהם תלמידי חכמים מפני שאין מברכין בתורה תחלה.

כי אף אם היו מברכין בפה, מ״מ דבר הזה שהוא נתינת התורה צריך לברך הש״י בכל לבו, ובזה יש לו האהבה הגמורה אל השי״ת.

ואף אם הוא תלמיד חכם והוא צדיק גמור, רחוק הדבר הזה שיברך הש״י בכל לבו על נתינת התורה כפי הראוי. ועוד כי התלמיד חכם לבו דבק אל

9. D'varim 6:5.
10. In Hebrew, "*Chazal*," חז״ל, "our sages of blessed memory."
11. N'darim 81a.

התורה כי חביבה התורה על לומדיה, ובשביל אהבתם לתורה דבר זה מסלק אהבת המקום בשעה זאת שבאים ללמוד, כי כאשר באים ללמוד תורה ואהבתם אל התורה, אין בלמוד שלהם האהבה אל השם יתברך במה שנתן תורה, כי אין האהבה לשנים, כי כל אהבה היא דבקות בנאהב ואם דבק בזה אינו דבק באחר, ולפיכך אהבת התורה שהיא חביבה עליהם, דבר זה מסלק שאין הברכה בכל לבו אל השי"ת במה שנתן התורה. וזה שאין מברכים בתורה תחלה, ולפיכך אין יוצאים מהם תלמידי חכמים.

כי אלו היו אוהבים אותו במה שהתורה נמצא מאתו יתברך, היה השם יתברך ג"כ סבה לתורה לצאת מהם תלמידי חכמים, ועתה שהם דבקים ורודפים אחר התורה עצמה בלבד, ואינם דבקים בו יתברך במה שהוא יתברך סבה לתורה, לא היה יוצא מאתם תלמיד חכם שיש בו תורה, שאין כאן הסבה המשפיע את התורה הוא התלמיד חכם.

needs to bless Hashem with all one' s heart and thereby one has complete love for Hashem.

Even if a person is a Torah scholar[12] and a completely righteous person, it is still rare that he blesses Hashem with all his heart (as is suitable) about the giving of the Torah. Moreover, a Torah scholar's heart actually bonds with the Torah because Torah is loved by those who learn it, and their love for Torah removes the love of Hashem at the time that they come to learn. [This happens] because, when they come to learn Torah, their love is for the Torah and they don't have love for Hashem for giving the Torah – because it is impossible to love two things simultaneously.[13] The reason for this [not being able to love two things simultaneously] is that every love is actually a bonding with the beloved; and if a person is so joined to one thing, he cannot be bonding with something else simultaneously. Therefore, the love of Torah (which is so dear to them) removes from them the ability to bless Hashem with all their heart for giving them the Torah. This is what it[14] means that they didn't make the blessing first over the Torah. Therefore, these sages do not produce other sages.

But if the [teaching] sages loved Hashem through the fact that the Torah is maintained by Hashem, then Hashem would also be the reason for the continued existence within them of the Torah, and therefore, they would produce disciples who became sages. But now that they are bonding with and pursuing Torah for its own sake and do not bond with Hashem as the reason for the Torah, they cannot produce disciples who are sages because the reason which is generating the Torah [i.e., Hashem] is not present [but rather] the sage is bestowing [the Torah on the student and Hashem is not bestowing the Torah on the student.]

12. In Hebrew, "*talmid chacham*," תלמיד חכם, "a sage."
13. See the Commentary, Introduction § Point 5.
14. The Gemara.

The Maharal returns to explaining the Gemara in N'darim based on the principles he has laid down. Firstly he explains how the verse cited there actually fits the Gemara.

וזה שאמר הכתוב (ירמי' ט') ולא שמעו בקולי נגד התורה עצמה, ולא הלכו בה שלא לקחו התורה עם סבתה, כי לקיחת התורה עם סבתה נקרא הליכה בתורה לגמרי.

This is what the Torah means when it says, "They did not listen to My voice,"[15] which refers to the [fact that the Jews at the time of the destruction of the First Temple did not observe the] Torah itself; while, "and they did not walk in it" refers to the fact that they [additionally] didn't take the Torah along with its reason and cause [i.e., Hashem], because taking the Torah along with taking G-d is called "complete walking in the Torah."

The Maharal continues his explanation (begun above) as to why no one but Hashem knew why the First Temple was destroyed, applying his central principles.

ומפני זה לא היו יודעים דבר זה לא חכמים ולא נביאים ולא המלאכים, כי דבר זה מגיע אל הסבה הראשונה בפרט ואין מגיע אל המסובב, וכל אלו הם עלולים ומסובבין ולכן פרשה הקב"ה בעצמו.

This is also the reason that no one understood that this was the cause of the destruction of the Temple – not the sages, the prophets nor the angels – because this [i.e., the status of the loving relationship or lack thereof between human beings and Hashem] reaches all the way up to the reason of Torah – G-d Himself – and has nothing to do with anything G-d created (and the sages, prophets and angels are all creations and effects). Therefore, G-d alone could answer the question [as to why the destruction occurred].[16]

The Maharal continues his explanation (begun above) as to why certain sages do not produce disciples who themselves become sages. Here, too, he applies the key principles. He again makes use of the metaphor of the tree from which fruit is detached, in which case the fruit will rot.

15. For further reference, see the Gemara as we cited it in its entirety earlier in the Introduction. This quote from Yirmiyahu 9:11 is cited there in its entirety.

16. The question was brought in the Gemara as to why the Land of Israel was destroyed. The answer the Maharal supplied earlier was that the people, even though they learned Torah, did not have a bond with Hashem through their Torah learning. The expansion brought here is that Hashem alone (and not angels, prophets or sages) knew that the people were not connecting to Him through the Torah since He alone knew whether He and they shared that intimate relationship or not.

וכן אם אין תלמיד חכם מברך בתורה תחלה, אין לוקח את התורה עם סבת התורה, ויש כאן הסרה והפסק, ואין יוצאין ממנו תלמידי חכמים, כמו מי שלקח אילן בלא שרש אשר ממנו האילן אז אין נמשך פרי ממנו, ולפיכך אם מברך בתורה תחלה יוצא מהם תלמיד חכם ועושה פרי.

So, too, if a sage doesn't make the blessing on the Torah first [before learning], he doesn't take the Torah with its Cause [i.e., G-d] and he has a removal and impediment and therefore he cannot produce [students who become] sages. This is the same as one who examines a tree which has no root [from which the tree stems] – it is clear that this tree cannot produce fruit. But if a sage makes the blessing on the Torah first, he would produce disciples who are sages, that is, he would produce fruit.

The Maharal returns to the questions with which he began this Introduction – how can one ensure that one reaches a true understanding of Torah as well as communicating it adequately? The answer is identical for both questions – the only way that Torah can be understood, communicated, maintained and transmitted to the next generation is if, and only if, a person learns Torah in the context of a loving relationship with Hashem.

ומפני כך כאשר האדם מכוין בתורה להש"י אשר נתן התורה, גם כן הש"י מציל אותו מן השגיאה ויאיר עיניו בתורתו.

Because of this, while he is learning, if a person concentrates on Hashem who gave the Torah, Hashem will save him from error and enlighten his eyes in Torah.

SUMMARY

Introduction: 2/4

I. Further analysis of the Gemara in N'darim 81a

A. The three levels of beings who were asked the reason for the destruction of the Temple:
   1. The three levels
      a. Sages: They live in this world but have an intellectual understanding which is beyond this world.
      b. Prophets: They live in this world but get information from spiritual worlds.
      c. Angels: They live completely in spiritual worlds.
   2. All three of these levels are caused and created, they are not the Cause. They are like branches on the tree. Therefore, the beings occupying these levels have no knowledge of what happens at the level of the Prime Cause, i.e., Hashem, since they do not exist at that level.
   3. Therefore, none of the sages, prophets or angels could arrive at an understanding of the true reason for the destruction of the land and Temple. They could see the symptoms (i.e., immoral behavior and sin), but they could not penetrate to the ultimate reason which was the lack of loving relationship between the Jewish people and Hashem. The only One who knows the status of this relationship is Hashem since it is so intimate and takes place directly between Hashem and individuals.

B. This is another application of the Maharal's principle that true Torah learning can only happen within the context of a loving relationship with Hashem.
   1. Learning Torah as a way of connecting to Hashem, actually forms that connection which serves to:
      a. Preserve Torah within a person.
      b. Ensure that even if one stumbles spiritually, that the Torah within them remains and helps return them to the correct path.

C. The Essence of the Blessing over Torah = loving Hashem for giving us the Torah
   1. This should be expressed by a complete love for Hashem.
   2. This complete love is suitable since the Torah is the ultimate goodness.

II. Why do some sages' disciples not become sages themselves?

A. Because those sages have the same problem as the Jews at the time of the First Temple:
   1. They say the words of the blessing on the Torah, but they do not completely, lovingly bond with Hashem through His giving of the Torah.

B. Why do some great sages not connect to Hashem through the Torah?
   1. They bond with the Torah in and of itself in an absolute and complete join which prevents them from bonding with Hashem.

C. The results of their connection to Torah superseding their connection to Hashem
   1. The reason for the Torah, i.e., G-d, is not part of them when they study Torah, therefore, their students connect to Torah through the sage alone and have no connection to Hashem, and without a connection to Hashem, they cannot connect to Torah.
   2. The sage is like a tree which is rootless and thus cannot produce fruit, and therefore, the sage cannot produce disciples who are sages.

D. This is another application of the Maharal's principle that true Torah learning can only happen within the context of a loving relationship with Hashem.

III. Explanation of the verse's phrasing: "walking in the Torah"

A. Walking in the Torah = taking the Torah along with Hashem as its reason

B. Without Hashem in the picture, a person has no flow from the reason of the Torah (Hashem) to the Torah itself to the person.

IV. Application of the principle in one's personal learning

A. Without a connection to Hashem during learning, a person will make errors and will misunderstand.

B. If a person is connected to Hashem while learning, Hashem will help the person avoid errors and will help him arrive at a true understanding.

INTRODUCTION

Part 3 of 4

The Maharal now begins a lengthy explanation of Tehillim 19,[1] in which he expands on the central theme we have seen thus far – the need for bonding with Hashem through Torah learning. He does all this within the context of addressing the two challenges facing the Torah scholar which he has raised previously: the need to reach truth and the need to communicate it effectively. As we will see, only at the very end of his extensive commentary on the Tehillim, does the Maharal arrive at King David's statements on these two challenges and thus it seems that the Maharal's intention is not simply to cite the view in Tehillim on these two issues, but rather to deepen our understanding of the way in which Torah assists one in bonding with Hashem (which forms the bulk of the Maharal's commentary here). Here, he addresses the issue from the opposite direction to that which he has examined thus far: not only is a bond with Hashem needed for Torah study, but Torah study enables and enhances this bond.

When King David saw these two things which we have mentioned (i) that a person should be concerned that he fail to understand words of Torah and (ii) that even if he does understand, he may not be able to communicate his understanding favorably to his fellow, he [King David] discussed this in the Tehillim [which begins,] "[For the conductor.] A Psalm [by David,] the Heavens relate the glory of G-d."[2]

First, he [King David] addresses the excellence of the Torah:

> The Torah of Hashem is perfect and innocent,[3] it restores the soul; [the tes-

וכאשר ראה דוד לפניו שני דברים אלו אשר זכרנו, האחד שהיה ירא פן יכשל בד"ת, והשני שלא יהיו דבריו לרצון לזולתו, נגד זה סדר דבריו במזמור השמים מספרים כבוד א-ל וגו' (תהלים י"ט).

הקדים תחלה לספר מעלת התורה שאמר:

> תורת ה' תמימה משיבת נפש פקודי ה' וגו'.

עד

> גם עבדך נזהר בהם בשמרם עקב רב.

ולפי מעלת הדבר צריך שיהיה נזהר שלא יכשל בו.

---

1. "*Tehillim*" is a Psalm. See the Commentary, Introduction § Point 15, for further commentary by the Maharal on this Tehillim.

2. Psalm 19.

3. In Hebrew, "*t'mimah*," תמימה. See the Commentary, Introduction § Point 1 for a note on terminology.

timony of Hashem is faithful, making the simple person wise.] The precepts of Hashem [are honest, rejoicing the heart; the commandment of Hashem is pristine, enlightening the eyes. The Awe of Hashem is pure, enduring for ever; the ordinances of Hashem are true, they are righteous altogether. They are more desired than gold, even more than much fine gold; sweeter also than honey and the honeycomb.][4]

Then he [King David] says,

Your servant is careful regarding the mitzvot, in keeping them is great reward,[5]

because according to the excellence and superiority of the Torah, a person must be careful not to fail in it.[6]

The Maharal now begins his analysis. First he questions why King David uses compound terms – "the Torah of Hashem," "the Testimony of Hashem" and so on. Here, the Maharal begins to examine his central theme, but from the opposite direction: Torah is the best channel through which one can bond with Hashem. As he says, the Torah itself is wedded to Hashem and thus it is the best medium for achieving one's own bonding with Hashem. It is even better than acquiring individual positive character traits.

וזכר ששה דברים ובכל אחד זכר השם לומר כי התורה מצורפת אל השם יתברך שנקראת תורת ה' עדות ה' וכן כולם, לומר כי על ידי התורה קונה האדם דבקות בו יתברך.

King David mentions six items above – Torah, Testimony, Precepts, Commandment, Awe, Ordinances – and coupled to each of these is Hashem's name.[7] The idea behind this is that the Torah is wedded to Hashem and therefore it is called "the Torah of Hashem," "the Testimony of Hashem," etc. This teaches us that via the Torah, a person acquires *bonding with Hashem*.[8]

---

4. Tehillim 19:8–11.
5. Tehillim 19:12.
6. As we will see later, this corresponds to the first concern – misunderstanding Torah. See the Commentary, Introduction § Point 16, for the Pachad Yitzchak's comment on this verse.
7. As it says, "the Torah *of Hashem*," "the testimony *of Hashem*," etc.
8. Here we see that the Maharal clearly states the reverse side of the equation we have seen thus far – he teaches us that Torah facilitates a bond with Hashem and this complements his previous teaching that a bond with Hashem facilitates the learning of Torah.

Next, the Maharal questions why King David uses six different terms, really synonyms, to discuss the effects of the Torah; we explore this more in the Commentary, Introduction § Point 11.

ומפני שבא לומר שהדבקות הזה הוא דבקות גמור לא דבקות בצד מה, כמו מי שהוא בעל מידות ע"י המידות קונה דבקות בו יתברך ואינו קונה רק הדבקות בצד מה כפי המידה אשר דבק בה, אבל ע"י התורה דבק בו יתברך לגמרי בכל צד.

ומפני שהצדדין המחולקים הם ששה והם ימין ושמאל פנים ואחור מעלה ומטה, וכנגד זה זכר ששה שמות שהוא דבק בו יתברך בכל צד ואינו נוטה מן השי"ת לא לימין ולא לשמאל לא לשום צד.

This bonding to Hashem [via Torah] is a complete bonding, not a resultant, secondary attachment. If a person acquires positive character traits, then via those character traits, a person acquires a resultant bond with Hashem, but he only acquires a bond through the perspective of the trait that he has perfected. But through the Torah, a person cleaves to Hashem completely through all perspectives.

In this world, there are six major perspectives (right, left, forwards, backwards, up and down). Therefore, King David mentions six items [above], parallel to these six perspectives, in order to teach that through the Torah, a person bonds with Hashem throughout all perspectives and deviates neither right nor left nor any way.

The Maharal now begins analyzing each of the six terms that King David mentioned. First he determines how the Torah assists one in becoming "tamim" (perfect and innocent). A person in such a state is bonded with Hashem, which restores one's soul through infusing him with the life-energy of Hashem, Who is the life of all worlds.

והתחיל לומר תורת ה' תמימה משיבת נפש כי כאשר התורה תמימה ע"י זה האדם ג"כ תמים, וכאשר הוא תמים האדם הוא עם השי"ת לגמרי וכדכתיב תמים תהיה עם ה' א-להיך (דברים י"ח) ופירשו ז"ל במס' נדרים (דף ל"ב ע"ב) כל המתמים עצמו הוא עם השי"ת.

ולכך אז"ל (ע' חולין צ"א) צורת תם

King David begins by saying, "The Torah of Hashem is perfect and innocent, it restores the soul."[9] Since the Torah is *tamim*, through it, a person also becomes *tamim*. And when a person is *tamim*, he is completely with Hashem, as the Torah says, "You shall be perfect and innocent with Hashem your G-d."[10]

9. In the citation from Tehillim 19 (above), which is the subject of the Maharal's comments.

10. D'varim 18:13. The verse is literally a commandment, "You shall be *tamim* [i.e., perfect and innocent] with Hashem, your G-d!" However, it can also be read as, "[If] you are *tamim*, you will be with Hashem your G-d." The Gemara is using the alternate reading.

חקוקה בכסא הכבוד כי יעקב נאמר עליו ויעקב איש תם (בראשית כ"ה), ולכך אמר משיבת נפש כלומר שהיא משיבת נפש להחיותו. כי התמים הוא עם השם יתברך כמו שאמרנו, וכתיב (דברים ד') ואתם הדבקים בה' א-להיכם חיים כלכם היום כי מצד הדבקות בו יתברך אתם חיים ולכך כתיב תורת ה' תמימה משיבת נפש.

Our rabbis, *z"l*,[11] explained in N'darim[12] as follows, 'Anyone who makes himself *tamim* is with Hashem'.

For this reason, our sages, *z"l*, said (see Chullin)[13] that the image of a *tamim* person is engraved on Hashem's throne of glory, since Ya'akov[14] [whose image is engraved there] is called an "*ish tam*."[15, 16] Therefore, the next phrase is "it restores the soul," since the *tamim* person is with Hashem, bonding to Hashem, and the Torah says, "And you, who are bonding to Hashem, are all alive today."[17] The verse means, "*due* to your bonding to Hashem, you are alive." This is why it says "The Torah of Hashem is *tamim*, it restores the soul."

Next, the Maharal elucidates the phrase, "The testimony of Hashem is faithful, making the simple person wise." The Maharal introduces a key concept in his thought – that of the "*sichli*."

ואחר כך אמר עדות ה' נאמנה מחכימת פתי.

פי' כי מה נחשב האדם שאין בו רק שכל האנושי, אבל עדות ה' נאמנה מחכימת פתי שעל ידי התורה נעשה חכם, כי התורה מעידה על הנמצאים לברר כל דבר והיא נאמנה מחכימת הפתי עד שנחשב שכלי ביותר.

Afterwards it says, "The testimony of Hashem is faithful, making the simple person wise."[18]

The explanation of this is that a human, having only human intelligence, is not really that noteworthy, but the Testimony of Hashem (i.e., the Torah) is faithful and makes wise the [human being who is fundamentally] simple: for through the Torah a person becomes wise because the Torah gives testimony

11. "*Z"l*" is an acronym for "*zichronam livrachah*," זכרונם לברכה, which means, "May their memory be a blessing."

12. N'darim 32b.

13. Chullin 91a.

14. "Ya'akov," יעקב, is Jacob.

15. Meaning, "a perfect and innocent man." See B'reishit 25:27.

16. The Maharal explains that the intention of the Gemara, when it says that Ya'akov's image is engraved on Hashem's throne, is that when a person reaches a state of being *tamim*, they are close to Hashem and with Hashem, as if their profile were engraved on His "throne," as it were.

17. D'varim 4:4.

18. In the citation from Tehillim 19 (above) which is the subject of the Maharal's comments.

about the [true reality of all] creations, clarifying all things; and the Torah is faithful, making the simple wise, until he is considered exceedingly *sichli*.[19]

Next, the Maharal discusses the phrase, "The precepts of Hashem are honest, rejoicing the heart."

Afterwards, King David says that the Torah further brings a person to a level where it gladdens one's heart.[20] The explanation of this is that when a person is complete, he is happy; and the opposite of this is when a person is in a state of lacking something – which is when he is, G-d forbid, in mourning. Therefore, when death strikes one of his close relatives, G-d forbid, a person mourns.[21]

ואח"כ אמר שעוד מביאה התורה את האדם אל המדרגה שהיא משמחת לב, פי' שנחשב האדם שהוא מציאות שלם על ידי התורה, ולכך היא משמחת לב האדם, שכאשר האדם הוא בשלימות הוא בשמחה והפך זה כאשר הוא בחסרון הוא באבילות, ולכך כאשר קרה לו המיתה מן שאר בשרו הוא באבילות.

Next, the Maharal explains the phrase, "Hashem's commandment is pristine, enlightening the eyes."

King David says further that "Hashem's commandment is pristine, enlightening the eyes."[22]

This means that by following Hashem's commandments, a person's eyes are illuminated so that he doesn't walk in the dark from the point of view of his actions[23] but rather, he does the mitzvot. This continues until a person is completely perfect in his mind and in his actions.

ועוד אמר מצות ה' ברה מאירת עינים.

ר"ל כי התורה מלמדת לאדם את המעשה אשר יעשה ולא נחשב שהולך בחושך, ולפני זה אמר מחכימת פתי על החכמה המחכמת אותו, וכאן אמר מצות ה' ברה מאירת עינים שלא ילך במעשיו בחושך רק יעשה המצוה, עד שהאדם הוא שלם לגמרי בין בשכלו ובין במעשיו.

19. The Maharal identifies beings which are "*sichli*," שכלי (lit. "cerebral" or "intellectual") with having spiritual substance. The more *sichli* a thing is, the more abstract and spiritual it is. For an examination of this, see the Commentary, Introduction § Point 1.

20. In the citation from Tehillim 19 (above), which is the subject of the Maharal's comments, where King David writes, "The precepts of Hashem are honest, rejoicing the heart."

21. Therefore, since the Torah brings one to a state of completion, one feels happy.

22. In the citation from Tehillim 19 (above), which is the subject of the Maharal's comments.

23. I.e., he isn't confused as to what he should do, practically.

Next, the Maharal elucidates the phrase, "The Awe of Hashem is pure, it stands forever."

ואח"כ יראת ה' טהורה עומדת לעד פי' שעל ידי התורה יקנה הנצחיות, ודבר זה רמזו בפרק במה מדליקין (שבת ל"א ע"א) על פסוק יראת ה' היא אוצרו כי על ידי היראה יקנה הקיום הנצחי ויתבאר זה בפרקים הבאים בעזה"י.

Afterwards, King David says that "The Awe of Hashem is pure, it stands forever."[24] The explanation of this is that through the Torah, a person acquires eternity. This is what our sages hinted at in [Tractate] Shabbat[25] regarding the verse, "The Awe of Hashem is His treasure house."[26] Because, through Awe of Hashem, one will acquire an eternal existence – this will be explained in coming chapters, please G-d.[27, 28]

Next, the Maharal elucidates the phrase, "The ordinances of Hashem are true, completely righteous."

ואמר משפטי ה' אמת צדקו יחדיו.

דבר זה עוד יותר על הכל שעל ידי התורה מתדמה אל השם יתברך במה שאפשר להתדמות אל בוראו, כי חותמו של הקב"ה אמת ומשפטי התורה ודרכיה אמת.

ואומר צדקו יחדיו כי כל הדברים יש בהם אמת בצד מה ומשפטי ה' אמת צדקו יחדיו כלומר שכולם שוים באמיתות, וזה מורה שהם אמת לגמרי לכך כולם שוים באמיתות שאל"כ לא היו כולם שוים באמיתות רק זה יותר מזה אבל מפני שהם אמת לגמרי לכך כולם שוים באמיתות.

Finally, King David says, "The ordinances of Hashem are true, completely righteous."[29]

This level is even above the others because through the Torah one becomes similar to Hashem (as much as it is possible to become similar to one's creator) because Hashem's signature[30] is *truth* and the ordinances of the Torah and its paths are true.

King David uses the term "completely righteous," in order to teach that they are all equal in truth which implies that they are all completely true – this

---

24. In the citation from Tehillim 19 (above), which is the subject of the Maharal's comments.

25. Shabbat 31a.

26. Y'shayahu 33:6.

27. See Chapter Ten.

28. For an exploration of the term "Awe of Hashem" and of these ideas in general, see the Commentary, Introduction § Points 1, 9 and 10 .

29. In the citation from Tehillim 19 (above) which is the subject of the Maharal's comments.

30. Lit., "seal" or "stamp."

is the reason they can all be equally true.[31] If they were not all completely true, they could not be equally true because one would end up having more truth than another. But since Hashem's ordinances are completely true, they are all equally true.

The Maharal has explained the first section of Tehillim 19, which contains six different expressions of the manner in which Torah enables one to bond with Hashem. In effect, the Maharal has now presented us with two interlocking ideas: one can only learn Torah successfully if one is doing so in order to bond with Hashem; and one can best bond with Hashem through the Torah. This creates a transcendent spiral of spiritual growth – the more one strives to bond with Hashem through Torah learning, the more one is able to comprehend Torah truly and communicate it, which in turn creates that very bond.

31. For an explanation of this idea, see the Commentary, Introduction § Point 12.

SUMMARY

Introduction: 3/4

I. The two issues of concern previously mentioned regarding Torah study

- A. Failure to understand truly.
- B. Failure to *communicate* one's understanding of the truth.

II. The Maharal explains that King David discusses these ideas in verse 8 and onwards of Tehillim 19

- A. The bulk of the Maharal's commentary on this Tehillim does not focus directly on these two issues, but rather views these two issues as symptoms of a deeper malady – the lack of connection to Hashem through Torah study.
- B. In his comments here, the Maharal discusses the superlative nature of Torah study and of mitzvot with an emphasis on the manner in which they help one connect with Hashem.
- C. The interlocking of these two ideas creates a transcendent spiral of spiritual growth – the more one strives to bond with Hashem through Torah learning, the more one is able to comprehend Torah truly and communicate it which in turn creates that very bond.

III. The difference between other methods of drawing near to Hashem and Torah

- A. Resultant Closeness vs. Essential Closeness
    1. Resultant Closeness: Through Positive Character Traits
        - a. The Maharal explains that when one acquires a positive character trait, one only (as it were) resembles Hashem in the limited aspect conferred by that particular character trait.
    2. Essential Closeness: Through Torah
        - a. However, the Maharal explains, through Torah, one can, as it were, resemble Hashem in all possible aspects without deviation.
- B. Six elements = All perspectives of this world
    1. King David lists six elements in the Tehillim which illustrate the aspects through which Torah allows one to bond with Hashem.
    2. There are specifically six listed, as there are six major physical dimensions (right, left, forwards, backwards, up and down). This teaches that Torah allows one to bond with Hashem in all manners possible within this physical reality.

IV. The six elements

Term	*Description*	*Result*
Torah of Hashem	Perfect and Innocent (תמימה)	Restores the soul
Testimony of Hashem	Faithful	Makes the simple person wise
Precepts of Hashem	Honest	Rejoice the heart
Commandment of Hashem	Pristine	Enlightens the eyes
Awe of Hashem	Pure	Endures forever
Ordinances of Hashem	True	Altogether righteous

A. The Torah of Hashem is perfect and innocent (*tamim*), it restores the soul.
   1. The Maharal explains that a *tamim* person is with Hashem and a person with Hashem gains life. Therefore, the verse says, "it restores the soul."

B. The Testimony of Hashem is faithful, making the simple person wise.
   1. The Torah gives one true wisdom, beyond normally attainable human intelligence.

C. The Precepts of Hashem are honest, rejoicing the heart.
   1. Happiness stems from completion and perfection. Mourning stems from lack and loss.
   2. The Torah brings one to completion and thus to happiness.

D. The Commandment of Hashem is pristine, enlightening the eyes.
   1. Torah is a guide to action in this world – enlightening one's eyes with guidance.

E. The Awe of Hashem is pure, enduring forever.
   1. Awe of Hashem is connected to eternity, an idea we explore further in the Commentary, Introduction § Points 9 and 10.

F. The Ordinances of Hashem are true, they are righteous altogether.
   1. This is the highest level – through Torah, one becomes as similar as is possible to Hashem.
   2. All mitzvot are equal in infinite truth.

INTRODUCTION

Part 4 of 4

The Maharal continues his analysis of Tehillim 19, explaining how King David explores the scope of the effects of Torah learning and mitzvot. First he addresses the positive consequences of Torah learning in both the physical and intellectual realms.

ואמר הנחמדים מזהב ומפז רב פי' כי המצוה יש בו שני דברים, האחד שהמצוה טוב לאדם הגופני שדבר זה מבואר לכל שכל המצוות שהם בתורה הם להשלים תקון האדם עד שהאדם הוא בטוב, והשני שהשכל ג"כ מחייב המצוות מצד סוד שכלי.

King David says that the mitzvot are "more desired than gold, even more than much fine gold, [sweeter also than honey and the honeycomb]."[1] The explanation of this is that there are two elements to a mitzvah [to which the above verse hints]: firstly, a mitzvah is good for a person physically[2] (this is clear to everyone that all the mitzvot in the Torah complete the perfection of a human until a human is "in goodness")[3] and secondly, the mind requires mitzvot[4] from the perspective of an intellectual secret.[5]

The superlative nature of the Torah's effect on the intellect.

ועל זה אמר כי מה שהמצוה יש בה סוד שכלי א-להי הם נחמדים מזהב ומפז רב, שהם נחמדים לראיית העין לבד ומצוות התורה הם יותר נחמדים לראיית השכל, שכמו שיפול לשון ראייה על העין כך יפול ראייה על השכל כי לשון ראה משמש כאחד לשניהם כמו שאמר רואה אני דברי פלוני לפיכך אמר כי השכל הא-להי בתורה יותר נחמד לראיית השכל מזהב ומפז שהוא נחמד לראיית העין.

From the point of view of the intellectual need for Torah, King David writes that the mitzvot are "more desired than gold, even more than much fine gold," both of which are pleasing to the *physical eye* only, while the Torah's commandments are more pleasant to the *mind's eye*. (Linguistically, the verb "to see" can be used for both physical sight as well as for mental perception and understand-

1. Tehillim 19:11 – continuing the analysis.

2. This is what the verse means when it says that the mitzvot are sweeter than honey, as the Maharal will explain later.

3. See the Commentary, Introduction § Point 13.

4. This is what the verse means when it says that the mitzvot are more desired than gold.

5. See the Commentary, Introduction § Point 13.

ing. The term, "to see," applies to both physical and mental perception – as a person says, "I see[6] your point of view.") Therefore, King David says that the G-dly intellect in the Torah is more pleasant to the mind's eye than gold and fine gold which are pleasing to the physical eye.

The superlative nature of the Torah's effect on one's physical existence.

ועל טוב הגופני שהתורה מעמיד הכל בטוב כי התורה תקרא טוב עז"א ומתוקים מדבש ונופת צופים שזה עריבות גופני.

But regarding the physical goodness which the Torah brings (for the Torah must bring goodness in all spheres since it is called "good,")[7] the Tehillim says that the Torah is "sweeter also than honey and the honeycomb," which relates to physical sweetness.[8]

The verse's double wording indicates that the Torah's benefit in both these realms is infinite.

ומה שכפל הדבר אצל כל אחד ואחד.

לומר מזהב ומפז ומתוקים מדבש ונפת צופים, שאם אמר הנחמדים מפז אפשר לומר שאינם נחמדים רק יותר מפז ועתה שכתיב הנחמדים מזהב ומפז יש ללמוד, כמו שאין פירוש מזהב ולא יותר שהרי גם כן נחמד מפז, כן פירוש מפז לא שהוא נחמד מפז בלבד רק שהוא נחמד יותר על כל.

וכך פירוש ומתוקים מדבש ונופת צופים.

Why does the verse double the metaphors ("more [desired] than gold, even more than [much] fine gold; sweeter also than honey and the honeycomb")?

This was in order to establish an infinite range of quality – for if the verse had only said "more desired than fine gold," one could understand that the Torah is more desired than fine gold [but not more desired than something more valuable than fine gold, for example, platinum]. But now that there is a double metaphor, the idea is that the phrase "more desired than gold" doesn't mean that there is an upper limit, because the Torah is desired "even more than fine gold"; rather, the phrase ["more desired than gold"] means that the Torah is more desired than anything [on the level of the intellect].

This is also the explanation of the phrase "sweeter also than honey and the honeycomb" [i.e., that the Torah is superlative for the body, too].

Due to the peerless nature of Torah and mitzvot, a person should therefore take great care in their fulfillment, which is how the Tehillim continues.

6. I.e., I understand.

7. As above, see the Commentary, Introduction § Point 13.

8. Since taste is a sensual, physical sense, the sweetness of the Torah refers to its physical benefits.

ועל זה אמר גם עבדך נזהר בהם לפי מדרגתם ומעלתם ראוי שיהיה נזהר בהם ובשמרם עקב רב לעוה"ב.

Therefore, the next verse says, "Your servant is careful regarding the mitzvot, in keeping them is great reward,"[9] because once you understand the incredible excellence and value of the mitzvot, it is suitable that one should be careful regarding them. In observing the mitzvot there is "great reward"[10] – in the World to Come.[11]

The Maharal continues his analysis of Tehillim 19 below. Here he finally arrives at the comments of King David which address the two concerns related to learning Torah: not understanding it truly and not being able to communicate it adequately.

ואח"כ אמר שגיאות מי יבין וגו'.

כלומר כי לפי מדרגת ומעלת הדבר צריך שיהיה האדם נזהר שלא יחטא, ולכך אמר שגיאות מי יבין נגד אם יטעה בדברי תורה שאי אפשר לגודל עומק שלהם שיבין כל הדברים על אמיתתם ולכך אמר מי יבין.

Next, the Tehillim states, "Who can discern his [own] errors? [Hashem, help me clean myself from hidden faults. Hold me back from presumptuous sins, that they may not have dominion over me; then I shall be faultless, and I shall be clear from great transgression.]"[12]

This means that according to the excellence and quality of the mitzvot, a person should take care in them, that he should not sin. Therefore, King David says, "Who can discern his own errors?" – this relates to learning Torah. If a person errs in his understanding of the Torah, it is impossible to discern [the error] due to the depth of Torah;[13] therefore, King David wrote, "Who can discern his own errors?"

Before the Maharal addresses the second concern (not being able to communicate Torah), he discusses the idea in Tehillim that Hashem can help one repair any damage caused to oneself through unintentional sins.

ואח"כ אמר מנסתרות נקני על שגגת מעשה שלא ידע מן העבירה.

Afterwards, King David continues, "cleanse me from hidden [faults]," which is a request that Hashem cleanse us from the negative effects exerted on us by performing a forbidden

9. Tehillim 19:12.

10. As the verse concludes.

11. For more on this, see the Commentary, Ch. 5 § Point 4 . The Maharal seems to be hinting here to two different ideas: firstly, that the mitzvot are their own reward since they refine the human being and enable him to bond with Hashem; and secondly, that they earn one merit for the World to Come.

12. Tehillim 19:13–14, continuing the analysis.

13. This refers to the difficulty in understanding the Torah correctly.

action even inadvertently – where one doesn't even know of the prohibition.[14]

Now, the Maharal explains how King David addresses the second concern: being unable to communicate Torah effectively. He explains King David's words both in Tehillim 19 and in a Midrash.

ואח"כ אמר יהיו לרצון אמרי פי כדי שיהיה לו זכות שישפיע תורה לאחרים ועז"א יהיו לרצון אמרי פי שיהיו מקבלים את דבריו.

ובמדרש (שו"ט וילקוט שם):

יהיו לרצון אמרי פי שיעשו לדורות ויחקקו לדורות ואל יהיו קורין בם כקורין בספר המירום פי' ספרי המינים, כמו ספרי המירום אינם מטמאים דמסכת ידים (פרק רביעי) רק יהיו קורין בהם ונוטלים עליהם שכר כנגעים ואהלות.

אמר רבי ירמיה בשם רבי יוחנן אגורה באהליך עולמים וכי ס"ד שדוד מבקש דירה בשני עולמים אלא יהיו קורין ומזכירין אותי בבתי כנסיות ובבתי מדרשות כאלו אני קיים.

Thereafter, King David writes, "Let the words of my mouth be acceptable . . ."[15] Here King David finally refers to the second concern relating to Torah study:[16] this verse is a prayer that a person gain the merit to connect to others and influence them with Torah. This is why it says, "Let the words of my mouth be acceptable . . ." meaning that others should accept one's words.

In the Midrash (see Midrash Shocher Tov and Yalkut [Shimoni] on Tehillim 19), the following comment is made:[17]

> What does the verse mean when it says, "Let the words of my mouth be acceptable . . ."?[18] It means that King David is praying that his words will last for generations and be written down for generations and that people will not read them like they read a Book of Mirus (which is a book of heresy – this can be proved from Tractate Yadayim[19] which refers to the fact that this book does not cause one's hands to become ritually unfit[20]) rather, King David prayed that

14. Previously in the Introduction, we learned that if one is bonded with Hashem, Hashem will help one return to the path of Torah even if one has veered off it. Here, the Maharal extends this idea to Hashem's helping one repair spiritual damage which one has inadvertently inflicted upon oneself. See the Commentary, Introduction § Point 14 for a clarification of the connection between this idea and that which precedes and proceeds it.

15. Tehillim 19:15, the last verse in the Tehillim.

16. This refers to the difficulty in communicating Torah, even if one understands it truly.

17. Yalkut Shimoni, Tehillim 1:613, 19:678; Midrash Shocher Tov 19 (shortened form).

18. Tehillim 19:15.

19. Yadayim 4:6.

20. As the Rambam explains (Commentary on the Mishnah, Yadayim 3:3), sacred

people would learn his words and receive reward for that learning just as one receives reward for learning the laws of [skin] impurities and Structures.[21,22]

Rabbi Yirmiyah said in the name of Rabbi Yochanan, "Another verse in Tehillim says,[23] 'Hashem, I will dwell in Your tent forever.'[24] What did David mean by using the plural form [of the word 'forever']? Did he think that he would live in both worlds simultaneously [both this world and the World to Come – which is impossible?] Rather, David prayed, '[Even after my death, may my Tehillim be] learned and mentioned in synagogues and places of learning, and this would be as if I am still alive in this world.' "

ולכך אמר יהיו לרצון אמרי פי אל הבריות,

For this reason, King David writes [in Tehillim 19, in the final verse,] "Let the words of my mouth and the meditation of my heart be acceptable before You, Hashem, my Former, and my Redeemer." The first part of the verse, "Let the words of my mouth be acceptable . . ." refers to other human beings – that they should accept his words of Torah.[25]

The Maharal now focuses on the last section of the final verse of Tehillim 19. This, he says, relates to the concern that one will misunderstand Torah.

והגיון לבי לפניך רוצה לומר כי כל לבבות דורש הש"י וידעת שכוונתי לשם ה' ולכך ידריך אותי בדרך אמת.

The second part of the verse, "Let the meditation of my heart be acceptable before You, Hashem, my Former, and my Redeemer," refers to the fact that

---

texts were, at one stage, stored with certain foodstuffs, a practice which caused the texts to be eaten by pests drawn by the food. In an effort to discourage this, our sages decreed that holy texts render certain foods ritually unfit, *tamei*. The Maharal uses this decree as an illustration that a Book of Mirus is secular at the very least, since this book does not render anything *tamei*.

21. This refers to the laws regarding a structure which, if built over a grave, causes the entire area thereunder to gain the same halachic status as the grave so that, for example, a *kohein* (priest) would be unable to enter the structure.

22. The idea is that King David's prayer was that he be able to communicate his Torah so effectively that people would continue to learn it forever (which indeed is what happened). The laws to which he refers – skin impurities and structures over graves or corpses – despite the fact that they are not that "attractive," are parts of the eternal Torah.

23. Tehillim 61:5.

24. In Hebrew, the word for "forever" is "*l'olam*," לעולם, which literally means "for the world." Here the verse uses a plural form "*l'olamim*," לעולמים, which is a poetic form of "*l'olam*" also used to denote "forever"; however, literally it means, "for the worlds," in the plural.

25. This addresses the one concern: being unable to communicate Torah truths.

"Hashem searches out all hearts."[26] King David is saying to Hashem, "Hashem, You know what is in my heart – that my intention is for You only, therefore, guide me in the way of truth."[27]

The Maharal has now explained how the last verse of Tehillim 19 encapsulates within it the concern for the two possible pitfalls in Torah learning: the inability to grasp the truth, as well as the inability to communicate it. The Maharal sees King David's supplication to Hashem for His assistance in these two areas as the solution to these two pitfalls. Only closeness to Hashem can circumvent them.

ה' צורי וגואלי כלומר כי אחר שאתה יצרתני אין אתה מואס ביצוריך, ואם אחר שיצרתני מעשי גרמו להרחיק אותי הרי אתה גואלי מכל דבר אף כי רוחקתי עד שאני לרצון.

The last words, "Hashem you are my Former[28] and Redeemer," are addressing Hashem, saying, "Hashem, since You are the One who formed me, You do not despise Your creations, and even if after You formed me, my actions caused me to be distanced from You, You are my redeemer – You continue to redeem me from anything [which pulls me away from you], even if I have become distanced [you continue to draw me close], until I find favor in Your eyes."[29]

The Maharal concludes the Introduction by echoing King David's supplication to Hashem for guidance and support.

ובכן התפלה אל מי שאינו מואס בשפלים ואינו מרחיק לשהיו רחוקים, שיהיו לרצון אמרי פי לפני כל ויורני דרך אמת ויסעדני בימין צדקו נצח אמן.

And so, this is [my] prayer to the One [i.e., Hashem] Who does not despise the lowly and does not further distance those who were distant already, that my words will find favor before everyone and that He will teach me the path of truth and that He will support me with His right hand of righteousness, forever, Amen.

---

26. 1 Divrei Hayamim, 28:9.

27. This addresses the other concern: being unable to understand the Torah truthfully.

28. In Hebrew, "*tzur*," צור, is usually translated as, "rock," but it does come from the same root meaning "to form," thus it can be translated as "Former."

29. This prayer – that Hashem should redeem a person even if they have distanced themselves – is a reprise of the theme of the necessity for bonding with Hashem as a preservative for Torah. As the Maharal explained at the beginning of this introduction, if a person is bonded with Hashem, even if they err and distance themselves, since Hashem, the reason for the Torah, is with them, that will preserve the Torah within them and Hashem will assist them in returning to the ways of Torah.

Lastly, the Maharal explains his choice of title for this work.

The name of this book is *The Splendor of Israel*, Tiferet Yisrael,[30] because it is a book which deals with the Torah which is the splendor of Israel, as the verse says, "What other nation is there which has righteous ordinances and statutes [like you have, Israel]," "and the nations of the world will say, 'Only this great nation is wise and understanding.'"[31]

We already explained in the Introduction[32] to the book, G'vurot Hashem[33] that it is due to this that the sages said, '"Splendor"[34] refers to the giving of the Torah.'[35]

ושם החבור הזה נקרא תפארת ישראל כי הוא חבור על התורה שהיא תפארת ישראל כדכתיב (דברים ד׳) ומי גוי גדול אשר לו חקים ומשפטים צדיקים וגו׳ ואמרו רק עם חכם ונבון הגוי הגדול הזה.

וכבר בארנו בהקדמה של חבור גבורת ה׳ שבשביל כך אמרו במסכת ברכות בפרק הרואה (נ״ח ע״א) והתפארת זו מתן תורה.

30. In Hebrew, תפארת ישראל.

31. D'varim 4:8, 6. The Maharal cites this verse which demonstrates that the splendor of the Jewish people in the eyes of the nations will be accrued through the Torah.

32. In the third introduction to G'vurot Hashem.

33. In Hebrew, גבורות ה׳.

34. 1 Divrei Hayamim, 29:11. The Gemara is elucidating the meaning of this verse, which states, "Yours, Hashem, are greatness, power, splendor, eternity, grandeur – everything in the heavens and earth; Yours, Hashem, are majesty and pre-eminence over all." The Gemara examines each term, "greatness," "power," etc., and explains that each of them is referring to a particular event or object. Its explanation is that the word "splendor," in the verse, refers to the Torah.

35. B'rachot 58a.

SUMMARY

Introduction: 4/4

I. The Torah is more desired than gold and fine gold, and sweeter than honey and honeycomb

A. The two benefits of mitzvot
   1. *Sichli* / Intellectual benefit
      a. This is represented by gold, which is pleasing to the physical eye.
      b. "Sight" is also a mental faculty and in this sense we say that the Torah is pleasing to the mental eye.
   2. Physical benefit
      a. This is represented by the sweetness of honey – taste being a physical sensation.

B. The repetition of the metaphors
   1. Each of the above metaphors are repeated:
      a. Torah is more desired than gold and fine gold
      b. Torah is sweeter than honey and the honeycomb
   2. The reason for the repetition is to establish that there is no upper limit on either of these two levels – that Torah brings the greatest possible *sichli* benefit as well as the greatest possible physical benefit.

II. King David's prayer for the gift of understanding Torah truly

A. King David writes, "Who can discern his own errors?" The Maharal explains that the meaning of this is that Torah is so profound, it is often impossible to detect one's error in understanding it. Therefore, one needs Hashem's help to attain truth.

B. This relates to the first concern regarding learning Torah and the solution reprises the Maharal's central theme – that one needs an intimacy with Hashem in order to understand Torah.

III. King David's prayer for the removal of the negative consequences of hidden faults

A. King David writes, "Cleanse me from hidden faults." The Maharal explains that this is a prayer that Hashem help us repair the spiritual damage we do to ourselves even when done in ignorance of the harmful nature of the act.

B. This again raises the central theme of the Maharal – that when one is bonded with Hashem, Hashem guides one back to Torah. Here we ask for Hashem's help even in areas of which we are unaware of any negativity at all.

IV. "Let the words of my mouth be acceptable and [let] the meditation of my heart [be acceptable] before You, Hashem . . ."

A. This is the last verse of the Tehillim and it addresses both concerns regarding Torah learning

B. Communication of Torah to others

1. "The words of my mouth" refers to the communication of Torah to others.
2. King David's response to the concern that he would be unable to communicate Torah adequately to others is a prayer that Hashem assist him, again reprising the central theme of the need for a close relationship with Hashem in order to communicate Torah.
3. Yalkut Shimoni; Midrash Shocher Tov
   a. The Midrash explains that King David's prayer, implicit in the words, "Let the words of my mouth be acceptable," is that Hashem aid him in the writing of Tehillim so that people will forever learn his Torah as they do other parts of Torah – that he be able to communicate the truths of Torah in his Tehillim.

C. Understanding the Truth of Torah

1. "The meditation of my heart" refers to attaining a true understanding of Torah.
2. When learning Torah, a person must only desire to join to Hashem. Hashem knows our intent and this will help a person secure Hashem's assistance in arriving at the truth.
3. Once again, this idea is central to the entire Introduction – in order to understand Torah, one must be bonded with Hashem.

V. "Hashem You are my Former and Redeemer"

A. The Maharal explains that these final words hint at an additional level of prayer. He says that King David is saying that Hashem, as our Former and Creator, knows that we are fallible and as such He also acts as our Redeemer, because even when we do fail, as long as we are bonded with Hashem, He will redeem us even if we are the ones who have strayed. As the Maharal mentioned earlier, this is the power of being connected to Hashem through the Torah.

VI. The Maharal's prayer

A. The Maharal now implements these ideas himself. He prays that Hashem help him understand the Torah truly and communicate it to us, those learning his Torah.

VII. The title of the book

A. The title of the book is "The Splendor of Israel" because the Torah is the splendor of Israel.

CHAPTER 1

CHAPTER 1

Part 1 of 2

The Maharal begins his exploration of the purpose of Torah and mitzvot by examining the connection between activities performed in this world and the beings that perform them. The Maharal teaches that each being has a unique essence which is expressed through some particular action unique to that being.

Those creations which Hashem, may He be Blessed, created in His world, all act within the world in which they were created and each one of them, according to its unique specialty and importance, increases its activity.

The heavens and all the hosts of heaven[1] all act – they rotate the firmament and influence the lower creations – just as Hashem, may He be Blessed, created them and arranged them. So, too, the lower creations all act. The earth acts and produces its growth; the earth produces everything which emerges from the earth. So, too, water acts – sating the thirst of the ground and vivifying it. The wind also helps to develop everything, as is known. Fire, too, like the sun, warms and nurtures everything. So, too, all animals and all species on earth – "Hashem did not create them for nothingness,"[2] rather, about them it was said, "Be fruitful and multiply and fill the earth,"[3] [and they do this] till the point that not one of them is idle and each of them acts in the world in which it was created.

הנבראים אשר ברא ה' יתברך בעולמו כולם הם פועלים בעולם אשר נבראו בו וכל אחד לפי מעלתו וחשיבותו גודל פעולתו.

הנה השמים וכל צבא השמים כולם פועלים מסבבים הרקיע ופועלים בתחתונים כמו שבראם השם יתברך וסדר אותם. וכן התחתונים כולם פועלים. הארץ היא שפועלת ומוציאה צמחה וכל אשר הוא יוצא מן הארץ היא פועלת. וכן המים פועלים מרוים ומצמיחים האדמה, והרוח גם כן מגדל הכל כמו שהוא ידוע, וכן האש כמו החמה מחמם ומגדל הכל, וכן כל בעלי חיים וכל המינים שבעולם לא לתהו בראם רק נאמר עליהם (בראשית א') פרו ורבו ומלאו את הארץ עד שאין אחד בטל והכל פועלים בעולם אשר נבראו בו.

וכל פעולה היא מתיחסת אל הפועל כי החמימות אשר הוא פעולת האש מתיחס אליו, וכן הקרירות מתיחס אל המים אשר פועלים הקרירות, וכן בכל הדברים מתיחסת הפעולה אל הפועל. ומעתה האדם אשר הוא נבדל מכל שאר בעלי חיים מצד הנפש שאין נפשו נפש בהמית רק נפשו נפש שכלית לא

1. Which are the stars.
2. Y'shayahu 45:18.
3. B'reishit 1:22.

כמו שאר בעלי חיים הטבעיים שאין נפשם רק טבעית מחויב שיהי' לו פעולות מתיחס' אל נפשו השכלית הא-להית ויהיו לו פעולות שכליות א-להיות, שכבר אמרנו כי כל פעולה צריך שתהיה מתיחסת אל הפועל.

Now, every activity is related to the agent which implements it.[4] Warmth, which creates fire, is related to it. So, too, coolness is related to water which it causes. So, too, in all things, the activity is related to the agent which causes it. Therefore, humanity must have activities related to its G-dly, intellectual soul [since] humanity is differentiated from all other animals through its soul:[5] a human's soul is not an animalistic soul[6] but rather a *sichli* soul,[7] unlike the other natural animals which have only a natural soul.[8] This is because, as we have already noted, any action must be related to its agent.

The question which the Maharal has raised is: given that the defining characteristic of humanity is our G-dly, intellectual soul, and given that every creation has actions which flow from its essence, what then is the action flowing from the essence of the human being? What activity is our defining activity?

ומפני שתמצא האדם משתתף עם שאר בעלי חיים הטבעיים בהרבה פעולות, ודבר זה בודאי מצד הנפש החיוני אשר באדם אשר בו משתתף עם שאר בעלי חיים הטבעיים, אבל אי אפשר שלא יהיו לו פעולות גם כן מתיחסים אל נפשו השכלית הא-להית כי לא יגרע כחו.

כי מה שהאדם הוא בנאי ונגר ועושה מלאכת האפיה והבישול וכיוצא בזה מתיקון הבגדים שודאי אף כי דברים אלו צריכים לו נפש השכלית, מי הוא ערב לי שהדבר הזה הוא מצד שלימות שבו, והרי ראוי ומחוייב שיהיו לו פעולות א-להיות שיפעול בעולם אשר בראו כפי מעלת נפשו הא-להית,

Even though you will find humans have many activities in common with other natural animals – something which undoubtedly flows from their similarity to animals in that they all have a vital soul[9] – nevertheless, it is impossible that humans not have activities which relate to their G-dly, intellectual soul, because this power cannot be diminished.

When a person is a builder, carpenter or when he practices baking, cooking or tailoring, there is no doubt that these actions require a G-dly, intellectual soul; but who can guarantee me that a person does these things as part of his becoming perfect?[10] Rather, it is suitable

4. Meaning that the action reflects an aspect of the object's essence.
5. The Maharal explains that the defining essence of humanity lies in the nature of the human soul.
6. See the Commentary, Ch. 1 § Point 2.
7. See the Commentary, Ch. 1 § Point 2.
8. See the Commentary, Ch. 1 § Point 2.
9. Meaning, a soul which confers vitality. See the Commentary, Ch. 1 § Point 2.
10. I.e., both due to one's intellectual soul and also as part of self-perfection.

ואולי כל הדברים האלה אשר זכרנו הם מצד חסרון שבאדם.

and required that a person have G-dly actions which will act in the world which Hashem created according to the exaltedness of his G-dly soul. Perhaps engaging in all of these professions which we mentioned is actually a deficiency in human beings.

The Maharal now examines whether the use of our intellect to control nature in the pursuit of subsistence could be the essential action of humanity. He explores this question using the Gemara in Kiddushin as a springboard.

ובסוף קדושין (פ"ב ע"ב):

We learn at the end of [Tractate] Kiddushin as follows,[11]

תניא רבי שמעון בר' אלעזר אומר מימי לא ראיתי צבי קייץ וארי סבל ושועל חנוני והם מתפרנסים שלא בצער.

והם לא נבראו אלא לשמשני ואני נבראתי לשמש את קוני ומה אלו שלא נבראו אלא לשמשני מתפרנסים שלא בצער ואני שנבראתי לשמש את קוני על אחת כמה וכמה אלא שהריעותי את מעשי וקפחתי את פרנסתי שנא' עונותיכם הטו אלה וגו' עד כאן.

> We learned in a *B'raita*,[12] "Rabbi Shimon ben Elazar says, 'I have never seen a deer drying figs in the field, or a lion carrying heavy loads, or a fox opening a store, and yet all of them make their living without anguish.
>
> 'Now all of these animals were only created to serve me.[13] If so, how is it possible that they make their living without anguish and yet I, a being who was created to serve my Creator,[14] make my living in anguish?[15] It must be that it was intended originally [by G-d] that I make my living in a similarly easy fashion, but that I sinned and so I ruined my livelihood. This is what the verse means, "Your sins have abrogated [the laws of nature, so that you are punished with drought] and your sins have prevented you from receiving goodness".'"[16]

11. Kiddushin 82b.

12. A *b'raita* is an early text from the time of the Mishnah which was excluded for various reasons from the official body of Mishnah.

13. I.e., humanity. For an exploration of this idea, see the Commentary, Ch. 1 § Point 3.

14. I.e., G-d.

15. The idea is: if they are only created to serve me, surely I should have all the benefits they have. In particular, since they manage to subsist without pain and suffering, surely I, the master, should be able to as well.

16. Yirmiyahu 5:25. Refer to the verse in context and see Rashi's comments ad loc. The verse indicates that there has been an abrogation of what is natural. Rabbi Shimon's deduction is that subsistence should be natural and if it is not, it can only be through evil altering the natural course of events. For an exploration of these assumptions, see the Commentary, Ch. 1 § Point 5.

הרי שבארו כי הפעולות והמלאכות שעושה האדם לצורך פרנסה אינם מצד מעלת האדם אבל הם לו מצד פחיתות וחסרון, וכשנברא האדם לא נבראת עמו המלאכה ותקון בגדים ובנין הבתים רק בגן עדן היה בלא דברים אלו, ואם כן אין אלו הפעולות לאדם מצד השלמות שלא נמצא בבעלי חיים אלו הפעולות והם מתפרנסים בלא דברים אלו. אם כן פעולות אלו הם לאדם מצד חסרון שחטא וקפח פרנסתו ולולא זה לא היה צריך לדברים אלו.

Here we see that our rabbis explained that professions and trades which are performed by humans are not signs of the superiority of humanity but rather they flow from the diminution and lack [of perfection] which is found in humanity. Thus, when human beings were created, no profession, clothing or building was created with them. Rather, they lived in the Garden of Eden without these things. If so, these activities are not part of human life due to our perfection (since animals make do without them and they subsist without these).[17] Therefore, these activities come to a person due to his imperfection [which is] due to his sinning and losing his livelihood – if he had not sinned, he would not need any profession.[18]

The Maharal delves deeper into the Gemara he cited above, explaining that it is referring to all three components of a human being: body, soul and intellect; teaching that none of these should be a slave to subsistence.

וזכר ג׳ דברים כי באדם ג׳ דברים, הגוף והנפש והשכל ובכל שלשתן משמש האדם בהם לצורך חיותו. ואמר כי אין שלמות האדם במה שהוא משמש לצורך פרנסתו הן בגופו הן בנפשו הן בשכלו.

וזה כי הארי יש לו גוף חזק כאשר נודע מענין הארי והרי אין משמש בכח גופו שיש לו לצורך פרנסתו, לכך אין לחשוב מה שעושה האדם בגופו הוא שלמות לו שהרי בבעלי חיים לא נמצא דבר זה שיהיה צריך אליו.

וכנגד הכח הנפשי שהתנועה היא

If you examine the *B'raita* brought above, you will see that Rabbi Shimon mentioned three different examples because human beings consist of three components: the body, soul and intellect.[19] Human beings use all three for the purpose of their sustenance. The *B'raita* is teaching us that it is not a sign of perfection that humans use any of these (body, soul or intellect) for the purpose of earning a livelihood.

The lion, as is known, has a powerful body and yet the lion doesn't use *the*

17. See the Commentary, Ch. 1 § Point 5.

18. As we mention in the Commentary, Ch. 1 § Points 5 and 6, the reference to the idea of the requirement for professions stemming from sin does not primarily refer to each individual human, but rather it refers to all of humanity, subsequent to the sin of Adam and Chavah (Eve). However, there are certain of our sages who believe that it applies to individuals as well.

19. The examples are the deer, the lion and the fox. The Maharal will explain the parallels between these three animals and the three components of a human being.

מן הנפש על זה אמר שהצבי שיש בו מהירות התנועה מאד הרי יש לו כח זה ביותר, והרי אינו משמש בכח זה לצורך פרנסתו ולפיכך אמר ולא ראיתי צבי קיץ דהיינו שיהיה מתקן מזונותיו בקיץ וצריך לזה כח התנועה להכנים את פירות הקיץ לבית.

וכנגד השכל אמר לא ראיתי שועל חנוני, כי השועל הזה יש בו חכמה מכל חיות השדה ואין משמש בכח זה לצורך פרנסתו, להיות חנוני בעל משא ומתן.

וכיון שלא נמצא בבעלי חיים שישתמשו בכחות אלו לצורך פרנסתן, אם כן מה שהאדם פועל בכח גופו וזיעת אפו ונושא משא גדול לצורך פרנסתו, אין זה מצד שלמות האדם שהרי אין צריך דבר זה לבעלי חיים שהוא יותר פחות מן האדם. ודבר זה התחייב לו מצד חטאו שאין לאדם מנוח בגופו ביום ובלילה רץ אחר פרנסתו כצבי ומשמש לזה כח נפשי שלו ואין זה מצד השלמות שהרי לא נמצא זה בבעלי חיים שהם למטה הימנו. וכן אין שלמות השכל של אדם לשמש בו אל פרנסתו כיון שלא נמצא שצריך דבר זה הבעל חי שהוא פחות מן האדם.

power of his body for the purpose of his livelihood.[20] Therefore, one shouldn't think that what humans do with their bodies [for the purposes of earning a living] is a sign of perfection – since animals have no need of this.

Parallel to the power of the soul, Rabbi Shimon mentioned the deer. This is because vitality and alacrity are products of the soul, and a deer champions these virtues. Rabbi Shimon said that a deer is exceptionally blessed with these virtues but does not use *this power* for the purpose of its livelihood;[21] therefore, he said, "I have never seen a deer drying figs in the field," meaning that one never sees a deer preparing its food in the summer and utilizing its *power* of speed for this purpose – to gather the food and store it in a home.

Parallel to the power of the intellect, Rabbi Shimon said, 'I have never seen a fox act as a shopkeeper.' He mentions the fox particularly, since a fox is shrewder than any other wild animal. Yet, the fox doesn't use *this power* for the purpose of his sustenance,[22] acting as a shopkeeper and closing business deals.

Now since we find that in the animal world, animals do not use their *powers* for the purposes of their livelihood, the fact that a human uses the *power* of his body and the sweat of his brow – carrying a great burden in pursuit of subsistence - is not due to the perfection of humankind (since even animals, which are inferior to humans, do not require this). Rather, humans became required to act in this way after the sin [of Adam and Eve]. Now [after the sin,] the human has no respite for his body – day and night he runs after his livelihood like a deer and uses the *power* of his soul for this end. All this is not due to human perfection, since animals, which are inferior to humans have no need of such behavior. Similarly, it is not the perfection of the intellect [which requires it] to serve a person in his search for livelihood, since we

20. See the Commentary, Ch. 1 § Point 4.
21. See the Commentary, Ch. 1 § Point 4.
22. See the Commentary, Ch. 1 § Point 4.

ואם כן מה שהאדם משובח מכל שאר בעלי חיים וראוי שיהיו לו פעולות מיוחדות, אין הפעולות המיוחדות ההם הפעולות שהם המלאכות והבנינים, כי דבר זה אינו לא לשלמות רק לחסרון ולפחיתות בשביל שחטא ונעשה בעל חסרון ולכך צריך לכל הדברים האלו.

see that animals, which are inferior to humans, have no need for this.

Indeed, humans are more praiseworthy than other animals and they should have actions which are allied to their essence. However, these actions [which demonstrate the essence of the human] are not professions or constructions [or any of the other non-essential activities mentioned above]; rather, all such non-essential pursuits are signs not of human perfection, but of human lack and diminution due to humanity sinning and becoming flawed. This sin and incompletion is why people engage in such activities for the purpose of livelihood.

> Seeing that normal human occupations cannot constitute the essential activity of human beings, the Maharal returns to his original question: what is this essential activity? His answer: the mitzvot.

וכבר בארנו כי אי אפשר שלא יהיו לאדם פעולות אשר הם מתיחסים אל נפשו אשר יש לו נפש א־להית, ואם כן נשארה השאלה איזה הם הפעולות המיוחדות לו המתיחסות אל מעלתו במה שיש לו נפש שכלי, לא ישאר לומר רק כי הפעולות המתיחסות אל מעלת נפשו הם הפעולות הא־להיות והם מצוות התורה, והם הם מיוחדים אל האדם לפי מעלת נפשו הא־להית ודבר זה בודאי הם פעולות המיוחדות אליו וראוים לו.

We have already explained that it is impossible that a human not have actions which are essentially related to the soul he possesses – the G-dly soul – and therefore, the question remains: what activities which humans perform are unique to humans and are functions of their excellence (which is possession of an intellectual soul)? The only possible answer is that the actions which are functions of the superiority of the human soul are G-dly actions: the mitzvot of the Torah. These are unique to the human being according to the excellence of his G-dly soul and they are definitely actions unique to him and suitable for him.

SUMMARY

Chapter 1: 1/2

I. Activities which express the essence of a creation

A. All creations perform activities in this world due to their being creative and productive creations of Hashem.

B. Each creation has actions associated with it which reflect its essence.

C. Therefore, *every* creation must perform certain actions which are functions of its unique essence. This includes human beings. The question is, which of all human activities falls into this category?

II. The essential activity of human beings

A. The essential uniqueness of a human being is his G-dly, intellectual soul.

  1. Humans share a vital, animalistic soul with animals, but the unique human essence is conferred on them through the possession of this G-dly, *sichli* soul.

B. The Maharal raises the possibility that human professions could be the actions which flow from the unique human excellence. His discussion on professions centers on the Gemara in Kiddushin:

  1. Kiddushin 82b
    a. The parable
      (1) One never sees a:
        (a) Deer drying figs in the field
        (b) A lion carrying burdens
        (c) A fox acting as a shopkeeper
    b. Rabbi Shimon's explanation
      (1) Animals do not need to perform activities which cause them "anguish" in order to gain their livelihood.
      (2) Animals were created only to serve humans and thus humans, by right, should have at least as easy a time gaining a livelihood as the inferior animal kingdom.
      (3) Therefore, it must be due to human sin that human livelihood is produced through painful means.
      (4) He cites a verse to prove this – Yirmiyahu 5:25.
  2. The Maharal's commentary on the Gemara
    a. Each of the animals represent one of the human being's component parts:
      (1) Lion: Body
      (2) Deer: Soul
      (3) Fox: Intellect

   b. The idea is that none of these animals need to use the *power* of their unique essence (which is parallel to one of the human being's component parts) for the purpose of making a living.
   c. So too, the fact that humans exploit their uniqueness (their G-dly, intellectual soul) for subsistence and have to utilize the powers of their body, soul and intellect in this campaign, cannot be a positive sign. This is his conclusion.

C. Understanding the Maharal's comments
   1. Please see the Commentary, Ch. 1 § Points 4, 5 and 6 for a discussion of these ideas.

D. The Maharal concludes that the actions which are functions of the superiority of the human soul are G-dly actions: the mitzvot of the Torah.

CHAPTER 1

Part 2 of 2

The Maharal questions why it is that mitzvot do not come to human beings naturally, if they are indeed our "essential" actions.

ואם תשאל ותאמר אם כן הרי כל הפעולות המיוחדות לכל אחד ואחד מן הנבראים הפעולות מתחייבות ממנו מעצמו ואינו משנה פעולותיו, ולמה לא נמצאו גם כן פעולות הא־להיות הם המצוות מן האדם מעצמו.

One could ask that if it is true [that the pursuit of professions by human beings is not an expression of their essential, unique G-dliness and only the mitzvot of the Torah are actions which reflect this essence, since] all other creations automatically have to perform the actions which reflect their essence and they never alter these actions, why then are the mitzvot *not* performed by human beings automatically and naturally?[1]

The Maharal now answers his question, explaining that there is one other specification of the human race which counters the requirement that mitzvot naturally flow from people, and that is: freedom of choice.

דבר זה אין שאלה כי אם ראוי שיהיו אלו הפעולות באות מן האדם הלא יצר הרע שברא באדם הוא מביאו אל הפעולות הרעות שבאות ממנו מצד יצר הרע שבו.

This is not really a question, because even if it is suitable for these actions to flow naturally from a human, the [human] inclination to [choose] bad, which [Hashem] created in [each] human, brings him to evil actions which are performed due to the inclination for bad within him.[2]

1. The Maharal cited examples (in the first section of Chapter One) of actions reflective of a creation's essence, such as the fact that warmth causes fire or the fact that lions have strength. Such actions flow automatically from the creation's essence. But he claimed there that mitzvot are the characteristic actions of humans – the problem is that humans do not automatically perform these. For a discussion of this issue, see the Commentary, Ch. 1 § Point 7.

2. The Maharal (and the Torah) do not hold that humans are essentially evil, G-d forbid. Rather, we believe that the essence of human beings is our freedom of choice to be G-dly. The mitzvot present us with these choices, but human beings must be perfectly poised between the possibility of doing mitzvot (and being G-dly) or the opposite, G-d forbid. If the mitzvot flowed naturally from us, we would have

ועל זה הוכיח משה רבינו ע"ה את ישראל ואמר (דברים ל"ב) האזינו השמים וגו' כמו שיתבאר בפרקים הבאים להודיע שאין זה לפי הסדר כלל, כי לפי הסדר השכלי ראוי שיתחייבו הפעולות מן כל נברא ונברא כפי מה שראוי, ואל האדם שנפשו א־להית שכלית ראוי לו פעולות מיוחדות והם פעולות המצוות שבתורה רק כי היצר הרע מעכב.

Regarding this, Moshe our Teacher, peace be upon him, rebuked Israel and said, "Listen Heavens and I will speak . . ."[3] (as will be explained in the coming chapters.)[4] Now Moshe said this to teach us that [the fact that people sin] is completely against the [natural] order.[5] [This is] because, according to the *sichli* order, it would be suitable that each creation would be obligated to perform those actions which are suitable to it. Special actions are suitable for humans, who possess a G-dly-intellectual soul; these actions are the mitzvot in the Torah, except that the inclination to [do] bad can prevent them.

The implication of the Maharal's answer is that human beings have varying levels of spiritual actualization – depending on how each person channels his inclinations to do good (or bad, G-d forbid). The Maharal now discusses these variations and the innate receptivity which people and nations possess (see the Commentary, Ch. 1 § Point 1).

אמנם כל המין מבני אדם אי אפשר שיהיו שוים כולם במעלת נפשם, ועם שכל מין בני אדם שוים בתאר פניהם ובעניניהם, אינם שוים במה שיש חלק מהם יותר א־להי מזולתם.

כמו שידוע כי הנבואה ורוח הקודש והשכינה היו מיוחדים בו העם אשר בחר בו השם יתברך משאר העמים עכו"ם, ואין ספק כי הנבואה הכנה בנפש האדם ותמצא הכנה הזאת

However, it is impossible that every member of the human species be equal in the excellence of their souls.[6] Even though all humans are equal in the [general] design of their faces[7] and [bodily] activities, they are not equal in that some of them are more G-dly than others.

[For example,] as is known, prophecy, divine spirit and G-d's presence were more prevalent in the nation which

no freedom of choice. See the Ramchal's Derech Hashem 1:3:1.

3. D'varim 32:1.

4. For further study, see later in Chapter Four.

5. This should be compared to what the Maharal writes in Chapter Four. The Maharal's answer is that the commandments should naturally flow from people except that they have freedom of choice to choose evil over good, but the actions that match their essence are good.

6. For further study, see the Commentary, Ch. 1 § Point 8.

7. The Maharal chooses the example of the human face for a variety of reasons, foremost amongst them because the human face is the unique identifier of individual human beings, but despite this, the variation in facial structure between humans is quantitative, not qualitative. See B'midbar Rabbah 21:2.

מיוחדים בה העם אשר בחר ה' יתברך, ומזה תראה כי העם הזה היה יותר נפשם א־להית מצד ההכנה הזאת.

וגם זה מוכרח לומר, וזה כי העולם הזה אשר בו מין בני אדם הוא עולם הטבע, ולפיכך הדבר אשר הוא טבעי ראוי שימצא בכל המין בשוה במה שהעולם הזה הוא טבעי בכללו, ואם ימצא שנוי בהם מפני שנוי המקומות דבר זה אינו נחשב שנוי כלל, אבל הא־להיות לא ימצא בשוה לכל המין שאם היה נמצא לכל המין בשוה היה עולם הזה עולם נבדל מאחר כי בכללותו נמצא הא־להיות. אבל העולם הזה הוא עולם הטבע ואינו עולם הנבדל, וד"ז מחייב שאין נמצא הא־להיות לכל המין בשוה כי אם בחלק ממנו.

Hashem, may He be Blessed, chose,[8] than in the other, idol worshipping nations. There is no doubt that prophecy [requires] a readiness in the soul of a person and you will find that the nation which Hashem chose, may He be Blessed, is distinct [in possessing] this readiness. From this you can see that the soul of this nation (due to this potential) was more G-dly.

In fact, one is bound to say this[9] because this world, in which the human species [lives], is a natural world. Therefore, it is fitting that the entire species be equal in the physical aspect [since the world is physical]; and if one finds differences in them due to the differences in geographical locations, these are not considered to be [qualitative] differences. But G-dliness is not found equally in the entire [human] species, for if it were, then this world would in fact be the transcendent [spiritual] world since G-dliness would be generally located in it.[10] However, this world is the natural world [and not the spiritual world] and this requires that G-dliness not be found equally throughout the entire species, but only in a section thereof.

The Maharal now explains that humans were all given certain commandments, due to their basic humanity and befitting their G-dly soul.

ומפני כי עכו"ם הם מן העולם הטבעי לכך היו שבעים אומות, כי עולם הטבע נברא בשבעת ימי בראשית, וכנגד שבעת ימי עולם הטבע היו שבעים אומות כנגד כל יום עשרה.

Now, since idol worshippers are part of the physical world, therefore, there were seventy nations [created],[11] since the natural world was created in the seven days of nature and there were ten nations corresponding to each day [of creation].[12]

8. I.e., the Jewish people.

9. That people must have differing spiritual potentials.

10. Regarding this, see the Commentary, Ch. 1 § Points 8 and 10.

11. Throughout the Oral Torah, there is a repeated assertion that there are 70 archetypal gentile nations. For example, see B'reishit Rabbah 66:4; Sifrei Ha'azinu 6; Sukkah 55b.

12. Thus rendering 70 times 10 which equals 70. See the Commentary, Ch. 1 §

However, the Torah was specifically given to the Jewish people and the Maharal now begins explaining that this is because the Jewish people, like the Torah, are above nature.

והאומה היחידה היתה על הטבע והיא כנגד השמיני כי השמיני הוא על הטבע, ולכך ראויה לישראל התורה שהיא על עולם הטבע, והתורה נבראת קודם שנברא העולם הטבעי וישראל נבראו גם כן קודם שנברא העולם הטבעי, לכך כל ענין התורה שהיא בשמיני כי הטבע היא תחת מספר שבעה ומה שהוא על הטבע הוא שמיני כמו שיתבאר בפרק שאחר זה.

ולכך היא לאומה הישראלית, אשר בחר ה׳ יתברך לחלקו והם הם נתיחדו בפעולות הא־להיות שהם מצוות התורה לפי מדריגת נפשם הא־להית במה שהיו מוכנים לנבואה ורוח הקדש ולהיות השכינה ביניהם, ועכו״ם לפי מעלתם נתן להם ז׳ מצוות שהם שבע מצוות בני נח.

But the unique nation [Israel], is *above* nature and she corresponds to the eighth day, because eight is above nature [which was created in the framework of seven days of creation], therefore, it is suitable that Israel would get the Torah which is above the world of nature. [Additionally,] the Torah was created before the natural world was created[13] and [the nation of] Israel was created before the natural world was created,[14] therefore, the whole essence of the Torah is that it should be [associated with] the eighth because nature is subsumed under the number seven and anything above nature is the eighth (as will be explained in the following chapter).[15]

Therefore, the Torah is [given] to the Israelite nation, which Hashem chose as His portion, and they [the Jewish people] were uniquely signified by the G-dly actions which are the commandments of the Torah, according to the level of their G-dly soul (which is capable of prophecy and divine spirit-illumination and of having the divine presence dwell among them), but Hashem gave idol worshippers, according to their level, seven commandments,[16] which are the seven commandments of a Noahide.[17]

Point 9.

13. B'reishit Rabbah 1:4.

14. For further reference, see B'reishit Rabbah 1:4 where it states that the nation was not physically created then, but the concept of Israel was created before the world.

15. We have already investigated this in the Commentary, Introduction § Point 15.

16. Gentiles, due to their physical perfection, received 7 mitzvot since the number 7 represents physical perfection.

17. The Torah terms all gentiles as "Noahides," meaning, a person who is descended from No'ach (Noah), from whom the world was populated after the flood. For a listing of these 7 mitzvot, see the Commentary, Ch. 1 § Point 10.

The Maharal now cites a Gemara and a Midrash which he uses to explain further the reason that the Jewish people specifically were given the Torah. He explains that the essence of the idol worshipping nations is not primed to accept all the mitzvot, only the seven with which they were commanded. However, the Jewish nation is primed for the whole set of mitzvot.

ובפרק קמא דע"ז (ב' ע"ב):

ה' מסיני בא וזרח משעיר למו הופיע מהר פארן מאי בעי בשעיר ומאי בעי בפארן מלמד שהחזיר הקב"ה התורה על כל העולם, ולא רצו לקבלה עד שבאו ישראל וקבלוה.

ובמדרש (ספרי ברכה):

אמר מלמד שהחזיר הקב"ה את התורה לבני עשו ואמר להם רוצים אתם לקבל התורה ואמרו לו מה כתיב בה אמר להם לא תרצח אמרו לו כל ברכות של אותו איש ועל חרבך תחיה אין אנו רוצים לקבלה, אמר לבני ישמעאל רוצים אתם לקבל התורה אמרו לו מה כתיב בה אמר להם לא תגנוב אמרו לו כל ברכותיו של אותו איש והוא יהיה פרא אדם ידו בכל ויד כל בו אין אנו רוצים לקבלה, ע"כ.

In the first chapter of Avodah Zarah it says,[18]

The Torah states, "Hashem came from Sinai and shone from Se'ir to *them*;[19] He appeared from the mountain of Paran."[20]

[The Gemara asks,] but what was Hashem doing in Se'ir and what was He doing in Paran?

[The Gemara answers,] it teaches us that Hashem offered the Torah to every nation in the world,[21] but they didn't want to accept it. The only nation to accept it was Israel.

In the Midrash it states,[22]

This verse[23] teaches us that Hashem offered the Torah to the children of Eisav[24] and they said to Him, "What is written in it?"

Hashem replied, "It includes the commandment, 'Do not murder!'"[25]

They replied, "All that we were blessed with by that man [Yitzchak][26] was,

18. Avodah Zarah 2b.
19. The Midrash will elucidate that the "them" is the Jewish people.
20. D'varim 33:2
21. This is the idea of Hashem coming from Se'ir and Paran to Sinai – that first He went to Paran and Se'ir (headquarters of different gentile nations) to offer the gentiles the Torah. Only thereafter did He come to Sinai to offer it to the Jewish people.
22. Sifrei, V'zot Hab'rachah 2.
23. D'varim 33:2, cited above in the Gemara.
24. Esau, Jacob's brother.
25. Sh'mot 20:13.
26. I.e., Isaac. In B'reishit 27, we learn that Ya'akov [Jacob] disguised himself as his older brother, Eisav, in order to receive the blessing of their father, Yitzchak.

'By your sword shall you live!'[27] We do not want the Torah!"[28]

Then Hashem said to the sons of Yishma'el, "Do you want to accept the Torah?"

They said to Him, "What is written in it?"

He said to them, "It includes the commandment, 'Do not steal!'"[29]

They replied, "All that we were blessed with by that man[30] was, 'He[31] shall be a wild man, his hand shall be on everyone, and everyone's hand on him.' We do not want to accept it!"[32]

באר ו בזה הדברים אשר אמרנו כי מצוות התורה שהם הפעולות הא־להיות מתיחסות אל ישראל, שלפי מעלת נפשם הם מוכנים אל הפעולות הא־להיות והם ביחוד להם, אבל עכו"ם מצד חסרונם ופחיתותם אינם ראויים לפעולות הא־להיות שהם המצוות.

וזהו שהיה מחזיר התורה על כל אומה ולשון ועצם נפשם ממאן לקבל הפעולות הא־להיות כי אם ישראל היו מוכנים לתורה מצד מעלת נפשם.

Our sages illustrated through this [Gemara and through the Midrash] exactly what we explained about the fact that the commandments of the Torah are the G-dly actions which relate to Israel; because, due to the level of Israel's soul, they are receptive towards G-dly actions, [in fact] they are particularly suited to them. However, idol worshipping [nations], due to their lack and diminution are not suited for [the complete set of] G-dly actions, that is [all 613] mitzvot.[33]

This is the meaning [of the idea brought in the Midrash] that Hashem offered the Torah to each nation but their essential language[34] and selfhood refuses to accept G-dly actions; only Israel was receptive to the Torah due to the level of their soul.

Eisav pleaded afterwards for another blessing but Yitzchak refused. Eisav continued pleading until Yitzchak finally relented and blessed him with the blessing, "By the sword shall you live."

27. B'reishit 27:40.

28. The children of Eisav interpreted the blessing that Eisav received from Yitzchak to mean that they were "blessed" with the ability to murder.

29. Sh'mot 20:13. Halachically, this refers to kidnapping, but in the Midrash, it seems to be understood by Yishma'el as a prohibition against ordinary theft.

30. B'reishit 16:12. This verse describes the blessing that Yishma'el was given (while still in vitro) by an angel. According to the Midrash, Yishma'el understood this blessing to mean that he was destined to become a robber.

31. Yishma'el.

32. The sense of the Midrash is that both Eisav and Yishma'el felt that they had received blessings making them solely capable of acts which the Torah forbids – such as murder and theft.

33. See the Commentary, Ch. 1 § Points 10 and 12.

34. See the Commentary, Ch. 1 § Point 11.

The Maharal explains that the Midrash's position is that furthermore, idol worshipping nations have essences which are opposed to the Torah.

אמנם במדרש ביאר כי לא בלבד שהם אינם מוכנים לתורה שהם פעולות א-להיות אבל יש בהם הכנה אל הפך זה, ורצה לומר כי עשו וישמעאל היו מוכנים אל פעולות שהם הפך התורה וזה מצד ההכנה שבהם, כי אין ספק שברכתם לפי מה שהם היו מוכנים אליה בעצמם.

However, in the Midrash it is explained that not only do the idol worshippers lack receptivity to Torah (which are G-dly actions) but the idol worshipping nations are actually primed for the opposite of Torah.

Eisav and Yishma'el were receptive to actions that are the opposite of the Torah – this is from the point of view of that to which they are receptive, in potential, because there is no doubt that their blessings were [given] according to that for which they were suited in their essence.

The Maharal describes the essential problem with the idol worshipping nations – that their potential is inclined to a particular extreme. He explains that such a fundamental imbalance – the inclination to any extreme – culminates in evil.

ומה שזכר הכתוב הזה עשו וישמעאל, לומר כי עכו"ם ההם נפשם נוטה אל הקצה וכל שנוטה הכנת נפשו אל הקצה הוא רע.

וזהו ה' מסיני בא וזרח משעיר למו הופיע מהר פארן, כי הש"י ראה כי פעולות התורה הם הם הדרכים הישרים הם דרכי ה', ראוים לאשר להם הכנה ממוצעת והיא התכונה הישרה, לא אל אשר תכונת נפשו נוטה אל הקצה ופעולות שלהם אינם ישרים.

וזכר בשביל כך עשו וישמעאל שיש בכל אחד קצה אחד, כלומר כי אלו שתי אומות עכו"ם תכונת נפשם נוטה מן האמצע כל אחת לקצה אחד לכך הם ממאנים לקבל התורה. וזהו שאמר כי האחד ברכתו על חרבך תחיה לרצוח, וישמעאל ידו בכל בכח ובחזקה על הבריות ואלו שניהם תכונות רעות מחולקות כל אחד ואחד נוטה לקצה

And why did the Midrash mention Eisav and Yishma'el in particular? This is to teach that the soul of these idol worshipping nations is inclined to an extreme extent [towards these anti-Torah actions] *and anyone who has the receptivity of his soul inclined to any extreme, is evil.*

This is why the verse brought is, "Hashem came from Sinai and shone from Se'ir to them; He appeared from the mountain of Paran,"[35] to teach that Hashem, may He be Blessed, saw that the actions of the Torah are unwavering paths, these are the ways of Hashem, appropriate for those who have well-balanced potential which is the straight, honest characteristic. The Torah is inappropriate for one whose soul is inclined to an extreme and whose actions are thus not straight.

35. D'varim 33:2.

אחד כאשר ידוע לחכמי אמת, ובשביל כך היו תכונתן ממאן לקבל התורה.

אמנם בגמרא לא אמרו רק שהם לא רצו לקבלה, והכוונה בזה כי אין ראוי להם התורה והמצוות שהם הפעולות והמעשים הא־להיים שאין נפשם מוכן לזה, כי אם ישראל מצד נפשם הא־להית ומפני זה ראוי להם הפעולות הא־להיות והם מצוות התורה.

The midrash therefore mentioned Eisav and Yishma'el since each one has an extreme: the characteristic of these two idol worshipping nations inclines away from the balanced mean – each one to a different pole. Therefore, they refuse to accept the Torah. This is why the Midrash has the one[36] saying that his blessing is, "You shall live by your sword"[37] [which Eisav interpreted to mean] that they would murder; and Yishma'el [says that his blessing was] that his hand would be on everyone [which they interpreted to mean] against the will of others [in acts of robbery]. These two have negative characters which each incline to a different extreme (as is known to the scholars of truth), and therefore their characters refused to accept the Torah.

In the Gemara,[38] however, it was only stated that they didn't want to accept the Torah [as opposed to the Midrash which records their active opposition to the Torah]; the intention of which is that the Torah and mitzvot (which are the G-dly activities and actions) are not suitable to them since their soul is not prepared for it. Only Israel is prepared for it, due to their G-dly soul, and therefore G-dly actions (the mitzvot of the Torah) are suitable for them.

The Maharal explains the title, "Adam." He teaches us that it relates to the potential of a nation to accept a maximum number of mitzvot.

והוא עצמו מה שאמרו ז"ל (יבמות ס"א ע"א) אתם קרוים אדם ואין עכו"ם קרוים אדם.

ביאור ענין זה שההבדל המיוחד אשר בין האדם ובין שאר בעלי חיים מה שהאדם יש לו נפש א־להית והנה אותם אשר יש להם נפש א־להית הם מוכנים לדברים א־להיים כמו הנבואה ורוח הקדש ודבר זה לא תמצא רק בעם אשר בחר בו השם יתברך לכך

This is exactly what our sages said,[39] "You [Israel] are called '*adam*' and idol worshippers are not called '*adam*.'"[40]

The explanation of this is that the special difference between man and the other animals is that man has a G-dly soul. Those who have a G-dly soul are receptive to G-dly things such as prophecy and Divine spirit; but this you will only find in the nation which Hashem

36. Eisav.

37. B'reishit 27:40.

38. This Gemara was the first source cited above by the Maharal – the Gemara in Avodah Zarah 2b.

39. Y'vamot 61a.

40. "*Adam*," אדם, was the name of the first human being, Adam. It is also the Hebrew word for "human."

הם קרוין אדם בפרט מפני שיש בו בשלימות, במה שיש בהם כל אשר ראוי להיות לאדם שנקרא אדם בפרט מפני שיש בו מעלה א־להית ואינו טבעי ולפיכך אתם קרוים אדם.

ומפני זה המצוות שהם הפעולות הא־להיות מתיחסות בפרט לישראל בשלימות כאשר יתבאר עוד.

(may He be Blessed) chose. Therefore, Israel in particular, is called "*adam*" since they possess a perfection in that they have *everything* that is suitable to suffice to be called "*adam*": they have a G-dly excellence which is not natural; therefore, they are called "*adam.*"

Therefore, the commandments, which are G-dly acts, relate *completely* to Israel in particular, as will be explained further.[41]

The question is now raised – if there is such a fundamental uniqueness to the Jewish soul, how is it that gentiles can convert?

ואל יקשה אם כן הגר איך אפשר שיהיה מקבל התורה כאשר יש לו תכונה נפשית שאינה טובה, אין זה קשיא כלל כי מאחר שבא להתגייר הנה יש לו תכונה ישראלית, וכאשר נתגייר נעשה טפל לאומה הישראלית והרי הוא כמוה.

ועם כל זה אמרו (נדה י"ג ע"א) קשים גרים לישראל כמו ספחת כי הספחת מזגו אינו טוב ומקלקל הבשר שיש לו מזג טוב.

Do not find a difficulty [with the above concept] due to the fact that a gentile can [convert to Judaism and] accept the Torah when he has a spiritual character trait which is not positive. This is no difficulty at all, since from the fact that he has come to convert, he [must now] have[42] an Israelite character and when he actually does convert, he becomes attached to the Israelite nation and he is like her [the Jewish nation].

And despite this, our sages said, "Converts are as bad for Israel as a *sapachat* plague."[43, 44] This is because a *sapachat*'s nature is that it itself is not good and it destroys the body's flesh (which has a good nature).[45]

Another question is now raised – if the Jewish people have such a unique and positive character, how is it that they were so enamored of idolatry?

41. See Chaps. Two, Five and Twelve.

42. The Maharal does not explicitly state whether such a convert previously had an "Israelite character" or whether this character is attained upon conversion. Rabbi Hartman (Chap. 1, p. 43, n. 94) suggests the former.

43. *Sapachat* is a type of metaphysical malady which manifested as a skin disease. See Vayikra 13.

44. Niddah 13a.

45. See the Commentary, Ch. 1 § Point 13. According to the Maharal, the parallel here is that the Gemara seems to be saying that converts, like the *sapachat*, are negative in and of themselves, and also have a negative influence on the healthy, i.e., the Jewish people.

ואל יקשה הרי נמצא כי ישראל היו העם הנבחר עם התכונה הטובה שהיתה להם היו להוטין ביותר אחר עבודה זרה מכל האומות, כי דבר זה יתבאר עוד באריכות בפרקים הבאים.

[Also] do not find it difficult that Israel, which was the chosen nation and despite its positive spiritual nature, was still more gluttonous for idol worship than all the other nations; this matter will be explained more at length in the coming chapters.[46]

46. Rabbi Hartman (Chap. 1, p. 45, n. 99) states that he has no knowledge of where else in *Tiferet Yisrael* the Maharal discusses this, however he points to Netzach Yisrael, Chapters Three, Twelve and Twenty-Five.

SUMMARY

Chapter 1: 2/2

I. Mitzvot are the actions suited to humans due to their exalted spirituality (continuation from Part 1)

- A. The Maharal's question
  1. All other beings' essential actions flow naturally and automatically from them (e.g., fire from warmth). If it is true that humans' essential actions are mitzvot, why do they not flow naturally from humanity?
- B. The Maharal's answer
  1. The mitzvot should flow automatically, except that humans must also have freedom of choice (bestowed upon them due to the existence within them of an inclination towards bad) and this choice allows humans to choose alternative actions, i.e., evil.

II. There is a difference in spiritual potential between nations

- A. The Maharal states that Israel has greater receptivity to spirituality since:
  1. Prophecy was more prevalent amongst Israel.
     - a. Prophecy is a function of the receptivity to spirituality which is due to a greater spiritual potential.
  2. People cannot be equal in spirituality.
     - a. Physically, people are equal and the minor differences due to geographical variations are insignificant.
     - b. Spiritually, people cannot all be on the same level, since if they were, this world would be fundamentally spiritual and it is not – it is physical.
       - (1) Idol worshipping nations are part of the physical world (therefore there are seventy of them – ten for each day of creation, which signifies physical completion).
       - (2) Israel is above the physical world and therefore corresponds to the number eight. The Torah is also above the physical world and thus the Torah was given to Israel.
       - (3) Idol worshipping nations received seven mitzvot since they are more rooted in the physical world and do not have the required receptivity for more mitzvot. Seven is the number representing physical perfection (as explained in the Introduction.)
- B. This concept is illustrated in the Gemara (Avodah Zarah 2b) as well as the Sifrei (V'zot Hab'rachah 2).

1. Hashem offered the Torah to all the nations in the world, who refused it.
2. In particular, Eisav and Yishma'el refused it because:
    a. Eisav: felt that their blessing from Yitzchak bestowed the ability to murder, which the Torah prohibits.
    b. Yishma'el: felt that their blessing from Avraham bestowed the ability to steal, which the Torah prohibits.
3. The general idea is that the "rejection" of the Torah by the nations of the world is due to their lack of spiritual suitability for it.
4. In particular, anyone who possesses an extreme in any character trait will be unable to accept the Torah since the Torah is "straight" and balanced.
    a. Eisav and Yishma'el had extremes in different directions, but their extremism ensured that they could not, by nature, accept the Torah.

C. Difficulty: converts
1. The Maharal asks: if there is this inherent spiritual difference, how can gentiles convert?
    a. The Maharal answers that such gentiles have Israelite spiritual potential.
2. Despite this, the Maharal seems to be saying that converts are a negative force.
    a. They are compared to a *sapachat* plague which is negative and destroys the healthy flesh around it (please see the Commentary, Ch. 1 § Point 13 for more on this).

D. Difficulty: Jews pursued iol worship more than other nations
1. If the Jews have this spiritual edge, why were they so addicted to idol worship?
    a. The Maharal will explain this later.

CHAPTER 2

CHAPTER 2

Part 1 of 1

In this chapter, the Maharal presents a general outline of the nature of Torah and mitzvot and their relationship to human beings.

התבאר לך כי הפעולות הא־להיות שהם מצוות התורה הם ראויים לאדם לפי מדריגת נפשו הא־להית שהיא בקרבו, והפעולות האלו הם השלמת האדם שבהם יושלם עד שהוא הבריאה אשר בה רצון בוראו. ויתבאר בפרקים הבאים דבר זה באריכות בעזרת נותן התורה. ובזה הפרק יתבאר דרך כללות בקצור.

It has become clear to you that the G-dly actions (which are the mitzvot and the Torah) are suitable for a person due to the level of his G-dly soul which is within him. These actions encompass the perfection of a person through which he will be perfected until he becomes the creation which the Creator desires. This will be explained at length in the coming chapters, with the help of the One Who bestows the Torah [but as an introduction, all this] will be explained concisely, in this chapter, in terms of general rules.

The Maharal explains that Torah and mitzvot are the spiritual means which enable human beings, who all possess spiritual potential, to perfect themselves.

שהאדם יציר כפו של הקדוש ברוך הוא מבחר התחתונים חסר, עד שהוא נשלם על ידי מעשה עצמו, ועל ידי מצוות התורה יגיע האדם אל ההשלמה, כי מצד שיש בו נפש א־להי שיש בו הכנה א־להית לכך אין השלמתו בדבר שהוא טבעי אבל השלמתו בתורה ובמצוה שהוא על הטבע.

The human being is the handiwork of the Holy One, Blessed be He, and humans are the chosen ones of all the lower creations, but they are [created] imperfect and they can [only] be perfected through their own actions. Through the mitzvot of the Torah, humans can reach perfection. Due to humans possessing a G-dly soul, which has G-dly potential, a person's perfection cannot be attained through physical means; rather, his perfection is through Torah and mitzvot which transcend nature.

The inherent spirituality of Torah and mitzvot is also expressed through the numerical values with which they are associated. Physicality is encompassed within seven dimensions while the metaphysical corresponds to the eighth level. Thus, Torah and mitzvot are expressed by the eighth dimension.

ודבר זה מבואר במקומות הרבה שמצוות התורה הם יותר במדריגה ובמעלה מן הטבע.

ובמזמור (תהלים י"ט) השמים מספרים כבוד א-ל וגו' ואחר כך התחיל לומר תורת ה' תמימה וגו' עד סוף המזמור. ויש מן תחלת המזמור עד תורת ה' תמימה שבעה פסוקים ואחר כך תורת ה' תמימה. כי הנהגת הטבע נברא בשבעה ימי בראשית ואלו התורה היא על הטבע והיא מדריגה שמינית.

ועל פי טעם זה מזמור אשרי תמימי דרך שהוסד על התורה, יש בו שמונה אלפ"א בית"א שהתורה היא מדריגה שמינית שהיא על הטבע שנברא בשבעת ימי בראשית. וכן כל דבר שהוא על הטבע והוא תיקון מה שחסר הטבע הוא אחר השבעה.

וזה טעם מילה בשמיני כי האדם מצד הטבע נברא עם הערלה והוא פחיתות הטבע, והמילה היא תיקון הטבע ולפיכך תיקון הזה הוא ביום השמיני לפי שהוא אחר הטבע שנבראת (בששת) [בשבעת] ימי בראשית.

This idea is clarified in many places: that the mitzvot of the Torah are higher in level and stature than nature.

[For example,] in Tehillim 19 it says, "The heavens tell of Hashem's glory . . ."[1] and afterwards it begins to state "The Torah of Hashem is perfect . . ."[2] [and the descriptions of the Torah's superlatives continue] until the end of the Tehillim. From the beginning of the Tehillim, where it discusses nature, until the verse where it begins describing the Torah, are seven verses. And then in verse eight it starts talking about the Torah. This is because the natural world was created in the seven days of creation while the Torah transcends nature; and [therefore] it is the eighth level.[3]

For the same reason, in Tehillim "Happy are those who are *tamim*[4] on the path,"[5] each letter of the *Aleph-Beit*[6] has eight verses [beginning with it], because this whole Tehillim is about the Torah[7] and the Torah is the eighth level which is above nature which was created in the seven days of creation. So, too, anything which is above nature and is a mending of something which is

1. Tehillim 19:2.
2. Tehillim 19:8.
3. There are six directions in the physical world: up, down, left, right, forwards and backwards. Including the origin (the central point) there are a total of seven. So, eight is above the natural world. This is part of the Maharal's numerology – see at length in the Commentary, Introduction § Point 15.
4. We explored the term, "*tamim*," in the Commentary, Introduction § Point 1. As we explained there, this word appears in Tehillim 19, to which the Maharal also refers here. In Tehillim 19 it states, "The Torah of Hashem is *t'mimah*." We explained that "*tamim*" means, "pure," "innocent" and "complete."
5. This is Tehillim 119. The Maharal references it through the opening words of the first verse.
6. The Hebrew alphabet.
7. As it says in Tehillim 19, "The Torah of Hashem is *tamim*" and Tehillim 119 is an ode to those "who are *tamim* on the path, who walk in the Torah of Hashem" (Tehillim 119:1).

lacking in nature must come after the seventh level.

This is the reason that *milah*[8] is performed on the eighth day, because humans were created with a foreskin which is a natural imperfection, and *milah* is a repair and elevation of nature. Therefore, this perfection of nature is performed on the eighth day since it is above nature which was created in the seven[9] days of creation.[10]

The Maharal now summarizes his position – that humans were created intentionally with inbuilt physical and spiritual imperfections which exist for us to perfect. There is a complete correspondence between human beings, who, though physical, have spiritual potential; and the mitzvot, which though performed physically, have a spiritual result.

ומעתה תדע כי המצוות שהם הפעולות הא־להיות והם מעשה האדם יגיע בהם האדם למדריגה שהוא על הטבע. וראוי שיהיה כך כי מעשה האדם במה שהוא בעל שכל הוא יותר במעלה מן הטבע שהרי הטבע הוא כח חמרי בלבד ואלו האדם הוא שכלי.

You now know that through the mitzvot, which are G-dly activities but are actualized through the actions of humans, a person can reach a level above nature. And it is fitting that it should be so because the actions of humans, due to the fact that humans possess the power of the intellect, are higher in stature than nature, since the natural world is a purely physical element; while humans are *sichli*.[11]

The Maharal now poses a fundamental question which is the subject of the remainder of the chapter: surely, since nature is a direct outgrowth of Hashem's will, it must be closer to Hashem and in fact, more spiritual, than any act of a human being which is generated by mere human will. The answer the Maharal gives to his question is that as much as nature is a product of Hashem's will, so is human intellect and human choice. So nature and humanity are at least on the same level. Moreover, the intellect is, by definition, more transcendent than physicality and thus, when human beings perform mitzvot (utilizing their choice and intellect), their actions are superior to nature.

If one would say that the power of nature acts through a power from Hashem, may He be Blessed, we can [answer this challenge and] say that since humans

8. "*Milah*," מילה, means "circumcision."

9. Textual emendation as per Rabbi Hartman, vol. 1, 48.

10. This is part of the Maharal's numerology – see at length in the Commentary, Introduction § Point 15.

11. As noted previously, the Maharal identifies *sichli* reality almost synonymously with the spiritual realm. See the terminology entry in the Commentary, Introduction § Point 1.

are *sichli*, they act through the power of the intellect which Hashem gave them. Therefore, the G-dly mitzvot are suitable for humans, who are *sichli* (with an intellect above nature) since they are actions which are not natural and through them a person will reach the highest level which is above nature – the transcendent world.

ואם יאמר כי כח הטבע פועל בכח שהוא מן השם יתברך, נאמר גם כן כי האדם שהוא שכלי פועל בכח השכל שנתן לו השם יתברך. ולפיכך ראוי אל האדם שהוא שכלי והשכל הוא על הטבע המצוות הא־להיות שהם המעשים שאינם טבעיים, ועל ידם יגיע האדם אל מעלה עליונה שהוא למעלה מן הטבע הוא עולם הנבדל.

The Maharal now cites a Midrash which addresses the purpose of the mitzvot and the relationship between the physical and transcendent realities. In it, Turnus[12] Rufus, a Roman general, challenges the idea of *milah* (circumcision).

And in the Midrash (Tanchuma, Tazri'a) it says:[13]

Turnus Rufus the wicked [Roman General] asked Rabbi Akiva, "Whose deeds are better? Hashem's or human beings?"

Rabbi Akiva answered, "Human beings!"

Turnus Rufus said to him, "Consider the sky and earth – do you think you could manage anything like it?"

Rabbi Akiva said, "Don't talk to me of things beyond human capabilities. Let's discuss comparable things, which human beings can also make."

Turnus said to him, "Why do you circumcise yourselves?"

Rabbi Akiva said, "I knew you were going to ask that question! That's why I answered you before that people's deeds are better than Hashem's." Rabbi Akiva continued, "Bring me fresh ears of wheat and some cake." [Then he said to Turnus,

ובמדרש (תנחומא תזריע):

שאל טורנוסרופס הרשע איזה מעשים נאים של הקדוש ברוך הוא או של בשר ודם?

אמר לו של בשר ודם.

אמר לו טורנוסרופס הרשע ראית השמים והארץ יכול האדם לעשות כיוצא בהם?

אמר לו רבי עקיבא לא תאמר לי בדבר שהוא למעלה מן הבריות שאין שולטים עליו אלא אמור דברים שהם מצוין בבני אדם.

אמר לו למה אתם מולים?

אמר לו אני הייתי יודע שעל דבר זה אתה שואלני ולכך הקדמתי ואמרתי לך שמעשה בני אדם נאים משל הקדוש ברוך הוא. הביא לו רבי עקיבא שבלים וגלוסקאות. [(הבא בסוגריים אלה ליתא במהר"ל אבל איתא בגירסתנו במדרש) א"ל אלו מעשה הקב"ה ואלו מעשה ידי אדם א"ל אין אלו נאים יותר מן השבלים?]

אמר לו טורנוסרופס הרשע אם

12. "Turnus" is understood by some to be a variant of the Latin, "*Tyrranus*," tyrant. See Rabbi Jonathan Sacks, *To Heal a Fractured World* (Continuum, 2005), p. 80.

13. Tanchuma, Tazri'a. Some versions of the Midrash have this as subsection five, six or seven. As per the two footnotes below, we will reference the Buber edition of the Midrash (Vilna: 5645) which has it as Tazri'a 7.

הקדוש ברוך הוא רוצה במילה למה אינו יוצא הולד מהול ממעי אמו?

אמר לו רבי עקיבא ולמה טיבורו יוצא עמו והוא תלוי בבטנו ואמו חותכתו ומה שאתה אומר למה אינו יוצא מהול שלא נתן הקדוש ברוך הוא המצוות אלא לצרף האדם בהם לכך אמר דוד כל אמרת א־לוה צרופה ע"כ.

"So which of these is better? The fresh wheat which is Hashem's work, or the cakes which are people's?"][14]

Turnus retorted, "Well if Hashem wants you to be circumcised, why aren't you born that way?"

Rabbi Akiva asked, "Well why don't you ask about the umbilical cord which comes out with the baby and hangs from his stomach? We are definitely not meant to have that and yet we are born with it and our mothers have to cut it off! So why aren't we born circumcised? [Both of these anomalies have the same reason, which is reflected in the very concept of mitzvot] because Hashem only gave the mitzvot to Israel in order to refine them. Therefore, David said,[15] 'All the statement of Hashem is refined.'"[16]

The issue raised above is whether the product of human actions can ever be superior to that of nature, which is G-d's handiwork. Turnus Rufus believed that such a state of affairs would be impossible, thus rendering the act of circumcision purely an act of destruction. The Maharal now explains Rabbi Akiva's first response to this question.

וביאור זה כי טורנוסרופס היה סבור כי מעשה האדם פחותים מן מעשה הטבע במה שהטבע פעל א־להי, לכך אמר שהמילה היא יותר פחותה מן הערלה שהיא מעשה הטבע שפעל השם יתברך ואלו המילה מעשה האדם.

והשיב לו שאין הדבר כך כי מעשה האדם במה שהוא פעל האדם שהוא בעל שכל יותר במדרגה מן הטבע

The explanation of this is that Turnus Rufus believed that human actions are inferior to natural ones, since nature is made by G-d; therefore, he said that having a circumcision is inferior to [possessing] the foreskin, which is a work of G-d, while circumcision is an act of man.

Rabbi Akiva answered him that the

14. This bracketed section is not in the Maharal's text but is in our version of the Midrash.

15. There seems to be a printer's error here. There are two similar verses in the Tanach (see next note). One is in Mishlei which begins with the word "All," which is what we have cited in the Maharal. The other similar verse is in Tehillim which just states "the statement of Hashem is refined," omitting the word "All." King Solomon wrote Mishlei while King David wrote Tehillim. Thus, there is a printer's error either in the citation or in the attribution. It seems more likely that the error is in the addition of the word "all," as in the Buber edition of the Midrash, this word is omitted and thus the verse is from Tehillim 18:31. We have translated "*tz'rufah*" as "refined" as per the M'tzudat David ad loc.

16. See previous note. This verse is either Mishlei 30:5 or Tehillim 18:31. In either case, this verse can also be understood as "The statement of Hashem *only* comes to purify," which is how it is being interpreted by the Midrash.

שהוא כח חמרי בלבד וכמו שהוכיח לו מן החטים שהוא פעל הטבע והוא חסר עד שיושלם על ידי אדם השכלי שמזה תראה כי פעל השכל הוא על הטבע.

matter is not so: a human action (in that it is a function of a human who possesses an intellect)[17] is above nature which is a physical power only. This is as Rabbi Akiva proved to him from the wheat, which is a product of nature but is lacking until it is completed by the *sichli* human. From this you see that the results of the intellect are above those of nature.

The second issue raised by Turnus Rufus is that even if we could say that the product of human actions could be superior to nature, can one say that nature, G-d's creation, is deficient? The Maharal explains that the Torah believes that in comparison to human beings, nature *is* flawed.

והוסיף עוד לשאול אם כן למה אין התינוק יוצא מהול אחר שהשם יתברך חפץ במילה ואינו רוצה כלל בערלה?

כי עדיין חשב אף כי פעל האדם הוא יותר במעלה במה שהוא פעל האדם בעל שכל, מכל מקום אין לומר שפעל הטבע הוא בחסרון ואם היה חפץ במילה והערלה היא רע אם כן למה לא השלים השם יתברך את הטבע ויצא התינוק ממעי אמו מהול.

ודבר זה לא יספיק התשובה מן החטים, שאף כי הגלוסקא פעל בעל שכל יותר נבחר מכל מקום גם השכלים שהם מעשה הטבע טובים רק שפעל בעל השכל יותר משובח אבל אין לומר שפעל הטבע הוא חסר.

Turnus Rufus continued and asked, "If so, why doesn't a baby emerge from the womb already circumcised, if it is true that Hashem wants a circumcision and doesn't want the foreskin at all?"

He asked this because he still believed that even if human actions are superior (through their being performed by one possessing an intellect), nevertheless, one cannot say that nature is lacking;[18] and if G-d wanted circumcision and if the foreskin is bad, why didn't Hashem, may He be Blessed, perfect nature and then the baby would exit his mother's womb already circumcised?

[The reason the Midrash continues with the conversation and that the "wheat" example was not conclusive enough to decide the argument is that]

17. As mentioned numerous times, the Maharal is not using the terms "intellect" and "intellectual" in the sense that they are usually employed. He does not mean that any product of the normal human mind is by necessity spiritual and holy and superior to nature – quite the opposite, the products of many human minds are often completely banal and depraved. Rather, he explains that the spiritual world is populated by "intellectual" beings – meaning that they exist on a rarefied level to which only the intellect can relate, when it is suitably refined and applied.

18. It would seem that the reasoning here is that since Hashem made nature, at the very least we cannot say that nature is lacking, we could only say that it is good as it is and that *sichli* action improves it.

the concession that Turnus Rufus made regarding the wheat [that human actions are better than natural ones] does not address this question; because even if we say that a cake is better than wheat (since the cake is a product of one possessing an intellect), nevertheless, the wheat (which is a product of nature) is also good; it's just that the product of the intellect is better – but one cannot say that the products of nature are flawed.

The Maharal explains that Rabbi Akiva's answer to this question is that indeed, we *do* say that nature is flawed even though Hashem created it – moreover, we claim that this was Hashem's intention in creation in the very first place. He cites a Midrash to prove this.

ועל זה השיב כי בודאי פעל הטבע הוא חסר גם כן כמו שתראה כי התינוק יוצא עם הטיבור והאם צריכה לחתכו עד שתראה מזה כי הטבע אין בו השלמה. וא"כ אין זה קשיא מה שיוצא התינוק עם הערלה כי אין פעל הטבע בשלמות כי אלו היה פעל הטבע בשלימות לא היה במעשה הטבע שנוי שהדברים אשר בהם השלימות אין שנוי בהם, אבל אין בו השלמה בפרט אל האדם השכלי שיש לו מעלה על הטבע מצד השכל.

To this, Rabbi Akiva answered that definitely, the product of nature is flawed, as one can see [from the fact] that the baby emerges with an umbilical cord and the mother needs to cut it off. One can see from this that nature does not possess perfection; if so, there is no difficulty from the question as to why a baby is born uncircumcised, because the products of nature are not perfect, for if the products of nature were perfect they would never change (for all things which are perfect cannot change.)[19] Rather, nature does not possess perfection, especially [when compared] to the *sichli* human who is superior to nature due to the intellect.

ובמדרש עוד, (ב"ר פ' י"א):

In the Midrash it is further stated,[20]

כל מעשה ששת ימי בראשית צריכים עשיה אחרת כגון חטים צריכים לטחון החרדל צריך להמתיק התורמוס צריך להמתיק ע"כ.

> All products of the six days of creation require further action [upon them], like wheat which requires grinding, mustard which requires sweetening and lupine which requires sweetening.

וכל זה מפני כי אין פעל הטבע בעל השלמה בעצמו אל האדם שיש בו השכל שהוא על הטבע וזהו מדרגת הטבע כמו שאמרנו, ולפיכך כל אשר נברא בששת ימי בראשית אין השלמה בו אל האדם.

All this is due to the fact that any product of nature cannot possess perfection in and of itself, especially in relation to humans who possess an intellect which transcends nature. This is the level of

19. Since change would imply that their original state was not perfect.
20. B'reishit Rabbah 11:6.

nature, as we have said. Therefore, anything created in the six days of creation does not possess perfection when compared to the human being.

The Maharal summarizes Rabbi Akiva's first answer to Turnus Rufus: that nature is created flawed and it is the task of humans to perfect the natural. The mitzvah of *milah* is a microcosm of this mission and thus, it encapsulates the message of the entire Torah.

ולכך אין זה שאלה אם נברא התינוק בלא מילה שזה שייך אל פעל הטבע במה שהוא פעל חסר, ואינו במדרגת ההשלמה אל האדם השכלי. ואילו נברא האדם בשלמות כאשר יצא מבטן אמו אם כן היה האדם טבעי בלבד, ולכך נתנה לו המילה שהיא השלמתו ביום השמיני כי כל השלמת האדם על הטבע לכן המילה שהיא השלמתו והיא על הטבע שקולה כנגד כל התורה.

Therefore, there is no difficulty in [the fact] that a baby is born uncircumcised since this [uncircumcised] state is a product of nature which is a flawed product and is not on a level of perfection when compared to the *sichli* human. Were a human to be born perfect as he exited his mother's womb, then he would be purely natural;[21] therefore, circumcision was given to the human since it is [the beginning of] his perfection [which is performed] on the eighth day because any perfection of the human is above nature and therefore, circumcision, which is a human's perfection and which transcends nature, is equivalent to all the Torah.[22]

The Maharal now addresses the philosophical concern one would have by saying (as he did above) that nature, a product of Hashem, is flawed. The Maharal's answer is that the system as a whole is perfect.

ואל תאמר כי יהיה חס ושלום בפעל השם יתברך דופי, אין זה כך רק הכל הוא בחכמה לפי אשר ראוי לעולם אשר יש בו הויה והפסד אשר אינו בעל השלמה ובפרט אל האדם השכלי

Now don't say, G-d forbid, that there is weakness within the product of Hashem, may He be Blessed; it is not so – in fact everything is [created] with wisdom according to that which is suitable to

21. As we explored in the Commentary, Ch. 1 § Point 8, the Maharal explains that there are only two ways for there to be no variability in the state of perfection of objects within this physical world – either those objects would have to be non-physical (impossible by definition), or they would have to be completely physical, with no potential for growth. Applying this principle here, if there were "nothing" to improve on in the human body, the body would remain only in its natural state, with no potential for perfection through the intellect. But now that the body is created somewhat flawed, it has the potential for improvement and thus there is room for humanity to exercise its creative abilities on itself.

22. For further study, see the Commentary, Ch. 2 § Point 1.

שהשכלי הוא על הטבע.

ולכך אל האדם אין הטבע בעל השלמה כי צריך לתקן מזונות שלו החטים לטחון והטבור לחתוך והערלה למילה.

a world in which there is [both] coming into being as well as loss [of being] and which does not possess perfection (especially when compared to the *sichli* human, since the *sichli* is above nature).[23]

Therefore, when compared to humanity, nature does not possess perfection because [human beings] need to prepare their food (that is, to grind the wheat) and to cut the umbilical cord and to remove the foreskin.

The Maharal now explains Rabbi Akiva's second answer to Turnus Rufus's question – that the mitzvot refine humanity.

ועוד השיב לו אף כי בודאי אין זה קשיא מה שאין יוצא התינוק מהול כמו שנתבאר, מכל מקום בזולת זה אין דבר זה ראוי לשאלה כי המצוה שציוה השם יתברך לבני אדם רוצה הוא יתברך לצרף את האדם.

כי מצד פעל השי"ת אין מילה וזהו מצד הבריאה שהשם יתברך ברא הכל על ידי הטבע ולפי הטבע ראוי הערלה, רק שנתן השם יתברך המילה לאדם שיהיה צירוף לאדם עד שיהיה בלתי טבעי שכאשר עושה המצוה הוא צירוף אל האדם מן הטבע.

Rabbi Akiva further responded to Turnus Rufus[24] that even though there is no philosophical difficulty presented by the fact that a baby is not born circumcised (as was explained),[25] nevertheless, even without this [previous answer] this matter is not even suitable to be posed as a question, because Hashem, may He be Blessed, gave humans the commandment [to circumcise themselves] in order to refine humanity.

From the perspective of the product of Hashem, may He be Blessed, there is [no requirement] for a circumcision since [from the perspective that] Hashem created the entire creation through nature and according to nature, the foreskin is suitable;[26] but Hashem gave

23. The Maharal's question is that it seems that since so much work is needed to perfect nature, this must mean that the product of Hashem's acts is not always perfect. His answer seems to be that the system as a whole is designed with Hashem's wisdom so that as a whole, it is perfect since Hashem also created humans who are the instruments of the perfection of this world.

24. This part of the Maharal explains the last section of Rabbi Akiva's response to Turnus Rufus, where Rabbi Akiva said, "Because Hashem only gave the mitzvot to Israel in order to refine them. Therefore, David said, '[All] the statement of Hashem is refined.'"

25. When examining nature in comparison to humanity, we say that nature is flawed, which is the first explanation of why circumcision is needed.

26. Nature only appears flawed when compared to human beings, but this world is a natural world (see the Commentary, Ch. 1 § Point 8) and thus the foreskin is entirely appropriate to this world, being a natural element of existence.

circumcision to humanity in order that there should be a refinement for the human being till the point that he rises above nature; since when a human performs a commandment, it is a refinement for him from [existing solely within] nature.

וזה אשר חפץ השם יתברך במילה, ואם היה נברא מהול לא היה צירוף אל האדם כי היו כל בני אדם כך שהטבע היא אחת לכל בני אדם ולא היה זה צירוף שאין הצירוף רק בדבר שאינו טבעי שהצירוף הוא הוצאה מן הטבע וזהו הצירוף כמו שיתבאר.

This is why Hashem wanted circumcision – and if a human were born circumcised there would be no refinement for humans [from this state] since all humans would be [formed] this way,[27] since nature is identical for all humans and thus, there would be no refinement.[28] [This is] because refinement only applies to something that is not natural (since refinement, by definition, means an exiting from the framework of what is natural) and this is [the very definition of] refinement, as will be explained.[29]

וכן כל המצוות שנתן השם יתברך הם צירוף לאדם שיהיה האדם פעולותיו ומעשיו הוצאה מן הטבעי ולא יהיו מעשיו של אדם שוים עם הבעלי חיים הטבעיים. כי מצד הטבע נחשב ונראה האדם כבהמה שהיא טבעית ואין כל אדם ראוי למעלה זאת כי אם העם אשר בחר בהם השם יתברך. ודבר זה עוד יתבאר.

So, too, all the commandments that Hashem, may He be Blessed, gave to humanity, are a refinement for humanity [in order] that the human's actions and activities will [lead towards] a transition out of [the framework of pure] nature and so that his actions will not be equal to those of natural animals (since, from the perspective of nature, the human is considered and seems to be like an animal which is [completely] natural.) But not every person is suitable for this level, only the nation which Hashem, may He be Blessed, chose. This matter will be explained further.[30]

27. I.e., circumcised.

28. As we explained above (as explored in the Commentary, Ch. 1 § Point 8), the Maharal explains that there are only two ways for there to be no variability in the state of perfection of objects within this physical world – either those objects would have to be non-physical (impossible by definition) or they would have to be completely physical, with no potential for growth.

29. See Chapter Three.

30. See Chapters Five and Seven of this work.

SUMMARY

Chapter 2: 1/1

I. Mitzvot as the only means to human perfection

A. Humans are created imperfect and their purpose is to perfect themselves through their own actions.

B. Since humans have a G-dly soul, their perfection cannot be through the physical world alone, since they are not purely physical; rather they have to use the Torah and the mitzvot, which are G-dly.

II. The Torah and mitzvot are above nature and are G-dly which is reflected in their numerology

A. Nature is the seventh level
   1. The physical world was created in seven days.
   2. Physical space is encompassed by the number seven: six directions and a central point.

B. The eighth level is the level above nature and represents the perfection of nature.

C. The Torah is on the eighth level and this is even reflected in the way that the Torah is presented:
   1. Tehillim 19
      a. The physical world's connection to Hashem is outlined in the first seven verses.
      b. The Torah is mentioned only in the eighth verse and onwards.
   2. Tehillim 119
      a. This Tehillim extols the Torah and is written in sections with eight verses each.
   3. This is the level of the Torah

D. Mitzvot are a combination of physical and spiritual
   1. Physical – they are performed by physical human beings.
   2. Spiritual – they are directed by an intellect.

III. The debate between Turnus Rufus and Rabbi Akiva according to the Maharal

A. The first stage of the argument
   1. Turnus Rufus's initial axiom is that nature, as a product of G-d's handiwork, is better than anything humanity could produce (which would be a product of a product.)
   2. Rabbi Akiva refutes this with the comparison between wheat and cake showing that human products are superior to nature's.

B. The second stage of the argument
   1. Turnus Rufus's next claim is that even if one concedes that the product of human beings is superior to nature's, surely nature, as the work of Hashem, cannot itself be flawed.
   2. Rabbi Akiva refutes this using the example of the umbilical cord.
   3. The conclusion is that indeed, in comparison to the *sichli* human being, the physical world is flawed.
      a. However, the system as a whole is perfect because humanity was created to perfect any flaw created within nature.

C. The third stage of the argument: The purpose of circumcision
   1. Circumcision was given to us as a mitzvah as a symbol of the perfection needed by the physical world and it is performed on the eighth day which connotes the level of Torah and mitzvot above nature.
   2. It combines both of the ideas above:
      a. That the acts of humanity are superior to those of nature.
      b. That nature, when compared to humanity, is flawed.

D. The fourth stage of the argument: Rabbi Akiva's second answer
   1. Rabbi Akiva's second answer is that the mitzvot were given to us to refine us.
   2. The Maharal takes this to be a separate refutation to Turnus Rufus's propositions.
      a. The whole framework of mitzvot exists only to ensure that humans are refined, by which is meant that they transition from an existence which is purely physical and attain an existence which transcends the physical. In other words, mitzvot enable people to attain spiritual existence.
      b. Thus, even if Turnus Rufus's assumptions all held true (i.e., that human products were inferior to natural ones and that nature was not flawed), there is still a cogent reason for circumcision and all the mitzvot – they enable transcendence.

CHAPTER 3

CHAPTER 3

Part 1 of 2

In this chapter, the Maharal discusses the infinite potential for greatness within every human being. He also raises the consequences of this idea. First he begins with the concept that a human being can never be a finished product as there is always more potential for growth within each of us. (See more on this in the Commentary, Ch. 3 § Point 4.)

As we've mentioned previously, humans alone have a G-dly soul, unlike all the lower creatures,[1] and so, the human being, with the excellence of his G-dly soul, must not accept the libel regarding himself which says that he has at some point achieved the final level of actualizing his potential. [Due to this potential,] the human being must not allow himself to think, "All will be well with me even if I sit idle without making any effort at all to grow," [believing that] his [innate] excellence and his [inherently elevated] status will protect him and will return him to his place and establish him and that he will enjoy that which he [already] has and that he has no need to acquire any further excellence.

All this is a revolting thought[2] which cannot be accepted and a person should never think this way, as it is an error within his soul. [The reason this is such an error is that] the final excellence of a human soul has not been actualized [while that person is still alive], and in fact, human beings alone, amongst all

האדם עם מעלת נפשו הא־להית אשר כבר אמרנו כי יש לו נפש א־להית בפרט שלא נמצא בכל נפשות התחתונים, אל יקבל אונאה בעצמו לומר כי יש לו מעלתו האחרונה בפעל, ויחשוב בנפשו שלום יהיה לי אף אם אני יושב בטל מבלי עמל כלל הרי המעלה שלו ומדרגתו יגן עליו על מקומו ישיבנו ועל כנו יחזירנו כי משלו יתן לו ואין צריך לקנות לו שום מעלה.

דבר זה מחשבת פגול לא ירצה ולא יחשוב כך כי הוא טעות בנפשו כי אין מעלת נפשו האחרונה בפעל, והוא מיוחד מבין כל הנמצאים עליונים ותחתונים שאין מעלתו האחרונה בפעל.

וכי יעלה על דעת האדם שיהיה נמצא לאדם מעלתו האחרונה בפעל כי זהו מדרגת העליונים שהם בפעל אבל התחתונים שהם בעלי חומר אינם בפעל. ודבר זה יכריח כי אין לאדם מעלתו האחרונה עד שנחשב מדרגתו בין העליונים ויהיה לו מהלכים בין העומדים האלה רק שנברא בכח ואינו בפעל שאין לו מעלתו האחרונה בפעל.

1. Lit., "souls."

2. Lit., "a thought of *pigul*" as per Vayikra 19:7. See the Commentary, Ch. 3 § Point 1.

upper and lower creations, are such that the final excellence of their souls is never actualized.

The thought that a human can have crystallized his final brilliance cannot seriously be entertained since this level [of complete attainment of potential] is that of the transcendent beings which are completely actualized; but the lower creations, which are physical, are not actualized. This [correct argument] leads to the understanding that a person can never have attained his final state of excellence until his level can be considered to be amongst the transcendent beings such that he "strides among those standing [angels]."[3] Rather, the human being was created with potential and not in [complete] final, actualized form.

The difference between the transcendent creations (for example, angels) and the physical creations is that the transcendent creations have fully actualized spirituality, while the lower creations are static. Humanity alone stands between the two with tremendous, self-actualizable potential, something no other creation has.

ונמצא לך ההפרש שיש בין האדם ובין כל הנמצאים התחתונים ועליונים. כי העליונים שלימותם בפעל ואינם צריכים להוציא שלימותם אל הפעל, והתחתונים זולת האדם אין להם גם כן יציאה אל הפעל כי מה שנבראו עליו אין השתנות ויציאה לפעל בהם. אך האדם הוא בכח ויוצא אל הפעל.

This leads one to the difference between human beings and all the lower and upper creations. The transcendent [upper] beings have their perfection already actualized and thus, they do not have any need to actualize it. The lower beings, except for humans, also have no actualization [of some potential perfection] since the state in which they were created is static and there is no change and no actualization.[4] But human beings alone *are* potential which can be actualized.

The Hebrew name for humanity, "*adam*," points to this uniqueness as it is derived from the word meaning "earth." The earth too is a vehicle for the conversion of potential to actual.

ויראה ששמו מורה על דבר העצמי לו, שהוא מיוחד בו האדם מכל. וזה שהוא נקרא אדם על שהוא עפר מן האדמה. ועתה יש לשאול וכי כל שאר הנמצאים

It would seem that the very name [of the human being] hints to this uniqueness in which the human being is unparalleled. A human being is called "*adam*"[5] since

3. Z'charyah 3:7.

4. As the Maharal states a little later, the other lower creations (besides humanity) also possess some perfection, but it is inherent and built-in from the moment of their creation.

5. In Hebrew, אדם, "*adam*," is derived etymologically from the word אדמה, "*ad-*

אינם מן האדמה שיקרא האדם ביחוד בשם אדם על שם שנברא מן האדמה.

אבל ענין האדם מתיחם ביותר אל האדמה, וזה כי האדמה היא מיוחדת בזה שהיא בכח ויש בה יציאה לפעל כל הדברים אשר יוצאים ממנה צמחים ואילנות ושאר כל הדברים והיא בכח לכל זה, וזהו ענין האדם שהוא בכח ויוצא שלימותו אל הפעל ולפיכך שמו ראוי לו שיהיה משתתף עם האדמה שהיא מיוחדת לצאת מן הכח אל הפעל בפירות וצמחים וכל אשר שייך אליה וכן הוא האדם יוצא כחו אל הפעל.

he was created from the dust of the earth.[6] Now one may ask, were not all the other creations also created from the earth?[7] Why should human beings alone be called "*adam*" just because they were created from the earth?

The answer is as follows: the essential concept of what the human being is, relates more closely to the earth than does that of any other creation. The earth is also unique in that it is also potential and can produce an actualization of that potential through all the creations which emerge from it: plants, trees and so on. The earth has potential for all these things and this is the [same] principle underlying humanity which also exists in potential and whose perfection can be transformed from potential to actuality. Therefore, the name, *adam*, is [most] suited to the human being in that he parallels the earth [in the act of transforming potential to actuality]. The earth is unique [amongst insentient beings] in that it brings forth fruit and plants from potential to actual; and so, too, human beings transform from potential to actual.

The Maharal continues discussing the comparisons between the earth and humanity: the perfection of humanity, like that of trees, is called "fruit."

ולכך שלימות האדם נקרא גם כן בשם פרי, וכדכתיב בקרא (ישעיה ג׳) אמרו צדיק כי טוב כי פרי מעלליהם יאכלו הרי שהזכות והשלימות יקרא פרי, וכמו שאמרו בפרק קמא דקידושין (מ׳ ע״א). ובפרק עגלה ערופה (סוטה מ״ו ע״א):

Therefore, the perfection of a human is also called "fruit," as it is written, "Say to the righteous that it is good, because they will eat the fruit of their deeds."[8] From here we see that human merit and completion are termed "fruits." As our sages, in the first chapter of Kiddushin[9] and in the chapter of *eglah arufah*, said,[10, 11]

amah" which means, "earth."

6. See B'reishit 2:7.
7. See B'reishit 1:24.
8. Y'shayahu 3:10.
9. Kiddushin 40a.
10. "*Eglah arufah*," עגלה ערופה, "a calf whose neck was severed." See D'varim 21, where the Torah teaches us that if a murder victim is found in a field and the judiciary cannot establish who the murderer was, an unblemished calf is to be killed in a ceremony which includes the leadership of the nearest town. The Maharal next

והורידו את העגלה אל נחל איתן.

אמר רבי יוחנן בן שאול מפני מה אמרה תורה הבא עגלה בנחל אמר הקדוש ברוך הוא יבא דבר שלא עשה פירות ויערף במקום שאינו עושה פירות בשביל מי שלא הניחו אותו לעשות פירות.

מאי פירות?

אילימא פריה ורביה אזקן ואסרים הכי נמי דלא ערפינן אלא מצוות ע"כ.

[Regarding the ceremony of the *eglah arufah*, the verse states,[12]] "They shall take the calf to a harsh valley."[13]

Rabbi Yochanan ben Sha'ul said, "Why does the Torah say to us, 'Bring a calf to the valley?' The Holy One, Blessed be He, is saying, 'Bring something[14] which never produced fruit and decapitate it in a place which doesn't produce fruit[15] for one[16] whom they[17] did not allow to produce fruit.'"

[The Gemara questions,] What are the "fruit" mentioned here by Rabbi Yochanan?

[The Gemara examines one option for the definition of the term, "fruit," a definition which it will subsequently reject.] If one takes this term literally to mean the fruits of one's body, that is, children, then if the one murdered were old [and childless and unable to father children] or if he were a eunuch, would we not follow the procedure of *eglah arufah*?[18] [The Gemara thus rejects this option since it leads to a contradiction.[19]

The Gemara therefore concludes that "fruit" here means something else. Rather, the "fruit" mentioned here are mitzvot.[20]]

הרי בשביל שלא הוציא שלימות שלו אל הפעל הוא כמו האדמה שלא עשתה פירות ולא הוציאה דבר אל

We see that since [the murder victim] was unable to transform his potential perfection to actuality, he is compared

discusses the ceremony and its significance.

11. Sotah 46a.

12. D'varim 21:4.

13. "Harsh valley" is the translation of נחל איתן according to Rashi.

14. The calf.

15. A harsh, barren valley.

16. The murder victim.

17. The murderers.

18. This is a rhetorical question, as the previously established law is that the procedure is carried out for all victims.

19. Rabbi Yochanan ben Sha'ul implies that the carrying out of the ceremony is dependent upon the victim's status as "one who was prevented from producing fruit." The Gemara has already established that the procedure is performed for all victims (even those unable to bear children) and thus the Gemara rejects the literal understanding of the term "fruit" which leads to the exclusion of certain victims.

20. Thus Rabbi Yochanan ben Sha'ul's statement is valid – the ceremony is held for any victim because any victim is considered to be one who did not produce the "fruit" he should have, i.e., the mitzvot he should have brought into the world.

הפעל ונשאר בכח, ולפיכך שמו שנקרא בשם אדם על שם אדמה נאה לו והוא נאה לשמו.

to the barren ground which has not transformed anything to actuality and only remains with potential. Therefore, the name for a human, *adam* (named after the earth), is suitable to him and he is suited to his name.

The difference between the term for humanity and that for the animal kingdom is now analyzed.

והבהמה נקראת בשם בהמה על שם ב"ה מ"ה, רצה לומר כי שלימות דבר שנברא עליו נמצא בה אף על גב שאינו שלמות גמור מכל מקום דבר זה נמצא עמה וזהו בה מה כי דבר מה נמצא עמה, הרי שכל אחד יורה שמו עליו.

Animals are called "*b'heimah*"[21] since the word *b'heimah* can be split into two component sub-words: *b'h*[22] and *mah*,[23] which together mean "Inside it is something." This is to say that some perfection is found in it and even if it is not absolute perfection, nevertheless, it is found within it. This is the meaning of *b'h mah* – because something is *already* in it[24] [and it has no further actualization]. We see that the names of humans and animals describe them suitably.

One might conclude that the only way a human being can truly be called "human" is when he has converted his potential greatness to actual greatness – that is, that it all depends on whether this goal has actually been achieved. The Maharal explains that really, the determining factor is the availability of a choice to perfect oneself as well as the choice itself; the actual result of the choice is secondary.

אמנם אל תטעה בדברים אלו לשלול השלמות ממי שאי אפשר לו שיוציא שלימותו אל הפעל אשר הלך לעולמו קודם שהוציא שלמות שלו אל הפעל, אין אנו שוללים העולם הבא ממנו כלל אם יש בו הכנה אל השלמות ומת שאנוס היה שלא הוציא שלמות שלו לפעל, כאמרם ז"ל (ברכות ו'):

However, do not be misled in these things by excluding someone from the possibility of attaining perfection just because it is impossible for that person to transform his potential perfection to actual perfection. For example, one who passed away before transforming his potential perfection to actuality – [in such a case,] we would not at all deny that such

21. "*B'heimah*," בהמה, means "animal," "beast" or "domesticated animal."

22. "*Bh*" or "*Bah*," בה, which means "in it."

23. "*Mah*," מה, which means "what" or "something."

24. The critical difference between all other physical creations and human beings is that all other creations possess all their perfection when they are first created – they have no potential for further spiritual growth and development. Humans, on the other hand, do.

a person can reach the World to Come as long as he has a receptivity and preparation for perfection when he died. [The reason for this is that] he was coerced not to transform his perfection to actuality [but he did not choose to remain untransformed]. As our sages said,[25]

> If a person intended to perform a mitzvah and was prevented from doing so by a force beyond his control, that person receives reward as if he had performed the mitzvah.
>
> חשב לעשות מצוה ונאנס יש לו על זה שכר כאלו עשה המצוה.

The reason for this is that the reward in the future (in the World to Come) is destined for the soul and when a person is prevented from performing a mitzvah by some force beyond his control, this delay is not due to the soul [which had decided to perform the mitzvah], but rather due to the body [which was unable to act]. Therefore, the soul is rewarded as if it had performed the mitzvah. But if a person with his mind and intellect, intentionally decided not to perform a mitzvah [and] this was due to the decision of the soul [and not the body] – such a person who had the capacity to transform his potential perfection to actuality and yet chose not do so [cannot reach his perfection since his soul has no receptivity to it.] This matter will be explained later in a more extensive and clear manner.[26]

וזה מצד כי השכר לעתיד הוא לנשמה וכאשר הוא אנוס לא היה עכוב זה מצד הנשמה רק לגוף, ולכך נותנין לנשמה שכר כאלו עשה המצוה, רק אם לא עשה במזיד בדעתו ובשכלו וזה היה מצד הנשמה, הכונה במי שאפשר להוציא שלמותו אל הפעל ולא הוציא שלמות שלו אל הפעל, ודבר זה יתבאר עוד בביאור רחב ובדברים ברורים.

The Maharal summarizes his position: human beings have infinite potential and therefore the only path open before them to greatness lies through the hard work of actualizing this potential.

It has now been explained to you that the excellence of the human being lies in his potential (as will be explained shortly) and therefore, he should never entertain any libel within his soul by saying that he should remain idle and he will nevertheless succeed eternally; rather his success will only be through [investing effort in] observing the Torah and mitzvot.

והתבאר לך כי מעלת האדם הוא בכח וכמו שיתבאר אחר זה, ול[פ]יכך לא יהיה אונאה בנפשו לומר שישב בטל ויצליח בהצלחה נצחית רק הצלחתו בקיום התורה והמצוות.

25. B'rachot 6a.
26. See Tiferet Yisrael 5.

SUMMARY

Chapter 3: 1/2

I. Human beings should not deceive themselves by thinking that they need invest no effort in order to achieve spiritual excellence

A. Transcendent beings are all actualized.

B. The lower beings, besides for humans, have no potential to actualize, their perfection is in-built.

C. Only human beings *are* potential which can be actualized. Only human beings can make the transformation. Thus a person who does not grow remains barren and unfulfilled.

II. The essence of humanity as reflected in the Hebrew term for humans, "*adam*"

A. Humans are called "*adam*" since the name is derived from the word "*adamah*" earth.

1. The parallel between the earth and humanity
    a. The earth transforms potential (seeds) into actual (crops, fruit).
    b. Humanity transforms spiritual potential into actuality.
    c. Thus the term for humanity is derived from that of earth.
2. Why do humans only bear such an affinity when all animals were created from the earth?
    a. Animals have no potential to transform, thus they do not parallel the earth.

B. The Hebrew term for human achievement is "fruit"

1. A physical fruit is the product of the conversion of potential within the earth to actuality.
2. Gemara Sotah 46a
    a. The Gemara speaks of a murdered person as one who "has not produced fruit."
    b. The Gemara concludes that these fruit are mitzvot which are the true fruit of the spiritual conversion of potential to actual.

III. The essence of the animal kingdom as reflected in the Hebrew term for animals, "*b'heimah*"

A. Animals are called "*b'heimah*" since this term is a contraction of two words: "*bah mah*, a thing is in it [already]."

B. The idea (as further explored in the Commentary, Ch. 3 § Point 3) is that animals are complete and have no potential to actualize. They have all they need within them from their very creation – *bah mah* – what they need is already in them.

IV. Involuntary unfulfillment

A. The question one may ask is: if indeed, when one reaches the World to Come, one cannot actualize any potential (since that world is complete actuality), what happens to a person who dies before their time, unfulfilled, G-d forbid. Are they imperfect and unactualized?

B. The Maharal's answer is that such a person never really decided *not* to fulfill their potential. To be unsuited for the World to Come, one must have had a real opportunity to choose to transform one's potential which one then refused.

   1. The Maharal brings the example of one who tries to do a mitzvah but is prevented from doing so by a force beyond his control. In such a case, he is rewarded as if he had performed the mitzvah. This is because the soul was in the process of actualization, the body's inability to actualize was what got in the way. However, the soul has actually undergone the process of actualization.
   2. The analogy is that a person only suffers from the bane of unfulfilled potential if that person's soul had the opportunity to fulfill that potential and, G-d forbid, chose not to actualize it. In the case of one who dies before gaining that opportunity, there can be no such negative ramifications.

V. The necessity for action

A. It is thus clear that one can only achieve perfection through the active striving for that perfection and the active transformation of potential goodness to actual.

B. One who is passive is not merely neutral – such a person is, in fact, choosing to forego all real opportunities for self-actualization.

CHAPTER 3

Part 2 of 2

The Maharal explains that human perfection is actually the unending process of mining one's flaws into the jewels of perfection: converting potential greatness to actual greatness.

ולהורות כי האדם חסר וצריך אליו השלמה, לכך אמרו בפרק חלק (סנהדרין צ"ט ע"ב):

In order to demonstrate that a human being is lacking and requires perfection, our sages said as follows in the chapter of *Chelek*:[1]

אדם לעמל יולד.

אמר רבי אליעזר איני יודע אם לעמל פה אם לעמל מלאכה כשהוא אומר נפש עמלה עמלה לו כי אכף עליו פיהו הוי אומר לעמל פה.

ועדיין איני יודע אם לעמל תורה אם לעמל שיחה כשהוא אומר לא ימוש ספר התורה הזה מפיך והגית בו יומם ולילה הוי אומר לעמל תורה, ע"כ.

The verse states, "A person will be born to toil."[2]

[Rabbi Eli'ezer questions the type of toil for which a person is born.] Rabbi Eli'ezer commented, "One might not know whether the verse refers to the toil of one's mouth[3] or to the toil of work.[4] Another verse comes to resolve this doubt – 'The hunger of a laborer works for him, for his mouth pushes him on.'"[5] [From this, Rabbi Eli'ezer concludes that humans are created for verbal toil.[6]]

[Rabbi Eli'ezer[7] clarifies exactly what type of verbal toil is meant.] "But still, one might not be sure to which type of 'toil of the mouth' the verse refers – it could be to the verbal toil of Torah or to the verbal toil of conversation. Another verse comes to resolve this doubt [as follows,] 'This book of the Torah shall not depart from your mouth and you will think of it day and night,'[8] this

1. Sanhedrin 99b.
2. Iyov 5:7.
3. I.e., verbal toil.
4. I.e., physical toil.
5. Mishlei 16:26.
6. It is beyond the scope of this work to explain how our sages make these hermeneutical deductions – whole chapters could be devoted to each such deduction!
7. For further study, see the Maharal's paraphrasing of this Gemara, cited in N'tivot Olam, N'tiv Hatorah 15.
8. Y'hoshu'a 1:8.

refers to verbal toil in Torah." [Rabbi Eli'ezer thus concludes that human beings are destined from birth for verbal toil in Torah.]

ובארו בזה הדברים אשר אמרנו, כי האדם הזה לא נברא בשלמותו האחרון והוא נברא להוציא שלמותו אל הפעל, וזה אדם לעמל יולד שהוא נולד ונמצא אל תכלית העמל דהיינו להוציא השלמות אל הפעל, ולא יגיע להיות נמצא בפעל לגמרי לעולם אבל תמיד יהיה עמל להוציא שלימותו אל הפעל וזה שלימותו האחרון.

ולפיכך אמר אדם לעמל יולד והעמל הוא היציאה אל הפעל, ותמיד הוא בכח עוד לצאת אל הפעל כי זה האדם הוא בכח ויוצא אל הפעל, וכמה שהוא יוצא אל הפעל נשאר בכח לצאת עוד אל הפעל תמיד.

Our sages [utilized the statement of Rabbi Eli'ezer as a vehicle to] explain the issues we have been discussing: that a person is not created in his final perfection and is, in fact, created in order to transform his perfection [from potential] to actual. This is the meaning of the verse, "A person will be born to toil": that a person is born and exists for the purpose of toil, which means to transform perfection [from potential] to actual. A person will never reach the state of complete actualization [of his potential] because no matter how much of his potential he transforms, there is always more.

Therefore, the verse uses the phrase, "will be born"[9] [implying that this birth is a constant activity] and the toil is the transformation [from potential] to actual. And [this perfection] always has more in potential to be transformed to actual because this is the definition of a human being – *a human is perfection held in potential*, waiting to be transformed to actuality; and no matter how much actualization occurs, there is always potential left to be actualized.

The Maharal now begins examining the various options which were considered in the Gemara. In the first instance, the Gemara seems to consider seriously the possibility that humans were created to transform to actuality their potential for physical perfection. The Maharal discusses how the Gemara could ever believe this to be the purpose of humanity.

ואמר ועדיין איני יודע אם לעמל פה או לעמל מלאכה.

Furthermore, Rabbi Eli'ezer says[10] "I still don't know to which type of 'toil' the verse refers – to the toil of one's mouth[11] or to the toil of work."

The reason [that this is a seriously considered option] is that even if a

9. This is the future form of the verb "to be born" and connotes the present continuous tense. This indicates that the process is never-ending, that a person toils in the past, present and future. See Rashi, Sh'mot 15:1.

10. Above, in the Gemara.

11. I.e., verbal toil.

כי אף אם נברא האדם בכח ולא בפעל, אולי הכח הזה הוא שייך לכח הגופני שאין ספק שהוא בכח ויש בו יציאה אל הפעל ובו שייך עמל, אבל כח הדברי שהוא יותר נבדל במה שלא נמצא בשאר ב"ח כי אם באדם לכך הכח הזה הוא יותר נבדל, ואפשר כי די הוא שיוציא מן הכח אל הפעל הכח הגופני ואין צריך להוציא כח הדברי אל הפעל שאין האדם נברא על זה.

ועל זה אמר כיון דכתיב נפש עמלה עמלה לו כי אכף עליו פיהו, הרי כי עמל הזה הוא עמל פה שהוא כח הדברי שכח זה צריך שיוציא אל הפעל ועל זה נברא האדם.

human is created in potential and not in [complete] actuality, perhaps this potential is for physical power (regarding which there is no doubt that it too resides in potential, requiring actualization and that the term "toil" applies to it). Further, one might claim that verbal potential is more transcendent than its physical counterpart in that verbal potential is found only in humans and not in any animal (therefore, this verbal potential is more transcendent) and therefore, one may claim that it is sufficient for humans to transform physical power from potential to actual and that there is no need to transform verbal power [from potential] to actual since humans were not created for this.[12]

In response to this [question], Rabbi Eli'ezer said that since the verse states, "The hunger of a laborer works for him, for his mouth pushes him on,"[13] this proves that the required toil is toil of the mouth, which is the human verbal capacity and it is this power that humans must transform from potential to actual and it is for this that humans were created.[14]

The Maharal now discusses the types of verbal communication which could be the purpose of human existence. In particular, he examines the possibility that we are here to perfect inter-human communication in general.

ואמר עוד ועדיין איני יודע אם עמל שיחה או עמל תורה.

כי אולי לא צריך שיוציא מן הכח אל הפעל רק כח הדברי שאינו שכל גמור אבל לא כח השכלי שהוא דבור של תורה וזהו שכל גמור.

כשהוא אומר לא ימוש ספר התורה הזה מפיך מזה נלמוד כי האדם על זה

Rabbi Eli'ezer said further,[15] "I still don't know whether this verbal power should be directed towards verbal toil in conversation or in Torah."

[He said this] because perhaps one only needs to actualize verbal potential which is not wholly *sichli* but one does not need to actualize the *sichli* potential

12. For an exploration of these ideas, see the Commentary, Ch. 3 § Points 5 and 6.

13. Mishlei 16:26.

14. It is difficult to understand how the Maharal answers his own question here. See the Commentary, Ch. 3 § Points 5 and 6.

15. Above, in the Gemara.

[entailed within] the communication of Torah, which is completely *sichli*.[16]

Therefore, Rabbi Eli'ezer cited the verse, "This book of the Torah shall not[17] depart from your mouth . . ."[18] [This illustrates that] since a human's perfection lies in potential, all his toil and activity should be in something which is his final perfection and for which he was created. As the verse says, "A person will be born for toil . . . ,"[19] which means that the purpose of humanity's superiority is for toil – the conversion of potential to actuality. This is the import of the verse, "This book of the Torah shall not depart [from your mouth and you will think of it day and night]."[20]

נברא שיוציא אל הפעל כח הדברי השכלי שהוא שכל התורה. ולפיכך אמר לא ימוש ספר התורה הזה מפיך כי אחר שהאדם שלמותו בכח צריך שיהיה כל עמלו ופעלו בדבר שהוא שלמותו האחרון אשר נברא בשבילו, כמו שאמר הכתוב אדם לעמל יולד, שר"ל כי תכלית מעלתו הוא אל העמל שהוא יציאה אל הפעל וזהו לא ימוש וגו'.

The Maharal addresses the question of whether one can ever be completely actualized. He cites a Midrash which illustrates the infinity of human potential and thus the never-ending task of human growth.

However, do not say that with the transformation of a human's perfection [from potential] to actual that this perfection could be *completely* transformed to actual [since] this is not a [possible] principle, because the nature of the human being is such that with the transformation of [any] potential to actual, there remains more potential (as we explained above); as the verse says, "A person will be born to toil . . . ,"[21] because a person is born to toil without pause and completion at all and even if a person transforms [some

אמנם אל תאמר כי עם יציאת שלמות האדם אל הפעל אפשר שיהיה יוצא שלמותו לגמרי אל הפעל, שזה אינו כלל כי זהו בריאתו שעם שהוציא שלמותו אל הפעל נשאר עוד בכח כמו שהתבאר לפני זה כמו שאמר אדם לעמל יולד, כי האדם נברא לעמל שאין לו שביתה והשלמה כלל.

ועם שהוא יוצא אל הפעל נשאר עוד תמיד בכח, שאם היה נמצא שלמותו בפעל לא היה נקרא זה עמל כי לשון עמל בא על דבר שאין לו הנחה ולא יבא אל תכלית הנחה, וכן האדם

16. This question assumes that one could entertain the real possibility that the purpose of human existence is to implement inter-human communication.

17. This verb is in the future tense – see n. 9 above.

18. Y'hoshu'a 1:8.

19. Iyov 5:7.

20. Y'hoshu'a 1:8.

21. Iyov 5:7. This is the future form of the verb "to be born" and connotes the present continuous tense. This indicates that the process is never-ending, that a person toils in the past, present and future. See Rashi, Sh'mot 15:1.

כל זמן היותו מחובר עם החומר אינו בשלימות בפעל עד אשר הוא נפרד מן החומר ואז נמצא בפעל.

of his potential] to actuality, he always has more potential.

[This is proved from the verse,] since if [at any point] a person were completely actualized, this [life] could not be called "toil" because "toil" refers to an action which has no cessation and will never fulfill the purpose of rest. So too as long as a person is joined to the physical, he is not complete in actuality [a state] which is only reached when he separates from the physical,[22] at which stage he exists completely in actuality.

ובמדרש (קהלת רבה פ"ו):

In the Midrash it states,[23]

גם הנפש לא תמלא.

לפי שהנפש יודעת שכל אשר תיגע לעצמה תיגע לפיכך אינה שבעה מצוות ומעשים טובים.

אמר רבי לוי משל לעירוני שהיה נשוי בת מלכים אף על פי שמאכילה כל מעדני מלך אינו יוצא חובתו למה שהיא בת מלכים כך כל מה שיפעול האדם עם נפשו אינו יוצא ידי חובתו למה לפי שהיא מלמעלה ע"כ.

"The soul will also never be satiated."[24]

[The meaning of this verse is] that the soul knows that however much it wearies itself in effort, it is working for itself, therefore, it never has its fill of mitzvot and good deeds.

Rabbi Levi said, "[One can understand this through a] parable of a townsman who was married to a princess.[25] Even if he provides her with all [the varieties of] royal delicacies, he never discharges his duty. Why? Because she is the daughter of kings. So too, no matter how much a person acts for his soul [in this world] he never discharges his duty. Why? Because his soul is from above . . ."

The analogy is that the soul is the princess, the body is the townsman, while Torah and mitzvot are the delicacies offered to the princess. The Maharal explains that the parable in the Midrash teaches us that even if a person immerses himself in Torah and mitzvot while in this world, his soul will never be completely satisfied, since its true place is in the transcendent world and it is constantly yearning to return. Even Torah and mitzvot only give the soul (while it is in this world) a taste of what it is missing.

22. I.e., when the soul leaves the body.

23. The source cited is Kohelet Rabbah 6:6. This seems to be a printing error. The correct source seems to be Vayikra Rabbah 4:2. See the Commentary, Ch. 3 § Point 7.

24. Kohelet 6:7. See the Commentary, Ch. 3 § Point 7.

25. Lit., "the daughter of kings."

וביאור ענין זה כי הנפש הזאת שהיא מלמעלה ועומדת בתחתונים, תמיד היא משתוקקת אל התורה ואל המצוות במה שהיא בתחתונים. ודבר זה לחסרון מדרגה נחשב לה שהיא עצם נפש א־להי מלמעלה עומדת בתחתונים, וכל דבר שהוא חסר משתוקק אל השלמה, והתורה והמצוה הם השלמה אל הנפש ובשביל כך משתוקקת הנפש אל התורה ואל המצוות לצאת אל הפעל ולהיות מושלם.

אמנם לא תשבע מצוות ומעשים טובים במה שהיא עומדת בתחתונים בגוף האדם, שדבר זה ממדרגת עצם הנפש שהיא מלמעלה ולכך אינה מושלמת בתחתונים בגוף החמרי, וכיון שאינה מושלמת אינה שבעה מצוות ומעשים טובים רק היא משתוקקת תמיד להיותה מושלמת לגמרי, ואינה מושלמת עד שתבא אל התכלית במה שהיא עצם א־להי מלמעלה.

וזה שהוא מדמה אותה אל בת מלך שנשאת לעירוני ועם שהוא נותן לה כל מעדני עולם אינו יוצא ידי חובתו עמה מפני שהיא בת מלך והיא מתחברת אל עירוני הזה, ואם כן תמיד היא חסרה כאשר היא עם העירוני הזה וכל אשר נותן לה סוף סוף היא עם העירוני שאינו זיווג שלה, ולכך לא יכול לעשות כפי הראוי לה שהיא בת מלך שעל כל פנים היא מתחברת לעירוני ולא מלך ולכך אינו יוצא ידי חובתו עמה.

The explanation of this matter is that this soul, which is from above, but which stands[26] amongst the lower [creations], is always longing for the Torah and mitzvot because it is [lodged] amongst the lower [creations]. This [yearning] is considered a lacking in the soul's level since, in essence, it is a G-dly soul from above which is stranded amongst the lower [creations] and anything which is lacking, yearns for completion. Torah and mitzvot are the completion for the soul and therefore, it yearns for Torah and mitzvot to transform itself from potential to actual and to become perfected.

Despite this, the soul cannot be satiated with mitzvot and good deeds since it is amongst the lower [creations, encased] in a human body [while fundamentally] it belongs in the transcendent world due to the level of its essence. Therefore, it cannot be complete in the lower worlds while encased in a physical body, and since it is not complete, it cannot be satiated [even] with mitzvot and good deeds, but rather it is constantly yearning to be completely perfect and it cannot be complete until it reaches [its] purpose, since it is a G-dly creation from above.

This is why the Midrash compares the soul to the daughter of a king who has married a townsman. And even though he gives her all the delicacies of the world, he has still not fulfilled his duty to her since she is the daughter of a king and [yet] is [still] bonding with this townsman. Therefore, she will always be lacking while she is with this city-dweller and no matter what he gives her, she is still with someone who is not her destined mate. Therefore, he can never do what is suitable for her since she is the daughter of a king

26. See earlier in this chapter where the Maharal cited the verse from Z'charyah (3:7) "strides among those standing angels," applying this to human beings. Also see the Commentary, Ch. 3 § Point 2 there where we analyzed this term.

who is nevertheless joined to a city-dweller (and not a king) and therefore, he can never fulfill his duty to her.[27]

So too, since the soul is from the transcendent world, even though mitzvot and Torah are its transformation from potential to actual, since the soul is standing[28] in the lower world within a human body and since the soul is a transcendent being from the upper worlds, the soul can never achieve completion. Therefore, it cannot be sated by the mitzvot and the soul is considered to be in potential for the entire period that it is with the body. This is what we wished to explain.

For one who knows the matter of the soul and its level (that it is from the upper world and is an unperfected essence and therefore, its perfection is through the Torah and mitzvot, as will be explained,[29] G-d willing), it is clear that [the soul needs] Torah from Heaven.[30] [This is] because Hashem gave the soul the greatest excellence above all others, which is the Torah, to fulfill its lack, since the soul is always yearning for completion because it is standing amongst the lower creations and is actually from the upper world; and that which is possible to perfect [within it] is perfected [through the Torah].

וכן כאשר הנפש היא מלמעלה ואף כי המצוות והתורה הם יציאה לה אל השלימות מכל מקום במה שהיא עומדת בתחתונים בגוף האדם והיא עצם נבדל מן העליונים לא תקבל השלמה, לכך אינה שבעה מן המצוות והיא נחשבת בכח כל ימי היותה עם הגוף וזה מה שרצינו לבאר.

ודבר זה מחייב תורה מן השמים למי שיודע ענין הנפש ומדריגתה שהיא מן השמים והיא עצם בלתי מושלם ולכך השלמתה על ידי התורה ומצוות כמו שיתבאר בעזרת השם יתברך, כי נתן לה המעלה היותר על כל היא התורה להשלים חסרונה, בעבור שהנפש משתוקקת תמיד אל ההשלמה מפני שעומדת בתחתונים והיא מן השמים ומה שאפשר להשלימה נשלמה.

27. The idea here is that the marriage is one which is not suitable, easy or ideal and this provides the context behind everything that the townsman does so that even were he to reproduce exactly her home environment and luxury, he cannot change himself to become what he is not. He is not a king but she was destined to be joined to a king. Their essences are at loggerheads – he a townsman, she a potential queen.

28. I.e., stuck.

29. See Chapter Seven.

30. The Maharal is emphasizing that the soul needs transcendent input to have any impact upon it at all – thus he emphasizes that the Torah which the soul needs, is from Heaven.

SUMMARY

Chapter 3: 2/2

I. The potential for perfection within a human being is infinite

- A. Gemara, Sanhedrin 99b
  1. Humans are born to toil.
     - a. Three possibilities for the type of toil:
     - b. Physical toil
     - c. Verbal toil
     - d. Verbal toil in Torah
     - e. Conclusion:
     - f. Verbal toil in Torah is the purpose of human life.
- B. The Maharal's understanding of the Gemara
  1. Toil
     - a. "Toil" means the conversion of potential perfection to actual perfection.
     - b. The verse uses the future tense "a person *will be born* to toil" because this process of conversion of potential to actual (within a human being) is never-ending – human potential is infinite.
  2. Are the three options mutually exclusive?
     - a. The Maharal understands that all three are needed, the question is which of them is primary.
  3. The possibility that people were created to perfect the physical aspect of the universe only
     - a. The Maharal's explanations of why this possibility is entertained
       - (1) As we learn in the Commentary (Ch. 3 § Point 5), this is not a hedonistic focus on glorifying the physical. Rather, it focuses on the perfection of the spiritual concepts which motivate and generate physicality.
       - (2) It is more attainable and more finite, whereas the alternatives are completely unlimited.
  4. The possibility that people were created to implement inter-human communication
     - a. The Maharal's explanations of why this possibility is entertained
     - b. As above, it is more attainable and more finite, whereas the alternatives are completely unlimited.
     - c. The Maharal explains the text used here to reject this option.
     - d. Parallel to the verse, "A person will be born to toil," the verse, "This book of the Torah shall not depart from your mouth," is also worded in the future tense.

e. Both verses depict an ongoing, never-ending process of toil – of transformation of potential to actual, even if that potential is infinite! Thus the Torah will be in our mouths forever, we shall never exhaust its possibilities and this is exactly the purpose of the creation of human beings – to convert potential to actual.
f. Human potential is never exhausted.

II. The soul yearns for Torah in order to achieve perfection

A. Midrash, Vayikra Rabbah 4:2
   1. The soul can never be satiated even with mitzvot and good deeds.
   2. The soul's situation can be compared to a townsman who married the daughter of a king – no matter what delicacies the townsman brings her, he will never fulfil his obligation to her, since she is the daughter of kings.

B. The Maharal's explanation of this Midrash
   1. The princess is a princess in essence which means that she should be a Queen, joined with a King. All the trappings associated with her lifestyle are functions of her inherent station. If her station remains unimplemented, the trappings are worthless. That is, if she does not become a Queen, joined with a King, the trappings are meaningless.
   2. So too, the soul is a transcendent being (which as the Maharal explained before, means that the soul's ultimate existence is on the level of actuality and not potential).
   3. While the soul is wedded to the body, it can never be fully actualized (by definition of it being transcendent), thus it yearns for the transcendent – in particular, pure transcendence. The problem is that while it is in the body, even transcendent things, such as Torah and mitzvot, cannot satiate the soul fully, since it still exists in potential and the potential within it cries out for more.

CHAPTER 4

CHAPTER 4

Part 1 of 3

In this chapter, the Maharal addresses the results of living the mitzvot – foremost of which is the refinement of the human being.

הדרכים והפעולות אשר הם מביאים אל ההצלחה הם מצוות התורה, שבזולתם היה נשאר בכח כמו שיתבאר עוד, והם הם כמו החבל שמעלין את האדם מבור התחתיות הוא העולם השפל אל עולם העליון להושיב אותו עם המלך ה' צבאות עין בעין וכמו שיתבאר ענין זה. כי המצוות הם צירוף האדם מן הגשמי עד שאין האדם טבעי חמרי בעל הויה והפסד כמו שהם הדברים הטבעים החומרים.

כי כל המצוות מחייב אותם השכל שכך וכך יעשה, וכאשר האדם עושה המצוה שהשכל מחייב הרי בזה יוצאה נפשו מן הטבע החמרית ודבקה בשכלי, כי השכל הא-להי מחייב המצוה וזהו צירוף וזיכוך נפשיי כמו שית'.

The paths and actions which lead one to success are the mitzvot of the Torah, without which [a person] would remain [solely] in potential,[1] as will be explained further. They [the Torah and mitzvot] are like the rope with which one raises a human from the lower pit (which is the lower world) to the elevated world, to seat him, eye to eye, with the King, Hashem [master of] Hosts, as will be explained in this regard. [This is] because the mitzvot are a [means to the] refinement of the human being from [having] a [purely] physical existence [and they continue refining a person] until he is no longer a [purely] natural and material [being] which comes into existence and deteriorates as do all natural, material things.

[This refinement occurs] because the intellect requires one to perform all the mitzvot[2] and when a person performs a mitzvah which the intellect has required, his soul leaves the [purely] physical [existence] and bonds with the *sichli* since the G-dly intellect has required [the performance of] the mitzvah and this is the spiritual refinement and purification, as will be clarified.[3]

The Maharal begins examining how the enumeration of the mitzvot in the two mitzvah-categories (*mitzvot lo ta'aseh* and *mitzvot aseh*) derives from the purpose of each category.

1. For more on this, see Chapter Three. Also see the Commentary, Ch. 4 § Point 1.

2. I.e., it is a logical necessity within this universe. The Maharal explains why there must be Torah and mitzvot in Chapter Sixteen of this work.

3. See the Commentary, Ch. 4 § Point 3.

ומספר המצוות שבהם נפשו יוצאה מאפילה לאורה כמו שאמרו ז"ל בסוף מכות (כ"ג ע"ב):

And the number of mitzvot through which a person's soul can exit from the darkness into the light[4] is as our sages said at the end of Tractate Makkot:[5]

דרש רבי שמלאי תרי"ג מצוות נתנו לו למשה שס"ה ל"ת כמנין ימות החמה רמ"ח עשה כמנין אבריו של אדם.

אמר רב המנונא מאי קראה תורה צוה לנו משה מורשה.

תורה בגימטריא הכי הוי? תורה שית מאה וחד סרי הוי אנכי ולא יהיה לך מפי הגבורה שמענום ע"כ.

> Rabbi Simlai expounded, "Six hundred and thirteen mitzvot were given [by Hashem] to Moshe. Of these, the 365 prohibitions[6] correspond to the days of the solar year and the 248 *mitzvot aseh*[7] correspond to the component-limbs[8] of a human being."
>
> Rav Hamnuna said, "What verse in the Torah alludes to this? The Torah says, 'Moshe commanded us [to keep] Torah, it is an inheritance [for the congregation of Ya'akov].'"[9]
>
> [The Gemara understands that Rav Hamnuna is using a numerological deduction – that the word "Torah" in the verse has the numerical value of 613, which is the number of mitzvot. The Gemara now points out that this calculation is incorrect.]
>
> But the numerological value of [the word] "Torah" is not 613, it's 611! So there is no allusion in this verse!
>
> [Rav Hamnuna answers,] "The first two commandments out of the Ten Commandments, 'I am the L-rd your G-d'[10] and 'You shall not have the gods of others[11] before me"[12] were not conveyed to us by Moshe[13] but we heard them directly from G-d!" [Thus, Rav Hamnuna's proof is that "Moshe com-

4. That is, from being exclusively physical, to becoming transcendent.

5. Makkot 23b.

6. See the Commentary, Ch. 4 § Point 2 and Introduction § Point 1 for notes on this terminology.

7. See the Commentary, Ch. 4 § Point 2 and Introduction § Point 1 for notes on this terminology. We also translate this as "initiative-action commandments," being actions one is required to initiate.

8. See the Commentary, Ch. 4 § Point 2 for notes on this terminology.

9. D'varim 33:4.

10. Sh'mot 20:2.

11. As per the Chizkuni's translation ad loc. See Rashi ad loc. and the other commentators.

12. Sh'mot 20:3.

13. This tradition, based on the grammar used in the first two commandments, is that the first two commandments were declaimed by Hashem directly to the Jewish people. However, after these two, the people requested that Moshe take over as it was too difficult for them to bear the divine voice. For further study, see Ramban on Sh'mot 20:7, Shabbat 88b and Rashi on Sh'mot 19:19.

manded us" only 611 commandments and the remaining two came directly from Hashem. This is why the word *Torah* has the numerical value of 611.]

ואין ספק שאין מספרם ומנינם של המצוות הא-להיות במקרה כי אין מקרה לכמו דברים אלו הא-להיים, ועוד שלא תלה המספר במקרה קרה רק שאמר על מצוות לא תעשה שהם כמנין ימות החמה ומספר מצוות עשה כמספר איבריו של אדם ומה ענינם לדברים אלו.

And there is no doubt that the number and accounting of the G-dly mitzvot are not accidental, as there can be no coincidence in such G-dly matters; and moreover, the Gemara did not pin the numbering on some happenstance, but rather said that the prohibitions correspond to the days of the solar year and the number of initiative-action commandments[14] correspond to the number of component-limbs in the human body – but what is the connection between each pair?

The Maharal now brings the explanation of Rashi for the parallels above and subsequently has difficulty with Rashi's opinion.

ואם נאמר כי מספר מצוות לא תעשה שס"ה שמזהירין את האדם בכל יום שלא לעבור לא תעשה, ומצוות עשה רמ"ח שמזהירים את האדם שבכל איבריו יעשה המצוות אם כן גם היה אפשר שיהיה בהפך זה, מצוות לא תעשה רמ"ח שמזהירים כל איבריו של אדם שלא יעבור לא תעשה, ומצוות עשה שס"ה שמזהירין כל יום שיעשה המצוות.

ומכל שכן שלא יהיה דבר זה רק רמז ואין ראוי בדברים הא-להיים שנמצאים כך לעצמם. ולכך המאמר הזה מן המאמרים העמוקים.

Now, if we say [as Rashi did][15] that the reason the number of prohibitions [parallels the number of days in a solar year] is that one is warned every day of the solar year not to transgress these prohibitions, and that [the reason] the number of initiative-action commandments [parallels the number of component-limbs in the body] is because one is warned that he should do the mitzvot [*aseh*] with all the component-limbs of his body, then it would also be possible to swap the explanation of each type of mitzvah! We could say that there are 248 prohibitions because we caution all the component-limbs of a person not to transgress the prohibitions, and we could say that there are 365 initiative-action commandments because a person is encouraged every day to do all these *mitzvot aseh*.

Even more problematic is the fact that this explanation just becomes some sort of hint [as an easy way to remember the number of mitzvot in each category] and this is inappropriate for G-dly things which should have

14. I.e., *mitzvot aseh*.

15. See Rashi's explanation in Makkot 23b, s.v. *ramach mitzvot aseh* and s.v. *shasah [mitzvot] lo ta'aseh*.

an essential connection.[16] Rather, this passage in the Gemara is [really] one of the [most] profound passages.

The Maharal has demonstrated that according to Rashi's explanation, there is nothing inherent tying the number of prohibitions (365) to the days of the solar year nor is there any inherent connection between the number of component-limbs of a person and the *mitzvot aseh* of the Torah (248). This type of casual connectivity is something he rejects.
He now brings his own "essential" explanation which is that the foundation of each category of mitzvah consists of certain spiritual fundamentals and this foundation generates the number of each type of mitzvah.

דע כאשר רצה השם יתברך לזכות את האדם שיקנה הנצחיות על ידי מצוות הא-להיות אי אפשר שיקנה אותו רק על ידי שני מיני מצוות.

החלק האחד שלא יהיה משנה את מציאותו אשר נברא עליו, כי אם משנה את מציאותו אשר נברא עליו הרי יש לו שנוי מה שהוא ראוי למציאות האדם ויבא הפסד למציאותו, ואלו הם מצוות לא תעשה שכל אלו המצוות הם שלא יצא האדם מן מה שהוא ראוי אל מציאותו.

כבעילת איסור וגזל וגניבה וכיוצא בהם מן המצוות. אף כי אנחנו לא נדע טעם המצוות מכל מקום נדע בהם שכל מצוות לא תעשה הם יציאה מן היושר המציאות מה שהשכל מחייב והיציאה מן היושר המציאות הוא הפסד ואבוד אליו.

You should know that when Hashem, may He be Blessed, wished to grant merit[17] to the human being so that humans could acquire eternity through the G-dly mitzvot, [it was clear] that humans could only acquire it through two types of commandments.

The first type [entails that] humans should refrain from altering the [ideal] reality in which they were created. [The idea is that] if humans alter the [ideal] reality in which they were created there would be a deviation from the reality that is suitable for humans and thus a loss would accrue to his reality. This type of mitzvah is the category we know as the prohibitions – all of which ensure that a human not exit the reality that is suitable for his existence.

For example, [the prohibitions against] forbidden sexual relations, theft, armed robbery and so on [all have this purpose]. Now even though it is true that we do not know the [the complete] reason for [each of] the [individual] mitzvot, we do know that, as a category, all the prohibitions [prevent] an exiting of a human being from the unswerving, honest reality [and consequently entering into a reality which entails] deficiency and loss for that person.

16. We have used Rav Hartman's explanation here, p. 69, n. 17.

17. Cf. Makkot 23b. See Chapter Five where the Maharal delves into the explanation of this idea.

החלק השני הם מצוות עשה, שכבר אמרנו כי אין האדם במדריגתו האחרונה הא־להית וכאלו הוא בכח בלבד וצריך שיקנה השלימות בפעל על ידי המצוות הא־להיות, וכמו שהתבאר לך למעלה בפרקים הקודמים שאף אם האדם קונה העולם הזה הטבעי החמרי לא קנה עולם הבא שאינו גשמי כי אם על ידי הפעולות הא־להיות ועל ידם יזכה לעולם הנבדל.

The second type of commandment is the *mitzvot aseh*. We have already explained that a person does not exist at his final, G-dly level [until he dies; but while he is alive] it is as if he exists as potential only and he needs to acquire perfection in actuality [which he does] through the G-dly mitzvot. And as was explained to you above, in the previous chapters, even if a person acquires [all the benefits of] this natural, material world, he will still not have acquired [any portion of] the World to Come, which is not physical. [Acquisition of the World to Come can only be achieved] through G-dly actions through which he will merit [a portion in] the transcendent world[18] [and this is the purpose of the *mitzvot aseh*].

18. The Maharal identifies a person's actualization of his/her spiritual potential with that person becoming more transcendent and thus compatible with and suited to the World to Come.

SUMMARY

Chapter 4: 1/3

I. Generalized purposes of mitzvot

A. Mitzvot bring about success for a person through allowing him to actualize his potential.

B. The mitzvot raise one to transcendent levels, allowing one to bond with Hashem.

   1. They do this by allowing human beings to connect to Hashem's intellect through performing the mitzvot which are determined by His intellect.

   2. This process of increasing transcendent existence is also a process of refinement of the human being wherein a person becomes less physical and more spiritual.

      a. The Maharal hints that death is also a function of physical existence and that the more refined a person is, the less the concepts of deterioration and death apply to him.

II. The number of mitzvot

A. Gemara, Makkot 23b

   1. 365 *mitzvot lo ta'aseh* (don'ts) correspond to the 365 days in the solar year.

   2. 248 *mitzvot aseh* (dos) correspond to the 248 component limbs in the human body.

B. Rashi's explanation of the correspondence

   1. For all 365 solar days a year, a person is cautioned not to transgress any of the 365 prohibitions.

   2. A person is cautioned to perform the 248 initiative-action mitzvot with all 248 component-limbs of his body.

C. The Maharal's rejection of Rashi's explanation

   1. In Rashi's explanation, there is no inherent connection between the concept of 365 solar days and the prohibitions, nor is there any substantial link between the 248 *mitzvot aseh* and the limbs of the body. It seems that the Gemara is just bringing some sort of convenient mnemonic device to recall the number of each category of mitzvot – so much so that there is no reason that one could not have made the opposite correspondence:

      a. 365 *mitzvot aseh* corresponding to solar days.

      b. 248 *mitzvot lo ta'aseh* corresponding to the component-limbs.

   2. The Maharal rejects this sort of casual connectivity.

D. The Maharal's explanation
   1. The purpose of the mitzvot is to allow us to reach a transcendent existence (as above).
   2. Purpose of *mitzvot lo ta'aseh*
      a. The prohibitions' purpose, in general, is to ensure that humans do not alter certain aspects of existence, which, in their current state, are conducive to the striving for transcendence.
      b. The prohibitions are the don'ts – preventing humans changing the way reality already is *and should remain.*
   3. Purpose of *mitzvot aseh*
      a. The *mitzvot aseh*'s purpose, in general, is to allow the human being to reach beyond his current status as a being in-potential, to actualize this potential and thus reach a transcendent status, which is his purpose in life.

CHAPTER 4

Part 2 of 3

The Maharal is in the midst of explaining the purposes of the two categories of *mitzvot* (*mitzvot aseh* and *mitzvot lo ta'aseh*) as well as the inherent connection between these purposes and the number of *mitzvot* in each category. Initially, he digresses to analyze the division of all of reality itself into two categories: humanity and everything else.

וכאשר תתבונן במציאות עולם הזה נחלק לב׳ חלקים כוללים כל המציאות.

When you consider the reality of this world, it is divided into two categories which include all of existence.[1]

The first category discussed is the "lower reality" which includes everything physical that exists. The sun is the symbol of this reality since it is the "king" of nature. The advantage of this category is that it is fundamentally incapable of deviating from the order in which it was set by G-d upon creation.

האחד הוא המציאות התחתון והוא בכללו מסודר תחת השמש והשמש כולל אותו, כי השמש מלך עולם הטבע ועולם הטבע מסודר תחתיו, וכמו שתמצא מבואר מן הכתוב שכאשר ירצה להזכיר כל העולם יאמר תחת השמש וכדכתיב (קהלת א׳) מה יתרון לאדם בכל עמלו שיעמול תחת השמש, וראיתי כל אשר נעשה תחת השמש וכן תמיד.

The first category is the lower reality which is, in general, "ordered under the sun" and the [term] "sun," includes all of it. [The reason that the sun is said to represent all of this lower reality is] because the sun is the king of the world of nature,[2] and the world of nature is ordered under it.[3] This is as you will find explained in the Torah – when the Torah wishes to refer to the entire world, it uses the term, "under the sun"; as is written, "What advantage does a person gain through all his toil under the sun"[4] and "I have seen all that is done under the sun,"[5] and so the term is always used.

1. For an exploration of this idea, see the Commentary, Ch. 4 § Point 2.
2. The Maharal seems to be using the terms "lower reality," "world of nature" and "this world" interchangeably.
3. For an exploration of these ideas, see the Ch. 4 § Points 4, 6 and 8.
4. Kohelet 1:3.
5. Kohelet 1:14.

[The reason that the sun is the symbol for nature is that] the sun is the [symbol of] maintenance of the order of nature through [the sun's] process and movement, by which it rules the world of nature; and just as the king enforces the orderliness [of his kingdom] by ensuring that nothing departs from its appropriate order, so too the sun rules this world, as it is written, "The sun which rules by day."[6] The sun preserves the order of the world [ensuring] that the order does not change or alter the appropriate arrangement [but rather that it] remains as it should be. This is well-known and there is no doubt about it. This is the first category.

והשמש היא שמירת סדר עולם הטבע במהלכה ובתנועתה במה שהוא מושלת בעולם הטבע, וכמו המלך שהוא השומר את הסדר לבלתי יצא אחד מן הסדר הראוי כך השמש שהוא המושל על עולם הזה, וכדכתיב (תהלים קל"ו) את השמש לממשלת ביום והוא השומר סדר העולם לבלתי יחליף וימיר את סדר הראוי ויעמוד על עמדו ודבר זה ידוע מאד ואין ספק בזה, זהו החלק הא'.

The second category discussed includes humanity only. Humanity is considered to be "king" over the lower creations, that is, the rest of creation. The advantage of this category is that humans have the ability to deviate from G-d's preset order and develop themselves for the better. This ability to deviate, however, can also be a liability in that humans can degenerate and destroy themselves, G-d forbid.

The second category [consists of] human beings only. This is the second category, ranged against the whole of the rest of reality. [The reason nothing else is included here is] that the human being exists on his own and is not included with the rest of those [objects] which exist, because everything was created for humankind: how could the servant[7] be included with his master[8] in the same category? Therefore, humankind is one category in and of itself.

החלק השני הוא האדם בלבד שהוא חלק שני נגד כל המציאות, שהוא בפני עצמו אינו נכלל עם שאר הנמצאים, שהרי בשביל האדם נברא הכל ואיך יהיה נכלל העבד עם אדוניו דבר זה לא יתכן כלל ולפיכך הוא חלק בפני עצמו.

Humankind is also differentiated from the [components of the] first category of existence due to the fact that the members of the first group do not change the order as part of which they

והוא גם כן נחלק מן חלק המציאות הראשון אשר לא ישנו סדרם אשר נברא עליו, אבל לא יקנו גם כן דבר מעלה נוסף על עצמם רק הם נשארים בהווייתם כמו שנבראו וכמו שנתבאר בפרק ג'.

והאדם הזה שהוא החלק השני אפשר שיצא מן הסדר הראוי אבל האדם הוא קונה מעלה יותר ממה שהיה לו.

וכמו שהשמש הוא מלך, גם כן האדם

6. Tehillim 136:8.
7. I.e., the rest of reality.
8. I.e., humankind.

were created, but [due to this] they also cannot acquire any further level above their original state, they simply remain in their existence as they were created (as was explained in the third chapter.)

The human being, who constitutes the [whole of] the second category, has the ability to deviate from the correct order, but he can [also, due to this ability,] acquire a greater excellence than he had [at the time of his creation].

The Maharal now explains that the human ability to perfect oneself and the world is actually the crowning glory of human beings, clearly designating him as king.

הוא מלך שהרי הכל נתון תחתיו, ומלכות האדם היא שהוא מוליך שלימות אל כל התחתונים כי הכל נברא לעבוד האדם ולשמשו ובזה הוא צורה אל כל התחתונים ומוליך שלימות אל הכל כמו המלך שהוא המשלים את הכל.

Just as the sun is the king, so is the human being the king, since *everything* is placed beneath him. The kingship of the human being is that he brings perfection to all the lower [creations] since everything was created to serve human beings and to cater to them, and in this way, the human being is the Form for all the lower [creations][9] and he brings perfection to them all just as a king completes everything.

The Maharal now explores the potential pitfall in human kingship: the ability to corrupt oneself and the world around.

והאדם הפך הנמצאים שכל הנמצאים תחת השמש אינם קונים מעלה על מה שנבראו אבל לא יצאו גם כן מסדר הראוי והאדם קונה מעלה יותר ממה שהיה אבל הוא יוצא מן הסדר. וכאשר הנביאים היו מוכיחין את ישראל היו מוכיחים אותם בדברים הטבעים כמו שאמר הנביא ישעיה (ישעיה א') ידע שור קונהו וגו', ומשה אדון כל הנביאים אמר (דברים ל"ב) האזינו השמים.

The human being is the antithesis of all the other [objects] which exist, for all the [objects] which exist under the sun do not acquire any excellence beyond that with which they were endowed on creation; but [on the other hand] they also do not deviate from the correct order. Meanwhile, the human being can acquire greater excellence beyond that [with] which he was [created] but he also [possesses the potential] to deviate from the order.[10] [For this reason,] when the prophets would criticize Israel, they

9. The idea, in brief, is that since the entire world was created for the sake of human beings, the spiritual DNA which characterizes the essence of the human being, also sheds light on the spiritual DNA of the rest of the world which is, in a sense, derived from it. This would be similar to the fact that the nucleus of a cell contains DNA detailing the details of the construction of all the non-nucleic components of the cell. For further development of this idea, see the Commentary, Ch. 4 § Point 4.

10. The very advantage of humanity contains within it the seed of our disadvan-

would rebuke them using natural metaphors, as the prophet Y'shayahu[11] said, "An ox knows its owner . . ."[12] and Moshe, master of all the prophets, said, "Listen heavens. . . ."[13]

ואמרו בספרי (שם) על זה:

And the sages said in the Sifri regarding this:[14]

אמר להם הסתכלו בשמים ובארץ וכל אשר בם אשר בראתי לשמש אתכם ואין להם שכר ועונש והם לא שנו מדתם ראיתם השמש הולך למזרח או שמא זרעתם את האדמה חטים והיא העלתה שעורים.

ואם אתם מקיימים תקבלו שכר ואם לאו תקבלו עונש על אחת כמה וכמה.

Moshe said to the Jews, "Contemplate the Heavens and Earth which I created to serve you – they have no reward or punishment, yet they do not deviate from their order. Have you seen the sun travelling to the east [instead of to the west]? Or perhaps you once sowed wheat seeds in the earth and instead the earth produced barley?

"But, if you [humans] fulfill [the commandments of the Torah] you will receive reward and if you do not, you will receive punishment. Thus, how much more should you observe the commandments [and not deviate from this divinely created structure.]"[15]

אמנם מעלתו על ידי המעשים הא-להיים וכמו שהתבאר למעלה ממעשה ידיו של אדם שהם יותר נאים ומשובחים ממעשה הטבע, שהם מעשה א-להיים ודבר זה מיוחד באדם.

However, the excellence of the human being is [gained] through [the performance of] the G-dly acts, and as was explained above, [it is also gained] from the works of human hands which are more pleasant and praiseworthy than the acts of nature since [human acts] are [potentially] G-dly acts. This is unique to humans.

---

tage. The rest of the natural world cannot deviate from what is ideal, which is how G-d created it. Only humanity, due to the very gift of freedom of choice, can be "unnatural" in both positive and negative senses: a human can rise above nature or, G-d forbid, sink below it.

11. Isaiah.

12. Y'shayahu 1:3. This prophecy criticizes the nation of Israel, claiming that they do not possess even the rudimentary sense of belonging that an ox does. He says that even an ox knows its owner, but the Jewish people abandon G-d, their owner, and forget Him.

13. D'varim 32:1.

14. Ad loc. 1, with variations.

15. The argument is á fortiori – if the insentient heavens and earth, with no thought of reward or punishment, do not deviate from the divinely ordained natural order, how much more so should humans, who will receive reward or punishment, not deviate.

The Maharal now explains the connection between the two categories of reality and the two categories of mitzvot. The prohibitions are linked to the "lower reality" ruled by the sun. The *mitzvot aseh* are linked to the 248 components of humanity. These linkages explain the numbers of mitzvot in each category.

וכאשר רצה השם יתברך לזכות את ישראל בב׳ מיני מצוות שהם לא תעשה ועשה.

And when Hashem, may He be Blessed, desired to grant merit to Israel,[16] [He gave them] the two types of mitzvot (which are the *mitzvot aseh* and the prohibitions[17]).

The prohibitions preserve the order of a human being's ideal reality, just as the sun preserves the order of the world. For this reason, there are 365 prohibitions, linked to the days of the solar year. Moreover, human reality is a microcosm of the universe and thus the preservation of the ideal human reality parallels the preservation of the balance within the universe in general.

שהמצוות ל״ת הם שישמור הסדר שלא יהיה לאדם יציאה מן הסדר, נתן לישראל מנין המצוות כמספר ימות החמה.

כי כבר אמרנו כי החמה היא שמירת סדר הנמצאים וימיה הם שס״ה ואלו שס״ה ימים הם משלימים אמיתת מלכות החמה כמו האברים לאדם, כי על ידי [ימות] החמה שהם שס״ה גומרת ממשלתה עד שמספר זה שהוא שס״ה מסוגל בעצמו לשמירת הסדר ובלתי יציאה מן סדר המציאות.

ולפיכך כאשר נתן השם יתברך תורה לישראל אשר ישראל נחשבו כל המציאות, כמו שהחמה והאדם הם כל המציאות, נתן להם שס״ה מצוות לא תעשה כמספר ימות החמה שהיא

The purpose of the prohibitions is to ensure the order [of the ideal reality of the human being]; that there be no deviation of humans out of the order, [so] He gave Israel prohibitions which numbered the same as the days of the solar year.

[The idea behind this is that] we have already said that the sun is [the symbol of][18] preserving the order of all [objects] which exist, and the sun's days are 365 and these 365 days complete the truth of the kingship of the sun,[19] just like a human's component-limbs [complete the human being]. For through the days of the solar year, which are 365, the sun completes[20] its kingdom [and this

16. Cf. Makkot 23b. See Chapter Five where the Maharal delves into the explanation of this idea.

17. *Mitzvot lo ta'aseh*.

18. See the Commentary, Ch. 4 § Points 4 and 6 for a discussion on the sun's role in the preservation of natural order.

19. Meaning that the order perpetuated by the sun is unbroken for 365 days which cycle back to the beginning.

20. Text as per Rav Hartman, 75.

link between the 365 days and the preservation of order is so strong] that this number, 365, is capable, in and of itself, of [becoming a symbol of] preserving the order and preventing deviation from the order of reality.

שמירת סדר המציאות, כי מאחר שסדר המציאות בכללו הוא על ידי מספר שס"ה שהם מספר ימות החמה נתן לישראל גם כן מספר שס"ה לא תעשה ועל ידם שמירת הסדר ובשמירת מצוות לא תעשה אין יציאה מן הסדר.

[Moreover,] Israel is considered as all of reality[21] (just as humanity and the sun encompass all of reality); therefore, when Hashem, may He be Blessed, gave the Torah to Israel, He gave them 365 prohibitions. This is the same as the number of days in the solar year, a number which is the preservation of the order of reality. [The inherent reason for this correspondence is that] since the order of reality as a whole is [preserved] through the number, 365 (which is the number of days of the solar year), Hashem also gave 365 prohibitions to Israel, through which there is a preservation of the order [of humanity and indeed the universe]; and through the observance of the prohibitions, there will be no deviation from the order.

The initiative-action mitzvot (*mitzvot aseh*) allow for the acquisition of perfection, something that only humanity (and nothing else) can do. The reason that humans can perfect themselves is because they were created in the "likeness of G-d," which is the human Form, consisting of 248 component-limbs. For this reason, there are 248 initiative-action mitzvot, linked to the 248 components of humanity.

Furthermore, Hashem gave them[22] another 248 initiative-action commandments which are the acquisition of [positive] action, through which a person acquires excellence and perfection.

This corresponds to the second part of reality which is humankind; for within humanity is found the [propensity for] acquisition of excellence – something which is not found within the first division [of reality] in which there is no acquisition [of excellence] at all and [in which] things stay exactly as they were created; while in humanity alone there is acquisition of excellence.

Now, the component-limbs of a

ונתן להם עוד רמ"ח מצוות עשה שהם קנין מעשה שעל ידם קונה מעלה ושלימות.

כנגד חלק המציאות השני שהוא האדם שנמצא באדם קנין מעלה שלא תמצא בחלק הראשון שאין בו קנין כלל רק נשאר על מה שנברא עליו והאדם בלבד יש בו קנין מעלה.

והאברים של אדם הם שלימות צורת האדם, כי אל תחשוב כמו שחשבו קצת בני אדם והם הרופאים, כי האברים של אדם הם טבעיים כמו שאר בעלי חיים, כי אין הדבר כך כלל כי רופאי אליל המה לא ידעו באמת תאר האדם ואיבריו שכולו א-להי, ולפיכך האיברים שלו הם שלימות

21. For a discussion of this idea, see the Commentary, Ch. 4 § Point 7.
22. The Jewish people.

האדם ועל ידי אבריו שהם רמ"ח נברא בצלם הא-להים, ומצד הזה הוא מלך בתחתונים שנאמר (בראשית א') נעשה אדם בצלמנו וגו' וירדו בדגת הים ובעוף השמים.

ולפיכך מספר המצוות שהם שלימות האדם כמספר אבריו שהם גם כן שלימות ומעלת האדם עד שהוא בצלם א-להים על ידי רמ"ח אבריו, ושלימות ומעלת המצוות נמשך אחר השלימות הזה מה שהאדם נברא בצלם א-להים שעל ידי זה האדם הוא שלימות כל התחתונים.

person are the perfection of the Form of the human. Do not think, as have some people ([that is] the "doctors,")[23] that the component-limbs of a person are [solely] natural as are animals', for the matter is not so! These are doctors of idols[24] and [therefore] they do not know the truth of the appearance of human beings and [the truth] of a human's component-limbs, which is that a human is completely G-dly. Therefore, a human's component-limbs are the completion of the human and through his component-limbs, which number 248, he is created in the likeness of G-d and through this he is the king over the lower [creations,] as the Torah says, "Let Us make humans *in Our likeness* . . . and they will dominate the fish of the sea and the birds of the heaven."[25]

Therefore, the number of [initiative-action] commandments, which are the perfection of human beings, corresponds to the number of a person's component-limbs which are also the perfection and excellence of the human being (to the extent that through his 248 component-limbs, he is in the likeness of G-d). And the completion and excellence of the mitzvot are a function of this perfection (that humankind is created in the likeness of G-d) since it is through this that humankind is the perfection of all the lower [creations].[26]

23. There is no direct indication to whom the Maharal was referring here. Clearly, it was some scholar or some school of scholars of the natural sciences.

24. I.e., idol worshippers.

25. B'reishit 1:26.

26. See the Commentary, Ch. 4 § Point 5 for an explanation of these ideas.

SUMMARY

Chapter 4: 2/3

I. Two categories of all existence

A. "Under the Sun"

1. Includes
   a. This category includes everything created (even human beings to a certain extent).
2. Ruled by
   a. The sun is the King of this category by virtue of its "maintenance" of the natural order.
3. Characteristics
   a. No deviation from the order set at creation.
      (1) Therefore, no improvement or degeneration possible of own volition.
   b. Created to serve the second category.
4. Defining number
   a. 365 = days of solar year.
5. Meaning of defining number
   a. The sun's rule is expressed in its completeness through the 365 days in the solar year during which order is maintained. This number thus connotes *maintenance of the suitable order for reality.*
6. Correspondence to mitzvot
   a. Corresponds to 365 *mitzvot lo ta'aseh* which similarly maintain an ideal human order.

B. "Humankind"

1. Includes
   a. This category includes humankind only.
2. Ruled by
   a. The Maharal doesn't say (but this would seem to be the ultimate choice of humanity, to crown Hashem king, or crown itself, G-d forbid).
3. Characteristics
   a. Deviation from the order set at creation is possible (for good or bad). Improvement is a possibility (as is degeneration, G-d forbid).
   b. Brings perfection to the first category.
   c. Is the Form of the first category.
   d. Made in the likeness of Hashem.

4. Defining number
   a. 248 = component-limbs of the body.
5. Meaning of defining number
   a. The rule of humanity is expressed in its completeness through the 248 component-limbs in the body, through which humanity gains the likeness of Hashem and thus gains perfection. This number thus connotes *perfection of everything under the sun.*
6. Correspondence to mitzvot
   a. Corresponds to 248 *mitzvot aseh* which allow humans (and vicariously, the universe) to gain perfection.

CHAPTER 4

Part 3 of 3

The Maharal continues his analysis of the two categories of reality (humankind and the natural world) and their correspondence to the two categories of mitzvot (*mitzvot aseh* and *mitzvot lo ta'aseh*). The Maharal first discusses the kingship of the sun and humankind.

ותעמיק יותר בענין זה ותדע ותבין שהשמש והאדם שני מלכים, כי השמש הוא מושל בעולם כמו שאמר הכתוב (שם) לממשלת היום. והאדם מושל בנמצאים גם כן כדכתיב (שם) וירדו בדגת הים ובעוף השמים ודבר זה מבואר.

And if you analyze this further, you will know and understand that the sun and humankind are both kings. For the sun rules the world, as the verse says, '[Hashem created the large luminary] to rule during the day";[1] while humankind *also* rules over those [objects] which exist, as is written, "And they will dominate the fish of the sea and the fowl of the heavens."[2] This matter has already been explained.

והמושל האחד הוא מושל הגשמי כי השמש היא גשמית. והמושל השני הוא נבדל כי האדם אינו גשמי גמור, הן בנשמתו הא־להית שיש לו נשמה קדושה והן מצד שנאמר בו כי בצלם א־להים עשה את האדם כי יש בצורתו ענין א־להי למי שיודע ברזי החכמה מכל מקום על כל פנים יש באדם ענין נבדל. הרי כי אלו שני דברים מחולקים האחד הוא המושל ויש לו חשיבת גוף. והשני יש לו ענין בלתי גשמי והוא נבדל יהיה הפירוש מה שיהיה בלשון צלם א־להים סוף סוף יש באדם דבר א־להי נבדל.

The one ruler[3] is the physical ruler, because the sun is physical and the second ruler [humanity] is transcendent because humankind is not completely physical, whether from the point of view of his holy soul or from the point of view of that which is said regarding him, "because [G-d] made humankind in the likeness of G-d"[4] (for there is in the human Form a G-dly matter for one who knows the secrets of wisdom). Either way,[5] humankind has a transcendent

והנה השמש והאדם היותר עליון בעולם הזה, כי העולם הזה יש בו

1. B'reishit 1:16.
2. B'reishit 1:26.
3. I.e., the sun.
4. B'reishit 1:27
5. Whether due to the holiness of his soul or being made in the likeness of Hashem.

facet. These two [rulers][6] are differentiated in the following manner: the one,[7] is a ruler and has physical import, while the second,[8] has a non-physical component and is transcendent (because whichever interpretation one chooses for the phrase, "likeness of G-d," in the end, humankind possesses a transcendent facet).

חומר וצורה נבדלת והחומר היותר עליון הוא לשמש כי יש לו חומר זך, ומעלת הצורה הנבדלת לאדם ולכך אלו שנים הם נחשבים מלכים מצד שהם עליונים בנמצאים בעולם הזה, והאדם נחשב צורה אל הנמצאים כולם אף אל השמש.

The sun and humankind are the more lofty [beings] in this world. This world contains material and [it contains] transcendent Form. The most elevated material in this world is the sun, for it has pure material, while the excellence of a transcendent Form is possessed by humankind. Thus, these two are considered kings from the point of view that they are the most superior amongst the [objects] which exist in this world and humankind is considered the Form for all [the objects] which exist, even for the sun.

The Maharal explains that a further reason for the correspondence between the number of prohibitions and the number of days in a solar year is that the sun is the king of the physical aspect of the world. On the other hand, when a person chooses to sin, it is because his physical aspect gains dominance. Therefore, the prohibitions prevent a person from sinning by placing boundaries on the physical aspect of human beings – they thus relate to the sun and the framework for physicality which it creates.

Now, it is known that sin flows from the material side [of a person] and not from the side of the Form, and therefore, the prohibitions [which entail a person] not committing a sin, correspond to the days of the solar year which brooks no deviation from the order even though it is material. And this matter will be clarified further in Chapter Thirteen, see there.

וידוע כי החטא הוא מצד החומר לא מצד הצורה, ולפיכך מצוות לא תעשה שלא יעשה חטא הוא כנגד ימות החמה שאין בה יציאה מן הסדר אף כי היא גשמית, ודבר זה יתבאר עוד בפרק י"ג ע"ש.

The Maharal now explains that there is a further correspondence between the male spiritual dynamic and "Form," as well as a correspondence between the female dynamic and "Matter." This creates a triple correspondence: "Form"–"*Mitzvot Aseh*"–"Male Dynamic"; "Matter–"Prohibitions"–"Female Dynamic."

6. I.e., the sun and humankind.
7. I.e., the sun.
8. I.e., humankind.

Therefore, women are also obligated in all prohibitions, just as are men, even though their[9] level is material, because the prohibitions are also [derived] from the physical aspect and on this matter we have spoken at length elsewhere.[10]

ולפיכך כל מצוות לא תעשה מחויבים בהם הנשים גם כן כמו האנשים אף כי מדריגתם חמרי, כי מצוות לא תעשה מצד החומר גם כן ובדבר זה הארכנו במקום אחר.

However, women are exempt from the *mitzvot aseh* which are time-bound.[11] This is because *mitzvot aseh* are derived from the aspect of Form, since the Form is the completion of humankind and humanity's [process of] becoming perfect is through the initiative-action commandments.[12, 13]

ואלו מצוות עשה שהזמן גרמא פטורין מהם הנשים כי מצוות עשה המצוה היא מצד הצורה כי הצורה היא שלימות האדם והשלמתו היא מצד מצוות עשה.

The Maharal explains that the number of solar days in a year and the number of component-limbs of a human being are essential and not incidental.

And you should have no doubt that the number of days in the solar year, which is 365, relates to the sun as it is[14] and so, too, that the number of component-limbs in a human relates to humanity in its essence – regarding all this, there is no doubt.[15]

ולא יהיה לך ספק כי מספר ימות החמה שהם שס"ה מתיחסים מספר ימיה אל החמה כפי מה שהוא. וכן מה שמספר אברי האדם הם רמ"ח מתיחסים מספר אבריו של אדם כפי מה שהוא אדם ואין בזה ספק.

9. I.e., women's.

10. See the Commentary, Ch. 4 § Point 9.

11. These are *mitzvot aseh* which are triggered by certain time factors. For example, one must recite the morning Sh'ma every day – once in the morning from daybreak till three halachic hours thereafter, and once at the night between nightfall and the next daybreak.

12. The Maharal taught earlier in this chapter that perfection (which is actualization of our Form) is achieved through the *mitzvot aseh*.

13. The Maharal's implication is that the male dynamic corresponds to "Form" while the female dynamic corresponds to "Matter." He has just explained that there is a further correspondence between Form and the *mitzvot aseh* on the one hand and Matter and the prohibitions, on the other. Both males and females share a little of both dynamics which is why they are both obligated to some extent in both categories but in general, these two correspondences would imply that the female dynamic has less connection to the *mitzvot aseh*; in particular, to the time-bound *mitzvot aseh*. For further study, see the Commentary, Ch. 4 § Point 9.

14. I.e., in its essence.

15. As before, the Maharal is saying that none of this is by chance: there is an essential connection between these numbers and the essence of the sun and humankind. He has already explained the essential connection of both categories of

The Maharal now finalizes his explanation of why the mitzvot of the Torah were compared to the sun and the human Form. He explains that the Torah really contains the ultimate, undiluted form of both the sun's attribute (maintenance of order) and that of the human Form (actualizing perfection). This is why the Torah is divided into two categories: prohibitions and *mitzvot aseh* – it is not that they mirror the sun and human Form, but the reverse: the sun and human Form mirror the two categories of mitzvot in the Torah.

We have already stated that these two (the sun and humankind) are the most superior [entities] in this world and they alone are considered [to be] kings and rulers in the world. The sun is the ruler and king and preserves the order [of the universe] so that it does not change, as is the function[16] of a [human] king. And humankind is also like a king who perfects the nation; so too, humankind perfects reality.

However, there is something even superior [to these two kings] and through it, "kings will reign."[17] This [superior entity] is the Torah, which is superlative in the world and through it "kings will reign."[18] Therefore, the Torah related to these two types of kings, the issue[19] of the first[20] is that there should be no deviation from the [suitable] order – this is the level of the prohibitions; the issue[21] of the second[22] is that of perfection –

וכבר אמרנו כי אלו שנים השמש והאדם הם ביותר עליון בעולם הזה והם בלבד נחשבים מלכים ומושלים בעולם, השמש הוא מושל ומלך ושומר הסדר שלא ישתנה כמו שהוא ענין המלך והאדם גם כן כמלך המשלים את העם כך האדם משלים את המציאות.

אמנם אשר הוא עוד יותר עליון אשר בה מלכים ימלכו היא התורה שהיא עוד יותר עליון בעולם ובה מלכים ימלכו ולפיכך התורה מתיחסת אל אלו שני מיני מלכים, אשר האחד ענינו בלתי יציאה מן הסדר במדרגת לא תעשה, והשני ענין השלמות שהוא משלים המציאות במצוות עשה.

כי דבר זה ראוי לתורה שיהיו בה מצוות לא תעשה אשר שומרים את הסדר שלא יהיה עובר החוק כמו שראוי למלך שהוא שומר העם שלא יצא מן הסדר, וגם יש בה מצוות עשה שהם השלמה לעולם כמו המלך שהוא השלמת העם ואלו שני דברים

mitzvot to these numbers. Commentary, Ch. 4 § Point 10.

16. I.e., matter.

17. Mishlei 8:15.

18. The Maharal has clearly repeated himself here, the purpose of which is unclear to us; but that there is a purpose is clear. See the the Commentary, Ch. 4 § Points 4, 5 and 7.

19. I.e., function.

20. I.e., the sun.

21. I.e., function.

22. I.e., humankind.

מתיחסים אל החומר והצורה, והדברים ברורים כשמש למי שמבין והארכנו במקום אחר בפירוש זה.

כלל הדבר כי השם יתברך נתן לאדם התורה שיהיה לאדם המעלה היותר עליונה שהיא בעולם, אם שיהיה בו המעלה היותר עליונה שלא יסור מן אשר נבראו עליו אל הרע ואל הפחיתות, ואם שיקנה השלמות היותר עליון על ידי מצוות עשה.

that he perfects reality through *mitzvot aseh*.

This is suitable for the Torah – that it should include prohibitions which preserve the [suitable] order that no-one transgress the law (as is suitable to a king who guards the nation that it should not deviate from the order) and that it should also contain initiative-action commandments which are the perfection for the world (just like a king who is the perfection of the nation). And these two aspects relate to the Matter and the Form. And the matters are as clear as the sun to one who understands, and regarding this explanation we have spoken at length in another place.[23]

The bottom line is that Hashem, may He be Blessed, gave the Torah to humankind [in order] that humankind should possess the most superior excellence[24] in the world – whether it be the most superior excellence in not deviating from [the order] under which humankind was created and [thus not reaching] evil and deficiency;[25] or whether it be that humankind [gains the ability to] acquire the most superior perfection through the initiative-action commandments.

The Maharal next explores a different correspondence between the numbers of mitzvot in each category and the human body.

ובמדרש (זוהר ח"א ק"ע ע"ב) אמרו כי רמ"ח מצוות עשה נתן השי"ת לישראל נגד אבריו של אדם ושס"ה מצוות לא תעשה נגד שס"ה גידין באדם.

וגם המדרש הזה פירושו כך, רק המדרש הזה נותן הכל באדם כי האדם הזה יש בו דבר נבדל א-להי ודבר שהוא בלתי נבדל הוא הגוף.

ולפיכך אמר שנתן רמ"ח מצוות עשה המשלימים את האדם נגד אבריו של אדם כי האברים הם צורתו שצורתו

In the Midrash,[26] our sages said that Hashem gave the 248 initiative-action commandments corresponding to the component-limbs of a human and [He gave] the 365 prohibitions corresponding to the 365 sinews in a human.

The explanation of this Midrash is the same [as that we gave above], except that this Midrash seeks to position all [of the levels of excellence] within humankind.[27] This is because humankind

23. See Chiddushei Aggadot to Makkot 23b and N'tivot Olam, N'tiv Ha'emunah 2.

24. I.e., level.

25. Which is the purpose of the prohibitions.

26. Zohar 1, 170b.

27. The Gemara cited previously (Makkot 23b) located the two types of kingship (ensuring non-deviation from order and perfection) in the sun and humankind

צלם א-להים נבדל כמו שהתבאר למעלה, וכנגד זה נתן לו רמ"ח מצוות עשה המשלימים האדם.

contains a transcendent, G-dly facet as well as a non-transcendent facet – the body.

ונתן לו שס"ה מצוות לא תעשה נגד גידין שלו שהגידין אינן צורתו של אדם אבל הם נותנים קיום לגוף האדם עד שהוא מקוים מבלי שינוי, ולפיכך הם שס"ה מצוות לא תעשה נגד גידין שלו שהגידין אינן צורתו של אדם אבל הם נותנים קיום לגוף האדם עד שהוא מקוים מבלי שינוי, ולפיכך הם שס"ה מצוות לא תעשה שלא יצא האדם מצד גופו מן הסדר הראוי ואין זה שלימות האדם.

Therefore, the Zohar said that Hashem gave humankind 248 initiative-action commandments which perfect the human and which correspond to the component-limbs of a person; since the component-limbs are a human's Form which is in the likeness of G-d and is transcendent (as was explained above), and corresponding to this Form, Hashem gave humankind 248 initiative-action commandments which perfect the human being.

Furthermore, Hashem gave humankind 365 prohibitions corresponding to his sinews because the sinews are not the Form of the human, rather they confer durability on the body so that it exists without change.[28] Therefore, there are 365 prohibitions in order that a person not deviate (from the point of view of his body) from the suitable order (as such a deviation would not be the perfection of the human being).

We now have two central correspondences regarding the numbers of mitzvot in each category. We have Rabbi Simlai in the Gemara who says that the 365 prohibitions correspond to the 365 solar days and that the 248 *mitzvot aseh* correspond to the 248 component-limbs of the body. On the other hand, the Zohar says that the 365 prohibitions correspond to the 365 sinews in the body, but agrees that the 248 *mitzvot aseh* correspond to the 248 component-limbs in the human body. The Maharal now compares these two correspondences.

ואין חלוק בין רבי שמלאי ובין זה המדרש, רק כי לדעת רבי שמלאי כל המציאות נחשב אחד וכל העולם נחשב כמו החומר אל אדם והאדם הוא שלמות וצורת כל המציאות, ולפיכך התורה היא נגד השמש והאדם.

There is no [substantive] difference between Rabbi Simlai[29] and this Midrash[30] except that in Rabbi Simlai's opinion, all of reality is considered one, but the whole world is considered as material (compared to the human being), while the human being is the perfection and

---

respectively. The Zohar here locates both of these within humankind.

28. I.e., deviation.

29. This was the correspondence from Makkot 23b, which drew the parallel between 365 prohibitions and the days of the solar year.

30. I.e., the Zohar.

ולדעת המדרש האדם מציאות נבדל לעצמו שקול נגד הכל, ולכך שס"ה לא תעשה ורמ"ח עשה הכל נגד האדם.

וראוי להבין דברים אלו שהם דברים גדולים מאד כי אי אפשר לכתוב יותר ועם שהם יותר עמוקים.

אבל הדברים האלו אין ספק בהם למי שידע להבין דברי אמת ויושר. והתבארו עוד במקום אחר והכל שורש אחד אמת וגזע צדק יוצא מפרדס החכמה. ועוד יתבאר.

the Form of all of reality; therefore, the Torah corresponds to the sun and the human [which between them, constitute all of reality].

But in the opinion of the Midrash [in the Zohar], the human being is a transcendent reality in and of himself and is weighed up[31] against everything and therefore, the 365 prohibitions and the 248 initiative-action commandments all correspond to the human being.

And it is worthwhile to understand these matters because they are very great, for it is impossible to write more even though they are even more profound.

But there is no doubt concerning these issues to one who knows how to understand words of truth and straightness. And these issues have been further explained in another place,[32] but it is all one root of truth and a trunk of righteousness which are sprouting from the orchard[33] of wisdom. And this will be explained further.[34]

31. I.e., is equal in value to the whole world. See the Commentary, Ch. 4 § Point 11.

32. See Chiddushei Aggadot to Makkot 23b and N'tivot Olam, N'tiv Ha'emunah 2.

33. The "orchard" is the sages' metaphor for the holistic understanding of the Torah, including the inner, hidden, Kabbalistic dimensions. It is to these mystical dimensions that the Maharal is referring.

34. See Chapters Seven and Twelve.

SUMMARY

Chapter 4: 3/3

I. Further aspects of the kingship of the sun and humankind

A. There are two components of the universe
   1. Material
      a. Of which the sun is king.
      b. The sun is the loftiest of this category.
   2. Transcendent Form
      a. Of which humanity is the king (and only member).
      b. Humanity is the loftiest of this category.

II. Further correlations between the number of mitzvot and the two kings

A. Prohibitions (*mitzvot lo ta'aseh*)
   1. Sin is due to the material side of existence.
   2. Since the sun rules this aspect, it is suitable that the number of mitzvot which prevent sin corresponds to the sun's kingship (that is, the preservation of order, which is the opposite of sin), which is expressed through the 365 solar days.
   3. Women are also obligated to observe the prohibitions.

B. Initiative-Action Commandments (*mitzvot aseh)*
   1. These commandments allow humanity to perfect itself. Such perfection is only possible due to humankind's Form (which is the likeness of Hashem, as explained previously in this chapter).
   2. Women are exempt from certain of these *mitzvot aseh* which are time-bound (an idea which the Maharal does not explain further).

III. The essential nature of these numbers

A. The reasons that the sun has a 365-day solar cycle and that human beings have 248 component-limbs are related to the essence of what the sun is and what humanity is.

B. The correlations between these numbers and the numbers of commandments in the various categories are similarly not coincidental.

IV. The Torah contains the essences of both the sun and humankind

A. Through the Torah, both the sun and humanity reign – meaning that the reason that they rule is because they represent one of the two aspects of kingship contained in the Torah.

B. The Torah includes two types of commandments

1. Prohibitions – relating to Matter – which preserve the suitable order of the universe.
2. *Mitzvot aseh* – relating to Form – which bring completion to humanity and thence to the universe.

C. Hashem gave the Torah to humanity to confer upon them the highest level possible:
1. In not deviating from the prescribed order.
2. In achieving perfection.

V. The Zohar's correspondence

A. The Zohar brings a different correspondence.
1. 248 initiative-action commandments correspond to 248 component-limbs (this is the same as above).
2. 365 prohibitions correspond to the 365 sinews in the human body (this is different).

B. The Maharal explains that the root of this correspondence is identical to the previous one.
1. Humanity has two components:
   a. Material – the body: non-transcendent
   b. Form: transcendent
2. The 365 prohibitions correspond to the 365 sinews because the sinews are that which prevents deviation within the human body, holding the body together.
3. The 248 initiative-action commandments correspond to 248 component-limbs which provide for humanity's perfection due to humanity's Form which is in the likeness of Hashem (as above).

VI. The difference between the two correspondences

A. In the first system (Makkot 23b)
1. The "world" is material.
2. Humanity is the transcendent element in creation.

B. In the Zohar
1. Humanity is transcendent in and of itself and is equivalent to everything else.
2. Both types of kingship (prevention of deviation as well as perfection) are located within the human being.

CHAPTER 5

CHAPTER 5

Part 1 of 3

The Maharal bases this chapter on the famous saying of Rabbi Chanani'ah ben Akashi'ah, who said that Hashem bestowed many mitzvot on Israel in order to increase their merit. The Maharal questions the traditional explanations of this aphorism and develops his own thesis.

המצוות שנתן השם יתברך לישראל יש לשאול עליהם, אם רבוי המצוות לטוב להם כמשמעות פשט הכתוב שנאמר (דברים ו') ויצונו ה' א-להינו לעשות [את כל] החקים האלה ... לטוב לנו כל הימים ... וצדקה וגו'.

ועם כי יש לומר שאין הכתוב מדבר ברבוי המצוות רק שהמצוות הם לטוב אל האדם שבקיום המצוה זוכה לחיים הנצחיים, מכל מקום כך מוכח פשט המאמר המפורסם (מכות כ"ג ע"ב):

One could ask [the following question] regarding the mitzvot which Hashem, may He be Blessed, gave to Israel: is the large number of mitzvot good for them, as is the simple meaning of the verse, "Hashem our G-d commanded us to perform [all][1] these decrees, for our good, for all days and it will be righteousness [for us] . . .'"?[2]

Even though one could explain that the verse is not addressing the large number of mitzvot, but [is] only [claiming that] the mitzvot are for the good of a person (since through the observance of the mitzvah, a person merits the eternal life), nevertheless, it is certain that the simple meaning of the [following] famous maxim is [relating to the large number of mitzvot]:[3]

> אמר ר' חנניא בן עקשיא רצה הקדוש ברוך הוא לזכות את ישראל לפיכך הרבה להם תורה ומצוות שנאמר ה' חפץ למען צדקו יגדיל תורה ויאדיר.

> Rabbi Chanani'ah ben Akashi'ah said, "The Holy One, Blessed be He, desired to accord merit to Israel, therefore, He multiplied Torah and mitzvot for them. As the verse states, 'Hashem desired his[4] righteousness, [therefore Hashem] enlarged the Torah and made [it] glorious.'"[5]

---

1. We have added the word "all," as per the cited source. Without it, the Maharal is difficult to understand.
2. D'varim 6:24–25.
3. Makkot 23b.
4. I.e., Israel's.
5. Y'shayahu 42:21, as per Rashi.

The Maharal questions the meaning of this saying.

ומעתה יש לשאול כי איך יאמר שה׳ חפץ לזכות את ישראל לכך הרבה להם מצוות, ודבר זה נגד השכל.

שהיה לו למעט במצוות כדי שלא יהיה צריך לשמור הרבה מצוות, ואז היה זוכה לעולם הבא על ידי מיעוט מצוות ממה שהוא מוסיף להם מצוות שאז אי אפשר לזכות כל כך לעולם הבא.

Now, one should ask how one can say that since Hashem desired to accord merit to Israel, therefore, He multiplied Torah and mitzvot for them – such a statement is illogical!

[If Hashem had really wanted to accord Israel merit] He would have reduced the number of mitzvot so that there would be no need to abide by [so] many mitzvot. Then, due to having fewer mitzvot, Jews would more easily merit [reaching] the World to Come than they would if Hashem added mitzvot for them, since [if they have more mitzvot] it is impossible to merit the World to Come to the same extent [as when there are fewer mitzvot].[6]

The Maharal now cites the Rambam's explanation of the saying.

והרמב״ם ז״ל פירש במסכת מכות וז״ל:

מעיקרי האמונה בתורה כי כשיקיים אדם מצוה מן תרי״ג מצוות כראוי וכהוגן, ולא שתף עם כונתה מכוונות העולם אלא שיעשה אותה מאהבה כמו שביארתי לך, הנה זכה לחיי עולם.

ועל זה אמר רבי חנניא כי המצוות בהיותם הרבה אי אפשר שלא יעשה האדם בחייו אחת מהנה על מתכונתה ועל שלימותה ובעשיית אותה המצוה תחיה נפשו באותו מעשה.

וממה שיורה על עיקר זה מה ששאל רבי חנינא בן תרדיון מה אני לחיי עולם הבא והשיב המשיב כלום מעשה בא לידך כלומר עשית מצוה כהוגן והשיב

The Rambam, *z"l*, explained [this saying in his commentary to] Tractate Makkot, as follows,[7]

> It is one of the principles of faith in the Torah that when a person performs any *one* of the 613 mitzvot suitably and correctly, and does not add any worldly intentions to its [proper] intention but only performs it out of love (as I have explained to you) [then] that person has merited eternal life.
>
> Regarding this, Rabbi Chanani'ah[8] said that since there are many mitzvot it is impossible that a person will not perform [at least] one of them in his lifetime in its

6. The Maharal's idea is clear – the increase in number of mitzvot simply allows for greater scope for violation thereof. If we only had one mitzvah, observing it would be simplicity in and of itself, as compared to the difficulty of observing 613 of them.

7. Peirush Hamishnayot, *Makkot* 3:16.

8. The author of the maxim regarding the merit conferred by an abundance of mitzvot.

כי נזדמנה לו מצות צדקה על השלימות וזכה בה לחיי עולם הבא עכ"ל.

[proper] way and in its perfection; and through the performance of that mitzvah, his soul will live [eternally] through that act.

Something that can shed light on this principle is that which Rabbi Chanina[9] ben Tradyon asked,[10] "Will I reach the World to Come?"[11] And the one[12] who responded to him answered, "Has no [positive] act ever come your way?" This means, "Have you never performed a mitzvah in the correct manner?" Rabbi Chanina responded that once he happened to perform the mitzvah of *tz'dakkah*[13] in its perfection; and [therefore, through this] he merited the World to Come.

The Maharal now questions the Rambam's explanation since it seems to contradict an earlier, more authoritative source.

ותימה על זה כי איך יסבלו דבריו הא דאמרינן בגמרא דראש השנה (ט"ז ע"ב) בהדיא דאליבא דכולי עלמא ברוב עבירות ליום הדין נדון בגיהנם, והתם איירי לעולם הבא דהא קאמר צדיקים גמורים נכתבים לחיי עולם הבא וכו' ואיך יסתור גמרא ערוך.

And this is astonishing! How can the Rambam's words suffer [the contradiction] with what we say explicitly in the Gemara in Tractate Rosh Hashanah,[14] [which is] that according to all opinions, a person is sentenced to *G'hinnom*[15] if a majority of his deeds are sinful. The Gemara there is addressing the World to Come, since it says, "Completely righteous people are inscribed for life in the World to Come . . ." Now, how can the Rambam contradict an [authoritatively] arranged Gemara [by saying that the majority of one's deeds are not the deciding factor, but rather whether one has managed to perform one deed superlatively]?[16]

9. Not to be confused with Rabbi *Chanani'ah*.
10. Avodah Zarah 18a. Cited later in the Maharal.
11. I.e., have I done enough to merit that reward?
12. Rabbi Yossi ben Kisma.
13. Jewish social outreach and support.
14. Rosh Hashanah 16b.
15. *G'hinnom* is a purification process for the soul after death. The process is painful as is all true growth, but has nothing in common with concepts of eternal purgatory.
16. The Maharal's question is that the Gemara in Rosh Hashanah states that one merits the World to Come only through a majority of one's deeds being righteous, while the Rambam seems to imply that one could achieve this through a single positive act (which is how the Rambam explains the saying of Rabbi Chanani'ah ben Akashi'ah in Makkot 23b). The Maharal understands that the opinion in Rosh Hashanah is a unanimous position in the Gemara and since the Gemara is an es-

The Maharal now brings a possible explanation of the Rambam, which he rejects for several reasons.

ואם יאמר דהא דאמרינן שאפילו במצוה אחת זוכה לעולם הבא היינו שעושה מצוה אחת אבל לא עשה שום עבירה אם כן אין כאן להגדיל שכר כלל, דסוף סוף כאשר יש להם הרבה מצוות אפשר שיעשה הרבה חטאים ויהיו החטאים מכריעים.

ואם רצה הרמב"ם ז"ל כאשר עושה מצוה ולא עשה שום חטא כנגד זה, בודאי כדבריו כן הוא. ודבר זה משנה פשוטה בפרק קמא דקידושין (ל"ט ע"ב):

One could say that the Rambam's intent, in saying that a person can merit the World to Come even through [the suitable performance of] just one mitzvah, is that [this will only hold true when] a person performs one mitzvah but transgresses no prohibitions at all. But then [if this is what he means] there is no [validity to the] concept of increasing reward at all,[17] since in the end [even] if the Jews have many mitzvot, it is possible that they will perform many sins and that the sins will determine [the final verdict through outnumbering the mitzvot].

And if the Rambam, *z"l*, had intended to say that when a person does one mitzvah but transgresses no prohibitions to counter this [mitzvah, that in such a case, a person would merit the World to Come], indeed it is [exactly] as his words [imply].[18] But [there is no reason for the Rambam specifically to write this, as] this idea is [learned from] a simple Mishnah in the first chapter of [the Tractate] Kiddushin,[19]

כל העושה מצוה אחת מטיבין לו ומאריכין לו ימיו ונוחל הארץ.

> Anyone who performs one mitzvah, gets goodness and his life is lengthened and he merits the Land.

ואף על גב דמוקי ליה שם כשעשה מצוה אחת יתירה על מחצה עונות, כל שכן שיש ללמוד מזה שאם עשה מצוה אחת ולא עשה שום חטא שזוכה לעולם הבא.

אך אם כן אין צריך לדבר זה מה שכתב שעשה מצוה אחת ולא שתף עמה כונה אחרת.

Even though the Gemara there explains that the context of this statement is that of a person who performed one mitzvah more than his sins, how much more so can one learn from this that if a person performed one mitzvah but transgressed no prohibitions, that such a person would merit the World to Come.[20]

---

tablished earlier authority, the Rambam cannot contradict it without support of an authority possessing equivalent eminence.

17. I.e., the idea that Hashem's giving us more mitzvot helps us gain merit.
18. That such a person would gain the World to Come.
19. Kiddushin 39b.
20. And therefore, the Rambam's supposed position is trivial, in the sense that

Also, if this is true,[21] then there is no need for the Rambam to write that [a person merits the World to Come if] he performs one mitzvah and "does not add to its [proper] intention" any other intention[22] [since even with a mixed set of intentions, when one has not performed any sins, one still merits the World to Come].

The Maharal concludes that the saying of Rabbi Chanani'ah cannot be as the Rambam explains it.

סוף סוף למדנו כי אין הדבר כמו שפירש הרמב"ם ז"ל דבמצוה אחת זוכה לחיי עולם הבא.

In conclusion, we have learned that the [meaning of the] matter[23] is not as the Rambam, *z"l*, explained, which was that with one mitzvah, a person could merit the life of the World to Come.

The Maharal now analyzes the case cited in the Rambam, regarding Rabbi Chanina ben Tradyon.

והא דרבי חנינא בן תרדיון הכי איתא התם (עבודה זרה י"ז [צ"ל י"ח] ע"א):

כשחלה ר' יוסי בן קסמא אמר לו רבי חנינא בן תרדיון מה אני לעולם הבא?
אמר לו כלום מעשה בא לידך?
אמר לו מעות של פורים נתחלפו לי במעות של צדקה וחלקתים לעניים.
אמר לו אם כן מחלקך יהא חלקי ומגורלך יהא גורלי ע"כ.

Now, regarding the case [cited by the Rambam] of Rabbi Chanina ben Tradyon, this is what is cited there:[24]

> When Rabbi Yossi ben Kisma fell ill, Rabbi Chanina ben Tradyon said to him, "Will I reach the World to Come?"
>
> Rabbi Yossi replied [rhetorically, in astonishment], "Has no [positive] act ever come your way?"
>
> Rabbi Chanina replied, "Once, I had money on Purim [set aside to pay for my feast on Purim] which was mistakenly switched with money set aside for charity and I disbursed my own money to the poor [but when I discovered my error, I didn't reimburse myself from the charity money]."[25]

---

there is no novel idea therein. The Maharal cannot accept that the thrust of the Rambam's comments would be to teach such a triviality.

21. That is, if we explain the Rambam's words to be addressing the case where a person performed only one mitzvah but no sins.

22. Since in such a case where a person has no transgressions, even if he didn't perform his sole mitzvah with completely pure intentions, nevertheless, he has not sinned and thus even with this non-ideal Mitzvah he would still merit the World to Come.

23. I.e., the saying of Rabbi Chanani'ah ben Akashi'ah.

24. Avodah Zarah 18a.

25. See Rashi ad loc.

Rabbi Yossi replied, "If so, may my portion [in the World to Come] be similar to your portion and may my fate be like your fate."

Contrary to the Rambam, the Maharal explains that this isolated mitzvah was not the cause of Rabbi Chanina's entry into the World to Come, but merely a barometer of his overall conduct.

ונראה לא שבשביל מצוה זאת יזכה לעולם הבא רק שראה בקיום מצוה אחת כתקנה מאד שהיה מחמיר בה, וכמו שכתב הרמב"ם ז"ל בעצמו שמזה המעשה ראה שקיים מצוה אחת כתקנה מזה היה יודע שהוא צדיק גמור בקיום כל המצוות והוא בן עולם הבא.

And it seems that it is not for the sake of this mitzvah that he would merit to the World to Come, but rather that he [Rabbi Yossi] saw that Rabbi Chanina kept this one mitzvah exactly as it should be done and that he was stringent in [observing] it. As the Rambam, *z"l*, himself wrote, from this act, Rabbi Yossi saw that Rabbi Chanina observed one mitzvah properly,[26] and from this he knew that Rabbi Chanina was a completely righteous man in observing *all* the mitzvot and [thus] he merited the World to Come.

26. The Rambam's phrase there is "he happened [to fulfill] the mitzvah of *tz'dakkah* in the way of perfection."

SUMMARY

Chapter 5: 1/3

I. Is the large number of mitzvot to the benefit of the Jewish people?

- A. Yes
  - 1. Two proof texts
    - a. Verses in D'varim 6:24–25
      - (1) This could be explained otherwise.
    - b. Gemara Makkot 23b
      - (1) Rabbi Chanani'ah ben Akashi'ah's saying.
- B. Question on this concept
  - 1. Surely having a larger number of mitzvot simply provides one with more opportunities for failure?

II. The Rambam's commentary on the Gemara in Makkot 23b

- A. A person can achieve the World to Come simply by performing one mitzvah in its ideal manner –which is: solely for the purpose of serving Hashem out of love.
- B. Therefore, the more mitzvot one has, the greater the chance that there will be at least one mitzvah to which a person can connect in such a fashion that he will be able to perform it in the correct fashion.
- C. Thus, having more mitzvot does actually benefit the Jewish people since it creates more opportunities for each person to find their unique mitzvah.

III. Maharal's questions on the Rambam

- A. The Rambam's main assumption is that a single mitzvah performance can assure a person of the World to Come if performed correctly. The Maharal questions this:
  - 1. The Gemara in Rosh Hashanah (16b) says that a person only merits the World to Come if his mitzvot outweigh his sins.
    - a. Thus ideal performance of one mitzvah can usually never tip the scales.
    - b. The only time that one mitzvah could determine one's fate is if it was the mitzvah which tipped the scales in favor of the mitzvot – that is, if both the mitzvot and sins were equal and then this mitzvah tipped the scales.
      - (1) But the Rambam doesn't say he is addressing such a case.
  - 2. Thus, the Rambam seems to be contradicting an explicit Gemara, which is unacceptable since the Gemara is a superior Halachic authority.

B. A possible explanation of the Rambam and consequent difficulties
   1. Possible explanation
      a. The Rambam is addressing the case of a person who has transgressed no prohibitions whatsoever, so the performance of this one mitzvah is enough to determine his fate.
   2. Difficulties with this explanation
      a. How would this explain the original difficulty – that more mitzvot means more opportunity to sin and fail? Just because there may be some people who manage to remain sin-free doesn't mean that for the whole nation having the mitzvot will be beneficial! In general, for the average person, the greater number of mitzvot *will* entail greater failure.
      b. If the situation we are addressing is of a person with no sins, why does the Rambam say that the scale is only tipped by a mitzvah done in the most exemplary fashion? If a person is sin-free, any mitzvah, even done in a non-ideal manner, will tip the scales.

C. Maharal's conclusion
   1. The explanation of the saying of Rabbi Chanani'ah ben Akashi'ah is not like the Rambam.

IV. Explanation of the case of Rabbi Chanina ben Tradyon

A. The Rambam's explanation
   1. Rabbi Chanina performed one mitzvah in an exemplary fashion and thus merited the World to Come through this performance.

B. The Maharal's explanation
   1. Rabbi Chanina's extraordinary diligence in performing this one mitzvah was a yardstick of his overall greatness.
   2. It was this greatness which assured him of his place in the World to Come.

CHAPTER 5

Part 2 of 3

The Maharal continues his rebuttal of the Rambam's thesis (mentioned at the beginning of the chapter) by presenting his own explanation of the Rambam's key proof (which was the statement of Rabbi Chanina ben Tradyon).

ועוד אני אומר כי מה שאמר כלום מעשה בא לידך לא שהיה רצונו לומר ממעשה מצוה אחת יזכה לעולם הבא שאין הדבר כך, רק היה שואלו כלום מעשה בא לידך שמן המעשה יש להבחין סימן בן עולם הבא?

ואמר מעות פורים נתחלפו במעות צדקה וחלקתי אותו לעניים.

I say further, that regarding[1] what he[2] said [to Rabbi Chanina ben Tradyon], "Has no [positive] act ever come your way?," [the meaning of this is as follows:] his intention was not to say that through the performance of only one mitzvah that a person would merit the World to Come, for this is just not the case; rather, he[3] was asking him,[4] "Has no [positive] act ever come your way through which you could determine some *sign* that [you are already worthy] of the World to Come?"

[In response] he said, "Once, I had money on Purim [set aside to pay for my feast on Purim] which was mistakenly switched with money set aside for charity and I disbursed my own money to the poor [but when I discovered my error, I didn't reimburse myself from the charity money]."

The Maharal now explains that Rabbi Chanina's act demonstrates his desire to have no share in the physical world at all but only in the World to Come.

והדבר רמז מופלג, כי מעות של פורים אינם עומדים רק לרבוי אכילה ושתיה ואלו היה יום הזה יום שיש בו קדושה לא היה הסעודה ענין גשמי לגמרי שהיה זה לכבוד היום ולמעלת קדושתו,

And this is a distant hint,[5] because the money for the feast on Purim is destined solely for increasing [physical] feasting and drinking – if this day [Purim] were a day which possesses sanctity, the feast

1. At the beginning of this chapter, the Maharal cited the Gemara in Avodah Zarah 18a which relates a conversation between Rabbi Yossi ben Kisma and Rabbi Chanina ben Tradyon.
2. Rabbi Yossi ben Kisma.
3. Rabbi Yossi.
4. Rabbi Chanina.
5. I.e., extremely profound.

אבל אין ביום זה קדושה כלל והאכילה והשתיה הוא דבר גשמי מענין העולם הזה שהוא כולו גשמי.

ונתחלף מעות אלו במעות עניים שמעות עניים הפך זה כי העני ידוע שאין לו עולם הזה כלל ואין נהנה מטובת עולם הזה, ונתחלפו לו מעות פורים שהוא הכל עולם הזה הפך זה במעות עניים שאין להם חלק בעולם הזה וחלק הכל לעניים.

ודבר זה רמז שהוא יחליף העולם הזה בעולם הבא ולא יהיה לו חלק כלל בעולם הזה וכל חלקו שיהיה ראוי לו בעולם הזה שמור לו לעולם הבא.

וכמו שהיה באמת לרבי חנינא בן תרדיון הצדיק הקדוש שהיה נשרף וספר תורה עמו ולא היה חלקו בעולם הזה רק הכל שמור לו לעולם הבא, ועל זה אמר אם כן מחלקך יהא חלקי כי סימן יש לו שחלקו שהיה ראוי לו בעולם הזה הוא שמור לו לעולם הבא.

would not be a completely physical event but would rather be a function of the holiness of the day and of the excellence of its holiness.[6] However, this day[7] possesses no sanctity[8] at all and the feasting and drinking [on it] are matters of this world which is completely physical.

[But in the case of Rabbi Chanina] the money for this [purely physical] purpose[9] was mixed with the money for the poor and the money for the poor is the exact opposite of this [money destined for physical purposes only], because the pauper knows that he has no portion in this world whatsoever and he doesn't enjoy the goodness of this world. And [when] the money for Purim (which is completely of this [physical] world) was mixed up with the money for the poor (which is the opposite of this, since paupers have no share in this world), he[10] distributed it all to the poor.

And this is a hint to the fact that [if he had his way] he would exchange this world for the World to Come and would not have any portion in this world and his entire portion (which would have been suitable to him in this world) is retained for him for the World to Come.

And this is, in truth, what actually happened to Rabbi Chanina ben Tradyon, the holy *Tzaddik*,[11] who was burned with a scroll of the Torah with him[12] and his portion was not in this world – it was all retained for him for the World to Come. Regarding this [striving for a portion solely in the

6. Unlike Torah festivals such as Pesach, Shavu'ot and others, the festival of Purim has no halachic, Torah-based sanctity; rather it is a rabbinically enacted festival with no inherent sanctity. The Torah-sanctity of a festival is expressed through amongst other things, requirements to say Kiddush (a prayer sanctifying the day at its inception) and prohibitions on *m'lachah* (halachically defined creative work), none of which exist on Purim.

7. I.e., Purim.

8. On a non-Rabbinic level.

9. I.e., the feast

10. Rabbi Chanina.

11. In Hebrew, צדיק, meaning, "a righteous person."

12. Avodah Zarah 18a.

World to Come], he [Rabbi Yossi] said, 'If so, may my portion [in the World to Come] be from your portion,' because Rabbi Chanina had a sign that his suitable portion in this world would be retained for the World to Come.

Having presented his own understanding of this Gemara, the Maharal explains that the Rambam cannot use it as a proof for his explanation (explored previously in this chapter) of the aphorism, "The Holy One, Blessed be He, desired to accord merit to Israel, therefore, He multiplied Torah and mitzvot for them."

ומעתה אין ראיה כלל וחזרה קושיין למקומה במאמר המפורסם רצה הקדוש ברוך הוא לזכות את ישראל לפיכך הרבה להם מצוות.

From here, there is no proof at all [for the Rambam's thesis of the meaning of the saying, "The Holy One, Blessed be He, desired to accord merit to Israel, therefore, He multiplied Torah and mitzvot for them,"] and our question returns regarding the [meaning of the] famous statement, "The Holy One, Blessed be He, desired to accord merit to Israel, therefore, He multiplied Torah and mitzvot for them."[13]

The Maharal now presents his own understanding of this maxim, which is that the mitzvot we are given are not a disconnected mass loaded onto us like a burden on a wagon; rather, whenever mitzvot are given to people, it is a requirement that the recipients are simultaneously blessed with an enhanced receptivity which enables proper acceptance and performance of those mitzvot. This is the great merit we gain through multiplication of mitzvot – multiplication of our receptivity to holiness.

ואני אומר כי לא קשיא כלל.

כי מה שישראל הם מוכנים אל התורה היא מדרגה בפני עצמה, כי מפני שהם מוכנים אל תורה כמו שהתבאר למעלה ואינם כמו עכו"ם שאין מוכנים לתורה, ואם נתן להם מעט מצוות לא היה הזכות שלהם כל כך כמו שיש להם זכות במה שיש להם תורה שיש בה מצוות הרבה ומוכנים אל הרבה מצוות.

And I say that there is no difficulty at all.

For the fact that Israel are receptive to the Torah is a [substantial spiritual] level in and of itself, since they are receptive to the Torah (as was explained above)[14] and are unlike the idolaters who are not receptive to the Torah. And if Hashem had given them[15] only a few mitzvot, they would not have had as much merit as they do when they possess Torah,

13. The Maharal explains that since the Rambam's explanation has fallen away, we are left once again with deciphering the meaning of the aphorism and explaining how it is that having more mitzvot is more beneficial, not less.

14. See Chapter One where the Maharal explains this at length. See also Commentary, Ch. 1 § Points 8, 9 and 10.

15. The Jewish people.

which includes within it many mitzvot, and [as] when they are receptive to many mitzvot.[16]

The Maharal now brings two arguments in favor of his explanation.

ואם לא היה מעלת ישראל במה שהם מוכנים אל התורה, באיזה צד נוכל לומר שאותם שלא היו יכולים לקיים מצוות התורה שמתו כשהם קטנים שיהיו בני עולם הבא, אבל הענין הוא במה שהם העם שיש להם תורה ומוכנים לתורה ומצוה בשביל הכנתם לתורה יזכו לחיי עולם הבא.

וכן חס ושלום לומר שאנחנו בני גלות ואין אנו יכולים לקיים הרבה מצוות התלוים בארץ, שלא יהיה לנו חלק באותן מצוות שלא נוכל לקיים, חס ושלום לומר דבר כזה למעט משלמות הדורות שמתו, אבל במה שאנו בני תורה ויש לנו הכנה אל התורה יש לנו שכר בכל התורה כולה, ודבר זה ברור ויתבאר דבר זה באריכות בעזרת השם.

Now, if the excellence of Israel were not to be found in this receptivity towards the Torah, how would we be able to say that those people who were unable to perform the mitzvot of the Torah (for example, because they died when they were children) [nevertheless] exist in the World to Come?[17] But the matter[18] is that since they [are of] the nation which has the Torah and are [thus inherently] receptive to the Torah and mitzvot, through this receptivity, they will merit the life of the World to Come.[19]

So too, G-d forbid should one say that we, dwelling in the exile,[20] who are unable to observe many of the commandments which are dependent on the land[21] [of Israel], do not have any portion in those mitzvot which we are unable to perform. G-d forbid that we should say such a thing, derogating from the perfection of the generations who have [already] passed away. But through the fact that we are *B'nei Torah*[22]

16. The Maharal is saying that the Jewish people are receptive to however many mitzvot they have. This pre-preparation is a positive reality in and of itself. Now, the extent of this receptivity is determined by the quantity (and perhaps quality) of mitzvot which the nation must perform; thus having a greater number (and quality) of mitzvot means that Hashem had to have given the nation a greater receptivity for them, á priori.

17. I.e., they reach the World to Come, despite not actually having physically performed the mitzvot.

18. I.e., the resolution of this problem.

19. Compare this with the Maharal's statements in Chapter Three regarding a person who is prevented from performing mitzvot due to externalities.

20. I.e., outside of the Land of Israel.

21. There are many mitzvot which can only be performed in the Land of Israel or on its produce. For example, one is commanded to separate certain tithes from one's crop every year (see Rambam, Laws of *T'rumot* 1:1).

22. In Hebrew, בני תורה. This term literally means "children of the Torah" but connotes people who are committed to and live by the Torah.

and we have the receptivity to the Torah, therefore, we have reward in the entirety of the Torah [even for those sections which cannot be practically implemented] and this matter is clear and it will be clarified at length,[23] with Hashem's help.

ועל זה אמר רבי חנניא דבריו כי רצה הקדוש ברוך הוא לזכות את ישראל ולפיכך הרבה להם מצוות הרבה והם מוכנים אל מצוות הרבה מאוד, וזהו זכות ישראל כאשר יש להם מצוות הרבה ביותר ולכך שכרם גדול יותר.

Regarding this, Rabbi Chanani'ah said his words, that the Holy One, Blessed be He, desired to accord merit to Israel, therefore, He multiplied many mitzvot for them and [thus] they are receptive to a great many mitzvot, and this is the merit of Israel, when they have so many mitzvot, therefore, their reward is greater.

The Maharal now deals with the problem that having many mitzvot itself creates so many opportunities for failure that surely this outweighs any benefit of having the mitzvot in the first place. The Maharal's counterargument is that the *definite* benefit of increased receptivity to Torah is preferable to the *possibility* of sin which is, after all, not definite.

ואל יקשה לך סוף סוף יהיה שכרם יוצא בהפסדם שאם לא יקיים רוב התורה יהיה רשע. זה אינו דסוף סוף מרויח בזה על ידי שיש לו הכנה אל התורה שיש בה מצוות הרבה. כי הדבר הזה שאפשר שיקיים המצוות או לא יקיים דבר זה הוא שקול כי אולי יזכה ויקיים המצוות וכיון שהדבר הוא שקול דבר זה מכריע מה שהוא מוכן אל תורה של רבוי מצוות ודבר זה הוא זכות גדול מאוד.

And do not find it difficult that, in the end, their[24] reward will be offset by their loss since if a person does not observe the majority of the Torah, he will be considered evil. This is false, since in the end, a person benefits through just having the receptivity to [a] Torah which includes many mitzvot [and not fewer]. [This is] because whether a person will observe mitzvot or not is undecided – perhaps he will observe [them]! And since this is undecided, this [other] matter, that is the preset receptivity to a Torah of many mitzvot, is that which tips the scales, for this[25] is a great merit.[26]

ודבר זה יתבאר לקמן כי זה מסגולת נפשם של ישראל שהם מוכנים אל המצוות, ואם היצר הרע מתגרה בהם מכל מקום מצד עצם נפשם מוכנים אל התורה. ולפיכך אמרו (סנהדרין צ' ע"א)

And this matter will be explained

23. Rav Hartman notes here that he could not find the correlate to this reference.

24. The Jewish people's.

25. The receptivity alone.

26. The Maharal says that since one's observance of mitzvot is an uncertainty (dependent on human choice), the certainty of the extra receptivity is considered an immediate benefit. This is reminiscent of the Talmudic rule, "certainty is preferable to uncertainty." See K'tubot 12b.

כל ישראל יש להם חלק לעולם הבא מפני הכנתם אל התורה ויותר מזה אמרו (שם ק"י ע"ב) שאפילו קטן שנולד יש לו חלק לעולם הבא כמו שיתבאר, ואין זה רק מצד שלמות בריאתו בעצמו שהוא מוכן אל התורה ולכך זוכה לעולם הבא.

ולפיכך אמר רצה הקדוש ברוך הוא לזכות את ישראל לפיכך הרבה להם תורה ומצוות שבמה שיש להם רבוי מצוות הוא זכות להם בודאי.

later,[27] for it is one of the virtues of the soul of Israel – that they are receptive to the mitzvot – and if the inclination to Evil incites them [towards evil], nevertheless, from the aspect of the essence of their soul, they are receptive to the Torah. And therefore, they [the sages] said,[28] "Every Jew has a portion in the World to Come," [which is] due to their[29] receptivity to the Torah. More than this, they[30] said,[31] that even a baby that is [just] born has a portion in the World to Come, as will be explained,[32] and this can only be due to the perfection of his creation in and of himself [without any growth or positive choice] in that he is receptive to [and capable of observing] the Torah and thus he merits the World to Come.

And therefore, [Rabbi Chanani'ah said that] "The Holy One, Blessed be He, desired to accord merit to Israel, therefore, He multiplied Torah and mitzvot for them," since due to the fact that they have a multitude of mitzvot, it is definitely a merit for them.

27. See the end of Chapter Twelve.
28. Sanhedrin 90a.
29. The Jewish people.
30. Our sages.
31. Sanhedrin 110b.
32. See the Introduction to Derech Chaim, the Maharal's commentary on Pirkei Avot (the Ethics of the Fathers). Also see the Maharal's comments above in Chapter Three.

SUMMARY

Chapter 5: 2/3

I. Explanation of "Has no positive act ever come your way": continued from earlier in the chapter

A. The Maharal's explanation is that the idea illustrated by the dialogue between Rabbi Yossi and Rabbi Chanina is not that one positive act alone can guarantee a person entry to the World to Come, rather, it is that certain acts are *indications* of the fact that the person doing them is so righteous that they have definitely already merited entry.

B. The Maharal now implements this idea in the story of Rabbi Chanina and Rabbi Yossi.

1. Rabbi Chanina's act was that his money for his Purim feast was swapped, in error, with charity money and he gave his money to the poor. When he discovered his error, he didn't reimburse himself from the charity money.
2. The Maharal explains the story as follows:
   a. Purim and its feast
      (1) Purim is a day without holy-day sanctity.
      (2) Therefore, the Purim feast is purely physical and is wholly of this world.
   b. Money for the poor
      (1) The poor have no portion in the physical world.
      (2) Money for the poor symbolizes the opposite of the physical, that is, the World to Come.
   c. The fact that Rabbi Chanina was prepared to swap his Purim-feast money (money of this world) for Charity money (money of the World to Come) showed that he was prepared to exchange all he had in the physical world for a portion in the World to Come. Such a person is clearly already a citizen of the World to Come.

C. Thus, this story does not support the Rambam's thesis that a single act can win entry to the World to Come, rather it shows how one act can shed light on a person's entire personality.

II. The Maharal's explanation of how more mitzvot equates to more merit for the Jewish people

A. The ability inherent within the nation to perform the mitzvot is implanted within them by Hashem according to the number of mitzvot that they are commanded to perform.

1. Hashem ensures that we have a receptivity to the mitzvot. So, the more mitzvot we have to do, the more He prepares us and implants within us the special receptivity to them and the spiritual capabilities to carry them out.
2. Therefore, if we have more mitzvot, we must have greater spiritual capacities which grants more merit.

B. The Maharal now brings two proofs of this idea
   1. A Jewish child just born gains entry into the World to Come without having performed any mitzvot – this must be due to the fact that the child's in-built receptivity already confers merit on him.
   2. Those Jews who live outside of Israel in the exile cannot be said to have no reward whatsoever from the mitzvot which can only be performed in Israel. Rather, since we immerse ourselves in Torah as a whole, we have this greater receptivity to all of the Torah, and due to our receptivity we gain some merit, at the very least, even for the mitzvot which we cannot perform for practical reasons.

III. Addressing the original difficulty

A. The original difficulty which the Maharal raised with the concept that "more mitzvot entails more merit" was that more mitzvot also entails more opportunity to fail.

B. The Maharal's explanation resolves this difficulty as follows:
   1. The receptivity to mitzvot which Jews have is a given and bestows immediate and definite beneficence and merit.
   2. The possible actualized fulfillment of mitzvot, or alternatively, the actualized failure in mitzvot is an unknown. Since it is dependent on human choice, the matter could swing either way and therefore, out of the two options, the definite one is dominant: definite merit bestowed by receptivity is seen to be preferable to questionable merit or demerit through actual success or failure.

CHAPTER 5

Part 3 of 3

Till this point, the Maharal has given his first explanation of Rabbi Chanani'ah's famous statement,[1] an explanation which focuses on the merit granted to Israel through their receptivity to mitzvot. The Maharal will now examine the simpler explanation for the statement of Rabbi Chanani'ah – which is that indeed, having more mitzvot bestows more merit through the actual performance of the mitzvot, not the receptivity to mitzvot.

ואפילו אם תאמר כמשמעו לא קשיא מידי.

And even if you will say [that the meaning of the saying is] as its [simple] meaning,[2] there is no difficulty at all.

First, the Maharal establishes that there is no shortcut to gaining merit – since G-d manages the world on the basis of justice, one cannot have more merit without achieving more.

שהרי אין לומר שיתן להם מעט מצוות ויהיה להם השכר הגדול שדבר זה לא יתכן כלל שלא היה זה משפט ישר כי לפום צערא אגרא. ומכל שכן לפי מה שנתבאר כי התורה הוא צרוף וזיכוך ישראל ולפי רוב המצוה הוא צירוף וזיכוך שלהם.

[Firstly,] one cannot say that Hashem should have given few mitzvot with much reward: this is impossible because this would not be honest justice – since [such actions would contradict the central premise of] "according to the pain [of toil] is the gain."[3, 4] And how much more so [does this hold true] since, according to what has been explained[5] that the Torah is the purification and

1. This was cited earlier in Chapter Five, that "The Holy One, Blessed be He, desired to accord merit to Israel, therefore, He multiplied Torah and mitzvot for them."

2. That the merit lies not in the preset receptivity to the mitzvot (which is more of a potential), but rather in the actual performance of the mitzvot. See the Commentary, Ch. 5 § Point 3 on the need for this second answer.

3. I.e., reward.

4. Avot 5:26. This idea is central to the Torah's morality – that one cannot receive reward unearned and that any demerit is directly proportional to one's misdeeds. See the Commentary, Ch. 5 § Point 5.

5. See Chapter Two.

refining of Israel, and [therefore] according to the increase in amount of mitzvot, so, too, is their purification and refinement.[6]

If so, it is definite that an increase of the mitzvot is good for them.

The Maharal now addresses the original question first advanced against this simple explanation and he brings two answers. The question was that more mitzvot also means greater scope for failure. The first answer to this challenge is that even if more mitzvot means greater challenge for some individuals, for the collective nation of Israel, it is still better to have more mitzvot and greater receptivity to Torah.

א"כ בודאי רבוי המצוות טובה להם.

ואם אתה אומר הרי יצא שכרן בהפסדן שכאשר לא יקיים המצוה יהיה לאדם עונש בודאי.

אילו אמר רצה הקדוש ברוך הוא לזכות את האדם היה זה שאלה שאפשר שאין זה זכות לאדם, אבל אמר רצה לזכות את ישראל כי אף אם היה יותר טוב לאדם הפרטי שלא יהיה לו הרבה מצוות אבל לכלל ישראל כבר אמרנו למעלה בפרק א' כי כלל ישראל מוכנים ומסוגלים לתורה, והוא יתברך נותן התורה לכל ישראל והוא זכות להם ואם יש אחד פורה ראש ולענה העולם נדון אחר הכלל וכלל ישראל מוכנים לתורה ומצוות מצד עצמם.

ומכל שכן שאין במציאות זה היחיד שלא היה חפץ במצוות, כי דור התורה אמרו נעשה ונשמע, והדורות הבאים אחריהם אותו אשר יאמר שאינו חפץ ה' אינו נחשב מן המציאות ואם כן בודאי חפץ ה' לזכות את ישראל ברבוי מצוות.

And if you say [as was raised earlier], "Their reward is offset by their loss [since having so many mitzvot also allows one so many more opportunities to fail and sin], since when a person will not observe the mitzvot, he will definitely be punished!"; [the correct response is as follows.]

This question would be pertinent had [Rabbi Chanani'ah] said, "The Holy One, Blessed be He desired to accord merit to *the human being*." But [he did not say this] rather he said, "[The Holy One, Blessed be He] desired to accord merit to *Israel*," for even if it would be better for the individual human being not to have many mitzvot [nevertheless] we have already said (above, Chapter One) that the congregation of Israel [as a collective] is receptive to [and capable of] the Torah. And Hashem, may He be Blessed, grants the Torah to all of Israel and this is a merit to them. If there is someone who is a "root flourishing with gall and wormwood"[7] [who will not choose to observe the mitzvot, despite his innate receptivity despite this] the world[8] is evaluated according to the community, and the community of Israel is receptive to [and prepared for] Torah and mitzvot in and of themselves.

And how much more so that such an individual [who rejects Torah and

6. See the Commentary, Ch. 5 § Points 1 and 4.
7. D'varim 29:17.
8. I.e., the situation.

mitzvot, despite his innate receptivity] is not considered as part of the reality [of the Jewish people], for the generation [which accepted] the Torah said, "We will do [what Hashem commands] and [then] we will hear."[9] So, if in the generations which proceed them, an individual arises who has no desire for Hashem, such an individual is not considered to be part of the reality [of "Israel"]. Therefore, definitely, Hashem desires to accord merit to *Israel* through multiplying mitzvot.[10]

The Maharal now brings his second answer which is that the merit that Hashem conferred on us (through giving us many mitzvot) can sometimes be against the will of particular individuals, but the merit is still bestowed even forcefully.

ועוד כי עיקר הפירוש שרצה השם יתברך לזכות את ישראל היינו שרצה לזכות אותם בעל כרחם ברבוי המצוות.

Moreover, the essence of the [above] explanation of [the statement that], Hashem, may He be Blessed, desired to accord merit to Israel is that He desired to accord them merit through multiplication of mitzvot [*even*] against their will.

ואף אם יש לחוש שלא יקיימו המצוות מכל מקום השם יתברך רצה לזכות אותם בעל כרחם ברבוי מצוות.

And even if one were to have misgivings that they [the Jewish people] would not observe the mitzvot, nevertheless, Hashem, may He be Blessed, desired to accord merit to them against their will, through multiplication of the mitzvot.

The Maharal now details the merit that Hashem conferred on us (through giving us many mitzvot): it is the opportunity to purify and uplift ourselves. This is not an external addition to our lives but rather it is a natural effect within a causal system: the more one actively attempts to perfect oneself, the more one is purified. Thus it is impossible to have less mitzvot and still reach the same level of elevation and enlightenment.

והשואלים שהיה ראוי למעט במצוות חושבים כי אפשר לזכות במעוט מצוות כמו ברבוי מצוות ודבר זה לא יקבל הדעת וימאן השכל, והוא דבר מוסכם

And those who ask that it would have been suitable [for Hashem] to minimize the number of mitzvot, think that it is as possible to accord [the same] merit

9. Sh'mot 24:7.

10. See the Commentary, Ch. 5 § Point 6. In short, the Maharal is saying that, as a collective entity, Israel definitely benefits from the larger number of mitzvot. Some individuals therein may not benefit, but by their choice not to connect to the destiny of Israel, they exclude themselves from the rubric, "Israel," and thus, the statement, "the Holy One, Blessed be He, desired to accord merit to Israel" does not apply to them anyway.

through a small number of mitzvot as through a large number of mitzvot. [However] this [idea] is unacceptable to the mind and the intellect rejects it and it is [an] agreed upon [principle][11] that "according to the pain [of toil] is the gain."[12]

And it will be explained in the chapter following this [one] that the mitzvot are a purification and refining of the human being, and a person will gain more refinement through [having] more mitzvot than he will gain through having less mitzvot, for this is the essence [of the reason] for the giving of the Torah and mitzvot – that the human being will have deeds and actions which refine his [material] soul[13] and [which will aim] to make the [material] soul pure and transcendent. For without this [aim], the "pre-eminence of humans over animals is nothing,"[14] for the human being would be [as] material-natural as an animal is.

If so,[15] how can this matter not be clear, that the large number of mitzvot is a merit for a human being? It is absolutely simple! And He, may He be Blessed, wished to accord them merit, as a father who admonishes and rebukes his child in order to grant him merit. And if the child says that he does not desire this, nevertheless, the father accords him the merit against his will. So too, Hashem desired to accord merit to Israel and therefore gave [them] the yoke of mitzvot in order to accord [them] a large amount of merit.

[Now] the question, regarding that which the sages[16] said, "The Holy One, Blessed be He, desired to accord merit to Israel, therefore, He multiplied Torah and mitzvot for them," has been resolved.

לפום צערא אגרא.

ויתבאר בפרק שאחר זה כי המצוות הם צירוף וזיכוך האדם ויותר יש לו צירוף ברבוי המצוות ממה שיש לו במעוט המצוות, כי זהו עיקר מה שנתנה תורה ומצוות שיהיו לאדם פעולות ומעשים אשר מצרפים נפשו החמרית ולעשות הנפש זך ונבדל ואם לא כן מותר האדם מן הבהמה אין כי היה האדם חמרי טבעי כמו הבהמה.

ואם כן איך לא יהיה הדבר הזה ברור כי רבוי המצוות הם זכות לאדם עד שהוא דבר פשוט בתכלית והוא יתברך רצה לזכות אותם כמו האב שהוא מייסר ומוכיח את בנו לזכותו ואם הבן אומר שאינו חפץ בזה מכל מקום האב מזכה אותו בעל כרחו וכך ה׳ רצה לזכות את ישראל לכן נתן עול מצוות כדי לזכות ביותר.

והותרה השאלה במה שאמרו רצה הקדוש ברוך הוא לזכות את ישראל ולפיכך הרבה להם תורה ומצוות.

11. I.e., axiom, as mentioned previously in the chapter.

12. Avot 5:26.

13. In Hebrew, "*nefesh*," נפש. See the Commentary, Ch. 5 § Point 7.

14. Kohelet 3:19.

15. That mitzvot are a means of refining and purifying the human being so that he can become transcendent.

16. Lit., "they."

SUMMARY

Chapter 5: 3/3

I. The Maharal's second explanation of Rabbi Chanani'ah's saying

A. The explanation

1. This explanation focuses on the simple level of meaning – that receiving more mitzvot to perform bestows more merit through the actual performance of the mitzvot.
2. The Maharal brings two reasons that there is no other way for Israel, the nation, to receive the merit it requires except through more mitzvot:
   a. Judaism rests on the principle of exact justice – that one receives reward commensurate with one's efforts only. Anything else is unjust. Thus one could never possibly have fewer mitzvot and earn the same merit.
   b. Mitzvot in essence are more than just merit-earning tasks, they are means to upliftment, empowerment and refinement. In this sense, the "merit" one receives is not some disconnected reward, but rather a *natural consequence*.
      (1) This is the more profound view of reward and punishment, seeing the idea of natural cause and effect being an echo of an ultimate spiritual cause and effect system. This spiritual cause and effect system gives rise to the positive and negative consequences of all human activity.
      (2) As such, there is no way that one can circumvent the requirement for greater effort in mitzvot to achieve the same refinement.

B. Dealing with the classical question

1. How does this second explanation deal with the question that as much as having more mitzvot *potentially* allows one to gain more merit, it *equally* allows one to gain more demerits through added opportunities for failure? At the very least, one should say that having more mitzvot adds more merit *and* demerit!
2. The Maharal offers two answers:
   a. His first answer is that Rabbi Chanani'ah's idea is expressed exactly, as: "The Holy One, Blessed be He, desired to accord merit to *Israel* . . ."
      (1) The claim is not that having more mitzvot bestows more merit on each *individual*: it could very well be that many individuals do not necessarily gain more merit through the

additional mitzvot. Rather, Israel the nation, as an organic composite-entity gains the merit.

(2) Moreover if an individual Jew rejects Torah, he is thus rejecting identifying himself with Jewish destiny (which is the playing out of the covenant made with G-d at Sinai) and is thus not included under the rubric, "Israel," and thus the statement "desired to accord merit to Israel" does not apply to him.

b. The Maharal's second answer is that the plain meaning of the statement is that Hashem "desired to accord merit to Israel" which implies that this happens even against the will of the individuals within the nation and possibly even to their detriment.

3. The Maharal deals with the question of whether it could have been possible to accord the same merit through fewer mitzvot.

a. The Maharal rejects this for three reasons:

(1) It is illogical.

(2) The other two reasons are cited above.

b. Hashem desired us to be refined (this is the merit we gain) and the mitzvot accomplish this for us. Just as a father, through setting appropriate boundaries and goals for a child, helps the child grow even against the child's will (if necessary), so too the mitzvot help refine us, even against our will.

CHAPTER 6

CHAPTER 6

Part 1 of 4

The Maharal now begins exploring how it is possible that mitzvot, which are comprised in part[1] of physical actions, could have such a tremendous effect on the human soul which is non-physical and transcendent. A second question is how mitzvot could generate reward in the non-physical World to Come. The Maharal makes it clear that these questions were originally posed by people he terms "philosophers" whose method he criticizes for its lack of reliance on Torah;[2] but he nevertheless is prepared to offer the Torah's response. This chapter is the first of a series stretching till Chapter Nine which discusses these issues.

יש מבני אדם והם אנשי חקרי לב ההולכים בדרכי הפילוסופים חוקרים מדעתם ושכולם על כל הדברים.

תמוה בעיניהם מאד בענין המצוות המעשיות שיזכה האדם הצלחה נצחית בעולם הנבדל על ידי המצוה שהוא גשמית.

ואמרו כי מה יועיל מעשה הגשמי אל הנפש לקנות על ידי זה שתחיה נצח בעולם הנבדל במקום שאין שם מעשה גשמי.

There are those people, the people who have searching hearts,[3] who walk in the ways of the philosophers [and] who investigate all things through their own opinion and mind.

In their eyes, the matter of [physically] practiced mitzvot is very bewildering: [they ask how it is possible] that a person should merit eternal success in the transcendent [non-physical] world through [the performance of] a mitzvah, which is physical.

[Secondly,] they have exclaimed, "How can a physical act aid the soul in acquiring eternal life in the transcendent world, which is a place in which there is no physical activity?"[4]

It is clear that some of the mitzvot have ethical and moral aims which are apparent to all and some of them are directed at the thoughts we think and the emotions we feel. It is possible to understand how such mitzvot could affect the soul through the values they seek to implant. The perplexing question is how other mitzvot, which do

---

1. The other components of a mitzvah are one's intentions, thoughts and feelings at the time of performing the mitzvah.
2. See the Commentary, Ch. 6 § Point 4.
3. Cf. Shof'tim 5:16.
4. The question is how physical acts could affect one's spiritual destiny. See the Commentary, Ch. 6 § Points 3 and 7.

not have such aims explicitly, can have an effect on the soul. Another question is that if certain mitzvot prevent the acquisition of negative values, it would be impossible to find exceptions to them, but we do find such exceptions.

Moreover, they are astonished [by the following]: *if* the mitzvot were *all* [aimed at implanting] positive values within the soul of a human, like the mitzvah of *tz'dakkah*,[5] and [like] the mitzvah not to hate one's fellow in one's heart, and [like the mitzvah] not to stand [idly] by the blood of one's fellow and so on (which are all positive character traits which are positive values in the soul of the one who performs them), then it would be possible to say that [even though the mitzvot are physical acts,] a person would acquire positive values through them and would distance himself from evil. Then we could say that Hashem, may He be Blessed, confers reward upon those in whom is found goodness and [on the other hand, Hashem] repays evil to one who does evil.[6]

ויותר מזה הם מתמיהים כי אלו היו המצוות כולם תכונות טובות בנפש האדם כמו מצות צדקה ומצות לא תשנא אחיך בלבבך ולא תעמוד על דם רעך וכיוצא בהן מן המידות הטובות שהם תכונות טובות בנפש העושה, אפשר לומר דמכל מקום יקנה האדם על ידיהן תכונות טובות ומתרחק מן הרע, ונאמר כי השם יתברך נותן שכר טוב למי שנמצא בו הטוב ומשלם רע לעושה הרע.

אבל מצות שעטנז וכלאי זרעים, ומצות שחיטה מן הצואר ולא מן העורף ובמקדש מליקה מן העורף ולא מן הצואר.

אם מן העורף הוא מעשה רע למה נאסר השחיטה מן הצואר במקדש, ואם מן הצואר הוא טוב אם כן למה במקדש נמצא הפכו.

However, the mitzvot of *sha'atnez*[7] and *kilayim*,[8] and the mitzvah to slaughter an animal at the throat and not from the [back of] the neck, and [the mitzvah] in the Temple to slaughter a bird from the [back of the] neck and not at the throat [are not mitzvot which focus on the acquisition of positive traits. Therefore, how do they affect the soul]?

[Moreover,] if slaughtering from the [back of the] neck were evil [if that is why, in general, we are commanded to slaughter at the throat], why was slaughtering at the throat forbidden in the Temple [for birds, which could only be slaughtered at the back of the neck]? And if slaughtering at the throat is good, why do we find the opposite of this in the Temple?[9]

---

5. The commandment to provide Jewish social support; usually mistranslated as "charity."

6. But since mitzvot are not all focused on the acquisition of internal, positive character traits, such a position is untenable, which is what the Maharal goes on to explain.

7. The prohibition against wearing garments made of mixtures of wool and linen.

8. The prohibition against sowing mixed seeds in one patch of ground.

9. I.e., slaughtering birds from the back of the neck.

The Maharal explains why he feels no real need to answer the philosophers' question – since they do not have a self-contained and sufficient system for explaining anything. Moreover, even if they could explain natural phenomena consistently, the Torah is still transcendent and thus their system of explanation wouldn't apply anyway.

Behold, they[10] have tunneled out many ways to give a reason or hint [as to how physical mitzvot affect the soul] according to their opinion (which is far from the ways of the Torah); however, the ways of the sages and the secrets of Torah and the truth were revealed only to those who know the Torah.

And even though it is appropriate not to respond to their question at all, for what they seek to do is to give a [necessary and] sufficient reason for all of reality and if we could see that they could assign a reason even to the lower, natural elements [of existence], then it would be our duty to pay attention to their question [but they cannot, therefore, there is no reason to be mindful of their question]. And [furthermore] even though there is as much a difference as the height of the heavens above the earth between natural elements [of existence] (which are on the earth) and the Torah (which you will not even find in the heavens but rather is from the transcendent realm), nevertheless, it would still be our duty to heed their question [if they could provide reasons for even the natural elements]. But, matters do not stand so, since the philosophers cannot give us a reason or taste even for the natural elements [of existence] such as animals and even plants. How could one even entertain the idea that the philosophers could give a [necessary and] sufficient reason for the number of sinews and component-limbs within every animal – the reason and unique description for each one! So too for the plants.

והנה הם חתרו דרכים הרבה לתת סבה וטעם כפי דעתם אשר הוא רחוק מדרכי התורה ומדרכי החכמים, ויודעי התורה אליהם בלבד נגלו מצפוני החכמה והאמת.

ואף כי מן הראוי שלא להשיב על שאלתם כלל, כי ד"ז מה שרוצים לתת סבה מחייבת בכל הדברים, אילו היינו רואים שנתנו לנו סבה בכל הדברים הטבעיים הפחותים מאד היה מוטל עלינו לתת לב על שאלתם, ועם כי הבדל יש כגבוה שמים מעל הארץ, כי הדברים הטבעיים הם בארץ והתורה לא תמצא אף בשמים כי אם מעולם העליון, מכל מקום היה מוטל עלינו לתת לב על השאלה. אך אין הדברים כך כי הדברים הטבעיים כמו הבעלי חיים ואף הצמחים אין נותנים לנו סבה וטעם, כי איך יעלה על הדעת שיתנו סבה מספקת לכל בעל חי מספר גידיו ואבריו לכל אחד סבה ותארו המיוחד וכן לצמחים.

ואל תשגיח ברופאים ובחכמי הטבע שאם נתנו סבה הוא לאחד מני אלף, ואף אשר נתנו אין כן האמת הברור כמו שידוע למי שיעיין בדבריהם.

10. I.e., the philosophers.

And pay no attention to the doctors and the sages of nature, for if they have given reasons, it is for one [element of existence] out of a thousand; and even the reasons that they gave are not the clear truth, as is known to one who ponders their words.

The philosophers attempted to discover a theory explaining the essential reason for the existence of every element in creation.[11] The Maharal is saying that since the philosophers cannot explain simple, material matters, there is no need to try to humor them by providing an explanation of mitzvot which belong to an infinitely higher, transcendent realm. This is because their method and assumptions are problematic and answering questions flowing from these assumptions may not necessarily be fruitful.

ואם הדבר הזה הוא בדברים הטבעיים כל שכן בדברים א־להיים והם המצוות הא־להיות אשר חייב האדם לפעול, למה יעשה פעולה זאת ולא יעשה פעולה אחרת, כשם שלא נדע גופו ותוארו אשר הוא קיומו בעה"ז לא נדע על השלמות, ואם לא היה נברא על זה התאר לא היה לו חיותו ושלמותו הגופני שיהיה מקוים וכל שכן פעולות הא־להיות המביאים את האדם אל החיים הנצחיים אף אם לא נדע באיזה ענין ולמה הם בענין הזה אין זה פלא.

והנה לא היתה זאת שאלת החכמים שמחויבים אנחנו בתשובתה, אם לא שהיו נותנים לנו סבות בכל הדברים הטבעיים באדם ובצמחים ודבר זה אינו נמצא.

אבל דרכי החכמים יודעי התורה ומצפוניה לא נעלים ובזה תעמוד על דרכי התורה.

If this is the case regarding natural elements [of creation], how much more so does it hold true for G-dly elements which are the G-dly mitzvot which a person is obligated to perform, that is, why a person should perform one action and not another. Just as we do not completely know [and understand] the body and description [of the human being] (which constitutes one's existence in this world) and if a person had not been created with this description, he would not have existence and bodily completion (which allows him to exist); how much more so [do we not understand] G-dly actions which bring a person to eternal life.[12] Even if we do not understand some [spiritual] matter and why [the mitzvot are as] they are, it is no wonder that this is the case [since we understand so little even about earthly, physical matters].

Now, we would be obligated to answer this question of the wise men[13] [how physical mitzvot can have spiritual effects] if they could offer reasons

11. Compare with the Rambam's Moreh N'vuchim (The Guide for the Perplexed) 3:13.

12. As opposed to physical life.

13. I.e., philosophers.

for all natural elements in humans and fauna, but they cannot [offer such reasons].[14]

However, we will not hide the ways of the sages who know the Torah and its secrets, and through this you will ascertain the paths of the Torah.

The Maharal now embarks on a lengthy exposition of the reason, in general, for Hashem's giving us the mitzvot. He uses the Mishnah and Gemara in B'rachot as a springboard to explain his views.

תנן בפרק אין עומדין (ברכות ל"ד: [צ"ל ל"ג:]):

We have learned in a Mishnah,[15] in the Chapter, "One doesn't stand" as follows,[16]

האומר על קן צפור יגיעו רחמיך ועל טוב יזכר שמך מודים מודים משתקין אותו ע"כ.

We should tell a person to be silent if he says, "Your[17] mercy extends [even] to the nest of a bird!"[18] or [if he says,] "Your name will be remembered for the good [that You do]!" or if he says, "We thank, we thank!"

וקאמר בגמרא:

The Gemara explains there,[19]

בשלמא מודים מודים מחזי כשתי רשויות.

ועל טוב יזכר שמך נמי דמשמע על הטובה ולא על הרעה ותנן חייב לברך על הרעה כשם שמברך על הטובה.

אלא על קן צפור יגיעו רחמיך מאי טעמא [לא] פליגי בה תרי אמוראי במערבא ר' יוסי בר אבין ור' יוסי בר זבידא חד אמר מפני שמטיל קנאה במעשה בראשית.

The reason that we tell a person to be silent for saying, "We thank, we thank," is clear, since it sounds as if the person were addressing two different [divine] powers[20] [and thus denying G-d's singularity].

Similarly, it is clear regarding one who says, "Your name will be remembered for the Good [that You do]!"; [we silence a person who says this] since it implies that one will remember G-d's name for

14. And therefore, we have no need to answer their questions.

15. B'rachot 5:3.

16. The citation in the text of the Maharal is B'rachot 34b, but this seems to be a printing error as the actual source is 33b.

17. I.e., G-d's.

18. The reference to G-d's Mercy on a bird's nest refers to the mitzvah which regulates one's actions when stumbling across a bird's nest in the wild. It is a mitzvah to chase away the mother bird and take the chicks. It is prohibited to take both the chicks and the mother bird. See D'varim 22:6–7.

19. B'rachot 33b.

20. This smacks of heresy, since G-d is the One and Only.

וחד אמר מפני שעושה מידותיו רחמים ואינם אלא גזרות ע"כ.

the good but not for evil;[21] however, we have learned in a Mishnah,[22] "A person is obligated to make a *b'rachah*[23] over evil just as he makes a *b'rachah* over good."[24]

However, it is unclear why we silence one who says, "Your mercy extends [even] to the nest of a bird!" There were two sages of the Talmud, in Israel, who disputed one another on this point – Rabbi Yossi Bar Avin and Rabbi Yossi Bar Z'vida. One said, "The reason is that [if one says 'Your mercy extends [even] to the nest of a bird!'] he is placing jealousy in the creation of the world [by saying the Hashem has mercy on some species but not on others]."

The other said, "[The reason one shouldn't say such things is that] such a person is making Hashem's attributes [due to] mercy when, in fact, they are exclusively decrees!"

The Maharal explains the dispute of Rabbi Yossi bar Avin and Rabbi Yossi bar Z'vida regarding a person who says, "Your mercy extends [even] to the nest of a bird!" First, the Maharal explains the position of Rabbi Yossi Bar Avin. Rabbi Yossi posits that the problem is that such a person is claiming that this mitzvah is generated by Hashem's attribute of Mercy. This further implies that Hashem is selectively merciful. Rabbi Yossi disputes both of these points, claiming that Hashem's Mercy extends to all of creation and that furthermore, the mitzvot are decrees from Hashem, not outgrowths of His Mercy.

וביאור ענין זה שא"ל על קן צפור יגיעו רחמיך, דמשמע כי המצוה הזאת צוה השם יתברך מצד שהוא מרחם על קן צפור, ובזה עושה חלוק ופרוד בין הנמצאים עד שאין העולם אחד כי למה ירחם על קן צפור ולא ירחם על מינים אחרים?

The explanation of this matter[25] is that one cannot say "Your mercy extends [even] to the nest of a bird!" because it implies that Hashem commanded this mitzvah since He has mercy on the nest of the bird and thus Hashem is creating a difference and separation between all that exists to the point that the world is no longer unified! Why should He have mercy on the nest of birds and not on any other species of animal?

Clearly, however, if they[26] are [exclusively] decrees which He decreed in

21. This also implies that G-d is not responsible for evil occurrences but that some other power is. Such a view is also heretical since G-d alone is responsible for everything in this world – both good and evil.

22. B'rachot 9:5.

23. Benediction, ברכה.

24. A *b'rachah* is an acknowledgement of the source of an event – both good and evil are acknowledged equally as having their source in G-d.

25. I.e., the first opinion

26. I.e., mitzvot.

His wisdom, there is no such difficulty, for [one could say that] this is the matter of the decree: that He decreed regarding this species only and not regarding any other; just as the species themselves are differentiated, that this is one species and that is another, so too one can say that one law applies to this species and another law applies to the other species.

However, regarding the attribute of [Hashem's] Mercy, [we believe that] all of Hashem's works are equally suitable for [receiving] mercy and if so, why did Hashem take mercy specifically on this species?[27] This would be a separation and differentiation in the species – that one species would have this thing from Hashem, may He be Blessed, while other species would not.

דודאי אם הם גזרות שגזר בחכמתו כך אין זה קושיא, כי כך ענין הגזרה שגזר בזה דוקא ולא באחר, כמו שהמינים מחולקים בעצמם שזה מין זה וזה מין אחר, כך יש לומר במין זה נוהג ד"ז ובמין זה נוהג ד"א.

אבל מדת הרחמים כל מעשיו ראוים לרחמנות בענין אחד ואם כן למה ריחם על זה דוקא והיה זה פרוד וחלוק במינים שיש דבר במין זה אצל השם יתברך מה שאין כן במינים אחרים.

The Maharal now explains that according to Rabbi Yossi bar Z'vida, the problem with a person who says, "Your mercy extends [even] to the nest of a bird!" is that such a person is claiming that Hashem's Mercy is the central factor in directing the universe, whereas in fact, it is Hashem's attribute of Justice which is the primary director. It is crucial to differentiate between these two concepts. "Justice" is what *must* happen in the world since Hashem, as the ultimate lawmaker, has created laws for the natural world as well as the moral world: there are exact and consistent consequences to particular actions. Thus in the world of Justice, all goodness is the natural consequence of good actions and all bad is the automatic consequence of bad actions. "Mercy" describes a paradigm in which Hashem may bestow goodness on an undeserving recipient.

When the Maharal states that the mitzvot flow from the attribute of "Justice", he means that mitzvot are part of what is appropriate, right and necessary in the world.

According to [the second opinion, that is] the one who says "The reason is that such a person is making Hashem's attributes [due to] Mercy when, in fact, they are exclusively decrees!", the explanation [of this] is that it is not suitable that the [primary] attribute by which Hashem consistently directs His world be Mercy; rather [He should direct] only through Justice and Decree.

ולמאן דאמר שעושה מידותיו רחמים ואינם אלא גזרות, פירוש שאין ראוי שיהיו מידות השם יתברך אשר הוא מנהיג עולמו בתמידות על ידי רחמים רק בדין ובגזרה.

כי הגזרה הוא לפי חכמתו יתברך ודבר זה ראוי למלך אשר מולך על הכל להנהיג באמת וביושר, אבל הרחמנות אין בו מדת אמת כי מרחם אף שאינו ראוי. ועם כי הוא יתברך עושה בודאי

27. I.e., birds.

רחמים עם הבריות מכל מקום עיקר המידה שהיא בתמידות הוא מדת הדין שבה מנהיג את עולמו.

ולכך תמצא בכל מעשה בראשית שם א־להים לפי שבראו בדין ומנהיגו בדין, רק ראה הוא יתברך שאי אפשר לעולם לעמוד בדין שתף עם הדין מדת רחמים, ומכל מקום הנהגה התמידית היא דין לפי שהוא יושר ודבר זה ראוי.

והאומר על קן צפור יגיעו רחמיך הוא עושה מידותיו שהוא יתברך מנהיג בהן עולמו רחמים שהוא מנהיג עולמו בתמידות ברחמים ודבר זה הוא יציאה מן היושר מה שאין ראוי.

This is because Hashem's decree flows from His wisdom, may He be Blessed, and such a thing is suitable for a king who rules over everything – that He direct through truth and honesty. But Mercy has no truth in it, for He has mercy even on those who are not worthy of it. Even though He, may He be Blessed, definitely has mercy on the creations, nevertheless, the central [single] attribute which operates constantly is the attribute of Justice, through which He directs His world.

Therefore, you will find throughout the whole of [the description of] the act of creation [that the name of G-d used in the description is] the name "*Elokim*,"[28] since G-d created the world through [His attribute of] Justice and He directs it through Justice. However, Hashem, may He be Blessed, saw that the world would be unable to continue to exist through Justice alone, therefore, He joined to it the attribute of Mercy.[29] Nevertheless [even after the merger of attributes], the [sole] *constant* attribute is Justice, since it is honesty and this is what is suitable.

However, one who says, "Your [G-d's] mercy extends [even] to the nest of a bird!" is changing Hashem's attributes through which He, may He be Blessed, constantly directs the world, into Mercy; and such a thing is a deviation from honesty, which is inappropriate [since G-d mainly directs the world through Justice which is "honest"].

---

28. See the Commentary, Ch. 6 § Points 5 and 6. As Rashi (B'reishit 1:1) points out, the name of G-d, Elokim, א־לוהים, is the name alluding to G-d's attribute of Justice.

29. Rashi (B'reishit 1:1) explains that the reason that the second chapter of B'reishit only refers to G-d by the compound name, Hashem-Elokim, יקוק-א־לוהים, is for the reason cited here in the Maharal, that the world needed a compound providential direction by the joint attributes of Mercy (designated by the name, Hashem, יקוק) and Justice (designated by the name Elokim, א־לוהים) because pure Justice would be too demanding a standard for fallible humans.

SUMMARY

Chapter 6: 1/4

I. The questions of the philosophers

A. The first two questions
   1. How can mitzvot, which are physical acts performed by physical beings, affect one's soul?
   2. How can such physical mitzvot generate reward in the spiritual, transcendent World to Come?

B. Partial solution
   1. Certain mitzvot clearly aid a person in acquiring positive character traits, for example, *tz'dakkah*. For these mitzvot, one could explain that due to the acquisition of positive traits, and distancing from evil, Hashem would reward a person in the World to Come.

C. The next two questions
   1. Not all mitzvot seem to focus on the acquisition of positive character traits. How do we explain these other mitzvot, for example, *sha'atnez* and *kilayim*?
   2. If we do claim that even these mitzvot ensure the acquisition of proper character traits, how do we explain that they allow one type of action in one context and forbid it in another – surely the action itself, when performed, will create the positive/negative trait.

II. The Maharal's rejection of the question

A. The question is part of a general endeavor on the part of philosophers to find a self-contained, rational, necessary and sufficient "reason" (or set of reasons) for everything in the world.
   1. They cannot, however, give such reasons for many of the lowest types of physical objects and phenomena.
   2. If they could assign such reasons even to the lowest of the physical, then the Maharal would feel duty-bound to answer their question regarding mitzvot, however they cannot.

B. The Maharal seems to be saying that it is clear that the method the philosophers are using is not actually working since they cannot explain even the simplest of things. Thus, he feels no need to explain mitzvot on their terms. He hints that the reason that this method can never reach the full truth is that it intentionally employs "pure" reason alone to arrive at conclusions but without Torah knowledge (which contains ultimate truth), it cannot arrive at truth.

C. Moreover, the mitzvot are in a completely different league to explaining mere physical objects, so even if they could explain every physical thing, it would still not create any obligation to use their method to explain mitzvot.

III. The Maharal agrees to explain the rationale behind the mitzvot according to the Torah

A. Mishnah B'rachot 5:3 (33b) and the Gemara there
   1. The Mishnah teaches us that we silence one who praises Hashem for having mercy on the mother bird (through His mitzvah not to take the mother bird and the chicks).
   2. The two explanations given in the Gemara (B'rachot 33b) for the need to silence such a person:
      a. Rabbi Yossi Bar Avin: such a person is placing jealousy in creation since he implies that Hashem has mercy on one species but not on the rest.
      b. Rabbi Yossi Bar Z'vida: such a person is explaining Hashem's mitzvot as results of His Mercy, as opposed to His decrees.

B. The Maharal's explanation of the Mishnah and the dispute between the two rabbis
   1. Rabbi Yossi Bar Avin: Placing jealousy
      a. Such a person is creating a differentiation between the components of Hashem's creation. This would not pose a problem if one accepted that Hashem's mitzvot were purely decrees as this would simply comprise one other differentiation between species akin to the natural differences He created; however, if a person is claiming that Mercy is the mechanism behind mitzvot, then it is difficult to understand why Hashem should only have mercy on one species, thus we silence him.
      b. He thus claims that Hashem is merciful to all His creations and that the mitzvot are not outgrowths of mercy, but are decrees.
   2. Rabbi Yossi bar Z'vida: Explaining Hashem's actions as functions of Mercy and not Justice
      a. Mercy doesn't operate consistently or truthfully since Hashem is merciful even to those undeserving thereof. Therefore, Hashem doesn't use Mercy as the primary means of directing the universe. Rather, Hashem directs the world through His Wisdom and Justice which are consistent and truthful.
      b. This is why the name of Hashem which appears in the description of the creation (in B'reishit, Chapter One) is "Elokim," which is the name of G-d alluding to His attribute of Justice. Even though the compound form, "Hashem-Elokim" (which is a com-

bination of Justice, "Elokim"; and Mercy, "Hashem"), appears in Chapter Two of B'reishit, it is only because Hashem foresaw that humans would not survive on unalloyed Justice.

c. A person who declaims that Hashem is running the world through mercy only is misrepresenting reality and thus we silence him.

CHAPTER 6

Part 2 of 4

The Maharal continues his discussion on the purposes of mitzvot. First he examines the comments of the Rambam on the Mishnah and Gemara in B'rachot which he cited previously in this chapter. This Mishnah and Gemara dealt with the mitzvah that enjoins one, when chancing upon a nest, not to take both the chicks/eggs and the mother bird, but rather to send away the mother bird first and then take the chicks/eggs. The Mishnah recorded the censure we direct at someone who comments regarding this mitzvah, "Your mercy extends [even] to the nest of a bird!"

The Rambam, *z"l*, wrote in his book, The Guide to the Perplexed, that,[1]

> . . . the reason for [the mitzvah of] sending away the mother bird is that most of the time, the eggs on which the mother [bird] is nesting and such young chicks which still require their mother, are not fit for consumption . . . and therefore, the majority of the time this will cause one to desist [and not take any eggs or chicks] since most of the time one will end up taking something unfit for consumption.
>
> And if the Torah took mercy upon the spiritual pain of animals and birds, how much more so for human beings. Do not question this by citing the statement [of the sages],[2] "We should tell a person to be silent if he says, "Your mercy extends [even] to the nest of a bird!" since this statement is only according to one of the two opinions which we have mentioned – the opinion that holds that there is no reason for the Torah except G-d's will.[3] However, we have followed the second opinion.

והרמב"ם ז"ל כתב בס' מו"נ (ח"ג פמ"ח):

כי טעם שלוח הקן כי הביצים ששוכבת אמם עליהם והאפרוחים הצריכים לאמם על הרוב אינם ראוים לאכילה וכו' ועל הרוב יהיה סבה להניח הכל כי מה שלוקח ברוב הפעמים אינו ראוי לאכילה.

ואם אלו הצערים הנפשיים חסה התורה עליהם בבהמות ועופות כל שכן בבני אדם. ולא תקשה על אמרם האומר על קן צפור יגיעו רחמיך וכו' כי הוא לאחד מב' דעות אשר זכרנו רצה לומר דעת מי שחושב שאין טעם לתורה אלא רצון הבורא יתברך ואנחנו נמשכנו אחר הדעה הב' ע"כ.

---

1. Moreh N'vuchim 3:48. See the Commentary, Ch. 6 § Point 9 for the complete text. See also the Commentary, Ch. 6 § Point 2 for the difference between the two key Rabbinic luminaries cited in this chapter, the Ramba*m* and the Ramba*n*."

2. Mishnah B'rachot 5:3. This was discussed at length by the Maharal previously in this chapter.

3. See the Commentary, Ch. 6 § Point 8. Also see the Commentary, Ch. 6 § Point

The Rambam explains that there is a dispute amongst sages as to whether one can say that there is any reason at all for mitzvot. The Rambam believes that one can ascribe some sort of reason for mitzvot, while some other sages believe that one can only say that mitzvot are a product of G-d's will. The Rambam's view is that the Mishnah is authored by sages holding the latter view who therefore censure a person who seems to give any type of reason for a mitzvah. The Rambam explains that we do not rule according to this latter view and therefore, we also do not espouse the need for censure expressed in the Mishnah. The Maharal now questions the Rambam's standpoint.

האמת כי יש להפליא הפלא ופלא על דברים אלו.

לומר על משנה שנויה בלי מחלוקת וגם היא שנויה בלשונה במסכת מגילה (כ"ה ע"א) והאמוראים פרשוה בטעמא ולא ראינו ולא שמענו פוצה פה ומצפצף נגדה ולומר על הכל שאינו הלכה וכל שכן דבר שהוא מגיע לאמונה.

The truth is that one should be completely astounded at these words [of the Rambam]!

How can the Rambam dismiss the halachic authority of this Mishnah which is brought without dispute and which is cited in its exact language in Tractate Megillah[4] and for which the *Amora'im*[5] actually gave explanations [which they would not have done if they disputed it, instead they would have marshalled arguments to prove its falsehood] and against which we have never even heard of anyone opening their mouths and even chirping! How can the Rambam[6] say that it is not the Halachah and how much more so when it comes to matters of faith!

As we saw, the Mishnah contained no opinion disputing the requirement to silence a person who says, "Your [G-d's] mercy extends [even] to the nest of a bird!" The only dispute we saw was in the Gemara in that there were two reasons given for this law but no-one disputed the law itself. The Maharal shows that the Mishnah is supported by the Amora'im's attempts to explain its reasoning as well as by its citation elsewhere without any counter-argument. In this light, the Rambam's declaration that the whole Mishnah is only one half of a widespread dispute is difficult to understand. The Maharal now continues with an exploration of the opinion of the Ramban[7] (not to be confused with the Rambam).

1 for a note on the terminology used here.

4. Megillah 25a.

5. The sages whose collective teachings on the Mishnah form the body of the Gemara.

6. Lit., "he."

7. Rabbi Moshe ben Nachman, otherwise known as Nachmanides. He lived from 1194 till 1270.

And the Ramban, *z"l*, in Parshat Ki Teitzei spoke at length on this matter and said that the reason for the mitzvah of sending away the mother bird is so that *we* do not become cruel (as he discussed at length there).[8] And this is his opinion [in general] regarding the mitzvot that Hashem, may He be Blessed, commanded to the nation whom He chose [that the purpose of the mitzvot is] to instill within them good character traits to benefit them; and Hashem, may He be Blessed, does not receive any benefit from this, rather it is only to benefit us and so on. This is the foundation of his opinion.

והרמב"ן ז"ל בפרשת תצא האריך מאד בענין זה ואמר כי טעם שלוח הקן שלא נתאכזר כמו שהאריך שם, וכן פירש טעם אותו ואת בנו שלא נתאכזר וזה דעתו במצוות שצוה השם יתברך להעם אשר בחר לקבוע בהם מידות טובות להטיב להם מבלי שהוא יתברך מקבל דבר טובה מזה רק להטיב לנו וגו' זהו יסוד דעתו.

The Maharal now questions the Ramban's opinion. The Maharal's question is that the Ramban's explanation (that the purpose of mitzvot is for humans to learn good traits) is not compatible with both opinions in the Gemara,[9] only the second one.[10] Each opinion presented a different principle which is violated when a person declares, "Your mercy extends [even] to the nest of a bird!" The problem is that it would seem that, according to the Ramban, this mitzvah in and of itself, without the person declaring anything, violates the first principle every time it is fulfilled.

According to the second opinion in the Gemara which says one should not "make Hashem's attributes into Mercy," the Ramban works well – the mitzvot are not because Hashem has mercy on birds, but because He decreed that *we* learn mercy, therefore Hashem, in His decree, can be selective and command us regarding birds only and not regarding other species.

But the Ramban's explanation doesn't work according to the first opinion. The principle cited there states that one should not "place jealousy" and create divisions between the creations. If the mitzvot are for us to learn mercy (as the Ramban claimed), whenever we fulfill this mitzvah, we are being selectively merciful and thus discriminating against certain species and violating this first principle.

Now even though it is not entirely appropriate to critique the great Rav, *z"l*,[11]

ועם כי אין ראוי להשיג על הרב הגדול ז"ל מכל מקום תורה היא וללמוד אנו צריכים.

8. Commentary on D'varim 22:6. See the Commentary, Ch. 6 § Point 10 for the full text of the Ramban.

9. These are the two opinions cited previously in this chapter – that of Rabbi Yossi bar Avin and Rabbi Yossi bar Z'vida – regarding why we censure a person who says, "Your [G-d's] mercy extends [even] to the nest of a bird!"

10. The Maharal does not explain why he feels that the Ramban cannot adopt only one of these two positions.

11. The Ramban.

כי גם בזה לא נחה דעתי ולא שקטה רוחי בקרבי, כי לא יתורץ למאן דאמר שלא יטיל קנאה במעשה בראשית שלא יעשה חלוק ופירוד בין הנמצאים שציוה שלא נתאכזר עם זאת ולא ציוה עם זאת.

nevertheless, this is Torah and we need to learn![12]

For my mind also cannot rest regarding this[13] and my soul is restless within me. [This restlessness is] because, according to the Ramban's explanation, there is no accordance with the [first] opinion in the Gemara which says that [the reason we silence a person who says "Your mercy extends [even] to the nest of a bird!" is because] "he is placing jealousy in the creation of the world" – which is implying that we should not make a differentiation and separation between the creations. [If we wish to preserve this principle,] how, according to the Ramban, could Hashem have commanded us [in the first instance] not to be cruel to certain species but then not commanded us regarding others? [Surely, if we are selectively kind, we are differentiating between the creations and thus violating this first opinion in the Gemara.]

The Maharal now suggests that one could deflect this criticism of the Ramban by saying that the first explanation, "placing jealousy in the creation of the world," is only a problem if Hashem is creating the jealousy; but here, Hashem isn't, humans are. If so, the Ramban's explanation fits with both opinions in the Gemara.

ואם כי יכול לומר שאין זה קנאה במעשה בראשית כיון שאין זה מצד השם יתברך רק מצד האדם, שציוה על האדם שלא להתאכזר עם זאת ולא ציוה על זאת.

The Ramban could answer that this is not "[placing] jealousy in the creation of the world" since, from Hashem's point of view, there is no distinction, just from the point of view of the human being who is only prohibited from this type of cruelty to one type of animals [birds] and not to others.

The Maharal is not completely satisfied with this solution and continues to question why any inter-species distinction would be needed. More particularly, the Maharal lists a host of contradictions between the reasons ascribed to certain mitzvot and what actually happens in practice. In so doing, he is questioning the entire enterprise of giving homocentric reasons for mitzvot.

---

12. This phrase, "It is Torah and we need to learn" is a paraphrase of a similar phrase which appears in B'rachot 62a regarding the actions of certain sages who, in their pursuit of Torah knowledge from their teachers, observed their teachers' behavior in private situations. Their explanation for such seeming disrespect was that, on the contrary, they only observed their teachers out of the utmost respect for the holiness and rectitude of their most minute actions in all circumstances. Here, too, the Maharal says that his dissent is borne of true respect.

13. I.e., the opinion of the Ramban.

אבל מכל מקום לא יצאנו ידי קושיא זאת כי למה ציונו על בריה זאת ולא צונו על אחרת. וכן באותו ואת בנו שגם כן נתן הרמב"ן ז"ל הטעם כדי לקבוע בנו מדת הרחמנות שלא נתאכזר עם בעלי חיים, אם כן קשיא דלמה אסר לנו בשור ושה והתיר לנו בחיה לשחוט אותו ואת בנו, והנה אין טעמו עולה בכל.

וכן ציוה אותנו שלא נתאכזר לשחוט אותו ואת בנו ביום אחד ואם שחט אחד בסוף היום ואחד בתחלת הלילה מותר ויש בזה אכזריות יותר מאחד שחרית והשני במנחה שאסור.

וצוה אותנו שלא נתאכזר אם האם יושבת על האפרוחים או על הביצים והתיר אם היא מעופפת על הקן.

ועוד באותו ואת בנו אם הטעם שלא נתאכזר למה התיר לנו בן פקועה כדאיתא במסכת חולין (ע"ד ע"א) וכי האכזריות מותר בו יותר וכן חלב בן פקועה מותר ושאר חלב אסור.

Nevertheless, we have [still] not escaped this difficulty – why did Hashem command us regarding this creature[14] and not others? So, too, regarding the [commandment not to slaughter] a mother animal and its offspring on the same day, for which the Ramban[15] also offered the reason [that the mitzvah comes] to set within us the trait of mercy – that we should not be cruel to animals: if so, there is a difficulty – why did Hashem prohibit us from behaving this way to cattle and sheep but allowed us this behavior with a kosher non-domesticated animal?[16] The Ramban's reason doesn't [seem to] fit all the situations.

So, too, Hashem commanded us that we should not become cruel by slaughtering a mother animal and its offspring on one day; however, if one would slaughter the one at the end of the day [at sunset] and then slaughter the other at the beginning of the night immediately following [which constitutes a different day halachically],[17] it would be permissible: but such an act contains more cruelty than slaughtering the one in the early morning and the other in the afternoon which is prohibited.

And Hashem commanded us that we should not become cruel [only] if the mother bird is nesting on the chicks or eggs, but He did permit them to us when the mother bird is hovering above the nest.

Moreover, regarding the commandment not to slaughter an animal and her progeny on the same day: if the reason was that we should not become cruel, why did the Hashem permit us to slaughter a female domesticated animal as well as its calf delivered [alive] after its death (as is cited in Tractate

---

14. I.e., not to be cruel to birds.

15. Commentary on D'varim 22:6.

16. See D'varim 14:5 where several non-domestic mammals are mentioned as being kosher, e.g., deer.

17. The Jewish day ends at nightfall, when the stars emerge and the next day begins then. Thus, the prohibition of slaughtering a cow and her calf on the same day would not apply if one killed the animals an hour apart as long as the one is killed before the end of the day and the other after the stars emerge.

Chullin 74a)?[18] Also, the *cheilev*[19] is permitted from such a calf delivered after the mother's slaughter but all other *cheilev* is forbidden.

The Maharal has pointed out that the reason given by the Ramban for many similar mitzvot (such as chasing away the mother bird and not slaughtering a domesticated animal and her progeny on the same day) does not necessarily explain the details of the mitzvot or why they entail distinctions between species. This seems to indicate the inadequacy of the Ramban's reason which is that these mitzvot seek to implant traits of kindness in us and to prevent us becoming cruel. In the end, the Maharal concludes that the reasons supplied by the Rambam and Ramban are not conclusive.

הא למדת כי הטעמים האלו שהם סברת הלב כאלו מצוות התורה הא־להיות כספר המידות בלבד אין בו ממש, כי לטעם אשר פירש הרמב"ן [עפ"י הרב הרטמן] ז"ל אין טעם לחלק.

We learn from this that these reasons are [merely] rationales [which are products] of the heart, as if the G-dly mitzvot of the Torah are merely like a book of [instruction as to how to acquire] good character traits but that the Torah has no real substance to its mitzvot, because, according to the reason which the Ramban explained, there is no reason to make a distinction [in all the cases which the Maharal cited above in his questions on the Ramban].

The Maharal continues his critique of the Ramban's position. He now examines how the Ramban explains the comments in the Gemara in B'rachot, in particular, the sub-phrase, "such a person is making Hashem's attributes [due to] Mercy." The Maharal points out that the Ramban's explanation does not fit with the complete phrase which concludes, "when, in fact, they are exclusively decrees!"

ומה שאמרו שאין מידות השם יתברך רחמים פירש הרמב"ן ז"ל כי אין מונע מאתנו לקיחת בעלי חיים לצרכנו.

דבר זה אין סובל הגמרא כלל מה שאמרו שעושה מידות השם יתברך רחמים ואינם אלא גזרות והוה ליה למימר שעשה ה' לרחם על הבהמה במקום שאינו מרחם.

The Ramban explained the position of our sages[20] [who said] that it is false that "Hashem's attributes [are due to] Mercy" by pointing out that Hashem does not prevent us from taking animals for our needs [which He would have done if He was acting out of mercy].

[However,] this explanation does not fit at all with the Gemara's language,

18. In the case where an animal was slaughtered and after slaughtering, it was found to contain a live calf, if that calf is delivered alive, the prohibition not to slaughter an animal and its calf on the same day does not apply.

19. Certain fats of kosher animals which are usually forbidden for consumption.

20. In the Gemara cited earlier in the chapter.

which explains, "[The reason we censure[21] is that] such a person is making Hashem's attributes [due to] Mercy *when, in fact, they are exclusively decrees!*" And if the Ramban's explanation were correct, the Gemara should have said, "The reason is that such a person is claiming that Hashem has mercy on animals, *when in fact, He does not.*"[22]

The Maharal now explains that the Ramban had an easier option for explaining this complete phrase.

אמנם מה שאמרו ז"ל שעושה מידות השם יתברך רחמים ואינם אלא גזירות לא קשיא כלל אף לפירושו.

וגם הרמב"ם ז"ל שהקשה מדבר זה ונדחק לומר כי המשנה אינה הלכה כמו שתראה מדבריו שדחה משנה ערוכה, אבל לא קשיא.

כי יש לפרש כי מה שאמרו חכמים ז"ל שאין מצוות השם יתברך רחמים ואינם רק גזירות, כלומר מה שציוה השם יתברך עלינו המצוות לא שיהיה השם יתברך מרחם על קן צפור וציוה בשביל כך שישלח האם, וכן אפילו באדם כאשר ציוה השם יתברך על הצדקה לא שהיה מרחם השם יתברך על העני וצוה לפרנסו, זה אינו שאם היה השם יתברך מרחם אפשר לו שירחם בעצמו ואין צריך לצוות את האדם רק המצוה גזר בגזירתו על האדם.

ומעתה נוכל לומר שהשם יתברך גזר בגזירתו שלא יתאכזר האדם רק האדם ירחם כי לא היה כונת רז"ל רק שלא יעשה מידות השם יתברך רחמים לומר כי המצוה על האדם בשביל שהיה הוא יתברך מרחם על קן צפור או שמרחם על העני ומכל מקום אפשר הוא ויכול להיות שגזר בגזירתו על האדם שלא יתאכזר האדם ולא קשה כלל. וכך פרשנו גם כן בחבור

However, [actually] there is no difficulty at all for the Ramban's explanation from the statement of our sages, *z"l*, that, "[The reason is that] such a person is making Hashem's attributes [due to] Mercy *when, in fact, they are exclusively decrees!*"

[Even though] the Rambam, *z"l*,[23] found this statement [so] difficult that he was forced to say that this Mishnah is not halachically authoritative (as you will see from his words)[24] and he rejected a set Mishnah, there is no problem from this [sub-phrase for the Ramban].

The reason [that the Ramban has no difficulty with this sub-phrase] is that one can explain that the intention of the sages', *z"l* (when they said that Hashem's mitzvot, may He be Blessed, are not [due to] Mercy but [are] Decrees) was that Hashem commanded us [to perform] the mitzvot *not* so that Hashem [can express His] Mercy on the nesting mother bird by commanding us to send away the mother. Similarly, even regarding humans, when Hashem, may He be Blessed, commanded us regarding the mitzvah of *tz'ddakah* [He did so] *not* because Hashem, may He be Blessed,

21. A person who says, "Your [G-d's] mercy extends [even] to the nest of a bird!"
22. See the Commentary, Ch. 6 § Point 11.
23. Maimonides, not to be confused with Ramba*n*, Nachmanides.
24. Cited above.

גור אריה בפרשת חקת.

had mercy on the pauper and therefore commanded us to support him. All such [reasoning] is false, for if Hashem had mercy [in these instances] he Himself could take mercy and He would have no need to command human beings. Rather, [the reason He commanded us to perform these mitzvot was *not due to His desire to express Mercy, but rather that] Hashem decreed the mitzvot on humanity through His decree.*

[If we posit that the mitzvot are generated purely as decrees,] we can say that Hashem decreed (through His decree) that we should perform the mitzvot in order that humanity should not become cruel and so that humanity should become merciful. The intention of our sages [when they said] that a person should not make Hashem's attributes [due to] mercy is to say that [one should not] claim that the mitzvot are placed upon humans *because Hashem has mercy* on the bird's nest and *because He has mercy* on a pauper. Nevertheless, it is possible and it could be that He decreed (by His decree) on human beings, that we should not become cruel. Thus, there is no difficulty at all. This is how we commented in our work, Gur Aryeh, on Parshat Chukat.[25]

The purpose of the entire previous paragraph was to show that the Ramban would have no issue with the text which states "in fact, they are exclusively decrees!" The Ramban's claim is that the purpose of these mitzvot is to help people become merciful and thus he would explain this text as saying, "The mitzvot are not an expression of Hashem's mercy on the beneficiary of the mitzvah (the bird or pauper) but they are an expression of His decree that human beings become merciful."[26]

ולפיכך אין אנו נוטים מפירוש הרב ז"ל מפני שקשה עליו המשנה האומר על קן צפור יגיעו רחמיך משתקין אותו, דזה לא קשיא כלל, רק כי פירושו אינו עולה כמו שהתבאר למעלה.

וכך מה שפירש הרב ז"ל שטעם המצוה לקבוע בנו הטוב שלא נתאכזר וכל המצוות הם לקבוע בנו מידות טובות וזהו ענין המצוות, גם כן אינו עולה.

Therefore, we do not deviate from the explanation of the Rabbi, *z"l*,[27] because he has difficulty with the Mishnah which says, "We should tell a person to be silent if he says, 'Your [G-d's] mercy extends [even] to the nest of a bird!'" because this is no difficulty at all. Rather, [the reason the Maharal rejects the Ramban's explanation is because] his explanation doesn't sit well as we explained above.

So, too, his explanation that the reason for this mitzvah is to set goodness within us so that we not become

25. Gur Aryeh on B'midbar 19:2.

26. See the Commentary, Ch. 6 § Points 11 and 12 for further exploration of these ideas.

27. The Ramban.

cruel and that the reason for all mitzvot is to set within us good character traits and that this is the substance of the mitzvot – [all this] doesn't fit [as we explained above].

The Maharal finally rejects the Ramban due to all the questions he asks above on the Ramban's position.

SUMMARY

Chapter 6: 2/4

I. **Understanding the rationale behind mitzvot: views of the Rambam and the Ramban**
   A. The Rambam's understanding of the mitzvah of sending away the mother bird
      1. The Rambam's view
         a. The Rambam claims that the mitzvah's rationale is because Hashem took mercy on the mother bird.
         b. This directly contradicts the Mishnah which states that we should tell anyone who says such a thing to be silent. The Rambam says that this Mishnah represents the viewpoint of those sages who declare that mitzvot have no rationale at all, while he is weighing in on the side of those who say that mitzvot do have rationales.
      2. The Maharal's rejection of the Rambam's view
         a. The Gemara never gives any indication that this Mishnah is part of the dispute the Rambam mentions. On the contrary, the Mishnah is:
            (1) Cited without dispute elsewhere in the Gemara.
            (2) Explained by two *Amora'im* who are supporting it and giving their understandings of the Mishnah's reasoning.
         b. If the Mishnah were disputed, the Gemara would say so as it does everywhere else!
   B. The Ramban's understanding of the mitzvah of sending away the mother bird
      1. The Ramban's view
         a. The Ramban claims that the mitzvah's rationale is to prevent human beings becoming cruel and so that we develop positive character traits such as mercy.
      2. The Maharal's questions on the Ramban's position
         a. Why does the Ramban contradict the first opinion in the Gemara?
            (1) The Ramban is at odds with the first opinion in the Gemara ("he is placing jealousy in the creation of the world"). The Ramban's explanation that we are commanded to send away the mother bird in order for us to learn mercy directly creates "jealousy" within the world by elevating one species (birds) above all others.

(2) A possible rebuttal of this problem
   (a) It is true that from the perspective of human beings, recipients of the mitzvot, there is a division created between species through this mitzvah. However, from Hashem's perspective there is no division.

b. According to the Ramban, why did Hashem command us not to be cruel only to certain types of animals?
   (1) This problem extends to the mitzvah of sending away the mother bird and to the prohibition against slaughtering a female kosher domesticated animal and its progeny on the same day.

c. If the purpose of these mitzvot was to prevent cruelty, why don't all the details of the mitzvot reflect this?
   (1) There are conditions within each of these mitzvot which, if not fulfilled, exempt one from the mitzvah and thus allow one to behave in a manner which is still ostensibly cruel. If the purpose of the mitzvah was to prevent cruelty, the mitzvah would not be so tightly constrained and would apply to wider situations.

d. The Ramban's explanation transforms the Torah from having independent substance into a book guiding a person, to a limited degree, in the acquisition of positive traits.

e. The Ramban explains that the second opinion in the Gemara ("such a person is making Hashem's attributes [due to] mercy when, in fact, they are exclusively decrees!") is supported by the fact that G-d allows us to take animals' lives, so we cannot say that the mitzvot are motivated by Hashem's mercy. However, his explanation ignores the final phrase, "when, in fact, they are exclusively decrees!"
   (1) A possible rebuttal of this problem
      (a) Even mitzvot which encourage the development of mercy were not commanded by Hashem due to His desire to take mercy on the object of the mitzvah. For example, Hashem did not command us to give charity to the pauper due to His mercy on the pauper. Rather, Hashem decreed that we perform the mitzvot so that we not become cruel and *this is a decree* (as opposed to an expression of Hashem's Mercy).

C. The Maharal rejects the Ramban's view due to these unanswered questions on the Ramban.

CHAPTER 6

Part 3 of 4

The Maharal continues his exploration of the general "reason" for mitzvot. The central question is whether Hashem decreed the mitzvot upon humans for human benefit or not. The Maharal claims that mitzvot were decreed because they are necessary and just, not out of Hashem's mercy on humanity. Nevertheless, the mitzvot do confer goodness and success on us.

אבל מדברי חכמים נראה שאין לומר כי המצוות שנתן השם יתברך בשביל המקבל שהוא האדם, רק הם גזירות מצד השם יתברך הגוזר על עמו גזירות כמו מלך הגוזר גזירה על עמו.

אף כי האמת ימשך מזה מצד שהוא מקיים הגזירה שגזר עליו הטוב וההצלחה שאין אחריה הצלחה. מכל מקום אין התחלת הגזירה שנתנה לטוב אל המקבל.

However, from the words of the sages, it seems that it is incorrect to claim that the mitzvot given by Hashem, may He be Blessed, are for the recipient (which is man); rather, the mitzvot are decrees emanating from Hashem, may He be Blessed, Who promulgates decrees on His nation, just as a king decrees a diktat on his nation.

Even though it is true that goodness and success (a success above all others) will flow from a person's fulfilling the decree which Hashem has decreed; nevertheless, the initiation of the decree is not for the purpose of benefitting the recipient.[1]

The Maharal now addresses several Torah sources which seem to contradict his idea above and which seem to claim that the actual reason for the mitzvot is, as the Ramban claimed, to benefit human beings.[2]

ומה שאמר הכתוב (דברים ו׳) ויצונו ה׳ א-להינו לעשות החקים האלה לטוב לנו, אין הפירוש שהוא יתברך צוה המצוות בשביל להטיב לנו שאין זה כך, רק הוא יתברך צוה עלינו כמלך הגוזר רק שהגזירה הזאת היא לטוב לנו לחיותנו כיום הזה אם נקיים המצוות

[On the other hand,] the Torah does say, "Hashem, our G-d, has commanded us to carry out these laws *for our good*,"[3] but this doesn't mean that Hashem, may He be Blessed, commanded us to do the mitzvot *in order* to benefit us – this is untrue; rather He, may He be Blessed,

1. I.e. human beings.
2. The Maharal explored the Ramban's position earlier in this chapter.
3. D'varim 6:24.

ולא שתחלת הגזירה הוא לטוב לנו.

ומה שאמר רצה הקדוש ברוך הוא לזכות את ישראל לפיכך הרבה להם וכו' פירוש כי בשביל שיש להם הרבה גזירות בשביל כך יש הרבה זכות.

commanded us as a King does! However, if we fulfill the mitzvot, then [as a by-product of our performance of the mitzvot] this decree will be for our good, "to sustain us [with vitality and life] as this day,"[4] but the initiation of the decree is not to benefit us.

[Similarly,] regarding the statement, "The Holy One, Blessed be He, desired to accord merit to Israel, therefore, He multiplied Torah and mitzvot for them,"[5] the meaning is [not that *the reason* that Hashem gave us the mitzvot is so that we would gain merit and benefit, but rather] that since Israel has many decrees, therefore, they have much benefit [as a by-product].[6]

The Maharal's view is that there are two separate stages in the issuing of mitzvot to human beings. There is the seminal motivation for Hashem's acts – which is a royal decree. However, subsequent to the mitzvot-decrees being issued is the second stage: the effects that Hashem's commandments have, when undertaken properly. One of the many results of His decree and its fulfillment is benefit bestowed on those who are the agents of that fulfillment, but one cannot state that this benefit is and was the reason for the mitzvot. The Maharal now cites several proofs of his explanation.

ודבר זה מוסכם בגמרא בכמה מקומות והוא עיקר שורש גדול בגמרא עליו נבנו כמה הלכות שאמרו במקומות הרבה.

מצוות התורה לאו ליהנות נתנו אלא בשביל גזירות נתנו. ולפיכך אמרו (ראש השנה כ"ח ע"א):

המודר הנאה מן השופר מותר לתקוע בו
והמודר הנאה מחבירו מותר לתקוע לו
והמודר הנאה מן המעין טובל בו
טבילת מצוה.

This principle is accepted in the Gemara in several places and it is a central principle and root on which several Halachot[7] are founded, Halachot which are mentioned in many places.

[For example, there is a principle of Halachah that] "Mitzvot were not given [to people] for benefit."[8] Therefore, our sages said,[9]

One who is prevented, through an oath,[10]

4. D'varim 6:24.

5. Makkot 23b. This statement was explored at length by the Maharal in Chapter Five of this work.

6. See Tiferet Yisrael Ch. 5 and Derech Chaim ad. loc.

7. In Hebrew, הלכות, "laws."

8. Eiruvin 31a, Rosh Hashanah 28a–b and elsewhere.

9. Rosh Hashanah 28a.

10. The idea of the Hebrew term מודר הנאה is that a person can forswear *hana'ah* accrued from particular objects as well as categories of objects as well as from certain people. This does not mean a person can take an oath not to fulfill a mitzvah, such

> from *benefitting* from a *shofar*[11] is nevertheless permitted to blow that *shofar* [and will fulfill his obligation to hear the *shofar* through that blowing and will not be considered to have violated the oath.][12]
>
> And one who is prevented, through an oath, from giving benefit to his companion is nevertheless permitted to blow the *shofar* for his companion [and his companion fulfills his obligation to hear the *shofar* and he is not considered to have violated the oath.]

and

> One who is prevented, through an oath, from benefitting from a natural spring, is nevertheless permitted to immerse himself in that spring if the immersion is required to fulfill a mitzvah.[13]

וכהנה רבות בגמרא, והטעם בכולם מפני שמצוות התורה לא נתנו ליהנות בעולם הזה רק לעול על האדם.

ואל תאמר כי פירוש לאו ליהנות בעולם הזה רק לטוב לנו לעולם הבא, דאם היה תחלת נתינת המצוה לישראל להטיב להם בעולם הבא אם כן מצוות ליהנות נתנו, ואם הדבר הוא כמו שפירש הרמב"ן ז"ל שתחלת המצוה היא לטוב לנו, אם כן לא היה הדין הזה כך שיהיה מותר לתקוע לו תקיעה של מצוה והוא מודר הנאה ממנו.

There are many such examples in the Torah and the reason given in all of them is that the mitzvot of the Torah were not given for benefit in this world, but rather as a yoke on human beings.

Don't say that the meaning of the phrase, "[mitzvot] were not given [to people] for benefit" means that they were not given for benefit in this world, but they were given to benefit us in the World to Come! If this were true – that the seminal purpose of the giving of the mitzvot to Israel was to benefit them in the World to Come – then we would be forced to say that mitzvot *were given for benefit* [since their original reason and purpose was for benefit, regardless of the world in which that benefit would be enjoyed]. And if this matter was [true, that the mitzvot were given for benefit, in whichever world, which is the same] as the Ramban *z"l* explained, that the original reason for the

---

oaths have no force, as our commitment to mitzvot precedes (both chronologically and axiologically) any oath we may take.

11. The ram's horn used to fulfill the mitzvah of hearing *shofar*-blasts on Rosh Hashanah.

12. The common theme in all these examples is that the oath-taker is not allowed to bestow a particular *benefit* on a particular person. Nevertheless enabling the latter to fulfill a mitzvah is still allowed since, halachically, we do not consider mitzvot to be "benefits."

13. At certain times, men and women are required by the Torah to immerse in a suitable body of water, such as a natural spring. In our case, not only is the immersion permitted, but the person is not considered to have violated his oath.

אבל בודאי המצוה עלינו כמלך הגוזר על עמו וכמו שבארנו ולכך אמר שמותר בכל אלה.

[giving of the] mitzvot was to benefit us, then the law would not be that one is allowed to sound the *shofar* to fulfill one's mitzvah [obligation] when one is forbidden by an oath to benefit from that *shofar* [since, in the end, mitzvot were given for benefit and such a benefit would violate the oath].

Rather, it is definitely true that mitzvot rest upon us as [the decree of] a King who decrees upon his nation, as we have explained. This is the reason that in all the cases cited above one is permitted [to perform a mitzvah with objects from which one is forbidden to "benefit"].

The Maharal has used the principle that "Mitzvot were not given [to people] for benefit," as an illustration of his thesis that the á priori reason for the giving of the mitzvot was not to benefit humans, but rather as a decree; for if it were true that the mitzvot were given to benefit humans, then in all the above cases, where a person was forbidden from "benefitting" from some object or person, then fulfilling a mitzvah through the agency of that object or person would also constitute "benefit" and would therefore be a violation of the oath. We see that in all these cases, the oath is not violated, therefore, it must be that there was no "benefit" accrued. The Maharal now deals with the fact that in many cases, the Torah makes statements which seem to imply that the mitzvot are for our benefit.

ואם נכספה נפשך לומר כי מצוות השם יתברך עלינו לטוב לנו כל הימים כפשט הכתוב ויצונו ה' א-להינו לעשות את כל החקים האלה לטוב לנו כל הימים לחיותנו כהיום הזה נוכל לומר כך, אבל באופן הזה שיהיה דבר זה גם כן בגזירה ולא כמו מי שרוצה להטיב לאחד ואם אינו רוצה לקבל הגזירה אז המקבל יכול להפטר.

If your soul yearns to say that [surely] Hashem's mitzvot are upon us for our good for all days, as is the simple meaning of the verse, "Hashem, our G-d, has commanded us to carry out these laws *for our good* for all days, to sustain us as on this day,"[14] we *can* say this, but only in such a manner that this matter [that is, the mitzvot,] will *also* be a decree [and is primarily a decree]. But this is not like a situation where someone wants to give benefit to another and the recipient has the ability to refuse the benefit if he doesn't want it [rather, mitzvot may be there to benefit us, but if we don't want them, we have no ability to refuse them, they are decrees.]

על דרך (יומא ס"ט ע"ב):

כלום נתת לנו רק לקבל שכר לא איהו בעינא ולא שכרו בעינא.

The Gemara cites a case [where someone raised a similar idea, saying,][15]

Did You, G-d, not give us the physical drives [including those which urge one to worship idols] in order to enable us to earn reward [by overcoming the

14. D'varim 6:24.
15. Yoma 69b.

urges of those drives]? [But we didn't ask for this!] We don't want these inclinations and we don't want their reward either![16]

שדבר זה אינו רק שהטוב ההוא בעצמו גזירה על ישראל.

ויהיה פירוש ויצונו ה' א־להינו לעשות את כל החקים האלה לטוב לנו וגו' כי השם יתברך גזר עלינו המצוות מפני שגזר עלינו הטוב, ומכל מקום כיון שהטוב הזה הוא גזירה בעל כרחו של אדם יאמר בזה מצוות לאו ליהנות נתנו כי לא נתנו על דעת המקבל ובשביל כך המצוות הם עול על האדם.

Such an idea [that the benefit of mitzvot can be refused,] is false – rather, that goodness is itself a decree on Israel.

Thus, the [correct] explanation [of the verse cited above,] "Hashem, our G-d, has commanded us to carry out these laws for our good . . ."[17] is that Hashem, may He be Blessed, decreed that we perform the mitzvot because He decreed goodness upon us [but in the end, it's still a decree]. However, since this goodness is a decree and is compulsory, one can still say, "Mitzvot were not given [to people] for benefit," since the mitzvot were not given from the perspective of the recipient[18] and therefore, they are [in essence, from Hashem's perspective,] a yoke on humanity.

The Maharal now explains that the Ramban's explanation can easily slot into his own.

ובודאי דעת הרמב"ן ז"ל תבין על ענין זה כי המצוות שלא נתאכזר.

המידה הזאת גזר ה' על האדם וכן שאר המצוות כולם הם לקבוע באדם מידות טובות והם גזירות על האדם.

You can surely understand the opinion of the Ramban, *z"l*,[19] on this issue [where he claims] that the mitzvot were given to prevent human beings from becoming cruel [in the same way].

This character trait[20] was decreed upon humanity by Hashem, and so too all the other mitzvot are all to set good character traits within human beings, but all these character traits are decrees on humanity.[21]

---

16. The idea is one with which the Maharal dealt extensively in Chapter Five of this work – that mitzvot may confer upon the human being the challenge and opportunity for great growth and its attendant rewards; however, they also grant one the opportunity to fail and suffer loss and punishment. Some people feel they would like to forfeit the chance for reward because such an action would definitely prevent their failure and loss.

17. D'varim 6:24.

18. I.e., humans, who benefit from the mitzvot.

19. Cited earlier in this chapter.

20. Not to become cruel.

21. See the Commentary, Ch. 6 § Point 13.

The Maharal now compares his own explanation to that of the Ramban and poses another question to the Ramban: that it seems that the Ramban would agree that the reason that Hashem commanded us to be kind to humans is due to Hashem's Mercy on human beings. The Maharal explains that if we accepted such an explanation regarding human-centered mitzvot, we would be able to apply it similarly to mitzvot directing us to be kind to animals. In this case, we would end up with the same difficulty with which we began – contradicting the view in the Gemara which holds that we cannot say that G-d's mitzvot are due to His Mercy.

However, the Ramban[22] explained that the opinion which holds that a person [should not] "make Hashem's attributes into Mercy when, in fact, they are exclusively decrees,"[23] is claiming that G-d did not have mercy on the nest of the bird and His mercies did not reach the cow and its progeny, for Hashem's mercies do not reach animal life to the extent of His preventing us from making use of animals for our needs. For if it were true [that Hashem's mercies reached the mother bird and the cow] then Hashem would have prohibited us from slaughtering animals [ever].

Rather, [the Ramban explains that this opinion holds that] the prevention [of taking the mother bird and its eggs or slaughtering a dam and its calf] is to instill within us the trait of mercy – that we should not become cruel and so on. From these words of the Ramban,[24] it is implied that only regarding animals one should not say this[25] but regarding humans it is possible to say [such a thing].

אבל מה שפי' (הרמב"ם) [הרמב"ן, (עפ"י ר' הרטמן)] ז"ל טעם מי שאומר שעושה מידות הקדוש ב"ה רחמים ואינן אלא גזירות, לומר שלא חס הא־ל על קן צפור ולא הגיעו רחמיו על אותו ועל בנו שאין רחמיו מגיעים בבעלי נפש הבהמית למנוע ממנו צרכנו, שאם כן היה אוסר השחיטה.

אבל טעם המניעה ללמד אותנו מדת הרחמנות שלא נתאכזר וכו'. ומדבריו אלה משמע שדוקא במין בעל חי אין לומר כך אבל באדם כגון הצדקה אפשר לומר שהשם היה מרחם על העני ולכך צוה לתת צדקה.

דבר זה אינו גם כן כי אין מדת הצדקה דרך רחמנות כי כל הדברים הם בגזירת הדין ולא מצד הרחמים שהוא יתברך מרחם על העני, רק כי גזר על האדם כך שיהיה האדם מרחם, לא שיהיה ה' מרחם על העני וצוה בשביל כך שיפרנס אותו האדם, כי לא הביט אל העני מצד דחקו כלל.

ומזה הטעם אין לומר גם כן כי השם יתברך היה מרחם על קן צפור כי גזירות שלו דין על האדם והם גזירות

22. Cited earlier in this chapter. Textual emendation as per R. Hartman, p. 108. The original text reads, "Rambam" which clearly doesn't work within the context.

23. An attitude displayed when such a person says, "Your [G-d's] mercy extends [even] to the nest of a bird!"

24. Textual emendation as per R. Hartman, p. 108. The original text reads, "Rambam."

25. That Hashem has commanded mitzvot out of mercy on the animals.

התמידיות שהוא מנהיג בהם עולמו.
ואם אפשר לומר כי השם יתברך מרחם
על האדם לעשות צדקה כך אפשר
לומר כי השם יתברך מרחם על הבעלי
חיים שלא נתאכזר אף אם מונע אותנו
מצרכינו.

רק כי לא נתנה לאדם המצוה בשביל
שהיה מרחם רק כי המצוה גזירה עלינו,
ולא הביט השם יתברך מה שהמקבל
חפץ ורוצה רק הכל גזירה עלינו.

For example, regarding the mitzvah of *tz'dakkah*, one *could* say that Hashem is being merciful to the pauper and therefore commanded [us] to give *tz'dakkah*.

Such an idea, however, is also false, for the mitzvah of *tz'dakkah* is not generated through [Hashem's] Mercy, since all the mitzvot are [a function of] the decree of Justice and not through Mercy (that is, that He, may He be Blessed, is having mercy on the pauper), but rather that He has decreed on humans that humans should have mercy (but not that Hashem has mercy on the pauper and therefore commanded us, due to this, that we should support that pauper) because Hashem did not look at the pauper from the perspective of his[26] need at all.[27]

Due to this reason, it is also not suitable to say that Hashem, may He be Blessed, would [command us about sending away the mother bird because He would] have mercy on the bird's nest, for His decrees are Justice on humanity and they are the constant decrees through which He directs His world.[28] And if it is possible to say that Hashem, may He be Blessed, has mercy on a person to provide charity [for him], so too is it possible to say that Hashem, may He be Blessed, has mercy on animals that we should not be cruel [to them] even if He should [therefore] prevent us from satisfying our needs [through animals].

However, [it is not true that Hashem prevents us from utilizing the animal world and additionally,] mitzvot were not given to humanity due to Hashem's having mercy, rather, the mitzvot are decrees on us and Hashem, may He be Blessed, did not examine what the recipient [of the benefit bestowed by mitzvot] desires, rather they are all exclusively decrees on us.

The Maharal now summarizes his own thesis – that the creation of the world and of Torah and mitzvot are all a function of Hashem's Justice.

26. The pauper's.

27. See the Commentary, Ch. 6 § Point 12 where we dealt with this idea earlier in the chapter. The Maharal does not mean that Hashem is indifferent, G-d forbid, to the pauper's need, he says explicitly (Gur Aryeh, B'midbar 19:2, as cited in the Commentary) that Hashem is without doubt deeply pained; rather, he means that the reason for Hashem's commanding us to support the pauper is not generated by Hashem's Mercy.

28. See the Commentary, Ch. 6 § Point 13.

וכמו שברא השם יתברך את העולם ועם שכל אשר ברא הכל הוא בטוב וכדכתיב (בראשית א׳) וירא א־להים את כל אשר עשה והנה טוב מאוד, מכל מקום לא ברא את העולם להטיב אל העולם רק בגזירת הדין נברא וכדכתיב בכל מעשה בראשית שם א־להים.

וזה עצמו בתורה עם שכל דרכיה דרכי נועם מכל מקום נתינתה לעולם הכל בגזירת דין.

Just as Hashem, may He be Blessed, created the world and even though everything He created is good (as it is written, "G-d saw everything He had made and it was very good"),[29] *nevertheless He did not create the world to give goodness to the world*, rather it was created through the decree of Justice, as [can be seen from the fact that] the name of G-d written throughout the Torah's description of the creation of the world is *Elokim*.[30]

This is true for the Torah as well – even though "All her[31] ways are ways of pleasantness,"[32] nevertheless, the giving of the Torah to the world was completely through the decree of Justice.

The Maharal now explains once again that the Ramban could easily have altered his explanation to fit in with the Maharal's view. Thus instead of the Ramban holding that the reason for the mitzvot is that we learn positive traits, he would say that the *reason* for the Mitzvot is that Hashem decreed them. What did He decree? That we learn positive traits. This may seem to be a semantic difference, however, the Maharal's entire thrust is that the world, the Torah and the Mitzvot are not some arbitrary whim of Mercy; but they *have* to exist due to what is right and just.

ולא היה צריך אל הרמב״ן ז״ל לדחוק כלל, דאף לפי סברתו שסובר כי השם יתברך רצה לקבוע בנו מדת הרחמנות, יש לפרש מה שאמרו על קן צפור יגיעו רחמיך משתקין אותו מפני שעושה מידות השם יתברך רחמים כאלו השם יתברך הוא מרחם על קן צפור ואין מידות השם יתברך רק גזירות ולא רחמים.

רק שגזר עלינו הרחמים שלא נתאכזר, ואם אומר על קן צפור יגיעו רחמיך כאלו הוא יתברך מרחם על קן צפור ודבר זה אינו.

And the Ramban, *z"l*, did not have to contort himself at all [in his attempts to explain the Gemara and the Mishnah], because even according to his reasoning (which is that Hashem, may He be Blessed, wanted to set within us the trait of mercifulness), one can explain the statement of our sages [as follows]: when they said that we should silence one who says, "Your mercy extends [even] to the nest of a bird!" because such a person is making Hashem's attributes [due to] Mercy when, in fact, they are exclusively decrees, they meant that [the reason we silence him is because] it is as if [he

29. B'reishit 1:31.

30. As we outlined in the Commentary, Ch. 6 § Points 5 and 6 at the beginning of Chapter Six, this name of Hashem indicates Hashem's attribute of Justice.

31. I.e., the Torah's.

32. Mishlei 3:17.

is implying that] Hashem, may He be Blessed, is having mercy on the nest of the bird, while in reality, Hashem's attributes are exclusively decrees and not Mercy.

[In essence, the Ramban would be saying that] Hashem decreed upon us that we should be merciful and not become cruel. But one who says, "Your mercy extends [even] to the nest of a bird!" is implying that Hashem, may He be Blessed, is having mercy on the nest of the bird [and is implying that this is the reason for the mitzvah], which is false.

SUMMARY

Chapter 6: 3/4

I. The Maharal's own view on the purpose of mitzvot

A. The Maharal's position

1. The Maharal's own view on the reason for mitzvot is not for the benefit of the "recipients." Rather, they are decrees flowing from Hashem's attribute of Justice.
2. Benefit will flow from the fulfillment of Hashem's decrees, but this benefit is an added bonus, not the *reason* for the mitzvot.

B. Torah sources which seem to contradict this idea

1. The sources
   a. "Hashem, our G-d, has commanded us to carry out these laws for our good." [D'varim 6:24]
   b. "The Holy One, blessed be He, desired to accord merit to Israel, therefore, He multiplied Torah and mitzvot for them." [Makkot 23b]
2. The Maharal's solution
   a. In both cases, the idea is not that the *reason* for the giving of the mitzvot is the benefit and merit, but rather that these benefits accrue from the fulfillment of the mitzvot despite the fact that they are *not* the reason for the mitzvot.

II. The halachic principle that "Mitzvot were not given [to people] for benefit."

A. The principle is used in several case studies in the Gemara where the idea is raised that the fulfillment of a mitzvah might also be considered a personal benefit for that person. In each case the Gemara says that this is not the case, as mitzvot were not given for benefit.

B. The Maharal uses the fact that this is an accepted halachic principle to buttress his claim that the initial reason for the giving of the mitzvot is not for any benefit of the recipients (human beings); for if it were, this principle would be inoperable.

C. Example

1. When a person takes an oath not to gain benefit from an object, he is still nevertheless allowed to use that object to fulfill a mitzvah because, "Mitzvot were not given [to people] for benefit."

D. Benefit in the World to Come

1. The Maharal also rejects the idea that the principle, "Mitzvot were not given [to people] for benefit," could imply that the mitzvot were

not given to benefit people in this world but were given to benefit people in the World to Come. The Maharal believes that such a case would still, nevertheless, constitute benefit and would invalidate the principle.

III. Mitzvot as a decreed benefit

A. Question on the Maharal's theory

1. The plain meaning of the verse, "Hashem, our G-d, has commanded us to carry out these laws for our good for all days, to sustain us as on this day" [D'varim 6:24] is that the reason for mitzvot is the benefit humans derive from them.

B. The Maharal's solution

1. One can say that mitzvot are a decreed benefit which means that one cannot refuse the mitzvot since they are a decree.
2. The verse above thus means that the decree Hashem made was that He decreed goodness upon us. From the human perspective, mitzvot are all benefit, but that is not the reason for their giving; rather, from Hashem's perspective, they are all decrees.

IV. Reconciliation of the Maharal's views with the Ramban's

A. The Maharal interprets the Ramban's views as being compatible with his own.

B. When the Ramban says that the mitzvot were given to prevent cruelty and to foster the trait of mercy, the Maharal understands that he could mean that Hashem decreed that we become merciful and veer away from cruelty.

C. Question on the Ramban

1. The Ramban seems to imply that one cannot say that Hashem acted out of mercy on animals when commanding us regarding the mother bird and other mitzvot, since Hashem allows us to take animal life. But this implies that he would agree that the mitzvot promoting kindness to humans (like *tz'dakkah*) are due to Hashem's mercy.
2. The Maharal rejects this reasoning since, in essence, once one has admitted G-d's Mercy as being the prime operator in the generation of any mitzvah, this would be operable in the case of the mother bird and we would once again be in conflict with the Gemara's principle that we should not make G-d's attributes into Mercy as they are purely decrees.

V. The purpose of the creation of the world

A. The Maharal states that the world was created through a decree of Justice and it was not created so that Hashem could give goodness to the world.

CHAPTER 6

Part 4 of 4

The Maharal continues his exploration of the general "reason" for mitzvot. He explained previously that mitzvot are decrees flowing from Hashem's attribute of Justice but now adds that this does not mean that mitzvot have no tangible benefits.

ועם כל זה שהמצוות הם גזירות על ישראל הם לטוב לנו, כי לא יבא מאתו יתברך רק הטוב הגמור כי כל מעשיו הם הטוב הגמור רק כי הטוב הזה גזר עלינו ולא שיש כאן שום צד רחמנות רק הכל דין.

Despite the fact that the mitzvot are a decree on Israel, they are definitely good for us; because only absolute goodness flows from Hashem, may He be Blessed, since all His actions are absolute goodness. It's just that He decreed this goodness on us and there is no aspect of Mercy here at all, only Justice.

The Maharal now cites a dispute between Rabbi Yochanan ben Zakai and a sect of Jews called Baytosim[1] which illustrates the Maharal's contention.

וזה בעצמו תשובת רבי יוחנן בן זכאי לבייתוסים כדאיתא במנחות פרק רבי ישמעאל (ס"ה ע"א):

This itself is the answer of Rabbi Yochanan ben Zakai to the Baytosim as is brought in [the Gemara, Tractate] M'nachot, Chapter Rabbi Yishma'el:[2]

שהיו בייתוסים אומרים עצרת אחר השבת.

The Baytosim used to say that the festival of Shavu'ot took place the day after Shabbat.[3,4]

נטפל להם רבי יוחנן בן זכאי ואמר להם שוטים מנין זה לכם?

ולא היה אדם אחד שהיה משיבו חוץ

1. The Baytosim, or Boethusians, were a sect of Jews in the time of the Second Temple. They broke away from Torah regarding certain central beliefs in the unity of the Written and Oral Torah, life after death and others. They derive their name from the teacher, Baytos who (perhaps unwittingly) spawned the sect through his teachings. See Avot D'Rabbi Natan 5:2.

2. M'nachot 65a.

3. I.e., on Sunday.

4. They claimed it would always be on a Sunday, while the Torah mandates that the festival falls on the fiftieth day after the beginning of Pesach (counted from the second day of Pesach) so that Shavu'ot can fall on any of 4 days in the week. This dispute with the sages is one of the key examples of their rejection of the authority of the Oral Torah.

מזקן אחד שהיה מפטפט כנגדו ואמר משה רבינו אוהב ישראל היה ויודע שעצרת יום אחד הוא ותקנה לאחר שבת כדי שיתענגו שני ימים.

קרא עליו מקרא זה אחד עשר יום מחורב דרך הר שעיר ואם משה אוהב ישראל היה למה איחרן במדבר ארבעים שנה ע"כ.

Rabbi Yochanan ben Zakai joined their discussion and said to them, "Fools! From where do you learn this?"[5]

But there was not one of them who could answer him except one elderly Baytos who was mocking him and said, "Moshe our teacher loved the nation of Israel and he knew that Shavu'ot is a festival lasting only one day,[6] so Moshe decreed that it should fall on the day following Shabbat so that Israel would have two days in succession on which to enjoy themselves."[7]

Rabbi Yochanan cited the following verse to disprove the Baytos's claim, "It was an eleven-day journey from Mount Sinai [to the Land of Israel], via Mount Se'ir."[8] [Rabbi Yochanan said,] "If Moshe loved Israel so much, why did he prolong Israel's wanderings in the desert for forty years [if it should only have been an eleven-day journey]?"[9]

וביאור ענין זה, כי הבייתוסי הזה היה סובר כי החגים והמועדים והשבת גם כן כולם לטובת ולעונג ישראל ואינו גזירת דין, ואמר כי משה היה אוהב ישראל ועל ידו נתנה התורה לישראל שיהא לטוב להם ולפיכך יש להם להתענג ב' ימים.

The explanation of this matter is that this Baytos believed that the festivals, sacred times and Shabbat were also all [ordained] for the good and pleasure of Israel and that they are not a decree of Justice. And he said that Moshe loved the nation of Israel and that the Torah was given through him to Israel in order that it be good for them and therefore, they should enjoy themselves for two days.

וראה והבן מדברי הבייתוסי שאמר משה אוהב ישראל היה ולא תלה הדבר כי הקדוש ברוך הוא אוהב ישראל ונתן להם שיתענגו שני ימים, שאין הבייתוסים כופרים בתורה שלא מצאנו זה רק שהם כופרים בתורה שבעל פה, אבל גם הבייתוסים היו יודעים כי מידות השם יתברך וגזרתו דין.

Now see and understand [that this is the true explanation] from the words of this Baytos since he said, "Moshe . . .

5. I.e., that Shavu'ot must fall on a Sunday.

6. Outside of Israel, our rabbis instituted that Shavu'ot be celebrated for two days (due to the time delay in communicating the precise date from the central court in Jerusalem to Diaspora communities), but the Torah mandates only one day of celebration.

7. As per Avot D'Rabbi Natan 5:2 cited above, the Baytosim denied the existence of the World to Come and thus were intensely hedonistic.

8. D'varim 1:2.

9. The Jewish people at the time rejected their opportunity to enter the Land of Israel and thus they wandered the desert for forty years until that generation died out and their children were the ones to enter. See B'midbar 13, 14.

רק אמר בשביל שהתורה נתנה על ידי משה רבינו עליו השלום ולכך נתנה על ידו כמו שהמקבל מוכן והוא היה אוהב ישראל ונתן על ידו שיתענגו ב' ימים.

ועל זה השיב רבי יוחנן אחד עשר יום מחורב ורצה בזה כי מעשה משה היה מדתו היושר והיה אצלו הכל בדין ויושר, ולכך ניתנה תורה של דין על ידו, ואם היה מוכן משה לטובת ישראל שתנתן תורה על ידו שהיא לטובת המקבל ולא במדת הדין למה הוליכן במדבר ארבעים שנה והוא היה מנהיג שלהם, נמצא שלא היה משה מוכן לענג אותם ולהנאותם רק משה היה מוכן אל היושר והאמת וכאשר לא זכו בדין היה מאחר ומנהיג אותם במדבר ארבעים שנה כי כל הנהגתו בדין. וכן התורה שנתן השם יתברך על ידי משה הכל במדת הדין וביושר ולא יאמר בזה שהוא להנאת המקבל, ודבר עמוק מאד השיב רבי יוחנן בן זכאי.

loved the nation of Israel" and he did not explain his beliefs by saying that the Holy One, Blessed be He, loves Israel and therefore ensured that they would enjoy themselves for two days. [The reason that the Baytos explained that it was Moshe's act and not Hashem's is] because the Baytosim do not deny the written Torah, we only know that they deny the Oral Torah, but even they know that the attributes of Hashem, may He be Blessed, and His decree are all due to Justice [therefore, they explained that it was Moshe's desire to benefit Israel, but Hashem gave the Torah through Justice.]

Therefore, the Baytos said that since the Torah was given through Moshe our teacher, peace be upon him; therefore, it was given in such a way that it would suit him (the [intermediary] recipient) and he loved Israel and he gave it so that they should enjoy themselves for two days.

To this, replied Rabbi Yochanan ben Zakai, "It is eleven days' journey from Sinai"; and he wanted to imply through this that Moshe's activity was all according to his attribute of Honesty and everything which he did was according to Justice and Honesty. Therefore, the Torah of Justice was given through Moshe. For if Moshe was primed for the goodness of Israel [primarily] – that the Torah should be given through him so that it should be for the benefit of the recipient[10] and not that it should be given through the attribute of Justice – why then did he [Moshe] lead the Jews in the desert for forty years when he was their leader? We see that Moshe was not primed to pleasure them and to give them benefit; rather, Moshe was primed for honesty and truth and when they [the Jews] did not merit [to enter the Land of Israel] according to what was Just, he then delayed them and led them in the desert for forty years, because all his behavior was through Justice. So too, the Torah which Hashem, may He be Blessed, gave through Moshe is all through the attribute of Justice and Honesty and one cannot say about it that it is for the enjoyment of the recipient. [We see that] Rabbi Yochanan gave a profound rejoinder.

10. I.e., Israel.

The Maharal summarizes his position: Torah is a decree – a function of Hashem's attribute of Justice – but it is decreed goodness.

אמנם אין הכונה פה חס ושלום שאין עם דברי התורה הטוב והנועם כי כל דרכיה דרכי נועם וכל נתיבותיה שלום שזה דבר ברור וכמו שיתבאר, רק הכונה פה כי לא מצד הזה נתנה תורה להנאתם רק נתנה תורה בדין וביושר.

ועם זה הכל לטוב לנו כי אין ראוי אל אשר הוא הטוב האמתי שיבוא ממנו רק טוב ולפיכך התורה היא לטוב לנו, אך הצואה היא גזירה שגזר עליהם המצוות וזה שאמר שעושה מידות הש"י רחמים ואינם אלא גזירות. ועוד יתבאר.

However, our intention here is not to say, G-d forbid, that Goodness and Pleasantness do not accompany words of Torah, for "All her[11] ways are ways of pleasantness and all her paths are peace,"[12] for this is clear (as will be explained). Rather, our intention is that the Torah was not given *due* to this aspect – for their[13] enjoyment – but that the Torah was given in Justice and Honesty.

Nevertheless, it is all for our good because it is suitable that only goodness come from Him Who is the true good and therefore, Torah is for our good; however, the commandments are a decree which He decreed the mitzvot on them and this is the meaning [of the opprobrium indicated by the Gemara][14] when it says, "he makes Hashem's attributes, may He be Blessed, into Mercy when they are exclusively decrees." And this will be explained further.[15]

11. Torah's.
12. Mishlei 3:17.
13. I.e., humans'.
14. B'rachot 33b. This is the Gemara cited at the beginning of this chapter which forms the backbone of the Maharal's comments throughout the chapter.
15. See Chapters Seven, Eight and Nine.

SUMMARY

Chapter 6: 4/4

I. **Although mitzvot are due to Hashem's Justice, they are, nevertheless, absolute goodness**
   A. The Maharal's position
      1. The Maharal clarifies that although the mitzvot were given through Hashem's attribute of Justice, since they flow from Him, they are goodness, since He is absolute goodness. It's just that His attribute of Mercy is not the *reason* for the giving of the mitzvot in the first place.
   B. The Maharal's proof text: The dispute between the Baytosim and Rabbi Yochanan ben Zakai
      1. The dispute
         a. The Baytosim, a sect which existed at the time of the Second Temple and which denied the validity of the Oral Torah, believed that an ambiguous phrase in the Written Torah set the date of the festival of Shavu'ot on a Sunday. They denied the Oral Torah's explanation of this ambiguity. The Oral Torah explains that Shavu'ot's date is variable, fifty days after the beginning of Pesach (counted from the second day of Pesach).
         b. When Rabbi Yochanan asked one of the Baytosim for their reasoning, their response was that Moshe, through whom the Torah was given, was a great lover of Israel and therefore ensured that Shavu'ot would fall on a Sunday – Moshe's reasoning being that since Shavu'ot lasts only one day, making it on a Sunday gives the Jewish people two consecutive days of rejoicing: Shabbat and Shavu'ot.
         c. Rabbi Yochanan's rejoinder was that if indeed Moshe was such a great lover of the Jewish people, why did he allow the Jews to wander the desert for forty years as a punishment for the sin of the spies?
      2. The Maharal's explanation of the dispute
         a. The Baytosim's position
            (1) The Baytosim believed that, in general, the Torah was given through Hashem's attribute of Justice. However, they believed that the festivals were Mitzvot given for the benefit of the Jewish people.
            (2) They also believed that the Torah had to be in sync with

the person who received it and passed it on to the Jewish people. This person was Moshe and they believed that his essential nature was one of mercy.

(3) Therefore, they believed that the festivals were Mitzvot which came through Moshe and they, in particular, were in sync with Moshe and were thus given for the benefit of the Jews.

b. Rabban Yochanan Ben Zakai's position

(1) He (and the faithful Torah Jews of the time) disagreed with the Baytosim (in this instance) on two points:

(a) He understood that all of the Torah is given through Hashem's decree of Justice, including the festivals.

(b) He understood that Moshe's basic character was justice, not mercy.

c. Therefore:

(1) The Torah does fit Moshe's character – Justice.

(2) Moreover, the reason Moshe led the Jews in the desert for forty years was because it was a just punishment and he, as a man of justice, accepted the verdict and did not attempt to overturn it or circumvent it out of misplaced mercy.

C. In summary

1. There is no intention to say that the Torah has no benefit or goodness. Just that this benefit and goodness are not the *reasons* the Torah was given.
2. The Torah comes from Hashem who is ultimate goodness and therefore, it must also be good.

CHAPTER 7

CHAPTER 7

Part 1 of 4

The Maharal continues his discussion of the reasons for mitzvot by analyzing the Rambam's explanation in Moreh N'vuchim.[1] In order to understand this chapter fully, one should familiarize oneself with the positions of the Rambam[2] and the Ramban[3] from the previous chapter. In short, the Rambam's stance is that each mitzvah has a reason but that not every detail within a mitzvah has a reason.

אחר שבארנו לך כי מידות [נ"ל צ"ל מצוות] השם יתברך גזרות על ישראל כמלך הגוזר על עמו, אין עליך לחשוב כמו שחשב הרמב"ם ז"ל בפירוש המאמר הזה שדעת חז"ל שגזר עלינו המצוות ואין להם טעם, רק שהם גזרה לנסות ישראל ולצרף אותם אם ישמרו

After we have explained to you that the mitzvot[4] [given by] Hashem, may He be Blessed, are decrees on Israel, like a king decreeing on his nation, you should not think, as the Rambam did[5] (in his explanation of this saying)[6] that the opinion of [some of] our sages, *z"l*, is that Hashem decreed the mitzvot upon us[7] and that they have no reason except to test Israel and to refine them [to test] whether they would keep His commandments.[8] The Rambam

1. The central citations which outline the Rambam's views are cited in full in the Commentary, Ch. 6 § Point 9.
2. Maimonides.
3. Nachmanides.
4. In the original Hebrew, the word here is מדות which means "attributes." It seems to me from the context, that this is a misprint and that the word should be, מצות meaning "mitzvot" and that the ד should be a צ.
5. Moreh N'vuchim 3:48.
6. The saying referred to here is from the Mishnah, B'rachot 5:3. This Mishnah is cited in full at the beginning of Chapter Six of this work.
7. This is indeed the way the Rambam explains the opinion of the sages in the Mishnah. In Moreh N'vuchim 3:48, the Rambam explains that he disagrees with these sages and sides with those sages (for whom he gives no source, as the Maharal pointed out in Chapter Six of this work) who dispute the Mishnah. The Rambam explains that these latter sages are those who opine that mitzvot do have reasons, a position held by many sages (but this dispute is not cited by the Gemara as being a factor regarding the Mishnah or Gemara in B'rachot).
8. The Maharal seems to be conflating two separate statements of the Rambam, since the about-to-be-cited Midrash was not cited at all in the Rambam's comments in Moreh N'vuchim 3:48, which is where the Rambam explained the Mishnah in

את מצוותיו, והביא לזה מאמרם בב"ר (ויקרא רבה פ' י"ג):

וכי מה אכפת להקדוש ברוך הוא אם שוחט מן הצואר או שוחט מן העורף הרי לא נתנו המצוות אלא לצרף בהן הבריות שנאמר כל אמרת א-לוה צרופה ע"כ.

ופירש הרמב"ם ז"ל בזה כי השם יתברך נתן המצוות לנסות ולצרף בהן הבריות.

ודעתו ז"ל בהמשל כי לכל מצוה ומצוה אין ספק שיש בה טעם למה ציוה במצוה זאת, אבל לדברים הפרטיים שהם במצוה כי כל מצוה ומצוה יש בה דברים פרטיים אין להם טעם, ועל זה אמר וכי מה אכפת להקב"ה אם שוחט

cited[9] their[10] statement in B'reishit Rabbah[11] as follows,

> Does it matter to the Holy One, Blessed be He, whether one slaughters from the throat or the [back of the] neck? Rather, the mitzvot were only given to refine humans, as the verse says, "All[12] the statement of Hashem is refined."[13, 14]

The Rambam explained this [Midrash] to be saying that Hashem, may He be Blessed, gave the [details of the] mitzvot to test and purify humans.

His opinion,[15] for which he gives examples, is that there is no doubt that

---

B'rachot 5:3. Rather, this Midrash is cited by the Rambam in Moreh N'vuchim 3:26 as a support for his views where there is no mention of the Mishnah in B'rachot at all.

9. Moreh N'vuchim 3:26. This is cited in full in the Commentary, Ch. 6 § Point 9.

10. The sages'.

11. B'reishit Rabbah 44:1 with variations. See also Vayikra Rabbah 13:3.

12. There seems to be a printer's error here. There are two similar verses in the Tanach, one in Mishlei 30:5 which begins with the word "All," which is what we have cited in the Maharal. The other similar verse is in Tehillim 18:31 which just states "the statement of Hashem is refined," omitting the word "All." It seems more likely that there is an error in the addition of the word "all" as in the Vilna edition of the Midrash in B'reishit Rabbah (which is the source cited in the text of the Maharal), this word is omitted and thus the verse is from Tehillim 18:31. See Chapters Two and Six, where this verse was similarly cited.

13. As the Maharal goes on to say, the Rambam understands that the word "refined" is used here in the sense of being tested and tried through the process of refinement.

14. Tehillim 18:31. This verse can also be understood as "The statement of Hashem *only* comes to purify," which is how it is being interpreted by the Midrash. See also Chapter Two where this verse is cited in the famous Midrash Tanchuma (cited by the Maharal there) relating the discussion between Rabbi Akiva and Turnus Rufus. In the citation in our chapter (in the Midrash currently under discussion), the interpretation of this verse seems to be at variance with how it is interpreted in the Tanchuma. Here it seems to be saying that Hashem's statements refine through the simple obedience a person displays through submission to G-d's decree, whereas in the Tanchuma there seems to be a clear understanding that mitzvot help us perfect ourselves in this world.

15. Which the Rambam believes is opposed to that espoused in the Mishnah.

מן הצואר או מן העורף כי שחיטת צואר דבר פרטי כי מצות שחיטה שישחוט ולא ימלוק יש בו טעם אבל שישחוט מן הצואר ולא ישחוט מן העורף לדבר הזה אין לו טעם כך הם דבריו.

every mitzvah has a reason (due to which Hashem commanded it), but as regards the details of the mitzvah [the Rambam believes that] in each mitzvah there are details which have no reason. [According to the Rambam] it is regarding this [latter idea, that the details have no reason] that the Midrash said, "Does it matter to the Holy One, Blessed be He, whether one slaughters from the throat or the [back of the] neck?," because slaughtering at the throat is a detail [of the mitzvah to slaughter]. Now the mitzvah to slaughter and not to sever the back of the neck does have a reason, but there is no reason specifically to slaughter at the throat and not the [back of the] neck. These are his words.

The Maharal now explains why he disagrees with the Rambam's claim that the details of the mitzvot have no reason. The Maharal cites several verses which show that external observers will comment that the mitzvot were all crafted with wisdom – something which could not happen if the mitzvot or their details were inexplicable.

ובודאי אין טעם לפי' הזה, כי על כל התורה אמר הכתוב (דברים ד') כי מי גוי גדול אשר לו חקים ומשפטים צדיקים ככל התורה הזאת ואמר עוד ושמרתם ועשיתם כי הוא חכמתכם ובינתכם לעיני העמים אשר ישמעון את כל החוקים האלה וגו'.

והרי כי כל דבר שבתורה בכלל ובפרט הכל דברי חכמה, ולא כמו שחשב הוא כי לדברים הפרטיים אין טעם כלל כי לא היה זה תורה של חכמה.

However, there is definitely no reason for this explanation, because it was regarding the whole[16] Torah, that the verse states, "But which nation is so great that it has righteous decrees[17] and ordinances like all this Torah"[18] and it states, "Because it[19] is your wisdom and understanding in the eyes of the nations who will hear all these decrees[20] [and they will say, 'This nation is only a wise and understanding people.']"[21]

This teaches us that everything in the Torah, whether the generalities or the details, all are words of wisdom and this is the opposite of what he[22]

16. Including the details.

17. *Chukim*, חוקים, decrees – those laws which are seen to be the most impenetrable.

18. D'varim 4:8.

19. The Torah.

20. *Chukim*, חוקים, decrees – as above.

21. D'varim 4:6. The section in brackets is not cited by the Maharal but is germane.

22. The Rambam.

thought – that the details have no reason – [for if the details had no reason] the Torah would not be a Torah of wisdom.

The Maharal now examines how the Ramban dealt with the Midrash (cited above) which the Rambam found so problematic. The Ramban's explanation of the Midrash is that our mitzvot are not intended to benefit Hashem but they are for us.

והרמב"ן פירש בזה כי מה שאמר וכי מה אכפת להקדוש ברוך הוא וכו' רצה לומר על דרך ואם צדקת מה תפעל לו (איוב ל"ה) אבל בודאי הקדוש ברוך הוא צוה המצוה לתועלת ולטוב להם כל הימים.

The Ramban explained[23] that when the Midrash stated,[24] "Does it matter to the Holy One, Blessed be He, whether one slaughters from the throat or the [back of the] neck?" it is conveying [an idea] along the lines [of the verse] "And[25] if you are righteous, what have you given Him [G-d]?"[26] Rather, [the Ramban explains that] the Holy One, Blessed be He, definitely commanded each mitzvah for a purpose and for their[27] good for all days.[28]

The Maharal now explores the Ramban's position further.

ומדרש חכמים בילמדנו פרשה זאת החיה (תנחומא שמיני):

[The Ramban cited] a Midrash of our sages in the Y'lamdeinu,[29] in the section of "This is the animal . . ." as follows:

וכי מה אכפת להקדוש ברוך הוא בין שוחט בהמה ואוכל או נוחר ואוכל כלום אתה מועילו או כלום אתה מזיקו.
וכי מה אכפת להקדוש ברוך הוא אם אוכל טהרות או טמאות.
אם חכמת חכמת לך הא לא נתנה תורה אלא לצרף הבריות שנאמר אמרות

> Does it matter to the Holy One, Blessed be He, whether one slaughters an animal and then eats or whether one stabs it and then eats? Neither of these [methods] benefits Him and neither of these [methods] harms Him.

---

23. Commentary to D'varim 22:6. This is cited in full in the Commentary, Ch. 6 § Point 10.

24. B'reishit Rabbah 44:1, cited above.

25. This would seem to be a printer's error, as the original source does not have the word "And," in it.

26. Iyov 35:7. This verse conveys the idea that even if a person performs positive acts, he cannot affect G-d Who is perfect. Thus the import of the Midrash is that it "doesn't matter" to G-d how we slaughter from the point of view that none of our actions change Him.

27. The Jewish people's.

28. Cf. D'varim 6:24.

29. Tanchuma, Sh'mini 8.

ה׳ אמרות טהורות וגו׳ ונאמר כל אמרת א־לוה צרופה.

Similarly, does it matter to Him whether one eats *tahor*[30] [food] or whether one eats *tamei*[31] [food]?

Rather, "If you have gained wisdom, you have gained wisdom for yourself"[32] and the mitzvot were only given to refine humans, as it says, "The statements of Hashem are pure statements [like purified silver, clear to the world, refined sevenfold]"[33] and it says, "All[34] the statement of Hashem is refined[35] [it is a shield to all who take refuge in Him]" . . .

כמו שלא יצטרך הוא לאורה של מנורה ולקטורת וכיוצא בזה, רק נדע האמת ונזכה בו עד שנהיה ראויים להיות הוא יתברך מגין עלינו, כי רוב כבודנו וספורנו בתהלותנו לאפס ותהו נחשבו.

[The Ramban continued, saying that] just as G-d does not need the light of the *m'norah*[36] or [the aroma of] the incense[37] and so on; [so too for all the mitzvot, their purpose is] only that *we* should know the truth and *we* should merit it until we become worthy of having Him, may He be Blessed, protect us;[38] because all our honoring [of G-d] and our relating His praises are considered as nothing and null!

---

30. In Hebrew, טהור, "*tahor*." Something which is *tahor* is compatible with the Temple and its functions. The opposite of this is *tamei*. Occasionally, the word *tahor* is used to indicate something which is halachically acceptable, in particular, kosher food.

31. In Hebrew, טמא, "*tamei*." Something which is *tamei* is incompatible with the Temple and its functions. The opposite of this is *tahor*. Occasionally, the word *tamei* is used to indicate something which is halachically unacceptable, in particular, non-kosher food.

32. Mishlei 9:12.

33. Tehillim 12:7. The section in parentheses is omitted by the Midrash but is pertinent to the idea of the refinement which the mitzvot perform.

34. There seems to be a printer's error here. There are two similar verses in the Tanach, one in Mishlei 30:5 which begins with the word "All," while the other similar verse is in Tehillim 18:31 which just states "the statement of Hashem is refined," omitting the word "All." It seems more likely that there is an error in the addition of the word "all," as in the Vilna edition of the Midrash in B'reishit Rabbah (which is the source cited in the Rambam), this word is omitted and thus the verse is from Tehillim 18:31. In any event, the section in parentheses occurs in both sources but is not cited in the Midrash or the Maharal, but is pertinent.

35. The Ramban cites the full version of the Midrash, while the Maharal ends here.

36. The golden candelabrum placed in the Tabernacle and Temple.

37. This was an incense offering brought every day in the Temple.

38. This is a reference to the language found at the end of the Midrash Tanchuma, cited partially (above) by the Maharal, but cited in full by the Ramban.

He brought a proof regarding this from [the Midrash cited above describing] one who slaughters from the throat or the [back of the] neck, which implied that they[39] are all for our benefit and not for G-d's, "for what does He care[40] . . ." Rather, they are for us, to guide us in the paths of mercy even at the time of slaughtering.

He[41] brought a further proof [from the Midrash], asking if it matters to Him[42] whether one eats *tahor* [foods] (that is, which are permissible) or whether one eats *tamei* [foods] (that is, which are forbidden, regarding which, the Torah said, "They will be defiled for you.")[43] Rather, [the mitzvah to eat kosher food] comes "to ensure we are pristine of spirit, wise and understanding the truth."[44]

על זה מביא ראיה מן השוחט מן הצואר או מן העורף לומר שכולם לתועלת לנו ולא להקב"ה כי מה אכפת ליה וכו' אלא לנו הם להדריכנו בנתיבות הרחמים אף בשעת שחיטה.

והביא ראיה אחרת או מה אכפת אם אוכל טהרות והם המאכלים המותרים לאכול או טמאות והם המאכלות האסורות שאמרה בהם התורה טמאים הם לכם רק שהוא להיותנו נקיי הנפש חכמים משכילים האמת כו'.

The Maharal now cites a similar Midrash to that cited by the Ramban.

Furthermore, [we find] in the Midrash in the Y'lamdeinu[45] in the section of "This is the animal . . ." [as follows],

ועוד במדרש בילמדנו בפרשת זאת החיה (שם):

> So did [King] David state, "G-d, His way is perfect and innocent;[46] the statement of Hashem is refined,"[47] – in order to refine humans . . . but does it matter to the Holy One, Blessed be He, if Israel eats [meat] without [the correct method of] slaughter

> כך אמר דוד הא־ל תמים דרכו אמרת ה' צרופה בשביל לצרף את בריותיו מה אכפת להקדוש ברוך הוא שיאכל ישראל בלא שחיטה או שיהא ישראל נוחר ואוכל שוחט מן הצואר ומן העורף?
> תדע שלא נצטוו על השחיטה אלא לצרף את ישראל כי לעתיד לבא עושה

39. All the mitzvot.

40. As the Ramban explained (his comments in full are cited in the Commentary, Ch. 6 § Point 10), G-d definitely cares about the pain of animals; however, His care does not extend to the point of preventing our taking of animal life for a higher purpose. Rather, the method of slaughter is only to benefit us, not G-d.

41. The Ramban.

42. G-d.

43. Vayikra 11:28. This verse is dealing with those foods which are forbidden to eat – in particular, non-kosher animals.

44. From the Ramban's language there.

45. Tanchuma, Sh'mini 7.

46. See the Commentary, Introduction § Point 1 where the term *tamim*, תמים, is introduced and explored. We translate it as "perfect and innocent."

47. Tehillim 18:31.

or whether Israel will stab [or whether the slaughter is performed] at the throat or the [back of the] neck?

סעודה לצדיקים ואין שם שחיטה וכו' עד אלא בשביל לבדוק ולצרף את ישראל ע"כ.

Know this, that they[48] were only commanded regarding [the correct method of] slaughter in order to refine Israel. For in the future, [Hashem] will make a feast for the righteous and there, there will be no slaughter . . . [we thus learn from this[49] that the laws of slaughtering] are only to test and refine Israel.

As he stated clearly in Chapter Six, the Maharal disagrees with the Ramban on the key element of the Ramban's explanation – that all Mitzvot come to refine humans by developing positive character traits within them. The Maharal now reintroduces his objections.

וכבר אמרנו שאי אפשר לומר שיהיו מצוות התורה על דרך שפירש הרמב"ן ז"ל לקבוע בנו מידות טובות, כי לא תוכל לפרש כך כי רוב מצוות לא נדע טעמם ואם כן איזה דרך ישכון אור המצוות?

But we have already stated[50] that it is impossible to say that the mitzvot of the Torah will function in the way that the Ramban explained – that is, to set within us good traits. One cannot say this since we do not know the reason[s] for most of the mitzvot and therefore, how can the light of the mitzvot dwell [within us if we do not learn any positive trait from most of the mitzvot]?[51]

The Maharal now explains his understanding of the Midrashim which seem to support the Ramban's contention that all mitzvot come to refine humans by developing positive character traits within them. The Maharal's view is that it is not the acquisition of positive traits which refine, but rather the very act of performing any mitzvah causes the refinement. He will expand on this in the continuation of this chapter.

48. The Jews.

49. The Midrash emphasizes that at the end of days, at the feast of the *Livyatan* (the so-called Leviathan), there will be no ritual slaughter required on the *Livyatan*. Thus we see that these laws are needed only to refine Israel. The Maharal will expand on his understanding of what this "refinement" is.

50. Tiferet Yisrael 6.

51. As the Maharal explained in Chapter Six, "if the mitzvot were all [aimed at influencing] positive values within the soul of a human, like the mitzvah of *tz'dakkah* . . . then it would be possible to say that a person would acquire positive values through them and would distance himself from evil . . . But, the mitzvot of *sha'atnez*, *kilayim* and the mitzvah to slaughter an animal at the throat and not from the [back of] the neck . . . [are not mitzvot which focus on the acquisition of positive traits]."

אמנם מה שאמר לא נתנה תורה רק לצרף הבריות, אין הפירוש כי המצוות הם מצרפים האדם במה שידריך האדם עצמו במידות הטובות וההגונות, שבזה יקשה כמו שכתבנו למעלה כי דבר זה היה הגון במצוות אשר נדע טעמם אבל במצוות שנעלם מאתנו טעם שלהם לא נוכל לומר כך.

אבל המצוות בעצמם מצרפים נפש האדם להשיב אותה אל ה׳.

However, when the Midrash[52] stated, "the Torah[53] was only given to refine human beings," the meaning of this was not that the mitzvot refine a human through guiding him in [the acquisition of] good and appropriate character traits – this understanding would encounter the difficulties we raised above. Such an explanation would [only] be suitable regarding the mitzvot the reasons for which we know, but regarding the mitzvot for which we do not know the reasons, we would be unable to supply this [explanation].

Rather, the mitzvot themselves refine the soul of a person, to return it to Hashem.

52. Cf. B'reishit Rabbah 44:1; Tanchuma, Sh'mini 8.

53. This phrase, containing the word "Torah" is not found in any of the Midrashim cited thus far, nor is it in the text of the Ramban. Rather, the phrase cited in all these sources is, "the mitzvot were only given to refine. . . ."

SUMMARY

Chapter 7: 1/4

I. The Maharal continues his explanation of the Rambam's (Maimonides's) Opinion

- A. The Rambam's statements are in Moreh N'vuchim 3:26.
- B. B'reishit Rabbah (44:1)
  - 1. The Rambam cites this Midrash which states that:
    - a. It doesn't matter to Hashem what *detailed* method of slaughter is used in kosher animals' slaughter, but the reason He commanded us to use a specific method was to refine us.
  - 2. The Rambam's explanation of the Midrash
    - a. All mitzvot have reasons.
    - b. The details of the mitzvot do not have reasons and come to refine human beings through teaching them obedience to Hashem.
- C. The Maharal's objection to the Rambam's position
  - 1. The Maharal believes that even the details have reasons.
    - a. The Torah (D'varim 4:8) states that it is self-evident from the mitzvot themselves that they have reasons.

II. The Maharal examines the Ramban's (Nachmanides's) explanation of this Midrash

- A. The Ramban's explanation (in his commentary to D'varim 22:6) of this Midrash:
  - 1. The Ramban explains that the Midrash's intent is not to say that there is no reason or purpose behind the details of the mitzvot, but rather that, in general, no mitzvah we perform can ever affect G-d. The mitzvot are not for G-d, they are for humans – their purpose is to develop within us positive traits.
- B. The Maharal cites another Midrash (Tanchuma, Sh'mini 7) which seems to support the Ramban's position.
- C. The Maharal reiterates his objection to the Ramban's position:
  - 1. One cannot say that the mitzvot's purpose is to develop positive traits within humans because there are too many mitzvot, the reasons for which are unknown, from which we therefore learn no positive traits.

III. The Maharal's explanation of how mitzvot cause refinement of human beings

A. The Maharal does say that the mitzvot refine a person, but not through inculcation of positive traits within him or her.
B. Rather, the very performance of the mitzvot themselves is the catalyst of that refinement (which will be explained further in the continuation of this chapter).

CHAPTER 7

Part 2 of 4

The Maharal now expands the idea he introduced previously in this chapter – that the simple performance of the mitzvot is what causes refinement of the human being, not the acquisition of any positive character traits thereby. First he examines how the prohibitions effect this refinement.

ולכך סדר השם יתברך מצוות לא תעשה כי על ידי סדר הזה האדם אינו יוצא מן הסדר כלל. ולהורות כי מצוות לא תעשה נותנים לאדם סדר שלא יצא מן הראוי, נתן לאדם מיד ז' מצוות כולם מצוות לא תעשה כמו שבארנו ענין אלו שבע מצוות בחבור גבורת ה' ע"ש.

Therefore, Hashem, may He be Blessed, arranged prohibitions – because through this arrangement the human being does not deviate from the [optimal] order at all.[1] And to illustrate that the Prohibitions confer upon a human an order [which ensures] that he not deviate [from the ideal arrangement, upon creation], Hashem immediately[2] gave humanity seven mitzvot which are all prohibitions; as we have explained in the work, the G'vurot Hashem,[3] see there.

The Maharal explains that there are seven facets in which all creations can vary. Thus there are seven dimensions in which a human being's behavior can deviate from the ideal and therefore, Hashem gave humans the seven Noahide laws in order to curb all possible deviation. The Maharal's idea is that even if we do not understand the consequences of the transgression of any prohibition, such a transgression causes us to deviate from the ideal cosmic order. This is true even if we do not see

---

1. See above, Tiferet Yisrael 4, where the Maharal explains this idea in depth.

2. See Sanhedrin 56b. There, the sages of the Gemara analyze the verse describing the first command given by Hashem to Adam. Their analysis shows that this command included the seven basic mitzvot which are incumbent on all human beings; in particular: "Laws," cursing G-d, idol worship, murder, sexual immorality, tearing a limb from a living animal and theft. However, for a different understanding, see Rambam (Laws of Kings 9:1).

3. G'vurot Hashem 66. Written by the Maharal, the name means "the mightinesses of Hashem," an admittedly cumbersome phrase – the translation of the Hebrew, "*g'vurah*," has no exact translation to English. See the Commentary, Ch. 7 § Point 4 here where we cite this chapter from G'vurot Hashem in full.

ourselves acquiring any negative trait through such a transgression. As he explains in G'vurot Hashem,[4] such deviations prevent human beings from bonding with G-d, and such bonding is the purpose of creation.

וזה כי כבר אמרנו שהאדם יש לו סדר בעצמו, וכל אשר הוא מסודר היציאה מן הסדר שלו הוא בו' פנים, כמו שתאמר הנקודה הזאת המיוחדת במקום זה יש לה יציאה שיוצאת מן היחוד והסדר שלה לימין או לשמאל או לפנים או לאחור או למעלה או למטה, ואלו ו' דברים הם מה שיש לה נטיה מן היחוד והסדר שלה, אבל הבטול לגמרי הוא דבר זולת זה והוא ענין שביעי נמצא שהדבר יש לו יציאה בשבעה דברים.

ואם כי זה שייך ברחקים הגשמיים שיש אל הגשם ששה צדדים אלו אשר אמרנו, אבל בדברים הנבדלים לא שייך כל זה, מ"מ תמצא ג"כ ימין ושמאל בדבר שאינו גשמי כמו שכתוב (דברים י"ג [צ"ל י"ז]) לא תסור מכל הדברים אשר יורוך ימין ושמאל, הרי תמצא ימין ושמאל אף שלא בדבר הגשמי רק הוא נאמר בבחינת הדבר המיוחד והמסודר שלא יהיה יציאה לו מן היחוד והסדר.

וכמו כן שייך לומר בכל הששה צדדין עד שיהיה נשאר בסדר וביחוד שלו, ואין לו יציאה בשום בחינה מן היחוד והסדר לשום צד על ידי אלו ז'

This is, as we said, because a human being has his own order and [in general] any deviation from his order can occur in any one of six ways. This is [the same] as one can say regarding a specific point in a specific place – it can deviate from its uniqueness [in position and from its] order, to the right, left, forwards, backwards, up or down [a total of six deviations]. And these six are the aspects from which it[5] can deviate from its uniqueness and order. However, that which causes absolute negation [of the uniqueness and the order of the point] is the seventh factor.[6] Therefore, every thing has seven factors through which it departs [from the ideal].

Now, although this applies to physical distances (since in physical space, these six dimensions exist), and despite the fact that all such concepts do not exist in the transcendent realm,[7] nevertheless, you do find the concepts of "right" and "left" in non-physical things, as is written, "You may not turn aside from any of the things that they will teach you, neither right nor left."[8] One sees that there is a right and a left even in non-physical matters, but these [references in the verse cited above] refer to a lack of deviation from that which is

4. Cited in full in the Commentary, Ch. 7 § Point 4.

5. The point.

6. For further reading, see the Commentary, Ch. 7 § Point 2 and Introduction § Point 15.

7. See the end of Tiferet Yisrael 18 where the Maharal explains that although time is also a physical concept, our time is really an analogue of a higher, transcendent concept of time. One can deduce the same for space.

8. D'varim 17:11.

מצוות בני נח שהם לא תעשה כי פעם יוצא בדבר זה מן יחודו ופעם בהפכו ופעם הוא בטול אליו לגמרי.

ומי שהוא מבין יבין באלו ז' מצוות אשר הם שומרים ומעמידים את האדם על יחודו ועל סדר שלו כמו שהתבאר בחבור גבורת השם, כי יחודו וסדר שלו עומד על ידי שבעה כי אי אפשר בפחות לכך היו לו ז' מצוות מעמידים אותו על יחוד שיש לו.

unique and ordered – that there should be no such deviation from uniqueness and order.

Similarly, it is appropriate to speak of all six dimensions so that a person will remain in his order and uniqueness and have no deviation in any aspect from uniqueness and order, in any way. [This lack of deviation will be ensured] through these seven Noahide mitzvot, which are all prohibitions,[9] because sometimes a person deviates from his uniqueness in one matter and sometimes in the opposite matter and sometimes his uniqueness is completely annulled.

And one who is perceptive will understand [that it is] these seven mitzvot which guard and preserve the human being in his uniqueness and his order, as has been explained in the work, G'vurot Hashem.[10] [This is] because his[11] order and uniqueness exist through these seven [factors] since it is not possible with fewer [than seven factors]; therefore, these seven mitzvot preserve him in his uniqueness.

The Maharal now expands this idea to explain the reason that the Jewish people have more mitzvot than just the seven Noahide laws. He explains that there is a directly proportional relationship between the degree to which a nation's destiny is wholly focused on G-d's will and the minimum allowable degree of deviation from the ideal order. Since Israel is completely set aside to serve G-d, they have far less margin for error and thus require more prohibitions to prevent deviation.

אמנם ישראל עם ה' אשר בחר בהם ונתיחדו אל השם יתברך יותר ויותר, שיש להם נפש מיוחדת א-להית ביותר, נתיחדו עוד במצוות לא תעשה שהם שס"ה כפי אשר הם מיוחדים נתיחדו יותר שלא יצאו מן הסדר הראוי.

However, Israel, which is the nation which Hashem chose and who were consigned[12] largely to Hashem, may He be Blessed, [and] who possess a very special G-dly soul, were designated [to have] more prohibitions – totaling three

9. This statement seems to indicate that the Maharal concurs with the Ramban's interpretation of the commandment relating to "Laws" in the seven Noahide commandments. The Ramban, as opposed to the Rambam, holds that this commandment is a prohibition against the perversion of justice. See the Commentary Ch. 7 § Point 4, in the citation from G'vurot Hashem.

10. G'vurot Hashem 66.

11. A person's.

12. Or "dedicated." See the Commentary, Ch. 7 § Point 1 for more on this terminology.

hundred and sixty-five.[13] According to their uniqueness, they were set aside to a greater degree, so that they not deviate from the suitable order.

The Maharal turns his attention now to the "initiative-action" commandments: *mitzvot aseh*. He explains that these are needed for the Jewish people to be able to become more transcendent and therefore to bond with G-d. Thus, the prohibitions prevent the formation of any obstacles to bonding with G-d while the initiative-action Mitzvot are the means for proactively bonding with G-d. The manner in which the *mitzvot aseh* allow a person to bond with G-d is simple: by adopting the mitzvot as a guideline for one's actions, one is really adopting a transcendent framework of thought. Thus, one is joined to G-d's mind, as it were.

ועוד נתיחדו במצוות עשה שהם רמ"ח מצוות.

כי הנפש שהיא עומדת בגוף נוטה עצמה אל הטבע, והיא באמת נפש א-להית מלמעלה רק שהיא עומדת בגוף צריך להוציא אותה מן הטבע ולהיות לה דביקות בו יתברך.

וזהו על ידי המצוות אשר מעשה המצוות הוא לפי השכל אשר מסודר לאדם, ועל ידי שעושה המצוה שהוא סדר שכלי יש לאדם דביקות בשכלי ויוצא מן הטבע שהאדם חומד בו ואז יש לו דבקות בו יתברך.

They[14] were further designated through *mitzvot aseh* (numbering two hundred and forty-eight).

[The reason they need these extra mitzvot is] that the soul which exists in the body inclines itself towards the natural [physical reality] while the soul, in truth, is really a G-dly soul from above, except that it is placed in a body. [Therefore] it is necessary to draw it [away] from nature in order that it may bond with G-d, may He be Blessed. This [bonding] is achieved through the mitzvot [*aseh*].

[The mechanism through which the *mitzvot aseh* achieve this bonding with G-d is] that the actions of mitzvot are determined by the intellect (which is arranged for humanity) and through performing the mitzvot (which comprise a *sichli*[15] system), a human gains a bond with the *sichli* [reality] and [thereby] a person draws [himself] away from the natural [reality] which he [usually] desires. Then he achieves bonding with G-d, may He be Blessed.[16]

The Maharal returns to his analysis of the Midrash he cited previously in this chapter. There he took issue with both the Rambam and the Ramban's explanations of

13. See above, Tiferet Yisrael 4, where the Maharal explores the significance of there being 365 prohibitions.

14. The Jewish people.

15. As we noted already in the Introduction to this work, the Maharal identifies that which is *sichli* and intellectual with being transcendent and spiritual. See the Commentary, Introduction § Point 1 in the Introduction of this work.

16. See the Commentary, Ch. 7 § Point 3 for more on this.

this Midrash. The Rambam understood that this Midrash implies that there are no reasons for the details of the mitzvot. The Ramban understood that this Midrash implies that the mitzvot all have reasons (even the details) but that they have no benefit for G-d and are aimed instead at inculcating positive traits within humans. Like the Ramban, the Maharal disavows the Rambam's position that the details of mitzvot have no meaning and he concurs that the mitzvot only benefit humans and not G-d. However, the Maharal believes, unlike the Ramban, that the benefit accrued to humans through the mitzvot is not through the acquisition of positive character traits, but rather through creating a bond with G-d. This is because mitzvah performance is actually the physical implementation of a transcendent, *sichli* framework of ideas, as he explained above.

וזה שאמר ומה אכפת להקדוש ברוך הוא בין שוחט מן הצואר ובין שוחט מן העורף בין אוכל טהרות ובין אוכל טמאות.

ורצה לומר כי אין השם יתברך חפץ בשחיטה מצד השחיטה בעצמה שהוא דבר טוב, כי מה אכפת להקדוש ברוך הוא בשחיטה בעצמה כי אחר שהוא מפסיד הבעל חי מה לי אם מפסידו מן הצואר או מן העורף?

אלא לא נתנה תורה רק לצרף הבריות כדי שיהיה מעשה האדם כאשר נותן הסדר השכלי שלו מן השם יתברך, ודבר זה הוא צרוף וזכוך הנפש כאשר דבק בשכלי ואז יש לו דבקות בו יתברך.

וזה שאמר אמרת אלוה צרופה מגן הוא לכל החוסים בו ואמרו (תנחומא שמיני) למה שהיא מגין עליך, כלומר כאשר יהיה צרופה נפשו מן הטבע החמרית ובזה יש אל נפש האדם דבקות

This is what [the Midrash meant when it stated] "Does it matter to the Holy One, Blessed be He, whether one slaughters from the throat or the [back of the] neck?"[17] [Similarly], "Does it matter to Him whether one eats *tahor* [food] or whether one eats *tamei* [food]?"[18]

The Midrash's intent is that Hashem, may He be Blessed, does not desire [that we perform a specifically regulated ritual] slaughter for the sake of the slaughter because it is good in and of itself – for what does the Holy One, Blessed be He, care for slaughter itself? Because once one is destroying an animal, does it matter whether one destroys it from the throat or the [back of the] neck?

Rather [as the Midrash continues,] "the mitzvot were only given to refine humans,"[19] in order that human actions should be according to the *sichli* order from Hashem, may He be Blessed. And this thing is a refinement and purification of the soul (when it bonds with the *sichli* [reality]) and then he[20] attains bonding with G-d, may He be Blessed.

17. B'reishit Rabbah 44:1 with variations. Also see Vayikra Rabbah 13:3.
18. Tanchuma, Sh'mini 8.
19. B'reishit Rabbah 44:1 with variations. Also see Vayikra Rabbah 13:3.
20. The person.

אל השם יתברך, וגם השם יתברך עם האדם והוא מגן עליו סוכך עליו.

This is the intent of the Midrash[21] when it cites [the verse], "All the statement of Hashem is refined, it is a shield to all who take refuge in Him."[22] And they[23] said,[24] "Why should it be a shield for you?" Meaning, when one's soul is refined of the material nature, then the human soul has a bonding with Hashem, may He be Blessed, and [also] Hashem, may He be Blessed, is with the person and He protects and shelters him.

21. B'reishit Rabbah 44:1 with variations. Also see Vayikra Rabbah 13:3.

22. Tehillim 18:31. The words, "it is a shield to all who take refuge in Him" are not cited in the Midrash, but they are the second half of the verse which is cited in the Midrash.

23. Our sages.

24. Tanchuma, Sh'mini 8.

SUMMARY

Chapter 7: 2/4

I. **The Maharal's explanation of how mitzvot cause the refinement of human beings**
   A. The purpose of Prohibitions
      1. The prohibitions ensure that a human being does not deviate from the ideal order and arrangement of life for a human being
         a. Therefore there were originally seven prohibitions given to humankind (the seven Noahide Laws).
            (1) This is because there are six dimensions and the origin which together give the position of any object in this world. Therefore, all variation and deviation derives from a change in one of these seven variables.
            (2) Therefore, there were Seven Noahide Laws – preventing all possible deviation from the ideal human arrangement.
      2. The Maharal refers to his work, G'vurot Hashem where he explains in detail that all such deviations have amongst others, a common effect: they prevent human beings from being able to bond with G-d.
         a. The seven laws suffice to prevent humanity in general from losing their ability to join with Hashem.
         b. The Jewish people who are designated completely for G-d's purposes have less margin for deviation and thus require more than just seven prohibitions – they have three hundred and sixty-five.
   B. The purpose of *mitzvot aseh*
      1. These allow one proactively to bond with Hashem.
      2. Since the body naturally tends to the physical (since it is physical and natural), one requires the means to enable oneself to overcome this trend and bond with Hashem.
      3. These means are the *mitzvot aseh*.
         a. They allow one to bond with Hashem since the entire system of mitzvot is generated by the transcendent-spiritual-*sichli* reality.
         b. Thus, when one performs a mitzvah, one is replacing one's natural, physical set of motivations with this spiritual system as the determinant of one's personal actions. Immediately, this creates a bond between a person and this adopted spiritual reality and thereby with Hashem.
   C. The Maharal's explanation of the Midrash
      1. The Midrash which stands at the center of the dispute between the

Rambam, the Ramban and the Maharal stated, "Does it matter to the Holy One, Blessed be He, whether one slaughters from the throat or the [back of the] neck?"

2. The Maharal explains that this means that the act of slaughter in and of itself has no intrinsic value, but what is important is that human beings choose to perform this act in the manner that G-d has set down. This adoption of G-d's set of priorities and of a spiritual system of motivation is what causes refinement to the human being.
   a. This happens regardless of whether the particular mitzvah helps a person acquire a particular positive character trait.
   b. The very fact that a person has chosen the Torah as his compass and map is an act of refinement.

CHAPTER 7

Part 3 of 4

The Maharal now brings a second explanation as to how the mitzvot refine human beings – this is an extension of his first explanation. He explains here that human beings consist of a spiritual seed (the soul) planted within a physical substrate (the body). In nature, the only way that any seed can flower, grow and perfect itself is through actualizing its essence – which is its potential – by actually producing its leaves, branches and fruit in a particular way.

Similarly, in the case of the soul, the only way it can perfect itself is by actualizing its essence – which is spiritual potential – by actually performing mitzvot. Just as the seed and ground work together to actualize the seed's potential, so should the soul and the body collaborate in reaching spiritual actualization.[1]

And know further that the seed which is sown in the ground produces a tree, fruit, leaves and branches. And the leaves and fruit are in a unique form which is suited to the seed due [to] its unique nature. Do not say that it would be bad if it were to produce the branches and leaves in another fashion, because this is what the nature of the seed decreed.[2] And through this form and description the seed becomes completely actualized and it is [only] complete when it produces the leaves and fruit as is appropriate to the nature of the seed.

Similarly, the soul (which is from above) is pristine and pure and is placed in the body of a human below and he needs to actualize it just as the seed is actualized in the ground in which it is

ודע עוד כי הגרעין אשר נזרע באדמה הוא מוציא אילן ופירות ועלין והענפים, והעלין והפירות הם בצורה מיוחדת שראוי אל הגרעין מצד טבעו המיוחד לו, ואל תאמר שאם היה מוציא הענפים והעלין בצורה אחרת שהיה זה רע, רק כי כך גזר הטבע של הגרעין ובצורה זאת התאר הזה יוצא הגרעין הזה אל הפעל הגמור, והוא בשלמות כאשר מוציא העלין והפירות כפי מה שראוי אל טבע הגרעין.

וכמו כן עצמו הנפש שהיא מלמעלה היא זכה וטהורה ונתנה בגוף האדם למטה, וצריך שיוציא אותה אל הפועל כמו שהגרעין יוצא אל הפעל מן האדמה שנזרע בו, והיא יוצאת אל הפעל כפי מה שראוי לנפש, וכאשר יצאה הנפש אל הפעל היא בשלמות, ומצד השלמות שלה היא דבקה למעלה עם ה' כמו שהיא באה מלמעלה.

1. For more on the parallels between seed and soul, fruit and mitzvot, see Chapter Three of this work.

2. The Maharal's idea here is that what differentiates one seed from another is its "essence in potential" – what we would call DNA.

sown. And [the soul][3] is actualized [in a manner] as is appropriate to the soul and when it is actualized it is complete, and by virtue of this perfection it bonds with Hashem above, as it came from above.[4]

The Maharal now explores the inconsistencies within the parallel between human actualization and that of a seed. The process within botany is a natural one which, by definition, is automatic; however, within the human world, this process is volitional. Moreover, the results differ greatly – the seed's end-product remains within the world of botany, but the products of the soul transcend the physical world where they were generated and reach the transcendent realm.

רק כי זהו ההפרש, כי האילן הוצאת תואר הענפים והעלין וצורת הפירות הכל הוא טבעי, אבל האדם הכל מצד הנפש, כי אין מעלתו האחרונה טבעית כלל רק יש לאדם נפש א־להית מיוחדת, וכפי נפשו הא־להית נתן לו גם כן מצוות מיוחדות אשר ראוים לו, ולכך נתן השם יתברך התורה והיא בלתי טבעית ועל ידה יצא אדם לפעל השלמות כמו שיצא האילן לפעל השלמות, והוא אשר רמז הכתוב (דברים כ') כי האדם עץ השדה כמו שנתבאר במקום אחר.

The difference [between the seed and the soul] is that regarding the tree, the extension of the appearance of branches, leaves and the form of the fruit is all natural; but regarding a human, everything is from the soul [which is transcendent] because its final level is not natural at all since man has a special, G-dly soul. And according to his G-dly soul, Hashem also gave him special mitzvot which are suitable for him and therefore, Hashem, may He be Blessed, gave [humans] the Torah which is not natural and through it a person will actualize his perfection just as a tree actualizes its perfection. This is [the idea] to which the verse hinted [when it stated,] "For is a man a tree of the field?"[5] as is explained elsewhere.[6]

3. Lit., "it."

4. Chapters Two, Three and Four of this work provide background material for the ideas that the Maharal is now presenting. In those chapters, the Maharal develops his thoughts on the identity of a human being as a hybrid spiritual-physical being with a transcendent component (the soul) which is constantly yearning to return to the transcendent world and to reunify with Hashem; he also explains his idea that mitzvot are the only channel for the soul to achieve transcendence while in this world (by virtue of their being determined by the *sichli* reality, which is Hashem's will).

5. D'varim 20:19.

6. The Maharal explains the various parallels between humanity and the tree in many different places. Amongst them, Gur Aryeh: B'reishit 9:21, B'midbar 14:37 and D'varim 20:19; Derech Chaim: Introduction and 3:17, and elsewhere.

The Maharal now concludes his argument by explaining that "refinement" is simply the actualization of one's essence. This applies to a seed in the ground as well as to a soul in a body.[7] Since mitzvot are the only channel allowing the human "seed" to flower properly, they are the only path to such "refinement." The reason he addresses this question is because the Midrash[8] over which he, the Rambam and the Ramban are disputing stated that, "the mitzvot were only given to refine humans" – here he brings his own definition of this "refinement."

וכמו שבאילן הוצאת הענפים והפירות שלו לצרף את טבעו כאשר ראוי, ואם לא היה מוציא הענפים והעלין וצורת הפרי בודאי היה מקולקל כאשר ראינו שאינו מוציא שלמות שלו אל הפעל, כך הוא דבר זה אם לא היה מוציא פעולת המצוות אל הפעל היה נשאר בכח מוטבע בחומר, ודבר זה קלקול אליו כאשר נפשו מלמעלה והיא מוטבע בגוף אם כן הנפש היא נשאר בכח.

וצריך שתצא נפשו אל הפעל מן החמרית ואין זה רק על ידי מצוות א־להיות כמו שיצא לפעל זרע הנטוע בארץ ודבר זה צירוף נפשו כאשר יוצאת לפעל.

And just as with a tree, the extension of the branches and fruit [acts] to refine its[9] nature as is suitable, and without the extension of the branches, leaves and the form of the fruit, it would definitely be corrupted (as we see since it would not be actualizing its potential perfection); so too is the matter [regarding the soul]: if it did not actualize the activity of the mitzvot, it would remain as potential sunk in the physical, and this would be a corruption for it (since one's soul is from above and [when] it is sunk in the body it remains in potential).

[Therefore,] it is necessary that one's soul is actualized [by departing from a state of pure] physicality, which only happens through G-dly mitzvot, just as a seed sown in the ground is actualized – and this is a refinement for one's soul, when it is actualized.[10]

The Maharal explains that the parallels between the soul-body and the seed-ground; and between mitzvot and fruit are reflected throughout the words of our sages.

7. See all the Midrashim cited throughout Chapter Six and at the beginning of this chapter – many of which focused on the idea of the Torah's refining effects on human beings.

8. This Midrash, B'reishit Rabbah 44:1, is the central source in Chapters Six and Seven.

9. The seed's.

10. See Chapter Three of Tiferet Yisrael where many of these ideas are discussed at length. In particular, the Maharal there explains why it is that the only way that the soul can achieve its potential while in this world, is though Torah and mitzvot.

Therefore, [our sages], *z"l*, said in every context in which they discussed the reward for the mitzvot [as follows],[11]

ולכך אמרו ז"ל בכל מקום כאשר היו רוצים לדבר על שכר המצוות אמרו (פאה פ"א):

> These are the things[12] for which a person enjoys the *fruit* [of his labor] in this world, while the capital remains for him in the World to Come.

> אלו דברים שאדם אוכל פירותיהם בעולם הזה והקרן קיימת לו לעולם הבא.

[They used the metaphor of "fruit"] because a person actualizes his potential perfection through the mitzvot (since [he possesses] a soul drawn from above), just as a tree actualizes its potential perfection, [and this actualization continues] until a person acquires the ultimate excellence and bonds with Hashem, may He be Blessed.

מפני שהאדם על ידי המצוות יוצא אל הפעל השלמות, במה שהיא נפש אצולה מלמעלה, כמו שיוציא האילן לפעל השלימות שלו עד שקונה האדם המעלה העליונה ולהיות דבק בו יתברך.

The Maharal summarizes his two explanations as to how the performance of the mitzvot causes a refinement of the human soul. His first explanation was that when a person intentionally chooses to perform a mitzvah, he is replacing his natural, physical, selfish desires with a framework of priorities determined by Hashem's will and thus one automatically draws closer to Hashem (by adopting His will) and is refined. His second explanation was that since each human has a G-dly soul planted within him, it is impossible for that soul to reach its perfection (that is, its most refined status) except through actualization of its G-dly potential, a potential which is built into the soul's G-dly DNA. This G-dly potential is only actualized through G-dly actions, which are the mitzvot, and in this view one is not replacing one's natural desires with G-d's will, but rather one is revealing that the mitzvot are actually the deepest desires of one's own soul.

Therefore, you have no need to enquire why it is that a person achieves perfection in actuality [only] through mitzvot, because this is definitely not a difficulty!

ולכן אין לך לשאול למה על ידי מצוה הזאת האדם בשלימות בפעל, שודאי אין זה קשיא.

Just as one feels no need to question why a tree [only reaches] actual perfection when its form and appearance are [expressed] in a particular way and not when its form and appearance are [expressed] in another way [and the

כמו שאין עליך לשאול למה אילן זה בפעל השלימות כאשר צורתו ותוארו כך ולא היה צורתו ותוארו בענין אחר, רק כי דבר זה מתחייב לפי העצם הגרעין, וכך מתחייב, לפי נפשו אשר היא א־להית מלמעלה שהוא בעל השלימות כאשר הוא

11. Mishnah, Pei'ah 1:1.

12. I.e., mitzvot.

עושה מצוות אלו, והכל הוא לפי מה שנותן השכל שיהיה האדם בפעל מצד שיש לו נפש א־להית ומה שגוזר ענינו.
וזהו צירוף נפשו.

reason one feels no need to question is] because this is required due to the essence of the seed and this [development] is mandatory; so too since one's soul is G-dly, from above, it possesses perfection [only] when it performs the mitzvot, and all this is due to the demands of the *sichli* [reality] that a person be actualized from the aspect of his G-dly soul [and it is also due] to what its[13] nature decrees.

This is [what is meant by the term] "refinement of his soul."

13. The soul's.

SUMMARY

Chapter 7: 3/4

I. **The Maharal's explanation of how mitzvot cause refinement of human beings: continued**
   A. The parallels between a human and a tree
      1. A tree
         a. A tree is produced through a partnership between a seed and the soil.
         b. Each seed is programmed with a particular path to self-fulfillment.
         c. After being planted in the soil, the seed produces a tree – leaves, branches and fruit – according to its nature.
         d. This is the only path that a seed has to self-fulfillment and self-perfection.
      2. A human
         a. A human being is produced through a partnership between a soul and a body.
         b. Each soul is programmed with a particular path to self-fulfillment.
         c. After being planted in the body, the soul can only reach self-fulfillment through producing certain types of actions with the body. This is the nature of the soul.
         d. This is the only path that a soul has to self-fulfillment and self-perfection.
   B. The differences between humans and trees
      1. A tree
         a. The entire process is automatic.
         b. The entire process is natural. The seed, soil and the growth emanating from the seed are physical.
      2. A human
         a. The process is not automatic at all – a person must choose to actualize his perfection.
         b. The process is not all natural. The soul is drawn from the transcendent world and ultimately, it belongs there, not here. Thus the only types of actions that can bring it fulfillment are spiritual actions which allow it to transcend the purely physical and thus the soul's fruits are not natural and physical, they are transcendent.

(1) These spiritual actions are mitzvot – the embodiments of Torah – and they allow the soul to reach transcendence and bond with Hashem.

C. Refinement
1. We term something to be "refined" when it is self-fulfilled and self-actualized.
2. Thus, a seed is only refined when it has produced a tree.
3. Similarly, the soul can only be termed "refined" when it has become actualized. This can only happen through the mitzvot, which are the soul's deepest desire.
   a. This is the meaning of the Midrash which explained that only through mitzvot can a person be refined.

CHAPTER 7

Part 4 of 4

The Maharal now completes his explanation of the reason that mitzvot are the only means to the refinement of the human being. Harking back to Chapter Four, he reminds us that humanity exists within a context, a place. He explains that the 365 prohibitions correspond to the "place" of the human being, which is "under the sun" (an existence delineated by 365 days of the year), and these prohibitions ensure that one does not deviate from the ideal order and arrangement of life for a human being. On the other hand, 248 *mitzvot aseh* correspond to the human being himself, ensuring that he/she is perfected.

Now, because a human being is completed through [having] 248 component-limbs[1] and [because] the world is completed through [having] 365 days (through which it doesn't deviate from the [ideal cosmic] arrangement and instead remains in its order without budging); therefore, [Hashem] also gave the human being 248 *mitzvot aseh* for his completion, and He gave him 365 prohibitions that he should remain in his order and not deviate from the order in which he was created.

Elsewhere[2] we have explained further that the human being (who is the crux of the creations) [has] his place in this world, under the sun, and this is his home and place. And as we have stated regarding all the objects in the world, they are [all] "under the sun."[3] And every object in the world has a place,

ומפני כי האדם הושלם ברמ"ח אברים, והעולם שלא יצא מן הסדר, רק יעמוד בסדר שלו ולא ימוש הושלם בשס"ה ימים, ובשביל כך נתן לאדם גם כן רמ"ח מצוות עשה אל השלמתו ונתן לו שס"ה מצוות לא תעשה שיעמוד בסדר שלו שלא יצא מן הסדר שנברא עליו.

ובמקום אחר פרשנו עוד כי האדם שהוא עיקר בנבראים ומקומו בעולם הזה תחת השמש וזהו ביתו ומקומו וכמו שאמרנו שעל כל הדברים שהם בעולם יאמר שהם תחת השמש. וכל דבר בעולם יש לו מקום, כמו שאמרו (אבות פ"ד) אין לך דבר שאין לו מקום, כאלו היה המקום שייך לאדם עד שהמקום נכנס בגדר של כל דבר, ולכך צריך לכתוב בגט שם המקום. ובדבר זה הארכנו במקום אחר כי המקום שייך לאדם ונכנס בגדרו.

ולפיכך מצוות התורה אשר נתן לאדם כנגד האדם ועולמו אשר דר בו

1. See Chapter Four for the Maharal's explanation of how the human being is completed through his 248 limbs.
2. D'rosh al Hatorah. See the Commentary, Ch. 7 § Point 5.
3. For the Maharal's explanation on this, see Chapter Four of this work.

האדם והוא מקומו. והאדם בעצמו יש לו רמ"ח אברים שהם שלימות האדם וכנגד זה נתן לו רמ"ח מצוות עשה שהם שלימות האדם.

ויש לו מקום אשר הוא בו אשר המקום מגביל הדבר שלא יצא, וכבר אמרנו כי מקומו של אדם הוא תחת החמה וכך נתן לאדם שס"ה מצוות לא תעשה כנגד החמה שיש לה שס"ה ימים, ואלו שס"ה מצוות מגבילין את האדם שלא יצא חוצה ויעבור אלו שס"ה מצוות והם מקומו כמו שהחמה שס"ה ימים שנה הוא מקומו של אדם.

והבן הדברים האלו ופרשנו אותו במקום אחר.

כלל הדבר כי האדם יוצא לפעל על ידי אלו המצוות עד שהוא בשלימות הגמור.

as [our sages][4] stated, "there is no thing which has no place."[5] This is almost as if the place belongs to the person until the place is considered as a "thing"[6] and therefore, in a bill of divorce, one has to write the name of the place [of residence of the divorcees].[7] We explained this at length elsewhere[8] because "place" is appropriate to a person and is contained in the concept [of the person him or herself.]

And the human being himself has 248 component-limbs which are the perfection of the human being. Corresponding to these, [Hashem][9] gave [the human being][10] 248 *mitzvot aseh* which are the perfection of the human being.

And [the human being][11] has a place ([and any place] limits an object so that it doesn't stray [from its location]) and we have already said[12] that a person's place is "beneath the sun." Corresponding to the sun (which has 365 days), He also gave 365 prohibitions to the human being. These 365 [prohibiting] mitzvot regulate the human being so that he should not stray outside [through] violating these 365 mitzvot which are his place; just as the 365 days are the place of a human being.

Understand these concepts; we have explained them[13] elsewhere.[14]

---

4. Lit., "they."
5. Avot 4:3 – i.e., every *thing* has a place.
6. This seems to refer to the citation the Maharal brought from Pirkei Avot, "there is no *thing* which has no place."
7. This is a profound concept which deserves its own book – the extent to which our contexts nurture and generate our identities and modify our behaviors. Modern scholars, in particular within the framework of criminology, have begun to discuss this (see the writings of James Q. Wilson, George L. Kelling and Philip Zimbardo), but it is a concept which Torah has discussed for millennia.
8. See for example, Chiddushei Aggadot, Vol. 3, Sanhedrin 37b, s.v. "*galut m'chaperet*" (p. 147 in the standard edition of the Maharal).
9. Lit., "He."
10. Lit., "Him."
11. Lit., "he."
12. Above and in Chapter Four.
13. Lit., "it."
14. D'rosh al Hatorah. See the Commentary, Ch. 7 § Point 5.

The general rule is that a person is actualized through these mitzvot until he is completely perfect.

The Maharal explains that the purposes of the prohibitions and the *mitzvot aseh* are reflected in the famous verse describing the Torah, "Her ways are ways of pleasantness and all her paths are peace."

ועם כי בודאי כל דברי תורה דרכיה דרכי נועם וכל נתיבותיה שלום.

כלומר כי כל דרכיה של תורה הם טוב בעצמם וזה כנגד מצוות עשה.

וכל נתיבותיה שלום וזה כנגד לא תעשה, שכאשר (ישמור) [(עפ"י הר' הרטמן) ישאר] האדם (החוק) [(עפ"י הר' הרטמן) בחוק] שנתן לו השם יתברך שלא יעבור שס"ה מצוות לא תעשה ולא יצא האדם מן החוק המוגבל ואז יש לו שלום, וכאשר יעבור החוק ונכנס בגבול אחר שאינו ראוי לו אין שלום לו רק השלום כאשר ישאר כל אחד בגבול שלו.

There is no doubt that [regarding] all the words of Torah [we apply the verse,] "Her ways are ways of pleasantness and all her paths are peace."[15]

The meaning [of the phrase, "Her ways are ways of pleasantness"] is that all the ways of Torah are good in and of themselves, which corresponds to the *mitzvot aseh*.

[The phrase,] "and all her paths are peace," corresponds to the prohibitions; for when a person remains within the framework[16] which Hashem, may He be Blessed, gave him (not violating any of the 365 prohibitions and not deviating from the regulated framework) then he has peace. But when a person breaches the limit and enters a different context,[17] one unsuited to him, there is no peace. Peace is only found when each person remains within his [appropriate] space.[18]

The Maharal summarizes his position on the purpose of mitzvot: they refine us.

מכל מקום אין מה שציוה השם יתברך את האדם המצוה מפני שהוא טוב ורצה שיעשה הטוב, רק שהמצוות הם צירוף הבריות שיצא מן הטבע החמרית כמו שאמרנו.

In any event, Hashem, may He be Blessed, did not command humans [to perform] mitzvot because they[19] are good and He desired that humans do good; rather [the reason for the commandments is that] the mitzvot are a refinement of creations which will transcend material nature, as we have said.[20]

15. Mishlei 3:17.
16. Lit., "decree." See the Commentary, Ch. 7 § Point 1.
17. Lit., "border."
18. Lit., "border."
19. The mitzvot.
20. See the Commentary, Ch. 7 § Point 6 for more on this.

The Maharal brings another proof that mitzvot are not performed due to the innate value of their actions but due to their being a function of a Transcendent-intellectual (*sichli*) framework.

ולכך כמה מצוות שאם עשאן אחר חייב מיתה.

כמו שאמר (סנהדרין נ"ח ע"ב) גוי ששמר את השבת חייב מיתה, ואלו היה המצוה משום שהדבר הזה והמעשה הזה טוב בעצמו סוף סוף עשה הגוי מעשה הטוב?

רק שהמצוות הם אל המקבל כפי סדר השכלי אשר ראוי, ולזה נותן סדרו כך ולזה אין נותן לו סדרו כך, אבל אם סדר השם יתברך המצוות כפי הטוב סוף סוף היה המעשה ההוא טוב בעצמו, ולכך המצוות הם מצרפים אדם זה ואת זה ממיתים כי הכל לפי הסדר השכלי.

Therefore, if certain mitzvot are performed by another [type of person, that person sometimes] incurs a death penalty.

[We see an example of this] as is said, "A gentile who observes the Shabbat is liable for death."[21] Now if [the reason for] a mitzvah was because this thing and act was good in and of itself, when it comes down to it, the gentile has done something good [and therefore, why is he deserving of the death penalty?]

Rather, [the reason he is liable for capital punishment is that] the mitzvot relate to the recipient according to the suitable *sichli* order – for one person it prescribes a specific order and to another, a different one. However, if Hashem, may He be Blessed, ordered the mitzvot according to [what is] good, at the end of the day, each act would be good in and of itself. [But this is not how Hashem set the mitzvot and] therefore, the [same] mitzvot [can] refine one person, and [on the other hand, can] cause the death of another – because everything is according to the *sichli* framework.

The Maharal now returns full circle to the Midrash which initiated the discussion at the beginning of this chapter. He explains how the Midrash should be understood according to his position.

וזהו פירוש ומה אכפת להקדוש ברוך הוא בין שוחט מן הצואר ובין שוחט מן העורף.

כי בודאי מצד עצם הפעולה אין חלוק רק שכך ראוי אל המקבל לפי סדר השכלי.

This is the meaning of [the Midrash which stated] "Does it matter to the Holy One, Blessed be He, whether one slaughters from the throat or the [back of the] neck?"[22]

[The meaning of this is that] from the

21. Sanhedrin 58b with variations. Various other examples could be cited – for example, those who are not *Kohanim* are forbidden from performing the Temple service.

22. B'reishit Rabbah 44:1 with variations. Also see Vayikra Rabbah 13:3.

aspect of the essence of this activity,[23] it is certain that there is no difference [between the two methods of slaughter], rather, this is what is suitable for the recipient[24] [of the mitzvot] according to the *sichli* order.

The Maharal now summarizes his position – that the mitzvot refine a person because when one performs a mitzvah, one is implementing G-d's *sichli* framework in this world.

It has thus been explained that a person should not say that the mitzvot are that Hashem, may He be Blessed, wishes [the correct method of] slaughter in and of itself. Rather, the [correct method of] slaughter is an action [which is part of] a framework that is suited to the human being, not due to the essence of the slaughter; and it is this [conformance to that *sichli* framework] which is the refinement of the soul, as we have explained.

And therefore, in the future,[25] when Hashem, may He be Blessed, will make a feast for the righteous, there will be no slaughter at all because [the correct method of] slaughter [functions] to refine the human being and in the future, [humans][26] will not require refinement

והתבאר לך שאל יאמר האדם כי המצוות הם שהשם יתברך רוצה השחיטה בעצמה, רק מפני שהשחיטה הוא מעשה שראוי אל האדם סדר הזה לא מצד עצם השחיטה, וזהו בודאי זכוך הנפש כמו שבארנו.

ולפיכך לעתיד כאשר השם יתברך יעשה סעודה לצדיקים לא תהא שום שחיטה כלל מאחר כי השחיטה היא לצרוף האדם ולעתיד לא יהיה צריך צירוף, כי האדם יהיה אז בשלמות מעלתו.

ואלו היה השחיטה טובה וראויה מצד עצמה אם כן למה תהא השחיטה בטילה כי הדבר שהוא טוב מצד עצמו אין בטול לו, רק כי השחיטה היא לצרף האדם מצד כי מעשה השחיטה השכל מחייב זה שכך יעשה האדם ובזה האדם הוא בפעל השלמות, ולפיכך

23. I.e., slaughter.

24. I.e., human beings.

25. This refers to the Midrash cited by the Maharal at the beginning of this chapter. It is from the Tanchuma, Sh'mini 7 and reads as follows, "Know this, that they [the Jews] were only commanded regarding [the correct method of] slaughter [in order] to refine Israel. For in the future, [Hashem] will make a feast for the righteous and there, there will be no slaughter . . . [we thus learn from this, that the laws of slaughtering] are only to test and refine Israel."

This midrash and the Maharal's comments relate to the discussion regarding the validity of the mitzvot during certain eschatological periods, in particular, following the resurrection of the dead which will usher in an era beyond current human conception. Understandably, given the antinomian attacks made on Judaism by Christianity, Islam and later breakaway sects, this requires full and proper study in and of itself. The Rambam's Thirteen Principles of Faith (in particular the ninth principle) and the commentaries thereupon are a good starting point for this study.

26. Lit., "he."

המצוה הזאת היא צירוף נפשו שהיא מלמעלה, אבל מצד עצם השחיטה לא אכפת להקדוש ברוך הוא אם נוחר או מעקר שיהיה הנוחר רע בעצמו זה אינו, ולכך לעתיד שאין עוד צרוף אין שחיטה.

ודבר זה מבואר ביותר ועוד יתבאר זה.

since the human being will then be at the pinnacle of his excellence.

Were [the correct method of] slaughter good and suitable in and of itself, why would it be annulled, for a matter which is good in and of itself has no annulment? Rather, [the correct method] of slaughter is to refine the human being through the act of slaughter being determined by the [G-dly] intellect (that this is how a person should act) and through this a person actualizes [his] perfection. And therefore, this mitzvah is a refinement for his soul (which comes from on high) but from the aspect of the essence of [the method of] slaughter, it has no relevance to the Holy One, Blessed be He, whether one punctures or uproots [a blood vessel as the act of slaughter, because] it is false that the one who punctures is evil in and of himself. And therefore, in the future, when there is no [need for] refinement, there is no slaughter.

This idea [of the mechanism of the refinement caused by the performance of mitzvot] is well explained and will be further elucidated.[27]

27. In the next chapter.

SUMMARY

Chapter 7: 4/4

I. The Maharal's explanation of how mitzvot cause refinement of human beings: continued

- A. The Maharal explains the function of prohibitions and *mitzvot aseh*
  1. Prohibitions
     - a. Each object which exists (including human beings) has a "place."
       - (1) This is the set of boundaries needed by that object to fulfill its purpose.
     - b. When these limitations are set in an ideal fashion, that object doesn't deviate from its ideal state.
     - c. This is the purpose of the prohibitions – to ensure that the "place" of the soul (its ideal set of boundaries) is set in an ideal manner.
     - d. Thus, there are 365 prohibitions which parallel the 365 days of the year.
       - (1) The reason for this parallel is that the days of the solar year are the ultimate physical, material limit of the human being – curtailing his/her time.
       - (2) Thus there are an equal number of prohibitions, indicating that they too provide the ideal boundaries for the soul.
  2. *Mitzvot aseh*
     - a. These correspond in number to the number of component-limbs in the human being.
     - b. The idea here is that the human Form only reaches its perfection through these 248 component-limbs; and so too the human being can only reach his/her perfection through the *mitzvot aseh* (which also number 248).
- B. "Her ways are ways of pleasantness and all her paths are peace"
  1. The Maharal explains that this verse, which refers to the Torah, encapsulates the ideas above.
  2. "Ways of pleasantness"
     - a. These are the *mitzvot aseh.*
  3. "All her paths are peace"
     - a. This refers to the prohibitions since peace is only attainable when there is respect for healthy boundaries.
- C. Mitzvot are not good in and of themselves, they are only of value since they correspond to the *sichli* ideal

1. The Maharal cites a proof that mitzvot are not good in and of themselves, because for different people, the same action can be positive or negative:
    a. A non-Jew who keeps Shabbat is liable for the death penalty. If keeping Shabbat were good in and of itself, the non-Jew performed a good deed, thus why should he be sanctioned?
    b. We see that the only reason the act of keeping Shabbat is mandated is because it is a part of the ideal *sichli* Torah for a particular person.

D. The Maharal's explanation of the seminal Midrash
1. When the Midrash stated, "Does it matter to the Holy One, blessed be He, whether one slaughters from the throat or the [back of the] neck?" it meant as follows:
    a. The action of slaughtering is not good in and of itself; the only reason that we do it in that particular manner is because it is part of the *sichli* system of the Torah.
2. The reason that the mitzvot refine the soul is due to the actions of the mitzvot adhering to this ultimate transcendent system.
    a. Therefore, in the future, when there will be no need for refinement, when all of humanity is perfected, we are taught that there will be no slaughter.

CHAPTER 8

CHAPTER 8

Part 1 of 3

The Maharal drives home his point that although our sages might sometimes seem to imply that mitzvot were given for the purpose of some specific benefit, this is not the essential reason for the mitzvot. Rather, the truth is that although the mitzvot all have benefits flowing from them automatically, the reason we were commanded to do them is simply that they are a decree from Hashem and are thus part of His transcendent system of life-ideas[1] which serve to refine humanity and thus enable us to bond with Hashem. The Maharal's proof is that Rabban Yochanan ben Zakai, when pressed, divulged that this latter answer is the true one.

התבאר לך כי התורה היא צרוף וזכוך נפש האדם.

ובמדרש (במדבר רבה פרשה י"ט):

שאל גוי אחד את ר' יוחנן בן זכאי אילן עובדיא דאתון עבדין נראים כמין כשפים אתם מביאים פרה ושורפים אותה וכותשין אותה ונוטלין את אפרה ואחד מכם מטמא למת מזין עליו שנים ושלשה טיפין ואתם אומרים לו טהרת.

אמר לו נכנס בך רוח חזזית מימיך?

אמר לו לא.

ראית אדם שנכנסה בו רוח תזזית?

אמר לו הן.

אמר לו ומה אתם עושים?

אמר לו מביאים עיקרים ומעשנין תחתיו ומרביצין עליה מים והיא בורחת.

אמר לו ישמעו אזניך מה שאתה מוציא מפיך כך הרוח הזה רוח טומאה

It has become clarified for you that the Torah is a refinement and purification of the human soul.

And in the Midrash [the following is stated],[2]

> A gentile once asked Rabbi Yochanan ben Zakai, "Those religious services which you perform – they look like witchcraft! You bring a cow[3] and burn it and crush it and take the ashes and then if someone has become *tamei*[4] due to contact with a corpse, you sprinkle on him[5] two or three drops [of water mixed with those ashes] and then you say to him, "You have become purified."
>
> [Rabbi Yochanan ben Zakai][6] answered him, "Have you ever been possessed by a demon of madness?"

1. As was explained at length in the previous chapter.
2. B'midbar Rabbah 19:8.
3. This refers to the procedure performed with the Red Heifer. See B'midbar Chapter 19.
4. Ritually impure.
5. The person who has become impure.
6. Lit., "He."

דכתיב וגם את הנביאים ורוח הטומאה אעביר מן הארץ מזין עליו והוא בורח.
לאחר שיצא אמרו לו תלמידיו לזה דחית בקנה לנו מה אתה אומר?
אמר להם חייכם לא המת מטמא ולא המים מטהרים אלא אמר הקדוש ברוך הוא חקה חקקתי גזירה גזרתי אי אתה רשאי לעבור גזרותי דכתיב זאת חקת התורה ע"כ.

He responded, "No."

He asked him, "Have you ever seen a person possessed by the demon of madness?"

He answered, "Yes."

He asked him, "And what do you do for him?"

He answered, "We bring roots, and make them smoke under him, and sprinkle water upon the demon[7] and it flees!"

Rabbi Yochanan responded, "Let your ears hear what your mouth is saying! This spirit [which we attempt to banish with the procedure of the Red Heifer is] a spirit of impurity, as it is written, 'I will also remove the prophets and the spirit of impurity, from the earth.'[8] [In a process similar to your own,] water of purification is sprinkled upon the person made impure by contact with a corpse, and the spirit of impurity] flees."

When the gentile[9] had left, Rabbi Yochanan's disciples asked him, "You dismissed him with a weak response,[10] but what explanation do you have for us?"

Rabbi Yochanan[11] said to them, "By your lives! It is not the corpse that causes one to become *tamei*, nor is it the water that makes one *tahor*.[12] Rather, the Holy One, Blessed be He, declared, "A fiat[13] I have enacted, a decree I have issued; you may not violate my decree," as it is written, "This is the fiat of the Torah."[14]

הנה רבי יוחנן בן זכאי השיב לגוי כי מצוות התורה הם תועלת בעצמם על דרך זה שאמר, כי פרה אדומה היא מעברת רוח הטומאה, וכמו שחשבו קצת בני אדם כי התורה אסרה מאכלות האסורות מפני שהם מולידים מזג רע וכן נתנו טעם בדם ובחלב שכולם הם

Rabbi Yochanan ben Zakai responded to the gentile that the Mitzvot of the Torah have a utility in and of themselves, when he said that the Red Heifer removes the spirit of impurity; which is as some people have thought – that the Torah prohibited forbidden foods[15] because

7. Lit., "it."
8. Z'charyah 13:2.
9. Lit., "he."
10. In Hebrew, lit., קנה, "*kaneh*," "a stick."
11. Lit., "he."
12. Ritually fit.
13. In Hebrew, חקה, "*chukkah*," meaning "a decree" or "fiat." See Chapters Six and Seven for a discussion by the Maharal on the concepts of *chukkim* – so called "decrees," mitzvot, the reasons for which are difficult or impossible for humans to grasp.
14. B'midbar 19:2.
15. In particular, as he explains below, the Maharal is referring to animals which

מולידים מזג רע.

they cause one to develop a negative character. So too they gave reasons for [the prohibitions against consuming] blood and *cheilev*[16] – that they all cause one to develop a negative constitution.

וכל הדברים האלו אין בהם ממש לענין אסור שלהם.

But all such explanations[17] have no substance as regards [the real reason for] their prohibition.

The Maharal now brings an example from forbidden foods. We are taught that eating forbidden foods damages a person spiritually and in other ways. The Maharal explains that the reason we are forbidden to eat such foods is not because of the damage they cause – the Torah is not a book of spiritual or physical remedies! Rather, the reason for the prohibition is that G-d forbade them. He explains that such foods *do* have a deviant essence and it is also this essence which subsequently has damaging consequences on the human body or soul, but this is secondary to the essential reason for the prohibition.

ובפרק אמר להם הממונה (יומא ל"ט ע"א):

And in the chapter, "The one appointed said to them," [the Gemara comments regarding the verse in the Torah,] 'you shall become [spiritually] congested through them,"[18] [as follows],[19]

ונטמתם בם תנא רבי ישמעאל עבירה מטמטם לבו של אדם שנאמר אל תטמאו בהם ונטמתם בם אל תקרא ונטמאתם אלא ונטמתם בהם.

Rabbi Yishma'el taught, "*Sin*[20] congests the heart[21] of a person as it states, 'Do not render yourself *tamei*[22] through [ingesting] them[23] [because if you do eat them,] you will be congested[24] by them.'" [Rabbi Yishma'el pointed out that]

---

are forbidden for consumption.

16. *Cheilev* refers to particular fatty parts of kosher animals, which are prohibited.

17. Lit., "things" or "words."

18. Vayikra 11:43. This verse addresses the results of eating forbidden animals.

19. Yoma 39a.

20. The Gemara emphasizes that it is *sin* which causes spiritual congestion.

21. See Rashi's comment here (in his commentary to the Gemara, s.v. *m'tamtemet*) where he explains that the congestion of heart which is mentioned by the Gemara is that one's heart is prevented from acquiring wisdom. The thrust of the Gemara is that it is not the spiritually or physically unhealthy nature of the food which causes the congestion, but rather it is the fact that the food is simply prohibited by the Torah: it is the sin which causes the congestion, not the food.

22. In Hebrew, תטמאו, from the root טמא, which we translate approximately as "to become ritually impure."

23. I.e., non-kosher animals.

24. In Hebrew, ונטמתם, from the root טמם, "to become congested" or "to become clogged." This word is a homophone for the word ונטמאתם, which means "to be

the verse doesn't state "you will become congested"[25] but rather it says, "you will become congested through them."

We see from here that they only said that *sin* congests a person's heart and Rabbi Yishma'el[26] said that this congestion is a function of sin. [The reason for this is] because he [the sinner] transgressed the mitzvot which are suitable for a person (since his soul is a G-dly soul as we have said)[27] and therefore, sin congests the soul of a person, but [in this case] it is not due to the nature of the [forbidden] insects.

It is true that [the consumption of] any forbidden item induces a negative character, however, this is not the reason for the prohibition [against eating them]. Rather, the reason the Torah forbade them is because they are items which have a difference and deviation from all other foods which are *tahor*[28] and it is due to this [already inherent] difference that there is [also] a deviant nature present [in such forbidden foods], as we have described above. However, this is not the reason for prohibiting or allowing [such foods], for if it were, the Torah would [simply] be a medicinal book or a book of [the science of] nature.

And when Rabbi Yochanan ben Zakai responded[29] to the gentile that the mitzvah of the Red Heifer [functions] according to this [purely natural, practical]

הרי כי לא אמרו רק עבירה מטמטם לבו של אדם, ואמר כי הטמטום הזה מצד עבירה כי מפני שעבר המצוות אשר ראוי לאדם מצד אשר נפשו נפש א־להית כמו שאמרנו, ולכך העבירה מטמטם לבו של אדם אבל אין זה מצד הטבע של השרצים.

ואם כי האמת שכל הדברים האסורים מולידים מזג רע, אין זה טעם האסור, רק כי מה שאסרה התורה אותם בזה נראה כי הם דברים יש בהם שנוי ויוצאים מכלל שאר המאכלים שהם טהורים, ובשביל השנוי שבהם ימשך אחריהם טבע זר משונה גם כן וכמו שכתבנו זה גם כן למעלה, אבל אין זה טעם באיסור והיתר, שאם כן היתה התורה ספר רפואות או ספר הטבע.

וכאשר השיב רבי יוחנן בן זכאי לגוי כי מצות פרה אדומה על דרך זה והיא כמו פעולות הטבע או סגולה מן הסגולות, אמרו לו לזה דחית בקנה לומר לו כי מצוות התורה על דרך זה, אבל אנו שאנו יודעים כי אין מצוות התורה על דרך זה אם כן מה אתה אומר לנו. והשיב חייכם שאין המת מטמא ואין המים מטהרים.

פירוש כי אין בטבע שיהיה המת מטמא או שיהיו המים מטהרים, שאין כאן דבר טבעי במצוה זאת רק גזרה גזרתי אי אתה רשאי לעבור עליה.

rendered *tamei*."

25. The Maharal seems to have had a different reading of this Gemara. Our version states, "[Rabbi Yishma'el pointed out that] the verse doesn't state "you will become impurified" but rather it says "you will become congested."

26. Lit., "he."

27. See Chapter Seven of this work.

28. I.e., permitted.

29. In the Midrash cited above.

manner and that it is like natural actions or like some good omen, [his students][30] said to him, "You dismissed him with a weak response[31] in saying to him that the mitzvot of the Torah [function] in this manner but what will you say to us, who know that the mitzvot of the Torah do not function in this manner?" And he responded, "By your lives! It is not the corpse that causes one to become *tamei*, nor is it the water that makes one *tahor*."

The explanation of this is that it is not [a phenomenon of] nature that a corpse causes ritual impurity or that water causes ritual purity, because there is no natural phenomenon in this mitzvah. Rather ". . . a decree I have issued; you may not violate my decree."

The Maharal now reprises his previous explanation of the reason for mitzvot which, in his opinion, is what is being taught by both Rabbi Yochanan ben Zakai in the Midrash and Rabbi Yishma'el in the Gemara. For a deeper view of this, see the Commentary, Ch. 8 § Point 1.

והפירוש הוא כי הכל מצד הסדר שנתן השם יתברך לנו מצוה שכלית מתחייב כך, ובשביל כך המת מטמא את האדם והמים מטהרים.

והכל מחייב החכמה היא התורה שנתן השם יתברך לאדם, אבל שיהיה דבר זה טבעי דבר זה אינו רק כי כך הסדר של הש"י לאדם בחכמתו ומצד החוק שהוא שייך לאדם המת מטמא והמים מטהרים.

The explanation [of both the Midrash and the Gemara cited above] is that all [the mitzvot] are a function of the [transcendent] framework [of mitzvot]: that Hashem, may He be Blessed, gave us a *sichli* mitzvah. It is due to this [framework] that a corpse causes a person to become *tamei* and that water causes [a person to become] *tahor*.

And all [of this] is a function of Wisdom, which is the Torah which Hashem, may He be Blessed, gave to humanity. But it is impossible to explain that this [system of mitzvot] is natural;[32] rather this is the framework of Hashem, may He be Blessed, [which he gave] to humanity in His wisdom. And it is due to the decree which is suitable to humanity that a corpse causes ritual unfitness and that water creates ritual fitness.

30. Lit., "they."

31. In Hebrew, lit., קנה, *kaneh*, "a stick."

32. The Maharal is discounting any proposed explanation of mitzvot which seeks to explain that mitzvot operate solely within the "natural" world, by which he means the physical world. Certain opinions explain that mitzvot have certain practical, this-worldly benefits. Although the Maharal does not dispute this, he does argue against those who claim that such benefits are the reason for the mitzvot. In his view, detailed in Chapter Seven of this work, the mitzvot's source and reason lie in the transcendent, spiritual, *sichli* world. See however the Rambam's view cited in the Commentary, Ch. 8 § Point 4.

SUMMARY

Chapter 8: 1/3

I. Benefits of mitzvot vs. Their essence

A. Rabbi Yochanan ben Zakai and the purpose of the Red Heifer
   1. B'midbar Rabbah 19:8
      a. A gentile challenged Rabbi Yochanan ben Zakai as to the validity of the religious ceremony of the Red Heifer.
      b. Rabbi Yochanan responded that the ceremony drives away evil spirits which are generated by contact with a corpse.
      c. When Rabbi Yochanan's students challenged him on this response, he responded that the truth is that the reason for the mitzvah is that Hashem decreed it.
   2. The Maharal's explanation
      a. The truth is that mitzvot are due to one thing alone: Hashem has decreed upon us that we should do them.
      b. There may be side benefits to the observance of mitzvot and practical results flowing therefrom, but this is all they are secondary.

B. Eating forbidden foods
   1. Yoma 39a
      a. Our sages specifically pointed out that if one ingests forbidden foods, any negative consequences from such ingestion are not due to the nature of the food itself but rather to the transgression of the prohibition against the ingestion.
   2. The Maharal's explanation
      a. The reason that Hashem forbade certain foods is not because of negative consequences which flow from eating those foods.
      b. It is true that each forbidden food has a deviant nature and therefore eating such foods bears negative consequences. But this is not the cause of the prohibition.

C. Maharal's explanation of these two sources
   1. The Maharal explains that both of these sources accord with his explanation for mitzvot – as detailed in the previous chapter. There the Maharal explained that the mitzvot are all components of a transcendent-*sichli* framework through which a person can become transcendent and thus bond with Hashem.
   2. He explains that in both of the sources above, we are taught that

there is no practical reason for the mitzvot. Rather, they are G-d's decree – flowing from His wisdom as part of the framework of mitzvot. There may be practical side-effects of fulfillment of the mitzvot, but this is not their reason.

CHAPTER 8

Part 2 of 3

The Maharal continues the theme he introduced in Chapter Seven and continued at the beginning of this chapter: that the reason for mitzvot is not any utilitarian consideration, but rather that mitzvot are components of a transcendent-*sichli* framework created by Hashem. Therefore, when a person chooses to behave according to the guidelines set down by mitzvot in the Torah, he adopts Hashem's framework of thought and thus bonds with Him and this bond is formed even if a person does not understand Hashem's inner rationales for that mitzvah.

ומפני כך אין להרהר אחר זה כי עמוק עמוק מי ימצאנו.

כי אין התורה טבעית, שאילו היתה התורה טבעית היה זה קשיא מה ענין הטומאה והטהרה, אבל אין זה דבר טבעי כלל רק הוא סדר שכלי.

ואם כי אינו יודע ואינו מבין ענין החוק הזה, הלא התורה לא נתנה רק לצרף הבריות והצירוף הזה הוא לאדם בין יודע טעם של מצוה או לא ידע, רק כאשר מעשיו הם נמשכים אחר הסדר השכלי מה שראוי לו ובזה מעשיו כמו שראוי לפי השכלי והוא צירוף וזכוך נפשו מן הטבעי כמו שהתבאר.

Therefore, one should not question this[1] because it is "deep, deep, who can find it?"[2]

[This is] because the Torah is not natural – for if the Torah were natural, one would have a difficulty [explaining] the issue of ritual impurity[3] and purity.[4] But this[5] is not a natural matter at all, rather it is [part of] a *sichli* framework.

And even if one does not know or understand the reason[6] of this decree,[7] the Torah was only given to refine humanity and this refinement is enacted upon a person [who fulfills a mitzvah] whether he knows the reason of the mitzvah or whether he doesn't know [its reason]; [the] only [condition is] that his actions are a function of the *sichli* framework which is suitable to him and through this, his actions are suitable in light of the *sichli* [transcendent reality]. And

1. I.e., the reason for the mitzvot. The Maharal is explaining that one cannot understand the true depth and ultimate reason for the mitzvot because they do not flow from practical, natural considerations.
2. Kohelet 7:24.
3. In Hebrew, "*tumah*," טומאה.
4. In Hebrew, "*taharah*," טהרה.
5. I.e., *tumah* and *taharah*. The Maharal addressed this issue earlier in this chapter.
6. Lit., "matter."
7. In Hebrew, "*chok*," חק.

כי התורה היא סדר השכלי אשר ראוי לאדם במה שהוא אדם, ועל ידי המצוות דבק בשכלי ועל ידי זה דבק בו יתברך וזהו דכתיב (במדבר י"ט) זאת חקת התורה וגו'.

this is a refinement and purification of his soul from [remaining solely on] the natural [plane of existence], as has been explained.[8]

For the Torah is a *sichli* framework which is suited to a human being by virtue of his humanity and through the mitzvot, a person bonds with the *sichli* [reality] and through this he bonds with Him,[9] may He be Blessed. And this is as it is written, "This is the decree of the Torah . . ."[10]

The Maharal illustrates this idea with a comparison to the human body. Every component of the body has a reason and function but a human being can successfully use his body even though he is ignorant of these reasons. So too, the whole of creation, including the mitzvot, were arranged by Hashem in His wisdom and our ignorance of the reasons for the mitzvot cannot render them invalid or ineffective.

וכבר אמרנו שאף אם אין ידוע לנו טעם וסבה של כל דבר ודבר שנמצא באדם למה הוא כך, מכל מקום ידוע לנו שאין דבר אחד לבטלה וכך סדר השם יתברך בחכמתו כל הנבראים עליונים ותחתונים, וכן ענין המצוות למה הם כך בודאי ידענו שכך נותן הסדר שסדר השם יתברך התורה וכך מתחייב ממנו.

ולכך אין לשאול על טעם המצוות למה הם כך, כי כך גזר השם יתברך הסדר לפי חכמתו ואין דבר אחד לבטלה וכך חקק השם יתברך. והאדם העושה והשומר הסדר הזה אשר סדר השם יתברך דבר זה צירוף וזכוך נפש האדם, כי על ידי עשיית המצוות שהם הסדר השכלי הוא דבק בשכלי ועל ידי זה דבק בו יתברך.

And we have already said[11] that even if the explanation and reason for every thing found in the human [body] is unknown to us – [that is] why it is as it is – nevertheless, we do know that there is no thing [in the body] which is without reason. And in this way, Hashem, may He be Blessed, arranged all the creations ([both the] upper and lower [creations]) in His wisdom. And this is also the matter[12] regarding the mitzvot – why they are as they are – definitely we know that this[13] is a function of the order [in] which Hashem, may He be Blessed, arranged the Torah, and this [mitzvah] is entailed by that order.[14]

Therefore, one should not ask for the reason of the mitzvot – why they are such – because Hashem, may He be Blessed, decreed this according to His wisdom and there is nothing

8. See Chapter Seven as well as Chapters Two, Three, Four and Five.
9. I.e., Hashem.
10. B'midbar 19:2.
11. See the beginning of Chapter Six.
12. I.e., reason.
13. I.e., each mitzvah.
14. Lit., "it."

והעובר על המצוות הוא יוצא מן הסדר השכלי שסדר השם יתברך וכל אשר יוצא מן הסדר מביא לו זה אבוד הנפש לגמרי.

without reason and so did Hashem, may He be Blessed, legislate. And the human being who performs and observes [the mitzvot entailed within] this framework which Hashem, may He be Blessed, arranged – this is a refinement and purification for the soul of the person. [The reason for this refinement is] that through the performance of the mitzvot (which are [part of] the *sichli* framework) a person bonds with the *sichli* [reality], and through this he bonds with Hashem, may He be Blessed.

But one who transgresses the mitzvot is departing from the *sichli* framework which Hashem, may He be Blessed, arranged. And any [person] who departs [from] this framework causes a complete loss of the soul.

The Maharal now presents several mitzvot for which people have provided natural, utilitarian reasons. For each, he demonstrates a refutation of the "reason." The first example is the laws pertaining to kosher animals. The Maharal illustrates that if the sole reason for the prohibition against consuming non-kosher animals is that they are spiritual and physical pollutants, then how could there ever be an exception to this prohibition, as existed at certain points in history?

ולפיכך כל מי שנותן במצוות טעם על פי הטבע לומר כי לכך אסרה תורה חזיר מפני שהוא מוליד בגוף מזג רע וכן הוא בודאי האמת, וכן נתנו טעם באיסור חלב שהוא מוליד מזג רע וכן בדם ומכל שכן בשקצים ובעופות הטמאות.

בכולם נתנו טעם על פי הטבע וכאלו היתה התורה ספר מספרי הרפואות או

Therefore, anyone who ascribes a natural reason to the mitzvot, claiming that for this [natural reason] the Torah prohibited pork, since it generates a bad character in the body,[15] [is incorrect,[16] even though] it is definitely true [that such foods do have this negative consequence]. And so too they[17] gave a [natural] reason for [the prohibition against eating] *cheilev* – that it generates a negative character and similarly with [the prohibition against consuming] blood and even more so regarding *tamei*[18] insects and birds.

15. See the Commentary, Ch. 8 § Point 2.

16. I.e., he is incorrect that this is the reason for the mitzvah, even though the Maharal concedes that the consumption of non-kosher foods does have deleterious spiritual effects.

17. Those who ascribe natural reasons only to the mitzvot.

18. As we explained previously, the word "*tamei*," טמא, is often mistranslated as "impure." Sometimes, as in this case, it is used to refer to animals which we are prohibited to eat.

ספר הטבע, חס ושלום לומר כך. ואם היה הדבר כמו שאמרו הם הרי אמרו בפרק קמא דחולין (י"ז ע"א):

In all these [cases] they supplied a natural reason as if the Torah was one of the medical books or a book of nature – G-d forbid that we should say this. And if it were the case (as they say) [how is it that] our sages said in the first chapter of Chullin as follows,[19]

ובתים מלאים כל טוב אמר רבי ירמיה אמר רב כותלי דחזירי התיר להם.

[The verse states, "And it will be when Hashem, your G-d, brings you to the land which He swore to your fathers – to Avraham, to Yitzchak, and to Ya'akov[20] – to give to you large and good cities which you did not build] and houses filled with all manner of good [things, which you did not amass . . . and you will eat and be satisfied.][21]

[Rabbi Yirmiyah (in the name of Rav)[22] deduces from this verse (from the fact that it concludes, "and you will eat and be satisfied") that even the food contents of the houses in the conquered land of K'na'an[23] were permissible no matter what type of food was there.] Rabbi Yirmiyah said in the name of Rav,[24] "[We can deduce from this verse that] Hashem[25] permitted the Israelites[26, 27] [the consumption of] dried pork."[28]

ואם שורש האסור בשביל מזג רע האסור להיכן הלך?

Now if the root of the prohibition [against eating non-kosher animals] was due to [an attempt to prevent one acquiring a] negative character, how did the prohibition disappear [for those Jews entering the land of K'na'an]?

The second example is *cheilev* – forbidden fats – a prohibition to which there are also exceptions.

וכן חלב אם מזגו רע אם כן בן פקוע למה חלבו מותר? כדאיתא בפרק גיד

So too regarding *cheilev*, if its character is negative[29] how is it that the *cheilev* of

19. Chullin 17a.
20. Abraham, Isaac and Jacob.
21. D'varim 6:10–11.
22. In our editions of the Gemara, it is Rabbi Yirmiya bar Abba in the name of Rav.
23. Canaan.
24. In our editions of the Gemara, it is Rabbi Yirmiya bar Abba in the name of Rav.
25. Lit., "He."
26. Lit., "them."
27. The words, "He permitted them" do not appear in our editions of the Gemara.
28. As per Rashi ad loc.
29. Meaning, if consuming *cheilev* causes one to develop a negative character.

הנשה (שם ע"ד ע"א) מה טעם בזה?

a *ben paku'a*[30] is permitted (as is cited in the chapter "The Sciatic Nerve")?[31] What reason could there be for this?

The third example is the requirement for ritual slaughter – a prohibition to which there are also exceptions.

וכן אם אסר השחיטה שלא נתאכזר למה התירה התורה בן פקוע בלא שחיטה?

So too, if He forbade [eating meat without appropriate ritual] slaughter in order that we not become cruel, why did the Torah permit a *ben paku'a*[32] [which does not require ritual slaughter in all its details]?

The Maharal concludes that it is always inappropriate to supply naturalistic explanations for mitzvot. Rather, the reason for any mitzvah is that it is part of the transcendent-*sichli* framework which Hashem constructed. This also explains how at times, certain actions which are usually prohibited, are permitted – because the reason for the prohibition in the first place is not some inherent negativity in that action but because, in Hashem's framework, they are usually prohibited. But this same framework dictates that at times those very actions are permitted.

לכך אין ראוי לומר כך. ואף אמנם כי האמת הוא כי כל אלו יש בהם מזג רע ודבר זה ימשך בודאי במה שיש בהם שנוי רע גם כן, אבל אין זה עיקר טעם המצוה רק שאינם ראוים אל האדם כפי הסדר אשר סדר השם יתברך לכך הרחיקה אותם ולפעמים לא הרחיקתם התורה.

Therefore, it is not fitting to supply[33] such [natural explanations for any mitzvah, ever!] Even though it is true that all of these [prohibited foods and actions, if transgressed, induce] a negative character and this [negative character] is a function of their possessing an additional negative deviation; however, this [negative deviation] is not the essence of the reason of the mitzvah. Rather, [the reason for the prohibition, in each case, is] that they are unsuited to humanity according to the framework which Hashem, may He be Blessed, arranged. Therefore, [sometimes] the

30. A *ben paku'a*, בן פקוע, is an animal found in utero after the slaughter of its dam (where the dam is kosher). Many of the restrictions applied to the consumption of kosher meat do not apply to the *ben paku'a*; one of which is that while the *cheilev* of a regular animal is forbidden, that of the *ben paku'a* is not.

31. Chullin 74a. See Rashi there s.v "*umotzi et damo*."

32. As mentioned in the footnote above, a *ben paku'a* has certain restrictions related to consumption, relaxed. One of these is that it does not require ritual slaughter, in all its details.

33. Lit., "say."

Torah distanced [us] from them[34] and sometimes did not distance [us] from them.[35]

[In] this [case mentioned above] when Hashem, may He be Blessed, assured [us,] "you shall consume all the nations,"[36] the prohibition [against consuming forbidden foods] was not suitable [rather] in light of the circumstances at the time, it was suitable that [the verse] "and houses filled with [all manner of] good . . ."[37] would be fulfilled. And therefore, the Torah did not distance these [usually forbidden] items [at that time]. Just as the Torah prohibited [these actions] when it was suitable to prohibit (according to the *sichli* framework), so did the Torah permit it when it was suitable to permit – and everything is according to the transcendent-*seichel*[38] according to which it is suited that a person behave.

וזה אשר הבטיח השם יתברך ואכלת את כל העמים, לא היה ראוי הרחקה מצד שעתה ראוי שיהיה מקוים ובתים מלאים כל טוב ולפיכך לא הרחיקה התורה דברים אלו, וכמו שהתורה אסרה כאשר היה ראוי לאסור לפי הסדר השכלי כך התירה התורה אותו כאשר הוא להתיר והכל לפי השכל אשר ראוי שיהיה בו הנהגת האדם.

The Maharal brings a final proof from our sages that they reject natural explanations for mitzvot.

This is as our sages[39] say, *z"l*,[40]

> A person should not say, "I do not desire pork, I do not desire some [forbidden] thing." Rather [a person should say,] "I do desire [it]! But what can I do, for my Father in Heaven has decreed on me [that it is forbidden to me.]"

They illustrated through this [statement] that one should not say that the Torah is natural, for if it were natural

וזה אמרם ז"ל (תו"כ קדושים):

> לא יאמר אדם אי אפשי בבשר חזיר אי אפשי בדבר פלוני אלא אפשי ומה אעשה שאבי שבשמים גזר עלי.

הורו בזה שאין לומר כי התורה טבעית שאם היתה טבעית לא היה בה קבול שכר א-להי על דבר שהוא טבעי. ולכך יאמר אפשי מצד הטבע רק השם יתברך גזר עלי בחכמתו מה שאין ראוי אל האדם ומיוחד בו נפשו.

34. The ability to eat certain foods or perform certain actions.
35. The Maharal is answering the question he posed originally in Chapter Six, as well as in the current chapter, which related to the fact that certain actions are prohibited under certain circumstances and not only are they permitted in other circumstances, but they are even obligatory.
36. D'varim 7:16. See the Commentary, Ch. 8 § Point 3.
37. D'varim 6:11.
38. "*Seichel*," שכל, is the noun of "*sichli*."
39. Lit., "they."
40. Sifra, K'doshim 10. Also see Yalkut Shimoni, Vayikra 20:626.

there could be no G-dly reward for [keeping it if it is just] a natural thing.

And therefore, a person should say, “I do desire [to transgress the Torah] from a natural perspective, except that Hashem, may He be Blessed, decreed on me, in His wisdom [not to perform] that which is unsuitable to a human being (whose soul is unique).”

SUMMARY

Chapter 8: 2/3

I. **Natural vs. essential explanations for mitzvot**

A. All the mitzvot are components of the transcendent-*sichli* framework which Hashem has created

1. The Torah is not a natural system with natural explanations.
2. Rather, it is a transcendent-*sichli* framework.
    a. When a person observes a mitzvah, he is adopting Hashem's framework of priorities and volition as his own.
    b. Therefore, one does not need to understand the ultimate reasons for mitzvot.
    c. Therefore, when one performs a mitzvah, one is simply bonding with the *sichli* reality and thus with Hashem. This bond causes a human being to be refined.
3. Incomplete knowledge on our part does not mean there is no reason for mitzvot
    a. We do not know the reason for every component of the human body, yet we do know that there *is* a reason and we still continue to use our bodies.
    b. So too with the mitzvot, even if we don't know the reason for the mitzvot, there are still reasons.

B. Rejecting naturalistic explanations for mitzvot

1. Bad character
    a. Certain sages posited that the reason for the prohibitions against the consumption of blood, *cheilev* and non-kosher animals is that they induce a bad character in a human being. Similarly, some suggested that this is also the reason that we are required to perform ritual slaughter – because not doing so engenders a negative humor.
    b. The Maharal proves that such utilitarian considerations cannot be the *reason* for any of the mitzvot listed above since they all have exceptional conditions under which these prohibitions are waived. If the reason for these mitzvot was that they naturally, automatically, engender a negative character, there should never be any exceptions:
        (1) Upon entering the Land of Israel, the Jewish people were permitted the consumption of all foodstuffs in the houses of the vanquished populace, even those items which were non-kosher, including pork.

(2) *Cheilev* is permitted in a *ben paku'ah* (an animal found in utero after slaughter of its dam).

(3) One is not required to perform ritual slaughter on a *ben paku'ah*.

2. Our sages' saying
   a. Sifra, K'doshim 10
      (1) "A person should not say, 'I do not desire pork, I do not desire something [forbidden].' Rather, 'I do desire! But what can I do, for my Father in Heaven has decreed on me.'"
   b. The Maharal's explanation of this is that a person should always reject a naturalistic explanation for a prohibition (for example by saying that one dislikes pork) and instead proclaim that the sole reason for the prohibition is G-d's decree.

CHAPTER 8

Part 3 of 3

After proving conclusively that practical, natural reasons are not the reasons for any mitzvot, the Maharal discusses how one should respond to a person who inquires as to the reasons that certain mitzvot are required by the transcendent-*sichli* framework.

ואם יאמר האדם למה נותן הסדר השכלי שיעשה האדם אלו המצוות?

בודאי מצוות שנדע טעמם כמו מצות צדקה ותפלה ומצות כבוד אב ואם והרחקת גנבה וגזלה דבר זה יש לומר כי ראוי שיהיה האדם מיוחד במעשים אלו כי הם ראויים לאדם.

אבל המצוות שאין טעמם ידוע ונגלה הלא הם ידועים למשה ולשאר חכמים לפי מעלתם ומדרגתם.

עד שכל המצוות הם לפי סדר השכלי ראויים לאדם ולכך הם מזכים ומצרפים את נפשו עד שהיא צרופה וזכה.

If a person asks, "Why does the *sichli* framework determine that a person should do these mitzvot?" [the answer is as follows].

Regarding mitzvot, the reasons for which we know, such as the mitzvot of *tz'dakkah*[1] and prayer and the mitzvot of honoring [one's] father and mother and distancing [oneself from] theft[2] and robbery[3] – for such things one should respond [to the question above by saying] that it is suitable that a human being to be singled out by these actions since they are fitting for a human being.

However, regarding mitzvot, the reasons for which are unknown and unrevealed [we respond by saying that their reasons] are known to Moshe and the other sages [each] according to his stature and level.

[The end result is] that all the mitzvot are according to the *sichli* framework [and] are suitable to a human being and therefore, they purify and refine his soul until it becomes refined and pristine.

The Maharal refers back to the Midrash he cited earlier which he used as a proof that the mitzvot do not have natural, practical reasons.

---

1. Jewish social welfare. As we have noted earlier, this term is often mistranslated as "charity."
2. In Hebrew, "*g'neivah*," גנבה, which is theft conducted secretly.
3. In Hebrew, "*g'zeilah*," גזלה, which is robbery conducted openly, by force.

והתבאר לך בירור הדברים מה שאמר כי לא המת מטמא והפרה מטהר טמאים.

כלומר שאין זה דבר טבעי למת שהוא מטמא ודבר טבעי למי הנדה שהוא מטהר, רק השם יתברך חקק וסדר לאדם מעשיו כפי מה שחייב השכל שכך יקח לטהרתו אבל אינו דבר טבעי רק הכל שכל א-להי.

The statement[4] [of Rabbi Yochanan ben Zakai] that "it is not the corpse that causes one to become ritually impure," nor is it the [ashes of] the [red] heifer that makes one ritually pure, has now been explained.

[The meaning of this statement is] that it is not a natural phenomenon that the waters of a *niddah*[5] make one ritually pure, rather it is Hashem, may He be Blessed, Who decreed and ordered a person's actions according to what the [G-dly] intellect required [which was] that a person should take [the water and ashes] to purify himself. But this is not a natural phenomenon; rather the whole thing is [determined by] G-dly intellect.

The perspective of humans on the mitzvot is different from Hashem's. Often, we have no inkling of the rationale behind mitzvot. When that occurs, all we can say regarding the mitzvot is that they are Hashem's decrees. However, not knowing the reason for a mitzvah doesn't prevent a person from bonding with Hashem through its fulfillment since performing the mitzvah entails adoption of Hashem's thought-framework, as the Maharal explained previously.

ואל האדם הוא חוק וגזרה כאשר אינו עומד על טעם המצוה שהוא שכל א-להי, וכך הם כל המצוות שהם שכל א-להי ולא שכל אדם. ולפיכך האדם אשר יש לו נפש א-להית והיא עומדת בחומר על ידי מצוות השכליות הא-להיות כאשר הוא דבק בהם ועושה אותם הוא דבק בו יתברך ומוציאים את נפשו מן הטבע.

When a person cannot fathom the reason of a mitzvah (since it is [a function of] G-dly intellect), it is a decree and legislation [from the human perspective]. This is [true] regarding all the mitzvot, which are G-dly intellect and not human intellect. And therefore, the human, who possesses a G-dly soul which is embedded in the material [human body, needs to perform the mitzvot, because] when he performs and bonds with the G-dly, *sichli* mitzvot, through those mitzvot, he bonds with Him, may He be Blessed, and they[6] transition his soul from the [solely] natural [existence he had before, to a transcendent, *sichli* reality.]

4. Cited at the beginning of this chapter – B'midbar Rabbah 19:8.

5. Cf. B'midbar 19:13. This phrase "waters of a *niddah*" is used in the Torah to denote a *mikvah*. A *niddah* is a menstrual woman. The term "waters of a *niddah*" are used because menstrual women immerse in a *mikvah* in order to reverse their menstrual *tumah*.

6. The mitzvot.

ואף שלא ידע טעם המצוה הלא כאשר הוא עושה המצוה ודבק במצוה שהוא השכל א־להי, נדבק בו יתברך.

And even if a person doesn't know the reason for a mitzvah, when he does perform the mitzvah and bonds with the mitzvah (which is G-dly intellect), he is bonded with Him, may He be Blessed.

והבן הדברים האלו ודי בזה.

And understand these things – and this is enough [of an explanation].

SUMMARY

Chapter 8: 3/3

I. How should one respond when asked why it is that certain mitzvot are included in the framework of mitzvot?

- A. The Maharal differentiates between the appropriate response for different types of mitzvot
  1. Mitzvot for which we assume we know the reasons
     - a. We may respond that these mitzvot are fitting to a human being.
  2. Mitzvot for which we do not know the reasons
     - a. We respond that our sages, each in their own way, understood these mitzvot.
- B. General response
  1. All mitzvot are determined by Hashem's *seichel* and are part of a *sichli* framework which, when adopted by a human being, refine that person.

II. Recap of the purpose of mitzvot

- A. Rabbi Yochanan ben Zakai's statement
  1. Rabbi Yochanan stated that "it is not the corpse that causes one to become ritually impure," nor is it the [ashes of] the [red] heifer that makes one ritually pure.
- B. The meaning of this is that the mitzvot do not have natural effects and consequences, rather they are all part of the *sichli* framework determined by Hashem.

III. Does one need to understand a mitzvah in order for it to have the required effect – bonding with Hashem?

- A. The Maharal explains that if a person does not understand the reason for a mitzvah, when he performs the mitzvah, he nevertheless still bonds with Hashem through his adoption of the *sichli* framework which is set by Hashem's intellect.

CHAPTER 9

CHAPTER 9

Part 1 of 3

The Maharal now begins his answer to the question which began the last three chapters: how is it that physical actions (mitzvot) can have metaphysical consequences. He begins by describing the view of those sages who view the wisdom which a person acquires as the only means of attaining eternity. Such a view makes it difficult to understand the function of the mitzvot in helping one forge a spiritual, eternal destiny since many mitzvot have relatively little effect on one's intellect.

אחר שנתבאר לך דברים אלו נבאר עוד השאלה הראשונה איך יקנה האדם ההצלחה על ידי מעשה התורה.

אשר הלכו בדרך חכמי המחקר והם הפילוסופים אשר זכרנו למעלה, יתנו שם ותפארת אל השכל ועל ידי המושכלות יקנה האדם הנצחיות ויעשו המעשים הישרים והטובים כמו תכונה וסולם אשר יגיע בהן אל המושכלות.

After these matters have been elucidated for you, we will further clarify [the answer to] the first question[1] [which was,] "How can a person acquire [spiritual] success[2] through the [physical] acts of the Torah?"

Those who have walked in the path of the sages of enquiry (these are the philosophers whom we mentioned previously) assign importance and grandeur to the intellect and [believe that] a person acquires eternity through the Conceptualizations;[3] and [furthermore] they transform ethical and good acts into an attribute and a ladder[4] [through] which a person reaches the Conceptualizations.

---

1. The two questions were posed at the beginning of Chapter Six in this work. The first question was how physical actions could produce (eternal) effects in the spiritual world which is non-physical, or as the Maharal put it, "There are those people, the people who have searching hearts, who walk in the ways of the philosophers who investigate all things through their own opinion and mind. In their eyes, the matter of *mitzvot aseh* is very bewildering: [how is it possible] that a person should merit eternal success in the transcendent [non-physical] world through a mitzvah which is physical. They have exclaimed, 'How can a physical act aid the soul in acquiring eternal life in the transcendent world, which is a place in which there is no physical activity?'"

2. See the Commentary, Ch. 9 § Point 1. This is not to say that the Maharal believes that Torah brings spiritual success only, G-d forbid. As he emphasized in the Introduction to this work, the Torah is good for a person both spiritually and physically.

3. See the Commentary, Ch. 9 § Point 1.

4. In Hebrew, "*sulam*," סולם, lit., "ladder."

The Maharal begins his refutation of the belief outlined above.

However, it is from this [selfsame] ladder[5] that they have fallen and we, students of Moshe, our Master, peace be upon him, have arisen and encouraged ourselves[6] through the Torah of Hashem and [through] His mitzvot.

The principle which brought [these philosophers][7] to this [error] was that it was inconceivable to them that a physical act could encompass the success of [a] transcendent soul and therefore, they forsook the [physical] acts of the human being[8] and relied [instead] upon the intellect [only].

ומזה הסולם נפלו, ואנחנו תלמידי משה רבינו עליו השלום קמנו ונתעודד על ידי תורת ה' ומצוותיו.

והעיקר אשר הביאם לזה, שהיה רחוק מהם שיהיה המעשה הגשמי הצלחת הנפש הנבדל, ולכך עזבו את המעשה האדם ונשענו על השכל.

The philosophers would admit that certain mitzvot which undoubtedly have moral dimensions could have a spiritual effect.

Now it is not inconceivable that it would be possible for a person to acquire spiritual success through good deeds such as: prayer and supplication, taking mercy on people with *tz'dakkah*, performing law and justice, loving one's fellow, not worshiping the gods of others,[9] not cursing Hashem, [not] robbing, [not] extorting, [not] murdering, not accepting a bribe, [not having] forbidden sexual unions and so on. [This is because] the mitzvot which entail serving Hashem [through] prayer, supplication and distancing oneself from worshipping strange gods all [overtly produce] an attribute in the soul, refining it and purifying it from the vanity of physicality.

והנה לא רחוק הוא לאדם, שאפשר לקנות ההצלחה הרוחנית על ידי המעשים הטובים כמו התפלה והבקשה ולרחם על הבריות בצדקה ולעשות דין ומשפט ולאהוב את עמיתו ושלא לעבוד א-להים אחרים ושלא לברך את השם ושלא לגזול ולחמום ולשפוך דם ושלא ליקח שוחד ולגלות עריות וכיוצא בהם. שהמצוה שהיא לעבוד השם יתברך כתפלה ובקשה והתרחק מלעבוד אלהי נכר כולם תכונה לנפש לזכך אותה לטהר אותה מפחיתות החומר.

5. A pun on the *sulam* mentioned above.

6. Cf. Tehillim 20:9.

7. Lit., "them."

8. They denied that it was the mitzvot which generate spiritual success, but rather the intellect; and inasmuch as mitzvot are critically important, this is only since they positively influence the intellect.

9. Translation as per Chizkuni, Sh'mot 20:3.

The Maharal now begins explaining his thesis as to how physical mitzvot affect the soul. His first building block is the idea that the mitzvot allow one to bond with Hashem. This bond is the greatest success and joy which a person can experience; while the opposite, G-d forbid, being cut off from G-d, is the ultimate pain and failure.

וצריך להשיב הנפש בפעל ולעשות אותה רוחנית על ידי זכוך הנפש ולהדבק בו יתברך על ידי העבודה אליו.

שזהו תכלית ההצלחה כמו שמעיד עליו הכתוב (שמואל א' כ"ה) והיתה נפש אדוני צרורה בצרור החיים את ה' א-להיך.

והפך זה האבדון הוא הכריתה והפירוד ממנו יתברך כמו שאמר בכל מקום על האבדון הכרת תכרת ופירשו חכמים (שבועות י"ג ע"א) תכרת בעולם הבא.

נמצא השכר הוא הדבוק בו יתברך והעונש הוא הכריתה והפירוד ממנו.

ודבר זה ברור בלי ספק לכל אדם בעל דעת כי הנפש הזאת שהיא מן השם יתברך צריך להשיבה אל השם יתברך אשר נתנה וכמו שאמר הכתוב (קהלת י"ב) וישוב העפר על הארץ כשהיה והרוח תשוב אל הא-להים.

There is a need proactively to return the soul [to Hashem] and to make it [more] spiritual through the refinement of the soul [so that it may] bond with Him, may He be Blessed, through one's serving Him.

This [bonding] is the pinnacle of success, as the verse testifies, "And the soul of my master will be bound within the bond of life with Hashem, your G-d."[10]

The opposite of this is obliteration, which is when one is cut off and separated from Him, may He be Blessed. This is as the Torah[11] says consistently regarding being obliterated, "You shall *surely* be cut off,"[12] which our sages explained to mean, "you shall be cut off in the World to Come."[13]

Thus, the [true] reward is bonding with Him, may He be Blessed; while the [most severe] punishment[14] is being cut off and separated from Him.[15]

And this matter is clear, without a doubt to every sensible person – that the soul, which is from Hashem (may He be Blessed) must be returned to

10. 1 Sh'mu'el 25:29.

11. Lit., "it."

12. B'midbar 15:31. This is in fact the only place that this exact phrase occurs, however, the Maharal's intent is that the term "*kareit*," "being cut off," is that used to indicate complete oblivion, which is because when one is cut off from G-d, the source of all life, this is oblivion.

13. Shavu'ot 13a. The Gemara learns this from the double language in the verse, "*hikareit tikareit*," הכרת תכרת, which we have translated as "you shall *surely* be cut off." Since the Torah could have phrased this idea in a simpler fashion, using only one term, the Gemara learns that the second term teaches us an extra idea – that the severance mentioned refers to the World to Come.

14. See the Commentary, Ch. 9 § Points 1 and 3 for a note on terminology here.

15. See the Commentary, Ch. 9 § Points 1 and 3.

Hashem (may He be Blessed) who gave it. This is as the verse states, "The dust will return to the ground, as it was; and the soul will return to G-d."[16]

The Maharal explains next that the only way a person can achieve the ultimate in life (bonding with Hashem) is by refining oneself through adoption of a transcendent set of motivations and actions. This is of course the Torah and the actions entailed within it are the mitzvot. This is his general response to the question of how physical mitzvot affect the soul.

ודבר זה אינו כי אם בטהרה מפחיתות החמרי ומצרף ומזכך נפשו מן החמרי, וזהו על ידי המעשים שסדר השם יתברך אל האדם בסדר השכלי והם זכוך נפשו ומקרבים אותו אל השם יתברך עד שהאדם דבק בו יתברך.

But this [can only occur] when the soul[17] is purified of the vanity of the physical, which is [only] through the actions which Hashem, may He be Blessed, arranged for humans, within the *sichli* framework [of mitzvot]. And the mitzvot[18] [constitute] a refinement of his soul and draw him closer to Hashem, may He be Blessed, until the person bonds with Him, may He be Blessed.

The Maharal now relates directly to the philosophers' question by focusing on those mitzvot which have a clear moral and ethical dimension. With the Maharal's understanding of the purpose of life and of mitzvot, it becomes clear that those deeds which clearly possess a moral and ethical dimension, contribute to the ultimate spiritual goal of bonding with Hashem. This is because the more that one performs these actions, the more one comes to resemble G-d (as it were) since such actions are typical of how G-d acts in this world. Thus one has automatically generated a bond with G-d through this "resemblance."

וכל הדברים הטובים כמו הצדקה ולעשות משפט דבר זה אין צריך לפרש כי על ידם הוא זוכה אל הצלחה אחרונה. וזה כי בדברים ההם יש לו ההתמדות וההתיחסות אל השם יתברך במה שאלו הדברים הם דרכי

Now, it is unnecessary to explain that a person merits the ultimate success [of bonding with Hashem] through all the good deeds, such as *tz'dakkah* and performing justice. This is because these actions constitute a resemblance to and a relationship with Hashem, may He be Blessed, because these actions are the ways of Hashem, may He be Blessed: He performs kindness, justice and law on the earth.[19] And this relationship

16. Kohelet 12:7.

17. Lit., "it."

18. Lit., "they."

19. Yirmiyahu 9:23. Verses 22 and 23 read as follows, "Thus says Hashem, 'Let not the wise man glory in his wisdom, neither let the mighty man glory in his

השם יתברך שהוא עושה חסד משפט וצדקה בארץ, וההתיחסות הזה הוא הדבוק בו יתברך וכמו שאמרו בפרק קמא דסוטה (י"ד ע"ב [צ"ל ע"א]):

with Hashem is the bonding with Him, may He be Blessed. As they said in the first chapter of [Tractate] Sotah,[20]

אחרי ה' א־להיכם תלכו.
וכי אפשר להדבק בשכינה?
אלא הלוך אחר מידותיו.

> [The verse states,] "You shall walk after Hashem your G-d [. . . and bond with Him.]"[21]
>
> [The Gemara asks,] "But is it possible [for a physical human being] to bond with the [infinite, transcendent] divine presence?[22] . . .
>
> [The Gemara answers,] "Rather, [it means that] you should emulate[23] His attributes."[24]

הרי כי ההתדמות אליו במעשים מה שאפשר נקרא הליכה אחריו וההליכה אחריו הוא דבוק בו יתברך, כי ראוי ההתדמות באין ספק להביא החבור כאשר תמצא דברים הדומים יש להם חבור יחד והדברים אשר הם הפכים זה לזה אי אפשר שימצאו יחד, ודבר זה אין צריך ראיה.

וכמו כן הגזל והגנבה והרציחה והעריות באין ספק שהוא מביא העונש

This illustrates that resemblance to Him through actions (as much as possible) is termed, "walking after Him." And "walking after Him" is bonding with Him, may He be Blessed, because, without doubt, resemblance [in general] is suited to generate a bond [with the item resembled] as one finds with similar things which have a bond together. However, objects which are opposite to one another cannot be found together. This matter needs no proof.

Similarly, robbery, kidnapping,[25] murder and forbidden sexual relations

---

might, nor let the rich man glory in his riches; but let him that takes pride in anything, glory in this: that he understands and knows Me for I am Hashem who does kindness, justice and righteousness in the earth, because I have desired these . . .'" This verse is the main one cited by the Rambam (cited in the Commentary, Ch. 9 § Point 2) to indicate that the ultimate success comes through perfection of the intellectual "knowing" of G-d. The Rambam emphasizes the first half of the verse which speaks of a person who "knows Me" while the Maharal focuses on the last half of the verse which addresses the fact that Hashem acts in certain ways. See the Commentary, Ch. 9 § Point 2.

20. Sotah 14a, with variations. Our version reads, "'You shall walk after Hashem your G-d.' But is it possible to walk after the divine presence – it has already stated, 'For Hashem your G-d is a consuming fire'? Rather, one should walk after [i.e., emulate] the attributes of the Holy One, Blessed be He."

21. D'varim 13:5.

22. G-d is infinite, while we are finite! How could such a bond ever occur?

23. Lit., "walk after."

24. I.e., the way G-d acts.

25. As per Rashi, Sh'mot 20:13.

הנצחי מצד הזה שכל אלו הם רחוקים ומתועבים בעיני השם יתברך שהוא יתברך עצם היושר ובכל אלו שהם גזל וגנבה והרציחה הוא העולה אשר הוא מתועב בעיני השם יתברך, ואם כן אין ספק כי המעשים האלו מביאים הרחקה מן השם יתברך.

וכן העריות שהוא זנות והוא ענין חמרי ואין לו גדר קדושה הוא רחוק מן השם יתברך אשר הוא קדוש בתכלית הקדושה ולכך ראוי אליו הכריתה והפירוד ממנו יתברך.

והנה המצוות האלו ועם שהם מעשים גשמיים באין ספק שהם קונים אליו ההצלחה אחרונה מצד הדבוק בו יתברך כי הם צירוף הנפש כאשר יש לאדם ההתדמות לבוראו, והחוטא בהם מביא אליו עונש הכריתה והפירוד ממנו יתברך.

והנה אלו המעשים הטובים מיחדים נפש האדם האצולה מן השם יתברך להוציא אותה מן הטבע אשר משותף האדם עם שאר בעלי חיים.

כאשר יש לו על ידי מעשים אלו דבקות בו יתברך ויתעלה.

generate eternal punishment (in the sense explained [above])[26] without a doubt. [The reason for this is] that all of these [immoral acts] are distant from and repulsive in Hashem's eyes, may He be Blessed; for He, may He be Blessed, is the essence of morality. But all these (robbery, kidnapping and murder) are [the pinnacles of] injustice which is repulsive in Hashem's eyes, may He be Blessed. If so, there is no doubt that these [evil] actions generate distance from Hashem, may He be Blessed.

Forbidden sexual relations also [have this effect, since] they are a material action and have no boundary of sanctity [and thus] they are far from Hashem, may He be Blessed, Whose holiness is the pinnacle of sanctity. And therefore being cut off and separated [from Hashem] is suited [to one who has illicit sexual relations.]

Now the mitzvot, despite their being physical actions, undoubtedly acquire the ultimate success for a person from the point of view of bonding with Hashem,[27] may He be Blessed, because they are a refinement of the soul through the person resembling his creator. But one who transgresses them generates for himself the "punishment" of being cut off and separated from Him, may He be Blessed.

These good deeds make a person's soul unique [the same soul] which is [still] drawn[28] from Hashem, [and these good deeds aid it in] transitioning from the natural [world] which a human shares with the animals [and lead it to a transcendent existence].

26. I.e., not punitive reward and punishment, but rather the simple consequences of one's actions – drawing oneself closer to Hashem or the opposite, G-d forbid.

27. Lit., "Him."

28. In Hebrew, "*atzulah*," אצולה. The source of this word is "*eitzel*," אצל, which means "adjacent to." See Ramban, B'midbar 11:17 for a discussion of the various interpretations of this word. It seems that by his use of the intransitive form of the verb, the Maharal's meaning is "drawn down from."

[This happens] when a person has a bond with Him, may He be Blessed, and elevated, through these actions.

The Maharal has now explained how even the philosophers would concede that the types of mitzvot which allow one to come to "resemble" Hashem or which prevent one becoming repugnant to Hashem, can effect the soul.

ולכך אין בהם תמיה כלל איך המעשים האלו מביאים אל האדם הצלחה עליונה ועל ידי מעשה הרע מביא עליו עונש נצחי.

Therefore, there is no astonishment how it is that these [particular, moral and ethical] actions bring a person superior success and how [the opposite,] a negative act, brings upon him an eternal "punishment."

SUMMARY

Chapter 9: 1/3

I. The initial question from Chapter 6: How do physical mitzvot have metaphysical effects?

A. The Maharal cited a question raised by the "philosophers" which was: How can physical actions, such as mitzvot, have an effect on the eternal, spiritual destiny of a person?

B. The underlying assumption of the philosophers

1. The philosophers' central assumption is that the only eternal things which a person can attain are Conceptualizations of the truth.
2. As such, they can only view mitzvot which are a means to the acquisition of such Conceptualizations as having an eternal, spiritual effect.
3. Their focus is on the human intellect and not on human action.

C. Concession regarding certain mitzvot

1. Certain mitzvot (for example, prayer and supplication, taking mercy on people with *tz'dakkah*, performing law and justice, loving one's fellow, not worshiping false gods, not cursing Hashem, not robbing, not extorting, not murdering, not accepting a bribe, not having forbidden sexual unions) clearly distance one from the physical and allow one greater intellectual focus.
2. Therefore, the philosophers would concede that such mitzvot indeed contribute towards one's eternal, spiritual future.

II. The Maharal's understanding of "Reward and Punishment"

A. Every reward and punishment is a simple and direct consequence of the reality which every human chooses for him or herself.

B. The ultimate success, goodness and "reward"

1. The ultimate goodness and reward is to be bonded with and connected to Hashem.
2. The soul comes from Hashem and its destiny is to return to Hashem.

C. The ultimate failure, evil and "punishment"

1. The ultimate failure, evil and "punishment" is to be separated and cut off from Hashem.
2. This is the penalty of *kareit*, often mentioned in the Torah.

III. The purpose of mitzvot

A. In general, mitzvot enable one to bond with Hashem and prevent one distancing oneself from Hashem.

B. As explained previously in Chapters Six, Seven and Eight, the mitzvot constitute a *sichli* framework created by Hashem's wisdom such that when a person chooses to perform a mitzvah, he has aligned his will and desire with Hashem's, which creates a bond.

IV. How mitzvot enable one to bond with Hashem

A. Mitzvot which emulate G-d's attributes

1. Sotah 14a

a. We are taught in the Torah to bond with G-d. But this would seem to be impossible as we are finite and Hashem is infinite.

b. The Gemara explains that the directive to bond with Hashem means that we should *emulate* Hashem. The Torah teaches us how Hashem acts in the world and it is these actions (or attributes) which we should emulate.

2. This emulation of Hashem's attributes is termed, "walking after Hashem."

3. Examples of such mitzvot are mentioned above

a. *Mitzvot aseh*

(1) These allow one's actions to "resemble" Hashem's.

b. *Mitzvot lo ta'aseh*

(1) These ensure that one doesn't distance oneself from Hashem through attaching oneself to actions which are detestable in Hashem's eyes.

CHAPTER 9

Part 2 of 3

The Maharal now begins explaining how it is that mitzvot enable one to succeed spiritually even if one is completely ignorant of the reasons behind those mitzvot.

וכן המצוות שלא נדע טעמם באיזה צד הם הצלחת נפשו ויקנה בהם הצלחה עליונה, כבר אמרנו כי המצוות האלו ראוים אל האדם מצד כי המצוות כולם שכליות א־להיות, שכך סדר השם יתברך לא מה שחייב שכל האדם רק מה שסדר השם יתברך בחכמתו, ולכך הדבק במצוות דבק בשכלי והוא השכל הא־להי העליון ועל ידי זה יש לו דבקות בו יתברך ומוציאין אותו מן הטבע המשותפת ובזה נפשו צרופה ואז דבק בו יתברך.

וראוים מעשה האדם בפרט להוציא את האדם מן הטבע החמרית וכמו ששאל טורנוסרופוס הרשע לר"ע (מדרש תנחומא פ׳ תזריע) איזה מעשים יותר יפים מעשה השם יתברך או מעשה האדם כמו שהתבאר למעלה שהשיב רבי עקיבא אליו שמעשה האדם יותר נבחרים מן הטבע, וכמו שהארכנו למעלה כי האדם הוא על הטבע במה שיש לו נפש אצולה מן העליונים.

And similarly, regarding the mitzvot for which we do not know the reason ([that is we are ignorant of] which way they [contribute to] the success of one's soul and [we do not know how they assist] one [to] acquire ultimate success) we have already said that these mitzvot are suited to the human being from the perspective that they are all G-dly-*sichli* – that this is what Hashem, may He be Blessed, arranged. [They are] not what human intellect would require but rather what Hashem, may He be Blessed, arranged in His wisdom. And therefore, one who bonds with the mitzvot bonds with the *sichli* which is [in this case] the elevated, G-dly intellect. And through this, one has bonding with Him, may He be Blessed, [which] extracts [the person[1] performing the mitzvot,] from nature (common [to animals and humans]) and through this his soul is refined and then [it] bonds with Him, may He be Blessed.

And the deeds of the human being in particular, are suitable to extract a person from physical nature – as Turnus Rufus the wicked [Roman General] asked Rabbi Akiva,[2] "Whose deeds are better? Hashem's or human beings'?" As was explained above,[3] Rabbi Akiva responded to him that human acts are

1. Lit., "him."

2. Tanchuma, Tazri'a. Some versions of the Midrash have this as Subsection Five, Six or Seven. We reference the Buber edition of the Midrash (Vilna, 5645) which has it as Tazri'a 7.

3. See Chapter Two where the Maharal explained this Midrash at length.

preferred to natural [acts] and as we [explained] at length above that a person is above nature in that he has a soul drawn from the elevated [transcendent reality].

The question of the philosophers was the springboard for this chapter (and the entire series of chapters from Chapter Six till this point). The Maharal now summarizes his response to this question. His response is that fulfillment of mitzvot is, in and of itself, a bonding with the *sichli* framework which Hashem created in His wisdom. This bonding enables one to transport him/herself out of a purely physical existence and this constitutes a refinement of the human being. This simultaneously allows the soul to take one step closer back towards its source – Hashem.

ושוב לא יקשה כלל איך אפשר שיקנה האדם הצלחה העליונה על ידי מעשה המצוות, כי אין מעשה האדם מעשים טבעיים אבל מעשיו הם על הטבע, ולפיכך על ידי מעשים אלו דבק בסדר השכלי.

ובזה הותרה שאלתם לגמרי איך אפשר שיקנה האדם המדרגה הרוחנית על ידי המעשים הגשמיים, כי לא כמחשבותיהם מחשבותינו כי אנחנו אומרים כי הנפש הזאת היא אצולה מן השם יתברך והיא בת מלך שנשאת לעירוני, ומפני שעומדת בחומר צריכה השבה אל המלך שהוא אביה ואין צריכה השלמה אחרת, ועל ידי המצוות היא שבה אל בית אביה שאין חסר לה רק זה אחר שהיא בת מלך בעצמה.

[Therefore] it can never again be asked how it is possible that a person [could] acquire pre-eminent [spiritual] success through the [physical] acts of the mitzvot [since] human acts are not [constrained to remain only] natural acts but they [can be] above the natural,[4] and therefore, through these actions [a person] bonds with the *sichli* framework [of mitzvot which Hashem created.]

Through this [response], the question [of the philosophers][5] has been completely answered, [their question being] "How is it possible for a person to acquire a [superior] spiritual level through material actions?" For their thoughts are not like our thoughts,[6] for we say that this soul is drawn from Hashem, may He be Blessed, [and we say] that it is a princess[7] which married a townsman and since it is trapped in [a] material [body], it [always] needs to be returned to the King who is her Father and it needs no other completion. And through the mitzvot, she returns to her Father's house – which is the

4. If a person chooses to become more than an animal and chooses to let his soul guide his life, he will transcend nature.

5. See the Maharal's citation of this question at the beginning of Chapters Six and Nine.

6. Cf. Y'shayahu 55:8.

7. This metaphor was first explored by the Maharal in Chapter Three. The source is Vayikra Rabbah 4:2.

כי המצוות שהם הסדר השכלי מוציאים אותה אל הפעל עד שתצא מן החומר המוטבע ושבה אל בית אביה הוא המלך העליון כמו שאמרנו.

כי הנשמה היא מלמעלה והיא א־להית נבדלת, וכאשר האדם עושה המצוה שהיא מעשה השכלי הנה מתקרב בזה אל המעלה הנבדלת ומצרף נפשו מן הטבע החמרית הן גופו הן נפשו, כי המעשה של המצוה הוא מעשה א־להי שעושה על ידי גופו, ומכל שכן כאשר הוא עוסק בתורה השכלית שבזה מתדבק נפשו בשכלי לגמרי ובזה נפשו יוצאת מן הטבע החמרית.

only thing she lacks since she is, in her essence, a princess.

[The mechanism through which this occurs is] that the mitzvot are a *sichli* framework which transition her [from her potential] to her actualized [perfection] to the point that she leaves the material [in which she was] encased and returns to her father's house – He is the lofty King, as we have explained.

[This is] because the soul is from above and is G-dly-transcendent; and when a person performs a mitzvah (which is a *sichli* act), through this he approaches the transcendent level and refines his soul from material nature – [in fact, he refines] both his body and his soul. [The reason for this refinement is] that a mitzvah act is a G-dly act which one performs by means of one's body [thus the body is also refined.] How much more so [is a person refined] when he is immersed in the *sichli* Torah through which his soul bonds with the *sichli* [reality] completely; and through this, his soul exits material nature.

The Maharal explains why it is that the philosophers found it difficult to arrive at such a solution to their question.

ובודאי לדעתם שאינם מודים שהנפש בעצמה עצם א־להי הוקשה להם איך אפשר שעל ידי המצוות תשוב א־להית.

Definitely, in their opinion,[8] since they do not concede that the soul, in and of itself, is a G-dly object,[9] they find it difficult [to explain] how it is possible that through the [physical] mitzvot it[10] can become G-dly.

The Maharal reiterates his view – that the physical implementation of mitzvot must have spiritual ramifications – in particular, creating a bond with Hashem. The mitzvot are, in fact, the means by which finite humans can bond with Hashem Who is infinite (a bond which would otherwise be impossible). This bond is created through mitzvah

8. The philosophers'.

9. As we note in the Commentary, Ch. 9 § Point 2, the philosophers believed that the intellect, as opposed to the soul, is the part of the human being which can become G-dly.

10. The soul.

performance because such performance additionally[11] indicates that a person has accepted Hashem as King which creates a King-subject relationship.

אבל דעת התורה כמו שאמרו ז"ל שהיא בת מלך נשאת לעירוני והנפש מוטבעת בחומר ועל ידי המצוות יש לנפש דבוק וחבור בו יתברך ותשוב אל אביה.

ואיך לא יקנה מדרגה א-להית על ידי המצוות, כי המצוות כולם במה שהם מצוות השם יתברך על האדם אין ספק שזה התיחסות וחבור בין השם יתברך ובין האדם, כמו מלך הגוזר גזירה על עמו ואין ספק כי יש יחוס וחבור בין המלך ועבדיו המקבלים את הגזרה מצד שהוא מלכם גוזר עליהם והם מקבלים. ומאחר שכך הוא איך לא נאמר מה שמקבלים ישראל מצוותיו וגזרותיו עליהם שהוא יתברך אשר הוא נבדל יש לו יחוס אליהם וצירוף מצד שהם מקבלים גזרותיו אשר השכל מחייב אותם שבזה הצד מתקרבים ומתדבקים אל השם יתברך אשר הוא נבדל מהכל ויקנו בשביל כך ההצלחה העליונה בשביל החבור והדבוק הזה.

However, the view of the Torah is as [our sages], *z"l*, have stated – that the soul[12] is a princess[13] married to a townsman [which means that] the soul is embedded in the material [body]; but through the mitzvot, the soul has a bond and joining with Him, may He be Blessed, and [thus] returns to her Father.

And how could one not acquire a G-dly status through the mitzvot? Since the mitzvot are all the commandments of Hashem, may He be Blessed, [directed] at human beings, there is no doubt that this constitutes a relationship and bond between Hashem, may He be Blessed, and the human being, just like a king who makes a decree on his nation. And there is no doubt that there is a relation and bond between the king and those servants who accept the decree due to his being their king who decrees on them and they accept [his decrees]. And since this is so, how can we not say that through Israel's accepting His mitzvot and decrees, may He be Blessed, Who is transcendent [and separated], He [then][14] has a relationship with them and it[15] is a refinement [for them] due to their accepting His decrees which are a function of [His] intellect. And through this [acceptance] they

11. Besides the reason the Maharal has already mentioned: that when performing a mitzvah one has adopted Hashem's *sichli* framework.

12. Lit., "it."

13. As referenced above, this is cited by the Maharal earlier in Chapter Three, from Vayikra Rabbah 4:2.

14. The Maharal emphasizes that a priori, Hashem is transcendent and separate from human beings. It is the mitzvot which generate a bond between finite humanity and infinite G-d.

15. The relationship is generated through Israel's acceptance of Hashem's mitzvot. Once this acceptance has taken place, a bond is formed between Hashem and Israel. It is this bond with constitutes a refinement for Israel.

draw close to and bond with Hashem, may He be Blessed, Who is [originally] separated from everything, and thus they acquire superior success through this connection and bond.

There is no doubt that this is the bonding with Him, may He be Blessed, as it says in the verse, "and to bond with Him."[16] When a person does His will and accepts the decree of the King and [thus] is His servant – this in and of itself constitutes the join and bond with Him, may He be Blessed, and [it] extracts a person from the [purely] material [plane of existence] to bond with Him, may He be Blessed.

Now, comprehend with wisdom and analyze with understanding that the Torah extracts a person from nature and brings a person to bonding with Him, may He be Blessed. A metaphor for this is [as follows]: There are two paths before a person and [someone] says, "Walk on this path!" And the reason [for the choice of the one path over the other] is not that this path is better and more suitable in and of itself, but that this path is the one on which a person will reach his destination [and therefore, the person giving advice] places him before his [correct] path. And so too, the reason[17] for mitzvot is only that they are a clarification of the correct and straight path [which will take a person

כי אין ספק שזהו ההתדבקות בו יתברך כמו שאמר הכתוב (דברים ל"א [צ"ל, ל:כ או י"א:כ"ב]) ו[ל]דבקה בו כאשר האדם עושה רצונו ומקבל גזרת המלך והוא עבדו זהו עצמו החבור והדבוק בו יתברך ומוציא את האדם מן החמרי ולהיות דבק בו יתברך.

ועתה הבן בחכמה וחקור בבינה כי התורה מוציאה את האדם מן הטבע ומביא אותו אל הדבקות בו יתברך, דמיון זה שני דרכים לפני האדם ויאמר תלך בדרך הזה, ואין הטעם שדרך הזה דרך יותר טוב ויותר ראוי מצד עצמו, רק בשביל שזה הדרך שבו יגיע אל מחוז חפצו ומעמידו נוכח דרכו, וכן אין ענין המצוה רק שהמצוה היא בירור הדרך הנכון והישר, שבדרך התורה יבא להתדבק בו יתברך כמו שהתבאר למעלה וכמו שיתבאר לקמן וכמו שאין כל הדרכים מביאין את האדם אל מקום חפצו המיוחד לו, כך אין כל הדרכים והמעשים מביאים אותו אל הדבקות המיוחד, רק דרך המצוות הם מצרפים ומבררים את דרך הישר המיוחד אשר הוא נוכח ה' מבין שאר דרכים.

16. The Hebrew citation of the verse in the Maharal here seems to contain a printer's error. There are two possibilities for the source of this verse. It is either D'varim 11:22 which reads, "כִּי אִם שָׁמֹר תִּשְׁמְרוּן אֶת כָּל הַמִּצְוָה הַזֹּאת אֲשֶׁר אָנֹכִי מְצַוֶּה אֶתְכֶם לַעֲשֹׂתָהּ לְאַהֲבָה אֶת ה' אֶ-ל־הֵיכֶם לָלֶכֶת בְּכָל דְּרָכָיו וּלְדָבְקָה בוֹ", meaning, "For if you will surely cherish all this mitzvah which I command you to perform: to love Hashem your G-d, to walk in all His ways and to bond with Him." Or, it is D'varim 30:20, which reads, 'לְאַהֲבָה אֶת ה' אֶ-ל־הֶיךָ לִשְׁמֹעַ בְּקֹלוֹ וּלְדָבְקָה בוֹ כִּי הוּא חַיֶּיךָ וְאֹרֶךְ יָמֶיךָ לָשֶׁבֶת עַל הָאֲדָמָה אֲשֶׁר נִשְׁבַּע ה' לַאֲבֹתֶיךָ לְאַבְרָהָם לְיִצְחָק וּלְיַעֲקֹב לָתֵת לָהֶם', meaning, "To love Hashem your G-d, to obey His voice and to bond with Him; for He is your life and length of your days to dwell on the land which Hashem promised to your forefathers, to Avraham, to Yitzchak and to Ya'akov, to give [it] to them."

17. Lit., "the matter of."

וזהו שאמר לא נתנה תורה רק לצרף הבריות שיהיה להם דביקות בו ית' אבל שיהיה חפץ בעצם השחיטה זה אינו רק שהמצוה צירוף האדם להעמיד את האדם על דרך שהוא נוכח ה' עד כי יש לו דבקות עם השם יתברך.

to the ultimate destination – bonding with Hashem.] For on the path of the Torah so that he can obtain bonding with Him, may He be Blessed, as was explained above and as will be explained later.[18] And just as not all paths bring a person to his unique destination, so too, not all paths and deeds bring a person to the unique bonding [with Hashem] – it is only the path of mitzvot [which accomplishes this] refining and clarifying the straight and unique path (which is before Hashem) from amongst the other paths.

This is what was stated,[19] "the mitzvot were only given to refine humans" [which means that the mitzvot refine humans through] them bonding with Him, may He be Blessed. However, it is false to state that He desires the essence of [ritual] slaughter;[20] rather [it means] that the mitzvah is a refinement for the human being, standing him on the path which faces G-d to the extent that he obtains bonding with Hashem, may He be Blessed.

---

18. See Chapter Eleven.

19. Tanchuma, Sh'mini 8. This Midrash was cited earlier by the Maharal at the beginning of Chapter Seven.

20. This references the Midrash which the Maharal has just cited (Tanchuma, Sh'mini 8) where the Midrash states, "Does it matter to the Holy One, Blessed be He, whether one slaughters an animal and then eats or whether one stabs it and then eats! Neither of these [methods] benefits Him and neither of these [methods] harms Him." In Chapter Seven the Maharal explains that this means as follows, "The Midrash's intent is that Hashem, may He be Blessed, does not desire [that we perform a specifically regulated ritual] slaughter for the sake of the slaughter because it [the slaughter] is good in and of itself – for what does the Holy One, Blessed be He, care for slaughter itself? Because, once one is destroying an animal, does it matter whether one destroys it from the throat or the [back of the] neck? Rather [as the Midrash continues,] "the mitzvot were only given to refine humans," in order that human actions should be according to the *sichli* order from Hashem, may He be Blessed. And this thing is a refinement and purification of the soul (when it bonds with the *sichli* [reality]) and then he [the person] attains bonding with G-d, may He be Blessed.' See there for a fuller analysis.

SUMMARY

Chapter 9: 2/3

I. **How do mitzvot contribute to spiritual greatness if they are not understood?**
   A. The main thrust of the philosophers' difficulty is that if mitzvot are designed to affect the human intellect (this is their central assumption), how can it help to fulfill mitzvot which are not understood by the one performing them or which are beyond all human understanding?
   B. The Maharal's three answers
      1. Adopting G-d's *sichli* framework (the Maharal's previous answer)
         a. When one performs mitzvot one is adopting the framework of priorities and desires created by G-d.
         b. Thus when one performs a mitzvah one is assimilating G-d's will and thus one is bonding with his *sichli* will and thereby with Hashem himself.
         c. One's understanding of the mitzvah is not vital to the basic level of this process, only one's replacement of personal will with Hashem's.
      2. The value of physical action
         a. Since human beings possess a soul which is drawn from the transcendent world, human actions have the potential to be more than just physical activities.
         b. The metaphor used for this is that the soul is like the daughter of a king who marries a townsman. Her only desire is to return to her father since this is where she can achieve her personal completion and perfection.
         c. When one performs mitzvot one refines one's body and soul through bonding with the transcendent.
      3. Creating a relationship with the King
         a. The very fact that Hashem has issued a command and that we accept and obey it, creates a relationship and bond between us.
         b. This can be understood using a simple analogy:
            (1) If a king is accepted by his subjects as their king, it means that they will obey his laws, and it is this acceptance which generates the relationship of king and subject. If the subjects reject his laws, then there is no bond at all between the ruler and the ruled.
            (2) So too, when we accept Hashem as our King through performing his mitzvot (a term which literally means "com-

mandments") this, in and of itself, links us to Hashem as His subjects.

c. Due to the fact that we now have a bond with Hashem, Who is nominally transcendent and separate from this world, this bond glues us to the transcendent reality and thus causes us to become refined and less earth-bound, regardless of our understanding of the mitzvot.

II. The source of the philosophers' difficulty

A. The philosophers do not accept that the soul is a G-dly, transcendent object.

CHAPTER 9

Part 3 of 3

The Maharal now explains that the term, "Torah" was chosen because it indicates the essential task of the Torah – which is to guide one on the path to forming a bond with Hashem.

ויש לך להבין כי בשביל כך נקראת התורה בשם הזה, ולא נקראה בשם חכמה ותבונה ודעת שהרי על התורה נאמר (שם ו') כי היא חכמתכם ובינתכם לעיני כל העמים.

אבל לומר כי התורה אף שיש בה החכמה אין החכמה שהיא בתורה היא חכמה מחקרית, אבל החכמה שהיא בתורה, שהתורה היא מלמדת ומורה לך דרך החיים שהאדם יקנה ההצלחה האחרונה היא הדבקות בו יתברך שנפשו תהיה צרורה בצרור החיים את ה', ודבר זה שיבא אל הדבקות הזה הוא על ידי עשיית התורה.

And you should understand that this is the reason that the Torah was given the name ["Torah"] and it is not called, "Wisdom," "Understanding" or "Knowledge"[1] [which would not have been unreasonable] as it says, regarding the Torah, "For it is your wisdom and understanding in the eyes of all the nations."[2]

[The reason the Torah was given its name (which is related to the word "to guide")][3] is to say that even though the Torah does contain wisdom, it is not empirical[4] wisdom but Torah wisdom; for the Torah teaches and *guides* you on the path of life [through which] a person acquires ultimate success, which is bonding with Him, may He be Blessed: where his "soul is bound within the bond of life with Hashem."[5] And the means by which a person will arrive at this bond is through implementing the Torah.[6]

The difference between Torah and other wisdoms is that although all wisdoms allow a person to partake of the *sichli* due to their being intellectual pursuits, they are not qualitatively *sichli* enough to allow one to bond with Hashem through their study.

1. See the Commentary, Ch. 9 § Point 1.
2. D'varim 4:6.
3. The word "Torah," תורה, is a derivative of the verb להורות, "*l'horot*" which means "to teach" or "to guide." See, for example, B'reishit 46:28. As the Maharal explains, it is used in the sense of providing guidance, מורה דרך.
4. Meaning wisdom which can be discovered by human means.
5. 1 Sh'mu'el, 25:29.
6. I.e., performing the mitzvot.

וזהו ההפרש שיש בין התורה ובין שאר החכמות, כי שאר החכמות אינם מביאין את האדם אל הדבקות הזה אף כי בודאי על ידי החכמה גם כן האדם הוא שכלי, מכל מקום מה שקונה מן השכל אינו כדאי שיהיה דבק עם השם יתברך שהוא נבדל לגמרי מהכל.

אבל מה שמביא האדם אל הדבקות היא התורה שהיא מורה הדרך אל השם יתברך שעל ידי זה יהיה דבק בו יתברך.

And this is the difference between the Torah and other wisdoms. Other wisdoms do not bring a person to this bonding [with Hashem] even though through that wisdom a person also becomes *sichli*, but what he acquires from the intellect [in other wisdoms] is not sufficient to allow him to bond with Hashem, may He be Blessed, Who is completely transcendent above everything.

But the Torah is that which brings a person to the bonding [with Hashem and it is the Torah] which guides one on the path to Hashem, may He be Blessed, and through which a person will be bonded with Him, may He be Blessed.

The Maharal now addresses the question as to whether human beings are worthy of bonding with Hashem and if so, why.

ואין ספק כי האדם ראוי לזה מצד כי האדם נברא בצלם א-ל-הים בדמותו וזה הקירוב היותר כמו שאמר התנא הא־להי (אבות פ"ה) חביב האדם שנברא בצלם א־להים והדבקות הזה הוא על ידי התורה שמורה לאדם הדרך שהוא הדבוק.

ולכך מספר מצוות עשה הם כמספר אבריו של אדם שהם רמ"ח כי אבריו של אדם הם צורת צלמו שבשביל מעלה זאת ראוי אל הדבוק בו יתברך.

And there is no doubt that a person is worthy of this [bonding with Hashem] due to his being created in the "image of G-d,"[7] "in His Form"[8] which is the closest intimacy [that one can attain to Hashem] as the G-dly Mishnaic sage[9] said,[10] "Beloved is the human being, who was created in the likeness" of Hashem. And this bonding is accomplished through the Torah which teaches the human being the path which is [itself] the bond.

Therefore, the number of the *mitzvot aseh* corresponds to the number of component-limbs of a human (that is, 248) because the component-limbs of a human are the Form of his likeness and due to this excellence,[11] [the human being] is suitable to bond with Hashem,[12] may He be Blessed.[13]

7. B'reishit 1:26.
8. B'reishit 5:1.
9. A sage who lived at the time of the creation of the Mishnah, the central component of the Oral Law. The particular sage in question here is Rabbi Akiva.
10. Pirkei Avot 3:14.
11. I.e., the fact that the human being's Form in some way resembles Hashem's.
12. Lit., "Him."
13. See the Commentary, Ch. 9 § Point 4.

The Maharal now cites a Gemara which discusses those actions and attitudes which effectively prevent one from bonding with Hashem despite the inherent worthiness of each person to do so.

ובפרק קמא דשבועות (י"ג ע"א):

רבי אומר כל העבירות שבתורה בין עשה תשובה ובין לא עשה תשובה יום הכפורים מכפר חוץ מפורק עול ומגלה פנים בתורה שלא כהלכה ומפר בריתו של אברהם אבינו שאם עשה תשובה יום הכפורים מכפר ואם לא עשה תשובה אין יום הכפורים מכפר.

And in the first chapter of [Tractate] Shavu'ot [it states],[14]

> Rabbi [Yehudah Hanassi] says, "Yom Kippur[15] atones for all the sins in the Torah, whether or not a person did *t'shuvah*,[16] except for: one who rejects the yoke [of service of Hashem],[17] one who reveals facets of the Torah which are not according to the Halachah,[18] and one who annuls the covenant of Avraham our forefather.[19] [Regarding someone who transgressed one of these abovementioned three sins,] if he did *t'shuvah* then Yom Kippur atones [for him] and if he did not do *t'shuvah*, then Yom Kippur does not atone [for him].

והטעם באלו דוקא שהאדם יש לו חבור אל השם יתברך באמצעות התורה כמו שהתבאר, וכאשר המקבל אין מוכן לקבל החבור, או שאין לו אמצעי שעל ידו החבור, או אינו מודה בעלה שבו החבור הרי הוא נפרד מן העלה ואין לו קשור עם העלה.

And the reason for these [three sins having a more stringent requirement to gain atonement] is that a person possesses a connection to Hashem, may He be Blessed, by means of the Torah (as was explained) but when the recipient [of this bond with Hashem] is not

14. Shavu'ot 13a. Our version has slight variations.

15. As the Torah teaches us in Vayikra 16:30, the purpose of the day of Yom Kippur (the Day of Atonement) and its attendant service in the Holy Temple, was to grant atonement to the Jewish people. The Gemara here discusses whether this atonement is dependent upon the individual doing *t'shuvah* or not.

16. "*T'shuvah*," תשובה, is often mistranslated as "repentance" and better translated as "return." See the Commentary, Ch. 9 § Point 1.

17. Rashi (ad loc., s.v. *poreik ol*) explains that this refers to one who becomes a heretic.

18. Our versions of the Gemara do not have the phrase, "which are not according to the Halachah." Rashi (ad loc., s.v. *m'galeh panim batorah*) explains that this refers to one who approaches the words of Torah with disrespect and arrogance.

19. Our version reads, "one who annuls the covenant in the flesh." As Rashi explains (ad loc., s.v. *b'rit*) this refers to one who does not fulfill the mitzvah of circumcision (in the event that he was not circumcised as a child).

receptive to accept this bond, then [automatically] he is separated from the [Primal] Cause[20] and has no bond with it.

The Maharal explains how each of the acts mentioned above has this severing effect. Each of them, in their own manner, constitutes a decision to remain apart from and unbonded with Hashem and therefore, only after a process of t'shuvah, which is, in essence, a reconnection with Hashem, can they achieve atonement.

וכאשר הוא מפר בריתו של אברהם אבינו אין האדם מקבל בריתו של הקדוש ברוך הוא, וכאשר מגלה פנים בתורה שלא כהלכה הרי הוא כופר באמצעי שעל ידו החבור, וכאשר הוא פורק עול הוא כופר באותו אשר החבור בו הש"י שבו החבור.

ולכך אין יום הכפורים מכפר רק מי שלא נפרד בעצמו מן העלה, וכאשר הוא לא נפרד לגמרי רק שהוא נפרד במקצת על ידי יום הכפורים יש לו כפרה.

למה הדבר דומה לפרי המחובר בענף והענף מחבר הפרי לאילן, ואם יגרע דבר מה לפרי מכל מקום מה שהפרי הוא מחובר לענף והענף לאילן לכך הוא מעלה ארוכה, אך אם נכרת עד שאין הפרי מקבל החבור אז

When one annuls the covenant of Avraham our forefather, he cannot receive a covenant with the Holy One, Blessed be He.[21] And when one reveals facets of the Torah which are not according to the Halachah, he is denying [the validity] of the *means* by which [one acquires] the bond [with Hashem]. And when one rejects the yoke [of service of Hashem] he is denying [the very existence of] Him with Whom one bonds, that is, Hashem, may He be Blessed.

Therefore, Yom Kippur only atones for one who has not separated himself from the [Primal] Cause [unlike a person who has transgressed one of the above three sins, who has separated himself completely from Hashem. However,] Yom Kippur does atone for one who has not separated [himself] completely, but rather has just distanced himself a little.

To what can this be compared? To a fruit connected to a branch[22] which [in turn, by proxy] connects the fruit to the tree. If the fruit is somehow diminished, nevertheless, since the fruit is connected to a branch which is con-

20. I.e., Hashem. The Maharal here uses the term "Primal Cause" which he first introduced in the Introduction to this work. See the Commentary, Ch. 9 § Point 5.

21. The whole idea of a covenant is that one creates a bond between two parties, in this case, Hashem and a human being. When a person refuses to have a circumcision, they are exhibiting their decision not to have a covenant – i.e., not to bond with Hashem.

22. The Maharal reprises a theme he introduced originally in the Introduction to Tiferet Yisrael: that a person is like a fruit on the tree of life. See his explanations there.

נפסד הפרי, וכן אם הענף הוא נכרת באמצעיתו הרי אינו מעלה ארוכה ואף אם לא נכרת באמצעיתו והוא שלם רק נבדל מן העיקר עד שאין לו עיקר הרי אין תרופה לאותו פרי.

וכן זה בעצמו כאשר מפר בריתו של אברהם אבינו הרי נבדל האדם שהוא המקבל מן השם יתברך.

וכאשר מגלה פנים בתורה שלא כהלכה הרי אין לו אמצעי שעל ידו החבור בו יתברך.

וכאשר הוא פורק עול אין לו מי שהחבור בו.

ולפיכך דרש שם הכרת תכרת אחת קודם יום הכפורים ואחת אחר יום הכפורים.

nected to the tree [the tree] brings about healing [to the fruit]. But if the fruit[23] is severed [from the branch] so that the fruit no longer receives its bond [to the tree] then the fruit will decay. So too, if the branch is severed in the middle, the tree cannot heal [the fruit]; and even if the branch[24] is not severed in the middle and is whole except that it is separated from the trunk (to the extent that it no longer has a trunk) there is no remedy for that fruit.[25]

So too is the matter regarding one who annuls the covenant of Avraham our forefather – the person, who [potentially] receives [the bond] from Hashem, may He be Blessed, is detached [from Hashem, through his own actions].

And when one reveals facets of the Torah which are not according to the Halachah, he has no means by which [he can] bond with Him, may He be Blessed.

And when one rejects the yoke [of service of Hashem] he has no-One with Whom to bond.

And therefore, [the Gemara] learned there,[26] [from the verse] "You shall *surely* be cut off,"[27] [which has two consecutive terms denoting being "cut off," that] one [of the two terms] refers to [being cut off] before Yom Kippur and the other [of the two terms] refers [to being cut off] after Yom Kippur [implying that Yom Kippur does not prevent a person who has transgressed one of these three sins from being cut off.]

The Maharal summarizes his position: the Torah allows a person to bond with Hashem.

23. Lit., "it."

24. Lit., "it."

25. Note that the Maharal has mentioned three scenarios (fruit diminished, branch broken in the middle, branch whole but disconnected from the tree-trunk).

26. Shavu'ot 13a.

27. B'midbar 15:31. There is a double phrase in the verse, "*hikareit tikareit*," הכרת תכרת, which we have translated as "you shall *surely* be cut off." Since the Torah could have phrased this idea in a simpler fashion, using only one term, the Gemara learns that the second term teaches us an extra idea – that the severance is absolute, applying even after Yom Kippur.

הרי הדבר ברור כי התורה היא שעל ידה החבור בין השם יתברך ובין האדם ולפיכך הוסרה הקושיא לגמרי באיזה צד יש לאדם הצלחה האחרונה על ידי עשיית המצוה, והרי הדבר ברור כי ההצלחה היא על ידי עשיית המצוה במה שהם הקירוב והדבוק בו יתברך והוא ההצלחה האמתית.

The matter is clear that it is the Torah through which a bond exists between Hashem, may He be Blessed, and a person, and therefore, the difficulty (how it is possible that a person can attain ultimate [spiritual] success through performance of [physical] mitzvot) has been resolved. [The answer is that the mitzvot] constitute intimacy and bonding with Him, may He be Blessed, [something] which constitutes true success.

The Maharal cites an additional reason to reject the rationale of the philosophers – that their requirements for spiritual achievement are so exceptional that it disqualifies almost every human being.

ואלו בני אדם השואלין היו רוצים שיהיה לאדם הצלחה בעצמו והם המושכלות שהאדם קונה.

ולא שמו דעתם שעיקר הצלחה הוא הדבוק בו יתברך, ואף אם אמרו כי על ידי המושכלות הוא דבק בשכל הפועל עד ששכל האדם ושכל הפועל הוא אחד, אלו הם דברי הבאי כי לפי דבריהם לא תהיה רק לאחד או לשנים בדור וכי בשביל אלו העולם נמצא, לכן אלו דברים הם דברים שאין להם שורש ויסוד, ויתבאר עוד בפרק הסמוך.

והכל בשביל כי היה שפל בעיניהם שיהיה הצלחה א-להית ע"י מעשה האדם, והם לא עמדו בסוד ה' כי מעשה האדם הם למעלה מן הטבע וכמו שהשיב רבי עקיבא בעומק חכמתו איזה מעשה יפה יותר כמו שהתבאר.

And those people[28] who ask [how the Torah and mitzvot could contribute to a person's spiritual growth] would prefer that a person contain his [spiritual] success within himself – which would be the Conceptualizations which a person acquires [intellectually].

And they did not pay attention [to the idea that] the essence of success is bonding with Him, may He be Blessed; and even if they conceded that one bonds with the "Active Intellect"[29] through the Conceptualizations to the extent that the intellect of the person becomes one with the "Active Intellect," this is nonsense! [The reason it's nonsense is that] according to their words, this will only be [achieved] by one or two [people] in each generation – and does the universe exist just for these [one or two people]? Therefore, [it is clear that] these words have no root or foundation and it will be explained further in the next chapter.

And all [of this confusion came about] because it was degrading in the philosophers'[30] eyes that G-dly achievement be achieved through the [phys-

28. I.e., the philosophers.
29. See the Commentary, Ch. 9 § Point 1.
30. Lit., "their."

ical] actions of a human being; and they did not gain access to the secret of Hashem that human deeds are above nature, as Rabbi Akiva responded in the profundity of his wisdom [when he asked Turnus Rufus,] "Whose deed is better?" as has been explained.[31]

The Maharal summarizes his position one last time.

והתורה היא כמו אמצעי בין העלה ובין האדם, וכבר אמרנו כי התורה היא סדר השי"ת וכאשר האדם דבק בסדר הזה שסדר השם יתברך הוא דבק בו יתברך שמאתו הסדר הזה.

וזה הסדר נתן השם יתברך אל האדם אשר יש לו נפש א-להי ועל ידי שהוא שומר סדר הזה אשר סדר השם יתברך דבק בו יתברך, ולפיכך ראוי שיהיה בזה הצלחת האדם במה שהוא דבק בו יתברך וזהו תכלית ההצלחה כאשר יתבאר עוד בעזרת ה' נותן התורה.

And the Torah is like a link[32] between the [Primal] Cause and the human being. And we have already said that the Torah is the framework of Hashem, may He be Blessed, and when a person bonds with this framework which Hashem arranged, he bonds with Him, may He be Blessed, from Whom this framework [derives].

Hashem, may He be Blessed, bestowed this framework on the human being since he[33] possesses a G-dly soul; and through adhering to this order which Hashem, may He be Blessed, arranged [a person] bonds with Him, may He be Blessed. And therefore, it is suitable that a person's success will be through bonding with Him, may He be Blessed, and this is the pinnacle of achievement as will be further explained[34] with the help of Hashem, Who bestows Torah.

31. Tanchuma, Tazri'a 7. This is cited earlier in this chapter but primarily in Chapter Two. One of the central concepts the Maharal learns from Rabbi Akiva's arguments in this Midrash is that human deeds can transcend the natural.

32. Lit., "means" or "intermediary."

33. Humanity.

34. See Chapters Ten, Eleven and Twelve.

SUMMARY

Chapter 9: 3/3

I. The term, "Torah," denotes its purpose

A. Torah does contain wisdom but it is not empirical wisdom which is verifiable by human beings.

B. Torah is a guide

1. Therefore, the word "Torah" was chosen (as opposed to "wisdom," "understanding" or "knowledge") as the name for this communication from Hashem, because "Torah" comes from the word "to guide."
2. The Torah guides one on the path to ultimate success – which is bonding with Hashem.

II. All branches of wisdom are *sichli* but Torah is incomparably *sichli*

A. Every branch of genuine intellectual pursuit does have an element of the *sichli*.

B. The *sichli* element in Torah is qualitatively different – only Torah enables one to bond with Hashem through its study alone.

III. Why humans are worthy of bonding with Hashem

A. Humans are made "in the image of G-d" and "in His Form."

B. As discussed previously, the human Form consists of 248 component-limbs. This parallels the 248 *mitzvot aseh*. It is this Form which in some way is "in the image of G-d." Thus humans are inherently worthy of bonding with Hashem since they already share G-d's "Form."

IV. Activities which destroy the ability of a person to bond with Hashem

A. The only thing which can stop a person from bonding with Hashem is an active choice on the part of that person to disconnect from Hashem.

1. This disconnection is the consequence of the person's choice (and not a punitive reaction from Hashem, G-d forbid) and ultimately constitutes the greatest pain, failure and penalty.
2. Metaphor
   a. A good metaphor for this is a fruit which is on a branch on a tree.
   b. Should the branch be severed from the tree or the fruit be severed from the tree, the fruit will fall to the earth and rot.

B. Shavu'ot 13a

1. The Gemara lists three central actions of disconnection for which Yom Kippur alone cannot atone:

a. One who has a definite belief that G-d does not exist
   (1) Clearly one disconnects from Hashem if one believes He does not exist, G-d forbid.
b. One who denigrates the Torah
   (1) One cannot connect to Hashem except through Torah (as the Maharal has explained this entire chapter), and therefore, denigration of the Torah disconnects one from the only means to connect to Hashem.
c. One who does not give himself a covenantal circumcision
   (1) The covenant is the archetypal model of bonding with Hashem – similar to a marriage. One who rejects the covenant is rejecting the most basic level of bond.

2. The Maharal explains that Yom Kippur can only atone for a person who is not completely severed from Hashem, but one who has intentionally committed one of the above three acts has consciously cut himself away from Hashem and thus Yom Kippur cannot help him.

V. The philosophers' error

A. The Maharal explains that the reason for the philosophers' inability to comprehend how physical mitzvot could help one achieve spiritual greatness is that they did not accept that human actions have the potential to transcend nature.

B. Therefore, they insisted that spiritual perfection be encapsulated purely within the human mind – through the apprehension of fundamental truths. This *sichli* arena was one in which they felt that the transcendence of nature was automatic.

C. Because such an intellectual achievement is within the reach of perhaps only one or two people per generation, the philosophers' view additionally renders most of humanity as being without the ability to connect to Hashem, which is unacceptable in the Maharal's view.

COMMENTARY SECTION

COMMENTARY SECTION

Introduction

1. **Terminology**
   a. *Mitzvat aseh*
      i. Generally, we have left this phrase untranslated since there is no simple English term which captures its meaning, which is that this is a commandment requiring one to initiate some action.
      ii. It is often mistranslated by the phrase, "positive commandment." This does not capture the simple meaning and moreover implies that there is such a thing as a "negative commandment" (also sometimes used to mistranslate the next term), G-d forbid.
      iii. An example of a *mitzvat aseh* is the commandment to show respect and honor to one's parents, which requires one proactively to initiate a variety of actions, such as clothing and feeding one's parents.
      iv. Sometimes we have utilized the translation, "action commandment" or "initiative-action commandment" where the context emphasizes the action element of the commandment, but these phrases are unwieldy.

   b. Restraining Commandment or Prohibition, *mitzvat lo ta'aseh*
      i. We have used these two terms as translations of the Hebrew, מצוות לא תעשה, *mitzvat lo ta'aseh*. This is a prohibition, requiring one to restrain oneself from performing a particular action. For example, the prohibition against committing murder.
      ii. Often this term is translated by the phrase, "negative commandment," which as we have indicated is a mistranslation and also implies, G-d forbid, that a mitzvah could be negative.
      iii. On occasion, we have utilized the untranslated, *mitzvat lo ta'aseh*, again depending on the context.

   c. [Primal] Cause vs. Manifestations, results, consequences, effects
      i. The Maharal uses the paired Hebrew terms "*ilah*," עלה, and "*alul*," עלול.
      ii. Primal Cause – "*ilah*"
         1. We have translated "*ilah*" as "Cause" and when used to refer to Hashem, as "[Primal] Cause" or "Ultimate Cause."
      iii. Manifestations, results, consequences, effects
         1. An "*alul*" is the result of the "*ilah*," and as such we have translated

"*alul*" variously as "manifestation," "result," "consequence" and "effect."

iv. These two terms are quite central to the Maharal's thinking in general. For further study, see below.

d. "Perfect and innocent"

i. The term, **תמים**, "*tamim*," is used in this section of the Maharal. It has several different meanings, depending on the context. When we have translated it, we have used the phrase, "perfect and innocent" as there is no one English word which captures all its connotations.

ii. Instead of rendering this word into English, we will usually use the Hebrew, "*t'mimah*" (or the masculine form, "*tamim*"), and at times, as the context demands, we will use the translation, "perfect and innocent."

e. "*Sichli*"

i. The Maharal, throughout his works, uses the term, **שכלי**, "*sichli*," which literally means, "cerebral" or "intellectual."

1. When we have translated the term, we have used either of these two synonyms, but the Maharal's intention goes beyond both of them. The Maharal speaks of "intellectual" and "G-dly" items in the same breath – implying a strong connection between the transcendent, spiritual world and the intellect.
2. Therefore, we have often preferred simply to retain the Hebrew, "*sichli*" instead of translating it.

ii. Later in Tiferet Yisrael, the Maharal states,[1]

תפארת ישראל - פרק א

ומפני שתמצא האדם משתתף עם שאר בעלי חיים הטבעיים בהרבה פעולות, ודבר זה בודאי מצד הנפש החיוני אשר באדם אשר בו משתתף עם שאר בעלי חיים הטבעיים, אבל אי אפשר שלא יהיו לו פעולות גם כן מתיחסים אל נפשו השכלית הא־להית כי לא יגרע כחו. כי מה שהאדם הוא בנאי ונגר ועושה מלאכת האפיה והבישול וכיוצא בזה מתיקון הבגדים שודאי אף כי דברים אלו צריכים לו נפש השכלית, מי הוא ערב לי שהדבר הזה הוא מצד שלימות שבו, והרי ראוי ומחוייב שיהיו לו פעולות א־להיות שיפעול בעולם אשר בראו כפי מעלת נפשו הא־להית, ואולי כל הדברים האלה אשר זכרנו הם מצד חסרון שבאדם:

Tiferet Yisrael, Chapter 1

Even though you will find humans participating with other natural animals in many activities – something which undoubtedly flows from their

1. Tiferet Yisrael, Chapter 1.

similarity to animals in that they all have a vital soul[2] – nevertheless, it is impossible that humans will not have activities which relate to its G-dly, *sichli* soul, because this power cannot be diminished.

When a person is a builder, carpenter or when he practices baking, cooking or tailoring, there is no doubt that these actions require a G-dly, *sichli* soul, But who can guarantee that a person does these things as part of his becoming perfect?[3] Rather, it is suitable and required that a person have *G-dly actions* which will act in the world (which Hashem created) according to the exaltedness of his G-dly soul.

1. And as he says in Chapter Seven:

תפארת ישראל - פרק ז

ועל ידי שעושה המצוה שהוא סדר שכלי יש לאדם דביקות בשכלי ויוצא מן הטבע שהאדם חומר בו ואז יש לו דבקות בו יתברך.

Tiferet Yisrael, Chapter 7

And through doing a mitzvah, which is a *sichli* arrangement, a human bonds with the intellectual[4] and he transcends nature (in which a person is mere material) and then a person bonds with Hashem, may He be Blessed.

2. Both of these imply a strong connection between things which are *sichli* and those which are transcendent and G-dly.

iii. Later, the Maharal sharpens this definition and outlines the differences between ordinary *sichli* (cerebral) and *sichli Eloki* (G-dly cerebral).

1. Tiferet Yisrael, Chapter 9

תפארת ישראל - פרק ט

ויש לך להבין כי בשביל כך נקראת התורה בשם הזה, ולא נקראה בשם חכמה ותבונה ודעת שהרי על התורה נאמר (שם ו') כי היא חכמתכם ובינתכם לעיני כל העמים, אבל לומר כי התורה אף שיש בה החכמה אין החכמה שהיא בתורה היא חכמה מחקרית, אבל החכמה שהיא בתורה, שהתורה היא מלמדת ומורה לך דרך החיים שהאדם יקנה ההצלחה האחרונה היא הדבקות בו יתברך שנפשו תהיה צרורה בצרור החיים את ה', ודבר זה שיבא אל הדבקות הזה הוא על ידי עשיית התורה. וזהו ההפרש שיש בין התורה ובין שאר החכמות, כי שאר החכמות אינם מביאין את האדם אל הדבקות הזה אף כי בודאי על ידי החכמה גם כן האדם הוא שכלי, מכל מקום מה שקונה מן השכל אינו כדאי שיהיה דבק עם השם יתברך שהוא נבדל לגמרי מהכל, אבל מה שמביא האדם אל הדבקות היא התורה שהיא מורה הדרך אל השם יתברך שעל ידי זה יהיה דבק בו

2. I.e., a soul which confers vitality.

3. I.e., due to one's intellectual soul.

4. *Sichli*.

יתברך. ואין ספק כי האדם ראוי לזה מצד כי האדם נברא בצלם א־להים בדמותו וזה הקירוב היותר כמו שאמר התנא הא־להי (אבות פ"ה) חביב האדם שנברא בצלם א־להים והדבקות הזה הוא על ידי התורה שמורה לאדם הדרך שהוא הדבוק, ולכך מספר מצות עשה הם כמספר אבריו של אדם שהם רמ"ח כי אבריו של אדם הם צורת צלמו שבשביל מעלה זאת ראוי אל הדבוק בו יתברך:

Tiferet Yisrael, Chapter 9

You should understand that it is because of this that the Torah is called exactly this[5] and is not called, "wisdom and discernment" [which would have been an entirely appropriate alternative name] since it is said regarding the Torah, "For it[6] is your wisdom and discernment in the eyes of all the nations . . ."[7] [The reason that the name "Torah" was chosen instead is] to tell us that even though the Torah possesses wisdom, it is not analytical [human] wisdom; rather, the wisdom in the Torah is that the Torah teaches and guides us in the "path of life"[8] through which a person acquires the ultimate success – bonding with Hashem so that his soul "will be bound up in the network of life – G-d."[9] And that which leads one to this bonding is the implementation of the Torah.

This is the difference between the Torah and other wisdoms – other wisdoms do not lead a person to this bonding even if through this [alternate] wisdom a person is considered to be *sichli*. Nevertheless, what a person [who is immersed in an alternate wisdom] acquires from the intellectual [substance of that wisdom] is not sufficient that he should bond with Hashem, may He be Blessed, Who is completely transcendent above everything. However, that which draws a person to bonding [with Hashem] is the Torah which guides[10] [a person on] the path to Hashem, may He be Blessed – since through it a person will be bonded with Hashem.

iv. It would seem that the Maharal believes that the intellect is that which confers upon humanity the ability to transcend nature and reach the transcendent realm. However, not every intellectual pursuit allows one to bond with Hashem – only Torah can do this.

5. I.e., "Torah."
6. I.e., The Torah.
7. D'varim 4:6.
8. Mishlei 6:23.
9. Cf. 1 Sh'mu'el 25:29.
10. The word used here in Hebrew is "*moreh*," מורה, which means "to guide." It has the same root as "*torah*," תורה.

f. "Awe of Hashem"

   i. Throughout this translation, we will translate the term, יראת ה', "*yirat Hashem*," as "Awe of Hashem."

      1. The word יראה can be used to mean "fear"; this is, in fact, its primary usage. However, it also connotes "awe" and as we explain below, this is the Maharal's usage.
      2. In particular, it connotes an awareness that every element of one's being is an "extension" of Hashem. By "extension," we mean not that, G-d forbid, Hashem has different parts or that Hashem is physical, but rather that one (and in fact the entire universe) is completely dependent upon and grounded in Hashem. As we learn from the Nefesh Hachaim of Rabbi Chaim of Volozhin,[11, 12]

The Creator (Blessed be He, Who is Master of all, may His name be blessed), is the true place which bears and sustains the worlds and all of the creations; for if, G-d forbid, Hashem would remove His power from them[13] for even one second, there would be absolutely no place, no existence and no life for all of the worlds. This is as is written, "You sustain everything with life."[14]

a. As the Maharal describes it in N'tivot Olam,[15]

נתיבות עולם ב: נתיב יראת השם - פרק א

וזה כי כבר אמרנו כי עצם היראה מה שהאדם עלול אל העלה והוא אמיתת היראה, ובמה שהאדם הוא עלול אינו נחשב לכלום במה שהוא עלול תולה בעלתו ... כי העולם נברא על ידי זה שהוא ית' עלה אל העולם, כי אשר הוא עלה שייך אליו עלול הוא הנברא אשר הוא עלול ונברא מאתו, ואם אין כאן יראה בעולם כאלו אין עלול, כי היראה כמו שאמרנו שהאדם הוא עלול ואם כן אם אין יראה אין שייך בריאה בעולם ...

MAHARAL, N'TIVOT OLAM 2, N'TIV YIRAT HASHEM: 1

This is what we have said, that the essence of being in Awe of G-d is that the human being considers himself as an *effect* caused by the *Ultimate Cause* (Hashem) – this is the truth of Awe of G-d. When the human being

---

11. Rabbi Chaim of Volozhin (1749–1821) was a student of the famed Vilna Gaon and the founder of the first modern yeshiva – the famed Volozhin. His work, *Nefesh Hachaim*, is a classic of Jewish thought and character development which touches on mystical matters as well.
12. Nefesh Hachaim 3:1.
13. I.e., the worlds and creations.
14. N'chemyah 9:6.
15. N'tiv Yirat Hashem 1.

considers himself as an effect he removes all self-significance in that he considers himself as an effect merely grasping onto the Ultimate Cause . . . The world was created via the fact that Hashem is the Ultimate Cause of the world. Once Hashem is the Cause, it makes sense to talk of the world as His effect (i.e., the entire creation), but if there is no Awe of G-d in the world it is *as if* there was no effect at all from G-d's attempt to create, because as we said, Awe of G-d occurs when the human being views himself as an effect of G-d. Now if there is no Awe, it makes no sense to speak of a creation.

i. According to the Maharal, Awe of Hashem is a sense of connection to and total dependency on Hashem. Connection to Hashem is connection to the infinite. Moreover, creation itself is predicated on the fact that there will be a conscious acknowledgement of the reality of our being effects of Hashem, the ultimate Cause.

2. **Understanding the Maharal's View of the B'rachot on Learning the Torah**
   a. The Maharal has three topics which he intersperses throughout his discussion on the blessings on the Torah
      i. Reaching an understanding of truth vs. Immersion in Torah.
      ii. Not rejoicing at another's failure to reach an understanding of truth.
      iii. The reason that the First Temple was destroyed was due to the fact that people did not say the blessings on the Torah.
   b. The Maharal's repeated theme in all three of these topics is that Hashem is the giver of Torah every second and thus one can only receive Torah if one is connected to Hashem.
      i. One can only reach a true understanding of Torah, of truth, with Hashem's aid. It is never due *only* to one's striving. Thus, the only way to reach truth is to bond with Hashem.
      ii. Therefore, there is never a reason to bolster one's own ego and self-worth through one's success or another's failure. Rather, the more that one bonds with Hashem (as above), the more one will realize the futility of such emotions.
      iii. Moreover, Torah cannot exist without this bond to Hashem, Who is the reason for Torah. Without a bond to Hashem, one may seem to be pious but in fact, without this connection, every person will err and will be unable to recover. This is why the First Temple was destroyed.

3. **"Immersion" in Torah Means Verbalization**
   a. The Maharal's first explanation for the wording of the blessing on the Torah is that the phrase, "to immerse oneself in the words of Torah" reflects the fact that the act of learning Torah is to verbalize it.
   b. At first blush, it is difficult to understand the connection between the phrase, "to immerse oneself" and verbalization. However, this is only because we need to understand the Torah's profound view of the importance and weight of speech in and of itself. We explore this in depth in the Commentary, Ch. 3 § Points 6 and 5. For further reference, see there. In short, we learn from the Gemara and the Maharal's comments that the purpose of humanity is indeed to perfect itself and the world through (verbal) communication, and in particular, Torah communication.

4. **The Maharal's View of the Act of Learning Torah**
   a. The Maharal seems to be espousing a view that the purely intellectual exercises of thought, creativity and memory involved in the learning of Torah do not constitute a fulfillment of the commandment to learn Torah. He says that only by verbalizing the words of Torah that one is learning, does one fulfill this commandment.
   b. The Maharal has extensive thoughts on this subject, many of which are found in greater detail later on in Chapter Three. For further study, see the Commentary, Ch. 3 § Points 6 and 5 there for a wider treatment.
   c. We will spend some time below analyzing, from a purely halachic standpoint, the Maharal's ideas on the verbalization of Torah.
      i. Below we cite the central halachic sources in this discussion:
         1. The Gemara in B'rachot 20b
         2. Tos'fot, *ad loc.*
         3. Sefer Ha'agur, Tefillah 2
         4. Shulchan Aruch, Orach Chaim 47
         5. Mishnah B'rurah, Orach Chaim 47:5

      ii. B'rachot 20b

ברכות כ:

משנה. בעל קרי מהרהר בלבו ואינו מברך לא לפניה ולא לאחריה . . . גמרא. אמר רבינא, זאת אומרת: הרהור כדבור דמי. דאי סלקא דעתך לאו כדבור דמי, למה מהרהר? – אלא מאי הרהור כדבור דמי, יוציא בשפתיו! – כדאשכחן בסיני. ורב חסדא אמר: הרהור לאו כדבור דמי. דאי סלקא דעתך הרהור כדבור דמי – יוציא בשפתיו! – אלא מאי – הרהור לאו כדבור דמי, למה מהרהר? – אמר רבי אלעזר: כדי שלא יהו כל העולם עוסקין בו והוא יושב ובטל. – ונגרוס בפרקא אחרינא! – אמר רב אדא בר אהבה: בדבר שהצבור עוסקין בו.

B'rachot 20b

Mishnah:[16]

A *ba'al keri* must contemplate the Sh'ma[17] mentally[18] and he also does not make any blessing before doing so or afterwards . . .

Gemara:

Ravina said, "This teaches us that mental contemplation is equivalent to verbalization, for if it were not similar to verbalization, why does the Mishnah require the contemplation at all?"

[The Gemara questions Ravina rhetorically,] "Well if you are correct that mental contemplation is equivalent to verbalization, then why are we ruling that the *ba'al keri* should only do mental contemplation – if that is permissible, let him verbalize it and it should also be permissible since there is no difference between the two? [Clearly, since verbalization is forbidden, but contemplation is not, you are mistaken about the equivalence!]"[19]

[The Gemara answers its own question,] "This is exactly the same as that which happened at Mount Sinai!"[20]

---

16. The Gemara here is discussing whether or not silent mental contemplation has the same halachic effect as actual verbalization. There is a Torah requirement to *say* the Sh'ma twice daily. The question raised here is whether the requirement to "say" the Sh'ma can be fulfilled by mental contemplation alone. The second factor underlying this Gemara is the rabbinic enactment by Ezra the Scribe (Bava Kamma 82b) that a *ba'al keri* (a male who has experienced a seminal emission but has not yet immersed in a *mikvah* – a suitable, ritual pool) could not read words of Torah until he had immersed in the *mikvah* (see Rambam, K'ri'at Sh'ma 4:8). The Gemara is examining whether a *ba'al keri* simply doing silent, mental contemplation of the Sh'ma could fulfill his Sh'ma requirement without breaching the enactment against his reading words of Torah.

17. The Sh'ma is a prayer said three times daily. It is the central declaration of Jewish belief in G-d, His unity, the acceptance of the mitzvot and the facticity of the Exodus from Egypt.

18. But should not say it aloud as should normally be done.

19. The Gemara's question is that the contemplation and verbalization cannot be equivalent, since one is permitted (contemplation) and the other is forbidden (verbalization).

20. At Sinai, all the Jews were supposed to be in a ritually pure state in order to receive the Torah, but there were those who were not and they simply stayed silent and their attentive contemplation was sufficient. This answer implies that there is no absolute equivalence between contemplation and verbalization – verbalization is superior; but contemplation can be sufficient for certain purposes such as the acceptance of G-d as King and His commandments, something done at Sinai and repeated daily in the saying of the Sh'ma. Both at Sinai and on a daily basis, contemplation is thus sufficient.

Rav Chisda said, "Contemplation is not equivalent to verbalization, for if it were equivalent, a person would be allowed not only to contemplate but also to verbalize the Sh'ma when he is a *ba'al keri*!"[21]

[The Gemara questions Rav Chisda rhetorically,] "Well if you are correct that mental contemplation is **not** equivalent to verbalization, then why are we ruling that the *ba'al keri* should do mental contemplation – what does it accomplish?"[22]

Rabbi Elazar responded, "We rule that a person should do the silent contemplation [not because we think it has sufficient power to fulfill his obligation to read the Sh'ma but only] so that he will not be sitting idle while everyone else is immersed in saying the Sh'ma."

[The Gemara asks Rabbi Elazar,] "[If you are correct that the silent contemplation is only so that the *ba'al keri* not sit idle, why then does he have to contemplate the Sh'ma at that time,] let him contemplate some other chapter of the Torah?"

Rav Ada Bar Ahavah responded to this objection, "We rule that he should be doing what the community is doing."

1. In summary of the Gemara, we see two positions here.
   a. Ravina believes that contemplation and verbalization are fundamentally equivalent – not completely – but that whatever one can achieve minimally through verbalization, one can achieve through thought alone.

   b. Rav Chisda believes that the two are not equivalent at all.

iii. Tos'fot ad loc.

תוספות ברכות כ:

ורב חסדא אמר לאו כדבור דמי - ר"ח פירש דהלכה כרב חסדא . . . ולא יצא בקריאת שמע בהרהור.

Tos'fot B'rachot 20b

Rabbeinu Chananel explained that the Law is according to the view of Rav Chisda . . . and a person will therefore not fulfill his obligation to say Sh'ma by contemplation alone.

21. This was the question raised above against the position of Ravina.

22. The Gemara's question is that contemplation and verbalization must have some equivalence, else why would contemplation even be considered as a replacement for verbalization?

iv. Sefer Ha'agur Tefillah 2

ספר האגור הלכות תפילה סימן ב

ומי שמהרהר בלבו תורה קודם שברך בבית הכנסת א"צ לברך כי הרהור אינו כדבור לענין ברכה כמו שהוא הדין לענין ק"ש ותפלה שצריך הוצאה בשפתים.

SEFER HA'AGUR, TEFILLAH 2

A person who mentally contemplates Torah before he makes the required blessings on learning Torah [which are required before learning Torah] does not need to make these blessings first, because mental contemplation is not equivalent to verbalization for the purposes of requiring the blessing, as is the law for saying the Sh'ma and for prayer, both of which require verbalization with one's lips [in order to fulfill one's obligation.]

1. In the Sefer Ha'agur, we see the first expansion of the principle we learned in the Gemara. Here, the Agur claims that the principle we learned was not restricted to the reciting of the Sh'ma but in fact applies across the board: verbalization is not equivalent to contemplation.
   a. Thus, he rules that when learning Torah through contemplation alone, one is not fulfilling the mitzvah of learning Torah.
   b. He does not outline the source of his assumption that Torah study needs to be verbalized.

v. Shulchan Aruch, Orach Chaim 47

שו"ע אורח חיים סימן מז

א) ברכת התורה צריך ליזהר בה מאד: . . .
ג) הכותב בדברי תורה אע"פ שאינו קורא צריך לברך:
ד) המהרהר בדברי תורה אינו צריך לברך:

SHULCHAN ARUCH ORACH CHAIM 47

a. One must be exceptionally careful regarding the Blessing on the Torah . . .
c. One who writes words of Torah must make the blessing [before writing] even though he is not reading the words of Torah.
d. One who only contemplates words of Torah does not need to make a blessing [before the contemplation].

vi. Mishnah B'rurah Orach Chaim 47:5

(ה) אינו צריך - דהרהור לאו כדיבור דמי . . .

MISHNAH B'RURAH, ORACH CHAIM 47:5

One who only contemplates words of Torah] does not need to make a blessing.

[The reason that the Shulchan Aruch says this is] because silent meditation is not equivalent to verbalization . . .

vii. Conclusion
1. The *pos'kim*[23] from Rabbeinu Chananel (approximately 1000 CE) to the Tos'fot (1100–1300 CE) to the Sefer Ha'agur (approximately 1450 CE) to the Shulchan Aruch (mid 1500s CE) and finally to the Mishnah B'rurah (early 1900s CE) here display their adoption of the position of Rav Chisda as law: that silent meditation is not equivalent to verbalization.
2. They further implement this principle in the arena of Torah Study.
   a. In general, before one performs a *mitzvat aseh*, one pronounces a blessing over that mitzvah act.
   b. When it comes to the act of Torah learning, the *pos'kim* rule that the act is verbalizing the words of Torah, without which, one is not considered to have performed the act of the mitzvah of learning Torah.
   c. Therefore, if one does not verbalize one's learning but only learns through silent meditation, they rule that one need not make the blessing since the act of the mitzvah has not been performed.
3. We thus see that the view of the Maharal regarding the need for the verbalization of Torah study reflects the sentiment of the main corpus of halachic opinion.
4. The Bei'ur Halachah on the same section of the Shulchan Aruch, however, mentions that according to the Ga'on of Vilna, there is an additional mitzvah of learning Torah which one can indeed fulfill through silent contemplation alone.

d. Further Analysis
i. We can understand the Maharal's view using a method of analysis of mitzvot which divides each mitzvah into two components (a method of analysis which was first explored by R. Chaim Brisker, *zt"l*). Rabbi Yosef Dov Soloveitchik, *zt"l*, employs this in his analysis of various mitzvot). These two components are:
   1. The *ma'aseh* – action
   2. The *kiyum* – fulfillment
ii. In commandments which are primarily commandments of the heart or mind, Rav Soloveitchik, explains that although there will always be an external action to concretize the commandment, without the correct internal state, all that one has is an empty *ma'aseh*. In such

23. Sages who adjudicate halachic questions.

commandments, the inner state, the fulfillment, is vital to a complete performance of the commandment. He brings examples such as prayer, mourning and repentance.

iii. Thus, it may be that the Maharal is espousing a similar view here, with the *ma'aseh* being a verbalization of the words of Torah and the *kiyum* being the mental contemplation and understanding. Such an explanation could have other halachic objections raised against it, into which we will not delve here.

5. **The Impossibility of Loving Two Things Simultaneously**

   a. The Maharal makes several statements here which are difficult to understand at first. He says, "Moreover, a Torah Scholar's heart actually bonds with the Torah because Torah is loved by those that learn it, and their love for Torah removes the love of Hashem at the time that they come to learn . . . because it is impossible to love two things simultaneously. The reason for this [not being able to love two things simultaneously] is that every love is actually a bonding with the beloved; and if a person is so joined to one thing, he cannot be bonding with something else simultaneously . . ."

   b. The fundamental question is: Why does the Maharal believe that one cannot bond with or love two things simultaneously?

   c. In order to understand this, we will explore the Maharal's ideas on loving and bonding with Hashem from N'tivot Olam:

נתיבות עולם ב: נתיב אהבת השם - פרק א

כי האהבה שיש לאדם אל השם ית׳ במה שהאדם מצד עצמו אינו דבר רק מן השם ית׳ בא האדם ואליו האדם שב, כי הכל שב אליו ית׳ ואין דבר זולתו רק השם ית׳ והוא אחד ואין זולתו, ולפיכך אמרו ז״ל (שם ו. [צ״ל ה.]) אף על גב שקרא ק״ש בבית הכנסת צריך שיקרא ק״ש ג״כ על מטתו ואם ת״ח הוא אינו צריך מכל מקום צריך שיאמר פסוק אחד דרחמי כי בידך אפקיד רוחי, ומשמע אם יאמר קריאת שמע דהיינו שמע ישראל ה׳ א־להינו ה׳ אחד אין צריך שיאמר כי בידך אפקיד רוחי, והיכן אמר כי בידך אפקיד רוחי. אבל דבר זה שאמר ה׳ אחד שהוא ית׳ אחד ואין זולתו ומצד שהוא ית׳ אחד ואין זולתו הכל שב אליו, ובזה נשמתו הוא שב אל הש״י ומפקיד נשמתו ביד הש״י, ולפיכך ר״ע היה מאריך באחד עד שיצאה נשמתו, כי מה שהוא ית׳ אחד הנשמה אליו ית׳ תשוב, וכאשר היה מאריך באחד עד שיצאה נשמתו היתה נשמתו שבה אל הש״י לגמרי במה שהוא אחד, ומזה הצד נמצא האהבה, ולפיכך אמר ה׳ א־להינו ה׳ אחד ואהבת את ה׳ א־להיך וגו׳, כי מצד שהוא ית׳ אחד אין לשום נמצא בעולם הנפרד מאתו, כי הכל תלוים ודבקים בו יתברך כי הוא ית׳ עיקר הכל, ומפני כך שייך אהבה אל השם ית׳. ויותר שייך אהבה אל השם ית׳ ממה ששייך אהבה בשאר דברים, כי כל אהבה שיש בין האוהבים אף שהם דבקים זה בזה, מכל מקום יש לכל אחד ואחד מציאות בעצמו, אבל האהבה אל הש״י במה שהאדם שב רוחו ונפשו אליו לגמרי עד שאין לאדם מציאות בעצמו ובזה הוא מתדבק לגמרי בו וכדכתיב (דברים י״א) לאהבה את ה׳ א־להיכם ולדבקה בו, ובזה שייך אהבה גמורה. וכמו שאמר רבי עקיבא כל ימי הייתי מצטער על פסוק זה ואהבת

את ה' א-להיך בכל לבבך ובכל נפשך ועכשיו שבא לידי לא אקיימנו, כי זהו האהבה הגמורה כאשר מוסר נפשו אל ה' כי בזה דבק בו לגמרי והוא עצם האהבה, ויתבאר לך כי יותר שייך אהבה אל הש"י במה שהאדם מוסר נפשו אל הש"י ודבוק בו לגמרי והוא אמיתת האהבה:

N'tivot Olam 2, The Path of Loving Hashem: 1

For the love that a person should have for Hashem, may He be Blessed, is through the fact that a person, in and of himself, is nothing! Rather, human beings [and the whole of reality] derive from Hashem and to Hashem they will return because everything returns to Hashem, may He be Blessed, for there is nothing that truly exists but G-d[24] and He is One and there is nothing else. Therefore, our sages said,[25]

"Even though a person has recited the Sh'ma in the synagogue, he should

24. This idea is a fundamental of Jewish thought in both Kabbalistic and non-Kabbalistic circles. As the Rambam puts it (Y'sodei Hatorah 1:1–2), "The foundation of all foundations and the pillar of wisdoms is to know that there is one original reality (G-d) Who brings into existence all existence; and all that exists, from heaven to earth and that which is between them, can only exist due to the truth of G-d's existence. And if one were to contemplate the possibility that G-d did not exist, nothing else could exist." As the Derech Hashem (1:1:1) puts it, "Every Jew is required to believe and know that there is one original and eternal reality, Which is G-d, Blessed be He; and it is He that brought into existence and *continues to bring into existence* everything which exists . . . and He is the true reason for all things which exist and for all which happens to them . . ." and in Derech Hashem (4:4:2), "Hashem's existence, may He be Blessed, is not dependent on anything else at all and it has no relation to anything else because He is the required existence and He is perfect in and of Himself and He has no relationship at all with another – there is nothing above or below Him. This means that there is no reason which could explain Him at all, not as a cause or an accompaniment . . . He is the required existence in and of itself, as we have written. However . . . He desired and created creations, all of which are dependent on Him for their existence and all their aspects . . ." and in Derech Hashem (4:4:11), "Behold, every day, all of existence renews itself before Hashem, may He be Blessed. This happens in two ways. The first, is from the aspect of actual existence and continuous existence, because the divine [energy] flow is renewed to everything in order to ensure it exists and continues to exist . . ." Finally, as the Nefesh Hachaim (3:1) puts it, "the Creator (Blessed be He, Who is Master of all, may His name be blessed), is the true place which bears and sustains the worlds and all of the creations; for if, G-d forbid, Hashem would remove His power from them [i.e., the worlds and creations] for even one second, there would be absolutely no place, no existence and no life for all of the worlds. This is as is written, 'You sustain everything with life' (N'chemyah 9:6)."

25. B'rachot 5a. There is a printing error in the Hebrew text here which gives the source of this as "6a."

also recite it when going to bed. But if he is a talmid chacham,[26] there is no need to [recite it again before going to sleep] but nevertheless he should still say the following verse in prayer, 'For in your hand I place my soul'."[27]

The Maharal questions this Gemara's conclusion.

This Gemara implies that if a person said the verse,[28] "Listen Israel! Hashem is our G-d, Hashem is [the] One [and Only],"[29] then he would not need to say the verse, "For in your hand, I place my soul." But if this is true, where did he say "For in your hand, I place my soul"?

The Maharal's question is that the verse, "In your hand, I place my soul" is a specific idea which is not mentioned at all in the Sh'ma. If so, how can saying the Sh'ma exempt one from saying this verse – they embody two very different ideas?

However, when a person says, "Listen Israel! Hashem is our G-d, Hashem is [the] One [and Only]," the meaning is that Hashem is One and there is Nothing besides Him and from the perspective that He, may He be Blessed, is One and there is no other, everything returns to Him. And through this understanding, one's soul also returns to Him and one thereby places one's soul in the hand of Hashem, may He be Blessed.

The Maharal's explanation of the Sh'ma is that it is a declaration that Hashem is the only reality which truly exists and everything else only exists through Hashem's constantly maintaining it in existence. When one truly realizes this, one sees that there is nothing which exists separately from Hashem, and "everything returns to Him," i.e., everything is perceived, as it truly is, to be an expression of His will. One's soul, too, rests within Hashem's "hands," as it were.

Therefore, when Rabbi Akiva died [as he was saying the Sh'ma], he lengthened the pronunciation of the word "One [and Only]" until his soul left him, since Hashem, may He be Blessed, is One [and since everything therefore exists only by His will], thus one's soul will return to Him. And when Rabbi Akiva lengthened the pronunciation of the word "One" until his soul left him, his soul returned to Hashem completely though His Oneness.

26. Sage.
27. Tehillim 31:6.
28. I.e., the Sh'ma prayer.
29. D'varim 6:4.

It is from this perspective that one finds love [of G-d]. Therefore, the Sh'ma states, "[Listen Israel!] Hashem is our G-d, Hashem is [the] One [and Only!]" [and then the next verse is,] "You shall Love Hashem your G-d . . ."[30]

The Maharal now explains his understanding of Love, and in particular, Love of Hashem.

Now since Hashem, may He be Blessed, is One [and only], there is no object which exists separately from Him, because everything is dependent on Him and bonded with Him, because He is the mainstay of everything – therefore, Love is an appropriate concept with regards to Hashem. In fact, love is more appropriate towards G-d than it is towards anything else since when there is love between two beings, even though they are bonded to one another, each of them has a separate existence in and of itself; however, the love one has for Hashem is through the fact that a person's soul is completely part of Hashem, so much so that a person has no existence independent of Hashem, and therefore, a person bonds with Hashem completely. This is as the Torah teaches us, "To love Hashem your G-d [to walk in all His ways] and to bond with Him."[31] In such a case [only] is complete love appropriate.

The Maharal explains that "handing one's soul" over to Hashem means recognizing the reality that one's soul and entire existence are offshoots of Hashem. This is true even in moments of tragedy.

And as Rabbi Akiva said,[32] "How can it be possible that I would be pained, my entire life, by [my inability to fulfill the directive inherent within] this verse, 'You shall love Hashem your G-d with all your heart and with all your soul . . .' but now that the opportunity has come my way [to implement this as my reality], will I not take advantage?" For this is complete love – when a person hands over his soul to Hashem, through which that person can bond with Hashem completely, and this bonding is the essence of love.

The Maharal summarizes his position.

---

30. D'varim 6:5.
31. D'varim 11:22.
32. B'rachot 61b. The Gemara there records Rabbi Akiva's dialogue with his students as he was being tortured to death. Rabbi Akiva was saying the Sh'ma and his students questioned how he could speak about love for G-d at such a moment. The Maharal's explanation is that the Sh'ma is an expression of one's complete bond with Hashem and of one's existence completely being an expression of Hashem's will. This is true at even the most difficult and painful times.

Thus it is clear that love is more appropriate towards Hashem, may He be Blessed, when a person hands his soul to Him and thereby bonds with Him completely. This is the truth of love.

i. From all this, the Maharal's understanding of love emerges quite clearly. He says that to love someone or something is to be bonded with that thing, to have some degree of existential union.
ii. Based on this premise, it becomes clear that the greater the union, the greater the love.
iii. Therefore, the Maharal explains that the deepest possible love is one where the union that exists is complete, but the deepest possible union is one where a person's entire being and everything which makes them who they are, is constantly given freely to them by Hashem. Hashem's will and energy keep each physical and spiritual element in the universe in existence, every second. Moreover, our souls are, as it were, the breath of Hashem, as the Nefesh Hachaim teaches,[33]

The word "*n'shamah*" ["soul"] comes from the word "*n'shimah*" ["breath"] . . . the reason that it is named similarly to the word "*n'shimah*" [breath] is not because it is referring to human breath, but rather, as it were, to the breath of Hashem. As it says, "And Hashem blew into his nostrils, a soul[34] of life."

iv. This level of existential union, where a person's entirety is created constantly by Hashem, cannot be shared with anything else. We thus understand why the Maharal has posited that one cannot even love Torah at the same time as loving Hashem, because that would entail a union with Torah separate from our ultimate bond with Hashem and such a true love can only exist exclusively between two parties.

6. Purely Cognitive Torah vs. Existential Torah

a. The Maharal places an overwhelming emphasis on not conceding the emotional and intellectual connection to Hashem, no matter what Torah one is learning. The reasons that these connections are needed are:
   i. This connection is vital to the understanding of the Torah text. and
   ii. One is unable to transfer any connection to Hashem through Torah without this; therefore, it is vital for anyone trying to teach Torah.
b. Forging this connection is done through:
   i. Feeling a love for Hashem as He Who gave (in the past) us the Torah and as giver (right now) of the Torah.

33. Nefesh Hachaim 1:15.
34. The Hebrew word used here is "*nishmat*," נשמת.

   ii. Incorporating this feeling into the blessing one makes on the Torah.

c. The only two beings who really know whether or not this existential connection exists are Hashem and the person concerned – it is such an intimate love. Even the angels have no connection to this.

d. To claim that a Torah text can only be understood correctly when a person is connected to Hashem casts the concept and process of learning Torah in a completely different light.

   i. As opposed to the study, analysis, critique, summary and memorization of a text (hallmarks of academic scholarship), where the text is an object and the academic the subject, we are presented instead with a model more akin to an intimate, exclusive relationship communicated and continued partly through a text. Here the text is an intimate communication, a marriage document and love poem, a part of the relationship, as it were.

   ii. In an intimate relationship, when one party says something to the other, what is vital to the relationship is the fact that the relationship exists and secondarily, the intent behind the communication.

      1. The Maharal's warning is that in Torah learning one cannot forego the relationship for its message. The relationship is the bedrock of all communication that can take place.

      2. Secondarily, one can only decipher the meaning of the communication through intimacy with and proximity to the other partner in the relationship. The closer one is, the more one can understand the meaning of the message. The further one is, G-d forbid, the more one's understandings flow exclusively from one's own perspective and less from the perspective of the other, in this case, Hashem.

7. The Primal Cause and Its Effects

b. One of the Maharal's central concepts, mentioned throughout his works, is that Hashem is the Primal Cause of everything that exists. Moreover, being an Effect of Hashem and more importantly, *being aware* of one's being an Effect are central to the way he explains much of the meaning of life.

c. He explains in N'tivot Olam, as follows:

נתיבות עולם ב: נתיב יראת השם - פרק א

וזה כי כבר אמרנו כי עצם היראה מה שהאדם עלול אל העלה והוא אמיתת היראה, ובמה שהאדם הוא עלול אינו נחשב לכלום במה שהוא עלול תולה בעלתו . . . כי העולם נברא על ידי זה שהוא ית' עלה אל העולם, כי אשר הוא עלה שייך אליו עלול הוא הנברא אשר הוא עלול ונברא מאתו, ואם אין כאן יראה בעולם כאלו אין עלול, כי היראה כמו שאמרנו שהאדם הוא עלול ואם כן אם אין יראה אין שייך בריאה בעולם . . .

Maharal, N'tivot Olam 2, N'tiv Yirat Hashem: 1

This is what we have said, that the essence of being in Awe of G-d is that the human being considers himself as an *effect* caused by the *[Primal] Cause* (Hashem) – this is the truth of Awe of G-d. When the human being considers himself as an effect he removes all self-significance in that he considers himself as an effect merely grasping onto the [Primal] Cause . . . The world was created via the fact that Hashem is the [Primal] Cause of the world. Once Hashem is the Cause, it makes sense to talk of the world as His effect (i.e., the entire creation), but if there is no Awe of G-d in the world it is *as if* there was no effect at all from G-d's attempt to create, because as we said, Awe of G-d occurs when the human being views himself as an effect of G-d. Now if there is no Awe, it makes no sense to speak of a Creation.

ii. According to the Maharal, Awe of Hashem is a sense of connection and total dependency on Hashem. Connection to Hashem is connection to the infinite. Moreover, creation itself is predicated on the fact that there will be a conscious acknowledgement of the reality of our being effects of Hashem, the ultimate Cause.

d. The Maharal writes further, in G'vurot Hashem, that since human beings are the only beings who can choose to be aware or unaware of this reality, they are therefore the pinnacle of creation.

גבורות ה׳ ס"ו

ויש לשאול הנה השמים כסאו והארץ הדום רגלו ויהא שכינתו בעליונים ולמה בחר לשכון בתחתונים, ובדבר זה מעלין ולא מורידין יהיה א־להותו בעליונים למה צריך בתחתונים שהם עפר רימה ותולעה. אמנם אם נמצא שכל דבר המציאות תלוי בשכינתו בתחתונים ודבר זה הוא הכל מעתה הוסר השאלה, וכאשר תדע כי הוא יתברך מצטרף לנמצאים במה שהם עלולים, כי הוא יתברך שהוא עלת הכל רצונו בעלול וכאשר יש עלה יש כאן עלול נמצא, כי התקשרות הסבה הראשונה בנמצאים מצד שהוא יתברך עלה להם והנמצאים הם עלולים ממנו, וכבר הארכנו בקשור הנכבד הזה למעלה אצל ויקרא אליו מתוך הסנה. וכאשר התבאר זה אם כן אין עליך לומר שמיוחדים בזה העליונים כי אם התחתונים, כי במה שנקראים עליונים הם פועלים בתחתונים והם כמו עלה נחשבים ואין עיקר עצמם שהם עלולים, אבל התחתונים במה שהם תחתונים הם עלולים בעצמם, ולפיכך החבור האמתי שיש לסבה הראשונה שהוא עלה באמת הוא בתחתונים במה שהם עלולים באמת . . .

G'vurot Hashem 66

"Behold, the heavens are His seat and the earth is His footstool,"[35] and His dwelling is in the Upper Worlds. If so, why did Hashem choose to dwell

35. See Y'shayahu 66:1.

amongst the lowly [i.e., human beings]? In this matter, surely we should follow the principle that "we ascend [in holiness] and we do not descend,"[36] and therefore, His divinity should be amongst the transcendent; why does He need the lowly [humans] who are dust, maggots and worms?

However, if it is true that every element of reality depends on His presence dwelling amongst the lowly [human beings] and that this encompasses [the purpose of] everything, then there is no question! *And when you know that He, may He be Blessed, is bonded with the creations through their being Effects, for He, may He be Blessed, is the Cause of everything, then His will is vested within the Effect.* And when there is a Cause, then an Effect exists, for the connection between the Primal Cause [G-d] and the creations is through the fact that He, may He be Blessed, is a Cause for them and the creations are His Effects. And we have already discussed above at length regarding this important bond,[37] when we discussed the verse, "[G-d] called to him [Moshe] from within the [burning] bush."[38]

And now that this is clear, you shouldn't say that the transcendent beings are the elite, rather it is the lower beings [who are superior], because the transcendent beings act upon the lower ones and in this mode, the transcendent beings are considered as a Cause, and therefore, the *essence* of their being is not that they are [only] Effects [from G-d, but rather that they are both causes of other, lower realities as well as being effects from G-d]; however, the lower beings, through their being lower are, in their essence [only] effects and therefore, the truest connection with the Primal Cause [G-d] who is The Cause, in truth, is only shared with the lower beings through their being truthful Effects.

i. It is clear that the Maharal understands that the choice of a human being to accept the truth of his/her reality – that it is an effect of Hashem, is the foundation of the purpose of creation itself.
ii. The more that we feel ourselves viscerally as Effects of the Primal Cause (not just understanding it abstractly), the closer we will be bonded with Hashem.

8. **The Pachad Yitzchak's Insight into the Problem with not Making the Blessings on the Torah Properly**
   a. The Pachad Yitzchak offers a profound expansion of the ideas cited in the Maharal in this chapter.[39] We summarize the Pachad Yitzchak's ideas, but

36. See B'rachot 28a.
37. See G'vurot Hashem, Chapter 23.
38. Sh'mot 3:4.
39. Pachad Yitzchak, Shavu'ot 7.

this is a poor substitute for learning his awesome Torah firsthand, which we encourage all who can, to undertake.

b. In an article dedicated to explaining the vital necessity of gratitude in life, Rav Hutner explains (in brief) as follows:
   i. Human beings have the ability to resemble Hashem, as it were, to the extent that they approximate Hashem's nature as a source of life – a self-sufficient spring which replenishes itself constantly.[40]
   ii. It is thus impossible for a person to reach such a level of resemblance when he wishes to live a parasitic existence, constantly leeching off everyone around him.
   iii. The first person to reach a remarkably high state of resemblance to Hashem in this area was Avraham, our forefather, whose life ushered in an epoch of Torah.
      1. As the Mishnah in Pirkei Avot states,[41] "Beloved are Israel who were called 'children' of Hashem . . . Beloved are Israel to whom was given an object of delight [which is the Torah.]"
      2. We see, as the Maharal has explained thus far in this Introduction,[42] that there is a vital correlation between the level of one's closeness to Hashem and one's ability to receive the Torah. It is only because Israel were so close to Hashem, so resembled Him, as a child resembles a parent, that they were able to receive the Torah.

---

40. Of course, the only being or thing which possesses this property in total is Hashem. Everything else is dependent on Him for its existence, as we mention numerous times within this work. For example, see the Ramchal who writes in the Derech Hashem (4:4:2), "Hashem's existence, may He be Blessed, is not dependent on anything else at all and it has no relation to anything else because He is the *required existence* and He is perfect in and of Himself and He has no relationship at all with another – there is nothing above or below Him. This means that there is no reason which could explain Him at all, not as a cause or an accompaniment . . . He is the *required existence* in and of itself, as we have written. However, since He desired and created creations, all of which are dependent on Him for their existence and all their aspects, from this perspective, we call G-d, 'the Master of All' . . ." Or as the Nefesh Hachaim (3:2) states, "So is the matter with the entire sensate world which seems to have an existence in and of itself. Hashem, may He be Blessed, is the place of the world – which means that if there was no place in His will for the bringing into existence of all the world, how much more so [when compared to the lack of a physical space], would they all revert to nothing." The idea is that the only being which exists independently of anything else is Hashem. Everything else just has possibility, as they have no independent power to exist – only G-d does. Everything else that does exist, does so by virtue of Hashem willing it to exist.

41. Pirkei Avot 3:14.

42. The Introduction to Tiferet Yisrael.

3. Avraham our forefather reached this level of resemblance, as it were, due to his sterling, undistilled quality of *chesed*[43] – which was the channel through which Hashem created the world in His ultimate, altruistic act of giving.

iv. Therefore, we see that reaching a level of resemblance of Hashem is a prerequisite of receiving the Torah; but such a level entails that one be a giver, not a taker.

v. A person who is a parasitic taker is at the extreme opposite end of what is needed to receive the Torah. A person who is not as beholden to others is far closer to being able to receive Torah.

1. In particular, when a person receives something from someone else, the only method one has of not being cast as a "taker" (short of returning whatever one received) is through gratitude: a virtual, spiritual "repayment" of the favor or item received.

vi. Therefore, the Pachad Yitzchak explains, the Maharal's focus on the need to make the blessings on the Torah with the appropriate level of Gratitude, is vital. As the Maharal wrote above, "The Jews at that time, however, did not have this complete love for Hashem for His giving us the Torah – which was especially wrong since the Torah is the greatest goodness possible (therefore, a person should bless Hashem for this with all one's heart) – so they did not bless Hashem with all their heart, which they should have done in accordance with this superior goodness [which is the Torah]."

vii. Besides for being vital in all areas of life, appropriate gratitude is particularly necessary to receive Torah.

c. The Pachad Yitzchak elsewhere presents an even more profound reflection on the inherent link between Torah and the attribute of *chesed*, one which is beyond the scope of this work.[44]

9. "Fear of Hashem/Awe of Hashem" and the Connection to Eternity

a. Background from Maharal's N'tivot Olam[45]

נתיבות עולם ב: נתיב יראת השם - פרק א

וזה כי כבר אמרנו כי עצם היראה מה שהאדם עלול אל העלה והוא אמיתת היראה, ובמה שהאדם הוא עלול אינו נחשב לכלום במה שהוא עלול תולה בעלתו ... כי העולם נברא על ידי זה שהוא ית' עלה אל העולם, כי אשר הוא עלה שייך אליו עלול הוא הנברא אשר הוא עלול ונברא מאתו, ואם אין כאן יראה בעולם כאלו אין עלול, כי היראה כמו שאמרנו שהאדם הוא עלול ואם כן אם אין יראה אין שייך בריאה בעולם...

43. See Pachad Yitzchak, Rosh Hashanah 1. We inadequately translate "*chesed*" as "loving-kindness."

44. Pachad Yitzchak, Rosh Hashanah 2.

45. N'tivot Olam 2, N'tiv Yirat Hashem 1.

Maharal, N'tivot Olam 2, Yirat Hashem: 1

This is what we have said, that the essence of being in Awe of G-d is that the human being considers himself as an *effect* caused by the *[Primal] Cause*[46] – this is the truth of Awe of G-d. When the human being considers himself as an effect he removes all self-significance in that he considers himself as an effect merely grasping onto the [Primal] Cause . . .

The world was created via the fact that Hashem is the [Primal] Cause of the world. Once Hashem is the Cause, it makes sense to talk of the world as His effect (i.e., the entire creation), but if there is no Awe of G-d in the world, it is *as if* there was no effect at all from G-d's attempt to create, because as we said, Awe of G-d occurs when the human being views himself as an effect of G-d. Now if there is no Awe, it makes no sense to speak of a Creation.

b. According to the Maharal, Awe of Hashem is a sense of connection and total dependency on Hashem. Connection to Hashem is connection to the infinite. We now understand what the Maharal meant when he said (above in Tiferet Yisrael) that Awe of Hashem connects one to eternity – when one has Awe of Hashem, by definition, one is bonding with Hashem through affirming the status of oneself and of the world as a branch of the Infinite Root. Thus everything along that path from root to branch is vivified with the reality of Hashem's presence, which is of course, eternal.

10. The Maharal's Reference to Shabbat 31a

a. In his discussion of Awe of Hashem, above, the Maharal refers to the Gemara in Shabbat 31a. This Gemara discusses the importance of having Awe of Hashem. It hinges on explanations of the following verse,

ישעיה לג:ו

וְהָיָה אֱמוּנַת עִתֶּיךָ חֹסֶן יְשׁוּעֹת חָכְמַת וָדָעַת יִרְאַת ה' הִיא אוֹצָרוֹ׃

Y'shayahu 33:6 [as per Radak]

The faith of your times will be the refuge of salvations: wisdom and knowledge [and] the Awe of Hashem which is his treasure.[47]

b. The Gemara states as follows,

שבת ל"א. - ל"א:

אמר ריש לקיש מאי דכתיב והיה אמונת עתיך חוסן ישועות חכמת ודעת וגו' אמונת זה

46. I.e., Hashem.

47. "His" here refers to a person, meaning that a person's treasure is his Awe of Hashem.

סדר זרעים עתיך זה סדר מועד חסן זה סדר נשים ישועות זה סדר נזיקין חכמת זה סדר קדשים ודעת זה סדר טהרות ואפילו הכי יראת ה׳ היא אוצרו אמר רבא בשעה שמכניסין אדם לדין אומרים לו נשאת ונתת באמונה קבעת עתים לתורה עסקת בפריה ורביה צפית לישועה פלפלת בחכמה הבנת דבר מתוך דבר ואפילו הכי אי יראת ה׳ היא אוצרו אין אי לא לא משל לאדם שאמר לשלוחו העלה לי כור חיטין לעלייה הלך והעלה לו אמר לו עירבת לי בהן קב חומטון אמר לו לאו אמר לו מוטב אם לא העליתה: תנא דבי רבי ישמעאל מערב אדם קב חומטון בכור של תבואה ואינו חושש: אמר רבה בר רב הונא כל אדם שיש בו תורה ואין בו יראת שמים דומה לגזבר שמסרו לו מפתחות הפנימיות ומפתחות החיצונות לא מסרו לו בהי עייל . . .

Shabbat 31a–31b

Reish Lakish said, "What is meant by the verse,[48] 'The faith of your times will be the refuge of salvations: wisdom and knowledge [and] the Awe of Hashem is his treasure?'

[He explained each phrase in the verse as follows,]

"Faith" refers to the Order[49] of Plantings;[50]

"Your times" refers to the Order of Festivals;

"Refuge" refers to the Order of Women;

"Salvations" refers to the Order of Torts;[51]

"Wisdom" refers to the Order of Sanctities;

"Knowledge" refers to the Order of Purities.[52]

[Reish Lakish continued,] Yet despite this, 'The Awe of Hashem is his treasure.'

Rava said, "When a person is being brought in for Judgment [in the heavenly court], he is asked, 'Did you deal faithfully?[53] Did you set times for learning Torah? Did you engage in procreation? Did you hope for the redemption? Did you delve into wisdom? Did you understand one thing from another?' [Rava continues,] Yet despite this, if 'the Awe of Hashem is his treasure,' all is well, if not [it is] not [well]. This can be compared to a man who instructed his agent, 'Take up a *kor*[54] of wheat for me to the attic,' and he went and did so. [Later,] the man asked the agent, 'Did you mix in a

48. Y'shayahu 33:6, cited above.

49. In Hebrew, סדר, "*seder*," which means "order," is one of the six sections of the Oral Torah.

50. In Hebrew, זרעים, "*z'ra'im.*" This *seder* deals mostly with agricultural mitzvot.

51. In Hebrew, נזיקין, "*n'zikin*," which means "damages."

52. Which relate to the laws of ritual purity.

53. With honesty.

54. A measurement. A *kor* is a volume equivalent to about 7 bushels (246.2 metric liters).

kav[55] of *chumton*?'[56] The agent replied, 'No, I haven't!' The man said, 'Then it would have been better if you had not carried up the produce in the first place!'"

The School of Rabbi Yishma'el taught, "A person should mix a *kav* of *chumton* in a *kor* of grain, and then he will have no fear [of it rotting]."

Rabbah bar Rav Huna said, "A person who has Torah learning but has no Awe of Heaven is like a treasurer who has been given the keys [to the] inner [treasure chambers] but has not been given the keys to the outer [chambers through which one can gain access to the inner chambers]: How can he enter? . . ."

c. The Gemara presents several ideas relating to the importance of having Awe of Hashem. The first idea is that Awe of Hashem preserves one's wisdom. The second idea is that Awe of Hashem is a prerequisite to attaining inner wisdom, without which, one cannot truly arrive at the "treasure" of Torah.

d. The section to which the Maharal alludes (above in Tiferet Yisrael) is that dealing with the "*chumton*." *Chumton* is described here (as per Rashi) as some sort of preservative for produce and it is to this that Awe of Hashem is compared. The idea is that Awe of Hashem is the only "ingredient" which can preserve one's spiritual state, so that when one's spiritual accomplishments are evaluated (when one reaches the World to Come), if one lacks Awe of Hashem, one has no preservative for those accomplishments. Rashi (ad loc., s.v. *hi otzaro*) adds that Awe of Hashem is that which aids one in remembering one's Torah.

    i. We find this idea throughout the statements of the sages, principally in Avot (Ethics of the Fathers):

אבות ג: י"א

רַבִּי חֲנִינָא בֶּן דּוֹסָא אוֹמֵר, כֹּל שֶׁיִּרְאַת חֶטְאוֹ קוֹדֶמֶת לְחָכְמָתוֹ, חָכְמָתוֹ מִתְקַיֶּמֶת. וְכֹל שֶׁחָכְמָתוֹ קוֹדֶמֶת לְיִרְאַת חֶטְאוֹ אֵין חָכְמָתוֹ מִתְקַיֶּמֶת . . .

Avot 3:11

Rabbi Chanina ben Dosa says, "One whose fear of sin precedes his wisdom will have his wisdom *endure*. But one whose wisdom precedes his fear of sin will find his wisdom not enduring."

e. The Maharal above states that Torah leads one to eternity. He arrives at

55. A measurement. A *kav* is a volume equivalent to about 2.5 pints (1.4 metric liters).

56. Rashi (ad loc., s.v. *kav chumton*) explains that "*chumton*" was salty earth, the addition of which prevented produce from rotting.

this conclusion by explaining that Torah brings one to Awe of Hashem and Awe of Hashem leads one to eternity. As we explained above, Awe of Hashem, in the Maharal's view, is one's sense of connection to Hashem, the feeling that one is a leaf on the tree of existence which is rooted in Hashem. Being connected to Hashem, the eternal and infinite, confers upon a human some of that eternity and infinity.

i. The allusion the Maharal makes here is that *chumton* is a preservative and Awe of Hashem is also a preservative, but in a much more profound sense.

ii. Torah itself is "preserved" within a person (as Rashi says) only because of one's Awe of Hashem. This is one of the primary themes of the Maharal in this Introduction, as we have discussed already: that Torah on its own, cannot guarantee that a person will be righteous, nor is it self-sustaining. As the Maharal explained regarding the blessing on the learning of Torah (earlier in this Introduction), one has to be learning out of a conscious attempt to bond with Hashem, without which, one cannot hope either to understand the Torah in the first place, much less to sustain Torah within oneself. Such bonding is the ultimate result of Awe of Hashem, as we explained above. Thus we see that the Gemara in Shabbat is teaching both of these lessons:

1. As the Maharal explains later in Chapter Ten (the chapter to which he refers us above), if one has this bonding with Hashem, his Torah will be sustained. This is the concept of the *chumton* – preservative and is the first lesson taught here in the Gemara.
2. As we have already seen, without Awe of Hashem and bonding with Hashem, one cannot hope to understand the Torah. This is the second lesson taught here in the Gemara – the concept of the treasurer: without the outer key, the inner content is forever inaccessible.

11. The Perfection of Torah's Path and Possible Deviations

a. The Maharal says here, "But through the Torah, a person cleaves to Hashem completely through all perspectives. In this world, there are six major perspectives (right, left, forwards, backwards, up and down). Therefore, King David mentioned six items, parallel to these six perspectives, in order to teach that through the Torah, a person bonds to Hashem throughout all perspectives and deviates neither right nor left nor any way."

b. The question one may have is: what deviation could be possible? Secondly, the Maharal seems to use a redundant clause "neither right nor left nor any way." Surely the inclusive clause "nor any way" includes "neither right nor left."

c. A possible answer is as follows:
   i. There are two obvious types of possible deviations in one's striving to join with Hashem:
      1. One may omit a particular vital perspective and approach. This the Maharal addresses when he says, "through the Torah, a person bonds to Hashem throughout all perspectives."
      2. Once one is using a legitimate approach, another danger is that, at some point, one may lose one's way by overemphasizing or underemphasizing a particular perspective. This he addresses when he says, "deviates neither right nor left."
   ii. But what possible danger remains? What can the Maharal mean by, "nor any way"?
      1. A less blatant danger, and perhaps one more insidious, is the desire to simplify one's relationship with Hashem by working on only one perspective in isolation from all the others.
      2. One could affirm the necessity for using all valid perspectives and one could practice each of them correctly, but in isolation from the others. The Maharal, however, seems to imply that one needs to use all possible directions simultaneously, even if they are perhaps superficially opposing: right and left; back and forwards; up and down. This approach is more difficult and more complex.
      3. This is perhaps what he means when he says, "nor any way."[57]

12. Equal Truth = Complete Truth

a. The Maharal writes above, "Finally, King David says, 'The ordinances of Hashem are true, completely righteous.' This level is even above the others because through the Torah one becomes similar to Hashem (as much as it is possible to become similar to one's creator) because Hashem's signature is truth and the ordinances of the Torah and its paths are true. King David uses the term, 'completely righteous,' in order to teach that they are all equal in truth which implies that they are all completely true – this is the reason they can all be equally true. If they were not all completely true, they could not be equally true because one would end up having more truth than another. But since Hashem's ordinances are completely true, they are all equally true."
b. He seems to be presenting two opposite directions of reasoning:
   i. Since the teachings of the Torah are all equally true, therefore, they are all completely true.
      1. This is difficult to understand. For example, if I have five test re-

57. See a related comment by Rabbi Samson Raphel Hirsch in his commentary to B'reishit 1:31.

sults all of which are equal this doesn't mean that because they are all equal, they are all 100%. They could all be 30%!

- ii. Since the teachings of the Torah are all completely True, therefore, they are all equally true.
  1. This is easier to understand. For example, if I have five tests and for each test I have achieved the maximum possible grade, therefore, it is clear that the grades for all of the tests are equal at 100%.

c. We will attempt to explain the first line of reasoning which is more challenging.
   - i. The Maharal writes about his conception of truth in N'tivot Olam:

נתיבות עולם - נתיב אמת: א

ויש לפרש כי לכך חותמו של הקב"ה אמת מפני שהוא יתב' אחד ואין שני ולפיכך חותמו של הקב"ה אמת, כי אין דבר שהוא אחד רק האמת הוא אחד, ואי אפשר שיהיה האמת שנים שאם תשאל על האדם מה זה, הנה אם אתה אומר שהוא בהמה או חיה או עוף וכל הדברים אשר אתה אומר עליו הכל הוא שקר, והם רבים עד שאין קץ ואין תכלית אל השקר, ואלו האמת הוא אחד שהרי הוא אדם ולא ד"א, א"כ האמת הוא אחד, וכן כל דבר שקר הוא הרבה והאמת הוא אחד . . . רק יש לפרש מה שחותמו אמת כי כל הנמצאים אף על גב שכולם ברא הש"י באמת מ"מ יש בהם בחינה שהם נוטים חוץ מן האמת, שהרי כל הנמצאים אפשרים מצד עצמם ואינם מחויבים, אבל הש"י מחויב המציאות, וכבר התבאר כי ההפרש שהוא בין האמת והשקר שהאמת הוא נמצא לגמרי והשקר אין לו מציאות כלל, כי זהו ענין השקר ושאר הנמצאים אע"ג שהם נמצאים כיון שהם אפשרים מצד עצמם ומצד עצמם אפשר שלא יהיו נמצאים הנה אין אתם האמת הגמור. כלל הדבר כי הש"י הוא האמת הגמור שהוא מחויב המציאות בעצמו והוא עצם האמת ואין זולתו . . . כי הוא יתברך האמת הגמור שהוא מחויב המציאות ומאתו נותן קיום אל הכל, כי מכח אמת שלו שהוא אמת גמור שהוא מחויב המציאות בו מקוים הכל, וזה שאמר כי חותמו אמת עצמו יתב' האמת, והבן הדברים מאוד:

N'tivot Olam, N'tiv Emet 1

One can explain that the reason that the signature of the Holy One, Blessed be He, is Truth,[58] is because He, may He be Blessed, is One and there is no other. Therefore, the stamp of the Holy One, Blessed be He, is truth because there is only one, except for truth. It is impossible for the truth to be two. For example, if one asks, regarding a human being, "What is this creature?" If a person were to respond, "It is a domesticated animal, a wild animal, a bird" or whatever else a person might respond, it is all false. In fact, there is an infinity of falsehoods; the truth however, is only one because this creature is a human being and nothing else. If so, we see that the truth is one. Thus, falsehood is multiple and plural while Truth is one . . .

58. Shabbat 55a, "Rabbi Chanina said, 'The signature [lit., "seal"] of the Holy One, Blessed be He, is Truth.'"

One can [also] explain that the reason that Hashem's signature is Truth is because despite the fact that Hashem [whose signature is Truth], using Truth, created all the objects that exist, nevertheless, they all have some aspect in which they deviate from the truth. The reason for this is that all objects that were created are not required to exist in and of themselves, they are possibilities. However, Hashem, may He be Blessed, is The [Only] required existence.[59] And it has already been explained that the difference between truth and falsehood is that the Truth is completely real and exists; while falsehood has no [independent] existence at all – this is the definition of falsehood. But the other beings which exist, even though they do [truly] exist, since they are possibilities in and of themselves and it is possible that they may not exist, therefore, they cannot have The Complete Truth with them.

The general idea is that Hashem, may He be Blessed, He is the Absolute Truth which is the Required Existence, in and of Himself, and He is the essence of Truth and there is nothing else besides Him . . . Because He, may He be Blessed, is the absolute Truth which is the Required Existence and from Himself, He gives existence to everything else – because from the power of His Truth (which is absolute Truth, which is the Required Existence), through that power, everything is sustained. This is why he [Rabbi Chanina] said that His Signature, may He be Blessed, is Truth. Understand these things well!

---

59. As we saw earlier in this Introduction, this idea is a fundamental of Jewish thought. The phrase, "required Existence," used here by the Maharal to refer to Hashem, is used by many of our sages. As the Ramchal writes in the Derech Hashem (4:4:2), "Hashem's existence, may He be Blessed, is not dependent on anything else at all and it has no relation to anything else because He is the *required existence* and He is perfect in and of Himself and He has no relationship at all with another – there is nothing above or below Him. This means that there is no reason which could explain Him at all, not as a cause or an accompaniment . . . He is the *required existence* in and of itself, as we have written. However, since He desired and created creations, all of which are dependent on Him for their existence and all their aspects, from this perspective, we call G-d, 'the Master of All' . . ." As the Nefesh Hachaim (3:2) states, "So is the matter with the entire sensate world which seems to have an existence in and of itself. Hashem, may He be Blessed, is the place of the world – which means that if there was no place in His will for the bringing into existence of all the world, how much more so [when compared to the lack of a physical space], would they all revert to nothing." The idea is that the only being which exists independently of anything else is Hashem. Everything else just has possibility, as they have no independent power to exist – only G-d does. Everything else that does exist, does so by virtue of Hashem willing it to exist.

ii. The ideas that the Maharal presents here are truly profound. He explains that Hashem and Truth are intimately connected by their level of "required existence." Only Hashem exists without being dependent on anything else – He has independent existence. So too is Truth, which is one of His attributes. Thus, they are not only independently existent, they are also One.

iii. Falsehood and anything which is not Hashem, cannot have independent existence and similarly cannot be One and must be many. More than this, one can possibly understand that if two beings have exactly the same level of "Truth" that they would in fact be identical. The Maharal implies this when he says, "because from the power of His Truth (which is absolute Truth, which is the Required Existence), through that power, everything is sustained." Thus the level of Truth in anything is what gives it reality and sustenance!

iv. Herein lies a possible explanation of the Maharal's seemingly confusing statement (above in Tiferet Yisrael) that since Hashem's precepts are equal in righteousness, they are all completely righteous. He is hinting to the ideas taught in N'tiv Emet. If the precepts of Hashem are all equal in Truth, if they are not all completely true, they must have some degree of falsehood, and therefore, there must be many of them and they must be different in their level of truth. But since they are all equal in their level of truth, therefore, they cannot have any falsehood and must all be One and must all be completely true.

v. These ideas admittedly rest on deeper concepts which are beyond the scope of this work.

13. Goodness and Intellectual Secrets

a. The Maharal writes above, 'firstly, a mitzvah is good for a person physically (this is clear to everyone that all the mitzvot in the Torah complete the perfection of a human until a human is "in goodness") and secondly, the mind requires mitzvot from the perspective of an intellectual secret.'

b. This is the merest beginning of the Maharal's comments on the effects and purposes of the Torah and mitzvot. He explores these ideas in tremendous depth beginning in Chapter Six of Tiferet Yisrael. We will content ourselves with a few citations from Chapter Six to flesh out the Maharal's comments here:

תפארת ישראל - פרק ו

ועם כל זה שהמצות הם גזירות על ישראל הם לטוב לנו, כי לא יבא מאתו יתברך רק הטוב הגמור כי כל מעשיו הם הטוב הגמור רק כי הטוב הזה גזר עלינו ולא שיש כאן שום צד רחמנות רק הכל דין... אמנם אין הכונה פה חס ושלום שאין עם דברי התורה הטוב והנועם כי כל דרכיה דרכי נועם וכל נתיבותיה שלום שזה דבר ברור וכמו שיתבאר, רק הכונה פה כי לא מצד הזה נתנה תורה להנאתם רק נתנה תורה בדין וביושר ועם זה הכל

לטוב לנו כי אין ראוי אל אשר הוא הטוב האמתי שיבוא ממנו רק טוב ולפיכך התורה היא לטוב לנו . . .

Tiferet Yisrael, Chapter 6

Despite the fact that the mitzvot are a decree on Israel, they are definitely good for us; because only absolute goodness flows from Hashem, may He be Blessed, since all His actions are absolute goodness. It's just that He decreed this goodness on us and there is no aspect of Mercy here at all, only Justice . . .

However, our intention here is not to say, G-d forbid, that Goodness and Pleasantness do not accompany words of Torah, for "All her[60] ways are ways of pleasantness and all her paths are peace,"[61] for this is clear (as will be explained). Rather, our intention is that the Torah was not given due to this aspect – for their[62] enjoyment – but that the Torah was given in Justice and Honesty. Nevertheless, it is all for our good because it is suitable that only goodness come from Him, Who is the true good; and therefore Torah is for our good . . .

i. The fundamental assumption of the Maharal in Chapter Six as well as here, in the Introduction, is that since the Torah and mitzvot flow from Hashem, they cannot be anything but good, since Hashem is absolute goodness. This is an axiom of Judaism in general. As the Derech Hashem of the Ramchal writes:[63]

דרך ה׳ א : ב

הוא לבדו ית׳ הטוב האמיתי . . .

Derech Hashem 1:2

Hashem alone, may He be Blessed, is true goodness . . .

c. The intellectual secret

i. Furthermore, the Maharal writes above, "secondly, the mind requires mitzvot from the perspective of an intellectual secret."

60. I.e., Torah's.

61. Mishlei 3:17,

62. I.e., humans'.

63. Rabbi Moshe Chaim Luzzato (1707–1746), the Ramchal, was a trailblazing Torah scholar and author whose works on Kabbalah and character development are mainstays of Jewish thought. His work, *Derech Hashem*, The Way of G-d, is a unique compilation of sources from all of Torah on fundamental questions of the relationships between Hashem and the universe, and in particular how human destinies interoperate with Hashem's systems of justice.

ii. The question is, what does this mean? The Maharal explains his meaning in his work, Gur Aryeh, as follows:

גור אריה דברים לג:ה

... כי התורה נקראת בשתי שמות; נקראת בשם "חסד", "ותורת חסד על לשונה" (משלי לא, כו), ונאמר (משלי ג, יז) "דרכיה דרכי נועם", ונקראת בלשון "אמת", "תורת אמת היתה בפיהו" (מלאכי ב, ו). כי המצוה בעצמה עשייתה הוא הטוב ונועם ... וכאשר תשכיל במצוה תמצא אותו אמת ונכון הוא, כמו כבוד אב ואם. ושמירת שבת טוב ונועם הוא, וכאשר תשכיל בו נמצא שהוא ראוי ומחוייב לעשות....

Gur Aryeh, D'varim 33:5

. . . the Torah is described by two terms. It is called loving-kindness,[64] as in, "And the Torah of loving-kindness is on her tongue"[65] and as in, "Her ways are ways of pleasantness."[66] The Torah is also called, truth,[67] as in, "A Torah of truth was in his mouth."[68]

[The reason for this duality is] because the actual performance of a mitzvah in itself is goodness and pleasantness . . . but when you gain understanding in [the concept of] the mitzvah you will find that it is true and correct; for example, the mitzvah to honor one's father and mother. [Similarly,] guarding and cherishing the Shabbat is good and pleasant and when you gain insight into it, it's clear that it is suitable and it is obligatory to perform it . . .

1. Here the Maharal explains that there is a duality to the mitzvot. On the face of it, the mitzvot bring tremendous human benefit and one might be tempted to assume that this benefit and pleasure is the sole motivation for Hashem's giving us the mitzvot.
2. However, the Maharal explains that this is only a superficial understanding. In reality, mitzvot *have* to be – there is no possibility for them not to be, they are part of the fabric of the universe. This level of understanding is far deeper than the simple, accessible idea of pleasure and enjoyment and it is perhaps to this that the Maharal refers when he says that "the mind requires mitzvot from the perspective of an intellectual secret."
3. The Maharal extensively develops this idea over the next few chapters of this work. In Chapters One, Two and Three, the Maharal explores the idea that Torah and mitzvot parallel the

64. In Hebrew, "*chesed*," חסד.
65. Mishlei 31:26.
66. Mishlei 3:17.
67. In Hebrew, "*emet*," אמת.
68. Malachi 2:6.

physical and spiritual DNA of humanity – being the only avenue which allows humans to reach their true potential. Thus, when Hashem created humanity, Torah and mitzvot had to exist to allow the fulfillment of human destiny.

4. In Chapter Four, the Maharal begins to explore the cosmological necessity for the existence of Torah and mitzvot.

14. Unintentional Errors vs. Understanding and Communicating Torah

a. King David deals with the concept of being cleansed from unintentional errors as part of the introduction to his final prayer to understand Torah and to be able to communicate it effectively. What is the connection between the prayer and the need to be cleansed from unintentional errors?

b. Based on the ideas explored previously, the connection is clear:

   i. If a person is truly bonded with Hashem and draws closer to Hashem through the Torah, Hashem will certainly help a person return after unintentional errors. Previously, the Maharal dealt with the idea that Hashem would help one return from even more serious transgressions, as long as a person had this relationship – the lack of which allowed the descent of the Jewish people into immorality at the time of the First Temple.

   ii. However, on a deeper level, unintentional sins could perhaps reflect the *lack* of a deeper connection and bond to Hashem; for if one is more deeply bonded one would be unable to act in certain ways, even unintentionally. This is a theme that the Maharal develops in the following piece which relates to the mitzvah of lending money to a Jew in need. He discusses the need to have a more intimate integration of Torah with one's natural desires.

   iii. First we shall cite the verses and the Rashi on which the Maharal's comments are based.

שמות כ"ב:כ"ד

"אִם כֶּסֶף תַּלְוֶה אֶת עַמִּי אֶת הֶעָנִי עִמָּךְ לֹא תִהְיֶה לוֹ כְּנֹשֶׁה לֹא תְשִׂימוּן עָלָיו נֶשֶׁךְ:"

Sh'mot 22:24

If you lend money to my nation [to the] poor among you, you may not behave towards him like a moneylender – you may not make him pay interest.

רש"י על שמות כ:כב

רבי ישמעאל אומר כל אם ואם שבתורה רשות חוץ מג' ואם מזבח אבנים תעשה לי הרי אם זה משמש בלשון כאשר וכאשר תעשה לי מזבח אבנים לא תבנה אתהן גזית שהרי חובה עליך לבנות מזבח אבנים שנא' (דברים כז) אבנים שלמות תבנה וכן (שמות כב) אם כסף תלוה חובה הוא שנא' (דברים טו) והעבט תעביטנו ואף זה משמש בלשון

כאשר וכן (ויקרא ב) ואם תקריב מנחת בכורים זו מנחת העומר שהיא חובה ועל כרחך אין אם הללו תלוין אלא ודאין ובלשון כאשר הם משמשים:

Rashi, Sh'mot 20:22

Rabbi Yishma'el says, "Every time the Torah uses the word, 'if,' it means that the act is optional except for three times that the word, 'if,' is used, in which the acts are obligatory. These three are:

(1) 'If you build Me an altar of stone'[69] – here 'if' doesn't mean 'if' but '*when*' – so the verse should be read, 'when you build me an altar of stone' – because we have to build a stone altar to Hashem – there is no other choice. The Torah itself says elsewhere 'you must build an altar of whole stones.'[70]

(2) 'If you lend money . . .'[71] But there is no choice of whether you can or cannot lend a Jew money – you have to lend a Jew money if he needs it. The Torah says this elsewhere, 'You must surely lend him,'[72] – here too, 'if' really means, '*when*.'

(3) 'If you bring the offering at the beginning of the harvest.'[73] Again, the bringing of this offering - the *omer* offering brought on the second day of Pesach – is not an option, but a requirement.

"We now see that in each of these three cases, the word 'if' really means 'when' and it doesn't mean that we can choose to do them if we so desire, but that we are obligated to!"

iv. The Maharal comments on this Rashi as follows,

ספר גור אריה על שמות פרק כ פסוק כב

יש לפרש מה שכתב לשון "אם" אף על גב דחובה הם, מפני שאם יעשה מחובה כאילו מקיים גזירת המלך - אין הדבר לרצון להקב"ה, וצריך שיעשה מרצונו, ואז כשיעשה מרצונו הוא מרוצה. [ד]המעשה שהוא הכרחי וחובה אין צריך להביט אל שום טעם, רק הוא מקיים גזירת המלך, ואם עושה אלו שלשה דברים כאילו מקיים גזירת המלך - אין זה דבר. כי אם בונה מזבח, שזהו עבודתו יתברך להקריב עליו, והוא מקיים מכח גזירת המלך בלבד - אין זה עבודה, כי העבודה צריך שיהיה עובד לו מרצונו, ואז נקרא "עובד", אבל אם הוא מוכרח, אין זה עובד. וכן אם הלוה כסף כאילו מקיים גזירת המלך, אין זה מצוה, כי צריך שיהיה מצות הלוואה מרצונו בלב טוב . . . וכן הקרבת העומר, שציוותה התורה (ויקרא כג, יד) שלא לאכול חדש עד הקרבת העומר, ופירשו רז"ל (ויק"ר כח, א) כי הוא יתברך מעלה עננים ומוריד גשמים ומפריח טללים ומצמיח האדמה ומדשן הפירות, ואנו נותנים לו שכרו עומר הקרבן, וכל זה להודיע שהוא יתברך אשר הצמיח לנו הפירות ונתן לנו הכל, וזה צריך הודאה בלב, לא כמלך בשר ודם המכריח את האדם

69. Sh'mot 20:22.
70. D'varim 27:6.
71. Sh'mot 22:24.
72. D'varim 15:8.
73. Vayikra 2:5.

שיודה במלכותו, אבל צריך שיודה בלבו שמאתו ומידו נתן לנו, ואם הוא מקיים את המצוה כאילו הוא מוכרח מגזירת המלך, אין זה הודאה שהוא יתברך עשה את הכל, ולפיכך צריך לקיים כאילו הוא רשות:

Gur Aryeh (Maharal's commentary on Rashi) on Sh'mot 20:22

One must explain why the Torah would use the word "if" when it really meant "when" – "if" sounds like it's optional to do, but the Torah doesn't mean that they are optional – they are obligatory!

The reason for this [seemingly inappropriate use of the conditional, "if"] is that if a person does certain things *just* because Hashem has commanded him to do them, Hashem is not pleased by such actions. A person has to do them of his own will, and when he does them of his own will, only then is Hashem pleased. When a person performs an action which is compulsory, there is no need for him to examine the reason behind it – he is obeying the King's command! But these three actions, if they are done *solely* because Hashem said so, then it's as if a person has not done anything!

When you build an altar – which is a way to serve Hashem, by sacrificing on it – and you only do it because Hashem said you must – this is not called "serving Hashem": real service of Hashem is when you want to do it! Only then can it be called "service of Hashem." But if you are forced to do it, you are not serving Hashem.

Similarly, if you lend money to a poor person just because Hashem told you that it is the right thing to do, *this is not a mitzvah* – because the mitzvah of lending a person money has to be that you are doing it with a good heart . . .

Similarly, the bringing of the *omer* offering (which is actually a dual commandment in the Torah – not only that we must bring the *omer*, but that we are not allowed to eat of the new harvest until we bring it) our rabbis explained as follows – Hashem raises the clouds and draws down the rains and blesses the dew and makes the earth produce crops and ripens the fruit and we bring the *omer* . . . as a sacrifice to announce that He [Hashem] is the one who made our fruit grow and who has given us all we have. And this requires gratitude in the heart. This is unlike a human king who forces people to acknowledge his kingship. Rather, Hashem wants us to acknowledge Him in our hearts and to admit that everything comes from Him and that He has given us everything. But if a person does this mitzvah just because he was commanded to – this is not any admission that Hashem has made everything and therefore, a person has to observe this commandment as if it were optional.

1. Here we see the Maharal's directive that the Torah and mitzvot be integrated within the psyche and soul of a person. His

remarks are extremely pointed and he goes as far as to claim that if one lacks this integration, that the performance of certain mitzvot "is not a mitzvah."

2. Such a level of integration of the Torah's values and ideals is what the Maharal expects of every Jew and we can now understand that at such a level, one will even be guarded from "unintentional errors" for one will simply not be able to do certain things.

15. Further Exploration of Tehillim 19 and of the Maharal's Numerology

a. The Maharal uses Tehillim 19 as the backbone for his Introduction to Tiferet Yisrael. It is illuminating to compare what he writes here with what he says elsewhere about this Tehillim. A little further on in Tiferet Yisrael,[74] the Maharal continues his commentary on this Tehillim. We cite his words here (for easier comparison) and will, please G-d, repeat them later.

b. We first present the two relevant Tehillim and a Midrash.

ספר תהילים פרק יט

(א) לַמְנַצֵּחַ מִזְמוֹר לְדָוִד: (ב) הַשָּׁמַיִם מְסַפְּרִים כְּבוֹד אֵ-ל וּמַעֲשֵׂה יָדָיו מַגִּיד הָרָקִיעַ: (ג)
יוֹם לְיוֹם יַבִּיעַ אֹמֶר וְלַיְלָה לְּלַיְלָה יְחַוֶּה דָּעַת: (ד) אֵין אֹמֶר וְאֵין דְּבָרִים בְּלִי נִשְׁמָע קוֹלָם:
(ה) בְּכָל הָאָרֶץ יָצָא קַוָּם וּבִקְצֵה תֵבֵל מִלֵּיהֶם לַשֶּׁמֶשׁ שָׂם אֹהֶל בָּהֶם: (ו) וְהוּא כְּחָתָן יֹצֵא
מֵחֻפָּתוֹ יָשִׂישׂ כְּגִבּוֹר לָרוּץ אֹרַח: (ז) מִקְצֵה הַשָּׁמַיִם מוֹצָאוֹ וּתְקוּפָתוֹ עַל קְצוֹתָם וְאֵין נִסְתָּר
מֵחַמָּתוֹ: (ח) תּוֹרַת ה׳ תְּמִימָה מְשִׁיבַת נָפֶשׁ עֵדוּת ה׳ נֶאֱמָנָה מַחְכִּימַת פֶּתִי: (ט) פִּקּוּדֵי ה׳
יְשָׁרִים מְשַׂמְּחֵי לֵב מִצְוַת ה׳ בָּרָה מְאִירַת עֵינָיִם: (י) יִרְאַת ה׳ טְהוֹרָה עוֹמֶדֶת לָעַד מִשְׁפְּטֵי
ה׳ אֱמֶת צָדְקוּ יַחְדָּו: (יא) הַנֶּחֱמָדִים מִזָּהָב וּמִפַּז רָב וּמְתוּקִים מִדְּבַשׁ וְנֹפֶת צוּפִים: (יב) גַּם
עַבְדְּךָ נִזְהָר בָּהֶם בְּשָׁמְרָם עֵקֶב רָב: (יג) שְׁגִיאוֹת מִי יָבִין מִנִּסְתָּרוֹת נַקֵּנִי: (יד) גַּם מִזֵּדִים
חֲשֹׂךְ עַבְדֶּךָ אַל יִמְשְׁלוּ בִי אָז אֵיתָם וְנִקֵּיתִי מִפֶּשַׁע רָב: (טו) יִהְיוּ לְרָצוֹן אִמְרֵי פִי וְהֶגְיוֹן לִבִּי
לְפָנֶיךָ ה׳ צוּרִי וְגֹאֲלִי:

TEHILLIM 19
(COLLOQUIAL TRANSLATION ACCORDING TO THE MAHARAL)

(1) For the Conductor. A Psalm of David. (2) The heavens declare the glory of G-d, and the firmament shows His handiwork; (3) Day to day expresses speech, and night to night reveals knowledge; (4) There is no speech, there are no words, neither is their voice heard. (5) Their line goes out through all the earth, and their words to the end of the world. Through His words, Hashem set a tent for the sun, (6) which is as a bridegroom coming out of his chamber, who rejoices as an athlete to run his course. (7) His going forth is from the end of the heaven, and his running route reaches the ends of it; and there is nothing hidden from his heat. (8) The torah of Hashem

74. Tiferet Yisrael, Chapter 2.

is *t'mimah*, restoring the soul; the testimony of Hashem is faithful, making the simple person wise. (9) The precepts of Hashem are honest, making the heart rejoice; the commandment of Hashem is pristine, enlightening the eyes. (10) The Awe of Hashem is pure, enduring forever; the ordinances of Hashem are true, they are righteous altogether; (11) They are more desired than gold, even more than much fine gold; sweeter also than honey and the honeycomb (12) Your servant is careful regarding the mitzvot; in keeping them there is great reward. (13) Who can discern his own faults? Hashem, help me clean myself from hidden faults. (14) Hold me back from presumptuous sins, so that they may not have dominion over me; then I shall be faultless and I shall be clear of great transgression. (15) Let the words of my mouth [be acceptable] and the meditation of my heart be acceptable before you, Hashem, my Former, and my Redeemer.

ספר תהילים פרק קיט א-ט"ז

(א) אַשְׁרֵי תְמִימֵי דָרֶךְ הַהֹלְכִים בְּתוֹרַת ה':
(ב) אַשְׁרֵי נֹצְרֵי עֵדֹתָיו בְּכָל לֵב יִדְרְשׁוּהוּ:
(ג) אַף לֹא פָעֲלוּ עַוְלָה בִּדְרָכָיו הָלָכוּ:
(ד) אַתָּה צִוִּיתָה פִקֻּדֶיךָ לִשְׁמֹר מְאֹד:
(ה) אַחֲלַי יִכֹּנוּ דְרָכָי לִשְׁמֹר חֻקֶּיךָ:
(ו) אָז לֹא אֵבוֹשׁ בְּהַבִּיטִי אֶל כָּל מִצְוֹתֶיךָ:
(ז) אוֹדְךָ בְּיֹשֶׁר לֵבָב בְּלָמְדִי מִשְׁפְּטֵי צִדְקֶךָ:
(ח) אֶת חֻקֶּיךָ אֶשְׁמֹר אַל תַּעַזְבֵנִי עַד מְאֹד:

(ט) בַּמֶּה יְזַכֶּה נַּעַר אֶת אָרְחוֹ לִשְׁמֹר כִּדְבָרֶךָ:
(י) בְּכָל לִבִּי דְרַשְׁתִּיךָ אַל תַּשְׁגֵּנִי מִמִּצְוֹתֶיךָ:
(יא) בְּלִבִּי צָפַנְתִּי אִמְרָתֶךָ לְמַעַן לֹא אֶחֱטָא לָךְ:
(יב) בָּרוּךְ אַתָּה ה' לַמְּדֵנִי חֻקֶּיךָ:
(יג) בִּשְׂפָתַי סִפַּרְתִּי כֹּל מִשְׁפְּטֵי פִיךָ:
(יד) בְּדֶרֶךְ עֵדְוֹתֶיךָ שַׂשְׂתִּי כְּעַל כָּל הוֹן:
(טו) בְּפִקֻּדֶיךָ אָשִׂיחָה וְאַבִּיטָה אֹרְחֹתֶיךָ:
(טז) בְּחֻקֹּתֶיךָ אֶשְׁתַּעֲשָׁע לֹא אֶשְׁכַּח דְּבָרֶךָ:

Tehillim 119:1–16

ALEPH

(1) [א] Happy are those who are upright in the way, who walk in the Torah of Hashem.
(2) [א] Happy are those who keep His testimonies, who seek Him with a whole heart.
(3) [א] They do no unrighteousness; they walk in His ways.
(4) [א] You have ordained Your precepts, that we should observe them diligently.
(5) [א] Oh that my ways were directed to observe Your statutes!

(6) [א] Then I would not be ashamed, when I have regard for all Your commandments.
(7) [א] I will give thanks to You with uprightness of heart, when I learn Your righteous ordinances.
(8) [א] I will observe Your statutes; please do not forsake me [Hashem].

BET

(9) [ב] How shall a young person keep his way pure? By taking heed according to Your word.
(10) [ב] With my whole heart have I searched for You; please let me not err from Your commandments.
(11) [ב] I stored Your word in my heart, so that I might not sin against You.
(12) [ב] Blessed are You, Hashem; teach me Your statutes!
(13) [ב] With my lips have I told all the ordinances of Your mouth.
(14) [ב] I have rejoiced in the way of Your testimonies, as much as in all riches.
(15) [ב] I will meditate in Your precepts, and have respect for Your ways.
(16) [ב] I will delight myself in Your statutes; I will not forget Your word.

i. One should note that Tehillim 119 is written with eight verses dedicated to each letter of the Hebrew alphabet, in order.
ii. Next we cite the Midrash,

מדרש תנחומא (בובר) פרשת תזריע סימן ז

וביום השמיני ימול בשר ערלתו (ויקרא יב ג) ... שאל טורנוסרופוס הרשע את ר' עקיבא איזה מעשים נאים של הקב"ה או של בשר ודם, א"ל של בשר ודם נאים, א"ל טורנוסרופוס הרשע הרי השמים והארץ יכול אתה לעשות כהם, א"ל ר' עקיבא לא תאמר לי בדבר שהוא למעלה מן הבריות, שאין שולטין בהן, אלא בדברים שהן מצויין בבני אדם. א"ל למה אתם מולים, א"ל אף אני הייתי יודע שאתה עתיד לומר לי כן, לכך הקדמתי ואמרתי לך מעשה בשר ודם הם נאים משל הקב"ה, הביאו לי שבולים וגלוסקאות, [אמר לו אלו מעשה הקב"ה ואלו מעשה בשר ודם אין אלו נאים ... א"ל טורנוסרופוס הואיל הוא חפץ במילה, למה אינו יוצא מהול ממעי אמו, א"ל ר' עקיבא ולמה שוררו יוצא בו, לא תחתוך אמו שוררו, ולמה אינו יוצא מהול, לפי שלא נתן הקב"ה לישראל את המצות אלא כדי לצרף בהן.

Midrash Tanchuma, Parshat Tazri'a: 7

"And on the eighth day you will give [a male child] a circumcision."[75]

Turnus Rufus, the wicked [Roman General], asked Rabbi Akiva, "Whose deeds are better? Hashem's or human beings'?"

Rabbi Akiva answered, "Human beings'!"

75. Vayikra 12:3.

Turnus Rufus said to him, "Look at the sky and earth – do you think a person could manage anything like it!?"

Rabbi Akiva said, "Let's discuss comparable things – things which human beings can also make."

Turnus said to him, "Why do you Jews give yourselves circumcisions?"

Rabbi Akiva said, "I knew you were going to ask that question! That's why I answered you before that people's deeds are better than Hashem's." He continued, "Bring me fresh ears of wheat and some cake." Then he said to Turnus Rufus, "So which of these is better? The fresh wheat which is Hashem's work or the cakes which are peoples'?"

Turnus retorted, "Well if Hashem wants you to be circumcised, why aren't you born that way?"

Rabbi Akiva asked, "Well, why don't you ask about the umbilical cord? We are definitely not meant to have that and yet we are born with it and our mothers have to cut it off! So why aren't we born without it and why aren't we born circumcised? [The same reason applies to both -] because *Hashem only gave the mitzvot to Israel in order to refine them.*"

c. The Maharal comments on all of these sources as follows:

ספר תפארת ישראל - פרק ב

התבאר לך כי הפעולות הא־להיות שהם מצות התורה הם ראוים לאדם לפי מדריגת נפשו הא־להית שהיא בקרבו, והפעולות האלו הם השלמת האדם שבהם יושלם עד שהוא הבריאה אשר בה רצון בוראו . . . שהאדם יציר כפו של הקדוש ברוך הוא מבחר התחתונים חסר, עד שהוא נשלם על ידי מעשה עצמו, ועל ידי מצות התורה יגיע האדם אל ההשלמה, כי מצד שיש בו נפש א־להי שיש בו הכנה א־להית לכך אין השלמתו בדבר שהוא טבעי אבל השלמתו בתורה ובמצוה שהוא על הטבע ודבר זה מבואר במקומות הרבה שמצות התורה הם יותר במדריגה ובמעלה מן הטבע. ובמזמור (תהלים י"ט) השמים מספרים כבוד א־ל וגו' ואחר כך התחיל לומר תורת ה' תמימה וגו' עד סוף המזמור. ויש מן תחלת המזמור עד תורת ה' תמימה שבעה פסוקים ואחר כך תורת ה' תמימה. כי הנהגת הטבע נברא בשבעה ימי בראשית ואלו התורה היא על הטבע והיא מדריגה שמינית. ועל פי טעם זה מזמור אשרי תמימי דרך שהוסד על התורה, יש בו שמונה אלפ"א בית"א שהתורה היא מדריגה שמינית שהיא על הטבע שנברא בשבעת ימי בראשית. וכן כל דבר שהוא על הטבע והוא תיקון מה שחסר הטבע הוא אחר השבעה, וזה טעם מילה בשמיני כי האדם מצד הטבע נברא עם הערלה והוא פחיתות הטבע, והמילה היא תיקון הטבע ולפיכך תיקון הזה הוא ביום השמיני.

Maharal, Tiferet Yisrael: 2

You now understand that all G-dly actions (which are the mitzvot and the Torah) are suitable to a person according to the level of his G-dly soul (which is within him). These actions (i.e., the Torah and the mitzvot) are actually the completion and perfection [of a person] – through which he can become perfected so that he becomes the creation which Hashem originally wanted . . . because human beings – the work of Hashem – were created *imperfect* in order to become perfected by their own actions.

And it is via the mitzvot and the Torah that a human can reach perfection. Why is this? Well, humans have in them a G-dly soul which has G-dly potential (which is waiting to be fulfilled) so a human can never be completely perfected by just physical means. *Rather, human perfection can only be achieved through mitzvot and Torah which are above nature.*

This principle is explained in many places – that mitzvot and Torah are on a higher level than nature. [For example,] in Tehillim 19, the Tehillim starts talking about "the heavens . . ."[76] and then later it says, "The torah of Hashem is perfect . . ."[77] Now from the beginning of the Tehillim (where it talks about nature) until where it starts talking about the Torah is seven verses. And then in verse eight it starts talking about the Torah. This is because the natural world was created in the seven days of creation while the Torah is above nature. And it[78] is the eighth level.[79]

For the same reason, in Tehillim 119, each letter of the *Aleph-Beit*[80] has eight verses [dedicated to it] because this whole Tehillim is about the Torah and the Torah is the eighth level which is above nature, which was created in the seven days of creation. So too, anything which is above nature and is a repairing of something which is lacking in nature must come after the seventh level. This is the reason that circumcision is performed on the eighth day, because humans were created with a foreskin which is a natural imperfection, and the circumcision is an improvement of nature. Therefore, this perfection of nature is performed on the eighth day.

d. Putting it all together
   i. From the Midrash Tanchuma we learn that Hashem leaves the world unfinished in order to grant humans the mandate to perfect it. The result is a partnership (as it were) between humans and Hashem.
      1. This is true in the physical sense – that human intervention improves the physical, for example, wheat to bread. Here Hashem provided the physical substrate and humans use it to reach for greater perfection physically.
      2. This is even truer in the moral and spiritual sense where, through

76. Tehillim 19:1.

77. Tehillim 19:8.

78. I.e., the Torah.

79. There are six directions in the physical world: up, down, left, right, forwards, backwards. When one includes the center point we have seven. So, eight is considered to be above the natural world. We examine this numerology in greater detail later on.

80. The Hebrew alphabet.

the Torah and its mitzvot, humans and the physical world can reach physical and spiritual perfection.

3. In a certain way, the mitzvah of circumcision is a superb illustration of both these facets. There is a physical improvement,[81] but this physical improvement is an echo of the entirety of life's aim, which is to create spiritual improvement through the performance of mitzvot.[82]

ii. The Maharal's numerology of the Physical and the Metaphysical
   1. The number seven connotes the physical world (up, down, left, right, forwards, backwards and the center make seven.)
   2. Therefore, eight is above the physical world and denotes metaphysical means for perfecting the physical world.
   3. Illustrations of these concepts
      i. The mitzvah of circumcision
         1. Circumcision is performed on the eighth day because it is an improvement of the physical, perfecting it spiritually.
      ii. Structure of Tehillim 119
         1. It has eight verses for each letter in the alphabet. This Tehillim extols the virtues of the Torah which is the ultimate "8" – it is the container of all metaphysical means which enable one to perfect the physical.
      iii. Structure of Tehillim 19
         1. The first seven verses focus on the physical world.
         2. The eighth verse begins the series of verses which the Maharal uses as the backbone for the Introduction to Tiferet Yisrael. This is because the Torah is the ultimate "8" – the metaphysical means to perfect the physical world.

iii. Combining this with the Maharal's ideas in the Introduction to Tiferet Yisrael
   1. The Maharal's focus throughout the Introduction was on the duality of intimacy with Hashem, and the Torah as a means to achieve this. On the one hand, without intimacy one cannot understand the Torah and yet without the Torah, one cannot achieve true intimacy. We also discussed the fact that even one's unintentional sins are, in a sense, a barometer of the level

81. At the time of this writing, Israeli doctors are in Africa, performing free circumcisions on the male populace as the lowest-cost means to prevent the spread of AIDS.

82. This is what the Torah refers to as "circumcision of the heart" in D'varim 10:16.

of intimacy and that the Maharal requires an internalization of Hashem's will (expressed through the commandments in the Torah) to the extent that it becomes one's own will, not just an accepted commandment from Hashem.

2. Here we are led to understand why, in the Maharal's thought, the Torah occupies such a central role in the duality above. It is the bridge over the seemingly insurmountable chasm between our physical existences and the infinite G-d. On the one hand, we are trapped within the seven days of time and the seven "dimensions" of space – we are banality personified. On the other hand we can reach across infinity to gain closeness with Hashem. It is Torah, the eighth, which allows this relationship to be formed.
3. This centrality of Torah even defines the way that the verses of Tehillim 19 and 119 are structured. Not only does it communicate how Torah creates this bridge, but in the medium itself lies the message.

e. The seeming contradiction in the Maharal's numerology
   i. Earlier in the Introduction to Tiferet Yisrael, the Maharal wrote, "This bonding to Hashem is a complete bonding, not a resultant, secondary join. If a person acquires positive character traits, then via those character traits, a person acquires a resultant bond with Hashem, but he only acquires a bond through the perspective of the trait that he has perfected. But through the Torah, a person cleaves to Hashem completely through all perspectives. *In this world, there are six major perspectives (right, left, forwards, backwards, up and down).* Therefore, King David mentioned six items, parallel to these six perspectives, in order to teach that through the Torah, a person cleaves to Hashem throughout all perspectives and deviates neither right nor left nor any way."
      1. Here the Maharal seems to be saying that in this world there are six perspectives.
      2. But we have just seen (above) that the Maharal claims that: "This is because the natural world was created in the seven days of creation while the Torah is above nature. And it is the eighth level . . . and the Torah is the eighth level which is above nature which was created in the seven days of creation. So too, anything which is above nature and is a repair of something which is missing in nature must come after the seventh level."
      3. Here the Maharal seems to be claiming that in this world there are seven perspectives.
   ii. We find the resolution later in Tiferet Yisrael, Chapter Forty.

ספר תפארת ישראל - פרק מ

וכבר ידוע כי הגשם יש לו חלופי צדדים ששה ועל ידם הגשם שלם והם המעלה והמטה וארבעה צדדין שהם ארבע רוחות הידועים כי אין גשם שלם רק כאשר יש לו ששה צדדין . . . ויש עוד גבול נבדל לעצמו והוא האמצעי אשר הוא נבדל לעצמו ואינו נוטה לא לימין ולא לשמאל לא לפנים ולא לאחור רק עומד באמצע, ואין האמצעי הזה מתיחס לגשם כמו ששה צדדים כי הצדדים הששה יש להם רוחק והרוחק הוא גדר הגשם ולכך על ששה הצדדין יאמר שהם צדדין גשמיים אבל האמצעי מפני שאין לו רוחק לא יאמר עליו שהוא גשמי בעצמו ומתיחס אל בלתי גשמי.

Tiferet Yisrael Chapter 40

It is already known that the physical world has six *variable* dimensions and through these six, the physical world is complete. These six are: up, down, and the four dimensions which are the four known cardinal directions. Physicality is not complete without these six dimensions . . . *But there is another boundary which is separated on its own and this is the central point which is completely separate – it doesn't tend to the right, left, forwards or backwards, but simply remains stationary in the center. This central point is not related to the physical in the same way that the six dimensions are related to the physical world because the six dimensions have distance*[83] *and this distance is the defining element of the physical world. Therefore, we say that the six dimensions are really physical dimensions, but regarding the central point (which has no extensibility and is merely a point) we cannot say that it is truly physical in and of itself and it indeed has a relation to the non-physical.*

1. We thus see that the seventh point, the central point, is somewhat of a hybrid in that it is *not variable. The six dimensions vary, they have extensibility and variation, they can be large or small; whereas the central point has no variability.*
2. The Maharal says that, in essence, non-stasis, variability and quantity are what define the physical world. One cannot say that the seventh *is* physical, but one can also not say that it is metaphysical.
3. Thus, when the Maharal is discussing (in Tiferet Yisrael 2) the status of Torah, he clearly says that everything below "eight" is included within the definition of the physical world, since from the point of Torah which is the ultimate metaphysical object, even the central point, the seventh, is physical. However, when he discusses (in the Introduction) the *variable* means and perspectives in which a person can grow and develop, here there are only six relevant perspectives, since the seventh allows for no development or variation.

83. I.e., extension.

f. A hidden sub-theme in Tehillim 19
   i. The names of G-d in the Tehillim and their frequency:
      1. א־ל : appears only once – in verse 2.
      2. י־ה־ו־ה : appears seven times – in verses 8, 9, 10 and 16.
   ii. In total, there are eight names of G-d here – a clear parallel. But on a deeper level, the name א־ל is used in the sections referring to the physical world, while י־ה־ו־ה is used where referring to the metaphysical world. We have no business in hidden matters, but there is surely much hidden here to which the Maharal is only hinting.

16. "Your servant is careful regarding the mitzvot, in keeping them is great reward" – the Pachad Yitzchak's Explanation

a. The Pachad Yitzchak has a tremendously profound discourse on the meaning of this verse and the entire Tehillim.[84]
b. Once again, the précis which we offer here pales in comparison to the majesty of his explanations and we encourage all who can, to see there.
c. In the article, Rav Hutner explains (in brief) as follows:
   i. Initial question
      1. The Midrash[85] comments on this verse, "Your servant is careful regarding them,[86] in keeping them is great reward"[87],[88] that this refers to those mitzvot which are often disregarded as being unimportant.[89] The Midrash says that if a person is careful to observe such mitzvot, then the following verse applies, "How great is Your goodness which you have concealed for those who are in awe of You."[90]
      2. The Pachad Yitzchak deduces that the Midrash is teaching us that there are two different types of goodness (reward) – a revealed goodness and a concealed one.
      3. He questions why it is that one merits specifically a concealed reward through diligence in keeping mitzvot which are usually disregarded.
   ii. General answer
      1. The Pachad Yitzchak explains that there are two ways in which the Torah impacts the human soul:

84. Pachad Yitzchak, Shavu'ot 15.
85. Tanchuma, Eikev 1.
86. The mitzvot.
87. The word used here for "reward" is the Hebrew, עקב, "*eikev*," meaning "heel."
88. Tehillim 19:12.
89. See Rashi, D'varim 7:12, where he explains that people crush these mitzvot underfoot, with their heels.
90. Tehillim 31:20.

a. The Torah empowers the human mind to control all other human faculties, including emotions.
   i. This is indicated by the phrase, "Torah brings one to awareness."[91]
   ii. When the Torah affects one in this way, all one's conscious desires and faculties are controlled by a Torah mindset.
b. The Torah elevates the very faculty of pleasure itself so that it becomes a vessel for service of Hashem.
   i. This is indicated by the phrase, "The light within [Torah][92] can return a person in *t'shuvah*."[93]
   ii. He explains that this is a higher level than the previous one in that it includes all of the human being – affecting areas of the human being beyond the control of the volitional mind.
   iii. When the Torah affects one in this way, the Torah's effects extend even beyond one's conscious awareness to levels above and below that which we can usually control.

2. The definition of "mitzvot which are usually disregarded"
   a. These mitzvot are not intentionally disregarded, rather they are below one's conscious radar, to the extent that they are not even noticed.
   b. Thus, the only way one can reach and notice such mitzvot is through the second effect of Torah – that which elevates the very faculty of pleasure; for as soon as one takes pleasure in something, it becomes noticeable. However, this second effect is sub- and super-conscious – it is hidden.
   c. This then is the reason that one who manages to notice and fulfill such normally disregarded mitzvot merits a "hidden" reward, because the only method of reaching these mitzvot is a hidden method – one beyond conscious control.

iii. Structure of Tehillim 19
   1. Whereas the Maharal here only explicitly lists six levels of the effects of Torah, the Pachad Yitzchak notes that there are in fact eight – something which makes complete sense given the Maharal's explanation that the Torah exists on the eighth level.
   2. The Pachad Yitzchak's levels are divided into two groups:
      a. Six levels of Conscious control – which belong to the "Torah

91. Avodah Zarah 20b.
92. Lit., "it."
93. Eichah Rabbah, Introduction 2.

which brings one to awareness"

- i. "The Torah of Hashem is perfect and innocent (*tamim*), it restores the soul."
- ii. "The Testimony of Hashem is faithful, making the simple person wise."
- iii. "The Precepts of Hashem are honest, rejoicing the heart."
- iv. "The Commandment of Hashem is pristine, enlightening the eyes."
- v. "The Awe of Hashem is pure, enduring forever."
- vi. "The Ordinances of Hashem are true, they are righteous altogether."

b. Two levels of non-Conscious control
- i. Reaching Above the level of Conscious control
  1. "More desired than gold, even more than much fine gold, sweeter also than honey and the honeycomb."
- ii. Reaching Below the level of Conscious control
  1. "Your servant is careful regarding the mitzvot, in keeping them is great reward."[94]

d. Unintended *t'shuvah*
- i. Much of what the Pachad Yitzchak writes above links in directly to the Maharal's explanation of the fact that if one makes the blessings on the Torah, thus expressing one's gratitude for the Torah, and creating a relationship with Hashem through the Torah, then even if one sins, the Torah will help him return.
- ii. Although the Maharal does not explicitly cite the concept that "The light within [Torah] can return a person in *t'shuvah*," it is clear that he is relating to the same idea. In fact, the Maharal's discussion of how one can be prevented from unintentional sins, fits precisely with this.
- iii. Both of these concepts point out that the Torah can and should affect one sub- and super-consciously. Whether it is the fact that one simply cannot do certain sinful acts and cannot even conceive of doing them or whether it is the fact that if one has stumbled, one is almost compelled to return, both point to a deeper and higher effect of Torah, elevating a person in the innermost recesses of the heart, mind and soul.

94. This is the verse with which the Pachad Yitzchak began his explanation.

COMMENTARY SECTION

Chapter 1

1. Terminology

a. "Receptivity"

i. The Maharal speaks of the "*hachanah*," הכנה, that the Jewish people have for the Torah and mitzvot.

ii. This word literally means "preparation." The meaning here is closer to "receptivity" or "potential compatibility with." He refers to an inherent, spiritual quality.

iii. Generally, we have translated the word as "readiness" or "receptivity to," sometimes adding in brackets "[and preparation for]."

2. Varying Levels of Souls

a. The Maharal states here that animals have an animalistic, natural soul as opposed to humans who possess a *sichli* soul. The Maharal uses various terms to describe these different levels or types of souls. Although we have no business with hidden matters, some explanation is forthcoming. We bring below some sources on the matter and then a brief explanation:

בראשית רבה יד:ט

חמשה שמות נקראו לה נפש רוח נשמה יחידה חיה נפש זה הדם... רוח שהיא עולה ויורדת... נשמה זו האופיה דברייתא... חיה שכל האברים מתים והיא חיה בגוף יחידה שכל האברים משנים שנים והיא יחידה בגוף...

B'reishit Rabbah 14:9

There are five names for the soul: (1) *nefesh* (2) *ru'ach* (3) *n'shamah* (4) *y'chidah*[1] (5) *Chayah*. (1) *Nefesh* is the blood . . . (2) *Ru'ach* goes up and down . . . (3) *N'shamah* is the personality of the person . . . (4) *Chayah* – all the organs of a person die except for this one which lives in the body and so it is called *chayah*,[2] (5) *Y'chidah* – all the organs in the body come in doubles, except this one which is single[3] in the body.

---

1. Although in the first half of the Midrash, *Y'chidah*, is mentioned fourth, it actually comes last logically as is evidenced from the continuation of the Midrash, where the order is reversed.
2. In Hebrew, "*chayah*" means "alive."
3. In Hebrew, "*y'chidah*" means "single."

ספר נפש החיים - שער א - פרק טו

הלא שם נשמה פירושו הוא נשימה. והרי נראה לעין שנשימת האדם הוא ההבל העולה מהלב ממטה למעלה . . . ואינו בחי' עליונה. אמנם הענין שנקראת בלשון נשימה. אין הכונ' בחי' נשימת האד'. אלא כביכול נשימת פיו ית"ש. כמ"ש ויפח באפיו נשמת חיי'. וכבר המשילו רז"ל (בר"פ חלק) ענין השתלשלו' הרוח חיי' באדם לעשיי' כלי זכוכית . . . שכשנבחין בנשימת פי האומן בכלי הזכוכית בעת עשייתו. נמצא בו ג' בחי'. בחי' הראשונה הוא כשנשימת ההבל הוא עדיין תוך פיו קודם באו לתוך חלל השפופרת החלולה. אין לקרותה אז אלא בשם נשימה. והבחי' השנית כשנכנס ההבל ובא לתוך השפופרת ונמשכת כמו קו. אז נקרא רוח. והבחי' הג' התחתונה הוא כשיוצא הרוח מהשפופרת לתוך הזכוכית ומתפשטת בתוכה עד שנעשית כלי כפי רצון המזגג רז מכליא רוחו ונקרא אז נפש לשון שביתה ומנוחה: כן בדמיון זה. הוא ענין הג' בחי' נר"ן שמושפעי' כביכול מנשימת פיו ית"ש. שבחי' הנפש היא הבחי' התחתונ' שהיא כולה בתוך גוף האד'. ובחי' הרוח הוא בא דרך עירוי מלמעל'. שחלק וקצה העליון שלו קשור ונאחז למעל' בבחי' התחתונ' של הנשמה. ומשתלשלת ונכנסת גם בתוך גוף האד' ומתקשרת שם בבחי' העליונה של הנפש . . . אמנם בחי' הנשמה. היא הנשימה עצמה שפנימיות עצמותה מסתתרת בהעלם ומקורה ברוך כביכול בתוך נשימת פיו ית"ש. שאין עצמות מהותה נכנסת כלל בתוך גוף האדם. ואד"הר קודם החטא זכה לעצמותה. ובסיבת החטא נסתלקה מתוכו ונשארה רק חופפת עליו. לבד משרע"ה שזכה לעצמותה תוך גופו. ולכן נקרא איש האלקים . . . וזולתו לא זכה אליה שום אדם. . . . והיא הנותנת להאדם בינה יתירה להשכיל השכליות הפנימים הגנוזים בתו"הק . . .

Nefesh Hachaim 1:15

The word *N'shamah* comes from the word *n'shimah*.[4] One can see that a person's breath is the air which rises from the heart, from down, inside the chest, upwards . . . spiritually it is not a higher level. Rather, the reason that it is named similarly to the word *n'shimah* is not because it is referring to human breath, but rather, as it were, to the breath of Hashem. As the verse says [when describing the creation of the first human being], "And Hashem blew into his nostrils a breath of life."[5]

Our sages likened the process whereby the soul is drawn down into the living person to the creation of a glass vessel . . . because when we examine the breath of the craftsman at the moment that he creates the glass vessel we see that there are three stages. The first stage is when the breath of the craftsman is still inside his mouth, before it has entered the hollow tube. At that stage it is called *n'shimah*.[6] The second stage is when the air enters the hollow tube and is stretched out like a straight line. At that stage [since it is in motion] it is called *ru'ach*.[7] Then the third stage is the lowest stage and it is when the *ru'ach* leaves the tube and enters the glass and spreads

4. Meaning "breath."
5. B'reishit 2:7.
6. I.e., breath – while it is motionless but has the potential to move.
7. Which means "wind."

out into the glass until it is made into a vessel according to the desire of the glassmaker – the glass contains and imprisons the *ru'ach* and in such a state it is called *nefesh* – a word which comes from the root which means rest and stopping.[8]

This is exactly the comparison to the three levels of the soul – *n'shamah*, *ru'ach* and *nefesh* which are created by Hashem's breath, as it were. The *nefesh* is the lowest level of the soul and is entirely encapsulated within the body of the person. The *ru'ach* comes to the person from above like a liquid being poured from one vessel to another. The upper portion of the *ru'ach* is connected above to the bottom part of the *n'shamah* while the bottom section of the *ru'ach* flows down into the body and there it links with the upper section of the *nefesh* . . . However, the *n'shamah* section is the breath itself – the internal essence of which is concealed in hiddenness and its source is blessed, as it were, inside the breath of Hashem, as it were. Without it, a person could not be called a person.

i. We see that there are three lower levels of the soul (in ascending order):
   1. *Nefesh*
   2. *Ru'ach*
   3. *N'shamah*

ii. But what functions does each of these levels have?

ספר נפש החיים - שער א - פרק יד

ואלו הג' בחי' מעשה דבור מחשבה. הן כלל הבחי' פנימיות של האדם. שהם הג' בחי' נר"ן. כי המעשה הוא מבחי' הנפש כמ"ש והנפש אשר תעשה הנפשות העושות. והרב' כיוצא כי הדם הוא הנפש שהנפש שור' ומתלבש בדם האדם . . . ומרוצת הדם בכל פרטי חלקי האברים כלי המעשה הוא הנותן להם חיות התנועה והתעוררות שיוכלו לפעול ולעשות את אשר בכחם. ואם יומנע מרוצת הדם מאבר א' אותו האבר מתיבש ואין בו שום תנועה לעשות שום דבר. והוא אבר מת. והדבור הוא מבחי' הרוח כמ"ש (ש"ב כ"ג) רוח ה' דבר בי (ישעיה י"א) וברוח שפתיו. וכמו שת"א ע"פ (בראשי' ב') ויהי האדם לנפש חיה. לרוח ממללא. וכן נראה לעין שבכל דבור שהאדם מוציא מפיו יוצא רוח והבל מהפה. ומשכן הרוח עיקרו הוא בלב . . . ומחשבה היא בחי' הנשמה שהיא המלמדת לאדם דיעה ובינה בתו"הק. לכן איקר משכנה הוא במוח כלי המחשבה והוא הבחי' העליונה שבהם. וכן אמר בב"ר פי"ד חמשה שמות נקראו לה כו' נפש זה הדם כו'. רוח כו'. נשמה זו האופי' דברייתי. ר"ל דעתו ומחשבתו כמו שפי' הערוך ורש"י ז"ל:

Nefesh Hachaim 1:14

These three facets (action, speech and thought) are a synopsis of internal facets of the human being, which are the three facets of the soul: *nefesh*, *ru'ach* and *n'shamah*.

8. Since the air is no longer in motion, "*nefesh*" is an appropriate name for it.

Action flows from the facet of the *nefesh*, as the verse states, "And the soul[9] which acts . . . ,"[10] and "the souls[11] which act . . . ,"[12] and many other verses like these. [The reason that *nefesh* is associated with action is] because the blood contains the *nefesh*, because the *nefesh* is present in and is clothed by one's blood . . . and the flow of blood in all the detailed parts of the limbs (which are the agents for carrying out actions) is what confers upon the limbs the vitality of movement and arousal so that they will be able to act and execute that which is their potential. And if the flow of blood would be prevented from any limb, that limb will wither and there will be no movement within it to carry out any action and it will be a dead limb.

Speech flows from the facet of the *ru'ach*, as is written, "the *ru'ach* of Hashem *spoke*[13] through me . . ."[14] and "and in the *ru'ach* of His *lips* . . ."[15], [16] and as Unkelus[17] translates the verse "and the human being became a living *nefesh*"[18] [which he translates as], "[and the human being became a] *speaking ru'ach*." So too, it appears to the eye that with every speech that a person articulates is exhaled wind[19] and air from the mouth. And the primary dwelling place of the *ru'ach* is in the heart . . .

And thought is[20] the facet of the *n'shamah* which is what teaches a person knowledge and insight[21] in the holy Torah. Therefore, the primary dwelling place of the *n'shamah* is in the brain which is the agent of thought; and it is the highest element of them all. So too it says in B'reishit Rabbah,[22] "There are five names for the soul . . . *nefesh* is the blood . . . *ru'ach* . . . *n'shamah* is the

9. The word used in the verse to denote "soul" is the Hebrew, "*nefesh*."

10. B'midbar 15:30.

11. The word used in the verse to denote "souls" is the Hebrew plural of the word "*nefesh*," which is "*n'fashot*."

12. Vayikra 18:29.

13. In this verse, it is the *ru'ach* which is speaking.

14. 2 Sh'mu'el 23:2.

15. In this verse, it is the *ru'ach* which is associated with the lips – two of the main organs of speech.

16. Y'shayahu 11:4.

17. Unkelus was an early sage who translated the Torah into Aramaic.

18. B'reishit 2:7. It is important to note that the word used here, in the verse, is "*nefesh*" and that when the *nefesh* is "living" it becomes *ru'ach* in Unkelus's translation, gaining the power of speech.

19. The word "*ru'ach*," רוח, literally means, "wind."

20. Note the change in phraseology. Action and speech "flow from" the *nefesh* and *ru'ach* respectively, but thought *is* the *n'shamah*.

21. Cf. Y'shayahu 40:14.

22. Cited above, B'reishit Rabbah 14:9.

personality of the person." By personality, it means a person's knowledge and thought, as the Aruch[23] and Rashi, *z"l*, explained.[24]

iii. Here we see that the three sections of the soul parallel certain capacities:
   1. *Nefesh*: Action
   2. *Ru'ach*: Speech
   3. *N'shamah*: Thought

iv. Lastly, one might ask which of these (if any) are possessed by animals. The Maharal (in the Derech Chaim) and the Ramchal (in the Derech Hashem) concur as follows:

ספר דרך חיים - פרק ב משנה ח

וג' דברים יש באדם כי האדם יש בו נפש כמו שיש לכל שאר בעלי חיים . . .

Derech Chaim 2:8

There are three elements in a human being. A human being has a *nefesh*, just as other animals do.

דרך ה' א:ה:א

כאן צריך שתזהר שלא תטעה לחשוב שיהיה ענין שאר הבעלי חיים כענין האדם, כי אין נפש הבעלי חיים אלא דבר גשמי מן הדקים שבגשמיות, ומענינו נמצא גם כן באדם, בבחינת היותו בעל חי, אמנם זולת כל זה יש באדם נשמה עליונה, שהוא מין בריאה בפני עצמו, נבדל מן הגוף לגמרי ורחוק ממנו עד מאד, שבאה ונקשרת בו בגזירתו ית' . . .

Derech Hashem 1:5:1

Here one must take heed not to err in thinking that the state of other animals is equal to that of human beings. Rather, the *nefesh* of animals is actually a physical object even though it is one of the least physical of all physical objects. A soul of this type is found in human beings from the point of view that human beings are also living beings [and the animal soul confers life] however, besides all this, humans have a supernal *n'shamah* which is a type of creation in and of itself, entirely separate from the body and very distant from the body which nevertheless comes and is bonded to the body by the decree of Hashem, may He be Blessed . . .

v. From the explanation of Nefesh Hachaim, we see that the *nefesh* is that section of the soul which vivifies the body (conferring action and

23. Aruch, s.v. *apei* (2nd entry). The Aruch is an early dictionary of Torah terms written by Rabbi Natan ben Y'chi'el of Rome.

24. Rashi, B'reishit Rabbah ad loc., s.v. *n'shamah*.

movement) and is the lowest part of the soul. As the Maharal and the Ramchal teach, this is what is shared by humans and animals.

b. The Maharal's terminology
   i. The Maharal (above in the Tiferet Yisrael) uses various terms which are partly similar to those we explained above.
   ii. In other places, the Maharal uses other terms. Let us examine, for example, Derech Chaim 2:8.

ספר דרך חיים - פרק ב משנה ח

וג' דברים יש באדם כי האדם יש בו נפש כמו שיש לכל שאר בעלי חיים, ויש בו נפש המדברת נוסף על שאר ב"ח שאין להם נפש המדברת, ויש עוד לאדם שכל נבדל מן הגוף לגמרי, כי הנפש המדברת אינו שכל נבדל כי גם לתינוק יש לו שכל זה, רק קראו אותו שכל היוליאני בלתי נבדל כי הוא כח בגוף והתבאר זה למעלה אבל יש לאדם שכל נבדל גם כן.

Derech Chaim 2:8

There are three elements in a human being.

A human being has a *nefesh*, just as other animals do.

A human being also has a *nefesh-m'daberet*[25] in addition to [the *nefesh* possessed by] other animals which do not possess a *nefesh-m'daberet*.

A human being also has a transcendent-mind which is completely separate from the body.

The *nefesh-m'daberet* is not a transcendent-mind, because even a child has this [verbal] mind [and therefore, a child can speak even though he does not yet have a transcendent mind]. Therefore, they called this *nefesh-m'daberet*, "Hyle-mind,"[26] which indicates that it is not transcendent because it is a power of the body. This was explained above. However, a person also has a transcendent-mind.

   iii. In his Chiddushei Halachot (Shabbat 31b), he uses other terms and makes an explicit correlation with the more familiar terms we've seen:[27]

חידושי ההלכות שבת ל"א:

האדם יש לו ג' כחות שהם זה למעלה מזה... האחד הוא כח הגופני שהוא מוטבע בגוף.

---

25. Verbal *nefesh*.

26. "Hyle" is a Greek word which is used to connote "matter." The idea here is that the verbal-*nefesh* is somewhat physical, somewhat connected to matter, so it was termed, "hyle-mind" as opposed to "transcendent-mind" which is completely disconnected from physicality and is transcendent.

27. Citation and text as per Rav Hartman, p. 31, n. 29.

והשני כח נבדל מן הגוף, אבל הוא מצורף ומחובר אל הגוף, שאינו נבדל לגמרי. והכח הג' הוא נבדל לגמרי מן הגוף. ובדברי חכמים [ב"ר י"ד, ט] נקראו 'נפש' 'רוח' 'נשמה' . . .

Chiddushei Halachot 31b

A human being has three powers, each more elevated than the previous . . . the first [and most primal] is the physical power which is embedded in the body. The second is a power distinct from the body, but nevertheless connected and networked to the body, but not completely separated from the body. The third power is completely separate from the body. In our sages' terminology, they were termed, *nefesh*, *ru'ach*, *n'shamah*.

iv. In total, the Maharal uses the following terms:
  1. In our section of Tiferet Yisrael
     a. Animalistic Soul [*nefesh b'heimit*]
     b. *Sichli* Soul [*nefesh sichlit*]
     c. Natural Soul [*nefesh tivit*]
     d. Vital Soul [*nefesh chiyunit*]
     e. G-dly-*sichli* Soul [*nefesh sichlit Elokit*]
  2. In the citation from the Derech Chaim
     a. Soul [*nefesh*]
     b. Verbal Soul [*nefesh m'daberet*]
     c. Transcendent-mind [*seichel nivdal*]
  3. In the Chiddushei Halachot
     a. Physical Power [*ko'ach hagufani*]

v. Here we see the possible correlations between the terms we learned in the Nefesh Hachaim (which is more classical terminology) and in the Maharal:

<table>
<tr><th>Nefesh Hachaim's term</th><th>Associated faculty</th><th colspan="4">Maharal's Terminology</th></tr>
<tr><td>Nefesh</td><td>Action, movement</td><td>Animalistic Soul</td><td>Natural Soul</td><td>Vital Soul</td><td>Physical Power</td></tr>
<tr><td>Ru'ach</td><td>Speech</td><td colspan="4">Verbal Soul</td></tr>
<tr><td>N'shamah</td><td>Thought</td><td colspan="2">Transcendent Mind</td><td colspan="2">G-dly-Sichli Soul</td></tr>
</table>

  1. A question which is beyond the scope of this work would be why the Maharal uses four different terms for the *nefesh* and two different terms for the *n'shamah*.

3. Animals being Created to Serve Human Beings

  a. Many of our sages present a clear vision of the purpose of the universe as one which will be achieved through the medium of positive human choice. The universe is, in their view, a vast arena offering humans a variety of choices between good and evil.

b. This is clearly presented in a beautiful section of the Ramchal's M'silat Y'sharim.[28]

ספר מסילת ישרים פרק א - בבאור כלל חובת האדם בעולמו

ואם תעמיק עוד בענין תראה כי העולם נברא לשימוש האדם. אמנם הנה הוא עומד בשיקול גדול. כי אם האדם נמשך אחר העולם ומתרחק מבוראו, הנה הוא מתקלקל, ומקלקל העולם עמו. ואם הוא שולט בעצמו ונדבק בבוראו ומשתמש מן העולם רק להיות לו לסיוע לעבודת בוראו, הוא מתעלה והעולם עצמו מתעלה עמו... והנה על העיקר הזה העירונו זכרונם לברכה במדרש קהלת (רבה, ז) שאמרו... בשעה שברא הקדוש ברוך הוא את אדם הראשון, נטלו והחזירו על כל אילני גן עדן ואמר לו, ראה מעשי כמה נאים ומשובחים הן, וכל מה שבראתי בשבילך בראתי, תן דעתך שלא תקלקל ותחריב את עולמי.

M'silat Y'sharim 1

If you contemplate the matter further, you will understand that the physical world was only created for the use of human beings. Nevertheless, the world itself balances on a knife-edge. Because if a person is drawn after the world and is distanced from Hashem, both the person is corrupted and he corrupts the world with him. But, if a person controls himself and connects to Hashem and *uses the world as an aid in service of Hashem, both the person is elevated and the physical world is elevated with him* . . . Regarding this issue, our rabbis roused us in the Midrash Kohelet when they said, . . .[29] "At the time that Hashem created the first human being, He took him and showed him all the trees in the Garden of Eden and said to him, 'Look at all My creations, how nice and praiseworthy they are and everything I created, I created for you – make sure you don't corrupt and destroy My world'."

4. **The Discussion Regarding the "Use of Essential Faculties" by Animals Deserves further Elucidation**
   a. Two questions
      i. The Maharal's comments on the lion, deer and fox are puzzling. It is clear that all of the animals mentioned benefit exceptionally from their "essential excellences" – a lion gains its place in the pride via its strength (the female lions definitely use their strength in hunting). Similarly, the deer uses its speed to stay alive, even if not in the ac-

28. Rabbi Moshe Chaim Luzzato (1707–1746) was a trailblazing Torah scholar and author whose works on Kabbalah and character development are mainstays of Jewish thought. His work, *M'silat Y'sharim*, The Path of the Just, is the basic text for the study and practice of Jewish character development.

29. Kohelet Rabbah 7:19.

tual process of browsing. The fox too uses its brain in outwitting man and other predators. The Maharal clearly knew all this, so what does he mean when he says, "yet the lion doesn't use the power of his body for the purpose of his livelihood"?

ii. Our second question is as follows. The Maharal uses the phrases, "Rabbi Shimon said that a deer is exceptionally blessed with these virtues but does not use this power for the purpose of its livelihood; therefore, he said, 'I have never seen a deer drying figs in the field,' that is, one never sees a deer preparing its food in the summer and utilizing its essential excellence (speed) for this purpose to gather the food and store it in a home" and "Yet, the fox doesn't use this power for the purpose of his sustenance, acting as a shopkeeper and closing business deals." The obvious question here is – indeed we don't see the lion acting as a porter, the deer as a fig farmer or the fox as a shopkeeper! But we do see them using their power, speed and acumen in their natural setting! The fact that lions are not porters surely doesn't mean that they don't utilize their bodies' strength for their sustenance!

b. Possible answer

i. Rabbi Yehoshua Hartman also presents this question[30] and answers that the Maharal is claiming, as per the language of the *B'raita*, "[these animals] secure their livelihood without anguish," that these animals have no need to put in *extra* effort to make their livelihood through the use of their specialized, unique faculties.

ii. However, this explanation still seems difficult to me as it does not seem to fit in with the Maharal's words (cited above) which seem to exclude *any* use of these essential faculties.

c. Second possible answer

i. It originally seemed to me that there is a second solution[31] which Rabbi Hartman himself seemed to suggest elsewhere,[32] that the Maharal is specifically referring to the *power* behind these faculties, not the faculties themselves.

1. The Maharal seemed to hint this specifically in his Chiddushei Aggadot (however, as Rabbi Hartman suggested, this source does not relate particularly to humans):

מהר"ל, חידושי אגדות שבת קנ"ב:

וכל אשר אמרנו פה מן גוף אין הכונה כלל על גוף של בשר דודאי זה אינו, רק על כח

30. Tiferet Yisrael, p. 32, fn. 31.

31. The Maharal's comments in Chiddushei Aggadot, Shabbat 152b suggested this to me.

32. Tiferet Yisrael, Hartman Edition, vol. 1, p. 31, n. 29.

הגוף שאין ספק כי לגוף הזה של [אדם] יש לו כח שאינו בשר ודם, והוא נקרא גוף של [אדם].

Chiddushei Aggadot, Shabbat 152b

Every time we have discussed "the body," it does not connote the physical body, rather it refers to the *power of the body* because there is no doubt that the human body has a power which is not flesh and blood, but this power is nevertheless termed "the human body."

ii. However, it still seems to me that the Gemara and the Maharal are drawing a close parallel between the three animal facilities described here (in particular, "intelligence") and that of humans. This being the case, it seems that the Maharal might not be referring to the actual body, vivacity or intelligence of the lion, deer and fox respectively, but rather to the "power" behind them. This power is the abstract idea, the blueprint, a spiritual force which generates these faculties. For this reason, the Maharal uses the term "*power*" in all three cases in his comments in Tiferet Yisrael: "power of the body," "power of the soul" and "power of the intellect."[33]

iii. Let's explore this idea a little further:

1. When a person is using his physical strength to act as a porter, he is not just utilizing physical strength, but he has abstracted the idea of applying physical force to the extent that he can direct that strength towards external objects. Similarly the idea of drying figs is the abstraction of the concept of movement to that of transporting other objects, not just one's body. Similarly, the idea of being a businessman or shop owner is the abstraction of intelligence to work on *information* describing physical phenomena (as opposed to the physical phenomena themselves).
2. In each of these examples, the human being has abstracted the concept of strength, movement or intelligence to operate on external, third parties. This is primarily an intellectual capacity. But more than that, it is a meta-level – where the faculties do not just "operate" but rather where the human being has abstracted the faculties themselves so as to operate on externalities.
3. This meta-level is what the Maharal may mean when he speaks of the "power" behind the faculty. It is not just the faculty, but the generalized concept, the abstraction of that faculty. Not just brute strength, speed and intelligence but the abstraction of "strength," "movement" and "intelligence."

iv. This then is what the Maharal may be saying. The animals have had

33. The Hebrew word for "power," כח, "*ko'ach*" also means "potential."

no need to reach the level of abstracting their faculties. They simply utilize them.

1. The natural use of the lion's strength is to hunt prey which it does. It is unnatural for the lion to learn to use an abstraction of that strength to act on a third party which is not its prey.
2. The natural use of the deer's alacrity is for it to escape danger. It is unnatural for the deer to learn to use an abstraction of that alacrity by transporting anything else besides its own body.
3. The natural use of the fox's intelligence is for it to evade predators and capture its prey – it is manipulating firsthand survival data. It is unnatural for the fox to use that intelligence to analyze meta-data.
4. So too, the natural use of the human intellectual faculty would be learning Torah and understanding Hashem's universe[34] – intellectual gestures which gain their worth not by the utilitarian ends they achieve but rather by their very exercise. Humanity, however, is unable to survive through the exercise of pure intellect! Pure Mathematics cannot create a combine-harvester, only applied Mathematics and Engineering can. Thus it is only the human who cannot suffice by solely utilizing his faculties directly, but must resort to manipulating abstractions thereof.[35]

v. This then may be the "anguish" described in the Gemara – the anguish of being unable to be oneself, to be true to one's true identity and having to enslave one's natural, essential uniqueness to pragmatic necessities.

5. Natural Animal Subsistence vs. Humans' post-Sin

a. The Maharal states, "Thus, when human beings were created, no profession, clothing or building was created with them. Rather, they lived in the Garden of Eden without these things. If so, these activities are not part of human life due to our perfection (since animals make do without them and they subsist without these)."

b. The Maharal seems to prove that the reason that professions are a result of sin is because:

   i. We didn't need professions in Eden.

---

34. As the Maharal explains in N'tivot Olam, N'tiv Hatorah, Chapter 14.

35. On a deeper level, this may be related to the *type* of reasoning employed by Chavah when deciding to eat the forbidden fruit, which was almost entirely utilitarian (see B'reishit 3:6). It seems that she employed her intellect there in a purely utilitarian fashion, to analyze what the most *useful* action would be, as opposed to the most inherently moral. Perhaps this act was what stained human intellect, reducing it to being a utilitarian tool.

   - ii. Animals make do without them.
- c. The second part of this proof seems difficult! Just because animals make do without something doesn't render that thing a result of sin! Animals do not circumcise their young – does that make it a result of sin?
   - i. In fact, as the Maharal will explain in Chapter Two, that which is natural is below the level of the intellect, as he says there (specifically relating to circumcision), "This is as Rabbi Akiva proved to him from the wheat which is a function of nature but is lacking until it is completed by the intellectual human, from which you see that the functions of the intellect are above those of nature."
   - ii. Thus we see that the Maharal would view the act of baking bread (one of the professions he mentions above) as definitely being superior to eating plain wheat.
- d. What then is the Maharal's meaning here? We can glean some understanding of the Maharal's profundity from his comments on the Gemara in Kiddushin which serves here as the springboard for his thoughts:

חידושי אגדות, קידושין פ"ב:

פי' הפרנסה לאדם הוא קיומו, ואם היה אדם חסר פרנסה שהוא קיום מציאותו אין זה מפעולת הפועל שיפעל פעולה שאין לה קיום ועמידה, אבל מגדר הפועלה שלם שיהיה פעולתו בשלימות, ולפיכך נמצא בכל הנמצאים שיש להם פרנסה בלא טורח ובלא עמל כאשר ראוי, ומכ"ש היה ראוי דבר זה לאדם אשר הוא מבחר מן הנמצאים, וכן היה קודם שחטא האדם:

Chiddushei Aggadot, Kiddushin 82b

The explanation of this Gemara is as follows: the livelihood of a human being is his existence and if a person were lacking livelihood (which is the sustaining of his existence), this would not be the action of [Hashem] to perform an action which has no persistence and robustness.

Rather, the definition of the action of He who is Perfect[36] is that His action should be complete; therefore, all creations have a livelihood without worry and labor, as is suitable. Therefore, how much more so should this hold true for humanity which is the pinnacle of existence – and so it was before the sin of Adam [and Eve]."

   - i. Thus we understand here that the Maharal's comments (regarding something unnatural being the result of sin) are specifically limited to the sphere of self-sustenance.
      1. The fact that human beings do not seem to have as natural a method of self-sustenance as do animals is a serious theologi-

36. I.e., Hashem.

cal problem – it points to an absurdity – that G-d could possibly create an object which cannot subsist naturally.

ii. As we said above, it would seem that the question is that human subsistence is not attained through the unadulterated exercise of that which is uniquely human – the pure intellect – but rather, humanity must pervert the pure nature of the unblemished intellect in order to apply it to manipulating abstractions of the physical world, in order to attain self-sustenance. It is this which bothers the Gemara according to the Maharal – that the human being's intrinsic nature is not sufficient to sustain it.

iii. As the Maharal's final comments (cited above), "and so it was before the sin of Adam [and Eve]," prove, the comments that sin has caused the need for a profession are not directed to particular individuals, but rather to the human race.

e. If we examine the Gemara in Kiddushin, we find that the proof text which Rabbi Shimon uses says exactly this:

Your sins have abrogated [the laws of nature, so that you are punished with drought] and your sins have prevented you from receiving goodness.[37]

i. The idea is that there are laws of nature which should provide for human sustenance. That is what is natural. The only reason that such laws could be set aside, is human-generated evil.

6. Professions as a Result of Sin

a. The Maharal writes above, "Here we see that our rabbis explained that professions and trades which are performed by humans are not signs of the superiority of humanity but rather they flow from the diminution and lack [of perfection] which is found in humanity. Thus, when human beings were created, no profession, clothing or building was created with them. Rather, they lived in the Garden of Eden without these things. If so, these activities are not part of human life due to our perfection (since animals make do without them and they subsist without these). Therefore, these activities come to a person due to his imperfection [which is] due to his sinning and losing his livelihood – if he had not sinned, he would not need any profession."

b. There is much written on this topic by many of our sages – entire works have been devoted to this topic and thus we will cite just a few central sources.

i. Rabbi Shimon bar Yochai vs. Rabbi Yishma'el

37. Yirmiyahu 5:25, as per Rashi's comments.

ברכות לה:

תנו רבנן ואספת דגנך מה תלמוד לומר לפי שנאמר לא ימוש ספר התורה הזה מפיך יכול דברים ככתבן תלמוד לומר ואספת דגנך הנהג בהן מנהג דרך ארץ דברי רבי ישמעאל רבי שמעון בן יוחי אומר אפשר אדם חורש בשעת חרישה וזורע בשעת זריעה וקוצר בשעת קצירה ודש בשעת דישה וזורה בשעת הרוח תורה מה תהא עליה אלא בזמן שישראל עושין רצונו של מקום מלאכתן נעשית על ידי אחרים שנאמר ועמדו זרים ורעו צאנכם וגו' ובזמן שאין ישראל עושין רצונו של מקום מלאכתן נעשית על ידי עצמן שנאמר ואספת דגנך ולא עוד אלא שמלאכת אחרים נעשית על ידן שנאמר ועבדת את אויביך וגו' אמר אביי הרבה עשו כרבי ישמעאל ועלתה בידן כרבי שמעון בן יוחי ולא עלתה בידן.

B'RACHOT 35B

Our rabbis taught in a *B'raita*, "[The verse states] 'And you shall gather in your corn.'[38]

[The Gemara asks] What does this verse teach us?

[The Gemara answers,] Since the Torah states, "This book of the Torah shall not depart out of your mouth,"[39] I might think that this is to be taken literally [and that one should sit and study all day and not engage in a profession]; therefore, the Torah states, "And you shall gather in your corn,"[40] [which implies that] one should combine the study of Torah with a profession. This is the view of Rabbi Yishma'el.

Rabbi Shimon Bar Yochai states, "Is it possible that a man will plough in the ploughing season, and will sow in the sowing season, and will harvest in the harvesting season, and will thresh in the threshing season, and will winnow in the windy season? [If a person engages in this, his whole year will be taken up and then] what is to become of the Torah?

"Rather, [the ideal situation is as follows] when Israel perform the will of Hashem, their work is performed by others, as the Torah states, 'And strangers shall stand and feed your flocks . . .'[41] And when Israel do not perform the will of Hashem, their work is carried out by themselves, as it states, 'And you shall gather in your corn.'[42] Moreover, [when Israel is behaving incorrectly], not only do they have to do their own work, but they also do others' work, as it states, 'And you will serve your enemy.'"[43]

Abbayeh said, "Many have followed the advice of Rabbi Yishma'el, and have succeeded; others have followed Rabbi Shimon Bar Yochai, but were not successful."

---

38. D'varim 11:14.
39. Y'hoshu'a 1:8.
40. D'varim 11:14.
41. Y'shayahu 61:5.
42. D'varim 11:14.
43. D'varim 28:48.

1. The Gemara here presents two views, that of Rabbi Yishma'el and that of Rabbi Shimon Bar Yochai
    a. Rabbi Yishma'el's view is that one's life should be a combination of Torah learning and work.
    b. Rabbi Shimon Bar Yochai's view is that one should only study Torah and that if Israel, as a nation, fulfilled Torah and mitzvot appropriately, then sustenance would be provided for them by the other nations.
2. Neither of these views necessarily contradicts the Maharal's position as the Maharal is discussing the ideal position, before the sin of Adam and Chavah.
3. For a further discussion of this particular issue, see:
    a. The view of the Rambam in his: Commentary to Avot;[44] Yad, Laws of Torah Study.[45]
    b. The view of the Tashbetz.[46]

ii. The Ramban's view

רמב"ן על ויקרא פרק כו פסוק יא

והכלל כי בהיות ישראל שלמים והם רבים, לא יתנהג ענינם בטבע כלל, לא בגופם, ולא בארצם, לא בכללם, ולא ביחיד מהם, כי יברך השם לחמם ומימם, ויסיר מחלה מקרבם, עד שלא יצטרכו לרופא ולהשתמר בדרך מדרכי הרפואות כלל, כמו שאמר (שמות טו כו) כי אני ה' רופאך וכן היו הצדיקים עושים בזמן הנבואה, גם כי יקרם עון שיחלו לא ידרשו ברופאים רק בנביאים... אבל הדורש השם בנביא לא ידרוש ברופאים - ומה חלק לרופאים בבית עושי רצון השם, אחר שהבטיח וברך את לחמך ואת מימיך והסירותי מחלה מקרבך, והרופאים אין מעשיהם רק על המאכל והמשקה להזהיר ממנו ולצוות עליו: וכך אמרו (ברכות סד) כל עשרין ותרתין שנין דמלך רבה רב יוסף אפילו אומנא לביתיה לא קרא... והוא מאמרם (ברכות ס) שאין דרכם של בני אדם ברפואות אלא שנהגו, אילו לא היה דרכם ברפואות יחלה האדם כפי אשר יהיה עליו עונש חטאו ויתרפא ברצון ה', אבל הם נהגו ברפואות והשם הניחם למקרי הטבעים: וזו היא כונתם באמרם (שם) ורפא ירפא מכאן שנתנה רשות לרופא לרפאות, לא אמרו שנתנה רשות לחולה להתרפאות, אלא כיון שחלה החולה ובא להתרפאות כי נהג ברפואות והוא לא היה מעדת השם שחלקם בחיים, אין לרופא לאסור עצמו מרפואתו, לא מפני חשש שמא ימות בידו, אחרי שהוא בקי במלאכה ההיא, ולא בעבור שיאמר כי השם לבדו הוא רופא כל בשר, שכבר נהגו ועל כן האנשים הנצים שהכו זה את זה באבן או באגרוף (שמות כא יח) יש על המכה תשלומי הרפואה, כי התורה לא תסמוך דיניה על הנסים... אבל ברצות השם דרכי איש אין לו עסק ברופאים.

44. Avot 4:5.
45. Laws of Torah Study 3:10–12. See Kessef Mishnah ad loc.
46. Tashbetz 1:142–148.

Ramban on Vayikra 26:11

And the general rule is that when Israel are many and complete, *their affairs will not be managed by natural means*: not their bodies, their land, the whole community nor individuals. Because Hashem will bless their food and water and will remove all sickness from them until they have no need for doctors, *nor will they need to take any medical preventions*. This is what it says "For I am Hashem your healer."[47] And this is what the righteous people used to do at the time of prophecy – *even when a sin caused them to become ill, they did not go to doctors, rather they went to the prophets* . . . But a person who seeks Hashem will not seek doctors. In fact, how on earth can a doctor play any role in the life of one who does the will of Hashem? Hashem has promised that He will bless our food, water and remove sickness from us; while a doctor's key task is to supervise the intake of food and drink.

This is what the Gemara means in B'rachot,[48] "All twenty-two years that Rabbah Bar Rav Yosef was the *Nasi*,[49] they didn't call a doctor to his house." . . . And this is what the Gemara in B'rachot[50] means when it says that, "It is not the way of people to need doctors, but it has become the custom." It means that our way is not to need doctors – *people used to get sick as the punishment for a sin and people would get well by Hashem's will. However, nowadays that people have begun to use doctors, Hashem allows the random side of nature to affect them.* This is what the Gemara means there when it says that "permission has been given to the doctor to heal patients." *It doesn't say that permission has been given to patients to go to doctors!* Rather, since the patient has become ill and he comes to a doctor to get better (since he is not one of Hashem's chosen few) the doctor may not prevent himself from healing this person. The doctor may not fear the fact that the patient might die by his treatment (since the doctor is an expert) and the doctor may not say, "Hashem is the healer of all" and then refuse to heal the patient (since this person has already become accustomed to visiting doctors).

Therefore, after two people have been fighting and one has injured the other with his hand or with a weapon, the person who was injured gets compensation for the medical treatment he required, *because the Torah does not make its laws reliant on a miracle . . . but when Hashem is involved with a person's life, that person has no need for doctors.*

1. The Ramban paints a clear picture of whether a person need take practical, this-worldly steps for his own physical benefit. In

47. Sh'mot 15:26.

48. B'rachot 64b.

49. In Hebrew, נשיא, "*nasi*," meaning "officer" or "prince." The *Nasi* was the President of the Jewish Supreme Court, the Sanhedrin.

50. B'rachot 60a.

this case, the Ramban is addressing health and medicine, but presumably, his reasoning is general and applies to subsistence as well.

2. The Ramban explains that it all depends on the individual – if a person truly has a completely intimate relationship with Hashem and understands and lives the reality of Hashem's absolute control of the world and of nature's merely being a façade, then that is indeed the reality that he will experience and he would use spiritual input alone to address even physical needs.
3. On the other hand, if a person really chooses to view his life as being mainly constrained by the laws of the physical world and gives credence to nature and believes that natural law is real, then that will be his reality and indeed he will need to work for a living and go to doctors for healing.

7. Freedom of Choice

a. The Maharal's discussion of the status and uniqueness of humanity touches, albeit briefly, on the essence of how the Torah views man.

b. As the Maharal states later in Chapter Three, "This leads one to the difference between human beings and all the lower and upper creations. The transcendent [upper] beings have their perfection already actualized and thus they do not have any need to actualize it. The lower beings, except for humans, also have no actualization [of some potential perfection] since the state in which they were created is static and there is no change and no actualization.[51] But human beings alone *are* potential which can be actualized."

c. Furthermore, as the Maharal states later, at the beginning of Chapter Two, "The human being is the handiwork of the Holy one, Blessed be He, and humans are the chosen ones of all the lower creations, but they are [created] imperfect and they can [only] be perfected through their own actions . . ."

d. We understand therefore, that the purpose of human beings is to perfect themselves, but by their own choice. Thus, the placing of the metaphysical soul within the physical body of a human accomplishes two things:

   i. It creates the possibility for humanity to grow and become perfect – because we possess potential yet to be actualized (which is a nice way of saying we have both flaws and the ability to address them).
   ii. It places the choice for actualizing this possibility for growth within our hands. For if it were out of our hands, and our growth was as-

51. As the Maharal states a little later, the other lower creations (besides humanity) also possess some perfection, but it is inherent and in-built from the moment of their creation.

sured by Hashem's decrees, we would be no different from the angels and the other metaphysical beings.

e. Thus the fact that we can grow and the fact that this growth is volitional are completely interdependent. This explains why goodness cannot *automatically* flow from human beings but must rather be chosen.

8. Why Must There Be a Difference in Spiritual Potential between Different Human Beings?

a. The Maharal makes some statements here which are challenging.
   i. He says, "In fact, one is bound to say this because this world, in which the human species [lives], is a natural world. Therefore, it is fitting that the entire species be equal in the physical aspect [since the world is physical]; and if one finds differences in them due to the differences in geographical locations, these are not considered to be [qualitative] differences. But G-dliness is not found equally in the entire [human] species, for if it were, then this world would in fact be the transcendent [spiritual] world since G-dliness would be generally located in it. However, this world is the natural world [and not the spiritual world] and this requires that G-dliness not be found equally throughout the entire species, but only in a section thereof."
   ii. What does this mean? Why, if this world is a natural world, must there be qualitative differences between humans' spiritual potential but substantive similarity in their physical potential?

b. Possible answer
   i. Rabbi Hartman,[52] based on the Gur Aryeh,[53] explains that the Maharal's view is that the essence of an object is equally distributed within it. If so, since this world is essentially a physical world, physicality must be equally distributed within it. If spirituality were equally distributed within it, the world would no longer be physical, but spiritual.

c. Further exploration
   i. The status of the human being
      1. The Maharal states later in Chapter Three as follows, "This leads one to the difference between human beings and all the lower and upper creations. The transcendent [upper] beings have their perfection already actualized and thus they do not have any need to actualize it. The lower beings, except for humans, also have no actualization [of some potential perfection] since the state in which they were created is static and there is no change

52. Tiferet Yisrael, p. 35, fn. 53
53. Gur Aryeh, Vayikra 7:4.

and no actualization.[54] But human beings alone *are* potential which can be actualized."

2. We see that in the Maharal's view, human beings are an anomaly – a bridge between the transcendent world and the physical world – composed of both transcendent and physical components. The physical world is therefore not just some random stage on which the drama of life unfolds; rather, by definition, it is specifically created to be an environment where a being can exist in a state of potential actualization with the ability to choose to actualize its perfection or not, G-d forbid.

ii. Why then does the Maharal say that when it comes to physicality, humans must be essentially equal, but as regards their spiritual potential, they *must* be different? The answer is now clear.

1. There are three options for the type of reality humans could inhabit:
   a. Human are all solely physical beings, like all the other inhabitants of the physical world and are completely physical with no spiritual potential.
      i. This option is untenable, because as the Maharal explained (in the citation from Chapter Three), human beings, by definition, do have spiritual potential.

   OR

   b. Humans are all completely actualized and perfect – which would mean (as the Maharal explained above in the citation from Chapter Three) that they are all transcendent beings.
      i. Again, this contradicts the definition of a human being as one who is not completely actualized and therefore not completely transcendent, and therefore, this option must also be rejected.

   OR

   c. Human beings have variable spiritual potential.
      i. This is the only tenable option, which is what the Maharal accepts.

9. The Seventy Nations

a. The Maharal explains here that the reason that there were seventy gentile nations is because there were ten corresponding to each of the seven days of creation.
   i. As we saw in the Introduction, the Maharal explains that the number

54. As the Maharal states a little later, the other lower creations (besides humanity) also possess some perfection, but it is inherent and in-built from the moment of their creation.

seven represents physical perfection – reflecting the completion of all that was created in the seven days of creation.

b. Why were there ten created on each day?
   i. The Maharal, in G'vurot Hashem, says as follows:

גבורות השם יב

וזהו עשרה שנקראים רבוי . . .

G'vurot Hashem 12

. . . this is the number ten which indicates plurality . . .

   ii. Without delving into the Maharal's differentiation between the metaphysical concepts of unity and plurality,[55] it is clear that in the Maharal's view, the number ten is the embodiment of multiplicity which is the essence of the physical world.
   iii. Thus, combining the numbers ten and seven serves to concentrate the theme of physical perfection.

10. Understanding the Maharal's View of the Differing Spiritual Potential of Jews and Gentiles

a. The Maharal clearly states that there are differing spiritual potentials between Jews and non-Jews. He states it even more clearly in G'vurot Hashem, Chapter 72, as follows.

גבורות ה' ע"ב

הנה דבר ידוע אף כי ישראל והאומות הם שוים משתתפים בדבר הנגלה, ותראה שיש לכל בני אדם ראש ידים ורגלים אברים וגידין ובשר ופרצוף לאחד כמו השני, ואין חלוק ביניהם, אבל שלא יהיה שום חלוק בין ישראל לאומות בדבר הפנימי דבר זה אינו כלל, ואף חכמי האומות מודים בזה שיש לאומות מחולקות לכל אחת ואחת מזל בפני עצמו כמו שידוע מדבריהם. ואנו אין תולים החלוק הזה במזל וגלגל אבל אנו אומרים שיש לכל אומה ואומה שר מיוחד כמו שנזכר בכתוב (דניאל י:כ) שר פרס שר יון ובדברי חכמים הרבה, הרי כי האומות דביקים בכח מיוחד וישראל דביקים בכח קדוש הוא השם יתברך אשר הבדיל אותם מן העמים ולקחם אליו. ואין ספק כי יש לאומות הכנה פנימית שעל ידי אותה ההכנה מוכנים להתדבק בכח שלהם, ויש לישראל הכנה פנימית שעל ידי אותה ההכנה דביקים בו יתברך, ולכך אף אם כל בני אדם מתדמים בדברים המורגשים והחצונים מובדלים הם בכח פנימי . . .

G'vurot Hashem 72

Behold, it is well-known that Israel and the nations of the world share the revealed things. You will see that every human being has a head, arms, legs, organs, sinews, flesh and a face – each person has these and there is no difference between them.

55. For more details, see the full text from G'vurot Hashem 12.

However, there is no rule that Israel and the nations have no difference on an internal, spiritual level. Even the wise gentiles admit this – that different nations each have their own constellation[56] as is known from their words. However, we do not ascribe these differences to the zodiac and constellations; rather we say that every nation has a unique spiritual ministering angel, as is mentioned in the Torah,[57] "the ministering angel of Persia" and "the ministering angel of Greece." Such things are found numerously in the words of our sages.

Thus, the nations of the world bond with their special power and Israel bonds with its holy power which is Hashem, may He be Blessed, Who separated them from the nations and took them to Him. And there is no doubt that the nations have internal potential through which they are able to bond with their power; and Israel has an internal potential through which they bond with Hashem, may He be Blessed. Therefore, even if all humans resemble one another in perceptible, external things; they are separate as regards their internal potential.

b. It is impossible to explore the full length and breadth of the Torah's view of the distinctions between various nations. There is a sea of ideas in the halachic, philosophical and Kabbalistic realms and it is impossible to detail even a fraction of that here. However, there are some key points to delineate:
   i. Human beings are all created in the "likeness of G-d."[58]
   ii. A gentile who accepts upon him or herself the seven mitzvot which they are commanded by Hashem, gains the World to Come.[59] These mitzvot, according to the Rambam, are:[60]
      1. Prohibitions
         a. Idol worship
         b. Blasphemy
         c. Murder
         d. Sexual immorality
         e. Robbery
         f. Eating the limb of a living animal
      2. *Mitzvot aseh*
         a. Creation and maintenance of a legal system to enforce all of the above.

56. The Maharal refers to the belief that each nation had a representative sign of the zodiac which embodied the unique essence of that nation.
57. Daniel 10:20.
58. B'reishit 1:27.
59. Rambam, M'lachim 8:11.
60. Rambam, M'lachim 9:1.

11. "Essential Language and Selfhood"

a. The Maharal states, "This is the meaning [of the idea cited in the Midrash] that Hashem offered the Torah to each nation *but their essential language and selfhood* refuses to accept G-dly actions; only Israel was receptive to the Torah due to the level of their soul."
   i. The interesting point is that when describing the essence, so to speak, of a nation, he refers to "language" and "selfhood."

b. This idea, that "language" is somehow a determinant of the spiritual and moral make-up of a nation has its roots in the words of our sages in many places.
   i. As the Gemara says in Shabbat,[61]

שבת קיח:
אמר רב אלמלי שמרו ישראל שבת ראשונה לא שלטה בהן אומה ולשון . . .

Shabbat 118b

Rav said, "If Israel had just observed their first Shabbat [according to the requirements of the law], then no nation or language would have ruled over them."

   ii. Similarly, we say in our prayers on Festivals:

סדר תפלת שלש רגלים
אַתָּה בְחַרְתָּנוּ מִכָּל הָעַמִּים אָהַבְתָּ אוֹתָנוּ וְרָצִיתָ בָּנוּ וְרוֹמַמְתָּנוּ מִכָּל הַלְּשׁוֹנוֹת . . .

The order of the Prayer on the Three [pilgrimage] festivals

You [G-d] have chosen us from amongst all the nations. You have loved us and desired us and You have elevated us above all languages . . .

c. There are several salient and profound ideas to mention here, although they would require several works each to explore fully:
   i. Thought through language
      1. There is an age-old debate amongst philosophers and now psychologists and neurologists as to the primacy of language in allowing one to think at all.
      2. This has more recently become part of the debate regarding the Sapir-Whorf Hypothesis in linguistics. This hypothesis suggests that each language greatly determines the nature of thought of those people who speak it.

61. Shabbat 118b.

3. One clearly sees, implicit in the citations above and in the Maharal, that in the Torah's view, there is some substantial (and probably causal) relationship between broad national identity and language.[62]
4. An interesting statement in the Midrash[63] which perhaps supports this idea (to some degree) reads as follows:

מדרש תהילים מזמור לא

אמר ר' יונתן, שלשה לשונות [נאות] הן. לשון רומי, לקרב. לשון יוני, לדבר. לשון אשורית, לתפלה.

Midrash Tehillim 31

Rabbi Yonatan said, "There are three appropriate languages: Latin for war; Greek for speech; Ashurit for prayer."

ii. The Torah's view of cultural identity
1. Although one might be inclined to view the Torah's categorization of nations as based on "essential," immutable, transcendent spiritual differences, the ideas cited here mitigate somewhat against this approach.
2. It is very likely that when viewing the "identities" of nations, the Torah's view is that a large portion thereof is determined by their cultures and that such cultures are formed in large part through their language and mores. Such formative forces could be so powerful, as we briefly mentioned above, that an individual raised therein may be completely incapable of thinking in certain ways, as compared to a member of another culture.

12. The Torah as Marriage Document

a. The Maharal states, "due to the level of Israel's soul, they are receptive towards G-dly actions [in fact] they are particularly suited to them. However, idol worshipping [nations], due to their lack and diminution are not suited for [all the] G-dly actions, that is, mitzvot."
b. If we view this statement in light of the Maharal's extensive Introduction to Tiferet Yisrael and in light of the ideas we raised above, it becomes a lot clearer.

62. Two authors who explore these ideas (but in completely different contexts) are Samuel Huntington in his *Clash of Civilizations* (Simon & Schuster: 1998) where he posits language as one of the main factors in determining cultural affinities, and Oliver Sacks in his *Seeing Voices* (Vintage: 2000) where he explores the unique type of thinking of which deaf people are capable when taught Sign from an early age.

63. Midrash Tehillim 31.

i. As we explained in the Commentary, Introduction § Point 2, the Maharal views the Torah as the means for attaining intimacy with Hashem. On the other hand, he also says that without that intimacy, it is impossible to understand the Torah correctly.

ii. This addresses a common misapprehension of the nature of Torah. The Torah is not a text or a document to be read, understood, memorized, analyzed and summarized **only**. As our sages explain[64] regarding Moshe's breaking of the two tablets upon seeing the Jews worship the golden calf:

מדרש רבה שמות פרשה מו פסקה א

משל לשר שנטל אשה וכתב לה כתובה ונתנה ביד השושבין לאחר ימים יצא עליה שם רע מה עשה השושבין קרע את הכתובה אמר מוטב שתהא נדונית כפנויה ולא כאשת איש כך עשה משה אמר אם אין אני משבר את הלוחות אין לישראל עמידה.

Midrash Rabbah Sh'mot 46:1

This can be compared to a prince who married a woman and wrote her a marriage document and gave it to his counselor. After some time, a rumor [of infidelity] began to circulate about her – so what did the counselor do? He tore up the marriage document, saying, "It is better that she be judged as a single [as yet unmarried, promiscuous] woman and not as a married woman."

This is what Moshe did. He said, "If I do not break the tablets, Israel will have no chance to withstand [the judgment]."

1. Here we see a classical example where the Torah is compared to a marriage document – a vehicle for creating intimacy.
2. The implications of this are that one cannot view the Torah solely as an information-bearing text, but rather as the outgrowth and concretization of a relationship of love. As such, without access to that relationship, it becomes impossible to relate to the Torah correctly.

iii. Furthermore, the common metaphor used by the prophets for Israel's forsaking of the Torah is that of a spouse committing adultery, abrogating the covenant of marriage. As the prophet Y'shayahu says:[65]

ישעיה פרק א: כ"א

אֵיכָה הָיְתָה לְזוֹנָה קִרְיָה נֶאֱמָנָה מְלֵאֲתִי מִשְׁפָּט צֶדֶק יָלִין בָּהּ וְעַתָּה מְרַצְּחִים.

64. Cited in Rashi, Sh'mot 34:1.
65. Y'shayahu 1:21.

Y'SHAYAHU 1:21

How has the *faithful* city become a prostitute? Once she was filled with law, justice rested in her; but now [she is filled with] murderers!

c. Against this background, it becomes clear that the acceptance or rejection of Torah is not so much an acceptance or rejection of an externally imposed morality and of a chunk of information, but rather is comparable to the acceptance or rejection of a marriage partner, as it were. In the arena of marriage, one chooses one's spouse out of a deep sense of affinity of ideals, hopes, values and love. Thus, in the case of the nations and Israel, the question is whether there is a relationship with Hashem or not, prior to the presentation of the Torah, the marriage document. It is this relationship which determines their respective attitudes to Torah which is what is at the heart of what the Maharal is explaining.

d. As we explored in the previous point, these attitudes are deeply ingrained in the cultural fabric of each nation, which culture deeply affects part of the identity of most of the individuals reared in its embrace.

13. The Maharal's Attitude Towards Converts

a. The Maharal makes some very challenging statements regarding converts. He says, "And despite this, our sages said, 'Converts are as bad for Israel as a *sapachat* plague.' This is because a *sapachat*'s nature is that it itself is not good and it destroys the body's flesh (which has a good nature)."

b. It is enough to bear in mind that the great Rabbi Akiva,[66] who sustained the entire Jewish world after the destruction of the Second Temple, was held to be a descendant of converts, as was King David,[67] and as will be the Mashiach[68] (who will be a descendant of King David), to realize that the Maharal's statements cannot be read simplistically.

   i. Moreover, there are laws relating to the fact that one is forbidden from even mentioning to a convert the fact that he or she was once a convert.

      1. We learn,

בבא מציעא ד:י

...כך אונאה בדברים... אם הוא בן גרים לא יאמר לו זכור מעשה אבותיך שנאמר וגר לא תונה ולא תלחצנו:

66. B'rachot 27b and Rav Nissim Ga'on (ad loc.).

67. King David was a direct descendant of Rut (Ruth) who was originally a Moabite. For further reference, see Rut 4:17–22.

68. Messiah.

Mishnah Bava M'tzia 4:10

. . . So too there is speech which is considered, halachically, to be verbal abuse. For example . . . if a person is descended from converts, one is forbidden to say to him, "Remember your ancestors' deeds!" since the Torah states, "You may not verbally abuse a convert and you may not oppress him."[69]

   2. This is cited as Halachah in the Rambam.[70]
   3. Thus we must delve deeper into the Maharal's words.

c. It is important to understand the comparison cited fully.
   i. The Gemara compares converts to a *sapachat* plague. However, what is left implicit is that the Jewish people are the body on which the *sapachat* plague is found. This would mean that such a body is afflicted with the biblical *tzara'at*, often mistranslated as "leprosy." Thus, the Jewish people here are being depicted as being a *m'tzora* (one who has *tzara'at*).
   ii. Any person who was a *m'tzora* was not held to be in the best of spiritual states, the plague being a warning to the person to mend his ways in particular areas; to whit, speaking badly of other people.[71]
   iii. Thus the comparison of converts to a *sapachat* and of the Jewish people to a body which has contracted *tzara'at* is flattering to neither party. In fact, the *sapachat* is a result of a problem within the soul of the *m'tzora*.

d. The Maharal explains his position further in his D'rosh al Hatorah.

דרשות המהר"ל - הקדמה לדרוש על התורה

באין ספק כל הטוב שזוכים ישראל אליו הם זוכים מצד שהם בני אברהם יצחק ויעקב או מצד שהם אשר בחר בם אל, והגרים מבטלים דבר זה. לכך נקרא הגר ספחת שהוא דבר תוספת וטפילה על האדם והיא מבטלת עיקר תאר צלמו עד שאינו נחשב אדם שלם, כי האדם בצלמו ובתבניתו אין תוספת עליו ואין גרעון בו כלל . . .

Introduction to the Sermon on the Torah

There is no doubt that all the goodness which Israel merits, they merit due to their being descendants of Avraham, Yitzchak and Ya'akov and due to their being the nation which G-d chose.

But converts invalidate this [principle]. Therefore, a convert is said to be a "*sapachat*"[72] [which is a type of skin growth] since such a *sapachat* is an addition to a human being and is adjoined to a human being; therefore,

---

69. Sh'mot 22:20.

70. M'chirah 14:15.

71. See Rashi on Sh'mot 4:6, where Moshe, our teacher, *zt"l*, contracted *tzara'at* due to speaking ill of the Jewish people.

72. This is the "plague" mentioned in the Tiferet Yisrael above.

the *sapachat* invalidates the essential concept of the blueprint of the human being to the point that he is no longer considered a whole human being because a human being (from the point of view of the essential blueprint and of his structure) has no addition nor any omission at all.

i. We see from the Maharal here that he sees that the concept of anyone being allowed to add themselves onto the Jewish people must imply some sort of lack in the Jewish people. It is possible to understand that the implication of this is that the reason that converts can join the Jewish people is because there is some lack or imperfection which is what creates the possibility of the convert joining the Jewish people. There are, however, other ways to understand the Maharal.

ii. Thus we see that the Maharal's understanding of the maxim, "Converts are as bad for Israel as a *sapachat* plague,"[73] may be that the very fact that they can join the Jewish people shows that there is an imperfection within the Jewish people which is what is negative about the process.

iii. This idea is borne out by the simple understanding (as we cited above) of the comparison of the Jewish people to a *m'tzora*.

iv. See the Maharal's Netzach Yisrael (Chapter 32) for a wider exploration of these ideas. There he explains the necessity of including certain converts in Israel as revolutionary catalysts for national growth.

73. Niddah 13a.

COMMENTARY SECTION

Chapter 2

1. **Circumcision is Equivalent to the Whole Torah**
   a. The Maharal writes, "Therefore, circumcision was given to the human since it is his [beginning of] perfection [which is performed] on the eighth day because any perfection of the human is above nature and therefore circumcision, which is a human's perfection and which transcends nature, is equivalent to all the Torah."
   b. This statement is perhaps an entrée into the many statements of our sages to the effect that certain mitzvot are "equivalent to the all the mitzvot" or literally, "weigh the same as all the mitzvot."[1]
      i. It would seem that the idea is that *milah*, circumcision, is so pivotal to the entire world outlook of Torah that although Torah has many other necessary parts, *milah* undergirds the entire structure, almost as if it were a structural pillar, without which the entire superstructure would crumble.
      ii. Indeed, the Maharal uses *milah* as an archetype of the world of mitzvot in establishing three essential factors which he sees as being critical to understanding the purpose of Torah and mitzvot:
         1. The product of the act of a human being can be superior to that which exists naturally, without human intervention.
         2. When compared to humanity, nature is flawed and requires perfection.
         3. Mitzvot enable humans to transcend the physical world.
      iii. It would seem no co-incidence that Avraham, the progenitor of the Jewish people, received only one commandment for posterity – that of *milah* – since it exemplifies the entire world of mitzvot and Torah.
   c. The Maharal explains further in his Chiddushei Aggadot as follows:

חדושי אגדות חלק שני - מסכת נדרים

ששקולה כנגד כל המצות. גם דבר זה מבואר, וזה מפני כי כל המצות אינם רק שיהיה ברית וחבור בין הש"י ובין האדם, כי כל התורה היא הברית כאשר יודע, והמילה עצמה היא הברית ג"כ בין השם יתברך ובין האדם, ולכך המילה וכן השבת הם שקולים כנגד כל המצות. ואולי אם יאמר שכל זה קשיא, למה המילה ברית בין השם יתברך ובין האדם, כבר התבאר זה כי ראוי שתהיה התורה שהיא שלימת האדם . . . לכך אלו הם ברית בין השם יתברך והאדם, כי הברית הוא הצירוף והחיבור שיש בין השם יתברך ובין

1. N'darim 25a and M'nachot 43b regarding *tzitzit* and N'darim 32a regarding *milah*.

האדם . . . ויש ברית מצד המילה כי המילה השלמה לאדם מצד הגוף, וכל אחד השלמה בפני עצמו, כי התורה היא השלמה שכלית, השבת השלמה לנפש, המילה השלמת הגוף, ודבר זה יש לך להבין מאוד. וכאשר אלו הג' הם בשלימות, אז יש כאן ברית וחבור לאדם עם השם ית' מצד השלמת האדם:

Chiddushei Aggadot, N'darim 32a

[*Milah*] is equivalent to all the mitzvot. This is also clear since [the purpose of] all the mitzvot is only in order that there be a covenant and a bond between Hashem, may He be Blessed, and human beings. [This is] because the entire Torah is a covenant, as will be understood; and *milah* is itself also *the* Covenant[2] between Hashem, may He be Blessed, and humanity. Therefore, *milah* and Shabbat[3] are equivalent to all the mitzvot.

If a person will ask, "Why is *milah* a covenant between man and Hashem, may He be Blessed?" [The answer is that] it has already been explained that it is suitable that the Torah should be the perfection of a human being . . . therefore, it is suitable that these[4] be covenants between Hashem, may He be Blessed, and humans, because a covenant is a joining and a bond between Hashem, may He be Blessed, and humanity . . . and there is a covenant through *milah* because *milah* is the perfection of humanity from the point of view of the body. And each of these[5] is a perfection in and of itself: the Torah is *sichli* perfection, Shabbat is perfection for the soul, and *milah* is the perfection of the body. One should understand this well. When these three aspects are perfected, then there is a covenant and bond between humanity and Hashem, may He be Blessed, through the perfection of humanity.

i. The Maharal explains that the Torah, Shabbat and *milah* each confer a particular type of perfection on humanity, and in that perfection, a human being is able to partake in the infinite perfection of the Perfect one, Hashem; thus a bond and covenant is forged between finite man and Hashem.
ii. Thus, *milah* represents the entire purpose of Torah and mitzvot: to bond with Hashem.
iii. This parallel is further extended through the fact that both the Torah and *milah* exist at the eighth level. The Torah has the various associations with the number eight (as the Maharal described at the beginning of the chapter) and *milah* takes place on the eighth day.

---

2. The full title of *milah* is actually ברית מילה, "*b'rit milah*," "the covenant of circumcision," as per B'reishit 17:13.
3. Shabbat (the Jewish Sabbath) is also a covenant – as per Sh'mot 31:16.
4. I.e., Shabbat and *milah*.
5. The Torah, Shabbat and *milah*.

d. The Maharal's final point above is quite striking. He understands Rabbi Akiva as reversing his previous arguments and claiming that even if it were true that human actions were not superior to anything natural and that furthermore nature was not flawed, nevertheless, we would still perform mitzvot despite this. Why?

e. The Maharal explains that the purpose of our lives is to achieve transcendence – for us to reach above the physical-only world (into which we are born) so as to possess a spiritual life. This means that we need to perform acts which are not only-natural, we need to perform acts that are above nature, that are metaphysical.

f. *Milah* is such a perfect example of this because on the face of it, unlike the umbilical cord, the foreskin does not seem to be a hindrance and thus it is a clear symbol of the Torah's drive to enable humans to perform acts not entailed by natural necessity, but rather entailed by the striving for infinity.

COMMENTARY SECTION

Chapter 3

1. A "Thought of *Pigul*"

a. The Maharal refers to the belief that human beings have already actualized all their potential, as a "thought of *pigul*."

b. *Pigul* is the term which refers to a sacrifice offered in a particularly unacceptable manner.[1] That is, while the animal is being sacrificed, the owner has the intention not to complete the sacrificial process within the maximum proscribed time.[2] The term has connotations of being something abominable and revolting.

c. The idea of eating the sacrifice is that the very physical act is actually an act of service of Hashem. The Maharal is using this as a parallel to one's daily life. A person who believes that his maximum allotted time requires no active investment of effort is quite similar to one who does not see the necessity of serving G-d (through physical service of eating the sacrifice) within its maximum allotted time. Both display the casual belief that time is not really of the essence and that greatness may be achieved without any real investment of effort.

2. "Strides amongst the Standing [Angels]"

a. This quote from Z'charyah 3:7 is a wonderful encapsulation of the dichotomy the Maharal is explaining. As the Radak explains on the verse, angels "stand," meaning they are static and unchanging and exist forever. Human beings on the other hand are constantly in flux and are in a constant state of conversion of potential good into actual good – we are striding forward – or the opposite, G-d forbid.

b. It is a contradiction to be striding amongst these standing beings – in the spiritual world, all is actualized, striding is not possible. The idea is, however, that a human being who reaches such a high level is exactly that – one who has not always been there, but one who has made huge strides to get there.

3. The Perfection of the Animal Kingdom

a. The Maharal writes above, "This is to say that some perfection is found in it and even if it is not absolute perfection, nevertheless, this thing is found within it."

---

1. Vayikra 7:18, 19:7.
2. See Rambam, *P'sulei Hamukdashin* 13:1.

b. A more correct translation of this phrase is: "The perfection of a thing over which it is created, is within an animal, even though it is not a complete perfection, nevertheless, it is within it." The Maharal makes use of the phrase, "over which it is created" several times and its meaning is not clear to me.

c. The Maharal clarifies the meaning of this section in the *D'rosh* (sermon) on the Torah.

דרוש על התורה

. . . לא כן מסודרים בבריאתם על ענין זה כל שאר נבראים, שאינם בכח ויוצאים לפעל, כי כל מה שראוי שיהיה בהם נמצא בם מיד כשנבראו. ולכך נקראת היותר עצמות שבהם בהמה, כלומר בה מה כי מה שראוי שימצא בה הרי הוא מתחלה בה. שאם נברא השור לחרוש והחמור לישא משא הרי נמצא בהם בהבראם, ואין דבר בה בכח שיצא אחר כך אל הפעל . . . כי דמיון גמור יש לאדם אל האדמה. כי כמו אשר האדמה נזרע בתוכה חטים וכל מיני זרע נקי וטוב ונשרשים בה תוך העפר ומוציאה צמחיהם, כן נתן השי"ת הנשמה הטהורה והזכה חלק א-להי ממעל בגוף האדם ונשרשת שם ומוטבעת בגוף כאשר מוטבע החטה באדמה. ואם אין האדם מוציא צמחיו ופירותיו הטובות, אזי ידמה אל אדמה בורה ושדה בלתי נזרעת. ולכך החליטו חכמים לאשר איננו בעל תורה כנוי בור כשהוא כמו אדמה בורה שהובירה ואינה מוציאה דבר . . .

D'rosh al Hatorah

The other creations are not ordered in this manner in the same way [that human beings are] since the other creations are not categorized as having potential being actualized since everything that is suitable for them is found in them immediately when they are created. Therefore, the most independent of these lower creations is called "*b'heimah*," that is to say, "*bah mah*," that whatever is suitable to be within it is found in it from its very inception. For if the ox was created to plough and the donkey to bear loads, these capabilities are found within them when they are created and there is nothing in potential within them which needs to be transformed later into actuality.

There is an absolute analogy between humans and the earth. Just as the earth is sown with wheat and any good, clean seed which becomes rooted in the soil will thereafter produce its growth [from the soil], so too, Hashem, may He be Blessed, placed a pure and clean soul, a G-dly portion from above, within the body of a human and it takes root there and is imprinted on the body just as wheat is imprinted within the earth.

And if a person does not produce his growth and good fruit, he is compared to barren earth and to an unsown field. Therefore, our sages decided that one who possesses no Torah is called a "*boor*"[3] since he is like "*adamah boorah*"[4] which is barren and does not produce anything.

3. The English term is similar – a "boor."

4. I.e., barren earth.

4. Static Perfection?

a. The Maharal says of a human being, "He should never entertain any libel within his soul by saying that he should remain idle and he will nevertheless succeed eternally, rather his success will only be through observing the Torah and mitzvot."

b. There is something viscerally more attractive in the picture painted by Turnus Rufus[5] of a human being born perfect. The Maharal, however, disabuses us of this seeming attractiveness. Our very imperfection, our very flaws endow us with the ability to chart our own course towards self-perfection, towards our creation of ourselves. A static existence leaves a human's awesome and infinite potential barren and unutilized.

c. The Torah's contention (according to the Maharal) is that the *only* way for a person to reach true fulfillment is through active transformation of his potential perfection to actuality through the living of Torah and mitzvot.

5. Purposes of life

a. Citing the Gemara, the Maharal raises three possibilities as options for the purpose of human life:
   i. to perfect the physical;
   ii. to perfect inter-human verbal communication;
   iii. to perfect the verbal communication of Torah.

b. General comments
   i. The tendency would be to view these three options as being mutually exclusive. However, from what we have already learned in Tiferet Yisrael, it is clear that this is *not* the Maharal's position.
      1. In the debate with Turnus Rufus
         a. In Chapter Two, the Maharal cited the Midrash relating the debate between Turnus Rufus and Rabbi Akiva. In this Midrash, the concept of perfecting the physical is used as the paradigm for the approach of the Torah to life.
         b. Unlike the Greeks, we do not view the physical world as perfect in and of itself and we believe it must be perfected through human intervention. This is the first and most basic level of human interaction with the world but one which is definitely valid, required and desired; one which we encapsulate in the concept of *milah*, circumcision.
      2. Further, as the Maharal already said in the Introduction,

הקדמה לתפארת ישראל

ואמר הנחמדים מזהב ומפז רב פי' כי המצוה יש בו שני דברים, האחד שהמצוה טוב לאדם הגופני שדבר זה מבואר לכל שכל המצות שהם בתורה הם להשלים תקון האדם

5. Above in Chapter Two.

עד שהאדם הוא בטוב, והשני שהשכל ג"כ מחייב המצות מצד סוד שכלי . . . ועל טוב הגופני שהתורה מעמיד הכל בטוב כי התורה תקרא טוב עז"א ומתוקים מדבש ונופת צופים שזה עריבות גופני.

Introduction to Tiferet Yisrael

King David continues and says that the mitzvot are "more desired than gold, even more than much fine gold, sweeter also than honey and the honeycomb." The explanation of this is that there are two elements to a mitzvah: firstly, a mitzvah is good for a person physically (this is clear to everyone that the purpose of all the mitzvot in the Torah *is to complete the perfection* of a human until a human is in goodness) and secondly, the mind requires mitzvot from the perspective of an intellectual secret . . . But regarding the physical goodness which the Torah brings (for the Torah must bring goodness in all spheres since it is called "good"), the Tehillim says that the Torah is "sweeter also than honey and the honeycomb," which relates to physical sweetness.

   a. It is clear that the Maharal views "physical" perfection as part of the result of living the Torah.
   b. Something which must be emphasized is that the Torah's understanding of "perfection of the physical" is radically different from that of Greek or other philosophies even if they concur practically in certain areas.

3. Lastly, as we will see later, in citations from the N'tivot Olam of the Maharal, he explicitly states that he does not view these three as mutually exclusive.
4. Thus, it is clear that the Maharal's view is that these three purposes are not mutually exclusive. One's immersion in Torah should, as the Maharal put it, "bring goodness in all spheres" and that will include the sphere of interpersonal communication as well as the physical. Thus all three purposes will be achieved through Torah.
5. The question which the Gemara seems to be debating is which one of these three purposes is primary. One could ask how any goal, but the ultimate – Torah – could ever be considered?
   a. The Maharal suggests above that a possible rationale for even considering the first two options is that they are less transcendent and more finite than Torah and thus more attainable.
   b. In any event, the Maharal opines that humanity is not tasked with either of the two easier options but with the infinite, intangible option which never sates the soul completely – perfecting the world through the Torah. Whereas

many would be confounded and disheartened by such a task,[6] the Torah views it as the only one appropriate to the infinite potential within the human soul. Any lesser task would simultaneously entail a downgrading of human potential. Thus, not only is such a view non-tragic, it is, in fact, ultimately uplifting and redeeming.

c. At this point, we would like to spend a little time examining each of the three possible goals.
   i. Physical, bodily perfection
      1. How could this be the ultimate purpose of humanity?
         a. We raised the possibility above that the reason that consideration is given to this option is that it is more finite and attainable.
         b. The Maharal himself relates to this question in his Chiddushei Aggadot as follows:

ספר חדושי אגדות- מסכת סנהדרין

וג' דברים אמר עמל מלאכה עמל שיחה עמל תורה, וזה כי האדם יש בו נפש חיוני נפש המדברת נפש שכלי. ואמר שאל יחשוב האדם שלימתו האחרון הוא נפש החיוני שבאדם ... גם אל יחשוב כי שלימות האחרון שלו נפש המדברת, אבל שלימתו האחרון הוא הנפש השכלי הוא התורה:

Chiddushei Aggadot – Sanhedrin 99b

[Rabbi Eli'ezer] mentioned three options [for the purpose of life], the "toil of work," the "toil of communication" and the "toil of Torah."

[These three parallel the spiritual components of a human being.][7] A person has a vital soul, a verbal soul and a *sichli*-soul.

[Rabbi Eli'ezer] said that a person should not err in thinking that a human's final perfection is attained through the vital soul in a person . . . [He] also [said that one should not err] in thinking that a person's final perfection is attained through the verbal soul. Rather, a person's final perfection lies through the *sichli* soul, which is the Torah.

---

6. This could be easily reminiscent of the stories of the "tragic" Greek characters, Sisyphus and Tantalus; except that unlike Greek philosophy, the Torah does not engage in "tragedy" in the literary sense. Rather, the Torah views humanity as being tasked with becoming as G-dly as possible despite the fact that Hashem is infinite and beyond our grasp. Our reaction to this infinite goal is to feel uplifted by the fact that our potential matches that infinity – we are ebullient and overjoyed by the possibilities within each human being and our potential for greatness which makes us fit for an infinite goal.

7. See the Maharal's comments on the composition of the human soul in Chapter One and our comments in the Commentary, Ch. 1 § Point 2.

i. The Maharal explains here that there are three primary components of the human soul.

ii. The most basic component is the vital, animalistic soul which animals also share.[8] Despite this commonality, however, the Maharal has already taught us that only humans possess latent potential and thus only humans could perfect this animal soul; animals themselves cannot.

iii. We thus understand that this option – perfection of the physical world – is not some banal, hedonistic concept; rather it concerns the perfection of the spiritual precursor of physicality.

c. In N'tivot Olam, the Maharal writes:

נתיבות עולם א - נתיב התורה - פרק טו

ואמר איני יודע אם לעמל מלאכה אם לעמל שיחה, כלומר אם השלמת האדם במלאכה שהוא השלמת נפש החיוני בלבד, כמו שהוא אצל הבהמה שיש לה נפש חיוני והיא נבראת לעשות מלאכה, או שנברא אל עמל הפה פירוש השלמת נפש המדברת.

N'tivot Olam, *N'tiv Hatorah* 15

And Rabbi Eli'ezer stated,[9] "One might not know whether the verse refers to the toil of one's mouth or to the toil of work." The question here is whether the perfection of humanity will be through work which is the perfection of the vital soul *only*, similar to animals which possess a vital soul and which were created to perform work; or whether a human being was created for verbal toil, that is, to attain the perfection of the verbal soul . . .

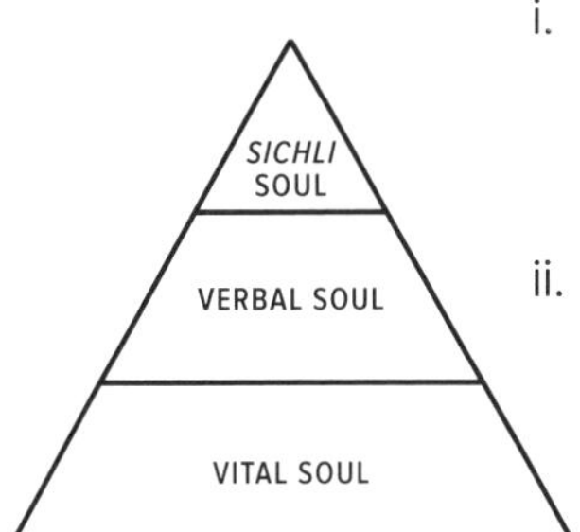

i. The use of the word "only," here, is tremendously instructive. The Maharal is saying that Rabbi Eli'ezer's question is whether to perfect the vital soul ***only*** or ***also*** to perfect the verbal soul.

ii. This may imply that the three levels are built in a pyramid, each layer resting on that beneath it.
   1. The bottommost layer is the vital soul.
   2. The next layer is the verbal soul which rests on the vital soul.
   3. The top layer is that of the *sichli* soul which rests on both of the previous two.

iii. In any event, the Maharal understands that at each level, there is a need to perfect the level in question and everything that preceded it.

8. As explored in the Commentary, Ch. 1 § Point 2.

9. In the Gemara cited in the Maharal above.

- ii. Verbal inter-human communicative perfection
    1. How could this be the ultimate purpose of humanity?
        a. As per the general approach outlined above, it could be that the argument which the Maharal proposes on behalf of even considering this as an option is that it is less transcendent and more attainable than its ultimate alternative.
            i. However, it seems that there could be a deeper possibility here. Please see the section below dedicated to the discussion of these ideas.
        b. The Maharal discusses this option in greater detail in N'tivot Olam, *N'tiv Hatorah*:

נתיבות עולם א - נתיב התורה - פרק טו

ועוד אמר ועדיין איני יודע אם השלמה הזאת השלמת נפש המדברת מצד הדבור בלבד, או אם השלמתו מצד התורה שהוא השכל הא-להי. ועל זה אמר כשהוא אומר לא ימוש ספר התורה הזה מפיך הוי אומר כי השלמתו הוא מצד הנפש המדברת והיינו בתורה, כי בזה יושלם האדם לא מצד הדבור בלבד...

N'tivot Olam, *N'tiv Hatorah* 15

Rabbi Eli'ezer said further,[10] "[We agree that the purpose of life is verbal toil, but] I am still unsure as to whether this perfection should be the perfection of verbal soul from the aspect of speech only, or if its perfection should be from the aspect of the Torah, which is the G-dly intellect. Regarding this, he responded that when the verse states, "This book of the Torah shall not depart from your mouth and you will think of it day and night,"[11] it implies that indeed, human perfection is through the verbal soul but specifically through the aspect of Torah. Through this, a human will be perfected and not *only* through the aspect of speech . . .

        c. The use of the word "only" here, as above, is once again tremendously instructive. The Maharal is saying that Rabbi Eli'ezer's question is whether to perfect the verbal soul through pure inter-human communication or if, *in addition*, such communication must be Torah communication.
    2. The Maharal has already mentioned some of his views on the issue of verbalization in general, and in particular, verbalization of Torah, in the Introduction to this work. In the Commentary, Introduction § Point 2, we cited several sources relating to his halachic ideas on the subject.

10. In the Gemara cited in the Maharal above.
11. Y'hoshu'a 1:8.

iii. Torah
   1. The verse cited here is, "This book of the Torah shall not depart from your mouth and you will think of it day and night."[12]
   2. Often it is beyond our abilities to understand our Sages' deductions from verses in the Torah, but if we examine the context of each verse cited in a Midrash or Aggadah to see how the verse, in context, relates to its didactic purpose in the Midrash or Aggadah, we can sometimes understand their train of thought.
   3. The context here is the first chapter of the book of Y'hoshu'a (verses 1 to 9).

ספר יהושע פרק א : א-ט

וַיְהִי אַחֲרֵי מוֹת מֹשֶׁה עֶבֶד ה׳ וַיֹּאמֶר ה׳ אֶל יְהוֹשֻׁעַ בִּן נוּן מְשָׁרֵת מֹשֶׁה לֵאמֹר: מֹשֶׁה עַבְדִּי מֵת וְעַתָּה קוּם עֲבֹר אֶת הַיַּרְדֵּן הַזֶּה אַתָּה וְכָל הָעָם הַזֶּה אֶל הָאָרֶץ אֲשֶׁר אָנֹכִי נֹתֵן לָהֶם לִבְנֵי יִשְׂרָאֵל: כָּל מָקוֹם אֲשֶׁר תִּדְרֹךְ כַּף רַגְלְכֶם בּוֹ לָכֶם נְתַתִּיו כַּאֲשֶׁר דִּבַּרְתִּי אֶל מֹשֶׁה: מֵהַמִּדְבָּר וְהַלְּבָנוֹן הַזֶּה וְעַד הַנָּהָר הַגָּדוֹל נְהַר פְּרָת כֹּל אֶרֶץ הַחִתִּים וְעַד הַיָּם הַגָּדוֹל מְבוֹא הַשָּׁמֶשׁ יִהְיֶה גְּבוּלְכֶם: לֹא יִתְיַצֵּב אִישׁ לְפָנֶיךָ כֹּל יְמֵי חַיֶּיךָ כַּאֲשֶׁר הָיִיתִי עִם מֹשֶׁה אֶהְיֶה עִמָּךְ לֹא אַרְפְּךָ וְלֹא אֶעֶזְבֶךָּ: חֲזַק וֶאֱמָץ כִּי אַתָּה תַּנְחִיל אֶת הָעָם הַזֶּה אֶת הָאָרֶץ אֲשֶׁר נִשְׁבַּעְתִּי לַאֲבוֹתָם לָתֵת לָהֶם: רַק חֲזַק וֶאֱמַץ מְאֹד לִשְׁמֹר לַעֲשׂוֹת כְּכָל הַתּוֹרָה אֲשֶׁר צִוְּךָ מֹשֶׁה עַבְדִּי אַל תָּסוּר מִמֶּנּוּ יָמִין וּשְׂמֹאול לְמַעַן תַּשְׂכִּיל בְּכֹל אֲשֶׁר תֵּלֵךְ: לֹא יָמוּשׁ סֵפֶר הַתּוֹרָה הַזֶּה מִפִּיךָ וְהָגִיתָ בּוֹ יוֹמָם וָלַיְלָה לְמַעַן תִּשְׁמֹר לַעֲשׂוֹת כְּכָל הַכָּתוּב בּוֹ כִּי אָז תַּצְלִיחַ אֶת דְּרָכֶךָ וְאָז תַּשְׂכִּיל: הֲלוֹא צִוִּיתִיךָ חֲזַק וֶאֱמָץ אַל תַּעֲרֹץ וְאַל תֵּחָת כִּי עִמְּךָ ה׳ אֱ-לֹהֶיךָ בְּכֹל אֲשֶׁר תֵּלֵךְ:

Y'hoshu'a 1:1–9

It was after the death of *Moshe*, the servant of Hashem. Hashem said to Y'hoshu'a, son of Nun, "*Moshe*, *My servant*, has passed away. And now, get up! You and all this nation must cross over this Jordan [river]! [And go to] the land which I am giving to them, the children of Yisrael. Every place on which the sole of your foot treads, I will give to you as I spoke to *Moshe* – from the desert and this Lebanon until the great river, the Euphrates, all the land of the Hittites until the great sea [in the west, where] the sun sets [all this will] be your border. No man will stand before you all the days of your life; as I was with *Moshe* I will be with you, I will not let go of you and I will not abandon you. Be strong and courageous because you will cause this people to inherit the land which I swore to their forefathers to give to them. Only be very strong and courageous to be careful to behave according to all the Torah which *Moshe* my servant commanded you. You must not deviate from it to the right or left in order that you will succeed in all [the ways] that you go. *This book of the Torah shall not depart from your mouth and you will think of it day and night*. Have I not commanded you, "Be strong and

12. Y'hoshu'a 1:8.

courageous"? [Therefore,] do not fear and do not be frightened because Hashem, your G-d, is with you in all [the ways] that you go.

a. With this context, the use of the verse in the Midrash is clarified.
b. The verses emphasize that Moshe, through whom we were given the Torah, Moshe, the servant of Hashem, is gone. Y'hoshu'a has large shoes to fill. Indeed, Y'hoshu'a has to conquer the entire land and give it to the children of Israel. His job would seem to be completely physical, pure conquest, as opposed to the task of Moshe, which was to teach (as we name him, *Moshe Rabbeinu*, Moshe, our teacher).
c. However, Hashem's message to Y'hoshu'a is clear. He will need much courage and strength but not in the area in which one would presume initially. He will need the courage and strength to ensure that he behaves completely in accordance with the Torah and to guarantee that its words never leave his mouth and mind. In the midst of what might have seemed to be a purely mundane and possibly violent life – conquest – Hashem teaches Y'hoshu'a that especially there, when engaged in acts which seem to be totally physical, the task of the Jew is to be meditating on and expressing the words of Hashem.
d. This hearkens back to the Maharal's opinion (above) that the living of a Torah lifestyle will bring success and perfection in the physical realms as well, and it paints the picture of a person who may indeed be immersed in this mundane world, yet whose purpose in life is to create a spiritual internet of humanity, bridged by the hypertext of inter-human, Torah communication.

4. Elsewhere in his works, the Maharal writes extensively on the importance of the verbalization of Torah. We cite these ideas in the following point.

6. The concept of Verbalizing Torah

a. The Maharal's view of the marriage of Speech and Torah, independent of speech as communication
   i. The Maharal explains his views on the verbalization of Torah in N'tivot Olam[13]:

13. N'tivot Olam, *N'tiv Hatorah* 4.

ספר נתיבות עולם א - נתיב התורה - פרק ד

ובכיצד מעברין (עירובין נ"ד ע"א) אמר רב אסי מ"ד כי נעים כי תשמרם בבטנך אימתי דברי תורה נעימים כי תשמרם בבטנך ואימתי תשמרם בבטנך בשעה שיכונו יחדו על שפתיך ר' זירא אמר מהכא שמחה לאיש במענה פיו אימתי שמחה לאיש בשעה שמענה בפיו רבי יצחק אמר כי קרוב אליך הדבר מאוד בפיך ובלבבך לעשותו אימתי קרוב אליך הדבר מאוד בפיך בזמן שבפיך ובלבבך לעשותו רבא אמר מהכא תאות לבו נתת לו וארשת שפתיו בל מנעת סלה אימתי תאות לבו נתת לו בשעה שארשת שפתיו בל מנעת סלה, פירוש דבר זה שבא לומר כי נעימות התורה כאשר התורה נמצאת אצל האדם בפועל כי אז האדם הוא שכלי כאשר התורה הוא עמו ואין נעימות למעלה מזה. וזהו כאשר אין התורה משתכחת ממנו, ואימתי אין התורה משתכחת מן האדם ונמצאת עם האדם כאשר דברי תורה על שפתיו תמיד שהוא למד בהם וחוזר עליהם ואז התורה עמו, ובלא זה לפי ריחוק התורה מן האדם אין נחשבת שהתורה היא עמו רק אם התורה היא על שפתיו אבל מי שלמד בעיון אין השכל עם האדם שהוא גשמי. ור' זירא למד דבר זה מדכתיב שמחה לאיש במענה פיו, כי ראוי שתהיה התורה השלמת האדם כי אין לאדם השלמה כי אם בתורה כמו שהתבאר למעלה כי לכך נקראת התורה אשה כי גם האשה השלמת האדם, ואי אפשר זה רק כאשר האדם בעל תורה בפועל כי הדבר שהוא בכח אינו נחשב שהוא נמצא, ולא נחשב שהוא בעל תורה בפעל השלימות רק אם תכף שישאל אותו האדם משיב על זה ובזה נראה שהוא בעל תורה בפעל השלימות, וזה שאמר שמחה לאיש במענה פיו, כי כל שמחה כאשר הוא שלם ואין לו חסרון ומפני השלימות נמצא השמחה, והפך זה ההפסד גורם אבל ותוגה שהרי יש אבל על מת שהוא הפסד. ומפני שהתורה שלימות האדם ועל ידה הוא שלם בפעל לכך אמר הכתוב שמחה לאיש במענה פיו, ר"ל כי שלימותו היינו שתכף מיד שישאל אותו האדם בדברי תורה תכף משיב לו ואצל זה התורה נחשב נמצא בפעל השלימות ואז התורה שמחה לו ר"ל שהתורה היא שלימותו שכל שמחה מצד השלימות, ולא כשמגמגם בדברי תורה כי אצל זה אין התורה בפעל רק בכח שצריך התלמיד חכם לחפש בספרים ממילא על ידי זה אינו נחשב שלם בפעל. ויש לפרש כמשמעו, כי האדם שלם בפעל כאשר התורה היא על שפתיו ומוציא הדבור אל הפעל זה נקרא שהוא בפעל כאשר מוציא התורה אל פעל הדבור, ועל זה אמר שמחה לאיש כי השמחה על השלימות והשלימות כאשר הוא בפעל וזהו כאשר מוציא התורה אל פעל הדבור, אבל ר' יצחק למד מן קרוב הדבר בפיך ובלבבך לעשותו, ודבר זה מצד אחר כי כאשר האדם התורה הוא בפיו ורגיל בה קרובה התורה לעשות אותה, כי גדול תלמוד תורה שמביא לידי מעשה וזהו כאשר התורה עמו, וכבר אמרנו למעלה שלא נחשב שהתורה עמו רק כאשר התורה היא עמו בדבור וכאשר התורה היא עמו אז קרוב גם המעשה. ודבר זה אנו רואים בעינינו שמיום שבטל דבר זה לא נמצאו בעלי מעשה והכל הוא הסבה הזאת. וכן לרבא הוא גם כן מצד אחר כי כאשר התורה עמו האדם קרוב אל השם יתברך מצד שהוא בעל תורה ואז בקשתו נעשה וכדכתיב ומי גוי גדול וגו'. כל הדברים אלו הם דברים גדולים וכל אחד מן החכמים נתן טעם מיוחד בפני עצמו, הראשון שאמר כי על ידי שהתורה עמו נחשב האדם שכלי אבל אם אין התורה עמו אין נחשב שכלי, וכן למאן דאמר כי כאשר התורה עמו הוא בפעל השלימות ואינו בכח כמו שהם כל עליונים שהם בפעל, וכן למאן דאמר כי כאשר התורה עמו הוא בפעל השלימות קרוב לעשות התורה וכלם הם דברים גדולים כאשר תבין הדברים על אמתתם: ועוד אמרו שם אמר ליה שמואל לרב יהודה שיננא פתח פומך תני כי היכי דתוריך חיין ותתקיים בידך שנאמר כי חיים הם למוצאיהם ולכל בשרו מרפא אל תקרי למוצאיהם אלא למוציאיהם בפה עד כאן. גם בזה בא לבאר באיזה ענין

יהיה למוד התורה ואמר שלמוד התורה אין ראוי שיהיה במחשבה בלבד רק בדבור. וזה מפני כי האדם הוא חי מדבר דכתיב (בראשית ב') ויהי האדם לנפש חיה ותרגם אונקלוס והוה אנשא לרוח ממללא, והתורה שעליה נאמר (דברים כ"ט) כי היא חייך ואורך ימיך כאשר מוציא התורה בדבור שהוא חיות האדם ואז הדבור שהוא החיים של אדם דבק בתורה שהיא אורך ימיו של אדם ועל ידי זה מאריך ימים. אבל אם עוסק בתורה על ידי המחשבה בלבד והמחשבה מקבל התורה, אין המחשבה היא החיים אצל האדם שיקבל על ידי התורה אורך חיים, רק כאשר מוציא התורה בפה שהוא הדבור שהוא חיים של אדם אז בוודאי דבק בתורה שהוא אריכות ימיו של אדם על ידי הדבור שהוא חיותו של אדם, וראוי להבין זה מאוד. ואמר ותתקיים בידך, דבר זה מבואר כי כאשר מוציא התורה לפעל על ידי הדבור ובשביל זה יש קיום אל התורה, כי אז יש לתורה זאת דביקות אל האדם עצמו שהוא חי מדבר, אבל כאשר הוא עוסק בתורה במחשבה בלבד כאילו אין האדם עצמו עוסק בתורה כי אין המחשבה הוא האדם רק הדבור. ולפי הנראה אין צריך לברך כלל על התורה כאשר עוסק במחשבה. ועוד כאשר מוציא הדבור מן הפה מקבל כח הזוכר את הדבור ונרשם בכח הזוכר כאשר מוציא הדבור מן הפה. לכך אמרו שם שיהיה העוסק בתורה מדקדק בלשונו שכאשר מדקדק בלשונו אז תורתו מתקיימת. וזה אמרם בני יהודה שהקפידו על לשונם תורתם מתקיימת בידם בני גליל שלא הקפידו על לשונם לא נתקיימה בידם. ומפרשים שם מתוך שהקפידו על לשונם מתנחי להו סמנים ונתקיימה תורתם בידם, דאמרינן שם אין התורה נקנית אלא בסימנים, כי צריך האדם להניח סימנים בתורתו ועל ידי זה התורה נתקיימת בידו כי אז נרשם הענין שלמד בכח הזוכר בשביל הסימן וזוכרו. ודבר זה עצמו הטעם שצריך להוציא הדבור מן הפה כי אז נרשם הענין שלמד בכח הזוכר המקבל.

N'tivot Olam, *N'tiv Hatorah* 4

In the chapter, "How does one make an *Eiruv*," we learn:[14]

The Gemara is discussing the excellence of Torah and how to preserve it within oneself. There are four opinions. The first is Rav Asi who says that Torah is only pleasant when it is "attached to one's lips."

> Rav Asi said, "What does the verse mean when it says, 'For it is a pleasant thing if you keep the words of the sages within your innards – let them be firmly attached together to your lips'?[15] [It means as follows.] When will the words of the Torah be pleasant? When you guard them in your innards! And when will you [manage to] guard them within your innards? At the time that they are firmly attached together to your lips!"

Rabbi Zeira says that Torah is only pleasant when one has the ability to respond immediately to a question on Torah.

> Rabbi Zeira said, "We learn this lesson from a different source – 'A person has joy through his mouth's response; and how good is a word spoken at

14. Eiruvin 54a.
15. Mishlei 22:18.

the right time!'[16] When does a person have joy? At the time that he has a response on his lips!"

Rabbi Yitzchak says that one must ensure he puts the Torah into practice.

Rabbi Yitzchak said, "[I disagree! We learn this lesson from a different verse as follows,] 'For the word[17] is very close to you – in your mouth and heart – to do it!'[18] When is the word very close to you in your mouth? At the time when it is in your mouth and heart to perform it!"

Rava says that Torah learning allows one to approach Hashem and achieve closeness to Him.

Rava said, "[I disagree! We learn this lesson from a different verse as follows,] 'You have given him the desire of his heart and have not withheld the utterance of his lips. Selah!'[19] When have you given him the desire of his heart? At the time that You have not withheld the utterance of his lips!"

The Maharal will now explain his deeper understanding of each of these views. He says that the first two views – those of Rav Asi and Rabbi Zeira – focus on the degree to which Torah is actualized within a person.

The explanation of this concept [according to the first opinion, that of Rav Asi] is that it comes to teach that the pleasantness of the Torah exists when the Torah is found in a person in actuality [as opposed to potential alone] for only then is a person considered to be *sichli*, that is when the Torah is with him. There is no pleasantness higher than this. But this is only true when the Torah is not forgotten by the person [who has learned it] and it thus exists with that person, which can only happen when the words of Torah are always on his lips – that he learns them and revises on them – and only then is the Torah with him. But without this, due to the distance of the Torah from the person, the Torah is not considered to be with him except if the Torah is on his lips. However, the Torah is not with one who [only] learns intellectually [without verbalization], since human beings are physical.[20]

---

16. Mishlei 15:23.
17. Lit., "thing."
18. D'varim 30:14.
19. Tehillim 21:3.
20. The Maharal seems to be saying that since the Torah is cerebral, there can

Rabbi Zeira [the second opinion] learned this same principle from the verse, "A person has joy through his mouth's response; and how good is a word spoken at the right time!"[21] For it is suitable that the Torah should encompass the perfection [and completion] of a person, for a person has no perfection except through Torah . . .[22] Therefore, Torah is also known as "a woman" since a woman also completes a man. But this [happiness due to the completion conferred by Torah] cannot exist except if a person is the owner of the Torah in actuality – for something which exists only in potential is not considered to exist [fully] – and a person is not considered to be the owner of the Torah in actuality until [he has reached the stage where] if someone asks him [a question regarding Torah], he is able to respond to that question [immediately]. In this way, he can be seen to be the owner of Torah in actual completion. This is what Rabbi Zeira [meant when he] said, "A person has joy through his mouth's response" because happiness exists when one is complete without lacking, and due to the completion, happiness exists. The opposite of this is loss which causes mourning and grief since there is mourning over the departed person who is now missed. And since the Torah is the completion [and perfection] of a person, through which he is perfected in actuality; therefore, the verse said, "A person has joy through his mouth's response," meaning, that his perfection exists through his ability to respond immediately when asked a question regarding Torah matters.

In this way, the Torah is considered to exist in actual perfection and then the Torah "is a joy to him," which means that at that point, the Torah is his perfection, since all happiness derives from perfection.

But when a person stammers over the words of Torah, it is not the case, since the Torah doesn't exist in actuality, only in potential, since the scholar needs to search [for the answer] in books – therefore, automatically he is not considered to be complete [and perfect] in actuality. And here one can explain as per the [simple] meaning [of Rabbi Zeira's statement] that a person is complete in actuality when the Torah is actually on his lips and he verbalizes the speech [taking it from potential] to actual. This is termed "actual existence," when he transfers the Torah [from potential] to

---

be no bridge between the physical human being and the cerebral Torah without verbalization creating such a connection.

21. Mishlei 15:23.

22. See later on in our citation from the Introduction to Tiferet Yisrael where the Maharal explained that happiness is an indication of being in a state of completion and wholeness; whereas sadness and mourning, G-d forbid, are due to loss and incompletion. The verse quoted here by Rabbi Zeira speaks of the happiness that a person experiences through Torah, which the Maharal links to the completion bestowed on a person by Torah.

the actuality of speech. Regarding this, Rabbi Zeira said that it is a joy to a person, because the joy derives from completion [and perfection] which exists in actuality but which only happens when he transfers the Torah to the actuality of speech.

Till this point, the Maharal has explained that both the statements of Rav Asi and Rabbi Zeira teach virtually the same lesson – that Torah only completes a human being when it exists in actuality, something that can only happen when a person has the ability to verbalize what he has learned. Rabbi Zeira adds that this requires a person to be able to remember all his learning and respond immediately as well. The Maharal now explains that the last two opinions – that of Rabbi Yitzchak and Rava – focus on the degree to which the Torah can be said to be part of a person.

However, Rabbi Yitzchak learned the idea from the verse, "For the word is very close to you – in your mouth and heart – to do it!"[23] This idea approaches the concept from a different angle.

When the Torah is in a person's mouth and he is familiar with it, it is close to being fulfilled, since "Studying the Torah is great because it brings one to performance [of the mitzvot]."[24] But this only happens when the Torah is with a person. We have already stated above that the Torah is only considered to be with a person when it accompanies a person in his speech; and when it is indeed with him, then the performance [of its mitzvot] is also at hand. We see this matter with our own eyes because since the day that this idea was nullified there have no longer been any people of action[25] and everything is due to this reason.

So too for Rava [except] he approaches the concept from a different perspective. He says that when the Torah is with a person, he is close to Hashem, may He be Blessed, due to the fact that the person is an Owner of Torah, and then such a person's requests are fulfilled as it is written, "For what great nation exists to which G-d is so close [to accept their prayers;] as is Hashem our G-d whenever we call to Him?"[26]

The Maharal summarizes the four opinions we have seen.

All of these ideas are weighty concepts and every one of the sages gave a unique reason in and of itself. The first[27] said that through the Torah being with him, a person is considered *sichli*, but if there is no Torah with

23. D'varim 30:14.
24. Kiddushin 40b.
25. Meaning, people who are exceptional in their performance of mitzvot.
26. D'varim 4:7 as per the translation of Unkelus.
27. Sage, i.e., Rav Asi.

him, he is not considered *sichli*. So too, the one[28] who said that when the Torah is with a person, he has actual perfection and not [only] potential perfection, which renders him similar to the transcendent beings which exist in actuality. So too, the one[29] who said that when the Torah is with a person, he has actualized perfection and is close to performing [the mitzvot of] the Torah. And all of these are great matters when you understand their truth.

The Maharal now examines another citation from the Gemara in Eiruvin which discusses the life-lengthening effects of Torah. The Maharal explains that for this to happen, there is an absolute need for the Torah to be verbalized. This is due to the essence of humanity which is defined through the faculty of speech.

They said further there,[30]

> Sh'mu'el said to Rav Yehudah, "Sharp one! Open your mouth and learn so that [your Torah] will endure within you and so that your life will be lengthened, as the verse says, 'For they[31] are life to those who find them and they are a remedy for all his flesh.'[32] [Sh'mu'el continued,] you can read the word "to those who find them"[33] with an alternative vowelization, as, "to those who verbalize them."[34]

Here, too, Sh'mu'el comes to explain how to learn Torah and he says that it is unsuitable that Torah learning be done through one's thoughts alone, but rather it must be verbalized. This is because the human being is a speaking life form. As it is written, "And the human being became a living soul,"[35] which Unkelus translates as, "And the human being became a speaking soul."[36] And the Torah [is described through the verse] "For it[37] is your life and the length of your days."[38]

---

28. Rabbi Zeira.
29. Rabbi Yitzchak.
30. In the Gemara Eiruvin 54a. Our version of the text varies slightly.
31. I.e., The words of Torah.
32. Mishlei 4:22.
33. In Hebrew, למוצאיהם, "*l'motzayhem.*"
34. In Hebrew, למוציאֵיהם, "*l'motz-i-ayhem.*"
35. B'reishit 2:7.
36. Op. cit. With variations.
37. I.e., the Torah.
38. There seems to be a printer's error in the text of the Maharal which cites D'varim 29 as the source. The phrase which the Maharal uses here is not in D'varim 29. There is a similar phrase in D'varim 30:20, "לְאַהֲבָה אֶת ה' אֱ-לֹ-הֶיךָ לִשְׁמֹעַ בְּקֹלוֹ וּלְדָבְקָה בוֹ כִּי הוּא חַיֶּיךָ וְאֹרֶךְ יָמֶיךָ", which means, "To love Hashem your G-d – to listen

[And the Torah possesses this power only] when a person verbalizes it through speech, which is the life-essence of a human being. At that point, speech, which is the life-essence of a human being, is bonded to the Torah, which is the length of his days, and through this, the person's days are lengthened. However, if one is immersed in Torah in thought alone, and one's thought receives the Torah, the Torah cannot bestow length of days [in such a situation] because thought is not the life-essence of a human being. But only when a person verbalizes Torah through speech (which is the life-essence of a human being) will a person definitely bond to Torah. This [process] is the lengthening of days of a human being though speech which is the life-essence of a human being. And it is suitable to understand this well.

The Maharal continues explaining the second statement in the Gemara above, which states that the Torah endures within a person when they verbalize it.

[In the Gemara above, Sh'mu'el continued] ". . . so that [your Torah] will endure within you." This matter is clear, for when a person transfers the Torah from potential to actuality through speech, the Torah gains endurance, because then this Torah has a bond to a human being itself who is a living, speaking being. However, when a person immerses himself in Torah through thought alone, it is as if a person himself is not immersing himself in Torah because thought does not define a person, speech does.

It seems [to me] that one doesn't need to make a blessing at all over the Torah if one is only immersing himself in Torah through thought.[39] Moreover, when one enunciates the speech from his mouth, he also attains the power to remember that which is spoken and the speech is inscribed in the faculty of the memory when a person verbalizes the speech. Therefore, they[40] said there[41] that a person who is immersing himself in Torah should be exact in his pronunciation for when he is, his Torah will endure.

This is what they said[42] "The Torah of the people who lived in Judah (and who were exact with their verbalization [of Torah]) endures, while the Torah of those who lived in the Galilee (and who were not exact in their verbalization,) does not endure." They explain there that since they

to His voice and to bond with Him. For it [lit., "He"] is your life and the length of your days . . ." The Ibn Ezra (ad loc.) brings those who understand this verse to refer to the voice of Hashem, i.e., the Torah, even though he and others disagree.

39. This is how the Shulchan Aruch, Orach Chaim 47:4 rules. See the Commentary, Introduction § Point 2.

40. Our sages.

41. Eiruvin 53a.

42. Eiruvin 53a.

[the people of Judah] were exact in their verbalization they were able to create mnemonics. As we say there,[43] "The Torah is only acquired through mnemonics." For a person must create mnemonics for his Torah through which it will endure within him; for if he does, the matter he learned is inscribed in the faculty of memory through the mnemonic and he thus remembers the matter. This is itself the reason that a person must verbalize [his Torah] through his mouth for then the matter he learned is inscribed in the receptive faculty of memory.

- ii. In the above selection, the Maharal explains, through two different citations from the Gemara, the reasons that one should verbalize one's Torah learning.
    1. From the first Gemara there are three clear ideas:
        - a. The Torah should exist within a person as actuality and not just potential.
            - i. The Maharal explains the views of Rav Asi and Rav Chisdah in this fashion.
            - ii. In his view they are both explaining that when Torah is verbalized by a person it becomes actualized. There is a large chasm between physical human beings and the Torah, which is *sichli* and is from the transcendent world. Therefore, the only way that one can ensure that the Torah exists within one is by verbalizing it – thus bridging the transcendent and physical worlds.
            - iii. Furthermore, if one has complete recall of one's Torah and one is able to verbalize any part of one's Torah immediately, it is even more present and actual.
        - b. The Torah should be so integral to a person that it is expressed in his actions as mitzvot.
            - i. One should be verbalizing Torah to the point that its ideas are so vivid that they are expressed as actions.
        - c. A person needs the Torah to be intimately close to him in order to be able to be close to Hashem.
            - i. The only way that a person can really acquire Torah is when it is constantly on his lips.
            - ii. This acquisition allows one to approach Hashem.
    2. The second Gemara introduces two ideas:
        - a. The verbal faculty is the life essence of humanity and must be married to the Torah which is the life essence of the world, in order to prolong one's life.
            - i. The Maharal's analysis of the essence of humanity

43. Eiruvin 54b.

1. Based on the Unkelus he cited above, the Maharal posits that the essence of humanity is the faculty of speech.

ii. The Torah itself is life-prolonging.

iii. When the Torah's life prolonging force is married to the human being's faculty of speech, the Torah has the power to touch that human essence and add life to it.

iv. Thus the human being gains endurance.

b. The verbal faculty allows the transfer of Torah from its potential state to an actual state thus giving it, in a sense, life.

i. Here it is the Torah which gains endurance.

ii. Moreover, it is stored in a human memory which is aided in its storage by the verbalization of Torah.

iii. The sum of these ideas

1. Taking the sum of these ideas produces a tremendously detailed vista of profound ideas.

2. In the Maharal's view, verbalizing one's Torah is part of a process to:

a. Transfer one's Torah from potential to actuality.

b. This transfer via the faculty of speech creates a life-giving bond between the Torah and the essence of the speaker and simultaneously gives the Torah an actual existence as it is stored in the speaker's memory.

c. This bond enables a person to bring the Torah to an even higher level of actualization as it is constantly on his mind and he is able to recall its details instantly and at this level of presence, the Torah affects one's actions so that they are constantly expressions of Torah.

d. At this level, a person acquires the Torah and thus gains an intimate closeness to Hashem.

e. This brings us back to the Introduction of this work where the Maharal taught that the Torah is the primary means to achieve bonding with Hashem. The Maharal has now explained why – since Torah connects the essence of a human to Hashem.

b. Torah speech as communication

i. Till this point, the Maharal has discussed the issue of verbalization of Torah without regarding this verbalization as a communication between two human beings but rather simply as a medium for enhancing one's own experience of Torah and closeness to Hashem. This is not to say that he does not examine the communicative aspect. We will examine this briefly.

ii. The discussion of the S'fat Emet[44] on the power of speech is a good basis for understanding the Maharal's views on the marriage of speech and Torah. We first cite two sources from B'reishit (Genesis) and Unkelus (the Aramaic translation of the Torah) which the S'fat Emet utilizes and which the Maharal cited above:

ספר בראשית פרק ב:ז

וַיִּיצֶר ה' אֱ-לֹקִים אֶת הָאָדָם עָפָר מִן הָאֲדָמָה וַיִּפַּח בְּאַפָּיו נִשְׁמַת חַיִּים וַיְהִי הָאָדָם לְנֶפֶשׁ חַיָּה:

B'REISHIT 2:7

Hashem-Elokim[45] created the human from the dust of the earth and He blew into his nostrils a breath of life and the human became a living entity.

תרגום אונקלוס שם

וברא ה' א־להים ית אדם עפרא מן אדמתא ונפח באפוהי נשמתא דחיי והות באדם לרוח ממללא:

UNKELUS'S TRANSLATION OF THE VERSE: B'REISHIT 2:7

Hashem-Elokim created the human [from] the dust of the earth and He blew into his nostrils a breath of life and the human became a speaking entity.

שפת אמת ספר ויקרא - פרשת בהר - שנת [תרס"ד]

דהנה עיקר יתרון המדבר מב"ח מה שיש להם צוותא זה לזה ע"י הדיבור . . . והוא מכח הנפש. וצריכין לשמור זה הכח שלא ישתנה ע"י כוחות הגוף. כי מצד הנפש כל הנפשות יש להם שורש אחד. ולכן בהר סיני שנעשו בנ"י אחדות א' כמ"ש כאיש אחד בלב אחד וקיבלו התורה כמ"ש מורשה קהלת יעקב. וכתי' אמרתי אלהים אתם. שהי' גובר כח הנפשות על הגוף. וכמו מה"ש שאין בהם קנאה ושנאה ותחרות שכל אלה מכוחות הגוף שהגופות מחולקים.

S'FAT EMET VAYIKRA – B'HAR 5664

Now the main advantage of Humans' power of speech over animals is the ability it gives us to *join together [in a society], which only happens via our speech* . . . and this ability to speak is derived from the power of the soul.

One needs to guard this power so that it should not become tainted through the powers of the body. [This is] because, from the perspective of the soul, all souls have one common root. Therefore, at Mount Sinai, when the children of Israel became one unity (as it says, "as one man with

---

44. The classic work of the second Gerrer Rebbe.

45. This is a combination of two of Hashem's names: Hashem and Elokim. Their individual and combined connotations are beyond the scope of this work.

one heart")[46] they received the Torah (as it says "Moshe commanded us the Torah, it is the inheritance of the congregation of Ya'akov").[47] And as it states, "I said, 'You are powerful spiritual forces.'"[48] [This verse refers to the receiving of the Torah] when the power of their souls overcame that of the body. They were like the angels who have no jealousy, hatred or competition since all of these are due to the body's forces, *since only physical things are separated.*

1. We see from the S'fat Emet that he views the ultimate superiority of human beings over animals in the human ability to use speech and communication to create unity. The reason that such unity confers superiority upon the human is that this unity is the underlying reality of the universe. Ultimately, all of creation is unified, since Hashem is one being and is the true source and matrix of all that exists, as the Midrash says, "Hashem is the place of the world but the world is not His place."[49] However, the only reason that it *seems* to humans that all is not unified is due to the fact that we are partly physical and it is the existence of the physical which causes separation. In fact, the S'fat Emet seems to indicate that this is indeed the purpose of the physical, to mask the ultimate unity of all that exists (allowing us to choose to reveal it).
2. Thus, when humans use their power of speech to overcome the superficial distinctions between them and to join to another being, they reflect their common spiritual heritage, since all human souls derive, ultimately, from one soul. This act demonstrates the ultimate reality of the universe and rips away the mask of the physical. This is indeed the purpose of creation of the universe. Thus through speech, humans have the potential to actualize the purpose of the world and it is this which confers upon them their superiority over the animal kingdom.

iii. We find similar sentiments in the Maharal, as follows.
   1. N'tivot Olam, *N'tiv Hatorah*

נתיבות עולם - נתיב התורה - פרק ו

כי כאן מדבר שהם מקשיבים כל אחד לדברי חבירו ונותן לבו על דבריו לכך הקדוש ברוך

---

46. See Rashi, Sh'mot 19:2. This phrase describes the level of unity attained by the Jewish people when they assembled at Mount Sinai to receive the Torah.
47. D'varim 33:4.
48. Tehillim 82:6.
49. B'reishit Rabbah 68:9.

הוא שומע לקולם גם כן . . . כי המקשיבים זה לזה יש להם חבור ביחד ביותר שמקשיבים זה לזה וכל אחד נותן לב על דברי חבירו וכאשר אין עושים כך כמו שהם דוחים החבור כך הקדוש ברוך הוא מסלק השכינה ונפרד מישראל, ודבר זה מבואר. ועוד כאשר הם נוחים זה לזה בתורה ומקשיבים זה לזה בתורה הם נעשים אחד לגמרי על ידי התורה שהיא אחת, וכאשר אינם מקשיבים זה לזה להיות מתחברין ביחד וכאלו היה חס ושלום חלוק בתורה לכך השכינה מסתלק מישראל, כי אין השכינה עם ישראל רק בשביל כי נתן להם תורה שהיא אחת לכך הקדוש ברוך הוא שהוא אחד הוא עם ישראל . . .

N'tivot Olam, *N'tiv Hatorah* 6

. . . here we are addressing a situation where two Torah scholars are each listening to the words of the other and each of them is giving his heart over the words of his fellow;[50] therefore, Hashem also listens to their voice . . . for those who listen to one another have an exceptional bonding with one another and each one is giving his heart[51] to the words of his companion. But when they do not behave in this way, just as they reject the bond with one another, so too Hashem removes His presence and is separated from Israel, and this is clear.[52]

Moreover, when these two scholars are pleasant to one another in their Torah learning and they listen to one another in Torah, they thus become absolutely unified through Torah which is one. But when they do not listen to one another to bond with each other, it is as if, G-d forbid, there is disunity in the Torah and therefore, the divine presence departs from Israel because the divine presence can only be in Israel through the agency of the giving of the Torah which is one, by virtue of which the Holy One, Blessed be He (who is One) is with Israel . . .

2. Here we find the Maharal echoing the words of the S'fat Emet in greater detail.
   a. The Torah is the agency through which humanity can con-

50. We have translated the phrase literally since its imagery is so evocative – the meaning of the phrase is that each one of the Torah scholars is paying attention to his fellow's opinion.

51. I.e., paying attention.

52. The intention is not that Hashem is behaving punitively, but as we explore later in the Maharal (in the Commentary, Ch. 5 § Points 4 and 5), that human beings have the ability to generate positive and negative consequences in the physical and spiritual worlds. The result of this power is that if a person creates a spiritual reality for himself consisting of disunity, separation and dissolution, this reality actually exists. It can be so powerful that if a person chooses not to have Hashem as part of their lives, Hashem will not be there as far as that person can perceive, G-d forbid (although Hashem is always there in ways that a person cannot perceive). Here, the idea is that if the two Torah scholars create disunity, they create an environment antonymous to Hashem, the ultimate unity.

nect with the transcendent and infinite which is simple and unified to a point unachievable in the fractious, physical world.

b. The very joining of two scholars, not through the adoption of identical views, *but through the validation of each other's different views*, is what truly brings G-d's presence into this world – it is an act which shows that beyond the seeming disunity of this world, underlying it all is Hashem's Torah, the blueprint of creation,[53] revealing the ultimate order and unity of the world.

c. When one combines all these ideas, it is breathtaking to see the breadth of the Maharal's vision of the entanglement of the verbal faculty, the communicative faculty and the Torah: a tripod upon which true intimacy with Hashem can be achieved.

7. The Midrash Cited which Relates the Parable of the Townsman and the Princess

a. "The soul will never be filled"
   i. Yearning is the expression of lack
      1. The Maharal expands on this in the Introduction to Tiferet Yisrael, where he writes,

תפארת ישראל, הקדמה

ואח"כ אמר שעוד מביאה התורה את האדם אל המדרגה שהיא משמחת לב, פי' שנחשב האדם שהוא מציאות שלם על ידי התורה, ולכך היא משמחת לב האדם, שכאשר האדם הוא בשלימות הוא בשמחה והפך זה כאשר הוא בחסרון הוא באבילות, ולכך כאשר קרה לו המיתה מן שאר בשרו הוא באבילות.

Tiferet Yisrael, Introduction

Afterwards, King David says that the Torah further brings a person to a level where it gladdens one's heart. The explanation of this is that when a person is complete, he is happy, and the opposite of this is when a person is in a state of lacking something – which is when he is, G-d forbid, in mourning. Therefore, when death visits one of his close relatives, G-d forbid, a person mourns.

   ii. The full text of this verse is completely appropriate even if the Midrash omits it. It reads:

53. See the Maharal later on, in Chapter Four in the Commentary, Ch. 4 § Points 4 and 5 for an expansion of these ideas.

קהלת ו:ז
כָּל עֲמַל הָאָדָם לְפִיהוּ וְגַם הַנֶּפֶשׁ לֹא תִמָּלֵא:

Kohelet 6:7
All the toil of a person is for his mouth, but the soul will never be filled.

b. Versions of this Midrash
   i. The Midrash relating the parable of the townsman who married the princess seems to be incorrectly sourced in the text. This is probably a printer's error as there are two very similar Midrashim, both dealing with the subject. We cite them both for comparison.
   ii. The version brought in the Maharal (with the correct sourcing).

מדרש רבה ויקרא פרשה ד פסקה ב
א"ר שמואל בר יצחק ... לפי שהנפש הזו יודעת כל שיגיעה לעצמה יגיעה לפיכך אינה שביעה למצות ומעשים טובים א"ר לוי משל לעירוני שהיה נשוי בת מלכים אע"פ שמאכילה כל מעדני עולם אינו יוצא ידי חובתו למה לפי שהיא בת מלכים כך כל מה שיפעל אדם עם נפשו אינו יוצא ידי חובתו למה שהיא מלמעלה ...

Vayikra Rabbah 4:2
"The soul will also never be filled."[54]

[The meaning of this verse is] that the soul knows that however it wearies itself in effort, it is working for itself, therefore, it never has its fill of [having performed enough] mitzvot and good deeds.

Rabbi Levi said, "[One can understand this through a] parable of a townsman who was married to the daughter of kings – even if he provides her with all [the varieties of] royal delicacies, he never discharges his duty. Why? Because she is the daughter of kings. So too, no matter how much a person acts for his soul [in this world] he never discharges his duty. Why? Because his soul is from above . . ."

   iii. The version sourced in the printer's error

מדרש רבה קהלת פרשה ו פסקה ו
א"ר חנינא בן יצחק ... וגם הנפש לא תמלא שהנפש יודעת כל מה שהיא עמלה לעצמה היא עמלה לכך אינה שבעה לא תורה ולא מעשים טובים משל למה"ד לעירוני שנשא בת מלכים אם יביא לה כל מה שבעולם אינן חשובין לה כלום למה שהיא בת מלך כך הנפש אילו הבאת לה כל מעדני עולם אינם כלום לה למה שהיא מן העליונים ...

54. Kohelet 6:7.

Kohelet Rabbah 6:6

Rabbi Chanina ben Yitzchak said, "The soul will also never be filled."[55] [The meaning of this verse is] that the soul knows that however it *toils*, it *toils* for itself, therefore, it never has its fill of [learning] Torah or [performing enough] good deeds.

"To what may this be compared? To a townsman who married a daughter of kings – even if he will bring her *everything in the world*, they are not important to her. Why? Because she is the daughter of a king. So too, even if you brought the soul all the delicacies of the world, they are nothing for her. Why? Because [the soul] is from above . . ."

c. There are a number of interesting differences here:
   i. The second version (V2) actually uses the world "toil,"[56], which is the key word of the Maharal in this section of Tiferet Yisrael (quoted above at the very beginning of the Maharal) while the first version (V1) uses the word "tire oneself out."[57]
   ii. V1 says the soul will never be sated with mitzvot and good deeds (omitting Torah). V2 speaks of a lack of satiation of Torah and good deeds (omitting mitzvot).
   iii. V1 speaks in terms of having "fulfilled one's duty" to the princess/soul. V2 speaks of whether physical things are "important" to the princess/soul.
   iv. V1 says that even if one brings the princess/soul "all the varieties of royal delicacies," it will not suffice. V2 says that even if one were to bring the princess/soul "everything in the world," it would not suffice.

d. V2 seems to be slightly more extreme than V1 and perhaps illustrates the Maharal's point slightly more conclusively than V1.
   i. V2 uses the keyword, "*amal,*" "toil," which immediately illustrates the Maharal's point regarding the conversion of potential to actual.
   ii. Moreover, V2 doesn't mention "fulfillment of duty," since this is not the issue. The issue is whether physicality is even noticed, if it even makes a difference at all. Thus, even if one were to bring "everything in the world" to the soul, it would scarcely notice it since its yearning is for so much more.

---

55. Kohelet 6:7.
56. In Hebrew, "*amal*", עמל.
57. In Hebrew, "*y'gi'ah*," יגיעה.

COMMENTARY SECTION

Chapter 4

1. **A Note on This Chapter**
   a. This chapter can be very challenging. Herein, the Maharal presents crucial and fundamental ideas about the universe, humanity, Kingship, Form and Matter. We have written as much as is suitable to provide a basis for understanding these concepts, but all this is merely the briefest glance into the Maharal's thought.

2. **Terminology**
   a. Categories of mitzvot
      i. The two categories of mitzvot are known in Hebrew as:
         1. *Lo ta'aseh*[1] – meaning "Do NOT act!" usually translated as "negative commandments." We will often leave this untranslated, but when we do translate, we usually use the term, "prohibitions."
         2. *Aseh*[2] – meaning "Do act!" usually translated as "positive commandments." Generally, we will leave this untranslated, but when we do, we usually translate it as "action commandment" or "initiative-action commandment."
      ii. See the Commentary, Introduction § Point 1 for more on this terminology.
   b. "Component-limbs"
      i. The Hebrew term used is "*eivarim*."[3] Some translators translate it as "limbs of the body," others translate it as "organs."
      ii. Since the Maharal is discussing the existence of 248 *eivarim*, it seems that it would be misleading to say that a human has 248 limbs or 248 organs since these two terms (in common usage) denote parts of the body which, even in combination, do not number 248.
      iii. For this reason, we have chosen either to leave the term untranslated or to use another compound noun: "component-limbs." The idea behind it being that they are smaller components of the body.
      iv. There is a large discussion around the exact correlation between the anatomy of a human and this concept of eivarim. The famous commentator on the Mishnah, Rabbi Ovadiah Bartenurah supplies the following definition:

---

1. In Hebrew, לא תעשה.
2. In Hebrew, עשה.
3. In Hebrew, איברים.

ר' עובדיה מברטנורא מסכת אהלות פרק א
האיברים - צריך שיהיה בהם בשר וגידים ועצמות, ובכך הוא נחשב אבר.

RABBI OVADIAH BARTENURAH COMMENTARY ON THE MISHNAH, OHALOT 1:7

The *eivarim* – it is only considered to be an *eivar*[4] if it has muscle[5], sinews or tendons[6] and bones.

v. The Derech Hashem[7] supplies a more kabbalistic explanation of the "*eivarim*" – that they are the underlying concepts of a human being, but this is beyond the scope of this work.

c. The two categories of existence
  i. The Maharal, as always, uses precise terminology, and in this chapter he describes the two categories of existence using two different terms.
    1. *Ha'adam*
      a. In Hebrew, **האדם**.
      b. This term literally means "the human," meaning the generic, abstract human. We have translated it as "humankind" or "the human being."
    2. *Sh'ar hanimtza'im*
      a. In Hebrew, **שאר הנמצאים**.
      b. This literally means "the rest of those [objects] which exist." This would seem to encompass everything else besides *ha'adam*. It may also include the physical component of humanity, that is our bodies.
  ii. Different terms describing various aspects of reality
    1. In this chapter, the Maharal uses eight different terms (excluding *ha'adam* and *sh'ar hanimtza'im*) to describe reality and its various aspects.
    2. Our translations are as follows:
      a. *Olam hateva*: "The natural world," **עולם הטבע**.
      b. *Olam hazeh*: "This world," **עולם הזה**.
      c. *Olam*: "World" or "universe," **עולם**.
      d. *Nimtza'im*: "[Objects] which exist," **נמצאים**.
      e. *M'tzi'ut* : "Reality," **מציאות**.
      f. *M'tzi'ut tachton*: "Lower reality," **מציאות תחתון**.

---

4. This is the singular form of *eivarim*.
5. Lit., "flesh."
6. The Hebrew term, "*gid*," **גיד** can refer to both sinews and tendons.
7. Derech Hashem 4:4:10.

            g. *Hakol*: "Everything," הכל.
            h. *Tachtonim*: "The lower [creations]," תחתונים.
    d. The two kingdoms
        i. The Sun's kingdom
            1. Different Phrases describing this kingdom
                a. The Maharal says that the sun is "king over":
                    i. *Olam hateva*.
                    ii. *Olam hazeh*.
                b. The Maharal says that the sun "rules over":
                    i. *Olam hateva*.
                c. The Maharal says that the sun "preserves the order" in:
                    i. The *olam*.
                    ii. *Olam hateva*.
                    iii. The *nimtza'im*.
                    iv. The *m'tzi'ut*.
                d. The Maharal says that the following are "ordered beneath the sun":
                    i. The *m'tzi'ut tachton*.
                    ii. *Olam hateva*.
        ii. Humankind's kingdom
            1. Different phrases describing this kingdom
                a. "Placed beneath" humanity:
                    i. *Hakol*.
                b. Humanity "brings perfection" to:
                    i. *Tachtonim*.
                c. Humanity is the Form of:
                    i. *Tachtonim*.
                d. Humanity is "king" over:
                    i. The *Tachtonim*.
            2. The Maharal says that humanity is also a king and we rule over the *tachtonim*, a term which literally means "the lower things" and which we have translated as, "lower [creations]."
                a. In particular, the Maharal cites a verse to illustrate what this kingdom is: "Let Us make humans in our likeness . . . and they will dominate the fish of the sea and the birds of the heaven."[8] This would seem to indicate that the kingdom over which humankind rules is composed of the other living beings.
                b. The use of the general terms, "*tachtonim*" and "*hakol*" would indicate that humanity is also king over the rest of the physical world.

8. B'reishit 1:26.

iii. It would seem from all of the above that the same objects (human beings included, at least the physical human body) are ruled over by both humankind and the sun. Each of these rulers supply a different, vital aspect of kingship, which we will now explore.

3. **Bonding with Hashem through the Mitzvot**
   a. In Tiferet Yisrael, Chapter Nine, the Maharal details the process through which the performance of mitzvot creates a bond between a human and Hashem. He writes there:

תפארת ישראל ט

כבר אמרנו כי המצות האלו ראוים אל האדם מצד כי המצות כלם שכליות א־להיות, שכך סדר השם יתברך לא מה שחייב שכל האדם רק מה שסדר השם יתברך בחכמתו, ולכך הדבק במצות דבק בשכלי והוא השכל הא־להי העליון ועל ידי זה יש לו דבקות בו יתברך ומוציאין אותו מן הטבע המשותפת ובזה נפשו צרופה ואז דבק בו יתברך . . . כי הנשמה היא מלמעלה והיא א־להית נבדלת, וכאשר האדם עושה המצוה שהיא מעשה השכלי הנה מתקרב בזה אל המעלה הנבדלת ומצרף נפשו מן הטבע החמרית הן גופו הן נפשו . . . ואיך לא יקנה מדרגה א־להית על ידי המצות, כי המצות כולם במה שהם מצות השם יתברך על האדם אין ספק שזה התיחסות וחבור בין השם יתברך ובין האדם, כמו מלך הגוזר גזירה על עמו ואין ספק כי יש יחום וחבור בין המלך ועבדיו המקבלים את הגזרה מצד שהוא מלכם גוזר עליהם והם מקבלים. . . .

Tiferet Yisrael Chapter 9

We have already said that these mitzvot are suitable for human beings due to the fact that the mitzvot are all G-dly-*sichli*; because this is what Hashem, may He be Blessed, arranged – not what human intellect requires, but only what Hashem arranged in His wisdom.

Therefore, one who bonds with the mitzvot is actually bonding with the *sichli* and this intellect is the highest, G-dly intellect. Thus, through this, a person acquires bonding with Hashem, may He be Blessed, and they[9] disentangle the person [who is performing the mitzvot] from the physical world which [humans] share [with animals] and through this his soul is refined and then he bonds with Hashem, may He be Blessed . . . Because the soul is from above and is G-dly and transcendent and when a person performs a mitzvah which is an intellectual act, through this, he approaches the transcendent level and he refines both his soul and his body from the material [world of] nature . . .

And how is it possible that a person would not acquire a G-dly level through the mitzvot? Due to the fact that they are the commandments of Hashem, may He be Blessed, to humans, there is no doubt that the mitzvot are all a relating to and a joining with Hashem, may He be Blessed, and

9. The mitzvot.

humans. This is like a king who decrees a decree on his people – there is no doubt that there is a relationship and a joining between the king and his servants *who accept the decree due to the fact that he is their king who decrees on them and they accept . . .'*

- b. The Maharal seems to bring two different rationales here:
  - i. Achieving transcendence
    1. The mitzvot derive from Hashem's transcendent will. They may be physical acts[10] but their source, description and motivation all lie within Hashem's transcendent wisdom.
    2. Thus, when one bonds with the mitzvot, one is bonding with a system which is ultimately transcendent, thus one bonds with the transcendent.
    3. Moreover, one is bonding with a system which originates in Hashem's "mind," and thus one is bonding with Hashem's "mind."
  - ii. Unifying with Hashem's will
    1. Just as it is regarding a human king, when one accepts the decree of the king (which is the statement of his will) and carries out his will as if the king's will were one's own, then purely because one accepts the king as leader, one is joined inextricably to the king. One has almost transplanted the king's will into one's own heart – His will is mine. It is clear that this could be a profound level of unity with the king, where I begin to feel his desires as my own.[11]
    2. This is also the function of the mitzvot: allowing one to implement the King's will and possibly to begin assimilating the King's will as one's own.

4. Two Views of Kingship

- a. In describing the sun as king and the human being as king, the Maharal highlights two characteristics of kingship.
  - i. Maintenance of a preset order amongst subjects
    1. The Maharal raises this when discussing the kingship of the sun.
  - ii. Development, advancement, completion and perfection of subjects
    1. The Maharal suggests this as the criteria for kingship of mankind.
- b. These two purposes, in their extreme forms, are clearly opposed. If a completely static order is maintained, perfection (in an imperfect system)

10. For further elucidation of this point, see the Maharal in detail in Chapter Nine.

11. Cf. Pirkei Avot 2:4.

is unattainable. Conversely, in a world of continuous improvement, a rigidly maintained order would fall away.

c. The Torah (and Israel)[12] is the system whereby these two facets of kingship are delicately balanced – allowing for positive development within a structure which maintains only the positive elements of boundary and stability.

5. The Kingship of Humanity

a. The Maharal writes above, "The kingship of the human being is that he brings perfection to all the lower [creations] since everything was created to serve human beings and cater to them, and in this way, the human being is the Form for all the lower [creations] and he brings perfection to them all just as a king completes everything." But he also states, "Therefore, a human's limbs are the completion of the human and through his limbs, which number 248, he is created in the likeness of G-d and through this he is the king over the lower [creations] as the Torah says, 'Let Us make humans in our likeness . . . and they will dominate the fish of the sea and the birds of the heaven.'"[13]
   i. Thus, he seems to be saying that there are two or three different reasons for humanity's kingship:
      1. Humanity brings perfection to the lower creations.
      2. Humanity is the Form of all the lower creations.
      3. Humanity is created in the likeness of Hashem.

b. There are many underlying concepts which require elucidation here. We will, please G-d, examine the ideas behind "Forms" as well as the relationship between these various components of humanity's kingship in an effort to reach a cohesive understanding of these three aspects of kingship.

c. "Forms"
   i. The concept of a "form," "*tzurah,*" צורה, is common to many of our sages. See, for example, the Rambam's Moreh N'vuchim[14] in which he examines the nomenclature for discussing "Forms."
   ii. This concept is also found in many of the Greek Philosophers, in particular, Plato, who developed an entire theory of Forms. One of the purposes of his theory was to explain, for example, how all tables are classified as tables when they clearly possess differences – that is, to answer the question, "What is the 'tableness' in which all tables share?"

---

12. See later in the Commentary, Ch. 4 § Point 7.
13. B'reishit 1:26.
14. Maimonides's Guide to the Perplexed 1:1.

1. As Plato writes,[15] "For neither does every smith, although he may be making the same instrument for the same purpose, make them all of the same iron. The form must be the same, but the material may vary, and still the instrument may be equally good of whatever iron made . . ."
2. Plato's idea was that a Form is like the blueprint of an object which exists beyond space and time and which determines the essence of that object.

iii. The Maharal's concept of "*tzurah*" goes beyond this, as we will see, please G-d.

d. Humans as the Form of All Creation

i. The Maharal here mentions a concept on which he expands elsewhere: that humans are the Form of all creation. We will study his Gur Aryeh commentary on B'reishit to gain further insight, but first we will examine some background to these ideas.

ii. The Torah begins with two parallel accounts of creation – B'reishit, Chapters One and Two. Our sages noted this, analyzed it and understood this duality as an immediate expression of a fundamental duality in the creation of the world.[16] An example of this duality is:

1. In the first chapter, the Torah states, "G-d *made*[17] the wild animals of the earth in their species and the domesticated animals in their species."[18]
2. However, in the second chapter, the Torah states, "Hashem-G-d *formed*,[19] from the earth, the wild animals in their species and the domesticated animals in their species."[20]
3. Rashi explains[21] the use of the word "formed" as follows, "In the midrashic works it is explained that the word 'formed,' in this context, means to suppress and conquer[22] . . . for Hashem conquered the animals [and placed them] under the control of humanity."

15. Cratylus as per B. Jowett's translation (available at classics.mit.edu/Plato/cratylus.html).

16. An examination of this duality is beyond the scope of this work. See, for example, Rashi's explanations and Rabbi J. B. Soloveitchik's *The Lonely Man of Faith* for initial study.

17. In Hebrew, ויעש, "He made," "*vaya'as*."

18. B'reishit 1:25.

19. In Hebrew, ויצר, "He formed," "*vayitzer*."

20. B'reishit 2:19.

21. Ad loc.

22. This explanation claims that the word "He formed," "*vayitzer*" is actually derived from the root, "*tzur*," צור, meaning to encircle and besiege.

a. There is a linguistic connection between the word "formed" and the Hebrew root denoting "conquest." However, the question is, is this connection accidental or fundamental?

iii. On this, the Maharal comments in Gur Aryeh as follows,

גור אריה, בראשית ב:ל"ו

ומפני שקשה דהוי למכתב "ויעש" כדכתיב לעיל (א, כה), דרשו רז"ל (ב"ר יז, ד) שהוא לשון כבוש . . . ואל תרחיק זה הפירוש עם שהוא נראה רחוק, כי כאשר תבין מאוד תמצא שהוא דבר נפלא, כי כל לשון "צורה" הוא בעצמו לשון רדוי וכבוש, כי הוא צר ועושה גבול וחוק לאותו דבר, וזהו כיבושו, שכובש את הדבר באותו צורה להיות לו גבול זה. ומתחלה כאשר לא היה האדם - נכתב (לעיל א, כה) "ויעש", ועכשיו שנברא האדם נכתב "ויצר", לפי שהצורה נותנת לדבר חוק וגבול, ולכך נקרא "צורה", וכאשר נברא האדם - היה כובשן שיהיו תחת האדם. שכל דבר שיש לו גבול הוא תחת אחר, ולפיכך צורתו זאת - הוא כבוש בעצמו תחת האדם . . .

Gur Aryeh, B'reishit 2:36

Since our sages had the question as to why the Torah wrote, "He formed"[23] as opposed to "He made"[24] (as was written in Chapter One of B'reishit), they learned that "He formed" connotes conquest . . .[25]

Now this explanation should not be rejected even if it seems distant [from the truth] because when you really understand it, you will find a wondrous thing. For the term, "form," itself, actually connotes suppression and conquest because [the idea of making a Form or mold is that] one restricts and creates a boundary and limit for that thing [for which one is making a form] and this is the conquest of that thing, for he is imprisoning it within that form which is a boundary for it.

So, initially [in the first chapter, where creation of the animals takes place] before humans had been created, it is written, "G-d made"; but in the second chapter where human beings were created already [before the animals],[26] the term used is "G-d formed,"[27] since the Form bestows boundaries and limits upon an object, and is therefore called "*tzurah*." And after humans had been created, Hashem conquered the animals that they should be under the human beings, because any object which has a border

23. B'reishit 2:19.

24. B'reishit 1:25.

25. As cited in Rashi ad loc.

26. As mentioned, there is a dual description of the creation of the universe in the Torah. These two descriptions of creation do have differences in chronology and this is one of them. In the first chapter, fish, fowl and beasts are created before humanity. In the second chapter, humanity is created first. As noted previously, we understand that these differences reflect two separate conceptions of the universe.

27. In Hebrew, ויצר, "He formed," "*vayitzer.*"

is under [the control of] something else and therefore, the actual Form of the animal is itself conquered under that of the human being . . .

1. The Maharal explains that certain Forms not only create the blueprint for one particular entity, but they prescribe the forms of other entities as well. It is as if one has Forms which are subsets of an overarching Form.
   a. A good example of this would be the blueprint for an automobile. The Form of the car will determine the Form of the front axle. The front axle is completely described by and due to the Form of the car.
   b. The axle "serves" the car and thus, in a sense, the Form of the Car dominates and rules that of the axle and all the other parts which are only there to "serve" the car.
2. Here too the Maharal explains that all of reality was created to serve humanity in our transformation of potential perfection to actual perfection. Thus the human being's Form is a microcosm which includes within it the plan, or Form, for the animal kingdom and indeed that of the entire natural world. Therefore, the rest of the lower creations are considered to be under humanity's rule, since the destiny and purpose of all these lower creations are but a function of humanity's. We will explore this idea further in the Commentary, Ch. 4 § Point 5.

e. Human beings are in the likeness of Hashem
   i. The Maharal says later,[28]

תפארת ישראל, ט

כי האדם נברא בצלם א־להים בדמותו וזה הקירוב היותר כמו שאמר התנא הא־להי (אבות פ"ה) חביב האדם שנברא בצלם א־להים והדבקות הזה הוא על ידי התורה שמורה לאדם הדרך שהוא הדבוק, ולכך מספר מצות עשה הם כמספר אבריו של אדם שהם רמ"ח כי אבריו של אדם הם צורת צלמו שבשביל מעלה זאת ראוי אל הדבוק בו יתברך:

Tiferet Yisrael 9

. . . the human being was created in the likeness of G-d, and this [being in Hashem's likeness] is the closest possible proximity [that one can attain to Hashem] as the G-dly Mishnaic[29] sage said,[30] "Beloved is the human being, which was created in the likeness" of Hashem.

---

28. Tiferet Yisrael 9.

29. A sage who lived at the time of the creation of the Mishnah, the central component of the Oral Law.

30. Pirkei Avot 3:14.

And this *bonding is accomplished through the Torah which teaches the human being the path which is [itself] the connection. Therefore, the number of the* mitzvot aseh *corresponds to the number of component-limbs of a human (that is, 248) because the component-limbs of a human are the Form of his likeness and due to this excellence*[31] *he is* **suited** *to bond with Hashem.*

1. The Maharal has clarified much of what is left unclear in our chapter.
2. The ultimate perfection in the world is Hashem and as the Ramchal[32] puts it, the only way for a human being to attain perfection is through the greatest possible resemblance and bonding with Hashem (Who is the ultimate in perfection). As he writes,[33]

מסילת ישרים א

וכשתסתכל בדבר תראה כי השלמות האמיתי הוא רק הדביקות בו יתברך . . .

M'silat Y'sharim 1

When you consider the matter you will see that the truest perfection [attainable by human beings] is bonding with Hashem, may He be Blessed.

3. The Maharal's view is that the Form of the human being is comprised of the 248 component-limbs and that it is this Form which is in Hashem's likeness.
4. Therefore, this Form on its own already confers a certain level of "resemblance" and bonding with Hashem. As the Maharal put it, "due to this excellence, he is *suited* to bond with Hashem," meaning that due to this resemblance, there is an underlying similarity, as it were. However, it is clear that the true resemblance and bonding can only be attained through a person's active choice to resemble Hashem, which is the purpose of the *mitzvot aseh* – to allow one to do this.

ii. The Maharal also explains (in the present chapter of Tiferet Yisrael) that the two parts of all reality are the physical and the transcendent but that the only transcendent thing present in this world is humanity. He writes there,

תפארת ישראל ד

והנה השמש והאדם היותר עליון בעולם הזה, כי העולם הזה יש בו חומר וצורה נבדלת והחומר היותר עליון הוא לשמש כי יש לו חומר זך, ומעלת הצורה הנבדלת לאדם ולכך

31. I.e., level of the human being.
32. Rabbi Moshe Chaim Luzatto.
33. M'silat Y'sharim 1.

אלו שנים הם נחשבים מלכים מצד שהם עליונים בנמצאים בעולם הזה, והאדם נחשב צורה אל הנמצאים כלם אף אל השמש.

Tiferet Yisrael 4

And the sun and humankind are the more lofty [beings] in this world. For this world contains material [beings] as well as [a] transcendent Form.

The most elevated material in this world is the sun, for it has pure material, while the excellence of a transcendent Form is possessed by humankind. Thus these two are considered kings from the point of view that they are the most superior amongst the [objects] which exist in this world *and humankind is considered the Form for all [the objects] which exist, even for the sun.*'

iii. Moreover, the Maharal implies later that the transcendent world is a world of Forms.

תפארת ישראל ד

כי האברים הם צורתו שצורתו צלם א-להים נבדל . . .

Tiferet Yisrael 4

. . . the component-limbs are a human's Form which is in the likeness of G-d and is transcendent . . .

f. Assembling all the ideas
   i. We now understand that the only true perfection is Hashem and that the only way to gain perfection is through proximity to, resemblance to, and bonding with Hashem.
   ii. The only beings in this physical world which have the capacity for such resemblance are human beings because they share a likeness with Hashem.
      1. This likeness lies (in its most basic form) in the Form of the human being. The human being's Form (being a blueprint of the human essence) is found in his 248 component-limbs.
      2. This Form is in the likeness of G-d.
      3. All such Forms exist in the transcendent world which is the spiritual reality.
   iii. Since we are in Hashem's Form, as explained above (that the Form rules those created by it), He is our King. Since we are the Form for the universe, we are the kings of the universe. Thus, being in Hashem's likeness (when He is the Form of everything), immediately confers kingship and dominion.[34]

34. This is perhaps the reason that the verse in B'reishit takes it for granted that

iv. As the Maharal explained previously,[35] the transcendent world is all actualized and only humanity has potential! Thus, our transition to perfection (more specifically, to actualized perfection) corresponds to a greater correspondence to our ultimate Form (which is completely actualized and exists in the spiritual reality) which is in Hashem's likeness.

v. Thus, as we move towards a greater actualization of this potential perfection, we become more perfect and since we are the world's Form, it too becomes more perfect. Thus, our being the world's Form and our having the ability to perfect the world are both expressions of our kingship over the world.

g. We now understand the relationship between the Maharal's three facets of Human Kingship, which are:

i. Humanity is created in the likeness of Hashem.

1. Therefore, our Form bears some resemblance to Hashem.
2. We are the only beings with this resemblance and the only beings perfectly poised to actualize the potential this Form bestows on us; therefore, everything else is created to serve us, since only through us can the rest of creation be perfected. Therefore . . .

ii. Humanity is the Form of all the lower creations.

1. As we progress towards perfection, everything which is a function of our Form (that is, the universe) also progresses towards perfection, therefore . . .

iii. Humanity brings perfection to the lower creations.

6. The Sun as King

a. The Torah has never ascribed any sort of divinity to the sun – all forms of nature worship being a particular anathema to Judaism. In fact, it is striking that when describing the sun and moon at its very outset, the Torah portrays them only as "the large luminary" and the "small luminary."[36] Such descriptions, reducing the sun and moon to their functions as luminaries alone, are the Torah's view of the sun and moon – viewing them as mere components of the natural order created and maintained by Hashem.

b. Thus we are left with the serious question of what the Maharal means when he says that the sun is a king.

c. The Maharal clarifies his views in G'vurot Hashem:

---

since we are in Hashem's likeness, we rule the world.

35. Tiferet Yisrael 3.

36. B'reishit 1:16. I first learned this from my teacher, Rabbi Mordechai Breuer, *z"l*.

גבורות ה׳, מ״ו

אמנם השנה משוער מן השמש שהוא המלך בצבא השמים וראוי למנות למלך . . . וכן החמה שהוא המלך מפני שעל ידה סדר המשך המציאות שהוא הזמן ולכך מונין השנה לחמה . . .

G'vurot Hashem 46

However, the year is calculated from the sun which is the king in the hosts of heaven and is suitable to be appointed king . . . and so the sun is the king *since through it, the order of the continuation of reality [is maintained]* ***and this is time*** *and thus we count each year according to the sun . . .*

i. From here, it becomes apparent that the Maharal understands the Torah's coronation of the sun ("the great luminary to rule by day")[37] as being due to the fact that the sun is the key factor in the determination of time (particularly, the length of the year).
ii. This also helps to clarify further the two categories into which the Maharal dissects reality.
    1. The first category, which is the natural world, could now be termed: time-bound.
    2. The second category, which is humanity, could now be termed: non-time bound (and this is a profound view of humanity).
iii. It would seem that the critical idea behind the type of kingship (as described previously) which is conveyed by being the Form of something else, is that it creates a framework which circumscribes everything within it. *Thus the creation of the framework itself is the kingship.*
    1. It is possible that in both the case of humanity and the sun, this formation of a delimiting framework is what creates the kingship.
    2. Regarding the sun, perhaps what the sun is creating is the actual framework of time itself (as far as humans perceive it). The sun is the original determinant of time – it rises and sets. The unit of twenty-four hours is the fundamental measure of time, as the Torah itself describes the sun and moon, "and they will be for signs and times, for days and years."[38] Thus, the sun assists fundamentally in creating within us the very awareness of time itself, our time-consciousness. Everything in our perception of the physical world is circumscribed by time. This then, is the sun's kingship.
    3. Perhaps this is what the Maharal means when he writes above

37. B'reishit 1:16.
38. B'reishit 1:14.

in our chapter, "the sun's days are 365 and these 365 days complete the truth of the kingship of the sun, just like a human's component-limbs [complete the human being]." Here there is a direct comparison between days and the component-limbs of a person – the component-limbs of a person collectively constitute a human's form. So too, the components of the sun are days.

4. Perhaps it is noteworthy that there is no measure of time mentioned in the whole story of Gan Eden (the Garden of Eden, in the second chapter of B'reishit) until the sin.
   a. After the sin, the Torah tells us in B'reishit:

בראשית ג:ח

וַיִּשְׁמְעוּ אֶת קוֹל ה' אֱ־לֹהִים מִתְהַלֵּךְ בַּגָּן לְרוּחַ הַיּוֹם וַיִּתְחַבֵּא הָאָדָם וְאִשְׁתּוֹ מִפְּנֵי ה' אֱ־לֹה־ים בְּתוֹךְ עֵץ הַגָּן:

B'reishit 3:8

And [Adam and Chavah][39] heard the sound of Hashem-G-d walking in the garden *in the direction of the day* and the human and his wife hid from Hashem amongst the trees in the garden.

   b. Rashi there comments

רש"י שם

לרוח היום - לאותו רוח שהשמש באה משם (ס"א לשם ודוק כי כן עיקר) . . .

Rashi ad loc.

"In the direction of the day" – [This means] from the same direction *from which the sun comes* (textual variants [in Rashi read]: "to which the sun goes") . . .

   c. The Maharal in the Gur Aryeh there comments:

גור אריה שם

[יד] שהשמש באה משם. נראה פירושו שהשמש באה לעולם, כלומר באותו צד שעומדת השמש, כי השמש נקרא "יום" בעבור שהוא עושה היום . . .

Gur Aryeh ad loc.

"From which the sun comes" – It would seem that Rashi's commentary means that *the sun is coming to the world*, that is, from that side on which the sun stands, *for the sun is called "day" because it makes day* . . .

39. Lit., "They."

5. This is not conclusive, but it would seem that the Maharal is hinting at the fact that:
    a. The sun's introduction at this point is not tangential but critical – indicating that at this point the sun is somehow introduced into the consciousness of humanity.
    b. Perhaps then it was after the sin that death and all the vagaries of time are introduced and humanity finds itself no longer the sole king of the material universe but also the subject thereof.

d. Another view
    i. Another way of understanding the kingship of the sun is as follows.
    ii. The Sun is a symbol of natural law and as such is consistent in its obedience to this natural law.
        1. It is a symbol of natural law.
        2. It is furthermore consistent in its obedience to this natural law.
    iii. In other words, not only does the sun rise and set in a manner predicted by law, but it follows this law consistently. This element of consistency is of course the framework of time which the sun itself "generates."
    iv. Thus, the sun becomes the symbol of the unwavering natural law which pervades the universe. Such a reality, that the universe should be subservient to Law in all times, is indeed a wondrous phenomenon – one which we would not automatically expect unless there was a Unity underlying the entire universe. This is the kingship of the Sun – the yoke of unceasing Law – which is testament to the existence of a Law-Giver, Hashem.[40]

7. Israel Is Considered Like the Whole of Reality

a. The Maharal writes above, "[Moreover,] *Israel is considered as all of reality* (just as humanity and the sun encompass all of reality); therefore, when Hashem, may He be Blessed, gave Torah to Israel, He gave them 365 prohibitions. This is the same as the number of days in the solar year, a number which is the preservation of the order of reality. [The inherent reason for this correspondence is that] since the order of reality as a whole is [preserved] through the number, 365 (which is the number of days of the solar year), Hashem also gave 365 prohibitions to Israel, through which there is a preservation of the [universe's] order; and

40. See Joseph Needham, *The Grand Titration: Science and Society in East and West* (Routledge: 2013), 237; Kenneth Miller, *Finding Darwin's God* (Harper Collins, 2007), 96; John D. Barrow, *Theories of Everything* (Fawcet Columbine: 1992) p. 22; Albert Einstein, *Letters to Solvine* (Carol Publishing Group: 1993), 132–133.

through the observance of the prohibitions, there will be no deviation from the order." Such a statement deserves elucidation.

b. The Maharal writes in N'tivot Olam,

נתיבות עולם, נתיב התורה א

כי דברי תורה תומכים ומאשרים כל העולם כולו . . . ומה שדברי תורה תומכין כל העולם, דבר זה מדברי חכמים שאמרו (שבת פ"ח ע"א) כי לכך הוסיף ה"א בששי לומר כי כל מעשה בראשית היו תלוים ועומדים עד ששי בסיון אם יקבלו ישראל התורה מוטב ואם לאו יחזור העולם לתוהו ובוהו. ואם כן דברי תורה מחזקים ותומכים הכל עד שיש לעולם קיום, וכל זה מפני כי התורה היא סדר האדם באיזה מעשה יהיה נוהג ואיך יהיה נוהג ואיך יהיה מסודר במעשיו וזהו ענין התורה. וכמו שהתורה היא סדר האדם, כך התורה היא סדר של העולם עד שהתורה היא סדר הכל, רק כי סדר האדם הוא נגלה ומפורש בתורה, כי אי אפשר זולת זה כי על האדם מוטל לשמור את הסדר הראוי לו ולכך הדבר הזה נגלה במפורש לאדם, אבל סדר כל העולם כולו גם כן הוא בתורה שאין התורה רק סדר מציאות העולם בכללו. וזה שאמרו במדרש (ב"ר פ"א) שהיה מביט בתורה וברא את עולמו, ר"ל שהתורה בעצמה היא סדר הכל, ולכך כאשר רצה השם יתברך לברא את עולמו ולסדר אותו, היה מביט בתורה שהיא סדר הכל וברא את עולמו.

N'tivot Olam, *N'tiv Hatorah* 1

For the words of Torah support the entire world . . . and the fact that the words of Torah support the entire world is [derived] from the words of the sages who said[41] that the Torah added a *hey*[42] to the word "*shishi*"[43] to teach us that the whole of the creation was waiting in suspense until the "*shishi*"[44] of Sivan to see if the Jewish people would accept the Torah – if they did accept it, all would be well; but if they didn't, the world would return to void and nothingness.

If so, the words of Torah strengthen and support everything to the point that the world has durability.[45] All this is because the Torah is the order of humanity regarding which act a person should perform and how he should perform it and how he should be organized in his actions and this is

41. Shabbat 88a.

42. The prefix of the letter *hey*, ה, in Hebrew, is the definite article.

43. This means, "sixth." The idea here is that in the first chapter of B'reishit, at the conclusion of each day of creation, the Torah uses the phrase "It was evening, it was morning, second day," "third day," etc. For each of the first five days the Torah never says "*the* second day" or "*the* third day." However, for the sixth day, the Torah describes it as "*the* sixth day," adding the definite article. The Gemara's idea is that the sixth day mentioned here is a specific, definite sixth day and is an allusion to the sixth of the Jewish month of Sivan, the date on which the Jewish people received the Torah from G-d.

44. I.e., sixth.

45. Implying that without the Torah, the world would not have durability.

the matter[46] of the Torah. And just as the Torah is the order of humanity, so is the Torah the order of the world to the point that the Torah is the order of everything. [The only difference is] that the order of humanity is revealed and explicit in the Torah (it could not be any other way because it is a human being's duty to preserve the order which is suited to him and therefore, this order is revealed explicitly to the human being); but [even though it is hidden] the order of the whole world is also in the Torah for the Torah is indeed the order of the existence of the entire world.

And this is what the sages said in a Midrash[47] that Hashem looked in the Torah and [then] created His world. This means to say that the Torah itself is the order of everything and therefore, when Hashem, may He be Blessed, desired to create His world and to order it, he looked in the Torah (which is the order of everything) and created His world.

c. The Maharal's explanation here is more explicit – the Torah's commandments do not merely correspond in number to various aspects of reality, they are actually the very blueprint of those aspects of reality.
d. We thus understand that the acceptance of the Torah, by the Jewish people, gave them direct access to the blueprint of reality and their bonding with Hashem (which is facilitated by the Torah) stamps this blueprint on their souls. They literally imbibe the blueprint of reality and, in a certain sense, encompass and embody reality.
e. There is also much written regarding the essential connection between the Jewish people and the Torah (beyond their choice to accept it), as the sages bring in many places, "The Torah, Israel and Hashem are one."[48]

8. The Sun's Material

a. The Maharal states that the sun is the superior body amongst all physical bodies in this world.
b. He expands on this idea in the N'tivot Olam as follows:

נתיבות עולם, נתיב הענוה א'

ידוע כי השמש שיש בה הזוהר העליון, וידוע כי אין לך בכל הנמצאים מסולק מן הגשמית כמו השמש עד שיש לו גוף זוהר עד שכמעט אין לו גשמית . . .

N'TIVOT OLAM, *N'TIV HA'ANAVAH* 1

It is known that the sun possesses the pre-eminent, superior radiance, for there is no other object in existence which is so removed from physicality

46. I.e., content.
47. B'reishit Rabbah 1:1.
48. Cf. Zohar 3, 73a.

as is the sun – [and it is so removed that] it has a radiant body which almost has no physicality.'

c. It would seem that the sun (and other stars) is categorized as being on the far end of the spectrum of matter since it is an obvious source of energy, in particular, light.[49]

d. We will not enter into the debate as to the extent to which the Maharal was reconciling his knowledge of Torah and Kabbalah with his extensive scientific knowledge. We have several sources attesting to the Maharal's possession of wisdom in all these areas and he was allegedly even consulted by the royalty of the day. The Maharal was seemingly also knowledgeable in astronomy as well. Such discussions arise with regard to other sages, for example, the Rambam and the Ramban and although such a discussion is germane, it is beyond the scope of this work.

9. Women's Exemption from Time-Bound *Mitzvot Aseh*

a. In several other places, the Maharal explains his ideas regarding the reasons for women's exemption from time-bound *mitzvot aseh*.

   i. In the Ohr Chadash, he writes,

אור חדש, דף קי"ד

ועוד יש לך לדעת כי הנושא אשה לש"ש כאלו ילדה שאמר במסכת סנהדרין (כב, ב) האשה גולם כלי עץ ואינה כורתת ברית אלא למי שעשאה כלי כלומר שאין האשה רק במדריגת החומר והאיש נחשב שהוא כמו צורה לה . . . ולכך מדמה האשה כמו גולם שהוא חומר בלבד ואין בו הצורה של כלי ואמר שאין האשה כורתת ברית אלא למי שעשאה כלי כלומר שאין לאשה חבור וברית רק לאיש שהוא נחשב צורה לאשה ואין לך חבור כמו חבור צורה לחומר שהם דבר אחד לגמרי והוא ידוע כי החומר אין מציאתו בפעל ומפני כי האשה נחשב כמו החומר ועל ידי האיש שנחשב כמו צורה לאשה נמצאת האשה בפעל ולכך נחשבת כאילו ילדה האיש והוציאה לפעל . . .

OHR CHADASH, P. 114

Furthermore, you should know that a man who marries a woman for the sake of heaven, it is as if he had given birth to her [in a conceptual sense].

For it states in Tractate Sanhedrin,[50]

> "A woman is the unformed material of a [potential] wooden vessel and she does not make a covenant with anyone except with a person who can form her into a vessel."

---

49. Light was the pre-eminent primordial physical creation, mentioned as being created by Hashem's utterance in B'reishit 1:3.

50. Sanhedrin 22b.

This is to say that woman has the exclusive status of Matter and man is considered to be a Form for her . . . Therefore, the Gemara compares a woman to unformed matter which is solely material and has no Form of a vessel in it and thus the Gemara says that a woman "does not make a covenant with anyone except with a person who can form her into a vessel," that is, that a woman has no connection and covenant except with the man who is considered a Form for her.

And there is no [other] connection which is comparable to the connection between Matter and Form, since they become absolutely one. It is known that the reality of matter does not exist in actuality. Since a woman is considered as matter and through the man (who is considered the Form for the woman) the woman exists in actuality, therefore, it is as if the man had given birth to her and brought her into actuality . . .

1. The Maharal here seems to be saying that in marriage male and female each contribute a vital part of reality, two components, which when fused are absolutely one:
   a. Matter: contributed by the woman.
   b. Form: contributed by the male.

ii. In Chiddushei Aggadot, the Maharal writes:

חידושי אגדות, מכות כ"ג:

ומעתה תבין כי האשה שהיא חמרית חייבת בכל מצות לא תעשה ואינה חייבת בכל מצות עשה, כי מדריגת האשה אינה מגיעה עד המעלה העליונה היא מדריגת מצות עשה שתהיה האשה בפעל לגמרי לפי שהיא חמרית, ואין לה [אלא] מעלת הצלם הזה שאליו מצות לא תעשה . . .

Chiddushei Aggadot, Makkot 23b

Now you understand that since woman is material, she is obligated by *all* the prohibitions and is *not* obligated in *all* the *mitzvot aseh* because the level of the woman does not reach the higher level which is the level of *mitzvot aseh* [which requires] that the woman be completely actualized [which she cannot be] since the woman is material and she [solely] possesses the level of Form to which the prohibitions are due.

1. Here the Maharal explains that there is a difference between the female and male dynamic. The female dynamic, being the material component, does not reach the level of actuality which only exists in the world of the Form, which is the male dynamic's contribution. He says that the level of *mitzvot aseh* is the level of actuality which is not completely attuned to the female component.

b. The purpose of this commentary is to clarify the Maharal's teachings. There are many sages, both before and after his time, who disputed his views and we have not cited them since this commentary is not comparative in general. However, we feel it would be beneficial, on this particular point, to cite the views of the greatest *Posek*[51] of the previous generation, Rav Moshe Feinstein, *zt"l*, who, in a responsum, addressed the reason for women's exemption from time-bound *mitzvot aseh*. Rav Feinstein writes,

שו"ת אגרות משה, חלק או"ח ד סימן מט

זה שהתורה פטרה ממ"ע שהזמן גרמה הוא מן התורה וגם רבנן לא חייבום כי לא ראו בזה שום צורך לחייבן ואדרבה משמע שהצורך הוא לפוטרן דוקא מהטעמים שפטרתן תורה, ולבד טעמי התורה שלא ידוע לסתם אינשי אף לא לת"ח גדולים ואנו מחוייבין להאמין שאיכא טעמים גדולים לקב"ה נותן התורה איכא גם טעמים גלוים לכל, כי סתם נשים בעולם אינם עשירות ועליהן מוטל גידול הילדים והילדות שהיא מלאכה היותר חשובה להשי"ת ולהתורה, וכן ברא השי"ת בטבע כל מין ומין דמבע"ח שהנקבות יגדלו את הולדות ואף את מין האדם לא הוציא מן הכלל בזה שגם טבע הנשים מסוגל יותר לגידול הילדים שמצד זה הקל עליהן שלא לחייבן בלמוד התורה, ובמ"ע שהזמ"ג =ובמצות עשה שהזמן גרמה=, שלכן אף אם ישתנה סדור החיים בעולם גם לכל הנשים ולעשירות בכל הזמנים ואף כשאפשר למסור הגידול לאיזה אינשי ונשי כבמדינתנו לא נשתנה דין התורה ואף לא דין דרבנן, ולא תועיל שום מלחמה כי אין שום כח לשנות אפילו בהסכם כל העולם כולו שום דבר . . . ושנית צריך לדעת כי אין זה בשביל שנשים פחותות במדרגת הקדושה מאנשים דלענין הקדושה שוות לאנשים לענין שייכות החיוב במצות שרק מצד הקדושה דאיכא בישראל הוא ציוי המצות וגם לנשים נאמרו כל הקראי דקדושה בין תחלת תנאי קבלת התורה והייתם לי סגולה ואתם תהיו לי גוי קדוש שנאמר לבית יעקב אלו הנשים ותגיד לבני ישראל אלו האנשים, ובין ואנשי קדש תהיון לי שבמשפטים והייתם קדשים דשמיני וקדשים תהיו והייתם קדשים שבפ' קדשים וכי עם קדוש אתה לה' שבפ' ראה ובכל מקום שנמצא ענין קדושה דישראל נאמר גם לנשים, ולכן גם הנשים מברכות בלשון אשר קדשנו במצותיו כמו האנשים אף על המצות שלא חייבתן תורה, ורק שהוא קולא מאיזה טעמי השי"ת שרצה להקל לנשים כדלעיל ולא מצד גריעותא ח"ו, ובהחיובים בין איש לאשתו איתא חיוב הכבוד על האיש לאשתו ועל האשה לבעלה בלא שום חלוק, והרבה מהנשים שהיו נביאות ויש להן כל דיני נביא שבאנשים, ובהרבה דברים נשתבחו בין בקראי בין בדברי חז"ל עוד יותר מלאנשים, וליכא שום זלזול בכבודן ובכל דבר בזה שנפטרו מלמוד התורה וממצות שהזמ"ג . . .

IGROT MOSHE, ORACH CHAIM 4:49

That the Torah exempted women from performing *mitzvot aseh* which are time-bound is an exemption found in the Torah, and the sages did not take the step to obligate them because they saw no reason to obligate them. On the contrary, it seems that there is a need to exempt women for the reasons that the Torah exempted them.

---

51. Halachic decisor.

Now besides for the reasons of the Torah (which are unknown to ordinary people and [are unknown] even to great scholars and we are obligated to believe that Hashem, giver of the Torah, has great reasons for everything) there are also reasons which we can understand.

For example, an average woman in the world is not wealthy and usually the responsibility of raising children is placed on them, which is the most important task in the eyes of G-d and the Torah. So too, in the natural world, in each species of animal, Hashem created [them in such a way] that the females raise the young and He did not exclude even the human species from this rule. Also the nature of women is more capable when it comes to raising children. So from this point of view, Hashem did not require women to learn Torah and to perform time-bound [active] commandments. So even if the conventions world-wide were to change for all women and wealthy women in all times and even if it is possible for a particular woman to hand over the raising of her children to hired men or women (as is done in the USA), this Torah law would not change and neither would the rabbinic law [which does not obligate women in these types of mitzvot.] No war will have any effect in this matter because there is no power in the world which can change any Torah law, even with the approval of all of humanity . . .[52]

Secondly, one also has to know that the reason that women are not obligated in these mitzvot is not because women are inferior to men in their level of holiness. As far as holiness goes, men and women are equal. In fact, a Jew's obligation in mitzvot, in general, derives from this essential holiness [in which women are equal to men.]

The proof of this is that every single statement in the Torah regarding holiness was said to both men and women:

- At the very beginning, when the Jews were offered the Torah and Hashem gave them certain conditions and said that they would be a "treasured nation" and that "the Jews will be a holy nation," it says, "Hashem commanded Moshe to speak to the House of Ya'akov and the Children of Yisrael."[53] We understand that this is not a tautology

52. Since Hashem did not obligate women, they are not obligated to perform time-bound commandments. It is vital to understand that Rav Moshe, *zt"l*, is addressing the fact that women are not *obligated* to perform time-bound commandments neither by the Torah nor by the rabbis. This doesn't mean that women cannot do them – he has not touched on that yet – all he is addressing is a simple question: are women obligated to do time-bound mitzvot or not. His answer is that the Torah does not and the rabbis have not to date obligated women, and Hashem has reasons for this that we do not know. We may adduce practical factors behind this exemption but these are not *the reasons* for the initial exemption, which only Hashem knows.

53. Sh'mot 19:3.

but rather that "the House of Ya'akov" refers to the women and the "Children of Yisrael" refers to the men.

- "You shall be a people of Holiness to Me"[54] in Parshat[55] Mishpatim was said to the men and women.
- "You shall all be holy"[56] in Parshat Sh'mini.
- "You shall be holy"[57] and "Holy shall you be"[58] in Parshat K'doshim.
- "For you are a Holy nation to Hashem."[59]

In fact, in every place where there is a reference to the Jews being a holy people, the words were said to both men and women. Therefore, women also say the same blessing as men, "Blessed are You Hashem . . . who *commanded us* in His mitzvot . . ." even for mitzvot which they[60] were not commanded to perform [but which they do voluntarily].[61] The only difference is that for Hashem's own reasons He wanted not to obligate women and it is not, G-d forbid, due to any inferiority.

[Proofs of this equality of holiness are many.] For example:

- In the obligations between husband and wife, there is an exactly equal obligation on a husband to respect and honor his wife as there is on a woman to respect and honor her husband.
- There were many women who were prophetesses and the laws applying to male prophets applied to them exactly.
- In fact, there are verses in the Torah and statements of our rabbis which praise women in many areas as being superior to men.

There is no disrespect at all to women due to the fact that they were exempted from studying Torah and performing time-bound mitzvot.[62]

10. The Essential Reasons for the Numbers of Solar Days and Component-limbs

a. The Maharal writes above, "And you should have no doubt that the number of days in the solar year, which is 365, relates to the sun *as it is* and so too that the number of component-limbs in a human relates to humanity *in its essence* – regarding all this, there is no doubt.

54. Sh'mot 22:30.

55. In Hebrew, פרשה, meaning, "portion," a section of the Torah, one of which is read each Shabbat as part of the morning prayer services, *Shacharit*.

56. Vayikra 11:44.

57. Vayikra 19:2.

58. Vayikra 20:7.

59. D'varim 14:2, 21.

60. The women.

61. Because the Jewish people as a whole were commanded and they share equally in this holiness.

62. Rav Feinstein's view is not the only one, however, and this is not the place for a complete discussion of this issue.

"We have already stated that these two (the sun and humankind) are the most superior in this world and they alone are considered [to be] kings and rulers in the world. The sun is the ruler and king and preserves the order so that it does not change, as is the matter[63] of a [human] king. And humankind is also like a king who perfects the nation; so too, humankind perfects reality.

"However, there is something even superior [to these two kings] and through it, "kings will reign"[64] – this is the Torah, which is even more superior in the world and through it "kings will reign."[65] Therefore, the Torah related to these two types of kings, the issue[66] of the first[67] being that there should be no deviation from the [suitable] order – this is the level of the prohibitions; the issue[68] of the second[69] is that of perfection – that he perfects reality through *mitzvot aseh*.

"This is suitable for the Torah – that it should include prohibitions which preserve the [suitable] order that no-one transgress the law (as is suitable to a king who guards the nation that it should not deviate from the order) and that it should also contain initiative-action commandments which are the perfection for the world (just like a king who is the perfection of the nation).

"And these two aspects relate to the Matter and the Form. And the matters are as clear as the sun to one who understands, and regarding this explanation we have spoken at length in another place."

b. What is the connection between the very first paragraph cited above and the two which follow it? The connection might be as follows:
   i. The Maharal states that the Torah is superior to both the sun and humankind and through it they actually gain their kingship.
   ii. Previously, we cited the Maharal in *N'tiv Hatorah*, where he writes,[70] "And this is what the sages said in a Midrash[71] that Hashem would look in the Torah and created His world. This means to say that the Torah itself is the order of everything and therefore, when Hashem, may He be Blessed, desired to create His world and to order it, he

63. I.e., function.
64. Mishlei 8:15.
65. The Maharal has clearly repeated himself here, the purpose of which is unclear to us; but that there is a purpose is clear.
66. I.e., function.
67. I.e., the Sun.
68. I.e., function
69. I.e., humankind.
70. N'tivot Olam, *N'tiv Hatorah* 1.
71. B'reishit Rabbah 1:1.

looked in the Torah (which is the order of everything) and created His world."

iii. It seems that here the Maharal is alluding to this concept. He says that one should not think that the link is simply casual between, on the one hand, the number of the sun's days and the prohibitions, and on the other hand, the number of the human's component-limbs and the *mitzvot aseh*. Then he says that both the sun and king can only rule through the Torah.

iv. The idea is, in essence, that the very concepts of "sun" and "humankind" are actually derived from the Torah and the sun and humankind were only created by Hashem using the Torah as a blueprint (as he writes in *N'tiv Hatorah*). Thus the reason the sun has 365 days in a solar year is because there are 365 prohibitions and not vice versa. Similarly, the reason that the human being has 248 component- limbs is because there are 248 *mitzvot aseh*. This is the true causality at work here.

11. The Difference Between the Correspondence of Rabbi Simlai and That of the Zohar

a. Rabbi Simlai
   i. There are two parts of reality which together make up the entirety of creation:
      1. The Material world.
      2. Humanity – the only transcendent being.

b. The Zohar
   i. The human being is considered a microcosm of everything and thus everything is included with him.
   ii. The Maharal states this concept elsewhere. He writes in N'tivot Olam:

נתיבות עולם, נתיב האמת ג'

כי האדם הזה הוא עולם קטן

N'tivot Olam, *N'tiv Ha'emet 3*

For this human being is a microcosm.

COMMENTARY SECTION

Chapter 5

1. **More Mitzvot as a Reward vs. Other Religions**
    a. In this chapter, the Maharal explores how it is that Hashem's laying the yoke of 613 mitzvot upon the Jewish people could be a sign of His favor and a merit for us.
    b. His arguments are profound and moving and once again reflect his understanding that Torah and mitzvot are not disconnected, impersonal directives from an ivory-towered CEO to a puny peon below. Rather, Torah and mitzvot are the warp and woof of our passionate, loving relationship with Hashem and thus the more mitzvot and Torah we have, the greater our scope for bonding with Hashem.
    c. It is important also to realize that the Maharal was writing against a background of criticism, emanating from both Christian and Muslim sources, focusing on the "burden" that G-d had placed on the Jews. Many such thinkers claimed that Hashem had punished us by laying upon us this onerous load of mitzvot which made our lives a misery and created further opportunity for us to fall and fail. For example, in the Koran, we find a statement such as the following, "And to those who were Jews we made unlawful every animal having claws, and of oxen and sheep we made unlawful to them the fat of both, except such as was on their backs or the entrails or what was mixed with bones: *this was a punishment we gave them on account of their rebellion*, and we are surely truthful."[1]
    d. Even though Jews today may feel less attacked in this arena, in previous generations, this was a commonly aired view by certain gentiles, and thus the Maharal's words had the added effect of answering these challenges.

2. **Understanding the Maharal's View of the Spiritual Potential of Jews**
    a. We addressed this in Chapter One. See the Commentary, Ch. 1 § Points 8, 9 and 10.

3. **Why Does the Maharal Bring His Second Answer?**
    a. The Maharal consistently answers the questions he poses with more than one answer. See, for example, the Maharal's two explanations for the wording of the blessing said on the Torah (which we learned at the beginning of the Introduction to Tiferet Yisrael.)

1. Al-Qur'an 6:146.

b. Each of his explanations clearly offers a new perspective on the question itself and its assumptions. In so doing, the Maharal teases out many of the threads of thought which, together, form the tapestry of Torah. Each of his answers is thus essential and they complement one another.

c. In this section, for example, his first and second answers both approach the issue at hand from different angles.
   i. The question he poses is: Why does the Torah's inclusion of many mitzvot result in Israel gaining merit? Especially in light of the fact that adding mitzvot is not by definition adding merit, but rather, adding the potential for either merit or demerit through the actual performance or non-performance of the mitzvot.
   ii. His first answer
      1. The first answer accepts the assumption of the question: that within this world, the world of action, the mitzvot confer neither merit nor demerit but rather the potential for either.
      2. He thus answers that the real merit is found within the predisposition and receptivity towards mitzvot which exists within the Jewish soul. Hashem prepares each human being with the receptivity towards the mitzvot which that person needs to fulfill. The more mitzvot a person must perform, the greater the spiritual fertility required. Thus the fact that Israel has many mitzvot means that Hashem must have given them a greater soul-preparation. This predisposition to mitzvot is a great merit.
      3. This answer functions at the level of each individual member of the nation of Israel (unlike the second answer).
      4. A shared theme of this and the next answer is that the merit is conferred without the choice of human beings and if necessary, even against their will. In this answer, the merit conferred is a pre-disposition to the spiritual and moral, something which happens without humans choosing it.
   iii. His second answer
      1. The Maharal's second answer rejects the very assumption of the question – that within this world, the world of action, the mitzvot confer neither merit nor demerit but rather the potential for either. Rather, this second answer claims that indeed, within the world of action, merit is conferred by the large number of mitzvot.
         a. Despite this difference in assumption with the first answer, he also uses the central principle of the first answer here – inbuilt receptivity.
      2. The Maharal explains here that if we focus on the nation as a whole and not on individuals, the idea is clear.
         a. The nation as a whole has receptivity towards mitzvot (as in the first answer).

   b. Any individual who rejects Torah is rebelling against his true nature which is receptive to Torah and by default, disconnects himself from the nation of Israel. Automatically, the statement "Hashem desired to accord merit to *Israel*" does not apply to him.
   c. The greater number of mitzvot does confer merit, since the nation as a whole will, in effect, accrue that benefit since the nation, as a whole, will observe the mitzvot! When we evaluate the ultimate effect of the mitzvot, we evaluate it as a whole, by the effect on the entire nation and not on individuals.
   d. This answer focuses on the national element of the observance of mitzvot. As with the first answer, the Maharal says here that this merit is conferred even against the will of the individual who may choose to reject it.

d. Together, these two answers create a striking complement, illuminating the purpose of the giving of the Torah and the mitzvot from the points of view of the individual and the community and examining the fundamental assumption of whether mitzvot confer merit on Israel in potential alone or also in actuality.

4. The Difference between Mitzvot as "Merit Earners" and "Refinements"

a. One of the major themes which arises in the Maharal's second explanation (see above) is the two different perspectives on mitzvot. In the first chapter of the classic Path of the Just, the Ramchal, *zt"l*,[2] discusses this:

מסילת ישרים פרק א

יסוד החסידות ושרש העבודה התמימה הוא שיתברר ויתאמת אצל האדם מה חובתו בעולמו ולמה צריך שישים מבטו ומגמתו בכל אשר הוא עמל כל ימי חייו. והנה מה שהורונו חכמינו זכרונם לברכה הוא, שהאדם לא נברא אלא להתענג על ה' ולהנות מזיו שכינתו שזהו התענוג האמיתי והעידון הגדול מכל העידונים שיכולים להמצא. ומקום העידון הזה באמת הוא העולם הבא, כי הוא הנברא בהכנה המצטרכת לדבר הזה. אך הדרך כדי להגיע אל מחוז חפצנו זה, הוא זה העולם. והוא מה שאמרו זכרונם לברכה (אבות ד): העולם הזה דומה לפרוזדור בפני העולם הבא. והאמצעים המגיעים את האדם לתכלית הזה, הם המצוות אשר צונו עליהן הא־ל יתברך שמו. ומקום עשיית המצוות הוא רק העולם הזה. על כן הושם האדם בזה העולם בתחלה כדי שעל ידי האמצעים האלה המזדמנים לו כאן יוכל להגיע אל המקום אשר הוכן לו, שהוא העולם הבא, לרוות שם בטוב אשר קנה לו על ידי אמצעים אלה. והוא מה שאמרו, זכרונם לברכה (עירובין כב א): היום לעשותם ומחר לקבל שכרם: וכשתסתכל בדבר תראה כי השלמות האמיתי הוא רק הדביקות בו יתברך, והוא מה שהיה דוד המלך אומר (תהלים עג): ואני קרבת א־לקים לי טוב. ואומר (שם כז): אחת שאלתי מאת ה' אותה אבקש שבתי בבית ה' כל

2. Rabbi Moshe Chaim Luzzato.

ימי חיי וגו', כי רק זה הוא הטוב. וכל זולת זה שיחשבוהו בני האדם לטוב, אינו אלא הבל ושוא נתעה. אמנם לכשיזכה האדם לטובה הזאת, ראוי שיעמול ראשונה וישתדל ביגיעו לקנותה, והיינו שישתדל לידבק בו יתברך בכח מעשים שתולדתם זה הענין והם הם המצות:

M'silat Y'sharim 1

The foundation of righteousness and the root of perfect service [of Hashem flows from] a person's clarification and verification of what his duty is in the world and the goal towards which he should direct his gaze and his aspiration in all of his labors, all the days of his life.

The Ramchal first examines mitzvot as "merit earners."

And what our sages, of blessed memory, have taught us is that humanity was only created for the purpose of taking pleasure in Hashem and enjoying the splendor of His Presence; for this is true enjoyment and the greatest pleasure that can be found. The place where this enjoyment [may be experienced], in truth, is the World to Come, which was created with the necessary preparation to provide it,[3] but the way to reach this, our desired destination,[4] is this world, as our sages, of blessed memory, have said, "This world is like a corridor to the World to Come."[5] The means which lead a person to this goal are the mitzvot, which we were commanded by G-d, may His name be Blessed. The place of the performance of the mitzvot is this world alone. Therefore, the human was placed in this world first - so that by these means, which were provided for him here, he would be able to reach the place which had been prepared for him . . .

The Ramchal next examines mitzvot as "refinements."

And when you look [more profoundly] into the matter, you will see that only bonding with G-d is true perfection, as King David said, "But as for me, the nearness of G-d is good for me,"[6] and "I asked one thing from G-d; that will I seek – that I may dwell in Hashem's house all the days of my life . . ."[7] *For this alone is the true good*, and anything besides this which people think is good is nothing but emptiness and false worthlessness. For a person to attain this good, it is certainly fitting that he first labor and attempt in his exertions to acquire it. That is, he should persevere so as to bond with

3. I.e., the pleasure of bonding with Hashem.
4. I.e., the World to Come.
5. Avot 4:21.
6. Tehillim 73:28.
7. Tehillim 27:4.

the Blessed One by means of actions which result in this end. These actions are the mitzvot . . .

- b. The Ramchal presents two different views of mitzvot here:
  - i. The first view is that the purpose of life is to achieve the bliss only offered in the World to Come and the passport which allows one entry there is the mitzvot.
    1. In this view, the mitzvot are more along the lines of being "merit earners" – clocking up merit to qualify one entry to the World to Come. The mitzvot, in this view, are not viewed as having a "natural" effect which is the reward, rather they are "merit earners" which do not produce the reward in a direct causal relationship, but merely entitle one to receive it.
  - ii. The second view is that the purpose of life is to bond with Hashem which constitutes that ultimate bliss.
    1. However, the way to bond with Hashem is to perform actions which *actually cause this bonding as a "natural" effect thereof.* The mitzvot, in this view, are viewed as being "natural" causes which produce certain natural effects in a direct causal relationship. Here the mitzvot directly cause the bonding with Hashem which is the reward itself.
- c. These two views are similarly mentioned here by the Maharal in his first two answers.
  - i. The second answer in the Maharal speaks of mitzvot in terms of the second view of the Ramchal – as having a refining and purifying effect which allows one to bond with Hashem.
  - ii. This view brings us in a full circle to the ideas raised by the Maharal in the Introduction to this work. There, the Maharal explained that, in essence, the primary function of Torah is to guide us in bonding with Hashem.

5. Justice and "Cause and Effect" in the World of Mitzvot

- a. The Maharal states here that according to his understanding of Rabbi Chanani'ah's statement, it is impossible to posit that we could gain more merit through having less mitzvot (which would help us avoid the potential pitfalls of increased opportunities to fail) because this is simply unjust.
- b. Underlying the discussion is the principle of Justice which Hashem teaches us, in the Torah, to be one of His prime attributes.
  - i. As we learn:

דברים לב :ד

הַצּוּר תָּמִים פָּעֳלוֹ כִּי כָל דְּרָכָיו מִשְׁפָּט אֵ־ל אֱמוּנָה וְאֵין עָוֶל צַדִּיק וְיָשָׁר הוּא:

D'varim 32:4

The Rock,[8] His work is perfect for all of His ways are Justice. He is a G-d of faithfulness without injustice, He is righteous and honest.

ii. As Rashi comments there:

רש"י שם

א־ל אמונה - לשלם לצדיקים צדקתם לעוה"ב ואע"פ שמאחר את תגמולם סופו לאמן את דבריו:

Rashi ad loc.

"He is a G-d of faithfulness" – to recompense the righteous for their righteousness in the World to Come, and even if He delays their recompense, in the end, He will verify His words.

iii. The principle which Rashi is delineating is that there is an unshakeable and irrevocable principle of justice – that all deeds have consequences. Good deeds have good consequences and the opposite, G-d forbid, have consequences which are not that good.
    1. Rashi further alludes to the profound question of why it might seem that in this world this principle is not operable. He says that there is a possibility of delaying the consequence – this holds for good consequences and the opposite, G-d forbid. This concept is profound and fundamental to Judaism's many approaches to theodicy.[9]

iv. The Ramchal also addresses both the issues which Rashi addresses at length in the fourth chapter of the *Path of the Just* as follows:[10]

מסילת ישרים פרק ד

כי הקדוש ברוך הוא אינו משלם אלא מדה כנגד מדה. אמנם הענין הוא, שלענין משקל המעשים כך עולות בכף הקלות כמו החמורות, כי לא ישכיחו החמורות את הקלות ולא יעלים הדיין עינו מהם כלל כאשר לא יעלים מהחמורות, אלא על כולם ישגיח ויפקח בהשואה אחת, לדון כל אחד מהם ולהעניש אחר כך על כל אחד כפי מה שהוא, והוא מה ששלמה המלך עליו השלום אומר (קהלת יב): כי את כל מעשה הא־לקים יביא במשפט וגו', כי כאשר אין הקדוש ברוך הוא מניח מלשכוח כל מעשה טוב קטן כמות שהוא, כן לא יניח מלשפוט ולהוכיח כל מעשה רע קטן כמות שהוא, ולהוציא מלב הרוצים להתפתות ולחשוב שלא יעלה האדון ברוך הוא בדיניו הדברים הקלים ולא יקח

8. See Hak'tav V'hakabbalah ad loc. who cites translations of this word rendering it as "creator."

9. Theodicy is the question of how G-d, being perfectly good, can allow seemingly bad things happen to seemingly good people.

10. The Ramchal deals with these issues at length there.

חשבון עליהם, אלא כללא הוא (בבא קמא נ): כל האומר, הקדוש ברוך הוא ותרן הוא, יתותרו מעוהי.

Path of the Just, Chapter 4

. . . for the Holy One, Blessed be He, only recompenses measure for measure. Indeed, the matter is that in relation to the evaluation of actions, those [actions] which are less serious are placed upon the balance just as the more serious ones are; for the more serious [transgressions] will not cause the less serious ones to be forgotten, nor will the Judge ignore them,[11] just as He will not overlook the weighty ones. But He will pay attention and attend to all of these equally, to evaluate each one of them and thereafter to mete out penalties for each one according to its nature. This is what King Solomon, peace be upon him, says, "For every act will G-d bring to judgment . . ."[12] Just as the Holy One, Blessed be He, does not forget any good deed, small as it may be, so does He not refrain from judging and admonishing any bad deed, however small . . . It is a general principle [cited in the Gemara as follows], "Whoever says that the Holy One, Blessed be He, overlooks [any deed] will have his innards[13] 'overlooked.'"[14]

c. All of this is summed up in the maxim which the Maharal quotes from Pirkei Avot, "according to the pain [of toil] is the gain."[15] This encapsulates the idea (explored in depth in the works of the Ramchal *zt"l*)[16] that human beings create their own reward or, G-d forbid, the opposite. There is no way to circumvent this basic dynamic of justice since it is a manifestation of Hashem's attribute of Justice, which is a prime force in the creation and maintenance of the universe.

6. An Individual Who Refuses Torah is not Part of the Reality of Israel

a. The Maharal introduces this idea and does not elucidate it. It is far-reaching and is worthwhile exploring.

b. The first principle which we should investigate is how a person would possibly "delist" from membership in the Jewish people.

   i. Although many have declared their desire not to be considered Jewish, there is no formal halachic ritual of such severance, and the

11. I.e., the less serious acts.
12. Kohelet 12:14.
13. I.e., his life.
14. Bava Kamma 50a.
15. Avot 5:26.
16. See particularly, Derech Hashem (The Way of G-d) 1:4:10–11.

Gemara makes the famous statement that even if a Jew sins, he is still a Jew.[17]

ii. On the other hand, the Torah explicitly describes a process called *kareit*, excision, from the Jewish people as a consequence of the performance of certain deeds. This *kareit* is understood variously by the different commentators, but the meaning of the word is that the person is "cut off" from the Jewish people in some way (this excision could take various forms).

iii. *Kareit*, for example, is incurred by a person who intentionally[18] does any of the following (in the absence of an halachic requirement to do so):[19] eats leaven on Pesach, eats food on Yom Kippur, or worships idols.[20]

iv. As delineated in previous notes on justice and reward, a central Torah view is that *kareit* (or any other "punishment") is not a divine, vindictive smiting for evil deeds; rather a person's acts have particular consequences. Certain acts definitively declare that the person wishes to have no part in the Jewish people, its destiny or identity. These acts are conclusive and serious enough that, *if performed with full intent*, constitute an act of severance and divorce to some extent. As such, the natural result of these acts is what is known as *kareit*. This does not preclude the possibility of later reconnecting through the process known as *t'shuvah*, literally meaning, "return."[21]

c. The Maharal explores these ideas further elsewhere:

נצח ישראל י"א

לכן אמר בפרשת אתם נצבים (דברים כט, יג-יד) "ולא אתכם לבדכם אנכי כורת את הברית הזאת כי את אשר ישנו פה וגו'". ומעתה איך אפשר שיכרות ברית עם אשר לא נולדו עדיין, ואינם בעולם. אבל הדבר ברור, לפי שכרת ברית עם אברהם מצד שהוא התחלת האומה בכלל, וכן בישראל הוא אומר (דברים כט, ט-י) שאין כורת ברית עמהם מצד שהם פרטים, אלא רק מצד האומה, דהיינו שם ישראל. ודבר זה כולל אותם שהם

17. Sanhedrin 44a.

18. In halachic terms, this includes the requirement, amongst others, that one have full knowledge of the prohibition and its punishment.

19. One could be required to perform such acts halachically, due to a superseding halachic principle. For example, in cases of danger to life, one would be required halachically to eat leaven on Pesach and to eat food on Yom Kippur. Idol worship is one of the three cardinal sins which supersede threat to life. All such questions must be addressed by a fully competent halachic authority.

20. In these cases, there would normally be a human, court-mandated penalty. But in the absence of the implementation of court-mandated punishments (for whatever reason), *kareit* would follow in the absence of repentance.

21. This term is often translated by the English term, "repentance."

עתה לפניו, וכן אותם שנולדו אחר כך, שכולם שם אומה ישראלית עליהם. ומאחר שכן הוא, איך יתכן לומר כי הפרטים אשר חטאו יבטלו הברית אשר היה חל על האומה הכללית, לא מצד אשר הם אלו בפרט, רק מצד הכלל בלבד:

NETZACH YISRAEL, CHAPTER 11

Therefore, Hashem said in the Torah portion of "You are standing [here today]" [as follows], "I am making this covenant and this oath not only with you alone, but [also] with those who are here [standing today with us before Hashem our G-d and (also) with those who are not with us today.]"[22]

Now, how is it possible that Hashem would make a covenant with someone not yet born[23] and who does not exist in the world?

But the matter is clear, because Hashem made a covenant with Avraham due to his being, in general, the progenitor of the nation. And so too does He say regarding Israel[24] that He is not making a covenant with them as individuals but rather the covenant is with the nation [as a single organic entity] – this is why the term "Israel" is used. And this matter[25] includes those who were at that time [standing] before Hashem as well as those who would be born afterwards, for on all of them the name, "Israel," devolves.

And since this is the case, how is it possible to say that the individuals who sin could ever annul the covenant which devolves on the general nation and [does] not [devolve] on those who are there as individuals but rather from the point of view of the collective alone.

i. Here, the Maharal explains that the covenant made between Hashem and Israel[26] was made between two parties: Hashem and Israel. Israel here is not a collection of individuals but rather a single, organic entity which is more than the sum of its individual parts.
ii. As such, through its Torah and mitzvot, this covenant bestowed upon Israel the merit conferred by those mitzvot. Israel is the beneficiary, the nation as an eternal nation, partnered with Hashem, not necessarily the individuals within it.

7. How Can One Have a "Material Soul"?

a. The Maharal makes reference to a "material soul," which he terms the *nefesh*. This seems to be an oxymoron – how can one have a soul (which seems to be, by definition, spiritual and non-material) which is nevertheless, material.

---

22. D'varim 29:13–14
23. Those who are "not with us today."
24. D'varim 29:9–11.
25. The covenant with the nation as a nation.
26. With Israel's part of the covenant consisting of the Torah and the Mitzvot.

b. We discussed this matter at length in the Commentary, Ch. 1 § Point 2.

c. Briefly, the Ramchal explains as follows:

דרך ה' א:ה:א

כאן צריך שתזהר שלא תטעה לחשוב שיהיה ענין שאר הבעלי חיים כענין האדם, כי אין נפש הבעלי חיים אלא דבר גשמי מן הדקים שבגשמיות, ומענינו נמצא גם כן באדם, בבחינת היותו בעל חי, אמנם זולת כל זה יש באדם נשמה עליונה, שהוא מין בריאה בפני עצמו, נבדל מן הגוף לגמרי ורחוק ממנו עד מאד, שבאה ונקשרת בו בגזירתו ית' . . .

Derech Hashem 1:5:1

Here one must take heed not to err in thinking that the state of other animals is equal to that of human beings. Rather, the soul of animals is actually a physical object even though it is one of least physical of all physical objects. *A soul of this type is found in human beings* from the point of view that human beings are also living beings [and the animal soul confers life].

However, besides all this, humans have a supernal soul which is a type of creation in and of itself, entirely separate from the body and very distant from the body which nevertheless comes and is bonded to the body by the decree of Hashem, may He be Blessed . . .

i. From the explanation of Rabbi Chaim of Volozhin, *zt"l*, in his work, Nefesh Hachaim, we saw[27] that the *nefesh* is that section of the soul which vivifies the body and is the lowest part of the soul. This is similarly reflected in the words of the Ramchal above.

ii. Thus, the Maharal terms it the "material soul."

27. In the Commentary, Ch. 1 § Point 2.

COMMENTARY SECTION

Chapter 6

1. **Terminology**
   a. Reason and Taste
      i. There are several words in Hebrew which are used to connote "the reason" for something.
      ii. Amongst these are:
         1. סבה (*sibah*), which is usually translated as "reason."
         2. טעם (*ta'am*) which literally means "taste" but is also used to connote "reason." Here the literal meaning (taste) is used metaphorically to describe the idea that one may get a taste of the concept at hand. Certain sources write explicitly that the central "taste" meaning of "*ta'am*" informs the alternative "reason" meaning, connoting that we merely have a taste of the underlying reason and we have not reached the essential reason. Thus, when both these words (*sibah* and *ta'am*) are used together we have translated *ta'am* as "taste" (also so as not to lose the sensory connotation).

2. **Acronyms**
   a. The Maharal in this section makes reference to two of the pillars of the Torah world in the Middle Ages: Maimonides and Nachmanides.
   b. As is the custom, he uses their "acronyms" which are very similar in both Hebrew and English:
      i. *RaMBaM*: *R*abbi *M*oshe *B*en *M*aimon – this is Maimonides (1135–1204).
      ii. RaMBa*N*: *R*abbi *M*oshe *B*en *N*achman – this is Nachmanides (1194–1270).
   c. Although the acronyms look almost identical, except for the final letters, they are two very different luminaries.

3. **Cause and Effect – Physical to Spiritual**
   a. The question of the philosophers picks up on one of the themes in the previous chapter – that a person generates, through their actions, their own reward, or, G-d forbid, the opposite. The question here is as to the mechanism whereby this occurs – how can a physical action have metaphysical consequences?
   b. The Maharal offers a partial solution which he rejects.
      i. This partial solution focuses on those mitzvot which help a person

acquire positive traits. The essence of the solution is that indeed, there is no direct cause-effect relationship between acts in this world and realities in the metaphysical, transcendent world. Rather, there is only an indirect connection: Hashem notes what traits one has acquired and rewards and punishes appropriately.

ii. This solution paints mitzvot more as "merit earners" – a way of clocking up merit points or of keeping score. Thereafter, Hashem rewards/punishes based on the score. Although there is no doubt that the positive character traits thus developed have value in and of themselves, these traits still do not generate metaphysical realities – Hashem has to do that post facto.

iii. The Maharal rejects this solution.

4. Why Does the Maharal Reject the Methods of the Philosophers?

a. The Maharal hints that the reason that this method can never reach the full truth is that it intentionally employs "pure" reason alone to arrive at conclusions, but without Torah axioms (which contain ultimate truth) it cannot arrive at truth.

b. This should be compared to the Maharal's statements regarding the verse in Tehillim 19, "The testimony of Hashem is faithful, making the simple wise" which we saw in the introduction to this work.

i. There he states categorically:

תפארת ישראל - הקדמה

ואחר כך אמר עדות ה' נאמנה מחכימת פתי. פי' כי מה נחשב האדם שאין בו רק שכל האנושי, אבל עדות ה' נאמנה מחכימת פתי שעל ידי התורה נעשה חכם, כי התורה מעידה על הנמצאים לברר כל דבר והיא נאמנה מחכימת הפתי עד שנחשב שכלי ביותר.

Tiferet Yisrael - Introduction

. . . it says, "The testimony of Hashem is faithful, making the simple person wise."[1] The explanation of this is that a person, having only human intelligence, is not really that noteworthy. But the Testimony of Hashem (that is, the Torah) is faithful and makes wise the [human being who is fundamentally] simple, for through the Torah a person becomes wise; because the Torah gives testimony about the [true reality of all] creations, clarifying all things, and the Torah is faithful, making the simple wise, until he is considered exceedingly *sichli*.

ii. Here he seems to imply that only Torah knowledge enables a person to become more *sichli*, that is, cerebral and transcendent.

1. Tehillim 19:8.

5. **Hashem's Different Attributes**
   a. The Maharal speaks of Hashem's "drives" for Mercy and Justice in this chapter, which may convey the mistaken assumption that indeed Hashem has separate drives or attributes, G-d forbid.
   b. It is essential to bear in mind the words of the Ramchal, *zt"l*, at the beginning of his Derech Hashem:

ספר דרך ה׳ א:א:ה

וכן צריך שידע, שמציאותו ית׳ מציאות פשוט בלי הרכבה וריבוי כלל ... אך האדון ית"ש איננו בעל כחות שונים, אע"פ שבאמת יש בו ענינים שבנו הם שונים, כי הרי הוא רוצה והוא חכם והוא יכול והוא שלם בכל שלימות. אמנם אמתת מציאותו הוא ענין אחד שכולל באמתתו וגדרו [פירוש - אמתת ענינו. כי אין שייך גדר בו ית׳ אלא על צד היתר לשון] כל מה שהוא שלימות. ונמצא שיש בו כל השלימיות לא כדבר נוסף על מהותו ואמתת ענינו, אלא מצד אמתת ענינו בעצמה שכוללת באמתה כל השלימיות, שאי אפשר לענין ההוא מבלתי כל השלימיות מצד עצמו. והנה באמת הדרך הזה רחוק מאד מהשגתנו וציורנו, וכמעט שאין לנו דרך לבארו ומלות לפרשו. כי אין ציורנו ודמיוננו תופס אלא ענינים מוגבלים בגבול הטבע הנברא ממנו ית׳, שזה מה שחושינו מרגישים ומביאים ציורו אל השכל, ובברואים הנה הענינים רבים ונפרדים. אולם כבר הקדמנו, שאמתת מציאותו ית׳ אינה מושגת, ואין להקיש ממה שרואים בברואים על הבורא ית׳, כי אין ענינם ומציאותם שוה כלל שנוכל לדין מזה על זה ...

Derech Hashem 1:1:5

You should also know that Hashem's existence, may He be Blessed, is simple without any composition or plurality at all . . . but the Master, may His name be Blessed, does not have different faculties – even though He contains matters which in ourselves are different [and multiple] for He has the faculty of will, He is wise and He is able and He is absolutely perfect; however, the truth of His existence is [that it is] one reality which includes in its truth and definition everything which is perfect. It emerges that He contains all perfections but not as additions to His essence or to the truth of His existence, but rather due to the truth of His existence in and of itself which includes in its truth all perfections – it is impossible for that existence without all perfections flowing from it.

In truth, this path is far from our abilities to comprehend or imagine and it is almost as if we do not even have the ability to explain it or the words to say it. This is because our creativity and imaginations can only grasp realities which are limited by the boundaries of nature which is created from Hashem, may He be Blessed, which is what our senses detect and thereafter transmit a representation thereof to our minds. And in the created beings, all these [above-mentioned] faculties are indeed many and separate.

However, we have already pre-empted this question by saying that the truth of Hashem's existence, may He be Blessed, cannot be comprehended and one may not deduce anything about the Creator, may He be Blessed, from what we see in the creations, since their matter and reality are not equal at all that we should be able to learn about one from the other . . .

i. The Ramchal explains that even though we might perceive Hashem's attributes as separate, this is only due to the limitations of our perception as human beings.
ii. A simple analogy for this is the wave-particle duality of light, a theory that developed within the context of quantum physics and quantum mechanics. In certain circumstances, light (and all matter and energy) behaves as if it consists of particles (little packages) whereas in other circumstances, it behaves like a wave. The problem is that it cannot be both a wave and a particle – those two states are mutually contradictory! The answer is that light is clearly something beyond both a wave and a particle, which we *perceive* as behaving like two different types of objects. The problem again is in our inability to perceive the unity within light. So too, as it were, with the attributes of Hashem.

6. Justice and Honesty – Constancy of Nature: Parallel between Natural Law and Spiritual Law

a. The Maharal above delves into some of the deepest ideas in Kabbalah: the relationship between Hashem's different attributes. In this work, we have no business in exploring these depths.
b. The one idea we would like to mention is that the Torah has long posited a parallel between the constancy of what we term "Natural Law" and Hashem's attribute of Justice.
   i. In many places, our sages point out that the words "*Elokim*" (the name of Hashem which signifies His attribute of Justice) and "*hateva*" (nature) are numerically equivalent.
      1. Each letter in Hebrew has a numerical value.
         a. *Hateva* = **הטבע** = 5 (ה) + 9 (ט) + 2 (ב) + 70 (ע) = 86
         b. *Elokim* = **א־להים** = 1 (א) + 30 (ל) + 5 (ה) + 10 (י) + 40 (ם) = 86
      2. The Maharal mentions this in many places, but in hints only since it is Kabbalah. For example:

ספר באר הגולה ז'

דהיינו שהנהגה המסודרת משם א־להים שגימטריא הטבע

B'er Hagolah 7

This is the method of governing the world which is ordered from the name "Elokim," the numerical value of which is "nature."

ii. However, the idea is not only that there is some quaint numerical equivalence; all of these *g'matri'ot*[2] seek to allude to a deeper parallel. Let us look, for example, at the idea presented by the Ben Ish Chai:

ספר בן איש חי - הלכות שנה שניה - פרשת כי תבא
אבל פעולות הטבעיות נעשים ע"י שם א-להים לכן תמצא א-להים גי' הטבע וכמ"ש המפרשים ז"ל ואמרתי בס"ד רמז שהנם נעשה ע"י שם הוי"ה . . .

Ben Ish Chai 2: Ki Tavo

But the natural actions are performed [by G-d] through the name, "Elokim." Therefore, the *g'matri'ah* of "Elokim" is "nature" as the commentators have noted. And I have given, with the help of Hashem a hint that any miracle is performed through the name "Y-H-V-H" [which refers to Hashem's attribute of Mercy].

iii. The ideas presented here briefly illustrate the Maharal's understanding of which attribute, or name, of Hashem is associated with which type of activity. The Torah teaches us that the name of Hashem which generates Justice and Law is *Elokim*, but that this is not only on the metaphysical level but on the purely physical level too. As we learned in Chapter Four, the underlying order of the universe, the law which we see in nature is, in the Torah's view, an expression of Hashem's actions as a Law-giver – whether physical or moral.

iv. Similarly, mercy, which is a deviation from, or perhaps a transcendence above, the constant law, is expressed in the world of justice and morality through not implementing the consequence of law. This is expressed by Hashem's name, Y-H-V-H. So too, the Torah teaches us that any deviation from physical law, which we term a miracle, is a function of this attribute of Y-H-V-H.

v. This beautiful parallel is one of the many examples of the Torah's view of the correspondence of the physical and spiritual worlds where what we see in the physical world is actually a representation of a metaphysical concept. We see apples falling down from the tree and view it as Hashem's attribute of *Elokim* commanding that law of gravity to exist in much the same way He says, "You shall not murder."

c. The question this raises is a profound one which many sages and scientists have asked: why is the cosmos so ordered and law abiding? Especially in our quantum era when the entire subatomic world seems to be governed by probability and chance, there are many who question

2. Numerical equivalences.

why the macro-atomic world rigidly obeys so-called laws of nature.[3]

i. The Maharal here raises the question as to why Hashem chose to guide the world with this attribute of Justice and Law as opposed to His attribute of Mercy. He says that Justice is a more appropriate attribute with which to govern the world because it is constant, unlike Mercy. He links this constancy to honesty but the explanation of this is beyond our scope.

ii. What we can say is that the world was created as a platform for human choice and that the way Hashem runs the world, the balance maintained here, makes that choice possible. For a wider exploration of this, see the Ramchal's Derech Hashem, Part One.

7. The Question of the Philosophers and Its Answer

a. The question

i. The question is a profound one which goes to the heart of the Torah's belief that a human being is somehow a dual citizen of the physical and transcendent worlds: what is the connection that allows physical deeds to affect one's fate in the spiritual world?

b. The answer

i. The Maharal here embarks on an answer to this question, an answer which encompasses this chapter as well as Chapters Seven, Eight and Nine.

8. Do Mitzvot "Have Reasons"?

a. There is an extensive discussion amongst our sages as to whether or not mitzvot "have reasons." This question is broad enough that a comprehensive answer would require many pages more than we have here. We will content ourselves with a brief overview of some of the main views and sources.

b. A caveat

i. Even those positions advocating that mitzvot have reasons and that we should delve into those reasons do not *in any way* link the obligation for performance of a mitzvah to one's prior understanding thereof. *Such attitudes are grave pitfalls to spiritual growth, changing the center of our lives from Hashem to ourselves, G-d forbid.* As the Rambam writes:

הלכות מעילה ח:ח

ראוי לאדם להתבונן במשפטי התורה הקדושה ולידע סוף ענינם כפי כחו ודבר שלא

3. For a fascinating taste of a scientist and Torah sage's view of this question, see Rabbi Aryeh Kaplan's *Faces and Facets*, pp. 72–79, in the essay entitled, "The Scientific Miracle."

ימצא לו טעם ולא ידע לו עילה אל יהי קל בעיניו . . . קל וחומר למצוה שחקק לנו הקב"ה שלא יבעט האדם בהן מפני שלא ידע טעמן . . . הרי נאמר בתורה ושמרתם את כל חקותי ואת כל משפטי ועשיתם אותם אמרו חכמים ליתן שמירה ועשייה לחוקים כמשפטים והעשייה ידועה והיא שיעשה החוקים והשמירה שיזהר בהן ולא ידמה שהן פחותין מן המשפטים והמשפטים הן המצות שטעמן גלוי וטובת עשייתן בעולם הזה ידועה כגון איסור גזל ושפיכות דמים וכיבוד אב ואם והחוקים הן המצות שאין טעמן ידוע . . .

Rambam, The Laws of Misappropriation of Sanctified Objects 8:8

It is fitting for a person to meditate upon the judgments of the holy Torah and to comprehend their full meaning as much as he can. But he should not trivialize a law for which he finds no reason and understands no cause . . . how much more so should a person take care not to reject a commandment decreed for us by the Holy One, Blessed be He, only because he does not understand the reason . . .

It is stated in the Torah, "Therefore, you must guard all My statutes, and all My judgments, and perform them."[4] The sages said, "[Why does the Torah mention both 'guarding' and 'performance' of the 'statutes' and 'judgments'? It is in order] to require 'guarding' and 'performance' of the 'statutes' [which do not have reasons or whose reasons are less accessible] just as much as [one would 'guard' and 'perform'] the 'judgments' [the reasons of which are clear]. The meaning of 'performance' is known, namely, that one should 'perform' the 'statutes.' And 'guarding' – that a person should take care regarding them, and not imagine that they are inferior to the 'judgments'."

'Judgments' are mitzvot, the reason for which is revealed and the benefit of whose performance in this world is clear; for example, the prohibitions against armed robbery and murder; the obligation to honor one's mother and father [and so on]. 'Statutes' are mitzvot, the reason for which is unknown.

c. There are several different positions that are taken and which could be taken:
   i. Regarding the reality of whether mitzvot have reasons:
      1. Mitzvot collectively and particularly have no humanly-understandable reasons, they are G-d's decrees.

      OR

      2. Mitzvot collectively have reasons but the individual mitzvot do not have individual reasons which a human can understand.

      OR

      3. Mitzvot as a whole and in particular have reasons, even if all the details of each mitzvah do not have reasons which a human can

4. Vayikra 19:37.

understand.

OR

4. Mitzvot as a whole and in particular have reasons, as do all their details and these are comprehensible to a human.

ii. Regarding how we should relate to such reasons:

1. Regardless of whether mitzvot have reasons, we should not delve into them.

OR

2. We should definitely delve into the reasons for mitzvot.

d. We'll now take a brief look at some of the central sources regarding whether mitzvot have reasons.

i. Mitzvot collectively and particularly have no humanly-understandable reasons, they are G-d's decrees.

1. The Rambam, in his Moreh N'vuchim,[5] mentions this opinion and links it to those who also believe that Hashem's acts are due to His pure will alone and not due to any wisdom or logic.

מורה נבוכים ג:כ"ו

כמו שחלקו אנשי העיון מבעלי התורה אם מעשיו ית' נמשכים אחר חכמה או אחר רצון לבד, לא לבקשת תכלית כלל, כן חלקו זאת המחלוקת בעצמה במה שנתן לנו מן המצוות. שיש מי שלא יבקש לזה סיבה כלל ויאמר שהתורות כולם נמשכות אחר הרצון לבד; ויש מי שיאמר שכל מצוה ואזהרה מהם נמשכת אחר החכמה...

Moreh N'vuchim 3:26

Just as the intellectual, inquiring people amongst Torah scholars, disputed whether Hashem's actions are due to wisdom or due to His will alone without any desire for a purpose, so too they had exactly the same dispute with regard to Hashem giving us the mitzvot. There are those who do not search for any reason at all and say that all of the laws are due to Hashem's will alone; and there are those who say that all mitzvot and prohibitions are due to wisdom.

2. The Rambam explains that those people who believe that anything that Hashem does is simply due to His will and has no relation to any type of wisdom must perforce believe that the mitzvot too have no reasons.

ii. Mitzvot as a whole and in particular have reasons, even if it may not be possible for a human to comprehend the reasons for all the details of each mitzvah.

5. Moreh N'vuchim 3:26. This is cited in full below.

1. The Rambam is the herald of this view:

מורה נבוכים ג:לא

מבני אדם אנשים שיכבד עליהם נתינת סיבה למצוה מן המצוות, והטוב אצלם - שלא יושכל למצוה ולאזהרה ענין כלל. ואשר יביאם אל זה הוא חלי שימצאוהו בנפשם, ולא יוכלו להגות בו ולא ידעו לומר אותו. והוא, שהם יחשבו, שאם היו אלו התורות מועילות בזה המציאות ומפני כך וכך נצטוינו בהם, ויהיו כאילו באו ממחשבת והסתכלות בעל שכל; אמנם כאשר יהיה דבר שלא יושכל לו ענין כלל ולא יביא לתועלת, יהיה, בלא ספק, מאת הא־לוה, כי לא תביא מחשבת אנוש לדבר מזה. וכאילו אלו חלושי הדעות - היה האדם אצלם יותר שלם מעושהו, כי האדם הוא אשר יאמר ויעשה מה שמביא לתכלית אחת, והא־לוה לא יעשה כן, אבל יצונו לעשות מה שלא יועילנו עשותו ויזהירנו מעשות מה שלא יזיקנו עשותו. חלילה לו, חלילה! אבל הענין בהפך זה! והכונה כולה להועילנו - כמו שבארנו מאמרו, "לטוב לנו כל הימים, לחיותנו כהיום הזה", ואמר, "אשר ישמעון את כל החוקים האלה ואמרו, רק עם חכם ונבון הגוי הגדול הזה" - כבר באר שאפילו ה"חוקים" כולם יורו אל כל הגוים שהם "בחכמה ותבונה", ואם היה ענין שלא תודע לו סיבה ולא יביא תועלת ולא ידחה נזק - למה יאמר במאמינו או בעושהו שהוא "חכם ונבון" וגדל המעלה ויפלאו מזה האומות?: אבל הענין כמו שזכרנו, בלא ספק, והוא, שכל "מצוה" מאלו ה"שש מאות ושלוש עשרה מצוות" היא - לנתינת דעת אמיתי או להסיר דעת רע, או לנתינת סדר ישר או להסיר עול, או להתלמד במדות טובות, או להזהיר ממדות רעות - הכל נתלה בשלשה דברים, בדעות ובמדות ובמעשי ההנהגה המדינית. ואשר חייב שלא נמנה המאמרים, כי המאמרים אשר זרזה התורה לאמרם או הזהירה מהם, מהם - מה שהוא מכלל המעשים המדיניים, ומהם - ללמד דעת אמיתי, ומהם - ללמד מדות. ומפני זה הספיק לנו באלו השלשה ענינים בנתינת סיבה בכל מצוה מן המצוות:

Moreh N'vuchim 3:31

There are some people who consider it problematic to give reasons for any mitzvah. It would be best in their eyes that the intellect would not find a meaning for any commandments or prohibition. What brings them to this is a sickness which they find in their soul, a malady which they are unable to contemplate and which they cannot articulate.

This sickness is that they think that if some laws were useful in this existence and had been given to us for a particular reason, it would be as if they came from the thought and the understanding of some intelligent being. However, if there is a thing for which the intellect cannot find any meaning at all and is not useful, it undoubtedly comes from G-d; for the thought of a human would not lead to such a thing. It is as if, according to these people of weak opinions, the human being is more perfect than his Creator because a human speaks and acts in a manner that leads to some intended goal but G-d does not act this way and instead commands us to do things that will not benefit us and He prohibits us from doing things that will not harm us. G-d forbid! G-d forbid! The matter is exactly the opposite!

The intention is completely [for the mitzvot] to benefit us, as we have explained G-d's saying,[6] "[Hashem has commanded us to perform all these Statutes, to be in Awe of Hashem, our G-d] to be good for us forever, to sustain us as we are this day." Hashem also said,[7] "[And you must guard and perform the Torah for it is your wisdom and insight in the eyes of the nations] who will hear of all these Statutes and they will say, 'This is only a wise and insightful nation!'" Here, Hashem has explained that even the 'statutes'[8] all teach all the nations that they are [commanded through] wisdom and insight. And if this were a matter for which no reason could be known and which would bring no benefit and which would not prevent any harm, why would anyone comment about one who believes in the Torah or performs it that he is 'wise' or 'insightful' and high of station? And why would the nations be impressed?[9]

However, the matter is as we have stated, that each mitzvah out of the 613 mitzvot was commanded to transfer a correct trait [to the one who performs the mitzvah] or remove a negative trait or to confer a correct order or to remove injustice, or to teach good values or to warn one of bad values . . .

a. Here the Rambam clearly outlines his belief that every single Mitzvah has a reason and benefit for human beings.

2. The Rambam explains elsewhere,

מורה נבוכים ג:כו

. . . אבל היות הקרבן האחד "כבש" והאחד "איל" והיות מספרם מספר מיוחד - זה אי אפשר לתת לו עילה כלל. וכל מי שמטריד עצמו לתת סיבה לדבר מאלו החלקים הוא בעיני משתגע שגעון ארוך ואינו מסיר בזה הרחקה, אך מוסיף הרחקות. ומי שידמה שאלו יש להם סיבה הוא רחוק מן האמת כמי שידמה שה"מצוה" כולה היא ללא תועלת נמצאת:

Moreh N'vuchim 3:26

It is impossible to give a reason at all why some sacrifices are of a lamb and others are of a ram and why there are some specific numbers [of

---

6. D'varim 6:24.

7. D'varim 4:6.

8. In Hebrew, "*chukkim*," חוקים. As we cited the Rambam above in the Laws of Misappropriation of Sanctified Objects 8:8, "*chukkim* are mitzvot, the reason for which is unknown."

9. The Rambam learns from the fact that even the *chukkim* inspire one with the feeling that the Torah is wise and insightful, that they must somehow be comprehensible and useful, otherwise why would they impress the nations? How much more so do other types of mitzvot have rationales!

animals] thereof. And, in my eyes, anyone who bothers himself to give a reason for any of these things is insane with a prolonged insanity and he doesn't remove distancing [from the truth] but rather adds distancing [from the truth]. One who believes that these details have a reason is far from the truth as much as is one who thinks that none of the mitzvot has any benefit.

a. Here the Rambam expresses his belief that some of the details of the mitzvot have no reasons.

iii. Mitzvot as a whole and in particular have reasons, as do all their details, all of which a human being could understand.

1. The Maharal asserts this, as we shall see, G-d willing, in Chapter Seven of Tiferet Yisrael:

תפארת ישראל פרק ז

...כי על כל התורה אמר הכתוב (דברים ד') כי מי גוי גדול אשר לו חקים ומשפטים צדיקים ככל התורה הזאת ואמר עוד ושמרתם ועשיתם כי הוא חכמתכם ובינתכם לעיני העמים אשר ישמעון את כל החוקים האלה וגו', והרי כי כל דבר שבתורה בכלל ובפרט הכל דברי חכמה, ולא כמו שחשב הוא כי לדברים הפרטיים אין טעם כלל כי לא היה זה תורה של חכמה.

Maharal, Tiferet Yisrael 7

. . . regarding the entire Torah, the verse stated,[10] "For who is such a great nation which has righteous statutes and judgments like this whole Torah . . ." And the verse stated further,[11] "And you must guard and perform the Torah for it is your wisdom and insight in the eyes of the nations who will hear of all these Statutes [and they will say, 'This is only a wise and insightful nation!'] . . ."

We see that everything in the Torah, the generalities and the specifics are all items of wisdom, not as the Rambam thought, that the specific items have no reason at all; for if this were so, it would not be a Torah of wisdom.

e. How should we relate to such reasons?

i. Regardless of whether mitzvot have reasons, ideally we should not delve into them,

1. This is the position of the Kuzari.[12]

---

10. D'varim 4:8.
11. D'varim 4:6.
12. Kuzari 2:26.

ספר הכוזרי ב:כ"ו

ואין אני טוען ואומר בהחלט חלילה לי מא־ל כי כונת העבודה הזאת היא הסדר הזה אשר אמרתי להפך אל נכון נעלם הדבר ונעלה מזה אומר אני תורת הא־להים היא ומי שקבלה בתמימות בלי התפלפלות ובלי התחכמות מעלה הוא מן המתחכם והחוקר אך מי שנטה מן המדרגה העליונה הזאת אל המחקר מוטב לו כי יבקש טעם לדברים האלה אשר יסודם בחכמה הא־לוהית מאשר יעזבם לסברות רעות ולספקות המביאים את האדם לאבדון:

Kuzari 2:26

I am not claiming at all, G-d forbid, that the intention of the [Sacrificial] service is as per the order which I have explained. On the contrary, the truth is that it is hidden and more elevated than what I have explained – I say that it is G-d's Torah. And one who accepts it in innocence without philosophizing and without being over-clever is on a higher level than the one who tries to be over-clever and who investigates.

However, one who has already deviated from this high level[13] and has turned to investigation, it is better for him to search for a reason for these things which have their foundation in G-dly wisdom than it would be to abandon them to evil rationales and doubts which lead a person to [spiritual] destruction.

ii. We should definitely delve into the reasons for mitzvot
    1. This is the position of the Rambam as we saw above.

9. The Full Text of the Rambam's Comments

a. The Rambam's comments on whether the mitzvot have reasons or not can be found primarily in three places:
    i. Moreh N'vuchim 3:48
    ii. Moreh N'vuchim 3:26
    iii. Moreh N'vuchim 3:31
b. The second source is cited partially above. The last of these is cited in full above. We shall cite the first two in full as follows.
c. Rambam, Moreh N'vuchim 3:48

ספר מורה נבוכים - חלק ג פרק מח

וזה הטעם גם כן ב"שילוח הקן", כי הביצים אשר שכבה האם עליהם והאפרוחים הצריכים לאמם על הרוב אינם ראויים לאכילה, וכשישלח האם ותלך לה, לא תצטער בראות לקיחת הבנים. ועל הרוב יהיה סיבה להניח הכל, כי מה שהיה לוקח ברוב הפעמים אינו ראוי לאכילה: ואם אלו הצערים הנפשיים חסר התורה עליהם בבהמות ובעופות, כל שכן בבני האדם כולם. ולא תקשה עלי באמרם "ז"ל", "האומר על קן צפור יגיעו רחמיך

13. I.e., innocent acceptance.

וגו'" - כי הוא לפי אחת משני הדעות אשר זכרנום - רצוני לומר, דעת מי שחושב שאין טעם לתורה, אלא הרצון לבד, ואנחנו נמשכנו אחר הדעת השני:

Moreh N'vuchim 3:48

This is also the reason for [the mitzvah of] sending away the mother bird. Because most of the time, the eggs on which the mother [bird] is nesting and such young chicks which still require their mother, are not fit for consumption and when he[14] sends away the mother and she leaves, she will not be pained by seeing the taking of her offspring. In the majority of cases, this will cause one to desist [and not take any eggs or chicks] since most of the time one will end up taking something unfit for consumption. And if the Torah took mercy upon the spiritual pain of animals and birds, how much more so for all human beings.

Now do not question me by citing the statement [of the sages], "We should tell a person to be silent if he says, 'Your [G-d's] mercy extends [even] to the nest of a bird!'" since this statement is only according to one of the two opinions which we have mentioned, that is the opinion that holds that there is no reason for the Torah except G-d's will. However, we have followed the second opinion.

i. The Rambam's view is that the mitzvah's purpose is to prevent an animal from experiencing the pain of seeing its progeny taken away.
ii. Secondarily, he mentions the need for sensitization of people towards paining other humans, through sensitization to the pain of animals.

d. Moreh N'vuchim 3:26

ספר מורה נבוכים - חלק ג פרק כו

כמו שחלקו אנשי העיון מבעלי התורה אם מעשיו ית' נמשכים אחר חכמה או אחר רצון לבד, לא לבקשת תכלית כלל, כן חלקו זאת המחלוקת בעצמה במה שנתן לנו מן המצוות. שיש מי שלא יבקש לזה סיבה כלל ויאמר שהתורות כולם נמשכות אחר הרצון לבד; ויש מי שיאמר שכל מצוה ואזהרה מהם נמשכת אחר החכמה, והמכוון בה - תכלית אחת, ושהמצוות כולם יש להם סיבה ומפני התועלת צווה בהם. והיות לכולם עילה, אלא שאנחנו נסכול עילת קצתם ולא נדע אפני החכמה בהם - הוא דעתנו כולנו, ההמון והסגולות. וכתובי התורה מבוארים בזה, "חוקים ומשפטים צדיקים". "משפטי ה' אמת, צדקו יחדיו". ואלו שנקראים "חוקים", כשעטנז ובשר בחלב ושעיר המשתלח", אשר כתבו עליהם החכמים "ז"ל" ואמרו, "דברים שחקקתי לך, ואין לך רשות להרהר בהם, והשטן מקטרג עליהן, ואומות העולם משיבים עליהן" - לא יאמין המון החכמים" שהם ענינים שאין להם סיבה כלל ולא בוקש להם תכלית - כי זה יביא לפעולות הבל (כמו שזכרנו); אבל יאמין המון ה"חכמים" שיש להם עילה - רצוני לומר, תכלית מועילה על

14. The one who finds the eggs and mother bird.

כל פנים, אלא שנעלמה ממנו, אם לקיצור דעותינו או לחסרון חכמתנו. כל ה"מצות", אם כן, יש להם אצלם סיבה - רצוני לומר, כי למצוה ההיא או לאזהרה יש תכלית מועילה, מהם מה שהתבאר לנו צד התועלת בהם. כאזהרה מן הרציחה ומן הגניבה, ומהם מה שלא התבארה תועלתם כמו שהתבאר בנזכרים, כאיסור ה"ערלה" ו"כלאי הכרם". והם אשר תועלתם מבוארת אצל ההמון יקראו "משפטים", ואלו שאין תועלתם מבוארת אצל ההמון יקראו "חוקים". ויאמרו תמיד, "'כי לא דבר רק הוא', ואם ריק הוא - 'מכם' - רצונו לומר, שאין נתינת אלו המצוות דבר ריק, שאין תכלית מועילה לו, ואם יראה לכם בדבר מן המצות שענינו כן - החסרון הוא מהשגתכם. וכבר ידעת הדבר המפורסם אצלנו ששלמה ידע סיבות המצוות כולן, מלבד "פרה אדומה"; וכן אמרם שהא-לוה העלים סיבות ה"מצוות" שלא יזלזלו בהם, כמו שארע לשלמה בשלש "מצוות" אשר התבארה עילתם - ועל זה העיקר נמשכו כל דבריהם, וכתובי הספרים יורו עליו:

אלא שאני מצאתי דבר לחכמים ז"ל ב"בראשית רבה" יראה ממנו בתחילת מחשבה שקצת ה"מצוות" אין להם עילה אלא המצוה בהם לבד, ולא כון בהם תכלית אחר ולא תועלת נמצאת - והוא אמרם שם, "וכי מה אכפת לו להקדוש ברוך הוא בין מי שהוא שוחט מן הצואר למי שהוא שוחט מן העורף? הוה אומר, לא נתנו המצוות אלא לצרוף בהן את הבריות - שנאמר, "אמרת ה' צרופה". ועם היות המאמר הזה נפלא מאד, שלא ימצא לו דומה בדבריהם, פרשתי אני בו פרוש תשמעהו עתה - עד שלא נצא מסדר דבריהם כולם ולא נפרד מהשורש המוסכם עליו, והוא - היות כל המצוות בוקש בהם תכלית מועילה במציאות, "כי לא דבר ריק הוא", ואמר, "לא אמרתי לזרע יעקב תוהו בקשוני, אני יי דובר צדק, מגיד מישרים". ואשר צריך שיאמינהו כל מי שדעתו שלמה בזה הענין הוא מה שאספרהו, וזה, שכלל ה"מצוה" יש לה סיבה בהכרח ומפני תועלת אחת צווה בה, אבל חלקיה הם אשר נאמר בהם שהם למצוה לבד. והמשל בו, שהריגת בעלי החיים לצורך המזון הטוב - מבוארת התועלת, כמו שאנחנו עתידים לבאר; אמנם היותה בשחיטה, לא בנחירה, ובפסיקת הושט והגרגרת במקום מיוחד - אלו וכיוצא בהם "לצרוף בהן את הבריות". וכן יתבאר לך ממשלם, "שוחט מן הצואר לשוחט מן העורף". וזכרתי לך זה המשל, מפני שבא בדבריהם "ז"ל", "שוחט מן הצואר לשוחט מן העורף". אבל אמיתת הדבר היא, כי כאשר הביא ההכרח לאכילת בעלי חיים כוון למיתה הקלה, עם קלות המעשה - שאי אפשר הכאת הצואר אלא בסיף וכיוצא בו, והשחיטה אפשר בכל דבר; ולברור מיתה קלה התנו חידוד הסכין. ואשר ראוי להמשיל באמת מענין החלקים הוא הקרבן - כי המצוה בהקרבת הקרבן יש לה תועלת גדולה מבוארת (כמו שאני עתיד לבאר), אבל היות הקרבן האחד "כבש" והאחד "איל" והיות מספרם מספר מיוחד - זה אי אפשר לתת לו עילה כלל. וכל מי שמטריד עצמו לתת סיבה לדבר מאלו החלקים הוא בעיני משתגע שגעון ארוך ואינו מסיר בזה הרחקה, אך מוסיף הרחקות. ומי שידמה שאלו יש להם סיבה הוא רחוק מן האמת כמי שידמה שה"מצוה" כולה היא ללא תועלת נמצאת:

Moreh N'vuchim 3:26

The Rambam establishes his central principle that all mitzvot have a reason, even those known as "chukkim," decrees.

Just as the sages who search [for the truth] were divided on the question whether the actions of Hashem, may He be Blessed, are the result of His wisdom, or of His will alone without being intended for any purpose at all, so they were also at odds regarding the mitzvot which Hashem gave us.

There are those who seek no reason for this [system of mitzvot] at all and say that all of the laws are functions of Hashem's will alone. Others say that every mitzvah and prohibition is a function of wisdom and serves a certain aim and that there is a reason for each of the mitzvot and that Hashem commanded [us to perform] them because they have a benefit.

The view of all of us, the masses as well as the elite [sages], is that there is a reason for every mitzvah, except that there are some for which we fail to understand the reason and for which we do not know the paths of wisdom. The verses of the Torah are clear on this when they say,[15] "Decrees[16] and ordinances which are righteous,"[17] "the judgments of Hashem are true, and altogether righteous."[18]

There are those [mitzvot] which are called "*chukkim*,"[19] such as [not wearing] *sha'atnez*,[20] [not eating] meat and milk, and the goat which is sent [into the desert on Yom Kippur].[21] Our sages said, regarding them, "[These are] things which I have decreed for you and you have no right to raise doubts about them; and the *satan*[22] lobbies against them and gentiles question them." The majority of the sages generally do not think that they[23] have no cause at all, and serve no purpose; for this would lead us to assume that Hashem's actions are purposeless (as we've mentioned [this is unconscionable]). Rather, [the majority of the sages] hold that they have a cause, that is, they have some beneficial purpose in some regard although it is hidden from us either due to the deficiency of our knowledge or the lack of our wisdom.

Therefore, all of the mitzvot have a reason: that is, each mitzvah or prohibition has a beneficial purpose and we understand that purpose for some of them, for example, [we understand the benefit of] the prohibitions against murder and stealing; and some of them for which we do not understand the purpose (like those examples mentioned above [and]) for

---

15. These verses imply that the mitzvot in general have a moral value and effect.
16. Implying that even the *chukkim*, the laws for which everyone agrees the reasons (if there are any) are challenging, are righteous.
17. D'varim 4:8.
18. Tehillim 19:10.
19. Decrees.
20. The prohibition against wearing clothing made from combined wool and linen. See Vayikra 19:19.
21. Vayikra, Chapter 16.
22. One's evil inclination.
23. The *chukkim*

example, the prohibitions against *orlah*[24] and *kila'ei hakerem*.[25] Those mitzvot for which the purpose is clear to the masses are called "*mishpatim*"[26] and those for which the purpose is not clear to the masses are called, "*chukkim*."

And they always say [citing the Torah],[27] "For this thing[28] is not an empty [thing from you]"[29] [which they explained as] "it is not empty" but if you do happen to find it [empty], it is "from you."[30] This means to say that the giving of these mitzvot is not something empty [of purpose] which has no useful function; and if it seems to you that this is the case regarding any mitzvah, the lack is due to *your* misunderstanding.

And it is already known to you that it is well-known amongst us that Sh'lomo[31] knew the reasons for all of the mitzvot except for the Red Heifer[32] and [you] also [know] their saying that G-d hid the reasons of the mitzvot so that people would not degrade the mitzvot (which is what happened to Sh'lomo[33] regarding the three mitzvot, the reasons for which were revealed).[34] Based on this foundation, all their[35] words were framed and the verses in the [holy] books prove this.

The Rambam now cites a Midrash which seems to contradict his principle, seemingly claiming that the mitzvot have no purpose for humanity and that they exist only so that we obey G-d.

24. The prohibition against eating the fruit of a fruit tree in its first three years of growth and the requirement to eat the fourth year's growth in Yerushalayim. See Vayikra 19:23–25.

25. The prohibition against sowing mixed seeds in one patch of ground. See D'varim 22:9.

26. Ordinances.

27. This saying is brought in the Talmud Y'rushalmi in many places. See, for example, Pei'ah 1:1 in the name of Rabbi Manna.

28. I.e., the Torah.

29. D'varim 22:47.

30. That the lack of understanding stems from you, but the mitzvot are not empty of reason.

31. King Solomon, *zt"l*.

32. Kohelet Rabbah 7:35.

33. For further reference, see Sanhedrin 21b. King Solomon, the sage who understood the reasons for all the mitzvot bar one, failed precisely in the 3 mitzvot for which the Torah gives the reasons explicitly. We learn from here that knowledge of the reasons for the mitzvot can be dangerous, since when one knows the reasons one can easily rationalize why the mitzvot do not apply in particular cases or to particular people. Such rationalizations lead to disaster.

34. These three mitzvot are the three things which were forbidden to a Jewish King in excess. See D'varim 17:16–17. The Torah itself supplies the reasons for these three mitzvot.

35. The sages'.

However, I have found a saying by the sages, *z"l*, in B'reishit Rabbah from which it seems initially that some of the mitzvot have no reason except for the command itself; and that Hashem had no intention in them for any other purpose and no utility. This is what they say there,[36]

> "Does it matter to the Holy One, Blessed be He, whether one slaughters from the throat or the [back of the] neck? Rather, the mitzvot were only given to refine humans, as the verse says, 'The statement of Hashem is refined.'"[37]

The Rambam now explains that this Midrash also fits his understanding.

Now despite the fact that this saying is truly amazing and has no parallel in their[38] words, I have explained it with a commentary (which you will hear now) which does not deviate from the order of their words and does not part ways with the principle[39] we agreed upon [above]. The explanation is as follows.

Since all mitzvot have a useful purpose in reality [as we have already proved from the verses,] "For this thing [the Torah] is not an empty [thing from you]"[40] and "I[41] did not say to the children of Ya'akov, 'Seek Me for nothing!' I am Hashem Who speaks justice and relates righteousness,"[42] [therefore] that which every whole-minded person must believe is as follows: in general, each mitzvah definitely has a reason and for that one purpose Hashem commanded it; however regarding the *details* of each mitzvah we say that their purpose is for the sake of commandment alone.

36. B'reishit Rabbah 44:1 with textual variations. See also Yalkut Shimoni, Vayikra 11:536.

37. Tehillim 18:31. This verse can also be understood as "The statement of Hashem ONLY comes to purify," which is how it is being interpreted by the Midrash. Also see Chapter Two where this verse is cited in the famous Midrash Tanchuma (cited by the Maharal there) which relates the discussion between Rabbi Akiva and Turnus Rufus. In the citation in our chapter (in the Midrash currently under discussion), the interpretation of this verse seems to be at variance with how it is interpreted in the Tanchuma. Here it seems to be saying that Hashem's statements refine through the simple obedience a person displays through submission to G-d's decree whereas in the Tanchuma there seems to be a clear understanding that mitzvot help us perfect ourselves in this world.

38. The sages'.

39. That all mitzvot have a purpose.

40. D'varim 22:47.

41. G-d.

42. Y'shayahu 45:19.

An example of this is the slaughter of animals for the purpose of [obtaining] good sustenance. In this case, the purpose is clear as we will explain later;[43] however, [the details of this commandment] that it should be through ritual slaughter and not stabbing, and that the esophagus and trachea need to be severed at a particular place – all such details are "to refine humans."[44] This is what becomes clear from their example [in the Midrash], "[Does it matter to the Holy One, Blessed be He, whether] one slaughters from the throat or the neck?"

I have mentioned this example because of their [exact] language [focusing on the detail of the mitzvah], "one slaughters from the throat or the neck?" However, the truth of the matter is that once one must consume a living creature, Hashem intended for the most painless death. For it is impossible to sever the neck without some sort of sword and slaughtering can be done with any implement but in order to select the most painless death, they created the required condition of having a sharpened knife.[45]

However, the best example in this matter is sacrifices. The mitzvah to perform sacrifices has a great, clear reason (as I will explain later), however, [the details of the sacrifice] that one sacrifice should be a lamb and the other a ram and that there should be a certain number of each [animal] – for these details it is impossible to give a reason at all. *And anyone who bothers himself giving a reason for any of these details is a madman in my eyes, sick with a protracted insanity. Through such actions he does not remove distance [between peoples' understanding and the truth] but actually adds distance.* And anyone who imagines that these have a reason is far from the truth, as much as the person who imagines that mitzvot in general have no existing purpose.

i. The Rambam's belief is that each mitzvah has a reason but that the details of each mitzvah may often simply be there to induce obedience to Hashem.
ii. He does continue (after the section cited) to explain that he has comprehended the reasons for most of the mitzvot and even some of the details.

10. The Full Text of the Ramban's Comments

a. The Ramban's comments can be found in his commentary to D'varim 22:6 which we cite here in full:

43. I.e., the purpose is to obtain healthy food.

44. Tehillim 18:31 as above. The Rambam is saying that obedience to the details of the mitzvot is for no reason besides obedience to G-d.

45. Here the Rambam explains one of the details of the laws of slaughtering – that the knife must be extremely sharp.

רמב"ן על דברים פרק כב פסוק ו

(ו) כי יקרא קן צפור לפניך גם זו מצוה מבוארת מן אותו ואת בנו לא תשחטו ביום אחד (ויקרא כב כח) כי הטעם בשניהם לבלתי היות לנו לב אכזרי ולא נרחם, או שלא יתיר הכתוב לעשות השחתה לעקור המין אע"פ שהתיר השחיטה במין ההוא, והנה ההורג האם והבנים ביום אחד או לוקח אותם בהיות להם דרור לעוף כאלו יכרית המין ההוא: וכתב הרב במורה הנבוכים (ג מח) כי טעם שלוח הקן וטעם אותו ואת בנו לא תשחטו ביום אחד, כדי להזהיר שלא ישחוט הבן בעיני האם כי יש לבהמות דאגה גדולה בזה, ואין הפרש בין דאגת האדם לדאגת הבהמות על בניהם, כי אהבת האם וחנותה לבני בטנה איננו נמשך אחרי השכל והדבור אבל הוא מפעולת כח המחשבה המצויה בבהמות כאשר היא מצויה באדם ואם כן, אין עיקר האיסור באותו ואת בנו רק בבנו ואותו, אבל הכל הרחקה ויותר נכון, בעבור שלא נתאכזר ואמר הרב ואל תשיב עלי ממאמר החכמים (ברכות לג:) האומר על קן צפור יגיעו רחמיך, כי זו אחת משתי סברות, סברת מי שיראה כי אין טעם למצות אלא חפץ הבורא, ואנחנו מחזיקים בסברא השניה שיהיה בכל המצות טעם והוקשה עליו עוד מה שמצא בב"ר (מד א) וכי מה איכפת לו להקב"ה בין שוחט מן הצואר לשוחט מן העורף, הא לא נתנו המצות אלא לצרף בהם את הבריות שנאמר (משלי ל ה) כל אמרת א-לוה צרופה:

וזה הענין שגזר הרב במצות שיש להם טעם, מבואר הוא מאד כי בכל אחד טעם ותועלת ותקון לאדם, מלבד שכרן מאת המצוה בהן יתברך וכבר ארז"ל (סנהדרין כא:) מפני מה לא נתגלו טעמי תורה וכו', ודרשו (פסחים קיט) ולמכסה עתיק, זה המגלה דברים שכסה עתיק יומין ומאי ניהו טעמי תורה וכבר דרשו בפרה אדומה (במדב"ר יט ג ד), שאמר שלמה על הכל עמדתי, ופרשה של פרה אדומה חקרתי ושאלתי ופשפשתי, אמרתי אחכמה והיא רחוקה ממני (קהלת ז כג), ואמר ר' יוסי בר' חנינא אמר לו הקב"ה למשה לך אני מגלה טעם פרה אדומה אבל לאחרים חקה, דכתיב (זכריה יד ו) והיה ביום ההוא לא יהיה אור יקרות וקפאון, יקפאון כתיב, דברים המכוסים מכם בעולם הזה עתידין להיות צפויים לעולם הבא, כהדין סמיא דצפי, דכתיב (ישעיה מב טז) והולכתי עורים בדרך לא ידעו, וכתיב (שם) אלה הדברים עשיתים ולא עזבתים, שכבר עשיתים לר' עקיבא הנה בארו שאין מניעות טעמי תורה ממנו אלא עורון בשכלנו, ושכבר נתגלה טעם החמורה שבהם לחכמי ישראל, וכאלה רבות בדבריהם, ובתורה ובמקרא דברים רבים מודיעין כן, והרב הזכיר מהן:

אבל אלו ההגדות אשר נתקשו על הרב, כפי דעתי ענין אחר להם, שרצו לומר שאין התועלת במצות להקב"ה בעצמו יתעלה, אבל התועלת באדם עצמו למנוע ממנו נזק או אמונה רעה או מדה מגונה, או לזכור הנסים ונפלאות הבורא יתברך ולדעת את השם וזהו "לצרף בהן", שיהיו ככסף צרוף, כי הצורף הכסף אין מעשהו בלא טעם, אבל להוציא ממנו כל סיג, וכן המצות להוציא מלבנו כל אמונה רעה ולהודיענו האמת ולזוכרו תמיד:

ולשון זו האגדה עצמה הוזכרה בילמדנו (תנחומא שמיני ח) בפרשת זאת החיה, וכי מה איכפת לו להקב"ה בין שוחט בהמה ואוכל או נוחר ואוכל כלום אתה מועילו או כלום אתה מזיקו, או מה איכפת לו בין אוכל טהורות או אוכל טמאות, אם חכמת חכמת לך (משלי ט יב), הא לא נתנו המצות אלא לצרף את הבריות, שנאמר (תהלים יב ז) אמרות ה' אמרות טהורות, ונאמר כל אמרת א-לוה צרופה, למה, שיהא מגין עליך הנה מפורש בכאן שלא באו לומר אלא שאין התועלת אליו יתעלה שיצטרך לאורה כמחושב מן המנורה, ושיצטרך למאכל הקרבנות וריח הקטרת, כנראה מפשוטיהם ואפילו הזכר לנפלאותיו שעשה שצוה לעשות לזכר ליציאת מצרים ומעשה בראשית, אין התועלת לו,

רק שנדע אנחנו האמת ונזכה בו עד שנהיה ראויים להיות מגן עלינו, כי כבודנו וספרנו בנפלאותיו מאפס ותוהו נחשבו לו:

והביא ראיה מן השוחט מן הצואר והעורף לומר שכולם לנו ולא להקב"ה, לפי שלא יתכן לומר בשחיטה שיהא בה תועלת וכבוד לבורא יתברך בצואר יותר מהעורף או הניחור, אלא לנו הם להדריכנו בנתיבות הרחמים גם בעת השחיטה והביאו ראיה אחרת, או מה איכפת לו בין אוכל טהורות והם המאכלים המותרים, לאוכל טמאות והם המאכלים האסורים, שאמרה בהם התורה (ויקרא יא כח) טמאים המה לכם, ורמז שהוא להיותנו נקיי הנפש חכמים משכילי האמת ואמרם אם חכמת חכמת לך, הזכירו כי המצות המעשיות כגון שחיטת הצואר ללמדנו המדות הטובות, והמצות הגדורות במינין לזקק את נפשותינו, כמו שאמרה תורה (שם כ כה) ולא תשקצו את נפשותיכם בבהמה ובעוף ובכל אשר תרמוש האדמה אשר הבדלתי לכם לטמא, א"כ כלם לתועלתנו בלבד וזה כמו שאמר אליהוא (איוב לה ו) אם חטאת מה תפעל בו ורבו פשעיך מה תעשה לו, ואמר (שם פסוק ז) או מה מידך יקח וזה דבר מוסכם בכל דברי רבותינו:

ושאלו בירושלמי בנדרים (פ"ט ה"א) אם פותחין לאדם בכבוד המקום בדברים שבינו לבין המקום, והשיבו על השאלה הזאת, אי זהו כבוד המקום כגון סוכה שאיני עושה לולב שאיני נוטל תפילין שאיני מניח, והיינו כבוד המקום, משמע דלנפשיה הוא דמהני, כהדא אם צדקת מה תתן לו או מה מידך יקח, אם חטאת מה תפעל בו ורבו פשעיך מה תעשה לו הנה בארו שאפילו הלולב והסוכה והתפילין שצוה בהן שיהו לאות על ידך ולזכרון בין עיניך כי ביד חזקה הוציאך ה' ממצרים, אינן לכבוד ה' יתברך, אבל לרחם על נפשותינו וכבר סדרו לנו בתפלת יום הכפורים, אתה הבדלת אנוש מראש ותכירהו לעמוד לפניך כי מי יאמר לך מה תעשה ואם יצדק מה יתן לך וכן אמר בתורה (לעיל י יג) לטוב לך, כאשר פירשתי (שם פסוק יב), וכן ויצונו ה' לעשות את כל החקים האלה ליראה את ה' א-להינו לטוב לנו כל הימים (לעיל ו כד) והכוונה בכלם לטוב לנו, ולא לו יתברך ויתעלה, אבל כל מה שנצטוינו שיהיו בריותיו צרופות ומזוקקות בלא סיגי מחשבות רעות ומדות מגונות:

וכן מה שאמרו (ברכות לג:) לפי שעושה מדותיו של הקב"ה רחמים ואינן אלא גזרות, לומר שלא חס הא-ל על קן צפור ולא הגיעו רחמיו על אותו ואת בנו, שאין רחמיו מגיעין בבעלי הנפש הבהמית למנוע אותנו מלעשות בהם צרכנו, שאם כן היה אוסר השחיטה, אבל טעם המניעה ללמד אותנו מדת הרחמנות ושלא נתאכזר כי האכזריות תתפשט בנפש האדם, כידוע בטבחים שוחטי השורים הגדולים והחמורים שהם אנשי דמים זובחי אדם אכזרים מאד, ומפני זה אמרו (קידושין פב) טוב שבטבחים שותפו של עמלק והנה המצות האלה בבהמה ובעוף אינן רחמנות עליהם, אלא גזירות בנו להדריכנו וללמד אותנו המדות הטובות וכן יקראו הם כל המצות שבתורה עשה ולא תעשה גזירות, כמו שאמרו (מכילתא בחדש ו) במשל המלך שנכנס למדינה אמרו לו עבדיו גזור עליהם גזירות, אמר להם כשיקבלו מלכותי אגזור עליהם גזירות, כך אמר הקב"ה קבלתם מלכותי אנכי ה' א-להיך (שמות כ ב), קבלו גזירותי לא יהיה לך וכו' (שם פסוק ג): אבל במדרשו של רבי נחוניא בן הקנה בשלוח הקן מדרש שיש במצוה סוד, אמר רבי רחמאי מאי דכתיב שלח תשלח את האם ולא אמר את האב, אלא שלח תשלח את האם בכבוד אותה בינה שנקראת אם העולם דכתיב (משלי ב ג) כי אם לבינה תקרא מאי ואת הבנים תקח לך, אמר רבי רחמאי אותם בנים שגדלה ומאי ניהו שבעת ימי הסוכה ודיני שבעת ימי השבוע וכו' והנה המצוה הזאת רומזת לענין גדול, ולכך שכרה מרובה למען ייטב לך והארכת ימים:

Ramban, D'varim 22:6

The Ramban first presents his position, which is that the reason for the various mitzvot requiring us to behave with compassion towards certain animals is in order that compassion and kindness become engrained within us.

"When you come across a bird's nest . . ."[46]

This mitzvah is also clarified through [the same idea behind the mitzvah of,] "You may not slaughter a [female] animal and its progeny on the same day."[47] In both of them, the reason is to prevent us becoming cruel and unmerciful. Or perhaps another reason is that the Torah does not allow us to perform an act of destruction and destroy an entire species even though it allows us to slaughter and eat a particular animal of that species, and someone who kills a female and its progeny on one day or who takes them when they are free to fly, partially destroys that species.

The Ramban now examines the opinion of the Rambam (Maimonides).

And the Rabbi[48] wrote in the Moreh N'vuchim[49] that the reason for the mitzvah of sending away the mother bird and for the mitzvah of "You may not slaughter a [female] animal and its progeny on the same day," is in order to take heed not to kill the progeny before the mother because there is no difference between the concern of a human [over a human child] to that of an animal over their children. This is because the love of the mother and her mercy on the children of her womb are not functions of the mind and [the faculty of] speech but are derived from the [rudimentary] power of thought which is found [even] in animals as much as it is found in people. If so, the essence of the prohibition against slaughtering an animal and its progeny is not because of the animal and its progeny but rather it is a precaution in order that we not become cruel. The Rambam said further,

> Do not question me by citing the statement [of the sages],[50] "We should tell a person to be silent if he says, 'Your [G-d's] mercy extends [even] to the nest of a bird!'" since this statement is only according to one of the two opinions, that is the opinion that holds that there is no reason for the Torah except G-d's will. However, we have followed the second opinion which holds that every mitzvah has a reason.

46. D'varim 22:6.
47. Vayikra 22:28.
48. The Rambam.
49. Moreh N'vuchim 3:48 cited in its entirety above.
50. Mishnah B'rachot 5:3.

And furthermore, the Rambam found difficulty with their[51] statement in B'reishit Rabbah [which states],[52]

> Does it matter to the Holy One, Blessed be He, whether one slaughters from the throat or the [back of the] neck? Rather, the mitzvot were only given to refine humans, as the verse says, "All[53] the statement of Hashem is refined."[54]

Now this issue which the Rabbi[55] decreed – that mitzvot have reasons – is very clear, because each mitzvah has a reason and a utility and improvement for the human being. This is besides the reward for the mitzvot from Hashem, may He be Blessed.

The Ramban now brings several proofs that mitzvot have reasons and that if we do not understand a mitzvah it is only due to our intellectual and spiritual shortcomings.

Our sages have already asked,[56] "Why were the reasons for the mitzvot not revealed?" [57,58] They deduced [the answer from a verse,] as follows,[59] "[To what does the verse refer when it states,] 'Elegant clothing'?[60] It refers to

51. Our sages'.
52. B'reishit Rabbah 44:1.
53. There seems to be a printer's error here. There are two similar verses in the Tanach, one in Mishlei 30:5 which begins with the word "All," which is what we have cited in the Ramban. The other similar verse is in Tehillim 18:31 which just states "the statement of Hashem is refined," omitting the word "All." It seems more likely that there is an error in the addition of the word "all," as in the Midrash in B'reishit Rabbah (which is the source cited in the text of the Maharal), in the Vilna edition, this word is omitted and thus the verse is from Tehillim 18:31. See Chapter Two where this verse was similarly cited.
54. As the Maharal states in Chapter Seven, he understands that the word "refined" is used here in the sense of being tested and tried through the process of refinement.
55. The Rambam.
56. Lit., "stated."
57. Sanhedrin 21b.
58. This Gemara clearly implies that the mitzvot have reasons, which were hidden for particular reasons. As the Gemara explains there, when people know the reasons for mitzvot, they often rationalize that the mitzvot do not apply to them and then fail egregiously.
59. P'sachim 119a.
60. Y'shayahu 23:18.

one who reveals matters which the Eternal One hid. And what are these matters? . . . These are the reasons of the Torah."[61]

And they [the sages] already deduced regarding the Red Heifer,[62] "That Sh'lomo said, 'I have comprehended everything and I have investigated and asked about and analyzed the portion of the Red Heifer, "I said I will gain wisdom, but it is beyond me".'"[63] Furthermore,[64] "Rabbi Yossi said in the name of Rabbi Chanina, 'The Holy One, Blessed be He, said to Moshe, "I am revealing the reason for the Red Heifer to you but for everyone else it will be a decree." As it is written, "On that day there will be no light but heavy clouds and thick."[65], [66] However, in the verse, the word "and thick"[67] is actually written "will become clear"[68] which indicates that things which are currently hidden from you in this world will be visible in the World to Come, like a blind man will see [at that time] as is written, "I will lead blind people in a way they do not know"[69] and as is written there,[70] "these are things I have done and not abandoned them" by which [Hashem] means, "I have already done them – that I revealed them to Rabbi Akiva [which implies that even though the reasons for many of the mitzvot may be concealed in general, certain unique sages merited to understand them]."'

Through all these examples they[71] have explained that the only obstacle preventing us from grasping the reasons of the Torah is the blindness of our minds and that the reason for the most challenging of the mitzvot was already revealed to the sages of Israel. There are many such examples in their words. And in the Torah and Scriptures there are many statements which teach this [principle] and the Rabbi[72] mentioned some of them.

The Ramban now explains the source (the Midrash in B'reishit Rabbah)[73] with which the Rambam had difficulty.

---

61. This source also implies that the mitzvot have reasons.
62. B'midbar Rabbah 19:3.
63. Kohelet 7:23.
64. B'midbar Rabbah 19:6.
65. In Hebrew, וקפאון, "*v'kipa'on.*"
66. Z'chari'ah 14:6. For further study, see the translation of the Ramban here in the edition of Rabbi Charles Chavel, *zt"l* (Judaica Press Incorporated: 2003).
67. In Hebrew, וקפאון, "*v'kipa'on.*"
68. In Hebrew, יקפאון, "*y'kipa'on.*" See the Maharzav ad loc.
69. Y'shayahu 42:16.
70. Y'shayahu 42:16.
71. Our sages.
72. The Rambam.
73. B'reishit Rabbah 44:1.

But those Midrashim with which the Rabbi[74] had difficulty, in my opinion, teach something altogether different. They teach that the mitzvot do not provide Hashem, may He be Elevated, with any benefit. Rather, the benefit is for human beings: to prevent themselves from being harmed or from [gaining] an evil belief or a disreputable character trait; or to remind themselves of the miracles and wonders of the Creator, may He be Blessed; and to [come to] know G-d.

This is the meaning of the phrase, "to refine"[75] – that humans should become like refined silver, because one who refines silver does not do so without reason, rather he does so in order to remove all dross [from the silver.] So too is it with the mitzvot – [their purpose is] to extract from our hearts any evil belief and to instruct us in the truth and to [help us] remember it forever.

But the language of this Midrash itself was cited in the Midrash Y'lamdeinu, in the section of "This is the animal . . ." as follows:[76]

> "Does it matter to the Holy One, Blessed be He, whether one slaughters an animal and then eats or whether one stabs it and then eats! Neither of these [methods] benefits Him and neither of these [methods] harms Him.
>
> "Similarly, does it matter to Him whether one eats *tahor*[77] [food] or whether one eats *Tamei* [food]?[78]
>
> "Rather, 'if you have gained wisdom, you have gained wisdom for yourself'[79] and the mitzvot were only given to refine humans, as it says, 'The statements of Hashem are pure statements [like *purified silver*, clear to the world, *refined* sevenfold,]'[80] and it says, 'All[81] the statement of

74. The Rambam.

75. In the "problematic" Midrash, "Does it matter to the Holy One, Blessed be He, whether one slaughters from the throat or the [back of the] neck? Rather, the mitzvot were only given to refine humans, as the verse says, 'The statement of Hashem is refined.'"

76. Tanchuma, Sh'mini 8.

77. In Hebrew, טהור, "*tahor*." Something which is *tahor* is compatible with the Temple and its functions. The opposite of this is *tamei*. Occasionally, the word *tahor* is used to indicate something which is halachically acceptable, in particular, kosher food. See the continuation of the Ramban below.

78. In Hebrew, טמא, "*tamei*." Something which is *tamei* is incompatible with the Temple and its functions. The opposite of this is *tahor*. Occasionally, the word *tamei* is used to indicate something which is halachically unacceptable, in particular, non-kosher food. See the continuation of the Ramban below.

79. Mishlei 9:12.

80. Tehillim 12:7. The section in parentheses is omitted by the Midrash but is pertinent to the idea of the refinement which the mitzvot perform.

81. There seems to be a printer's error here. See above, n. 53.

Hashem is refined [it is a shield to all who take refuge in Him].'[82] Why [does Hashem refine each person?] In order to protect you."

The Ramban uses this very similar Midrash to prove that the Midrash in B'reishit Rabbah does not imply that the mitzvot and their details have no meaning, but rather that they have no utility for G-d and, on the contrary, have much utility for human beings. He now analyzes this Midrash in depth.

Here we have [proven] explicitly that our sages [when using the phrase, "the mitzvot were only given to refine humans"] only came to teach us that there is no utility [in the mitzvot] for Hashem, may He be Elevated.

[For example, some might think] He needs light, as might be concluded from [the mitzvah to light] the *m'norah*;[83] or that He needs the food from the sacrifices or the aroma of the incense (as might be understood from the simple meanings [of the verses dealing with these mitzvot])[84] and even remembering His wonders which He did (which He commanded us to do as a reminder of the Exodus from Egypt and of the creation), in all of these, there is no benefit to Him! Rather it is so that we know the truth and merit it to the point that we merit to become worthy of Hashem shielding us. [The reason we understand that the benefit of mitzvot must accrue to ourselves is] because our honoring [of G-d] and our relating His wonders are considered nothing and worthlessness before Him.[85]

And the Midrash[86] cited the example of slaughtering from the throat or [back of] the neck in order to teach that all the mitzvot are for us and not for the Holy One, Blessed be He, because it is impossible to say that there will be more utility and honor for the Creator, may He be Blessed, [when one slaughters] at the throat than at the [back of the] neck or by stabbing. Rather, [it teaches us that] the mitzvot are for us, to guide us in the paths of mercy, even at the time of slaughtering.

And they[87] cited another proof [when they said,] "Similarly, does it matter to Him whether one eats *tahor* [food] or whether one eats *tamei* [food]?" that is, when one eats *tamei* foods which are the forbidden foods.[88]

---

82. As the Maharal says in Chapter Seven, he understands that the word "refined" is used here in the sense of being tested and tried through the process of refinement.

83. The golden candelabrum placed in the Tabernacle and the Temple.

84. See Sh'mot 29:25 and Rashi ad loc.

85. Cf. Y'shayahu 40:17.

86. In B'reishit Rabbah and in the Tanchuma.

87. Our sages in the Midrash Tanchuma.

88. Here the Ramban explains that the terms *tahor* and *tamei* are being used to

Regarding these, the Torah said, "They will be defiled for *you*."[89] And there is a hint [in the Midrash Tanchuma] that this [mitzvah to eat kosher food] is to ensure that *we* are pristine of spirit, wise and understanding the truth. [Further] they said [in the Midrash Tanchuma], "if you have gained wisdom, you have gained wisdom for yourself"[90] [by which] they taught[91] that the practical mitzvot, such as slaughtering at the throat are to teach us good traits and the mitzvot which restrict [the consumption of certain] species [of animals] are to purify our souls. This is as the Torah states, "so that you will not defile your souls through [non-kosher] animals, birds and anything which creeps on the earth which I have designated as being impure for you."[92]

Therefore, all of them[93] are for our utility alone and this is as Elihu said, "If you have sinned, what have you done to Him?[94] And if your misdeeds have multiplied, what have you done to Him?"[95] And he [Elihu] continued,[96] "What can He[97] take from you [to benefit Himself]?"

This is agreed upon in all the words of our sages.

The Ramban now brings a series of proofs from the Talmud and Tanach that the mitzvot are only given to improve human beings.

And they[98] asked in the Y'rushalmi in N'darim[99] [regarding the process

---

mean kosher and non-kosher respectively. This is common usage – see, for example, Mishnah Chullin 8:4.

89. Vayikra 11:28. This verse is dealing with those foods which are forbidden to eat – in particular, non-kosher animals.

90. Mishlei 9:12.

91. Lit., "mentioned."

92. Vayikra 20:25.

93. The mitzvot.

94. G-d.

95. Iyov 35:6.

96. Iyov 37:7.

97. G-d.

98. Our sages.

99. Y'rushalmi N'darim 9:1. This Gemara deals with the method used in annulment of vows. The process is complex, but in short, the source describes questions asked of a person who wishes to annul his vows. The questions seek to ascertain that the person would not have vowed had they been appraised (prior to vowing) of all the consequences of his/her vow. In this section, the Gemara is dealing with the damage a vow causes to one's parents' dignity or G-d's honor. The official conducting the annulment process asks the person who comes to annul his vows whether he would still have vowed had he known in full the affront his vow would cause to his parents' dignity. If the person acknowledges that they did not foresee such an

of annulment of a vow] whether one opens[100] [a breach in the vow by addressing the affront it caused to] the honor of G-d in a matter between the one who vows and G-d. They answered this question as follows,

> [The Gemara asks]What is [an example of a vow which we would annul on the basis that the one vowing did not realize it was an impugning of] G-d's honor?
>
> [The Gemara answers] For example, a person says, "I will not make a *sukkah*"[101] or "I will not take a *lulav*"[102] or "I will not put on *t'fillin*"[103]
>
> [The Gemara asks in astonishment] Is this G-d's honor?
>
> [The Gemara concludes] This teaches us that a person is benefitting himself and not G-d, as we learn [from the verse], "If you have been righteous, what can you give Him or what can He take from you [to benefit Himself]?"[104] and "If you have sinned, what have you done to Him [that is, G-d]? And if your misdeeds have multiplied, what have you done to Him [that is, G-d]?"[105]

[In this statement,] they explained that even the *lulav*, *sukkah* and *t'fillin* (which Hashem commanded as "a sign on your hand and a remembrance on your head, above the nose,[106] that Hashem redeemed you from Egypt with a strong hand")[107] are not for Hashem's honor, may He be Blessed; rather they are to take mercy on our souls. They[108] already composed

---

affront, there are grounds for the annulment. The question debated here is whether the affront caused to G-d's honor is grounds for annulment.

100. The term used to describe the annulment is "to open" – meaning that we open a breach in the binding nature of the vow.

101. A temporary dwelling. We are commanded to live in such booths for seven days a year during the festival of Sukkot. See Vayikra 23:42.

102. Lit., a palm branch. This term is the generic term used to refer to four species of plants and fruit (palm branch, willow and myrtle branches and a citron) which are bought and then used once a day during the festival of Sukkot. See Vayikra 23:40.

103. Phylacteries. See Sh'mot 13:9, 16.

104. Iyov 35:7.

105. See 35:6.

106. The Hebrew phrase is בין עיניך, which means lit., "between your eyes." Our sages explain that this was an idiom in biblical times to denote the entire median line running through the nose, "between the eyes," but not that it means literally on the bridge of the nose, between the eyes. In fact, the *t'fillin*, which are the remembrance referred to here, are worn above the hairline, but on the median line running through the nose.

107. Sh'mot 13:9.

108. Our sages.

[the following prayer] for us in the service of Yom Kippur, "Initially, you separated the human being and you recognized him to stand before you. Because who can say to you, "What are You doing?"[109] And even if such a person is righteous, what can he give You?"[110], [111]

Similarly, Hashem said in the Torah, "[And now, Israel, what does Hashem, your G-d, ask of you? . . . to cherish the mitzvot of Hashem and His decrees which I[112] command you today] *for your own good*,"[113] as I[114] explained.[115] Similarly [the same idea is understood from the verse which states,] "And Hashem commanded us to perform all these decrees, to be in Awe of Hashem our G-d, *for our own good*, forever."[116]

The import of this is that all of them[117] are for our good, not for His, may He be Blessed, and Elevated. Rather, everything that we have been commanded to do is in order that His creations be refined and purified without any drosses of evil thoughts or despised traits.

Similarly [the same idea is conveyed] when they said,[118] "[We should tell a person to be silent if he says, 'Your [G-d's] mercy extends [even] to the nest of a bird!' because] such a person is making Hashem's attributes [due to] Mercy when, in fact, they are exclusively decrees!"[119] [The reason our sages enacted this requirement was because] they meant that G-d does not take mercy on the nest of the bird[120] and His Mercy did not extend to an animal and her progeny [through the prohibition not to slaughter them both on the same day].

---

109. Cf. Iyov 9:12, Kohelet 8:4.
110. Cf. Iyov 35:7.
111. *N'ilah* Service, Yom Kippur.
112. Moshe.
113. D'varim 10:13.
114. The Ramban.
115. Commentary of the Ramban, D'varim 10:12.
116. D'varim 6:24.
117. The mitzvot.
118. Our sages.
119. B'rachot 33b. This is the citation which forms the backbone of this entire chapter of Tiferet Yisrael. See at the beginning of the chapter where it is cited in full and explained by the Maharal. Interestingly, the Ramban quotes this phrase from the Gemara in full, "[We should tell a person to be silent if he says, 'Your [G-d's] mercy extends [even] to the nest of a bird!' because] such a person is making Hashem's attributes [due to] mercy **when, in fact, they are exclusively decrees!**' and as we saw in the Maharal here, he challenges whether the Ramban's explanation relates to this last phrase, "when, in fact, they are exclusively decrees!" See further in the Commentary, Ch. 6 § Point 11 regarding this.
120. For an explanation of this concept at length in the Maharal, see here in Chapter Six.

This is because His Mercy does not extend to animal life forms [to the extent of] preventing us from using them for our needs; for if this was so,[121] Hashem would forbid slaughter [altogether]. Rather, the reason for the prevention[122] is to teach us the attribute of mercy: that we should not become cruel, because cruelty will spread in the human soul, as is known that the butchers who slaughter large oxen and donkeys are men of blood,[123] butchers of men[124] and very cruel. Because of this, they[125] said, "The best[126] of the butchers is the partner of Amalek."[127,128]

Now these mitzvot, which pertain to animals and birds, are not due to mercy on them [the animals and birds], rather they are *decrees* on us to guide us and teach us the good character traits.

The Ramban now proves that all mitzvot are termed, "decrees." This proves that the term "decree" does not indicate a lack of reason for the mitzvah, merely that they are compulsory and mandatory as a result of our being Hashem's subjects.

Thus, they[129] term all the mitzvot "decrees" (both *mitzvot aseh* and prohibitions), as they said,[130]

> This can be compared to a king who entered a country. His servants said to him, "Decree upon them[131] decrees!" [He responded to his servants,

121. That Hashem's mercy was completely extended to animals.

122. Requiring one to send away the mother bird and not to slaughter the animal and her progeny on the same day.

123. Tehillim 55:24.

124. Hoshei'a 13:2.

125. Our sages.

126. See Rashi's version of the text as opposed to that which we have in the Gemara (*kasher*, כשר, "the fittest").

127. See Sh'mot 17:8–16. The nation of Amalek attacked the Jewish people just after they left Egypt, while wandering in the desert. In particular, Amalek attacked the defenseless old and sick, and therefore, they are considered the epitome of cruelty.

128. Kiddushin 82a. The idea here, according to the Ramban, is that butchers share the quality of cruelty with Amalek despite the fact that the butchers are not genetic descendants of Amalek. The reason is, as the Ramban claimed, that cruelty diffuses throughout a person's character and thus even if a butcher starts out a sensitive human being, the process of repetitive slaughter will invariably desensitize a person and infuse him with a certain amount of cruelty which will spread throughout his character.

129. Our sages.

130. M'chilta, Bachodesh 6. The Ramban excerpts the citation, the full text of which is given in the footnote below.

131. I.e., the inhabitants of the country.

> "When they accept my Kingship, then I will decree upon them, because if they don't accept my Kingship, they will not accept my decrees."]
>
> So did Hashem say [to the Jewish people], "You accepted My Kingship [when you agreed to the first of the Ten Commandments, which states,] 'I am Hashem your G-d,'[132] therefore, now you must accept my decrees [the first of which is the second commandment,] 'You shall have not [have the gods of others[133] before Me] . . ."[134, 135]

The Ramban now brings a final proof that the mitzvah of sending away the mother bird, in particular, does have reasons. In particular, he cites a Kabbalistic understanding of the mitzvah to illustrate that these reasons may be hidden. This is clearly a paradigm for all mitzvot for which we do not understand the reasons.

However, in the Midrash of Rabbi N'chuni'ah ben Hakanah is a Midrash[136] regarding [the commandment of] sending away the mother bird [which explains] a hidden [aspect, as follows,][137]

> Rabbi Rachmai said, "What is the import of the verse which states, 'You shall surely send away the mother bird?'[138] Why did it not mention the father bird?
>
> "The answer is that [the mystical significance of this act is that] 'you shall surely send away the mother bird' in honor of that intuition[139]

132. Sh'mot 20:2.
133. As per the Chizkuni's translation ad loc. See Rashi ad loc. and the other commentators.
134. Sh'mot 20:3.
135. The full text of the Midrash is as follows, "This can be compared to a king who entered a country. His servants said to him, 'Decree upon them decrees!' He responded to his servants, 'When they accept my kingship, then I will decree upon them, because if they don't accept my kingship, they will not accept my decrees.' So did Hashem say to the Jewish people, 'I am Hashem your G-d [Who took you out of the land of Egypt.] You shall not have [the gods of others before Me.]' [The import of these first two commandments is as follows. Hashem was saying to them,] 'I am He Whose Kingship you accepted in Egypt.' The Jewish people responded, 'This is correct.' [Hashem continued,] 'Therefore, just as you accepted My Kingship; therefore, now you must accept My decrees [the first of which is the second commandment,]' "You shall not have [the gods of others before Me] . . .'"
136. This term, "'The Midrash of Rabbi N'chuni'ah ben Hakanah" is used by the Ramban to refer to one of the primary Kabbalistic texts, the Bahir.
137. Bahir 104 and 105.
138. D'varim 22:7.
139. This word is not found in the original text of the Bahir.

which is called 'the mother of the world' as it is written, 'Because *if*[140] you call intuition,'[141] [which can also be read as 'You shall call intuition, "mother."'] . . .

[Rabbi Rachmai continued,] "And what is the import of [the rest of that verse which states,] 'and you shall take the chicks for yourself?'[142]

"These are the children which she[143] raised. And what are these children? 'These are the seven days of the festival of Sukkot and the laws of the seven days of the week . . .'"[144]

One can see therefore that this mitzvah alludes to a profound matter, and therefore, its reward is great [as the verse continues] "in order that it may go well with you and your days will be lengthened."[145]

i. The Ramban here proves in exacting detail that:
   1. All mitzvot have reasons – concurring with the Rambam. However, if we cannot understand a mitzvah's reason, it is due to our intellectual and spiritual shortcomings.
   2. The mitzvot are all given to benefit man (here he somewhat disagrees with the Rambam) and do not benefit G-d at all. In particular, the mitzvah to send away the mother bird is not due to Hashem's mercy on animals[146] (for otherwise He would prevent our being able to take animal life at all), but rather to prevent us being cruel and to prevent us eradicating an entire species.
   3. The term "decree" is used to refer to mitzvot without implying that mitzvot have no reason, but rather implying that they are incumbent upon us due to our being Hashem's subjects.

11. The Maharal's Question on the Ramban

a. The Maharal questions whether the Ramban's explanation fits in with the Gemara. His question is as follows:

The Ramban explained the position of our sages[147] [who said] that it is false that "Hashem's attributes [are due to] mercy" by pointing out that

140. In Hebrew, this word is אִם, pronounced "*im*," meaning, "if." However, with a slight change of vowel, this word can be read as אֵם, pronounced, "*eim*," meaning, "mother."

141. Mishlei 3:2.

142. D'varim 22:7.

143. Referring to "intuition" as he taught in the first half of the Midrash.

144. The explanation of these Kabbalistic ideas is beyond the scope of this work.

145. D'varim 22:7.

146. As per the Rambam.

147. In the Gemara cited earlier in the chapter.

Hashem does not prevent us from taking animals for our needs [which He would have done if He was acting out of mercy].

[However,] this explanation does not fit at all with the Gemara's language, which explains, "[The reason we censure[148] is that] such a person is making Hashem's attributes [due to] mercy when, in fact, they are exclusively decrees!" And if the Ramban's explanation were correct, the Gemara should have said, "The reason is that such a person is claiming that Hashem has mercy on animals, **when in fact, He does not.**"[149]

However, [actually] there is no difficulty at all for the Ramban's explanation from the statement of our sages, *z"l*, that, "[The reason is that] such a person is making Hashem's attributes [due to] mercy **when, in fact, they are exclusively decrees!**"

[Even though] the Rambam,[150] *z"l*, found this statement [so] difficult that he was forced to say that this Mishnah is not halachically authoritative (as you will see from his words)[151] and he rejected a set Mishnah, there is no problem from this [sub-phrase for the Ramban].

The reason [that the Ramban has no difficulty with this sub-phrase] is that one can explain that the intentions of the sages, *z"l*, (when they said that Hashem's mitzvot, may He be Blessed, are not [due to] mercy but [are] Decrees) was that Hashem commanded us [to perform] the mitzvot **not** so that Hashem [can express His] mercy on the nesting mother bird by commanding us to send away the mother. Similarly, even regarding humans, when Hashem, may He be Blessed, commanded us regarding the mitzvah of *tz'ddakah* [He did so] **not** because Hashem, may He be Blessed, had mercy on the pauper and therefore commanded us to support him. All such [reasoning] is false, for if Hashem had mercy [in these instances], he Himself could take mercy and He would have no need to command human beings. Rather, [the reason He commanded us to perform these mitzvot **was not due to His desire to express Mercy, but rather that] Hashem decreed the mitzvot on humanity through His decree.**

b. However, as we saw above in the full citation from the Ramban, it seems that Ramban himself does indeed cite the complete explanation of the Gemara, and he also gives the same explanation as the Maharal offers for him. As the Ramban writes,

148. A person who says, "Your [G-d's] mercy extends [even] to the nest of a bird!"
149. See below in the Commentary, Ch. 6 § Point 12.
150. Maimonides, not to be confused with Ramban, Nachmanides.
151. Cited above.

Similarly [the same idea is conveyed] when they[152] said, "[We should tell a person to be silent if he says, 'Your [G-d's] mercy extends [even] to the nest of a bird!' because] such a person is making Hashem's attributes [due to] mercy **when, in fact, they are exclusively decrees!"**[153] [The reason our sages enacted this requirement was because] they meant that G-d does not take mercy on the nest of the bird[154] and His mercy did not extend to an animal and her progeny [through the prohibition not to slaughter them both on the same day] . . . Now these mitzvot, which pertain to animals and birds, are not due to mercy on them [the animals and birds], **rather they are decrees on us** to guide us and teach us the good character traits.

i. I am at a loss to explain the Maharal's comments here on the Ramban especially since in his work, Gur Aryeh[155] (cited later in the Commentary, Ch. 6 § Point 12), he seems to indicate that the Ramban's view is almost identical to his own.

12. If Hashem Had Mercy, He Would Act Himself

a. In the course of the Maharal's explanation of the Ramban, the Maharal raises the option of the Ramban holding that Hashem commanded us to perform the mitzvot "not because Hashem, may He be Blessed, had mercy on the pauper and therefore commanded us to support him – all this is false, for if Hashem had mercy [in these instances] he Himself would take mercy and He would have no need to command human beings."
b. Such a statement seems to present us with many problems:

---

152. Our sages.

153. B'rachot 33b. This is the citation which forms the backbone of this entire chapter of Tiferet Yisrael. See at the beginning of the chapter where it is cited in full and explained by the Maharal. Interestingly, the Ramban quotes this phrase from the Gemara in full, "[We should tell a person to be silent if he says, 'Your [G-d's] mercy extends [even] to the nest of a bird!' because] such a person is making Hashem's attributes [due to] mercy **when, in fact, they are exclusively decrees!"** and as we saw in the Maharal here, he challenges whether the Ramban's explanation relates to this last phrase, "when, in fact, they are exclusively decrees!" In fact, in explanation of this phrase, the Ramban continues here, "Now these mitzvot, which pertain to animals and birds, are not due to mercy on them [the animals and birds], rather they are decrees on us to guide us and teach us the good character traits." Thus, the Maharal's difficulty on this point in the Ramban seems to fall away.

154. The reference to G-d's mercy on a bird's nest refers to the mitzvah which regulates one's actions when stumbling across a bird's nest in the wild. It is a mitzvah to chase away the mother bird and take the chicks and it is prohibited to take both the chicks and the mother bird. See D'varim 22:6–7

155. Commentary to B'midbar 19:2:1.

i. There is the general issue of theodicy: if G-d is so good, why does He allow people or animals to suffer? How can He even allow or command people to inflict suffering on animals (as in the allowance of slaughter for consumption or the sacrificial service.)
ii. Furthermore, does the Maharal seriously consider it to be an option that G-d has no mercy on paupers or animals in suffering because if He did, He would act Himself?

c. Regarding the first question, theodicy, much has been written by our sages from the time of Moshe, our Master, and onwards, but this is not the forum for such a lengthy discussion.
i. What we will say is that the Gemara[156] teaches us that Moshe, our teacher, wrote the book of Iyov[157] which is one of Torah's direct wrestlings with the idea of theodicy and the Gemara[158] also teaches us that Moshe directly asked Hashem the question of why bad happens to some good people and good happens to some bad people. The Gemara explains that according to Rabbi Yochanan, Moshe received an answer from G-d; while Rabbi Meir says that Moshe did not receive an answer to this question.
ii. Suffice it to say that:
1. The sages[159] teach us, regarding one who is suffering, that G-d is "with one in anguish,"[160] not merely accompanying one, but actually suffering together with him, as it were.
2. Moreover, the Torah[161] teaches us that evil is a problem truly colossal in scope, but, is nevertheless something with which human beings must grapple and which we have the ability to banish.

d. The second issue we raised above is as challenging as the first and is deeply connected to it.
i. As the Rambam said above,[162] there were some of our sages who believed that whatever Hashem does is simply due to His will and not for any reason. This could be understood to mean that goodness and kindness are simply not G-dly traits but only human ones and that Hashem is above and beyond such things. The Rambam[163] rejects such an approach.

156. Bava Batra 14b.
157. Job.
158. B'rachot 7a.
159. See Sh'mot Rabbah 2:5, Tos'fot Chullin 65a, s.v. *af al pi*.
160. Tehillim 91:15.
161. See Derech Hashem, parts 1 and 2 and 4:7.
162. Moreh N'vuchim 3:26.
163. Moreh N'vuchim 3:13 and in 3:26.

ii. Alternatively, we could explain that it must be[164] that Hashem's not visibly directly intervening in the suffering of this world, is also due to His loving-kindness which is the primary driver for the creation in the first place and the only reason for the lack of His direct, empirically detectable interference is because it would destroy the very purpose of creation.

iii. The Maharal, however, in his reference[165] to his comments in Gur Aryeh, supplies us with the explanation of what he means:

גור אריה במדבר יט:ב

ואם תאמר, למה כתב בפרה אדומה לשון "גזרה היא מלפני", והלא כל המצות גזרות מלפני הקדוש ברוך הוא, כדאמרינן בפרק הרואה האומר "על קן צפור יגיעו רחמיך" משתקין אותו, מפני שעושה מדותיו של הקב"ה רחמים, ואינם אלא גזרות. ואם כן כולם גזרות הם מלפני הקדוש ברוך הוא (קושית הרא"ם). אין הפירוש שיהיו גזרות בלי טעם כמו שסובר הרמב"ם ז"ל (מו"נ ג, מח), דזה אינו, אלא הם גזרות שיש בהם טעם. ומה שנקראו "גזרות" אחר שיש לכל אחת טעם, היינו שלא יאמר האדם שהם של רחמים, שהקדוש ברוך הוא מרחם על הבריות ועושה דבר לרחמים, וזה אינו, שהתורה שנתן לנו הקדוש ברוך הוא כל דבר במדת הדין, שכך נותן הדין לעשות, ואינו משום רחמנות. ואפילו מה שאמרה התורה לאדם ליתן צדקה (דברים טו, יא) ומעשר (לעיל יח, כא), וכל הדברים אשר הם מגמילות חסד, כל המצות כולם הם גזרות במדת הדין, ואינם רחמים. כי מה שחייבה התורה בצדקה ובמעשר, שכן האדם מצד שהוא אדם חייב שיתן מעשר, כדי שיהיה האדם נפש טוב, ולא יהיה נפש רע. ואם כן, מה שצותה התורה היא בגזרתו של הקדוש ברוך הוא על המקיים המצוה, ולא יביט אל העני ונכה רוח - שיהיה מצווה על נתינת הצדקה כדי שיהיה מתפרנס העני, זה אינו, שאין המצוה אלא לעושה המצוה. אבל המצות אשר נתן לנו הקדוש ברוך הוא כולם הם לתועלת המקיים המצוה. ולפיכך הם כולם גזרות, אף אותם שהם רחמים. וזהו שאמר "מפני שעושה מדות הקדוש ברוך הוא רחמים ואינם אלא גזירות", כלומר שכך גזר הקדוש ברוך הוא במדת הדין, ואינם רחמים: ומה שתמצא שהקדוש ברוך הוא אמר "ואל זה אביט אל עני ונכה רוח" (ישעיה סו, ב), שהקדוש ברוך הוא עוזר דלים, אין הענין שיהיה בשביל כך מצוה לאדם לפרנס אותם בשביל שרחם על העני, שאין זה כן, אלא מה שהוא עוזר דלים ומרחם - הקדוש ברוך הוא בעצמו עושה זה לדלים ולאביונים במדת רחמים, וצוה הקדוש ברוך הוא במדת הדין לאדם שילך בדרכיו (דברים כח, ט). וזהו מגזרתו על האדם, ולא נתן הקדוש ברוך הוא המצות לישראל על צד הרחמים על הבריות, רק מפני גזירות. ובודאי טעם יש בכל מצוה ומצוה. וזהו פירוש נכון במאמר הזה, וכבר כתב זה הרמב"ן בפרשת תצא (דברים כב, ו) עיין שם, רק שהוא שינה בקצת פירושו, ופירוש זה נכון למשכיל:

Gur Aryeh, B'midbar 19:2

[The R'eim, a medieval sage, posed the following question on Rashi] "Why did Rashi, regarding the commandment of the Red Heifer, use the language 'it is a decree before me'? Are not all the mitzvot decrees before the Holy

164. See the Ramchal in the Derech Hashem 1:2:1–5.
165. He makes this reference above, in the text of the Tiferet Yisrael.

One, Blessed be He? As we say in the chapter of 'One who sees'[166] 'We should tell a person to be silent if he says, "Your[167] mercy extends [even] to the nest of a bird!"' because such a person 'is making Hashem's attributes [due to] mercy when, in fact, they are exclusively decrees!' If so, all of the mitzvot are decrees from before the Holy One, Blessed be He."[168]

[The Maharal answers as follows,] the explanation for this is that they are not "decrees" in the sense that they have no reason (which is actually what the Rambam, *z"l*, holds in Moreh N'vuchim)[169] because this is false; but rather that they are decrees which have a reason.

The only reason they are called "decrees" (despite the fact that each one of them has a reason) is so that people will not say that they are due to Mercy – that the Holy One, Blessed be He, has mercy on the creations and does a particular thing out of mercy, for this is false. In fact, the Torah which the Holy One, Blessed be He, gave us is completely derived from Hashem's attribute of Justice [as opposed to Hashem's attribute of Mercy]! [The reason we have to perform mitzvot is] because Justice demands that we behave this way, not Mercy. Even when the Torah commanded us to give *tz'dakkah*[170] and a tithe[171] and all commandments which are acts of loving-kindness, all of the mitzvot are decrees through Hashem's attribute of Justice and are not due to Mercy. *The reason that the Torah obligated one to give charity and a tithe is because a human being, due to his being a human being, is obligated to give a tithe, in order that he will be a good soul and not an evil soul.*

If so, what the Torah commanded is the Holy One's decree, Blessed be He, [which devolves] on the one who fulfills the mitzvah and one should not look at the [immediate beneficiaries of the mitzvah, that is, the] pauper and the person broken of spirit. For it is false to think that the mitzvah to give charity is so that the pauper will be sustained; *the mitzvah is for the one who performs it.* But the mitzvot that the Holy One, Blessed be He, gave us are all for the benefit of the person who performs them. Therefore, they are all decrees, even those which are merciful. This is the explanation of

166. This is the Mishnah cited by the Maharal here, throughout Chapter Six of Tiferet Yisrael. However, there seems to be a printer's error as the citation is not from the chapter, "One who sees" (B'rachot, Chapter Nine), but rather from the chapter "One doesn't stand" (B'rachot, Chapter Five).

167. I.e., G-d's

168. The question of the R'eim is that all mitzvot are decrees, so why does Rashi highlight the mitzvah of the Red Heifer in particular, as being a "decree"?

169. Moreh N'vuchim 3:48. The Maharal is not saying that the Rambam holds that mitzvot have no reason, just that the Rambam's explanation of the Gemara in B'rachot is that it is according to the opinion that the mitzvot have no reason.

170. D'varim 15:11.

171. A tenth of our crops to the Levi'im – see D'varim 18:21.

[the censure for one who says, "Your mercy extends [even] to the nest of a bird!"] "because such a person 'is making Hashem's attributes [due to] Mercy when in fact, they are exclusively decrees!'" *This means to say that this is how the Holy One, Blessed be He, decreed through His attribute of Justice and they are not due to His attribute of Mercy.*

Now, regarding that which you will find that the Holy One, Blessed be He, said, "To this person I will pay attention: to the pauper and the broken of spirit,"[172] which teaches us that the Holy One, Blessed be He, assists those in need; the meaning of this verse is not that since He has mercy on the pauper therefore He commands human beings to support those in need – this is false; rather, the meaning of this verse is that whatever Hashem does for those in need and His Mercy on them, all this He does *Himself* for those in need and for the paupers through His attribute of Mercy.[173]

Hashem commanded humanity through His attribute of Justice that "he should walk in G-d's ways,"[174] but this is His decree on humanity. And the Holy One, Blessed be He, did not give the mitzvot to Israel due to having Mercy on the creations, but rather they are decrees. And definitely there is a reason for each mitzvah. And this is the correct explanation of this statement and the Ramban already wrote this in Parshat Ki Teitzei[175] except that he changed his explanation slightly. But this explanation is correct for one who is wise.

iv. This answers most of our questions on his view.

v. He goes to great length to explain that the mitzvot do not flow from Hashem's own kindness (which exists more surely than our own) but are decrees. Later in this chapter we shall see him confront Torah texts which severely challenge his ideas. He goes to great lengths there to interpret these texts away from their most obvious explanations and he explicitly takes note that he is indeed pulling them away from what they seem to be saying. Why does he do this? The reasons he goes to these lengths are both technical and foundational.
   1. Technically, we have seen the difficulties the Maharal raised with the Ramban who seemed to be claiming that all the mitzvot are outgrowths of Hashem's own attributes of love and mercy.
   2. More fundamentally, however, the Maharal believes that the truth is that mitzvot do not derive from G-d's Mercy. When he

172. Y'shayahu 66:2.

173. The Maharal is explaining that the verse teaches us that Hashem is of course merciful, but that He Himself performs His own acts of mercy and doesn't require human proxies.

174. Cf. D'varim 28:9.

175. D'varim 22:6.

says that they are decrees, he doesn't mean, G-d forbid, that they are done without reason, but merely that they flow from Hashem's attribute of Justice and not from His Mercy.

a. Here, the Maharal gives us an incredible insight into the totality of mitzvot. He states that, of course giving charity is merciful, of course Hashem has mercy on all of his creatures, but that is not *why* Hashem commanded us to perform mitzvot – we are not some sort of proxy that Hashem, G-d forbid, needs to perform His merciful acts. Rather, the reason we must perform the mitzvot is because it is just and right to do so, and they flow from Hashem's strictest Justice. If we had a strong enough sense of pure Justice, we would realize this.

b. The idea that the mitzvot are decrees is echoed throughout the Ramchal's Derech Hashem. See, for example, in the first section[176] where, for almost that entire subsection, the Ramchal repeats again and again, "His wisdom decreed . . . ," "His wisdom decreed . . ." As we have said many times, we have no business in mystical matters, thus all we can say here is that the Maharal seems to be following a similar path – that everything that Hashem brought into being, especially the Torah and mitzvot, was done through the agency of this divine decree flowing from an ultimate wisdom and justice.

c. This discussion echoes one which appears in our sages' writings as well as in Plato's *Euthyphro*: does Hashem command goodness because it is independently good; or, do Hashem's commands become goodness by virtue of His having commanded them? This question is somewhat reminiscent of the medieval paradox questioning whether G-d can create a rock He cannot lift. Suffice it to say that for a variety of reasons, Torah has never been overly consternated by these questions. For further discussion on both issues, see Rabbi Jonathan Sacks, *To Heal a Fractured World*, and Rabbi Aryeh Kaplan, *The Aryeh Kaplan Reader*.[177]

vi. Now we are equipped to appreciate the breadth of the Maharal's claim here. A person may act beneficently and declare, "I've done a good deed! I've gone beyond what is right and expected!" The

176. Derech Hashem 1:2:1.

177. Rabbi Jonathan Sacks, *To Heal a Fractured World* (Continuum: 2005), pp. 162–174; Rabbi Aryeh Kaplan, *The Aryeh Kaplan Reader* (Mesorah Publications: 1999), pp. 131–138.

Maharal teaches us that one must realize that the performance of all mitzvot is first and foremost what *is* right and expected, not beyond the letter of the law! Even charitable acts are justice, first and foremost; and they serve our interests – we benefit, more than anyone by doing what is just.

vii. The Maharal's view of mitzvot which are acts of Kindness and reconciling this with G-d's Kindness

1. The Maharal says, in this citation from Gur Aryeh, that the motivating factor for such mitzvot as *tz'dakkah* is not Hashem's Mercy but His Justice. Initially, this is a startling idea – it really seems akin to those who opine that all of G-d's mitzvot are decrees which have no rationale at all and that there is no connection at all between what we humans perceive as Mercy and what G-d is.
2. But, as the Maharal goes on to say explicitly, this is *not* his position. There is no doubt that there is some overlap between Hashem's mercy or kindness and their human analogues, but the Maharal explicitly states that he is taking issue with those who understand that mitzvot *only* flow from this merciful center and not from anything beyond that.
3. In fact, throughout the Torah, we celebrate the fact that Hashem is in fact the source of human ideas regarding mercy and kindness.
   a. We learn in D'varim

דברים יא :כ״ב

כִּי אִם שָׁמֹר תִּשְׁמְרוּן אֶת כָּל הַמִּצְוָה הַזֹּאת אֲשֶׁר אָנֹכִי מְצַוֶּה אֶתְכֶם לַעֲשֹׂתָהּ לְאַהֲבָה אֶת ה׳ אֱ-לֹהֵיכֶם לָלֶכֶת בְּכָל דְּרָכָיו וּלְדָבְקָה בוֹ:

D'VARIM 11:22

For you must surely cherish all this mitzvah which I command you today, to do it and to love Hashem, your G-d: to walk in His ways and to bond with Him.

   b. Rashi questions what the verse could mean, "to walk in G-d's ways." His answer, based on the Sifri is:[178]

רש״י דברים יא:כב

הוא רחום ואתה תהא רחום הוא גומל חסדים ואתה גומל חסדים:

178. Eikev 13.

Rashi ad loc.

[What does it mean to walk in G-d's ways?] G-d is merciful, so should you be merciful; He bestows kindnesses, so should you.

c. The Rambam understands that this is actually a commandment in the Torah,[179] as he writes in The Laws of Character Traits and Values:

רמב"ם דעות פרק א: ה, ו

ומי שהוא מדקדק על עצמו ביותר ויתרחק מדעה בינונית מעט לצד זה או לצד זה נקרא חסיד כיצד מי שיתרחק מגובה הלב עד הקצה האחרון ויהיה שפל רוח ביותר נקרא חסיד וזו היא מדת חסידות ואם נתרחק עד האמצע בלבד ויהיה עניו נקרא חכם וזו היא מדת חכמה ועל דרך זו שאר כל הדעות וחסידים הראשונים היו מטין דעות שלהן מדרך האמצעית כנגד שתי הקצוות יש דעה שמטין אותה כנגד הקצה האחרון ויש דעה שמטין אותה כנגד הקצה הראשון וזהו לפנים משורת הדין ומצווין אנו ללכת בדרכים האלו הבינונים והם הדרכים הטובים והישרים שנאמר והלכת בדרכיו: כך למדו בפירוש מצוה זו מה הוא נקרא חנון אף אתה היה חנון מה הוא נקרא רחום אף אתה היה רחום מה הוא נקרא קדוש אף אתה היה קדוש ועל דרך זו קראו הנביאים לאל בכל אותן הכנויין ארך אפים ורב חסד צדיק וישר תמים גבור וחזק וכיוצא בהן להודיע שהן דרכים טובים וישרים וחייב אדם להנהיג עצמו בהן ולהדמות אליו כפי כחו:

Rambam, Dei'ot 1: 5–6

The early pious men would incline their character traits from the golden mean towards one of the two poles. Certain traits they would incline one way and other traits they would incline in the opposite direction and this is what is known as "beyond the line of the law."

We are *commanded* to walk in these golden means and they are the good and honest ways as it is said, "You shall walk in His ways."[180] Thus they learned in the explanation of this verse, "Just as He[181] is called merciful, so should you be merciful. Just as He is called compassionate, so should you be compassionate. Just as He is called holy, so should you be holy." And the prophets described Hashem in this fashion, using these descriptions "slow to anger," "great in kindness," "pious," "honest," "sincere," "heroic," "mighty" and so on [in order] to inform us that these ways are good and honest and *a person has an obligation to conduct himself in such ways and to become as similar to Hashem as he possibly can.*

viii. The Maharal is in complete agreement with these ideas in Rashi and the Rambam. He even quotes the same verse that the Rambam uses,

179. See his Book of Mitzvot, Asin 8.
180. D'varim 28:9.
181. Hashem.

"You shall walk in His ways."[182] Thus it seems that, in the Rambam's view, the Torah's basic understanding of the terms "mercy," "compassion" and "holiness" are derived, to a large extent, through our attempts at *imitatio dei* (emulating G-d).

ix. But what the Maharal wishes us to understand is that despite the fact that Hashem is commanding us to be kind (and He is also Kind), the essential reason for that commandment is beyond Hashem's Kindness and flows from what is Just and Right and Necessary in this world. This of course does not imply that the mitzvot are value-neutral (they are not, they are value-filled and value-imparting); it rather implies that their source is beyond mercy and kindness and is rooted in Hashem's Justice.

x. Moreover, the Maharal states that we are to emulate Hashem's kindness and mercy but we need to understand that He performs His own acts of kindness: when He has mercy, He does so Himself – our actions are not for His vicarious fulfillment, our actions are for our own benefit.

13. The Centrality of Hashem's Attribute of Justice especially in the Purpose of the Creation of the World

a. The Maharal in this section has placed the idea of G-d's decrees, created by His attribute of Justice, at the center. In particular, the Maharal claims that Hashem's Justice decreed both the creation of the world as well as the mitzvot.

b. At the beginning of Chapter Six, we saw the Maharal lay the groundwork for this idea. As he wrote there:

תפארת ישראל ו

ומכל מקום הנהגה התמידית היא דין לפי שהוא יושר ודבר זה ראוי, והאומר על קן צפור יגיעו רחמיך הוא עושה מדותיו שהוא יתברך מנהיג בהן עולמו רחמים שהוא מנהיג עולמו בתמידות ברחמים ודבר זה הוא יציאה מן היושר מה שאין ראוי.

Tiferet Yisrael 6

Nevertheless [even after the merger of Hashem's attributes of Justice and Mercy,] the [sole] constant attribute is Justice, since it is honesty and this is what is suitable. Now, the one who says, "Your[183] mercy extends [even] to the nest of a bird!" is changing Hashem's attributes through which He, may He be Blessed, constantly directs the world, into mercy; and such a thing is a deviation from honesty, which is inappropriate [because G-d mainly directs the world through Justice which is "honest"].

182. D'varim 28:9.
183. G-d's.

c. As we wrote in the Commentary, Ch. 6 § Point 1, it is difficult to grasp the Maharal's intentions, rooted as they are in the hidden depths of Torah.
   i. What seems to be clear (see the discussions in the Commentary, Ch. 6 § Points 5 and 6) is that the attribute of Hashem's Justice, *din* (in Hebrew), is by definition something which *must* be and it is not something optional. In Hebrew, the concept of doing something which is optional and beyond what must be, is called *lifnim mishurat hadin*, beyond the line of the law.
   ii. Thus, one of the basic concepts here being expressed may be that the creation of the world and the giving of the mitzvot were not whimsical expressions of Hashem's Mercy, the attribute which is not constant, but rather that this world flows from what is absolutely just.

d. The Maharal also sees no conflict between his stance and the fact that everything that Hashem does is good. As he writes in the continuation of this chapter:

תפארת ישראל ו

ועם כל זה שהמצות הם גזירות על ישראל הם לטוב לנו, כי לא יבא מאתו יתברך רק הטוב הגמור כי כל מעשיו הם הטוב הגמור רק כי הטוב הזה גזר עלינו ולא שיש כאן שום צד רחמנות רק הכל דין.

Tiferet Yisrael 6

Despite the fact that the mitzvot are a decree on Israel, they are definitely good for us; because only absolute goodness flows from Hashem, may He be Blessed, since all His actions are absolute goodness. It's just that He decreed this goodness on us and there is no aspect of Mercy here at all, only Justice.

   i. Thus the Maharal sees no contradiction between the idea that this world and the mitzvot were motivated by Justice and the idea that everything that Hashem does is good.
   ii. This can be understood in the following way. We have already discussed[184] that Hashem's attributes (Justice, Mercy and so on) may seem to us to be separate attributes, but in reality they are all one. Everything that Hashem does flows from this unified and incomprehensible reality, but the one thing that we do know is that whatever "attribute" seems to be acting, the essential motivation of that action is Hashem's goodness.

184. See the Commentary, Ch. 6 § Point 5.

COMMENTARY SECTION

Chapter 7

1. Terminology

a. "Dedication"

i. The Hebrew word used throughout this section is, נתיחד, which means "dedicated" in the sense of something that is set aside and designated for some exclusive use or function.

ii. We have translated it here as "dedicated," "consigned," "set aside" and "highlighted." However, the base meaning remains the same.

b. חק, "*chok*"

i. The usual translation of this word, "*chok*," is "decree." However, in this context, the meaning is closer to "boundary," "limit" or "framework" – all which we have used.

ii. This is reflected in the Maharal's works elsewhere:

ספר גבורות השם, הקדמה ראשונה

. . . במה שהעריות כולם התרחקות מדבר שאין ראוי החבור, ויהיו הנמצאים עומדים בחקם וגבולם שנתן השם יתברך להם. ולכך נקראים העריות חוק כדכתיב את חקותי תשמרו גבי עריות. וזהו סוד העריות, כי השם יתברך המציא הנמצאים ונתן להם חוק ולא יצאו מחקם . . .

G'vurot Hashem, first introduction

. . . in that the [prohibitions against] illicit sexual relationships are all precautions [distancing one] from that with which it is inappropriate to bond.

Thus [if people respect these precautions,] all [beings] that exist will remain in their framework[1] and their boundary, which Hashem, may He be Blessed, gave them. Therefore, the [prohibitions against] illicit sexual relationships are termed a *chok*, as is written regarding the [prohibitions against] illicit sexual relationships, "You shall guard my *chukkim*."[2] And this is the secret of the [prohibitions against] illicit sexual relationships – that Hashem, may He be Blessed, created all creations and defined for them a framework[3] that they should not deviate from their boundary . . ."[4]

---

1. "*Chok*" in Hebrew.
2. Vayikra 18:4.
3. "*Chok*" in Hebrew.
4. "*Chok*" in Hebrew.

iii. This is a usage similarly reflected in Tanach. For example,

תהילים קמח:א-ו

הַלְלוּיָ־הּ הַלְלוּ אֶת ה׳ מִן הַשָּׁמַיִם הַלְלוּהוּ בַּמְּרוֹמִים: הַלְלוּהוּ כָל מַלְאָכָיו הַלְלוּהוּ כָּל צְבָאָו: הַלְלוּהוּ שֶׁמֶשׁ וְיָרֵחַ הַלְלוּהוּ כָּל כּוֹכְבֵי אוֹר: הַלְלוּהוּ שְׁמֵי הַשָּׁמָיִם וְהַמַּיִם אֲשֶׁר מֵעַל הַשָּׁמָיִם: יְהַלְלוּ אֶת שֵׁם ה׳ כִּי הוּא צִוָּה וְנִבְרָאוּ: וַיַּעֲמִידֵם לָעַד לְעוֹלָם חָק נָתַן וְלֹא יַעֲבוֹר:

Tehillim 148:1–6

Praise Hashem! Praise Hashem from the heavens! Praise Him in the heights! Praise Him all His angels! Praise Him all His hosts! Praise Him sun and moon! Praise Him all the stars of light. Praise Him, heavens of heaven and the waters above the heavens! They will praise the name of Hashem, because He commanded and they were created; and He established them forever – He set a boundary[5] which they may not breach.

2. The Seventh Factor

a. The difference between the six variables and the seventh

i. The Maharal writes, "This is [the same] as one can say regarding a specific point in a specific place – it can deviate from its uniqueness [in position and from its] order, to the right, left, forwards, backwards, up or down [a total of six deviations]. And these six are the aspects from which it[6] can deviate from its uniqueness and order. However, that which causes absolute negation [of the uniqueness and the order of the point] is the seventh factor."

ii. Clearly the Maharal is drawing a distinction between the six axes of deviation along which a point can deviate (in Hebrew, "*n'tiyah*," **נטייה**) and the seventh. Regarding the seventh, he writes that it causes "absolute negation," in Hebrew, **הביטול לגמרי**.

b. What is this seventh factor?

i. We already examined this question in the Commentary, Introduction § Point 15.

ii. There we cited the Maharal's words later in Tiferet Yisrael and explained as follows.

ספר תפארת ישראל - פרק מ

וכבר ידוע כי הגשם יש לו חלופי צדדים ששה ועל ידם הגשם שלם והם המעלה והמטה וארבעה צדדין שהם ארבע רוחות הידועים כי אין גשם שלם רק כאשר יש לו ששה צדדין ... ויש עוד גבול נבדל לעצמו והוא האמצעי אשר הוא נבדל לעצמו ואינו נוטה לא לימין ולא לשמאל לא לפנים ולא לאחור רק עומד באמצע, ואין האמצעי הזה מתיחס לגשם כמו ששה צדדים כי הצדדים הששה יש להם רוחק והרוחק הוא גדר הגשם ולכך על

5. "*Chok*" in Hebrew.

6. The point.

ששה הצדדין יאמר שהם צדדין גשמיים אבל האמצעי מפני שאין לו רוחק לא יאמר עליו שהוא גשמי בעצמו ומתיחס אל בלתי גשמי.

TIFERET YISRAEL, CHAPTER 40

It is already known that the physical world has six variable dimensions and through these six, the physical world is complete. These six are: up, down, and the four dimensions which are the four known cardinal directions. Physicality is not complete without these six dimensions . . .

But there is another boundary which is separated on its own and this is the central point which is completely separate – it doesn't tend to the right, left, forwards or backwards, but simply remains stationary in the center. This central point is not related to the physical in the same way that the six dimensions are related to the physical world because the six dimensions have distance[7] and this distance is the defining element of the physical world.

Therefore, we say that the six dimensions are really physical dimensions but regarding the central point (which has no extensibility and is merely a point) we cannot say that it is truly physical in and of itself and it indeed has a relation to the non-physical.

1. We thus see that the seventh point, the central point, is somewhat of a hybrid in that it is not variable. The six dimensions vary, they have extensibility and variation, they can be large or small, whereas the central point has no variability.
2. The Maharal says that in essence, non-stasis, variability and quantity are what define the physical world. One cannot say that the seventh is completely physical, but one can also not say that it is completely metaphysical.
3. Thus in our current chapter (Chapter Seven) when the Maharal discusses how any object can leave the ideal order, the seventh factor must be mentioned, since there are, in total, seven ways in which an object can lose its unique, ideal status:
   a. It can *deviate* in one of six ways.
   b. It can completely lose its very existence – and this is the seventh factor.

3. The Mechanism by which the Torah Allows Humans to Bond with Hashem

a. The Maharal writes above, "[The mechanism through which the *mitzvot aseh* achieve this bonding with G-d is] that the actions of mitzvot are determined by the intellect (which is arranged for humanity) and through performing the mitzvot (which comprise a *sichli* system), a human gains a

7. I.e., extension.

bond with the *sichli* [reality] and [thereby] a person draws [himself] away from the natural [reality] which he [usually] desires. Then he achieves bonding with G-d, may He be Blessed.'

b. This idea is clearly expressed in the Tanya[8], as follows,

ספר התניא א:ה

הנה כל שכל כשמשכיל ומשיג בשכלו איזה מושכל הרי השכל תופס את המושכל ומקיפו בשכלו והמושכל נתפס ומוקף ומלובש בתוך השכל שהשיגו והשכילו וגם השכל מלובש במושכל בשעה שמשיגו ותופסו בשכלו ד"מ כשאדם מבין ומשיג איזו הלכה במשנה או בגמרא לאשורה על בוריה הרי שכלו תופס ומקיף אותה וגם שכלו מלובש בה באותה שעה. והנה הלכה זו היא חכמתו ורצונו של הקב"ה שעלה ברצונו שכשיטעון ראובן כך וכך דרך משל ושמעון כך וכך יהיה הפסק ביניהם כך וכך ואף אם לא היה ולא יהיה הדבר הזה לעולם לבא למשפט על טענות ותביעות אלו מכל מקום מאחר שכך עלה ברצונו וחכמתו של הקב"ה שאם יטעון זה כך וזה כך יהיה הפסק כך הרי כשאדם יודע ומשיג בשכלו פסק זה כהלכה הערוכה במשנה או גמרא או פוסקים הרי זה משיג ותופס ומקיף בשכלו רצונו וחכמתו של הקב"ה דלית מחשבה תפיסא ביה ולא ברצונו וחכמתו כי אם בהתלבשותם בהלכות הערוכות לפנינו וגם שכלו מלובש בהם והוא יחוד נפלא שאין יחוד כמוהו ולא כערכו נמצא כלל בגשמיות להיות לאחדים ומיוחדים ממש מכל צד ופנה.

TANYA 1:5

Behold, whenever a mind contemplates and comprehends any concept, that mind grasps the concept and embraces it and the concept is grasped and embraced and clothed[9] by the comprehending mind. But [simultaneously] the mind is clothed by the concept at the time that that mind comprehends and grasps [the concept].

For example, when a person properly and soundly understands and comprehends any Halachah in the Mishnah or the Gemara, his mind grasps and embraces it – and at the same time his mind is clothed by it. [The reason for this is that] this Halachah is the wisdom and will of the Holy One, Blessed be He, for it arose within His will that, for example, when Reuven makes a certain [legal] claim and Shimon another [legal] claim, that the verdict shall be such. And even if it never has and never shall come to pass that such a case, with respect to these claims and demands, shall be adjudicated, nevertheless, since this [verdict is what] arose in the divine will and wisdom (that if one makes a certain claim, and the other a certain claim, the decision shall be such) [then] when a person knows and comprehends this decision with his mind as a Halachah set forth in the Mishnah, the

8. Tanya 1:5.

9. Meaning "encapsulated" or "enveloped," like a person is enveloped by his clothing.

Gemara, or the *pos'kim*,[10] he comprehends and grasps and embraces (with his mind) the will and wisdom of the Holy One, Blessed be He, who is beyond [human] thought.

[And this embrace is] not through [the independent achievements of] his will and wisdom, but through their being clothed by the set Halachot before us and [then] also his will is clothed by them.

This is a wondrous unification unlike any other and there is no other with a similar value within the physical world [through which a human can become] one [with G-d] and dedicated [to G-d] from all perspectives.

i. The Ba'al Hatanya explains here that when one truly comprehends an idea in Torah, this allows one to unify with Hashem's wisdom and will which are the constant source of that idea. As one's mind cradles the idea and encompasses it, the idea, flowing from G-d's mind, also enwraps the person's intellect.
ii. The Ba'al Hatanya explains that this mutual embrace is the highest level of unification with Hashem.
iii. We can understand now how, when a person performs a mitzvah, they reach a similar level of unification with Hashem by virtue of their adopting G-d's will (as embodied in the mitzvah) as their own. When a person does this, he is literally joining with Hashem's will and to a certain extent, he is accustoming himself to will that which Hashem wills.

4. The Maharal in G'vurot Hashem

a. The Maharal references his work, G'vurot Hashem, Chapter Sixty-Six, several times in the section above. We cite this chapter in full as it sheds much light on the discussions here in Tiferet Yisrael.

ספר גבורות השם - פרק סו

אמר יהודה בן בצלאל זלה"ה כאשר לכל דבר יבוקש תכלית, ולפי ענין שלו יש לו תכלית, שאם היה הפעל פעל חשוב וגדול ראוי שיהיה לו גם כן תכלית חשוב, שאין ראוי שיהיה תכלית פחות ושפל לפעל חשוב, ומכל שכן פעל הא־ל שכל פעולותיו בחכמה והשכל, שכל פעולותיו ומעשיו הם הולכים לתכלית ראוי לפי הפועל. וכאשר ראינו ביציאת מצרים שפעל השם נוראות גדולות מאוד והוא בעצמו ובכבודו הוציאם ממצרים, אם כן ראוי שיהיה לפועל הזה תכלית ויהיה תכלית חשוב כפי ערך הפעל אשר פעל השם למען אותו התכלית. וכאשר מצאנו בכתוב שתכלית היציאה הוא שיהיה לישראל לא־להים וכדכתיב בתחלת היציאה (שמות ו') והוצאתי אתכם מתחת סבלות מצרים ולקחתי אתכם לי לעם והייתי לכם לא־להים, ובסוף פרשת תצוה (שם כ"ט) כתיב המוציא אתכם מארץ מצרים לשכני בתוכם, מוכח כי תחלת [אולי צ"ל תכלית] היציאה היה על מנת שיהיה להם לא־להים. ולפיכך יבאו הפרשיות כסדרן דמתחלה

10. Halachic decisors.

הוציאם ממצרים ואח״כ נתן להם י׳ דברות והתחלתם אנכי ה׳ א־להיך אשר הוצאתיך מארץ מצרים לא יהיה לך א־להים אחרים ואח״כ שאר דברות ופרשת אלה המשפטים. כי מאחר שהוא לא־להים להם צריכים לקבל את משפטיו כי כל אלהים יש לו משפט במה שהוא אלהים, ולפיכך המביא משפטו לפני ערכאות של עובדי ע״ז מייקר שם ע״ז שמקבל עליו משפט אלהי נכר שכל משפט שייך לאלהות, והרי בכל מקום אצל משפט כתיב אלהים (שם כ״ב) ונקרב בעל הבית אל האלהים וכן בכל מקום, ולפיכך אחר קבלת א־להותו מיד קבלת משפטיו שבזה הם עמו מה שמקבלים משפט א־להי ישראל שודאי א־להים נקרא המנהיג את העם וכדכתיב (שם ל״ב) עשה לנו אלהים אשר ילכו לפנינו, ואין הנהגה בלא משפט שהמשפט הוא הנהגת העם. ולפיכך תבין כמה גדול עון המביא משפטו בערכאות של עובדי ע״ז שיוצא ממשפט א־להי ישראל ונכנס תחת משפט אלהי נכר, כי כל אלהות יש לו הנהגה והמביא משפטו בערכאות מייקר הנהגת אלהות אחר, שהרי מיד אחר קבלת מלכותו בסיני נתן להם משפטים השייכים לא־להותו. ואח״כ היה רוצה לשכון ביניהם שהרי מיד אח״כ כתיב (שם כ״ה) ועשו לי מקדש ושכנתי בתוכם וגו׳, והנה התבאר כי תכלית היציאה שיהיה להם לא־להים ולהיות שכינתו ביניהם. ומעתה יש לעיין בתכלית הזה אם התכלית חשוב ראוי שיהיה בשבילו פעל גדול, ויש לשאול הנה השמים כסאו והארץ הדום רגלו ויהא שכינתו בעליונים ולמה בחר לשכון בתחתונים, ובדבר זה מעלין ולא מורידין יהיה א־להותו בעליונים למה צריך בתחתונים שהם עפר רימה ותולעה. אמנם אם נמצא שכל דבר המציאות תלוי בשכינתו בתחתונים ודבר זה הוא הכל מעתה הוסר השאלה, וכאשר תדע כי הוא יתברך מצטרף לנמצאים במה שהם עלולים, כי הוא יתברך שהוא עלת הכל רצונו בעלול וכאשר יש עלה יש כאן עלול נמצא, כי התקשרות הסבה הראשונה בנמצאים מצד שהוא יתברך עלה להם והנמצאים הם עלולים ממנו, וכבר הארכנו בקשור הנכבד הזה למעלה אצל ויקרא אליו מתוך הסנה. וכאשר התבאר זה אם כן אין עליך לומר שמיוחדים בזה העליונים כי אם התחתונים, כי במה שנקראים עליונים הם פועלים בתחתונים והם כמו עלה נחשבים ואין עיקר עצמם שהם עלולים, אבל התחתונים במה שהם תחתונים הם עלולים בעצמם, ולפיכך החבור האמתי שיש לסבה הראשונה שהוא עלה באמת הוא בתחתונים במה שהם עלולים באמת. ובמדרש רבות בפרשת בראשית (פ׳ י״ט) וישמעו את קול ה׳ א־להים מתהלך בגן לרוח היום מהלך אין כתיב כאן אלא מתהלך עיקר שכינה בתחתונים היתה כיון שחטא אדם הראשון נסתלקה שכינה לרקיע ראשון חטא קין נסתלקה לרקיע השני חטא דור אנוש נסתלקה שכינה לרקיע שלישי חטא דור המבול נסתלקה שכינה לרקיע רביעי חטא דור הפלגה נסתלקה שכינה לרקיע הה׳ עמדו סדומיים וחטאו נסתלקה שכינה לרקיע ששי עמדו מצרים בימי אברהם וחטאו נסתלקה לרקיע השביעי, ואח״כ עמדו ז׳ צדיקים והורידו השכינה בארץ אברהם יצחק יעקב לוי קהת עמרם משה דכתיב צדיקים יירשו ארץ וישכנו לעד עליה ורשעים מה הם עושים עליה וכי פורחים באויר אלא צדיקים ישכינו שכינה בארץ ע״כ. וביאור ענין זה כמו שאמרנו, כי מתחלה כאשר נברא העולם ואין פחיתות בעלול כלל, היה השם יתברך מתחבר כאשר ראוי חבור העלה בעלול, ואין התחברות רק בתחתונים במה שהם עלולים באמת, עד שנמצא חטא בנמצאים העלולים אז מפרידים הדבוק ההוא עד שאין כאן חבור העלה אל העלול. ואלו שבעה חטאים שחטאו העלולים, לפי שמתחלה בבריאת עולמו נתן להם אלו מצות אבר מן החי ברכת השם ע״ז גילוי עריות דינין גזל שפיכת דמים, הם ז׳ מצות שהם חבור העלה בעלול על ידי גזירותיו ומצותיו במה שהעלול מקבל גזירת ומצות העלה. ועוד יתבאר בספר תפארת ישראל, ולפיכך מיד כשנברא האדם נתן לו שבע מצות:

ואלו שבע מצות נראה שבחר באלו, כי חפץ השם יתברך שיהיה האדם טוב לשמים וטוב לבריות, ובאלו שני דברים הוא צדיק דכתיב (ישעי׳ ג׳) אמרו צדיק כי טוב כי פרי מעלליהם יאכלו, ובפרק קמא דקדושין (מ׳ ע״א) אמרינן וכי יש צדיק טוב ויש צדיק שאינו טוב אלא טוב לשמים וטוב לבריות הוא צדיק טוב טוב לשמים ואינו טוב לבריות צדיק שאינו טוב. ולכך נתן שלש מצוות שהם בינו ובין בוראו שלא יהיה רע לשמים והם גלוי עריות ברכת השם ע״ז, וג׳ מצות בינו ובין האדם והם גזל שלא יגזול אחר ודינין ושפיכת דמים שלא יהיה רע לבריות. והשביעי אבר מן החי הוא התחלה וסבה שלא יבא לידי אלו עבירות, וזה שהוא נגד יצר הרע נתן לו מצוה זאת שלא יחמוד לאכילה ויחתוך בהמה קודם שתצא נפשה בשביל יצרו וכדי לכוף ליצרו נתן לו מצוה זאת, וכמו שאמרו חכמים ז״ל (ביצה כ״ה ע״ב) נטיעה מקטעא רגליהון דקצביא ודבועלי נדות שהתורה נתנה שיעור לנטיעה שלש שנים יהיה לכם ערלים, והקצבים אינם יכולים להמתין לבהמה עד שתצא נפשה ודבועלי נדות אינם יכולים להמתין עד שתטבול, ולפיכך מצוה זאת אבר מן החי שלא ילך אחר יצרו שאם ילך אחר יצרו לבסוף יאמר לו יצרו עשה כך ולבסוף עשה כך עד שיעבור כל העבירות. וכן בעשרת הדברות בסופם לא תחמוד שהחטא של תאוה התחלת כל החטאים, והפייט יסד אלה המצות בלא תחמוד כלולים, לומר לך שכל המצות הם נכללים בלא תחמוד, שאם עובר חטא לא תחמוד הוא בא לכל החטאים, ולפיכך אבר מן החי שביעית. ולאדם שלא הותר לו הבשר כלל, נתן במקומו שלא יאכל מן עץ הדעת שנא׳ עליו שהוא טוב למאכל ותאוה לעינים שלא ילך אחר יצרו וזהו שגרם לו החטא כדכתיב בקרא שנמשך אחר יצרו ולפיכך נתן לו אלו מצות. ומה שנתן לו שלש מצות בינו לבין בוראו ושלש מצות בינו ולבין האדם, וזה כי האדם חלקיו הוא הגוף והנפש הם חלקי האדם, והאדם בכללו הוא כולל חלקיו כאשר מקבל על ידי החלקים צורת האדם, וזה דבר ג׳ כמו הבית שחלקיו הם העצים והאבנים ואח״כ נעשה ממנו הבית המורכב משניהם, והוא ענין זולת חלקיו ודבר זה נתבאר למעלה פעמים הרבה מאוד. וכנגד שלא יהיה חוטא בנפשו לשמים נתן לו ע״ז, כי כל החטאים א״א שיחטא בנפשו בלבד חוץ מע״ז דכתיב (יחזקאל י״ד) למען תפוש את ישראל בלבם וזהו בע״ז, וכדאמרינן בפרק שלוח הקן (חולין קמ״ב ע״א) ודלמא מהרהר בע״ז הוא דכל העבירות אין מצטרפת מחשבה למעשה חוץ מן ע״ז דכ׳ למען תפוש את ישראל בלבם, וא״כ החטא הזה בלבד הוא לנפש. וג״ע הוא לבשר מחמת יצרו שבגוף מתאוה לעריות, ודבר זה מבואר בכמה מקומות שחטא עריות הוא לגוף, וכמו שאמרה תורה בסוטה שיהא קרבנה שעורים שהיא עשתה מעשה חמור כך קרבנה יהיה מאכל חמור (סוטה י״ד ע״א) הרי כי חטא הערוה הוא ענין חמרי גופני ובכמה מקומות נתבאר דבר זה.

ברכת השם הוא לאדם במה שהוא אדם מחובר מגוף ונפש, כי ברכת השם הוא חוטא בלשון שמברך השם וגדר האדם שהוא חי מדבר, והנה הדבור הוא צורת האדם הכולל הגוף והנפש, ולפיכך ברכת השם בלשונו חטא האדם בכללו כמו שחטא עבודה זרה הוא בנפשו ועריות בגופו, ברכת השם בדבור הלשון שהדבור הוא כולל האדם. ועוד תדע והוא העיקר כי לכך חטא ברכת השם הוא בכלל האדם, כי בעל החטא הזה הוא כופר בעיקר שמברך השם וכיון שאין עיקר אין לו מציאות כלל והרי הוא חוטא בכלל האדם שמציאותו בטילה לגמרי, וכמו שכאשר הוא חוטא בגילוי עריות הוא חוטא בגופו ובע״ז החטא דבק בנפשו, מברך השם חוטא בעיקר שהוא הכל לכן החטא דבק באדם בכללו. וזה הטעם שאמרה תורה לסמוך ידיהם על ראש המברך ואומרים לו דמך בראשך, כלומר נתחייבת בעצמך ואנו לא גרמנו לך, כי כל שאר החטאים יש בו זכות מה ואם נתחייב בבית דין הרי ב״ד דנין אותו למיתה ומכל מקום יש לו קצת זכות לתלות בו ואין לומר עליו שהוא גורם לנפשו, אבל חטא ברכת השם שהוא כופר בעיקר אין לו שום

זכות, כי איך יהיה לו זכות מה והוא כופר בעיקר רוצה לעקור העיקר, לכך סומכין עליו ידיהם ואומרים לו דמך בראשך שאתה גרמת לך שהרי אין לך זכות כלל, ודבר זה נתבאר בספר גור אריה. וכנגד שלא יהיה רע לבריות שלש עבירות דינין גזל שפיכות דמים, דינין החטא הוא בנפשו שהוא מעוות משפט אמת והיושר אשר הוא בנפש האדם, כי האמת והיושר בנפשו הוא וזהו חטא הנפש כי אין יושר ומשפט רק בנפש השכלית, ועוד כאשר אין עושה דין הוא מפחיתות הנפש, שצריך כל אדם כאשר יראה דבר עולה אז נפשו מתעורר לעשות דין ולכך כל דיין צריך שיהיה לו לב אמיץ וחזק למשפט. ודבר זה ברור הוא שהדין הוא בא מן התעוררות הנפש וכאשר תשכיל בחכמה תבין איך הדין מפעולת הנפש, ובויקרא רבה בפרשת ויקרא (פ"ז) שני דברים הם בשמאלו של הקדוש ברוך הוא המשפט והנפש, המשפט דכתיב ותאחז במשפט ידי, הנפש כי בידך נפש כל חי וכל מקום שנאמר יד הוא שמאל אמרה תורה בראתי הנפש במקום המשפט והיא יצאת וחוטאת לכך כתיב ונפש כי תחטא וכו', לפיכך הנפש מבקש המשפט שהיא נבראת במקום המשפט ואם אין משפט הוא לחטא הנפש ודבר זה ברור ופשוט למבין.

ומצוה זאת נגד ע"ז שהיא מצוה שלא יהיה רע לשמים שהע"ז נקרא אלהים אחרים והדיין נקרא גם כן אלהים בכל מקום, ואמרו חכמים (סנהדרין ז' ע"ב) המעמיד דיין שאינו הגון כאלו נוטע אשירה וענין אחד הם בכל דבר, ולפיכך כנגד המצוה שנתן השם יתברך שלא יעבוד ע"ז שהוא חטא באלהי נכר ומצוה זאת היא בין האדם ובין בוראו, צוה בין האדם ואדם לעשות משפט אמת שלא יחטא בדבר שנקרא אלהים גם כן. וגזל הוא נגד עריות ובכל מקום אמרו חכמים גזל ועריות שנפש האדם מחמדתן הרי כי כל אלו שני דברים הם שוים, ועיקר גזל רדיפת הממון וחמדת העושר וההון מענינים הגופניים כמו עריות רק שדבר זה הוא בין האדם לחבירו, ואין עריות וגזל בכלל חמדה כי עריות שהוא רודף ומחמד נשים או הגזל שהוא רודף אחר העושר אין זה חמדה בלבד אבל הוא חמדה לדבר מיוחד שהוא לזנות או שהוא נבהל להון, אבל החמדה הוא שחומד דבר החסר לו ולא שיהיה חומד לדבר מיוחד רק שהוא חומד שהוא בעל תאוה, ודבר זה ענין אחר כמו שיתבאר שהוא מן החומר ודברים אלו ברורים. וחטא שפיכת דמים בין אדם לחבירו, וחטא הזה הוא שכל האדם הוא חוטא ואין החטא בחלק ממנו רק בכללו, וכמו שחטא ברכת השם הוא כופר בעיקר שהוא הכל כן זה השופך דמים הוא שופך דמו לגמרי לכך חטא זה גם כן בכלל כל אדם, לא כמו חטא דינין וחטא של גזל שאין החטא שכל האדם מקולקל רק הקלקול הוא בחלק, אבל שפיכת דמים כמו ברכת השם שהוא כופר בעיקר לגמרי כאלו אין השם יתברך ח"ו נמצא כך שפיכת דם האדם עשאו לאדם אינו נמצא לגמרי. והשביעי בחומר האדם שממנו החמדה ואינו יכול להמתין עד שישחוט, וזהו החמדה שהוא בא מן החומר שהוא חסר תמיד ולכך הוא תאב ומחמד להשלים חסרונו. ואמר בא אדם וחטא בחמדה שלקח הפרי שהוא נחמד לו נסתלקה שכינה לרקיע ראשון, בא קין וחטא בשפיכת דמים נסתלקה השכינה לרקיע ב'. בא דור אנוש וחטאו בע"ז כמו שאמרו חכמים בפ' כל כתבי (שבת קי"ח) כל שומר שבת מחללו וסמיך ליה אשרי אנוש יעשה זאת כל שומר שבת כהלכתו אפילו עובד ע"ז כמו דור אנוש מחול לו שנאמר מחללו אל תקרי מחללו אלא מחול לו ודורו היה הראשון שעבד ע"ז דכתיב אז הוחל לקרא בשם ה' נסתלקה שכינה לרקיע ג'. בא דור המבול וחטאו בגזל דכתיב בפירוש ותמלא הארץ חמס ואין חטא מפורש בהן רק זאת נסתלקה שכינה לרקיע רביעי. בא דור הפלגה וחטאו בברכת השם שאמרו נבנה לנו עיר ומגדל ונעשה עמו מלחמה וזהו ברכת השם נסתלקה שכינה לרקיע חמישי. עמדו סדומים וחטאו בדין כמו שמבואר ממעשיהם אשר סופר עליהם ומה שהיו דייני סדום עושים ואיך היו דנים נסתלקה שכינה לרקיע ששי. עמדו מצרים בימי אברהם וחטאו בעריות כמו שמבואר

ממעשה מצרים דכתיב (ויקרא י"ח) כמעשה ארץ מצרים וגו' ובשביל כך לא אמר פרעה הנה ארצי לפניך כמו שאמר אבימלך מפני שאמר המצריים שטופי זימה הם. נסתלקה שכינה לרקיע ז', בא אברהם שלא היה בעולם גדור בערוה כמו שהיה אברהם, וכמו שאמרו ז"ל (ב"ב ט"ז ע"א) עפרא בפומיה דאיוב שאמר ברית כרתי לעיני ומה אתבונן על בתולה באחריני לא מסתכל אבל בדידיה מסתכל ואילו אברהם בדידיה נמי לא מסתכל שאמר הנה נא ידעתי כי אשה יפת מראה את, שעד עתה לא הכיר ביופיה שלא נסתכל בה ולכך הוריד השכינה לרקיע ו'. עמד יצחק והיה צדיק בדין שקבל עליו מדת הדין באהבה שהרי פשט צוארו לישחט, והנה הוא הפך סדומים שקלקלו הדין ואין חלוק בין דין שמים ובין דין ב"ד של מטה הכל הוא הדין וידוע כי מדת יצחק הוא מדת הדין ולכך הוריד השכינה ברקיע ה'. בא יעקב והיה מקדש השם וכדכתיב קרא (ישעי' כ"ט) והקדישו את קדוש יעקב, וברכה ג' אתה קדוש ושמך קדוש מיוסד נגד יעקב, כי שלש ברכות ראשונות הם נגד אברהם יצחק ויעקב, ואף המלאכים מקדישים בשם יעקב כדכתיב ברוך א-להי ישראל וכמו שמבואר למעלה שהמלאכים מקדישים בשם יעקב, ולפיכך הוא נגד אנשי דור הפלגה שהיו מברכים השם והוריד השכינה לרקיע רביעי. לוי הפך גזל החומד ולוקח שאינו שלו ולוי הפכו, שהרי כל שבטו לא היה להם חלק בארץ ונחלה בביזה ה' הוא נחלתו, ולכך היה לוי נבדל מעניני הממון ורדיפת הממון ואפילו מה שראוי היה לחלקו לא היה לו, ואם לא היה מוכן שבט לוי לדבר זה לא נתן לו הקדוש ברוך הוא דבר זה, רק היה מסתפק בשלו, ואין לומר שבטו בלבד אבל לא הוא עצמו, שדבר זה לא יתכן כי אם לא זכה שבטו לזאת המדה מן אביהם לא זכה שבטו לזה, כי שם לוי לכל השבט לכך הוריד השכינה לרקיע שלישי. קהת נגד עבודה זרה משפחתו עובדים בגופם להשם יתברך שהם היו נושאי המקדש וכל זרעו היו עובדים אל השם יתברך בגופם, לא כמו בני גרשון ומררי שהיה להם עגלות אבל משפחת הקהתי בכתף ישאו וזהו נקרא עבודה דבר שיעבוד בגופו, וכן מזרעו הכהנים שעליהם העבודה בעצם ולפיכך הוריד השכינה לרקיע ב'. בא עמרם והיה צדיק גדול עד שלא חטא ועל ידו לא בא מיתה, ואמרו חכמים במסכת בבא בתרא (י"ז ע"א) שעמרם מת בעטיו של נחש, כלומר שלא היה ראוי לו המיתה רק בשביל הנחש שהביא המיתה לעולם, ולפיכך הוא נגד קין שהוא היה תופס אומנות של נחש הקדמוני והביא המיתה לעולם ואילו עמרם לא מת בשביל חטא עצמו, והרי הוא הפך קין לגמרי שקין הביא המיתה לאחר ועמרם אף מה שדרך העולם שמביא מיתה לעצמו על ידי חטא עצמו לא היה מביא, נמצא עמרם כולו חיים וקין כולו מיתה ודבר זה מבואר, לכך הוריד השכינה לרקיע הראשון. בא משה והיה צדיק שפירש מן האשה בזה תדע שלא היה החמדה עם משה, שאלו היה החמדה עם משה לא היה ראוי שיהיה פורש מאשתו כדי שלא יבא לידי חטא, לכך יש לדעת שלא היה נמצא אצלו החמדה ולכך היה נגד אדם הראשון שהיה בעל חמדה ולכך הוריד השכינה לארץ שהיתה השכינה שבה אל מקומה הראשון. ומכל מקום נדע מזה שהשכינה מקומה בארץ לטעם אשר התבאר, ועוד יתבאר מה שזכו התחתונים בפרט להיות שכינתו יתברך בתחתונים אם לא היה החטא המבדיל בין הנמצאים ובין העלה:

G'vurot Hashem 66

The Maharal posits that there is a directly proportionate relationship between the magnitude of an act and its purpose.

Yehudah son of B'tzalel[11] wrote as follows. Everything has a purpose – according to its matter it has a purpose. If [its] action is an important and great activity, it is suitable that it will also have an important purpose – for it is inappropriate that an important action have an inferior and lowly purpose. How much more so does this hold true of the action of G-d – for all His actions exist through wisdom and intellect[12] [and] all His actions and activities lead towards a purpose which is suitable according to the act.

The Maharal now explores the purpose of the Exodus from Egypt. Since the Exodus was such a momentous action on G-d's part, by the above reasoning it must have a correspondingly important purpose, which the Maharal explains to be that Hashem should be Israel's G-d.

And since we have seen, in the Exodus from Egypt, that Hashem performed very great and awesome deeds and that He Himself, in His glory, took them out from Egypt, if so, it is suitable that such an act will have a purpose which is as important as the act which Hashem performed to reach that purpose.

Now we have found in the Torah, that the purpose of the Exodus was that Hashem should be Israel's G-d, as is written at the beginning of the Exodus, "I shall remove you from under the burdens of Egypt . . . and I will take you to Me as a nation and I will be a G-d for you."[13] And as is written at the end of the Torah-portion "You will command," "[I am Hashem your G-d] Who removes you from the land of Egypt to dwell amongst you."[14]

It is therefore proved that the beginning[15] of the Exodus was in order that Hashem should be G-d for them [the Jewish people].

The Maharal notes that the order and content of the Ten Commandments and the mitzvot given to the Jewish people also reflect this purpose. He explains that the mitzvot are the decrees which flow naturally from Hashem being our G-d – since a central aspect of G-dliness is the creation of Law.

---

11. This is the Maharal; he refers to himself here in the third person.

12. In Hebrew, "*seichel*"; which, as we have explained before, does not refer simply to the intellect but to a transcendent, spiritual reality.

13. Sh'mot 6:6–7.

14. Cf. Sh'mot 29:46. It seems that there is a printer's error here. The correct reading is, 'They will know that I am Hashem *their* G-d Who removed *them* from the land of Egypt in order to dwell amongst *them*, I am Hashem *their* G-d.' It is important to note that to the Maharal's mind, Hashem's dwelling within the Jewish people is inherently connected with Him being their G-d.

15. Perhaps this word should be "purpose" as per the context. The Hebrew word for "beginning," תחלת, "*t'chilat*" is very similar to the word for "purpose," תכלית, "*tachlit*" and there may be a printing error here.

Therefore, all the sections [in the Torah, outlining the mitzvot] come in order: initially, Hashem removed them from Egypt and afterwards He gave them the Ten Commandments. The Ten Commandments begin with, "I am Hashem your G-d Who removed you from the land of Egypt. You shall not have the gods of others[16] before Me."[17] Afterwards the rest of the commandments follow along with the section of "These are the ordinances."[18] [The reason for this order is as follows.] Since Hashem is their G-d, they must accept His laws[19] because G-d has laws by virtue of Him being G-d.

The Maharal notes that a Jew who chooses to be judged in a court which runs according to the mores of idolatry is, in effect, exchanging G-d's Law (which animates a Jewish court) for Idolatry's Law. This underscores that the acceptance of G-d's Law is the acceptance of G-d as our G-d. There are thus two stages in our relationship to Hashem as our G-d: acceptance of His law and subsequently, His dwelling within us.

For this reason, one who brings his court case to the courts of idol worshippers increases the prestige of that idolatry through his acceptance upon himself of the law of strange gods, because all judgment is related to divinity. [We see proof of this in the Torah in that] in all places we find the term "*E-lo-him*"[20] written close to the concept of justice [for example,] "The homeowner will approach the *elohim*,"[21], [22] and so it is in all places.

And therefore, after the acceptance of Hashem being their G-d, the acceptance of His laws follows immediately, through which they[23] are

16. Translation as per the Chizkuni ad loc.

17. Sh'mot 20:2–3. As he has explained, the purpose of the Exodus was that Hashem should be our G-d; therefore, this is the first of the Ten Commandments.

18. The Ten Commandments are found in Sh'mot, Chapter 20. The next Torah portion is called "These are the ordinances" and spans Sh'mot Chapters 21–24. This portion contains a detailed list of social ordinances.

19. Lit., "ordinances."

20. In the Torah, the term "E-lohim," א־לוהים, means both "judge" as well as "G-d." One differentiates between the secular and holy uses of the word based on context. See the beginning of Tiferet Yisrael, Chapter Six, as well as the Commentary, Ch. 6 § Points 5 and 6, for an exploration of the ideas behind Hashem's different attributes, and in particular, the attribute of justice, signified by the divine name, "E-lohim."

21. The word used here means "judges." The Maharal's point is that the concepts of Law and G-dliness are so intertwined that the Hebrew word for "judges" is actually one of G-d's names.

22. Sh'mot 22:7.

23. The Jews.

Hashem's nation, through their acceptance of the laws of the G-d of Israel; because it is certain that G-d is called one who leads the nation, as it is written, "Make for us a god which will go before us,"[24] and there is no leadership without justice, because justice is the guiding of the nation.

And therefore you understand the gravity of the offence of bringing one's court case to the courts of idolaters – since one who does this is [willfully] foregoing the Justice of the G-d of Israel and is entering the justice of strange gods. For every [concept of] Divinity has a [parallel concept of] leadership and one who brings his case in the courts [of idolaters] grants recognition to the leadership of a strange god; since immediately after the acceptance of [Hashem's][25] kingship at Sinai, He[26] gave them laws appropriate to His Divinity. And after this He desired to dwell amongst them as is written immediately afterwards, "They will make me a sanctuary and I will dwell amongst them."[27]

Here it has been clarified that the purpose of the Exodus was that Hashem should be their[28] G-d and that His divine presence would be amongst them.

The Maharal now questions why Hashem would prefer, so to speak, to "dwell" amongst lowly human beings, when He is so exalted and transcendent.

Now we must examine the following. If we assume [as claimed above] that a great purpose requires a great action, then we should ask, "Behold, the heavens are His seat and the earth is His footstool,"[29] and His dwelling is in the Upper Worlds. If so, why did Hashem choose to dwell amongst the lowly [beings]?[30] In this matter, surely we should follow the principle that "we ascend [in holiness] and we do not descend"[31] and therefore, His divinity should be amongst the transcendent; why does He need the lowly [humans] who are dust, maggots and worms?

The Maharal's answer is that human beings, whose essence is completely comprised of being "caused by G-d" and being His effect, actually share a closer bond with G-d than the more transcendent, spiritual beings populating the upper realms, since the angelic beings are not only caused by G-d but they are also Causes themselves of lower realities.

24. Sh'mot 32:1.
25. Lit., "His."
26. G-d.
27. Sh'mot 25:8.
28. The Jewish Nation's.
29. Cf. Y'shayahu 66:1.
30. I.e., human beings.
31. Cf. B'rachot 28a.

However, if it is true that every element of reality depends on His presence dwelling amongst the lowly [human beings] and that this encompasses [the purpose of] everything, then there is no question!

And when you know that He, may He be Blessed, is bonded with the creations through their being Effects (for He, may He be Blessed, is the Cause of everything) then His will is vested within the Effect. And when there is a Cause, then an Effect exists, for the connection between the Primal Cause[32] and the creations is through the fact that He, may He be Blessed, is a Cause for them and the creations are His Effects. And we have already discussed above[33] at length regarding this important bond, when we discussed the verse, "[G-d] called to him[34] from within the [burning] bush."[35]

And now that this is clear, you shouldn't say that the transcendent beings are the elite, rather it is the lower beings [who are superior], because the transcendent beings act upon the lower ones and in this mode, the transcendent beings are considered as a Cause, and therefore, the *essence* of their being is not that they are [only] Effects [from G-d, but rather that they are both causes of other, lower realities as well as being effects from G-d]; however, the lower beings, through their being lower, are, in their essence, [only] effects and therefore, the truest connection with the Primal Cause[36] who is The Cause, in truth, is only shared with the lower beings through their being truthful Effects.

The Maharal now cites a Midrash to prove his thesis – that the divine presence can only truly rest in this world through humanity. Moreover, the Midrash illustrates that it is the mitzvot which enable Hashem's presence to rest within humanity by ensuring that this lower world is a suitable receptacle for the divine presence.

And [this principle is illustrated] in many Midrashim in the portion of B'reishit [as follows,][37]

"And they heard the sound of Hashem – Elokim[38] walking[39] [Himself] in

---

32. G-d.
33. See G'vurot Hashem 23.
34. Moshe.
35. Sh'mot 3:4.
36. G-d.
37. B'reishit Rabbah 19:7; B'midar Rabbah 13:2.
38. This is a double-barreled reference to Hashem. See the beginning of Tiferet Yisrael 6, as well as the Commentary, Ch. 6 § Point 5, for an exploration of the ideas behind Hashem's different attributes.
39. In Hebrew, מתהלך, "*mit-haleich*," lit. "walking oneself." It is important to note that when the Torah speaks of Hashem in anthropomorphic terms, it is a firm fun-

the garden in the direction of the sunrise."[40]

The word used [to denote G-d's strolling in the garden] is not "walking,"[41] rather it is "walking Himself."[42] This teaches that the essential dwelling place of Hashem's presence was amongst the lower beings.[43]

But when Adam sinned, the divine presence removed itself to the first firmament.[44] When Kayin sinned,[45] it removed itself to the second firmament. When the generation of Enosh sinned,[46] it removed itself to the third firmament. When the generation of the flood sinned,[47] it removed itself to the fourth firmament. When the generation of the dispersal sinned,[48] it removed itself to the fifth firmament. When the Sodomites stood up and sinned,[49] it removed itself to the sixth firmament. When the Egyptians stood up and sinned in the days of Avraham,[50] it removed itself to the seventh firmament.

And afterwards, seven righteous people stood and drew down the divine presence [back] to the earth: Avraham, Yitzchak, Ya'akov, Levi,

---

damental of Judaism that such terms are metaphors to allow humans some handle by which to grasp some concept of the Infinite One. In the words of our sages, "The Torah spoke in human language," (B'rachot 31b).

40. B'reishit 3:8.

41. In Hebrew, מהלך, "*m'haleich*," "walking."

42. In Hebrew, מתהלך, *mit-haleich*, "walking oneself." This is a reflexive verb – indicating that one is performing an action on oneself.

43. The Radal, *zt"l*, comments here (in his commentary to the Midrash in B'reishit Rabbah) that the verb "*m'haleich*" means to go from one place to another. Thus, had the Torah used this verb ("*m'haleich*"), it would have implied that Hashem had, so to speak, descended momentarily from the heavens to the Earth – He had gone to the garden. However, since the reflexive form is used ("*mit-haleich*"), it implies that Hashem was, so to speak, going from one place to another within the garden – that this was already His permanent dwelling place.

44. This Midrash reflects the view that G-d created seven different "firmaments" – aspects of Hashem's immanence. For further study, see Rosh Hashanah 32a and Tanchuma, Naso 16.

45. This is Cain who murdered his brother Hevel (Abel).

46. Enosh was the son of Sheit, son of Adam and Chavah as per B'reishit 4:26. As the verse says there, in his days, "humanity began to profane the name of G-d." Our sages (see Rashi ad loc.) explain that this is when idol worship began.

47. B'reishit, Chapters 6–10.

48. B'reishit, Chapter 11.

49. B'reishit, Chapter 19.

50. B'reishit 12:10–20.

K'hat[51], Amram[52] and Moshe.[53] As it is written, "The righteous shall inherit the earth and dwell[54] on it forever."[55] But if this is so [that the righteous will dwell forever on the earth] then what must the evil [people] do? Must they float in the air [since there is no place for them on the earth]? Rather, [read the word "dwell" with slightly different vowels[56] so that] the verse means that the righteous *will cause the divine presence to dwell*[57] on the earth."

The Maharal now explains how the seven "Noahide" laws are a natural result of the above idea. He says that these laws were actually given to Adam before No'ach because they are the only means humanity has of preventing the moral destruction of the universe – something which will make the universe unfit for Hashem's presence. Each one of these laws addresses a particular moral weak point – all listed in the Midrash above. If humanity succeeds, then they and this universe are clearly distinguished as the Effects of G-d and His presence dwells within them.

The explanation of this is as we have said. Initially, when the world was created and when there was no deficiency in the Effect[58] at all, Hashem, may He be Blessed, was connected [to the world] as is appropriate for the Cause to connect with its Effect. And there was only a connection to the lower beings, since [only] they are truly Effects.

[This continued] until sin was found amongst the lower beings which severed this bond until there was [almost] no connection between the Cause and the Effect. And these seven sins which the Effects committed [were so significant] because initially, when His world was created, [Hashem][59] gave them these commandments: [the prohibitions against] eating flesh from a living animal, cursing G-d, idol worship, sexual immorality; [perversion of] justice[60] and [the prohibitions against] stealing and murder.

---

51. Levi's son. See B'reishit 46:11.
52. K'hat's son. See Sh'mot 6:18.
53. Amram's son. See B'midbar 26:59.
54. In Hebrew, יִשְׁכְּנוּ, "*yishk'nu*," "they will dwell."
55. Tehillim 37:29.
56. In Hebrew, vowel sounds are not written as letters (as are consonants), but are rather separate diacritics added to consonants. Torah scrolls and scriptures are not vowelized, thus allowing several alternative vowelizations of each word.
57. In Hebrew, יַשְׁכִּינוּ, "*yashkinu*," "they will cause [them] to dwell."
58. I.e., the Universe, but in particular, human beings.
59. Lit., "He."
60. There is a dispute regarding the content of this mitzvah. The Rambam (Laws of Kings 9:14) holds that this mitzvah is to set up courts of justice. The Ramban (commentary to B'reishit 34:13) however, holds that this mitzvah is not to establish

These seven commandments are the bond between the Cause and the Effect through His decrees and commandments: [this happens] due to the Effect accepting the decree and the command of the Cause. This will be explained further in the work, Tiferet Yisrael.[61]

Therefore, immediately, when Adam was created, He gave him seven commandments.

The Maharal now explains the structure of the seven Noahide laws in detail. This is his first analysis, a slightly different one follows.

Three (the prohibitions against sexual immorality, idolatry and cursing G-d) regulate the relationship between man and G-d. Three others (the prohibitions against stealing, murder and the perversion of justice) regulate the relationships between humans and G-d. The last one (the prohibition against eating the limb of a living animal) is the lynchpin on which the others rest as it allows a person to master his/her physical impulses. In the case of Adam, this last mitzvah was different in detail (not to eat from the tree of knowledge of good and evil), but the purpose thereof was the same as the prohibition against eating the limb of a living animal.

It seems that [Hashem][62] chose these seven commandments because Hashem, may He be Blessed, desired that humanity would be good for the Heavens and good for the Creations and through both these aspects[63] a person is righteous, as it is written, "Say to the righteous that he is good,[64] because they will eat the fruit of their deeds."[65] And in the first chapter of [tractate] Kiddushin[66] [regarding the verse just cited], we say,

> [The Gemara asks] "And is there a righteous person who is good and one who is not good?

---

courts, but rather a prohibition against transgressing the Torah's civil laws. The Ramban holds that these civil laws are the same as those given to the Jewish people. The Ramban does concede that this transgression implies a need to set up a system of courts. It would seem from the Maharal's comments over the entirety of this citation that he agrees with the Ramban's opinion. We have therefore referred to this latter opinion's understanding of this mitzvah as "the prohibitions against perversion of justice."

61. See Tiferet Yisrael, Chapters Sixteen, Thirty-Five and Seventy.

62. Lit., "He."

63. Lit., "things."

64. This implies that there are some "righteous" people who are not necessarily considered "good."

65. Y'shayahu 3:10.

66. Kiddushin 40a, with variations.

> [The Gemara answers] "Rather, one who is good to heaven and to the creations is considered a righteous person who is good; one who is good to heaven and not good to the creations is considered a righteous person who is not good."

And therefore [Hashem] gave the three mitzvot which are between man and his Maker – in order that humanity not be "bad to heaven." These are [the prohibitions against]: sexual immorality, cursing G-d and idolatry. And [then He gave] the three mitzvot which are between man and his fellow, which are [the prohibition against] stealing (that one should not steal from another) [perversion of] justice and [the prohibition against] murder, in order that a person not be "bad for the creations."

And the seventh [mitzvah] is [the prohibition against eating] a limb from a living animal which is the beginning and reason that a person will not arrive at any of these prohibitions. [The reason this seventh mitzvah achieves this is that] it is set against the inclination to evil (which is why Hashem gave humanity this mitzvah), that he will not desire to eat and cut [a limb] off an animal before its soul has departed, because of his inclination. And this mitzvah was given so that a person could control his urges, as the sages said,[67]

> The planting[68] cuts the legs out[69] from under the butchers[70] and of those who have relations with *niddot*.[71]

[The explanation of this is that] the Torah gave a three-year [waiting] period for [consuming the fruits of] plants [as it is written,] "for three years it will

---

67. Beitzah 25b.

68. This refers to the prohibition to eat from the fruit of a tree during the first three years of its growth. See Vayikra 19:23.

69. I.e., this mitzvah combats the tendencies displayed by people who transgress the following prohibitions.

70. See Rashi ad loc. Rashi explains that certain butchers cannot bear to wait for an animal's internal organs to be checked for signs which would render the animal non-kosher, before they eat, with the result that sometimes they have already eaten and then the animal is found to be non-kosher.

71. A נדה, "*niddah*," is a woman who has menstruated but has not yet immersed herself in the *mikvah*, ritual pool. A husband may not have relations with his wife until after her immersion. See Vayikra 15:25. The idea here is that some people are so enslaved to their sexual urges that they cannot wait for their wives to complete the process of going to the *mikvah* and thus force themselves upon their wives beforehand, G-d forbid.

be sealed[72] up for you,"[73] and that the butchers cannot wait long enough for the animal's soul to depart and those who have relations with *niddot* cannot wait until they immerse [in the *mikvah*].

Therefore, this mitzvah (not eating the limb of a living animal) is to prevent a person following his inclination, because if he does, in the end, his inclination will tell him, "Commit the following [sin]!" and he will do it, eventually transgressing all the prohibitions. So too with the Ten Commandments, the final commandment is, "do not covet,"[74] because the sin of desire is the beginning of all sins. And the liturgist wrote as follows, "'These mitzvot'[75] are included in 'do not covet,'" meaning that all of the mitzvot are subsumed by [the prohibition,] "do not covet," for if one transgresses the prohibition of "do not covet," one will arrive at [a state where he performs] all sins.

Therefore, [the prohibition against eating] the limb of a living animal is the seventh [of the seven Noahide laws].

Now, Adam was not allowed to eat meat at all, and therefore, instead of this [prohibition against eating the limb of a living animal] [Hashem] gave him [the prohibition] that he could not eat from the tree of knowledge regarding which it is said, "It is good for eating and a desire for the eyes,"[76] to prevent [Adam] following his urges; and this [following after his urges] is what caused his sin, as the Torah writes – that he was drawn after his inclination. Therefore, [Hashem][77] gave him these mitzvot.

The Maharal now introduces a deeper, more detailed explanation of the internal structure of the two categories of the seven Noahide laws. The two categories are: between humans and G-d; and between each human and his fellow. Here he explains that in each of the two sections there are three mitzvot which parallel the structure of the human being: body, soul and whole person. The following are the sins of the soul: idol worship (between humans and G-d) and perversion of justice (between humans and their fellows). The sins of the body are: sexual immorality

72. See Rashi on this verse. This phrase, "sealed up," indicates that the plants may not be used in that 3-year period. It is noteworthy that the word used for "sealed up" is the same used to denote the physical foreskin, the removal of which our sages saw as part of developing sexual discipline, an idea also mentioned in this citation from the Gemara.

73. Vayikra 19:23.

74. Sh'mot 20:14.

75. B'midbar 36:13, Vayikra 27:34. This phrase connotes all of the mitzvot that Hashem commanded us.

76. B'reishit 3:6.

77. Lit., "He."

(between humans and G-d) and theft (between humans and their fellows). The sins which encompass the whole h-man are: cursing G-d (between humans and G-d) and murder (between humans and their fellows).
The final structure is:

	Sins of the soul	*Sins of the body*	*Sins of the whole person*
Between Humans and Hashem	Idolatry	Sexual immorality	Cursing G-d
Between Humans and one another	Perversion of justice	Theft	Murder

And the reason [Hashem][78] gave humanity[79] three mitzvot between him[80] and his Maker and three mitzvot between man and his fellow is because a human is comprised of [the following]: his sections are the body and the soul; while the human as a whole includes his parts when he receives through these parts, the Form[81] of the human being.[82] And this thing[83] is a third entity, just like a house's components are the stones and wood; and thereafter the house is built from the combination of both and it is an entity besides its components. And this idea was explained several times above.[84]

Idolatry – a sin between a human and G-d through the soul.

Hashem gave man [the prohibition against] idolatry in order that he shouldn't sin against his soul, because there is no sin with which one can sin against the soul exclusively besides idolatry, as it is written, "In order to catch Israel through their heart [that they have withdrawn from Me, all

78. Lit., "He."
79. Lit, "him."
80. Lit., "man."
81. For an exploration of the Maharal's concept of "Form" and "matter," see the Commentary, Ch. 4 § Point 5.
82. The Maharal explains that the human being is greater than the sum of his individual parts – the body and the soul – that there is a "Human Form" which includes but transcends these components.
83. The Human Form.
84. See G'vurot Hashem 43 and 60.

of them, with their idols],"[85] which refers to idol worship;[86] and as we say in the Chapter of "Sending away the mother bird,"[87] that perhaps he[88] was committing idolatry in his thought – because there is no sin where thought [alone] is considered an act [of sin] except for idolatry, as the verse states, "In order to catch Israel through their heart . . ."[89,90] Thus we see that it is [only] this sin[91] which is exclusively [a sin] of the soul.

Sexual immorality – a sin between a human and G-d through the body.

And sexual immorality is [a sin] of the body due to his [instinctual] inclination, which is located in the body, which lusts for sexual immorality. This idea is explained in many places, that the sin of sexual immorality is of the body, as the Torah said, regarding a *sotah*,[92] that the sacrifice she brings should be of barley, "since she committed the act of a donkey,[93] therefore, her sacrifice should be of the food of a donkey."[94] We see that the sin of sexual immorality is a material, physical matter. And this has been explained in several places.[95]

Cursing G-d – a sin between a human and G-d through the entire person.

The cursing of G-d relates to the human [as a whole entity] from the aspect

85. Y'chezkel 14:5. The section in parentheses is not quoted in the Maharal but is germane.
86. It is clear from the complete verse that the act of Hashem in catching Israel through their heart refers to apprehending them for the sin of idolatry.
87. Chullin 142a.
88. The Gemara is discussing a case where a person passed away while performing certain mitzvot which ostensibly have the reward of long life. The Gemara suggests that perhaps the reason for the tragedy was that as he was performing the mitzvah, he was simultaneously in the service of an idol, even if he was only thinking of such service.
89. Y'chezkel 14:5.
90. The Maharal cites this statement in the Gemara to prove that the verse he cited from Y'chezkel indeed refers to the sin of idolatry, in particular, to the fact that idolatry is the only sin that can be committed with thought alone.
91. Idolatry.
92. In certain cases, the Torah mandates a process of clarification of marital fidelity. If a husband requests his wife not to seclude herself with a particular man and she ignores this request and does so, the husband may initiate the "*sotah*" process. The woman is termed a *sotah*. For more details, see B'midbar 5.
93. I.e., sexual immorality.
94. Cf. Sotah 14a with slight variations.
95. See Derech Chaim 5:9 and N'tivot Olam, *N'tiv Ha'avodah* 2.

that he is comprised of a body and soul. [This is] because [when] cursing G-d, one sins with the tongue and the definition of a human is as "[a being who is] alive and speaks."[96] Therefore, speech is the Form of the human, which includes both body and soul and thus [when] cursing G-d with his tongue, a person has sinned with his entirety. Just as when he sinned through idolatry [he sinned] with his soul, and in sexual immorality [he sinned] with his body, when cursing G-d, it is through speech of the tongue, for speech includes [all of] the person.

You should also know, and this is the essential [idea], that cursing G-d includes the [whole] human being for the following reason – because one who performs this sin denies the Essence [of life][97] and since [for him] there is no essence, he has no existence at all, and therefore, he sins with all his humanity, since his existence is cancelled completely.[98] And just as when he sins through sexual immorality, he sins with his body; and through idolatry the sin cleaves to his soul; one who curses G-d sins essentially, which is everything, therefore, the sin bonds with the human in his entirety.

This is the reason that [when carrying out the death penalty against one who curses G-d, that] the Torah mandates that they[99] should place their hands on the head of the one who cursed and say to him, "Your blood is on your head,"[100] which means, "You have created this penalty, we have not caused you to suffer it." [This is] because [in] all other sins, he has some innocence[101] and if he is convicted by the court, it is the court which sentences him to death, but he nevertheless has some innocence by which he could depend and [therefore] we cannot say that he caused this [death penalty] to himself. However, [through] the sin of cursing G-d, a person denies the essence [of existence][102] [therefore] how could a person have any [iota of] innocence, since he denies the essence [of existence] and wishes to uproot this essence. Therefore, they [the witness and judges] place their hands on him and say to him, "Your blood is on your head, because you

---

96. See Unkelus on B'reishit 2:7, Moreh N'vuchim 1:51 and Kuzari 1:89, 5:20.

97. I.e., Hashem.

98. The idea here is that Hashem is literally the life-force enervating all of reality. Should one actually sever oneself from G-d, G-d forbid, existence is not possible. See the Rambam, Foundations of the Torah 1:1–2.

99. The witnesses and judges.

100. Rambam, Idolatry 2:10.

101. The Maharal is saying that with all other sins, the person still retains some iota of a claim of innocence within himself, and therefore, it is the court which is considered to have administered the death penalty. But here, since the person has literally severed himself from the source of all life, he has himself committed spiritual and essential suicide and there is no third party involved – the death penalty is simply the physical implementation of his own decisions.

102. I.e., Hashem.

have caused this to happen to yourself because you have no innocence." And this matter is explained in the book, Gur Aryeh.[103]

Now the Maharal explains the internal structure of the next three mitzvot (out of the seven Noahide laws), the purpose of which is to prevent one person being evil to another. These are: the prohibitions against perversion of justice, theft and murder.

And [as explained above,] in order that a person not be evil to [other] creations[104] [Hashem gave us] three prohibitions: [the prohibitions against perversion of] justice,[105] theft and murder.

Perversion of justice – a sin between a human and his fellow through the soul.

Regarding [perversion of] justice, the sin is through one's soul, since he distorts true justice and honesty, which are in the soul of the human being. [This is] because truth and justice are in his soul and thus this is a sin of the soul. [This is because] honesty and justice only reside in the Intellectual-soul,[106] as every person, upon seeing an injustice, requires that his soul will awaken to perform judgment, and therefore, every judge requires a courageous and strong heart for justice. This is clear – that justice arises from the awakening of the soul; and when you gain wisdom you will understand how it is that justice is one of the activities of the soul.

And in Vayikra Rabbah,[107] in the portion of Vayikra [we find,]

> There are two things in the [left[108]] "hand" of the Holy One, Blessed be He: justice and the soul. [We find textual proof for this location of] justice, as it is written, "My hand grasps justice."[109] [We find textual proof for this location of] the soul as it is written, "For in His 'hand' is the soul of all that lives."[110]

---

103. Gur Aryeh, Vayikra 24:14.

104. I.e., humans.

105. The fact that the Maharal refers to "justice" as a prohibition is a strong indicator that he concurs with the Ramban's understanding of this mitzvah, as mentioned above.

106. See the Commentary, Ch. 1 § Point 2 for a fuller explanation of the varying levels and types of souls.

107. Vayikra Rabbah 4:1 with variations.

108. In the Midrash itself, the word "left" is omitted. Instead, there is a distinction made between the "right hand" and "the hand." The Midrash thus demonstrates that it understands a reference to an unqualified "hand" to refer to the left hand.

109. D'varim 32:41.

110. Iyov 12:10.

And in every place that the term "hand" is used [without any qualification], it is the left hand. The Torah said, "I have created the soul in the same place as justice and it[111] goes out and sins; therefore, the verse says, 'When the soul[112] sins . . .'."[113] Therefore, it is the soul which seeks out justice because it[114] is created in the place of justice and if there is no justice, it is the sin of the soul. And this concept is clear and simple to one who understands.

And this mitzvah parallels [the prohibition against] idolatry,[115] which is a mitzvah which prevents a person being evil to heaven. [The reason for the parallel is that] idolatry is known as [the worship of] "the gods of others"[116] and a judge is also known as "*elohim*" in all places.[117] And our sages said, "One who appoints an unworthy judge is as if he has planted an *asheirah*[118] tree."[119] And they[120] have a common theme.[121] And therefore, parallel to the prohibition which Hashem gave that one should not worship idols (which is a sin of "gods of others")[122] which is between man and G-d, Hashem commanded [a mitzvah which is] between one human and his fellow – to create a true justice, that a person should not sin regarding something which is also called "*elohim*."[123]

Theft – a sin between a human and his fellow through the body.

111. The soul.

112. The Maharal cites this verse in particular because he wishes to emphasize that it is the soul specifically which sins, since it is the soul which has the capacity for recognition of justice and thus it is the component of the human being which is able to reject injustice and sin or to embrace them, G-d forbid.

113. Vayikra 5:1.

114. The soul.

115. This was also a sin of the soul, but between humans and Hashem.

116. Sh'mot 20:3, as per the translation of the Chizkuni ad loc.

117. For example, see Sh'mot 22:7, 22:8 and 22:27.

118. See D'varim 7:5. The *asheirah* tree was a form of idol worship which Israel was commanded to destroy upon entering the Land of Israel.

119. Sanhedrin 7b and Avodah Zarah 52a.

120. The prohibition against idolatry and that against the perversion of justice.

121. See the beginning of this chapter in the G'vurot Hashem, where the Maharal goes to great lengths to explain that one of the central aspects of Hashem being our "G-d" is that He defines our legal system. The connection between Justice and G-d, and injustice and idolatry, is thus even more profound than the Maharal discusses here.

122. See D'varim 31:16.

123. Compare this idea with the explanation which the Maharal brought at the beginning of this citation from G'vurot Hashem. There he explained that the court system is an embodiment of the will of G-d (if it is a Torah court) or, G-d forbid, of the will of idolatry (if it is an idolatrous court). The idea is that G-d's will is expressed directly through the laws practiced and enforced.

And [the prohibition against] theft parallels [the prohibition against] illicit sexual relations.[124] And in all places, the sages said, "The *nefesh*[125] of man desires [the fruits of] theft and illicit sexual unions."[126] Thus all of these pairs are equal.

And the essence of theft is the pursuit of money and the desire for wealth and riches – which are bodily matters, just like [the desire for] illicit sexual unions. The difference [between illicit sexual unions and theft] is that it [, theft,] is [a sin] between a human and his fellow [while illicit sexual unions is a sin between man and G-d].

Illicit sexual unions and theft are not included in [the abstract category of] "desire," because, regarding illicit sex, a person is pursuing and desiring women, while regarding theft, a person is pursuing wealth, and [therefore] this is not pure "desire" [as an abstract concept] but rather it is a specific desire for debauchery or that he is obsessed with money. However, if a person has "desire" in that he desires something which he lacks (and not that he desires a particular object), but rather that he is [simply] desirous – that he is lustful – this is a separate thing which will be explained as stemming from the material [nature of the human being].[127] And these things are clear.

Murder – a sin between a human and his fellow through the entire human.

And the sin of murder is between a human and his fellow. And this sin is that the entire human being sins and the sin is not through one of his components, but rather through his entirety. This is similar to the sin of cursing G-d,[128] in which one denies the Essence[129] [of reality] which is everything; so too, one who murders, kills the entire person; therefore, this sin also includes the entirety of the human being. This is unlike the sin of [perverting] justice and the sin of theft in which the sin is not that the entire person is corrupted, but rather the corruption lies in only one component [of the person]. But in murder, like cursing G-d, in which a person is denying the essence [of reality] completely, it is as if Hashem, may

124. Which the Maharal explained to be a sin of the body between man and Hashem.

125. *Nefesh* refers to the lowest part of the soul – the animalistic soul which both humans and animals possess. For more on this, see the Commentary, Ch. 1 § Point 2 where the different parts of the soul are explored.

126. Chagigah 11b and Makkot 23b.

127. See G'vurot Hashem 24 and Tiferet Yisrael 45.

128. Which the Maharal explained to be a sin of the entire person between man and Hashem.

129. I.e., Hashem.

He be Blessed, does not exist, G-d forbid; so too in murder, a person makes a fellow completely non-existent.[130]

Not eating the limb of a living animal – the mitzvah which regulates human desire.

And the seventh [mitzvah] relates to the material of the human being, from which flows the "desire" – [as we illustrated above,] that a person cannot wait until he slaughters an animal [but rather has such an overwhelming desire that he tears a limb off the animal before it is dead.]

And this is the desire which flows from the materiality (of a human being) which is always lacking, and therefore, the person always hungers and desires to fill his lack.

The Maharal now revisits the Midrash (which he cited above) which described the process whereby G-d's divine presence removed itself as a result of human sin and thereafter re-entered this world through the acts of righteous people. He shows that each sin is an example of one of the seven above.

The first sin was the general sin of desire – encapsulated in the eating of the forbidden fruit by Adam and Chavah.

And [the Midrash we cited above] stated that the human being[131] came and sinned through desire by taking the fruit which was "desirable"[132] for him and thereafter the divine presence removed itself to the first firmament.

The second sin was that of murder, exemplified by Kayin.

Then Kayin came and sinned through murder and the divine presence removed itself to the second firmament.

The third sin was that of idolatry, exemplified by the generation of Enosh.

---

130. The Maharal's profound words reflect a deeper idea. As the Torah teaches us, human beings are created "in the image of G-d" (B'reishit 1:27) and thus one who desecrates the human body is, in a sense, disrespecting G-d (see D'varim 21:23 and Rashi ad loc.). Moreover, one who, G-d forbid, murders a human being is, in a very real sense, rubbing out a "part" of G-d's immanence – that "part" which was reflected in that person.

131. I.e., Adam and Chavah.

132. Cf. B'reishit 3:6 where this term is used to describe the "forbidden fruit" and is given as one of the reasons that the first human beings decided to disobey G-d and eat of that fruit.

Then came the generation of Enosh, and they sinned through idolatry, as our sages said in the Chapter, "All the writings"[133] where the verse "[Anyone][134] who guards the Shabbat – not profaning it . . ."[135] is cited. [The Gemara there points out that] the second half of this verse is the phrase, "Praiseworthy is the *enosh* [person][136] who does this." The Gemara comments,[137]

> Anyone who guards the Shabbat according to its law is forgiven [for his sins] even if he worshipped idols like the generation of Enosh, as the verse says, "from profaning it."[138, 139]
>
> [The Gemara points out that the word "from profaning it" can be vowelized differently, producing a different reading for the verse:] Don't read the word as "from profaning it"[140] but rather as "he is forgiven."[141]

And his[142] generation was the first to worship idols, as it is written, "Then, to call in the name of Hashem became profaned."[143] At that point, the divine presence removed itself to the third firmament.

The fourth sin was that of theft, exemplified by the generation of the flood.

The generation of the flood came and sinned with theft, as it is written explicitly, "And the earth was filled with armed-robbery."[144] And there is no [other] sin specified for them besides this. Then the divine presence removed itself to the fourth firmament.

---

133. Shabbat 118b.
134. There seems to be a printer's error here as the word "anyone" is not in the text in Y'shayahu. It is in the text in the Gemara but not as a part of the citation of the verse.
135. Y'shayahu 56:2.
136. In Hebrew, אנוש, "*enosh*," means "person." It is also the name of the son of Sheit (who was the son of Adam) and the Gemara learns from this verse that the prophet is teaching us that it was in the generation of Enosh that idolatry began.
137. Shabbat 118b, with variations.
138. In Hebrew, מֵחַלְּלוֹ, "*meichal'lo*," "from profaning it."
139. Y'shayahu 56:2.
140. *Meichal'lo.*
141. In Hebrew, מָחוּל לוֹ, "*machul lo*," "he is forgiven." Thus the verse would read, "[Anyone] who guards the Shabbat – he is forgiven . . ."
142. Enosh's.
143. B'reishit 4:26. Translation courtesy of the *ArtScroll Tanach* (New York, Mesorah Publications: 2007), 11.
144. B'reishit 6:11.

The fifth sin was that of cursing G-d, exemplified by the generation of the dispersal.

The generation of the dispersal came and sinned through cursing G-d, when they said, "Come let us build a city and a tower[145] and we will make war with Him."[146] And this is the cursing of G-d. Then the divine presence removed itself to the fifth firmament.

The sixth sin was that of perverting justice, exemplified by the Sodomites.

The Sodomites stood up and sinned in [the perversion of] justice as is clear from their reported deeds and from what the judges of Sodom used to do and how they would judge.[147] [Then] the divine presence removed itself to the sixth firmament.

The seventh sin was that of sexual immorality, exemplified by the Egyptians.

The Egyptians stood up in the days of Avraham and sinned with sexual immorality as is clear from [the term] "the act of Egypt" as it is written, "[You shall not do anything] like the act of Egypt."[148]

And for this reason, Pharaoh did not say [to Avraham], "Behold, my land is open before you"[149] as did Avimelech.[150] [The reason Pharaoh didn't say this was] because he knew that the Egyptians were awash with

145. Till this point is a direct quote from B'reishit 11:4. The rest of the citation is the paraphrase which our sages gave to the words of the builders of the "Tower." See Rashi on P'sachim 94b, s.v. *shehimrid* and the Maharal in the Gur Aryeh on B'reishit 11:4.

146. I.e., G-d.

147. See Sanhedrin 109b where many of these incidents are related; and B'reishit Rabbah 50:3.

148. Vayikra 18:3. See the entire chapter there where this statement is the introduction to a long list of forbidden sexual relations, all of which were ascribed to the Egyptians.

149. B'reishit 20:15.

150. In B'reishit Chapter 20, we find the second of two incidents where Sarah, the wife of Avraham, was kidnapped to become a concubine or wife of a local tribal leader. The first incident is in B'reishit Chapter 12 and relates the story of Avraham's journey to Egypt and Sarah's abduction there. The second incident is in Chapter 20 regarding a similar abduction in the land of G'rar. In this second incident, the king, after realizing his error gives Avraham the key to the city, so to speak. In the first incident, in Egypt, Pharaoh sends Avraham and Sarah away. Our sages explain that Pharaoh did this because he knew that his population would be unable to prevent itself from repeating his sin, due to their promiscuity.

sexual immorality. Then the divine presence removed itself to the seventh firmament.

In summary:

Person/Populace	*Sin*
Adam	Unbridled Desire
Kayin	Murder
Generation of Enosh	Idolatry
Generation of flood	Theft
Generation of dispersal	Cursing G-d
Sodomites	Perversion of Justice
Egyptians	Sexual Immorality

The Maharal continues explaining the Midrash – now focusing on the people and the acts which succeeded in reversing the trend of the withdrawal of the divine presence from the world. This happens in the reverse order to which the withdrawals took place – sexual ***im***morality caused the divine presence to withdraw from the sixth to the seventh firmament, thus it is only through creating sexual morality that the divine presence is drawn back to the sixth firmament, and so on.

The one who bolstered sexual morality was Avraham and he caused the first reversal of the negative trend. This counteracted the Egyptians' licentiousness.

Then Avraham came, for there was no-one in the world who was as restrained [and disciplined] as Avraham in the area of sexual morality, as they[151] said,[152]

> Dust should be [placed] in Iyov's mouth because . . . [he said][153] "I have made a covenant with my eyes – why should I look at a virgin?"[154]
>
> [The Gemara explains that this implies that] he would not look at other [women] but he would look at his own [wife]. Avraham, however, would not even look at his own [wife], as it says, "Behold, please, I [now]

151. Our sages.
152. Bava Batra 16a.
153. These two words, "he said," are found in the Maharal's citation from the Gemara, but not in our version of the Gemara.
154. Iyov 31:1.

know that you are a beautiful woman . . ."[155] From this [verse] we learn that until that point, he [Avraham] did not know this!"

Therefore, he[156] drew down the divine presence [from the seventh firmament] to the sixth firmament.

The next positive trait was pursuit of justice which was embodied by Yitzchak. This counteracted the Sodomites' perversion of justice.

Yitzchak [then] stood up and was righteous in justice, for he accepted upon himself the attribute of justice with love, by stretching out his neck to be slaughtered.[157] He was thus the opposite of the Sodomites who perverted justice and there is no difference between the justice of heaven and that of a court below – both are justice. For the character trait of Yitzchak is the attribute of justice, and therefore, he brought down the divine presence to the fifth firmament.

The next positive trait was sanctification of G-d which was embodied by Ya'akov. This counteracted the desecration of G-d's name which was caused through the generation of the dispersal's cursing of G-d.

Ya'akov [then] came and sanctified G-d, as it is written in the verse, "They will sanctify the Holy One of Ya'akov."[158] And the third blessing [in the Amidah],[159] "You are Holy and Your name is Holy . . ." parallels Ya'akov. This is because the first three blessings [in the Amidah] parallel Avraham, Yitzchak and Ya'akov [respectively] and even the angels sanctify [G-d] in the name of Ya'akov, as it is written, "Blessed is the G-d of Israel"[160] and as

155. B'reishit 12:11. This is just before Sarah's abduction in Egypt. Our sages interpret this verse to mean that Avraham had been unaware till that point that Sarah was indeed strikingly beautiful.

156. Avraham.

157. This refers to the famous "Binding of Yitzchak" in B'reishit Chapter 22. Our sages interpreted many of the verses in the incident to indicate that Yitzchak (at some stage) became aware of his being destined to be sacrificed even before reaching the mountain and that he willingly submitted to this since G-d's attribute of Justice had so decreed. See, for example, Rashi on B'reishit 22:8 and B'reishit Rabbah 56:3 and 56:8.

158. Y'shayahu 29:23.

159. The main prayer recited three times daily by Jews

160. Israel was Ya'akov's second name. Hashem is often called, "G-d of Israel," see, for example, Sh'mot 5:1 and many others. For instances where Hashem is blessed as "the G-d of Israel," see 1 Sh'mu'el 25:32, 1 M'lachim 8:15, Yirmiyahu 45:2, Tehillim 41:14, Tehillim 72:18 and others.

is explained above,[161] that the angels sanctify [G-d] in the name of Ya'akov. And therefore he is contrasted with the people of the generation of the dispersal who cursed G-d and [therefore] he brought down the divine presence to the fourth firmament.

The next positive trait was disinterest in money and wealth, which was embodied by Levi. This counteracted the theft exemplified by the generation of the flood.

Levi reversed the theft of one who covets and who takes that which is not his. [This can be seen by the fact that] his entire tribe[162] did not have a portion in the Land [of Israel[163]] or a share in the plunder [of battles] because, "G-d is his portion."[164] Therefore, Levi was separated from matters of money and the pursuit thereof and he did not even have that in which it was suitable for him to share.

And if the tribe of Levi was not receptive [and prepared] for this, the Holy One, Blessed be He, would not have given it to them, instead, they would have simply sufficed with what they had.[165]

And one cannot say that the tribe only [possessed this trait] but that Levi himself did not. [The reason for this is that] this would be impossible – if [the members of] his tribe did not merit this character trait from their father,[166] they would not have had it [in the first place!].[167] [Moreover,] the name of Levi devolves on the entire tribe.[168]

---

161. G'vurot Hashem 44.

162. There were twelve sons of Ya'akov, of whom Levi was one. Several generations later, each of these sons had developed into a separate tribe, named after the original son.

163. See the next footnote. Unlike the other tribes, Levi did not receive a portion of the Land of Israel upon the conquest of the Land. Instead, Levi was apportioned several cities with plots of land around them. The tribe of Levi was dedicated to the service of G-d (see Rashi on D'varim 10:9).

164. D'varim 10:9 and 18:2.

165. The Maharal explains that indeed this receptivity was a self-developed trait – G-d did not impose a state of landlessness on the tribe of Levi. If they had not been intensely focused on such a way of life, Hashem would have simply let them have their portion, which would have been sufficient for them and they would have been happy as such.

166. I.e., Levi.

167. The Maharal explains that there is no way that the entire tribe would have simultaneously developed such an awareness. Rather, it was inherited from Levi himself which is why all the members of the tribe of Levi shared it.

168. The Maharal brings two short proofs that even though we do not have direct proof that Levi himself exemplified this trait, he must have done, since he is the common source of something shared by all the members of his tribe and

Therefore, he brought down the divine presence to the third firmament.

The next positive trait was dedication to Hashem which was embodied by K'hat. This counteracted the idolatry exemplified by the generation of the flood.

K'hat is contrasted with idol worship – since his family worships Hashem, may He be Blessed, with their bodies, in that they were the bearers of the sanctuary. And all of his descendants served Hashem, may He be Blessed, with their bodies, unlike the descendants of Ger'shon and M'rari who used carts.[169] But the family of K'hat "carried on their shoulders"[170] and this is termed "the service of something," that one serves with one's body. And also [descended] from him were the *Kohanim*[171] upon whom the service [in the Sanctuary] was essentially placed.

Therefore, he[172] drew down the divine presence to the second firmament.

The next positive trait was life, embodied by Amram. This counteracted the murder and death exemplified by Kayin.

Amram came and he was a profoundly righteous person – to the extent that he did not sin, and therefore, he did not experience death through sin. And our sages said in the Tractate of Bava Batra that "Amram only died through the snake's advice,"[173] meaning that death was unsuitable for him except for the fact that the snake had [already] brought death to the world.[174]

And therefore, he contrasts with Kayin who followed in the primordial snake's footsteps, and [also] brought death to the world; while Amram

---

moreover, they all share his name, which must reflect the essence of their shared tribal identity.

169. See B'midbar Chapters 4 and 7. These families, Ger'shon, K'hat and M'rari comprised all the families of the Levite tribe. The *Kohanim* were the descendants of Aharon (who was from K'hat). The rest of the Levites served in the Temple in various capacities. While the Tabernacle (a portable form of the Temple) was in use in the desert, the Levites carried all the components and vessels thereof. The K'hat family carried the most holy vessels on their shoulders. The other Levites used carts.

170. B'midbar 7:9.

171. The *Kohanim*, כהנים, actually performed the service in the Tabernacle and the Temple.

172. K'hat.

173. Bava Batra 17a. See Rashi ad loc.

174. See B'reishit 2:17 where Hashem explained to Adam that eating from the forbidden fruit would create the reality of death. Thus, through the snake's advice, death was brought into the world.

didn't die due to his own sin,[175] and therefore, he is the opposite of Kayin. Because Kayin brought death to another [human] while Amram, despite the fact that it is the way of the world to bring death to oneself through sin, he[176] did not do so. Thus Amram is completely [representative of] life while Kayin is completely [representative of] death. And this is clear.

Therefore, he[177] drew down the divine presence to the first firmament.

The next positive trait was lack of desire, embodied by Moshe. This counteracted the Desire displayed by Adam and Chavah when they ate from the forbidden fruit.

Then Moshe came and he was a righteous person who separated himself from women.[178] Through this you will know that no desire existed with Moshe, for if it did then it would have been unsuitable for him to separate from his wife (in order for him not to come to sin).[179] Therefore, you should know that no desire was found with him, and therefore, he contrasted with Adam who did have desire.

Therefore, he[180] drew down the divine presence to the earth so that it could return to its first place.

The Maharal summarizes his thesis.

In any event, from [all] this we know that the place of the divine presence is on the earth, for the reason we have explained. It will be further explained[181] how the lower realities in particular, merited to have His divine presence, may He be Blessed, were it not for the sin which divides between the creations and the [Ultimate, Divine] Cause.

---

175. See B'midbar 27:3 and B'rachot 33a, "A snake doesn't kill, sin kills." The snake here is metaphorical as well as literal.

176. I.e., Amram.

177. I.e., Amram.

178. See B'midbar Chapter 12 and Rashi ad loc. (12:1), where it is related that Aharon and Miriam, Moshe's siblings, discussed Moshe's actions in separating from his wife. They condemned his actions. As Rashi (B'midbar 12:4) explains, Hashem reacted forcefully against Aharon and Miriam for their slander and explained to them that Moshe, due to his capacity for prophecy at any time, had to be *tahor* at all times and thus separated from his wife. However, it is important to note that such behavior is not a Torah ideal for most people; see Shulchan Aruch, Even Ha'ezer 1:1.

179. The Maharal is saying that had Moshe felt any desire, it would have been incorrect of him to separate from his wife, as this would have led to a situation of frustrated desire and eventually, a sinful channeling of those desires.

180. I.e., Moshe.

181. G'vurot Hashem 67 and 70.

In summary:

Initial Downward Slide		Subsequent Regeneration	
Person/Populace	**Sin**	**Person/Populace**	**Correction**
1. Adam	Uncontrollable Desire	7. Moshe	Lack of desire
2. Kayin	Murder	6. Amram	Life
3. Generation of Enosh	Idolatry	5. K'hat	Dedication to Hashem
4. Generation of flood	Theft	4. Levi	Otherworldliness (ascetic trend)
5. Generation of dispersal	Cursing G-d	3. Ya'akov	Sanctifying G-d's name
6. Sodomites	Perversion of Justice	2. Yitzchak	Upholding Justice
7. Egyptians	Sexual Immorality	1. Avraham	Sexual Discipline

b. The breadth of the Maharal's analysis here is panoramic and awesome.
   i. Here he explains that the Torah's vision of morality is universal and was entrenched within creation from its very inception.
   ii. The very purpose of creation, which is Hashem's dwelling within humanity, can only be achieved through morality and the history of the world is that of the progressive deterioration of humanity's fitness to bond with Hashem, on the one hand, and the vigorous attempts by those heroes of Goodness who strove to reverse this trend.
   iii. What is possibly most striking is the all-inclusiveness of the Maharal's ideas – that all human beings are needed in the journey towards our ultimate goal and that the Seven "Noahide" laws are really possessed of an ultimately all-embracing structure to enable all of humanity to reach its destiny.

5. The Place of the Human Being

a. Above, the Maharal discussed the concept of a "place" of an object and of a human being. He expands on this idea in his D'rosh Al Hatorah as follows:

דרוש על התורה

ולכך כדי להשלים נפש החסירה נתן הש"י אל האדם שס"ה מצות לא תעשה כמנין ימות החמה ורמ"ח מצות עשה כמנין אבריו של אדם. כי האדם יחסר מצד שני דברים,

אם האחד כי נפש החיוני היא מן העליונים ויש לה חסרון במה שבאה אל התחתונים להורידה ממעלתה, הרי היא חסירה כשעומדת בתחתונים. וכמו שאמר במשל שנשאת לעירני הוא היושב בכפר זהו חסרון האחד מצד שעומדת בתחתונים והיא מן העליונים. אם החסרון השני שנתחברה בגוף האדם לגמרי שהוא חסר בתכלית . . . כי במה שנשאת לו היא מתחברת לו בחבור ודבוק גמור, הרי לך חסרון בשתי הבחינות. והנה האדם בעולם הזה הוא תחת השמש כדברי החכם בפסוק שהתחלנו בו מה יתרון לאדם בכל עמלו שיעמול תחת השמש. וכן בכל ספרו יכנה ויתאר דברי העולם הזה במה שהם תחת השמש. והשמש מקום ואהל לתחתונים. ובב"ב (דף כ"ה) על פסוק הולך אל דרום וסובב אל צפון אמר שם ר' יהושע שהעולם דומה לקובה, פירש בו רש"י ז"ל לאהל שכלו מוקף . . . הרי כי השמש הוא כמו אהל לאדם. ואהל זה הוא שמאהיל על האדם בשס"ה ימים . . . וכל דבר שיש לו מקום הוא שומר את מקומו ואינו יוצא ממנו ואינו עובר עליו. ולכך כדי להשלים מקומו של אדם באשר נשמתו מן העליונים ובאה אל התחתונים, כבת מלך שנשאת לעירני היושב בכפר, נתן הש"י שס"ה מצות לא תעשה שהם נחשבים מקום לנשמה, לבלתי תעבור את מקומה. כי מצות לא תעשה הם שלא לעבור אותם ולא לצאת מהם, הנה הם מקום לה כאשר לא יעבור עליהם האדם ויהיה לנשמה מקום קבוע בהם. וכמו שנתן הש"י רמ"ח אברים אל הגוף, אשר בהם יושלם ויוכלל גוף שלם והם עצם הגוף כמו שאמרנו למעלה כי על ידם הוא בשלימות, ככה השלים הש"י את הנשמה ברמ"ח מצות עשה. הרי כי כנגד מה שנעשית הנשמה חסירה כי היא בת מלך ונשאת לעירני, אם חסרונה מצד המקום שבאה לשם דהיינו לתחתונים, אם מצד שנתחברה לגמרי באדם שהוא בעל גוף, השלימה הש"י באלו שני דברים על ידי שנתן לה שס"ה מצות לא תעשה שהם השלמת מקום לה כנזכר, ורמ"ח מצות עשה המשלימים אותה מצד שעומדת לגמרי בגוף האדם הושלם ונגמר ברמ"ח אברים:

D'rosh Al Hatorah

And therefore, in order to perfect the incomplete soul, Hashem, may He be Blessed, gave the human being 365 mitzvot which parallel the number of days of a solar year; and He gave 248 *mitzvot aseh* which parallel the number of component-limbs of a human being.

[The reason for this is that] a person is incomplete from two aspects [as follows].

Firstly, the vital soul is from the transcendent [spiritual realm] and it is incomplete in that it comes to the lower [world and] is drawn down from its excellence; thus it is incomplete when it exists in the lower [world]. This is as is illustrated in the parable[182] [regarding the princess who marries the

182. See Chapter Three of this work, where this parable is cited. The source is Vayikra Rabbah 4:2 and it reads as follows, "'The soul will also never be satiated.' [The meaning of this verse is] that the soul knows that however much it wearies itself in effort, it is working for itself, therefore, it never has its fill of [having performed enough] mitzvot and good deeds. Rabbi Levi said, '[One can understand this through a] parable of a townsman who was married to the daughter of kings – even if he provides her with all the varieties of royal delicacies, he never discharges his duty. Why? Because she is the daughter of kings. So too, no matter how much a

townsman] in that she marries a townsman who lives in a village. This is the first lack in that she [the soul] exists in the lower [world] but is from the transcendent [realm].

Secondly, in a human being, she[183] is completely joined to the body which is absolutely lacking . . . [This is illustrated in the parable] in that she [the princess] is [actually] married to him [the townsman, through which] she is joined to him in an absolute join and bond.

This is the incompletion from both aspects . . .

And behold, the human being in this world is "under the sun," as [we see] from the words of the sage[184] in the verse with which we began, "What advantage does a human have in all his toil which he toils under the sun?"[185] So too, throughout his[186] book, he refers to and describes the matters of this world in that they are "under the sun." And the sun is the place and pavilion for the lower [creations].

And in [the Gemara in] Bava Batra,[187] regarding the verse, "[the sun] moves to the south and cycles round to the north,"[188] Rabbi Y'hoshu'a said that the world is similar to a cubicle. Rashi explained this as follows, "[A cubicle is] a tent which is completely enclosed." . . . we see that the sun is like a tent for the human being. And this tent is that which covers the human being with the 365 days . . .

And anything which has a place doesn't deviate from it and doesn't transgress against it. And therefore, in order to complete the place of the human being (in that his soul is from the transcendent [realm] and comes to the lower [world], like the daughter of a king who marries a townsman living in a village) Hashem gave [us] 365 prohibitions which are considered [to be] the "place" for the soul, that it not transgress its place. [This is] because prohibitions [exist] so [that the soul] not deviate from them or exit from them since they are a place for it [and] when [the human being] doesn't transgress them, they become a fixed place for the soul.

And just as Hashem, may He be Blessed, set 248 component-limbs in the body (through which [a person][189] is perfected and [reaches a] collectively complete body, and which are the essence of the body, as we said above) so too Hashem completed the soul with 248 *mitzvot aseh*.

---

person acts for his soul [in this world] he never discharges his duty. Why? Because his soul is from above . . .'"

183. The soul.
184. King Solomon.
185. Kohelet 1:3.
186. King Solomon's.
187. Bava Batra 25b.
188. Kohelet 1:6.
189. Lit., "he."

Therefore, in parallel with the imperfection caused to the soul (as the daughter of a king married to a townsman), whether it is a lacking due to the place to which it comes (that is the lower [world]) or whether it is due to its bonding completely within a person who has a body [parallel to these two imperfections] Hashem completed it[190] in these two areas by giving it 365 prohibitions (which are the perfection of a place for it[191] as we explained) and 248 *mitzvot aseh* which complete it[192] through the fact that it[193] exists completely in the body of a human being which is perfected and completed with 248 component-limbs.

i. The Maharal has explained here that the concept of a "place" is not in essence about physical location, rather a physical location embodies the concept of boundaries and limitations. Thus a "place" really refers to the limits and boundaries on anything.
ii. Everything in this world requires healthy limits, thus everything is said to have a "place." The physical limits that are placed upon a human being are called the "place" of the human being and these are paralleled by the 365 prohibitions. These limits ensure that a person does not cause him or herself any spiritual damage, G-d forbid.
iii. Secondly, besides for healthy limits, there are avenues for growth and development which need to be pursued if a person is to become more and better than he or she currently is. These avenues are the 248 *mitzvot aseh*, initiative-action commandments.

b. The linkage between a person and his place
   i. The Maharal explains that the concept of the place of a human being is linked inextricably to the essence of a person – so much so that certain documents have to specify the place of residence of a person in order to describe that person validly.[194]
   ii. Again, the idea is not that the physical residence is essential, but rather that it represents the set of limits within which a person operates, which reflects on that person's reality.

6. Mitzvot are Good, but that Is Not *Why* Hashem Gave Them

a. The Maharal writes above, "In any event, Hashem, may He be Blessed, did not command humans [to perform] mitzvot because they are good and He desired that humans do good; rather [the reason for the com-

---

190. The soul.
191. The soul.
192. The soul.
193. The soul.
194. As he explained above in the text of Tiferet Yisrael, regarding a bill of divorce.

mandments is that] the mitzvot are a refinement of creations which will transcend material nature, as we have said."

b. This is perhaps the Maharal's most extreme formulation of his view that the galvanizing first principle behind the mitzvot is ***not*** their essential goodness. It is important to stress once again that this does not mean that the mitzvot are not good, G-d forbid. As the Maharal wrote previously in Chapter Six, "Even though it is true that goodness and success (a success above all others) will flow from a person's fulfilling the decree which Hashem has decreed; nevertheless, the initiation of the decree is not for the purpose of benefitting the recipient. [On the other hand,] the Torah does say, 'Hashem, our G-d, has commanded us to carry out these laws for our good,' but this doesn't mean that Hashem, may He be Blessed, commanded us to do the mitzvot in order to benefit us – this is untrue; rather He, may He be Blessed, commanded us as a King does! However, if we fulfill the mitzvot, then [as a by-product of our performance of the mitzvot] this decree will be for our good, 'to sustain us [with vitality and life] as this day,' but the initiation of the decree is not to benefit us."

c. Once again, the Maharal stresses that the initial reason for Hashem's giving us the commandment flows from His justice, not His kindness or mercy; but since He is all-Good, the mitzvot which are generated by His justice are also good.

COMMENTARY SECTION

Chapter 8

1. *Sichli* vs. Order

a. The Maharal writes above, "The explanation [of both the Midrash and the Gemara cited above] is that all [the mitzvot] are a function of the [transcendent] framework [of mitzvot]: that Hashem, may He be Blessed, gave us a *sichli* mitzvah. It is due to this [framework] that a corpse causes a person to become *tamei* and that water causes [a person to become] *tahor*. And all [of this] is a function of Wisdom, which is the Torah which Hashem, may He be Blessed, gave to humanity. But it is impossible to explain that this [system of mitzvot] is natural; rather this is the framework of Hashem, may He be Blessed, [which he gave] to humanity in His wisdom. And it is due to the decree which is suitable to humanity that a corpse causes ritual unfitness and that water creates ritual fitness."

   i. The implication is that the reason that we are able to bond with Hashem is due to the fact that the framework determined by the Torah is one which is *sichli* – cerebral and transcendent – created by Hashem with His wisdom.

b. However, elsewhere the implication is slightly different. Later on, at the end of Chapter 9, the Maharal writes,

ספר תפארת ישראל - פרק ט

כבר אמרנו כי התורה היא סדר השי"ת וכאשר האדם דבק בסדר הזה שסדר השם יתברך הוא דבק בו יתברך שמאתו הסדר הזה, וזה הסדר נתן השם יתברך אל האדם אשר יש לו נפש א־להי ועל ידי שהוא שומר סדר הזה אשר סדר השם יתברך דבק בו יתברך, ולפיכך ראוי שיהיה בזה הצלחת האדם במה שהוא דבק בו יתברך וזהו תכלית ההצלחה...

Tiferet Yisrael – Chapter 9

We have already said that the Torah is the *arrangement*[1] of Hashem, may He be Blessed, and when the human being bonds with this *framework* which Hashem, may He be Blessed, arranged [then] a person bonds with Him, may He be Blessed, from Whom this *framework* derives. And this *arrangement* was given by Hashem, may He be Blessed, to humanity in that humanity has a G-dly soul; and through the preservation [and implementation] of

1. The word the Maharal uses here is "*seder*," סדר, which is usually translated as "order." We translate it variously as "order," "arrangement" and "framework."

this *framework* which Hashem, may He be Blessed, arranged, one bonds with Him, may He be Blessed.

And therefore, it is suitable that the success of a person will be achieved through this, by bonding with Him, may He be Blessed, and this is the pinnacle of success . . .

- i. Here, the Maharal seems to imply that it is the fact that the mitzvot are part of an *ordered framework* which allows one to bond with Hashem.
- ii. The word "סדר" meaning "framework" or "order" appears here six times. The emphasis seems to be on the ordering and design of the system of mitzvot rather than on the fact that this order is *sichli* – in fact, the word "*sichli*" doesn't even appear here.
  1. Thus, this citation would seem to indicate that it is the way that Hashem ordered the mitzvot – the system as a whole in its design and organization – which is what creates the channel for a person to bond with Hashem.
- iii. In the first citation above, however, the word סדר, "*seder*" does appear.

c. A possible resolution is to say that it is the order which Hashem gave to the mitzvot, the design and placement of the mitzvot which is a function of their being *sichli*; as opposed to saying that the mitzvot on their own are *sichli*. Alternatively, it could be a combination of both ideas: that both the mitzvot individually and their arrangement are *sichli*.

2. Sin Causes Congestion of the Heart

a. The Maharal above champions the idea that even if mitzvot have practical consequences – improving (or preventing harm to) one's quality of physical or spiritual life – this can never be the ultimate *reason* for a mitzvah.

b. The Ran[2] mentions a similar, fascinating idea regarding one who follows the directive of the Torah high court, allowing one to eat a specific food, which the court has mistakenly permitted. For the sake of some background, we first cite a Gemara which is the key text to which the Ran is referring.

תלמוד בבלי עירובין יג:

אמר רבי אבא אמר שמואל שלש שנים נחלקו בית שמאי ובית הלל הללו אומרים הלכה כמותנו והללו אומרים הלכה כמותנו יצאה בת קול ואמרה אלו ואלו דברי אלהים חיים הן והלכה כבית הלל וכי מאחר שאלו ואלו דברי אלהים חיים מפני מה זכו בית הלל

2. Rabbeinu Nissim of Girona, 1320–1380.

לקבוע הלכה כמותן מפני שנוחין ועלובין היו ושונין דבריהן ודברי בית שמאי ולא עוד אלא שמקדימין דברי בית שמאי לדבריהן

Eiruvin 13b

Rabbi Aba said in the name of Rabbi Sh'mu'el, "For three years the School of Shammai and the School of Hillel argued with one another – one claimed, 'The Law is according to our opinion!' The other claimed – 'No! The Law is according to us!' [Eventually] a voice from heaven rang out, 'Both of them are speaking the Words of The Living G-d – however, the law is according to the School of Hillel.'

"And why did the School of Hillel merit to have the law set according to them? Because they were gentle and patient and they would learn both their opinion and that of Beit Shammai. Not only that, but they would learn the opinion of Beit Shammai before their own."

דרשות הר"ן - הדרוש השביעי - והדרוש האחד עשר

איך נאמר ששתי כתות המחלוקת נאמרו ... מפי הגבורה, הנה שמאי והלל נחלקו? ... באמת, שאחד משני הדעות הוא דעת אמתית והשני הפכו, ואיך נאמר שיצא מפי השם דבר בלתי אמתי. אבל הענין כן הוא, שדבר ידוע שכל התורה שבכתב ובעל פה נמסרה למשה, כמו שאמר במגילה ... מלמד שהראהו הקב"ה למשה דקדוקי תורה ודקדוקי סופרים ומה שסופרים עתידים לחדש ומאי ניהו מקרא מגלה. דקדוקי סופרים, הם המחלוקת וחלוקי הסברות שבין חכמי ישראל, וכלן למדם משה מפי הגבורה, בלא הכרעה כל מחלוקת ומחלוקת בפרט. אבל מסר לו כלל אשר בו יודע האמת, והוא: אחרי רבים להטות ... הרי שניתן רשות לחכמי הדורות להכריע במחלוקת החכמים ... ונצטוינו לילך אחר הסכמתם הן שיסכימו לאמת או להפכו: וגם כן נאמין שאם הסכימו הפך האמת ונדע זה על ידי בת קול או נביא, אין ראוי שנסור מהסכמת החכמים ... לפי זה הדעת אם כן כשיסכימו החכמים בדבר אחד טמא שהוא טהור, מה יהיה, הלא הדבר ההוא יזיק אותנו ויפעל מה שבטבעו לפעול, ואע"פ שהסכימו בו החכמים שהוא טהור.... ואני סובר עוד, שאי אפשר שימשך ממה שיכריעו הסנהדרין הפסד בנפש כלל, גם כי יאכילו דבר האיסור ושיאמרו בו שהוא מותר. לפי שהתקון אשר ימשך בנפש מצד ההכרעה למצות החכמים מורי התורה, הוא הדבר היותר אהוב אצלו יתברך, כאמרו "הנה שמוע מזבח טוב", בתקון ההוא יסיר הרוע אשר הוא מעותד להתילד בנפש מצד אכילת הדבר האסור ההוא.

D'rashot Ha'Ran 7, 11

How can we say that both sides of the argument[3] were said . . . by Hashem? How is it that Hillel and Shammai could ever argue? . . . In truth, one of these two opinions must be true and the other must be false! How could it be that the Heavenly voice said that "they are both the words of the Living

3. The Ran is referring immediately to the halachic dispute cited above between two schools of Halachah – the School of Hillel and that of Shammai. He is seeking to understand the philosophical implications of any halachic dispute.

G-d" – is the false opinion also the word of G-d? How can it be? It's false!

But, the answer is as follows.

It is well-known that the entire Written Torah and Oral Torah was given to Moshe as it says in the Talmud in [tractate] Megillah[4] . . . "this teaches us that Hashem showed Moshe: the intricacies of the Torah, the intricacies of the sages and everything the sages would one day innovate – the latter being the requirement to read the *Megillah*[5] [of Esther]."

The "intricacies of the sages" are the disputes between the sages of Israel - all of which Moshe learned from Hashem *without a decision – every argument. But Hashem also gave him a rule by which he would [usually] know which side was true – that is: following the majority opinion . . . Thus we see that the sages in each generation were given permission to decide a dispute . . . and we have been commanded to follow their decision whether or not it is true. We must also believe that if they reached a false conclusion and we know that it is false via a voice from heaven or a prophet, it is incorrect that we stray from their decision . . .*

Now, according to this understanding, what would happen if all the sages agreed that a particular food was kosher, when in fact it was non-kosher?

There is no doubt that the non-kosher food would harm us and would have its normal [physical and spiritual] effects, whether or not the sages think it is kosher. . . .

I believe that in reality, we must say that there is no way that if a person obeys the Sanhedrin[6] that something negative would result, even if the Sanhedrin feeds one something non-kosher which they say is kosher. What happens is as follows – *due to one's following the ruling of the Sanhedrin, there is a positive effect on the soul. Now this listening to the sages, the teachers of Torah, is more beloved by Hashem, as the Torah says, "Listening to Hashem is better than sacrificing to Him."*[7] *This positive effect destroys the negative effect which should have resulted in the soul due to eating the non-kosher food.*

i. Here the Ran highlights clearly that the Torah's set procedures, the order of actions and legislations it mandates, are what is central. If one follows the Torah's command to institute the Sanhedrin – the High Court – and then one follows its halachic determinations, then one has obeyed Hashem and it is this adoption of Hashem's framework which is overriding – not practical considerations.

ii. The Ran takes things a step further and says that even if, due to

4. Megillah 19b.

5. On the Jewish festival of Purim, it is a rabbinically ordained mitzvah to read the Scroll of Esther which describes the historical and spiritual events of the original Purim. The Scroll of Esther is known as the "*megillah*," מגילה, meaning "scroll."

6. The Supreme Halachic Court.

7. 1 Sh'mu'el 15:22.

following Hashem's mitzvot, one would be spiritually harmed, G-d forbid, one should still obey and trust that Hashem will deal with such spiritual impairment.

3. The Concept of Consuming the Nations

a. The Maharal writes above, "[In] this [case mentioned above] when Hashem, may He be Blessed, assured [us,] "you shall consume all the nations," the prohibition [against consuming forbidden foods] was not suitable [rather] in light of the circumstances at the time, it was suitable that [the verse,] "and houses filled with [all manner of] good . . ." would be fulfilled. And therefore, the Torah did not distance these [usually forbidden] items [at that time]."

b. Elsewhere the Maharal elaborates on this idea as follows.

חדושי אגדות ג׳, בבא בתרא ע״ד:

אבל האדם הוא בענין הזה אשר יקבל הדבר והוא השלמתו שאינו עצמו ולפיכך באדם שייך שיקבל דבר ובאותו דבר שיקבל יש בו השלמה וזהו ענין אכילה שכל האכילה, ע״י האכילה מקבל השלמתו עד שאינו חסר. וענין האכילה והסעודה שהוא קבלת השלמה שתהיה לצדיקים לעתיד הוא ע״ד שאמר הכתוב ואכלת את כל העמים ואין הפי׳ שישמיד העמים כולם עד שלא יהיו נשארים דא״כ היה לו לכתוב והשמדתם את כל העמים אבל מה שאמר ואכלת כל העמים מפני שלא תמצא אומה שאין לה מדריגה מה ומעלה מה שהם מיוחדים בה, ואמר הכתוב ואכלת את כל העמים שהם ירשו את מדריגתם מה שהם מיוחדים ויהיה בטלים וישראל יושלמו באותה מדריגה . . .

Chiddushei Aggadot, Bava Batra 74b

A human being is such that he receives something and that [acceptance] is his completion [and that completion is derived from something] which is not himself.

And therefore, it is suitable for a human being that he receive something and through that thing he achieves completion – and this is the explanation[8] of eating; for through any [act of] eating, a person received completion to the point where he is [no longer too severely] lacking.

And the explanation[9] of the eating and feasting (which is a receipt of completion) by the righteous [which will take place] in the future[10] is in the same manner as the verse which states, "And you shall consume all the nations."[11] [The explanation of this is] that one cannot find a single nation which has no exclusive level or positive quality. The verse said, "And

8. Lit., "the matter."

9. Lit., "the matter."

10. This is mentioned in the Gemara in Bava Batra 74b which is the Maharal's source.

11. D'varim 7:16.

you shall consume all the nations,"[12] [meaning] that Israel[13] will inherit the nations'[14] unique level and they[15] will dissolve and Israel will become completed through that level . . .

c. The Maharal's understanding is that there is a unique positive quality in each nation in the world and that there is a process whereby the Jewish people assimilate these positive qualities into themselves.
d. In the section of the Tiferet Yisrael above, the Maharal seems to be saying that at the time that the Jewish people entered the Land of Israel, a process of active ingestion of these unique elements was taking place which was mirrored by the permission accorded to the Jewish people to consume the articles of food left behind in the homes of the seven nations of *K'na'an*.

4. **Naturalistic, medicinal explanations for the forbidden foods and for the requirement for ritual slaughter**
   a. The Maharal refers to certain sages who cited more naturalistic reasons for certain mitzvot. We have seen some of these sages' comments previously,[16] on which we will expand below.
   b. The Ramban states as follows,[17]

רמב"ן על דברים פרק כב פסוק ו

והביא ראיה מן השוחט מן הצואר והעורף לומר שכולם לנו ולא להקב"ה, לפי שלא יתכן לומר בשחיטה שיהא בה תועלת וכבוד לבורא יתברך בצואר יותר מהעורף או הניחור, אלא לנו הם להדריכנו בנתיבות הרחמים גם בעת השחיטה והביאו ראיה אחרת, או מה איכפת לו בין אוכל טהורות והם המאכלים המותרים, לאוכל טמאות והם המאכלים האסורים, שאמרה בהם התורה (ויקרא יא כח) טמאים המה לכם, ורמז שהוא להיותנו נקיי הנפש חכמים משכילי האמת ואמרם אם חכמת חכמת לך, הזכירו כי המצות המעשיות כגון שחיטת הצואר ללמדנו המדות הטובות, והמצות הגדורות במינין לזקק את נפשותינו, כמו שאמרה תורה (שם כ כה) ולא תשקצו את נפשותיכם בבהמה ובעוף ובכל אשר תרמוש האדמה אשר הבדלתי לכם לטמא, א"כ כלם לתועלתנו בלבד וזה כמו שאמר אליהוא (איוב לה ו) אם חטאת מה תפעל בו ורבו פשעיך מה תעשה לו, ואמר (שם פסוק ז) או מה מידך יקח וזה דבר מוסכם בכל דברי רבותינו:

12. D'varim 7:16.
13. Lit., "they."
14. Lit., "their."
15. The nations.
16. In Chapter Six.
17. See the Commentary, Ch. 6 § Point 10 for the complete citation.

Ramban, D'varim 22:6

And the Midrash[18] cited the example of slaughtering from the throat or [back of] the neck in order to teach that all the mitzvot are for us and not for the Holy One, Blessed be He, because it is impossible to say that there will be more utility and honor for the Creator, may He be Blessed, [when one slaughters] at the throat than at the [back of the] neck or by stabbing.

Rather, [it teaches us that] the mitzvot are for us, to guide us in the paths of mercy, even at the time of slaughtering.

And our sages[19] cited another proof [when they said,] "Similarly, does it matter to Him whether one eats *tahor* [food] or whether one eats *tamei* [food]?" that is, when one eats defiled foods which are the forbidden foods.[20] Regarding these, the Torah said, "They will be defiled for you."[21] And there is a hint [in the Midrash Tanchuma] that this [mitzvah to eat kosher food] is to ensure that we are pristine of spirit, wise and understanding the truth. [Further] they said [in the Midrash Tanchuma], "'if you have gained wisdom, you have gained wisdom for yourself'"[22] [by which] they mentioned that the practical mitzvot, such as slaughtering at the throat are to teach us good traits and the mitzvot which restrict [the consumption of] species [of animals] are to purify our souls. This is as the Torah states, "so that you will not defile your souls through [non-kosher] animals, birds and anything which creeps on the earth which I have designated as being impure for you."[23]

Therefore, all of the Mitzvot[24] are for our utility alone and this is as Elihu said, "If you have sinned, what have you done to Him?[25] And if your misdeeds have multiplied, what have you done to Him?"[26] And he continued,[27] "What can He take from you [to benefit Himself]?"

This is agreed upon in all the words of our sages.

i. Here, the Ramban explains that the reason for:
   1. *Sh'chitah* (ritual slaughter) – that we not become cruel even

18. In B'reishit Rabbah and in the Tanchuma.
19. Lit., "they." This refers to the Midrash Tanchuma cited previously.
20. Here the Ramban explains that the terms *tahor* and *tamei* are being used to mean kosher and non-kosher respectively.
21. Vayikra 11:28. This verse is dealing with those foods which are forbidden to eat – in particular, non-kosher animals.
22. Mishlei 9:12.
23. Vayikra 20:25.
24. Lit., "them."
25. I.e., G-d.
26. Iyov 35:6.
27. Iyov 35:7

when we need to consume meat.

2. Forbidden foods – that we not defile our souls.

c. The Rambam states as follows.

ספר מורה נבוכים - חלק ג פרק מח

ואומר כי כל מה שאסרתו התורה עלינו מן המאכלים – מזונם מגונה. ואין בכל מה שנאסר עלינו מה שיסופק שאין הזק בו רק החזיר והחלב; ואין הענין כן, כי החזיר יותר לח ממה שצריך ורב הפסולת והמותרות, ורוב מה שמאסתו התורה לרוב לכלוכו ומזונו בדברים הנמאסים. וכבר ידעת הקפדת התורה על ראית הלכלוכים, ואפילו בשדות במחנה - כל שכן בתוך המדינה. ואילו היתה מותרת אכילת החזיר, היו השווקים עם הבתים יותר מלוכלכים מ"בית הכסא" - כמו שתראה ארצות הצרפתים היום. כבר ידעת אמרם, "פי חזיר כצואה עוברת דמי": וכן חלב הקרב משביע, ומפסיד העיכול, ומוליך דם קר מדובק - ושריפתו היתה יותר ראויה מאכילתו. וכן הדם והנבלה קשים להתעכל ומזונם רע, וידוע שה"טרפה" תחילת נבלה היא": ודע שאילו הסימנים – רצוני לומר, העלאת גרה ושסיעת פרסה בבהמות, וסנפיר וקשקשת בדגים – אין מציאותם סיבת ההתר ולא העדרם סיבת האיסור, ואמנם הם סימן, יודע בו המין המשובח מן המין המגונה: וטעם "גיד הנשה" כתוב: ואמנם טעם "אבר מן החי" הוא היותו מקנה ומלמד אכזריות. ועוד שכן היו עושים אז מלכי ה"גוים"; וגם ל"עבודה זרה" היו עושים כן – רצוני לומר, שהיו חותכים מן הבהמה אבר ידוע ואוכלים אותו: ואמנם איסור "בשר בחלב" עם היותו מזון עב מאד, בלא ספק, ומוליד מלוי רב, אין רחוק אצלי שיש בו ריח "עבודה זרה", אולי כך היו אוכלים בעבודה מעבודותיה או בחג מחגיהם. וממה שמחזק זה אצלי – זכור התורה אותו שני פעמים תחילת מה שציותה עליו עם מצות החג, "שלש פעמים בשנה וגו'", כאילו אמר, בעת חגכם ובואכם לבית "י־י א־לוהיך" לא תבשל מה שתבשל שם על דרך פלוני, כמו שהיו הם עושים. זהו הטעם החזק אצלי בענין איסורו – ואמנם לא ראיתי זה כתוב במה שראיתי מספרי הצאבה: ואמנם מצות שחיטת בהמה היא הכרחית, מפני שהמזון הטבעי לבני אדם הוא מן הזרעים הצומחים בארץ ומבשר בעלי חיים, והטוב שבבשר הוא מה שהותר לנו לאכלו – וזה מה שלא יסופק בו רופא. וכאשר הביא הכרח טוב המזון להריגת בעלי חיים, כונה התורה לקלה שבמיתות, ואסרה שיענה אותם בשחיטה רעה, ולא יחתוך מהם אבר – כמו שבארנו: וכן אסר לשחוט -אותו ואת בנו" "ביום אחד" – להשמר ולהרחיק לשחוט משניהם הבן לעיני האם, כי צער בעלי חיים בזה גדול מאד, אין הפרש בין צער האדם עליו וצער שאר בעלי חיים, כי אהבת האם ורחמיה על הולד אינו נמשך אחר השכל, רק אחר פועל הכח המדמה, הנמצא ברוב בעלי חיים כמו שנמצא באדם. והיה זה הדין מיוחד ב"שור ושה", מפני שהם - מותר לנו אכילתם מן הביתיות הנהוג לאכלם, והם אשר תכיר מהם האם מן הולד: וזה הטעם גם כן ב"שילוח הקן, כי הביצים אשר שכבה האם עליהם והאפרוחים הצריכים לאמם על הרוב אינם ראויים לאכילה, וכשישלח האם ותלך לה, לא תצטער בראות לקיחת הבנים. ועל הרוב יהיה סיבה להניח הכל, כי מה שהיה לוקח ברוב הפעמים אינו ראוי לאכילה:

Moreh N'vuchim 3:48

I will say that all the foods which the Torah forbade us to eat have poor nutrition. And there is nothing amongst all [the foods] forbidden to us which is [only] speculatively harmful except pork and *cheilev*[28] [for everything else is definitely harmful.] But the matter [regarding pork and *cheilev* only being *possibly* harmful] is also not true [because pork and *cheilev* are actually *definitely* harmful, just like all the other forbidden foods.]

[The reason for this is] that pork contains more moisture than necessary and also [contains] much waste and unnecessary [substances]. And the majority of the Torah's loathing [of pork] is due to [a pig's] lack of hygiene and since its food consists of disgusting things. And you already know[29] of the Torah's insistence on [preventing] the visibility of loathsome things – even in the fields and the [military] camp, how much more so in inhabited areas. If consuming pork were permitted, the markets and homes would be dirtier than a toilet as you will see today in the French countries. You already know the sages'[30] statement,[31] "The mouth of a pig is like transient[32] feces."

So too, the *cheilev* of the stomach[33] satiates [a person in excess] and it disrupts digestion and draws cold, sticky blood. Burning it[34] [as a candle] would be better than eating it!

And so too, the blood and carcasses[35] are difficult to digest and have poor nutrition. And it is known that a *t'reifah*[36] is the beginning of a carcass [in that a *t'reifah* will die of its own accord and thus end up becoming a carcass; thus the same problem applies to a *t'reifah* as does to a carcass.]

[Furthermore, you should] know that these signs – chewing the cud, split hooves in domesticated animals and fins and scales amongst fish – are not the reason for [these animals] being permitted, nor are their absence the

---

28. Forbidden fats.

29. See Moreh N'vuchim 3:41 where the Rambam refers to the requirements (mentioned in D'varim 23:13–15) to ensure that even in a camp of war there be provision made that toilets are not situated within the body of the camp.

30. Lit., "their."

31. B'rachot 25a.

32. This statement is made in the context of a discussion regarding where a person can read the *Sh'ma*. Generally, the law is that one may not read the *Sh'ma* in the presence of feces. See Rashi ad loc. The meaning here is that a pig's mouth is likened to feces which are being removed from one place to another, which is considered less of an obstacle, halachically, to one's reading of the *Sh'ma*.

33. I.e., the forbidden type of animal fat.

34. The *cheilev*.

35. Animals which have died of disease or natural causes and have not undergone ritual slaughter. See Rambam, Forbidden Foods 4:8.

36. An animal with a terminal disease or injury. For further study, see Rambam, Forbidden Foods 4:8.

reason for [these animals] being forbidden. Rather, they are signs through which one may know which species is praiseworthy and which is detestable.

And the reason for [the prohibition against eating] the sciatic nerve is written[37] [in the Torah].

However, the reason for [the prohibition against eating] the limb of a living animal is that [doing so] teaches and makes a person acquire cruelty. Moreover, this is what the kings of gentiles used to do then.[38] Also they used to do so [as part of] idol worship, that is, they would cut off a certain limb from an animal [whilst it was still alive] and they would eat it.[39]

However, the prohibition [against eating a cooked combination of] meat and milk is because it is very coarse food, without a doubt, and it generates bloatedness.[40] In my opinion, it is not farfetched to say that it smacks of idolatry – perhaps they[41] would eat this [meat and milk mixture] in some idolatrous ceremony or on one of their festivals. What strengthens my opinion [that this is an issue related to idolatry] is that the Torah mentions it twice[42] at the beginning[43] of what the Torah commanded regarding the command of the festival, "Three times per year [shall all your males appear before the Master, Hashem],"[44] as if the Torah is saying, "At the time of your festival, when you come to the house of Hashem your G-d, you shall not cook whatever you cook there in the manner that the idolators[45] used to." This is the strongest reason in my opinion regarding its prohibition; however I have not seen this[46] written in what I have seen of the books of the *Tzaba*.[47]

However, the mitzvah of [ritually] slaughtering an animal is vital because the most natural food for humans is from the vegetation which grows in

37. B'reishit 32:32.

38. See N'darim 65a where the Gemara relates that Tzidkiyahu found N'vuchadnetzer (king of Babylon) eating a live rabbit.

39. See the Rambam's commentary on the Mishnah, Avodah Zarah 2:3.

40. See Rabbi Kapach's edition of the Rambam's Moreh N'vuchim (Mossad Harav Kook: 5756) where he indicates that the Rambam's intent here is that this food is difficult to digest and causes gassiness.

41. Idolaters.

42. The Torah mentions this prohibition three times in all – Sh'mot 23:19, 34:26 and D'varim 14:21. The first two occasions are the Rambam's focus.

43. Meaning that the Torah commanded us to abstain from eating cooked mixtures of meat and milk close to the beginning of the Torah's discussion of how we should behave on our festivals when Jews would pilgrimage to Yerushalayim.

44. Sh'mot 23:17 and 34:23 (with slight variations).

45. Lit., "they."

46. That meat and milk combinations were part of idolatrous practices.

47. See Rabbi Kapach's comments (p. 105, n. 15) where he explains that the *Tzaba* was a collection of idolaters concentrated in Babylon in the Rambam's times.

the earth and from the meat of animals. And the goodness which is in the meat is what was permitted for us to eat – no doctor will doubt this. Now that the necessity of good [quality] nutrition has required the killing of animals [since that is the only way we can obtain the necessary meat-based nutrition], the Torah intended for the easiest of deaths [when killing animals] and prohibited one from causing pain to them through a bad slaughter. And [similarly] one may not cut a limb from them [while they are still alive].

So too [the Torah] prohibited one from slaughtering "a dam and its offspring on one day,"[48] to guard and distance [one] from slaughtering both of them, the young in the sight of the dam. [This is] because the pain of animals in this [instance] is very great – there is no difference between the pain of a person over this and that of other animals, because the love of a mother and her mercy over her offspring is not a function of the mind but is rather a function of the power of the imagination (which is present in most animals just as it is found in humans). This law specifically applies to "an ox and sheep"[49] because they are permitted for consumption amongst the domesticated animals which it is customary to eat; and it is amongst them that a dam will recognize her young . . ."

i. Here, the Rambam explains the reasons for the following mitzvot:
    1. Prohibition against eating pork: poor nutrition and the raising of pigs contribute to the general lowering of hygienic standards.
    2. Prohibition against eating *cheilev*: almost dangerous to eat.
    3. Prohibition against eating blood: poor nutrition.
    4. Prohibition against eating carcasses: poor nutrition.
    5. Prohibition against eating the limb of a living animal: engenders cruelty and was possibly a part of idolatrous services.
    6. Prohibition against eating meat and milk: unhealthy food which causes bloatedness, and it was probably used in idolatrous services.
    7. Prohibition against slaughtering a dam and its offspring on one day: engenders cruelty.
    8. Requirement to perform ritual *sh'chitah* on an animal before eating it: prevents one from becoming cruel.

48. Vayikra 22:28.
49. Vayikra 22:28.

COMMENTARY SECTION

Chapter 9

1. **Terminology**
   a. "[Spiritual] success"
      i. The Hebrew term used is הצלחה, "*hatzlachah*," which means "success" or "achievement."
      ii. We have consistently inserted the word "spiritual" before "success" throughout this chapter when the Maharal is seeking to emphasize that the *physical* mitzvot can engender *spiritual* success and growth.
      iii. This is not to say that the Maharal believes that Torah brings spiritual success only; G-d forbid, as he emphasized in the Introduction to this work, the Torah brings both physical and spiritual success.
   b. "Conceptualizations"
      i. The Hebrew term used is מושכלות, "*muskalot*," which indicates something which is comprehended. We have used the term, "conceptualizations."
      ii. This term is used commonly by many of our sages (see, for example, the Rambam)[1] where it indicates an essential truth which a person can comprehend.
   c. "Punishment"
      i. The Hebrew term used is עונש, "*onesh*," the exact translation of which is "punishment."
      ii. However, as we explain below, this English term introduces a connotation which is quite foreign to the Torah way of thinking: that of a punitive, vindictive Entity meeting out demerits and pain.
      iii. A better translation would be "self-generated negative consequences"; however, we have retained the original due to the cumbersome nature of the alternatives.
   d. *T'shuvah*
      i. *T'shuvah*, תשובה, is often mistranslated as "repentance" and better translated as "return."
      ii. *T'shuvah* connotes an entire universe of ideas relating to the effects of sin and of unfulfilled potential as well as to the path back from these negativities. The fundamental concept is that the definition of

1. Moreh N'vuchim 3:54. Admittedly this is the Hebrew term chosen by the translators of the Rambam but it is employed generally by most translators including Rabbi Kapach, *zt"l*.

evil is distance from Hashem, and thus the reversal or repair of any evil requires a return to Hashem.

iii. Due to the breadth and depth of the meaning behind this word, we have left it untranslated.

e. Active Intellect

i. The Hebrew term used here is שכל הפועל, *"seichel hapo'el."* We have translated this as "active intellect."

ii. What exactly is this "active intellect?" The term is commonly used by the Rambam and other sages – we will cite the Rambam's use of the term as the Rambam is one of those sages whom the Maharal is citing here.

1. Moreh N'vuchim 2:4

מורה נבוכים ב:ד (אבן תיבון)

אמנם מאמר האחרונים מן הפילוסופים שהשכלים הנפרדים עשרה, מפני שהם מנו הכדורים שיש בהם כוכבים, והמקיף; ואף על פי שבקצת הכדורים ההם גלגלים רבים. והכדורים במספרם תשעה, המקיף בכל, וגלגל הכוכבים העומדים, וגלגלי השבעה כוכבים. והשכל העשירי - הוא השכל הפועל, אשר הורה עליו צאת שכלנו מן הכח אל הפועל, והיות הצורות הנמצאות ההוות הנפסדות, אחר שלא היו בחמרים שלהם אלא בכח. וכל מה שיצא מן הכח אל הפועל - יש לו מוציא בהכרח חוץ ממנו, וצריך שיהיה המוציא ממין המוצא

Moreh N'vuchim 2:4 (Ibn Tibbon translation)

The later philosophers assumed ten Intelligences, because they counted the spheres containing stars and the all-encompassing sphere, although some of the spheres included several distinct orbits. There are altogether nine spheres, viz., the all-encompassing sphere, that of the fixed stars, and those of the seven planets: nine Intelligences correspond to the nine spheres: the tenth Intelligence is the Active Intellect. The existence of the latter is proved by the transition of our intellect from a state of potentiality to that of actuality, and by the same transition in the case of the forms of all transient beings. For whatever passes from potentiality into actuality, requires for that transition an external agent of the same kind as itself.

a. It is clear from this that the Rambam viewed the "Active Intellect" as something external to the human being – as one of the ten spheres/Intelligences in his cosmological theory. However, it is of a similar type to the human intellect which enables it to catalyze our own intellectual actualization.

b. As we will see later in the Maharal, in Chapter 16, the Maharal understands that these intelligences are in fact what the Rambam considers to be "angels."

f. "Wisdom," "Understanding" or "Knowledge"

   i. The Maharal writes, "And you should understand that this is the reason that the Torah was given the name ['Torah'] and it is not called, 'Wisdom,' 'Understanding' or 'Knowledge' [which would not have been unreasonable,] as it says, regarding the Torah, 'For it is your wisdom and understanding in the eyes of all the nations.'"

   ii. These three concepts, "wisdom," "understanding" and "knowledge" have specific connotations.

   iii. Rashi explains them as follows,

רש"י, שמות לא:ג

בחכמה - מה שאדם שומע דברים מאחרים ולמד: ובתבונה - מבין דבר מלבו מתוך דברים שלמד: ובדעת - רוח הקדש:

Rashi, Sh'mot 31:3

"With wisdom" – [this refers to] those data which a person hears from others and learns.

"With understanding" – [this refers to a person who] understands something in his heart from [other] things which he learned.

"And with knowledge" – divine inspiration.[2]

1. Rashi's definition seems to be:
   a. Wisdom – information one learns from someone else, or perhaps the basic axioms of one's thought system.
   b. Understanding – the ability to deduce.
   c. Knowledge – knowledge gained only through G-d granting it.

   iv. The Maharal explains as follows elsewhere.

1. Derech Chaim 1:1

דרך חיים א:א

ותמצא בני אדם שהם טועים בחכמה שסברתם הפך הסברא האמיתית, ויש בני אדם אף כי יש להם סברא ישרה ונכונה, וכאשר הם באים להבין דבר מתוך דבר על ידי פלפול יש להם חסרון, והראשון נקרא חכמה שהוא סברת הלב, והשני הוא הפלפול ונקרא בינה שמוציא דבר מתוך דבר על ידי פלפול, ויש בני אדם חסרים דעת שאין יודעים דבר.

Derech Chaim 1:1

And you will find humans who err in their wisdom in that their logic is the opposite of true logic. And there are people who, even though they have honest and correct logic, have a deficiency when it comes to deducing one

2. Lit., "Holy spirit." This indicates knowledge gained directly from Hashem and not through intellectual achievement.

idea from another through deduction. The first [faculty] is termed "wisdom" which is the logic of the heart and the second [faculty] is deduction and is termed, "understanding" since he deduces one idea from another through deduction. And there are people who lack knowledge – that they don't know a thing.

a. Here we have clear definitions of "wisdom" and "understanding" which seem to concur with Rashi's definitions.
b. However, there is no clear indication of the definition of "knowledge."

2. The Maharal expands on this theme in N'tivot Olam, *N'tiv Hatorah* 14.

ספר נתיבות עולם א - נתיב התורה - פרק יד

ובמדרש (ילקו"ש משלי תתקל"ד[צ"ל תתקל"ב]) כי ה' יתן חכמה מפיו דעת ותבונה גדולה החכמה וגדול ממנה הדעת והתבונה הוי כי ה' יתן חכמה אבל למי שהוא אוהב מפיו דעת . . . ר"ל כי כל דבר שישיג נקרא חכמה ולפיכך לא כתיב רק כי ה' יתן חכמה, אבל אצל הדעת והבינה שהוא שכל עליון שכל אלהי נבדל לגמרי נאמ' מפיו דעת ותבונה, כי מפני כי הדעת והתבונה הוא נבדל א-להי לגמרי אמר מפיו כי ע"י דעת ותבונה הדבוק בו יתברך לגמרי פה אל פה ושני דברים שנושקים פה אל פה זה הדבוק הגמור. ומזה תדע כי הדעת והתבונה הוא יותר עליון מן החכמה, כי דבר זה הוא שכל נבדל לגמרי לא כמו החכמה שאין זה שכל נבדל לגמרי ובזה השכל אין חבור פה אל פה אל השי"ת. וכן תקנו חכמים בברכות אתה חונן לאדם דעת, כי במה שהוא אדם בעל גוף לכך הדעת שהוא השכל הנבדל אליו דרך חנינה, כמו מי שנותן מתנה לאחד דרך חנינה אף שהוא אינו ראוי מצד עצמו רק דרך חנינה, ולכך אמר לשון אתה, כי אל השם יתברך בפרט פעל זה . . .

N'tivot Olam, *N'tiv Hatorah* 14

And in the Midrash[3] it states, "'For Hashem will bestow wisdom, from His mouth [He bestows] knowledge and understanding.'[4], [5] Wisdom is great but knowledge and understanding are greater. This is [as the verse implies when it says,] 'For Hashem will bestow wisdom' but to one whom He loves [He bestows] 'from His mouth, knowledge and understanding.'" . . .

The explanation [of this Midrash is] that anything that a person

3. Tanchuma (Buber) Ki Tissa 10.

4. The Hebrew term used here for "understanding" is "*t'vunah*," תבונה, which is a variant on the word used by Rashi, "*binah*," בינה, but it is the same word that the Maharal uses in the section under discussion at the beginning of this section of the Tiferet Yisrael. In any event, we have translated both *t'vunah* and *binah* with the same English term, "understanding."

5. Mishlei 2:6.

understands is called "wisdom" and therefore, [the verse] only states, "For Hashem will bestow wisdom." But regarding "knowledge" and "understanding" which are [each a branch of the] superior intellect – G-dly intellect which is completely transcendent – [the verse states,] "from His mouth [He bestows] knowledge and understanding."[6] Since knowledge and understanding are completely transcendent and G-dly [the verse states that they come] "from His mouth" for through knowledge and understanding one gains complete bonding with Him, may He be Blessed – mouth to mouth [as it were]. And any two things joined mouth to mouth have a complete bond.

From this we know that knowledge and understanding are superior to wisdom because they are completely transcendent intellect – unlike wisdom which is not completely transcendent intellect and which doesn't confer a mouth-to-mouth bond with Hashem, may He be Blessed.

And so our sages instituted in the blessings [of the Amidah, the request for wisdom which is phrased as follows,] "You grace a person with knowledge" – since through a person being a bodily being, therefore, knowledge (which is transcendent intellect) [can only reach] him through [an act of pure] grace, like one who graciously gives a present to another who is not worthy thereof. Therefore, the [blessing] uses the term "grace" – since this action belongs exclusively to Hashem, may He be Blessed . . .'

3. Here it is clear that the Maharal concurs with Rashi that "knowledge" is the highest level – granted directly from Hashem in an act of pure grace.

2. The Beliefs of the Philosophers

a. The Maharal writes above, "Those who have walked in the path of the sages of enquiry (these are the philosophers whom we mentioned previously) assign importance and grandeur to the intellect and [believe that] a person acquires eternity through the Conceptualizations . . ."

b. The Maharal here is disputing the views of other sages, in particular, the Rambam and the Ralbag.[7]

c. The Rambam states as follows,

ספר מורה הנבוכים ג:נ"ד

וכבר השיגו החכמים ז"ל מזה הפסוק אלו העניינים בעצמם אשר זכרנום, ובארו לנו מה שבארתי לך בזה הפרק, שהחכמה הנאמרת סתם בכל מקום והיא התכלית, היא

---

6. The idea here is that knowledge and understanding come from Hashem's "mouth" as it were – meaning that they are intimately closer to Hashem.

7. Rabbi Levi ben Ger'shon (1288–1344). See in particular, Milchamot Hashem 1:11.

השגתו ית', ושאלו הקניינים שיקנם האדם שישימם סגולתו ויחשבם שלמות אינם שלמות, ושמעשי התורה כלם, ר"ל מיני העבודות וכן המדות המועילות לבני אדם כלם בעסקיהם קצתם עם קצתם, כל זה אין לדמותו אל התכלית האחרון ולא ישוה בו, אבל הם הצעות בגלל זה התכלית.

Moreh N'vuchim 3:54

Our Sages have likewise derived from this verse[8] the above-mentioned lessons, and stated the same theory that has been explained in this chapter – that the simple term "wisdom,"[9] as a rule, denotes the highest aim of humankind, which is the knowledge of G-d.

[They also explained] that those acquisitions which a person [usually] acquires, makes his peculiar treasure, and considers as his perfection, in reality do not include any perfection. [They also explained] that the religious acts prescribed in the Torah, that is, the various kinds of worship and the moral principles which benefit all people in their social intercourse with each other, do not constitute the ultimate aim of man, nor can they be compared to it, for they are but preparations leading to it . . .

i. It is clear from the Rambam's words here that he views the mitzvot as a means to the ultimate end which is "wisdom."

d. Further, the Ralbag writes,

מלחמות השם א:י"א

ובהיות הענין כן, הוא מבואר שלא יחויב מזה בשכל הנקנה שיהיה נפסד, אבל יחויב שיהיה נצחי, כמו שהתבאר בקודם:

Milchamot Hashem 1:11

Since the matter is so, it is clear that it is not required that the *acquired intellect* lose its existence [ever], rather it is required that it be eternal, as was explained previously.

i. The Ralbag makes it clear that it is the "acquired intellect" which is eternal.

e. The Maharal's thesis opposes the stance that the intellect is the eternal

8. Yirmiyahu 9:22–23, which states, "Thus says Hashem, 'Let not the wise man glory in his wisdom, neither let the mighty man glory in his might, nor let the rich man glory in his riches; but let him that takes pride in anything, glory in this: that he understands and knows Me, for I am Hashem Who does kindness, justice and righteousness in the earth, because I have desired these . . .'"

9. In Hebrew, חכמה, "*chochmah*."

facet of the human being and that the knowledge of G-d is the purpose of life. Rather, he holds that that soul is eternal and its bonding with Hashem is the purpose of life.

3. **Punishment vs. Consequence**
   a. As discussed previously in the Commentary, Ch. 5 § Points 1, 4 and 5, the general Torah approach to so-called "punishment" and "reward" is not that there is some system of merits and demerits assigned to those who act righteously and those who do not, G-d forbid. Rather, we understand that positive actions generate closeness to Hashem, which is the ultimate reward and pleasure, while negative actions distance one from Hashem, G-d forbid, which is the ultimate pain and "punishment."
   b. Thus, it is not Hashem who punishes or rewards like some punitive human, G-d forbid. Rather, He allows us the choice to make our own destinies – one close to Him, or if we so wish, disconnected from Him, G-d forbid.

4. **Humans in the Image of Hashem**
   a. The Maharal writes above, "And there is no doubt that a person is worthy of this due to his being created in the 'image of G-d,' 'in His Form' which is the closest intimacy [that one can attain to Hashem] as the G-dly Mishnaic sage said, 'Beloved is the human being, who was created in the likeness' of Hashem . . ."
   b. The Maharal has discussed this at length elsewhere – see Chapter Four. The Maharal writes there as follows,

תפארת ישראל ד

והמושל האחד הוא מושל הגשמי כי השמש היא גשמית. והמושל השני הוא נבדל כי האדם אינו גשמי גמור, הן בנשמתו הא־להית שיש לו נשמה קדושה והן מצד שנאמר בו כי בצלם א־להים עשה את האדם כי יש בצורתו ענין א־להי למי שיודע ברזי החכמה מכל מקום על כל פנים יש באדם ענין נבדל, הרי כי אלו שני דברים מחולקים האחד הוא המושל ויש לו חשיבת גוף. והשני יש לו ענין בלתי גשמי והוא נבדל יהיה הפירוש מה שיהיה בלשון צלם א־להים סוף סוף יש באדם דבר א־להי נבדל. והנה השמש והאדם היותר עליון בעולם הזה, כי העולם הזה יש בו חומר וצורה נבדלת והחומר היותר עליון הוא לשמש כי יש לו חומר זך, ומעלת הצורה הנבדלת לאדם ולכך אלו שנים הם נחשבים מלכים מצד שהם עליונים בנמצאים בעולם הזה, והאדם נחשב צורה אל הנמצאים כלם אף אל השמש . . . כי האברים הם צורתו שצורתו צלם א־להים נבדל . . .

Tiferet Yisrael 4

And the second ruler[10] is transcendent because humankind is not completely physical, whether from the point of view of his holy soul or from the point of

10. I.e., humanity.

view of that which is said regarding him, "because [G-d] made humankind in the likeness of G-d"[11] (for there is in the human Form a G-dly matter for one who knows the secrets of wisdom).

Either way,[12] humankind has a transcendent facet. These two[13] [rulers] are differentiated in the following manner: the one[14] is a ruler and has physical import while the second[15] has a non-physical component and is transcendent (because whichever interpretation one chooses for the phrase "likeness of G-d," in the end, humankind possesses a transcendent facet). . . . . . the component-limbs are a human's Form which is in the likeness of G-d and is transcendent . . .

c. For more on this, see the Terminology entry on "Component-limbs" at the beginning of the Commentary, Ch. 4 § Point 2.

5. The Primal Cause and its Effects

a. The Maharal writes above, "then [automatically] he is separated from the [Primal] Cause and has no bond with it." Here he refers to Hashem as *The [Primal] Cause* – a term he has employed rarely thus far in the Tiferet Yisrael.
b. He mentioned this idea briefly in the Introduction – for an analysis of the term, see the Commentary, Introduction § Point 1.

---

11. B'reishit 1:27.
12. Whether due to the holiness of his soul or being made in the likeness of Hashem.
13. The sun and humankind.
14. I.e., the sun.
15. I.e., humankind.

GLOSSARY

Adam	Human being
Adamah	Earth, ground
Aleph-Beit	Hebrew alphabet
Amora'im	Sages whose collective teachings form the body of the Gemara
Aruch	An early dictionary of Torah terms
Aseh	See *mitzvot aseh*
Avraham	Abraham
Ba'al keri	Male who has experienced a seminal emission but has not yet immersed in a *mikvah*, a suitable, ritual pool
Ben paku'a	An animal found in utero after the kosher slaughter of its dam
B'heimah	Animal, beast, domesticated animal
B'midbar	The biblical Book of Numbers
B'reishit	The biblical Book of Genesis
Beit Midrash	House of study of Torah
B'nei Torah	Literally, "children of the Torah." It connotes people who are committed to living a Torah lifestyle.
B'rachah	Blessing, benediction
B'raita	A *b'raita* is an early text from the time of the Mishnah which was excluded for various reasons from the official canon of Mishnah.
Chazal	Our sages, of blessed memory
Cheilev	Certain fats in a kosher animal which are nevertheless prohibited
Chesed	Loving-kindness
Chukkim	Literally, "decrees." Refers to a category of mitzvah, the reasons for which are less readily understood, if at all.
Chullin	A tractate of the Talmud
D'varim	The biblical Book of Deuteronomy
Eisav	Esau, Isaac's son
Emet	Truth
G'hinnom	*G'hinnom* is a purification process for the soul after death. The process is painful but has nothing in common with concepts of eternal purgatory.
G'matriah, pl. *g'matriot*	Each letter in Hebrew has a set numerical value and the corresponding values of different words are often compared as

	a manner of illustrating parallels between those words or the concepts that they represent.
Hachanah	Receptivity
Halachah, pl. *halachot*	Torah Law
Hashem	G-d
Kareit	Spiritual excision – the consequence of certain acts which sever one's relationship with Hashem
Kilayim	The prohibition against sowing mixed seeds in one patch of ground
Kohanim	Members of the tribe of Levi who actually performed the service in the Tabernacle and Temple – all direct descendants of Aharon.
Lav, pl. *lavim*	See *mitzvot lo ta'aseh*
Lo ta'aseh	See *mitzvot lo ta'aseh*
Lulav	Literally, a palm branch. This is the generic term used to refer to four species of plants and fruit (palm branch, willow, myrtle branches and a citron) which are used once a day during the festival of Sukkot.
Midrash	A collection of our sages' commentaries on the written Torah. It is a central component of the Oral Torah and contains both halachic and philosophical components.
Mikvah	Ritual pool
Milah	Circumcision
Mishlei	The biblical Book of Proverbs
Mishnah	The central component of the Oral Law. The Torah is composed of two sections: the Written Law and the Oral Law.
Mishpatim	Literally, ordinances. Mitzvot, the reasons for which are more readily understandable.
Mitzvot	Commandments in the Torah
Mitzvot aseh	A commandment where one is required to take the initiative and perform a particular action.
Mitzvot lo ta'aseh	A prohibitive commandment, where one is required to refrain from performing a particular action.
M'norah	The golden candelabrum placed in the Tabernacle and Temple
N'darim	A tractate of the Talmud
Nefesh	A "section" of the soul
Niddah	After a woman has undergone her menstrual cycle and has experienced a flow of menstrual blood, she is termed a *niddah*. It is forbidden for her and her husband to have relations until she has undergone a process lasting several days, culminating in immersion in a *mikvah*.
N'shamah	A "section" of the soul, also used to refer to the whole soul.
N'zikin	Literally, "damages" – one of the six *seder*s of the Oral Torah

Orlah	The prohibition against eating the fruit of a fruit tree in its first three years of growth and the requirement to eat the fourth years' growth in Yerushalayim.
Parshah	The Torah (the Pentateuch) is divided into sections, each of which is called a Parshah. A different Parshah is read in synagogue each week on Shabbat morning (in chronological order), so that over a year, the entire Torah is completed.
Pigul	Refers to a sacrifice offered in a particularly unacceptable manner. That is, while the animal is being sacrificed, the owner has the intention not to eat the animal within the maximum prescribed time. Such a sacrifice is halachically unacceptable and is termed, "*pigul.*"
Posek, pl. *pos'kim*	Decider of Halachah
Rambam	Maimonides, central medieval halachic decisor and philosopher.
Rashi	11th century commentator on Bible and Talmud. His commentary gained the greatest following and is still the central commentary used today.
Ru'ach	A "section" of the soul
Seder	Literally, "order" – the generic name for one of the six sections of the Oral Torah
Sha'atnez	The prohibition against wearing garments made of mixtures of wool and linen
Shabbat	The Jewish Sabbath which falls on Saturday
Sh'chitah	Ritual slaughter of kosher animals performed according to strict halachic guidelines
Sh'ma	A prayer said three times daily – the central declaration of Jewish belief in G-d, His unity, the acceptance of the mitzvot and the facticity of the Exodus from Egypt
Sh'mot	The biblical Book of Exodus
Shir Hashirim	The biblical Book of Song of Songs
Shofar	The ram's horn used as a musical instrument to fulfill the mitzvah of hearing it being blown on Rosh Hashanah.
Shul	Synagogue
Sichli	Literally denotes: cerebral, intellectual. The Maharal uses it to connote that which is spiritual, metaphysical.
Sotah	In certain cases, the Torah mandates a process of clarification of marital fidelity. If a husband requests his wife not to seclude herself with a particular man and she ignores this request and does so, the husband may initiate the *sotah* process. The woman is termed a *sotah*.
Sukkah	A temporary dwelling booth. We are commanded to live in such booths for seven days a year during the festival of Sukkot.

Tahor	Something which is *tahor* is compatible with the Temple and its functions. The opposite of this is *tamei*.
Talmid chacham	A sage
Tamei	Something which is *tamei* is incompatible with the Temple and its functions. The opposite of this is *tahor*.
Tamim	Perfect and innocent
TaNaCh	Hebrew acronym meaning, "the Bible," indicating its three textual components. *T* from the word *Torah*, the Pentateuch. *N* from the word *N'vi'im*, the Prophets. "*Ch*" from the word *Ch'tuvim*, the Writings.
T'fillin	Phylacteries
Tractate	A section of the Talmud
T'reifah	A kosher animal which is dying of a mortal disease or a mortal wound. Such animals may not be consumed.
T'shuvah	*T'shuvah* is often mistranslated as "repentance" and best translated as "return." *T'shuvah* connotes an entire universe of ideas relating to the effects of sin and of unfulfilled potential and to the path back from these negativities. The fundamental concept is that the definition of evil is distance from Hashem and thus the reversal or repair of any evil requires a return to Hashem.
Tzaddik	A righteous person
Tz'dakkah	The commandment to provide Jewish social support; usually mistranslated as "charity"
Tzurah	Form
Unkelus	An early sage who translated the Torah into Aramaic
Vayikra	The biblical Book of Leviticus
Ya'akov	Jacob
Yirmiyahu	The biblical Book of Jeremiah
Yishma'el	Ishmael, Abraham's son
Yitzchak	Isaac, our forefather
Yom Kippur	The Day of Atonement
Z'charyah	Zachariah, the prophet and eponymous author of the book in the Bible.
Z'ra'im	Literally, "seeds" – one of the six *seder*s of the Oral Torah.
Z"l	Acronym for *zichrono livrachah*, זכרונו לברכה, "may his memory be a blessing"; or alternatively (as per context), זכרונם לברכה, "may their memory be a blessing." Used as a postscript or suffix after mentioning the name of a righteous person who has passed away.
Zt"l	Acronym for *zecher tzadik livrachah*, זכר צדיק לברכה, "may the remembrance of the righteous be a blessing." Used as a postscript or suffix after mentioning the name of a righteous person who has passed away.

INDEX OF SOURCES

TORAH

B'reishit

Sh'mot

Vayikra

B'midbar

D'varim

N'VI'IM

Y'hoshu'a

MIDRASH

Chaim of Volozhin, R.

Chizkuni

Chofetz Chaim

Feinstein, R. Moshe

Halevi, R. Yehudah

Hartman, R. Yehoshua

Hirsch, R. Samson Raphael

Hutner, R. Yitzchak

Karo, R. Yosef

Landau, R. Ya'akov ben Yehudah

Maharal

Natan Ben Y'chi'el, R.

Nissim Ga'on, R.

Radak

Ralbag

Rambam

GENERAL INDEX

NAME INDEX

FREE EXTRA MATERIAL FOR EDUCATORS!

One of the goals of the writing of this work was to provide educators with a tool to teach better.

As an educator, I strive to provide my students, many of whom only have rudimentary (or non-existent) Hebrew and Aramaic language skills, with certain components to their Torah study:

1. A text and translation

Generally, I feel it is vital that students have both an original Hebrew text and a translation. Having only the English text often generates a feeling of distance from the original and I would like all my students to feel that not only is the original not distant, but that acquiring the skills to read it, should be a goal.

2. Summaries

Chazal go to great lengths to emphasize the necessity for *chazarah*, and summaries form a crucial part of this process, allowing one to assimilate the knowledge gained and sometimes more importantly, to integrate it within a broader context.

3. Discussion

When one learns any section of Torah, one is inevitably required to digress and explain other concepts which make an appearance within that particular *sugyah*. This is no different within the many topics which the Maharal discusses.

Because of all this, purchasing this work entitles educators to access the educators' program which you can find at: www.ravramon.net. To access the program, please go to the above website and follow the instructions there.

The program includes the following and more (*IY"H*).

- **Material**

Each subsection of each chapter exists as a standalone PDF unit for educators to use as a source sheet with attached summaries. Several chapters of this work are available there, divided into source sheets for the educator. Similarly, each Chapter Summary exists as a standalone hand-out. The Commentaries (chapter by chapter) are also available as PDFs for the educator – especially for those who would like to create further source materials for discussion.

- **Guides**

The guide contains suggestions (from myself and yourselves as well, *IY"H*) as to how the materials supplied can be used. For example, some educators will want to stick more closely to the text, while others will want to use the Maharal as a springboard to discuss some of the ideas which he raises, perhaps utilizing the sources within the Commentary section.

- **Shiurim**

My own audio shiurim on the Maharal will be posted there too, G-d willing.

ABOUT THE AUTHOR

Rabbi Ramon Widmonte was born in Johannesburg, South Africa. He attended Yeshivat Har Etzion in Alon Shvut, Israel, where he was privileged to learn from Rabbi Yehuda Amital, *z"l*, Rabbi Aaron Lichtenstein, *z"l* and להבחל"ח Rabbi Mosheh Lichtenstein, *shlit"a*. He also holds a degree in Mathematics and Computer Science. He directs Mizrachi South Africa and is the co-founder and Dean of the Academy of Jewish Thought and Learning (www.TheAcademy.org.za), a cutting-edge adult education program. Rabbi Widmonte and his wife, Julie, are blessed with are blessed with three children, Batya Chaya, Yonatan Ya'akov Yitzchak and Aryeh Tzvi, נ"י. You can read more of Rabbi Widmonte's writings on the website, www.RavRamon.net.